ALL ■ IN ■ ONE

CompTIA

Linux+™ Certification

EXAM GUIDE

Second Edition (Exam XK0-005)

ABOUT THE AUTHORS

Ted Jordan (MS, CompTIA Linux+, CompTIA Security+, CompTIA Cloud+, CISSP, CSSLP) has over 25 years of UNIX, IRIX, Solaris, and Linux engineering experience. He studied coding and UNIX as a graduate student of the University of California, Berkeley and Kettering University. During Mr. Jordan's engineering career, he coded in C/UNIX for General Motors, Silicon Graphics, Fakespace CAVE Virtual Reality, and Sun Microsystems. He is the founder and president of successful technical ventures, Funutation, Inc., and JordanTeam LLC, both providing Linux coding and education. He has taken and passed all CompTIA Linux+ exams since 2001 and has successfully trained hundreds of others to attain their Linux+ certifications. Follow him on Twitter and YouTube @JordanTeamLearn.

Sandor Strohmayer is a trainer and curriculum developer who has been teaching and writing Linux and UNIX training material for more than 20 years. Mr. Strohmayer began as a hardware and operating system instructor for Sun Microsystems. Since then he has developed and taught UNIX, Linux, and other training programs for schools, corporations, and the military, using study guides and blended learning techniques supplemented with individually paced learning via a learning management system. Mr. Strohmayer also offers study, Linux, and other IT hints on LinkedIn (www.linkedin.com/pub/sandor-strohmayer/4/702/765).

About the Technical and Developmental Editor

Kenneth "Ken" Hess is a practicing senior system administrator and a technology author, blogger, columnist, editor, and podcaster. Ken has written hundreds of technology articles on topics that cover Linux, open source software, Windows, Mac, mobile devices, databases, and cryptocurrencies. He also reviews technology products and is an avid photographer and filmmaker.

ALL ■ IN ■ ONE

CompTIA

Linux+™ Certification

EXAM GUIDE

Second Edition (Exam XK0-005)

Ted Jordan
Sandor Strohmayer

New York Chicago San Francisco
Athens London Madrid Mexico City
Milan New Delhi Singapore Sydney Toronto

McGraw Hill books are available at special quantity discounts to use as premiums and sales promotions, or for use in corporate training programs. To contact a representative, please visit the Contact Us pages at www.mhprofessional.com.

CompTIA Linux+™ Certification All-in-One Exam Guide, Second Edition (Exam XK0-005)

1 2 3 4 5 6 7 8 9 LCR 28 27 26 25 24 23

Library of Congress Control Number: 2023933885

ISBN 978-1-264-79896-4
MHID 1-264-79896-2

Sponsoring Editor
Lisa McClain

Editorial Supervisor
Janet Walden

Project Editor
Rachel Fogelberg

Acquisitions Coordinator
Caitlin Cromley-Linn

Technical Editor
Kenneth Hess

Copy Editor
William McManus

Proofreader
Lisa McCoy

Indexer
Ted Laux

Production Supervisor
Thomas Somers

Composition
KnowledgeWorks Global Ltd.

Illustration
KnowledgeWorks Global Ltd.

Art Director, Cover
Jeff Weeks

This book is dedicated to my parents, Gwendolyn and Theodore Jordan, who helped me find my passion for technology and teaching others "how to fish."

—Ted Jordan

CONTENTS AT A GLANCE

CONTENTS

ACKNOWLEDGMENTS

Thank you to my wife, Cheryl, and my children, Theo and Aria, for allowing Daddy to toil, peacefully, in the basement, alone, to complete this work.

Also I would like to thank my Cass Technical High School teachers Mr. Max Green and Mr. Walter Downs, a Tuskegee Airman who felled 6 ½ enemy aircraft in WWII, for giving me my "serious fun" teaching style.

Dr. David "Doc" Green and Dr. Duane McKeachie of Kettering University showed me how to simplify difficult concepts for students.

Dr. Larry Stark and Dr. Masayoshi Tomizuka of the University of California at Berkeley introduced me to UNIX, which has taken me further than I imagined.

—Ted Jordan

INTRODUCTION

Congratulations on your decision to become CompTIA Linux+ certified! By purchasing this book, you have taken the first step toward earning one of the hottest certifications around. Being CompTIA Linux+ certified provides you with a distinct advantage in today's IT job market. When you obtain your Linux+ certification, you prove to your employer, your coworkers, and yourself that you truly know your stuff with Linux.

The new CompTIA Linux+ exam, XK0-005, is an expanded version of the previous CompTIA Linux+ XK0-004 exam. In addition to Linux, it covers some DevOps, virtualization, and cloud topics. The Linux portion of the test includes SELinux and other security topics as well as device management firewall and server commands used in a multiserver environment.

The XK0-005 exam is designed for those with at least 12 months of hands-on experience working with Linux servers as a Linux, cloud, or DevOps support engineer. The exam includes both multiple-choice and performance-based questions, requiring a working knowledge of the topics listed in the CompTIA Linux+ exam objectives, described later in this introduction.

We first need to introduce you to the nuts and bolts of this book and the CompTIA Linux+ certification program. We'll look at the following topics:

- Who this book is for
- How to use this book
- How this book is organized
- Special features of the All-in-One certification series
- The CompTIA Linux+ certification exam
- Tips for succeeding on the Linux+ certification exam

Let's begin!

Who This Book Is For

Before you start this book, you need to be aware that we have two primary goals in mind:

- To help you prepare for and pass the Linux+ exam offered by CompTIA
- To provide you with the extra skills and knowledge you need to be successful on the job after you are certified

How to Use This Book

We suggest you use the virtual machine image supplied with the book (see Appendix B for more details). Although it is a large download, the image contains everything you need to study for the test offline. The image is CentOS 7–based, but it also contains Docker images to review the material specifically related to Fedora, openSUSE, and Debian. We have also included an Ubuntu image. Each of these images may be opened by executing the `fedora`, `opensuse`, `debian`, or `ubuntu` commands.

Prior to working with the image, make a clone. Before experimenting, make a snapshot so that if you mess up you can just roll it back. Don't be afraid to trash the image. That is what learning is about.

There are two users on the system: `root` and `student1`. To log in as `root` from the graphical interface, select Unlisted and then use the username `root` and the password `password`. To log in as `student1`, select `student1` and supply the password `student1`.

We have also provided a directory called `/LABS`. This directory contains lab files for specific chapters. Each chapter directory contains a `source` directory and a `work` directory. We suggest you practice with the copy in the `work` directory; if you make a mistake or want to start over, you can easily copy the original lab files from the `source` directory to the `work` directory.

As you are reading, use the Linux image to test what you have read. Read a section and then try the commands in the section. These actions will help you remember the material better and also improve your problem-solving skills. Most chapters also include one or more exercises. When you encounter an exercise, do each step. Don't just scan the exercise—understand what each step does. Anticipate what your actions will affect and then verify the results. If something unexpected happens, try to understand why, and try again.

The activities help you understand the material better *and are similar to the exam's performance-based questions*. So don't just read the activities or watch the videos; perform them so that you can pass the exam the first time.

In some exercises we have not supplied all the steps. We are not trying to trick you. We want you to build the assessment skills that you will need not only when taking the CompTIA Linux+ exam but also in real life. Always ask, what do I have to complete? What do I need for this function to work? Examine pertinent variable or parameter settings as well as related configuration files. If you are having difficulty, each exercise has an accompanying video available in the online content that demonstrates how to perform the exercise.

Take your time studying. The object of the CompTIA Linux+ exam is to certify that you know what you are doing, not that you can pass a test. Rome wasn't built in a day. Take the time to prepare. If you can explain concepts, can complete the exercises while understanding them, and can discriminate why a question's answer is correct whereas other choices are incorrect, you are ready to take the exam.

How This Book Is Organized

The CompTIA Linux+ exam objectives, as currently published, are organized by topic. They aren't organized into a logical instructional flow. As you read through this book, you'll quickly notice that we don't address the CompTIA Linux+ objectives in the same order as they are published by CompTIA. All the objectives are covered; however, we've reorganized them such that we start with the most basic Linux concepts first. Then, as we progress through the book, we address increasingly more advanced CompTIA Linux+ objectives, building on the skills and knowledge covered in preceding chapters.

The Exam Objective Map in Appendix A has been constructed to help you cross-reference the official exam objectives from CompTIA with the objectives as they are presented and covered in this book. The exam objectives are listed in the left column of the table exactly as CompTIA presents them, and the right column identifies the corresponding chapter(s) in which each exam objective is covered.

Special Features of the All-in-One Certification Series

To make the All-in-One Certification series exam guides more useful and a pleasure to read, McGraw Hill has designed the series to include several conventions that you'll see throughout this book.

Icons

To alert you to an important bit of advice, a shortcut, or a pitfall, you'll occasionally see Notes, Tips, Cautions, and Exam Tips peppered throughout the text.

NOTE Notes offer nuggets of especially helpful stuff, background explanations, and information. They also define terms occasionally.

TIP Tips provide suggestions and nuances to help you learn to finesse your job. Take a tip from us and read the Tips carefully.

CAUTION When you see a Caution, pay special attention. Cautions appear when you have to make a crucial choice or when you are about to undertake something that may have ramifications you might not immediately anticipate. Read them now so that you don't have regrets later.

EXAM TIP Exam Tips give you special advice or may provide information specifically related to preparing for the exam itself.

End-of-Chapter Reviews and Questions

An important part of this book comes at the end of each chapter, where you will find a brief review of the main points, along with a series of questions followed by the answers to those questions. Each question is in multiple-choice format.

The questions are provided as a study aid to you, the reader and prospective CompTIA Linux+ exam taker. We cannot guarantee that if you answer all of the questions correctly you will absolutely pass the certification exam. But we can guarantee that the questions will provide you with an idea about how ready you are for the exam.

Online Content

This book comes with access to virtual machine files you can download and use to set up your very own Linux system to practice with. It also includes access to video clips from the authors demonstrating many of the exercises you'll find within the book's chapters, as well as TotalTester practice exams to prepare you for the real certification exam. Read more about the online content and how to access it in Appendix B.

The CompTIA Linux+ Certification Exam

Now that you understand how this book is organized, it's time for you to become familiar with the CompTIA Linux+ certification program and the associated exam. Let's review the following topics:

- About the CompTIA Linux+ certification
- Taking the CompTIA Linux+ exam

About the CompTIA Linux+ Certification

The CompTIA Linux+ certification is an excellent program! It is a vendor-neutral certification designed and administered by the Computing Technology Industry Association, affectionately known as CompTIA.

The CompTIA Linux+ certification is considered "vendor neutral" because the exam is not based on one specific vendor's hardware or software. This is somewhat unique in the information technology industry. Many IT certification programs are centered on one particular vendor's hardware or software, such as those from Microsoft, Cisco, SUSE, or Red Hat.

The CompTIA Linux+ certification, on the other hand, is designed to verify your knowledge and skills with the Linux operating system in general, not on any one particular distribution. The following is according to CompTIA (at the time of writing):

> *CompTIA Linux+ validates the skills administrators need to secure the enterprise, power the cloud and keep systems running. The new certification ensures that IT professionals, software developers, cybersecurity engineers and penetration testers have these necessary skills to support today's tech systems.*

CompTIA Linux+ is the only job-focused Linux certification covering the latest foundational skills demanded by hiring managers. Unlike other certifications, the new exam includes performance-based and multiple-choice questions to identify the employees who can do the job. The exam covers tasks associated with all major distributions of Linux, setting the foundation for advanced vendor/distro-specific knowledge.

As previously mentioned, CompTIA has published objectives for the exam that define the CompTIA Linux+ certification. These exam objectives specify what a Linux system administrator should know and be able to do. The CompTIA Linux+ exam objectives (along with practice exams) are available at https://comptia.org/certifications/linux, upon submitting a brief registration form. To be CompTIA Linux+ certified, you must be able to perform the tasks contained in these objectives.

Taking the CompTIA Linux+ Exam

The CompTIA Linux+ exam is a timed exam and delivered electronically on a computer. The exam is composed of 90 questions and must be completed within 90 minutes. (A countdown timer is provided in the upper-right corner of the screen.)

NOTE You might actually see fewer than 90 questions on the exam because performance-based questions (PBQs) carry more weight. Expect to see about 5 PBQs. The more PBQs on the exam, the fewer total questions provided. Partial credit is granted on PBQs.

The exam interface is fairly straightforward. Items are displayed one at a time on the screen. You are presented with a question along with a series of responses. You mark the appropriate response and then go to the next question. You are allowed to go back to questions that you've marked for review.

Each exam is composed primarily of multiple-choice items. Most of the multiple-choice questions require only one answer; however, some will require the selection of multiple correct responses. If you forget to select one, the exam will warn you that your answer is incomplete.

After you complete the exam, the computer will immediately evaluate it and your score will be printed out. To pass, you need a minimum score of 720 points out of a possible 900. If you do not pass, your score printout will list the objectives where you missed questions. You can use this information to review and prepare yourself to retake the exam.

To make the exam globally available, CompTIA administers the CompTIA Linux+ exam through its testing partner, Pearson VUE (https://home.pearsonvue.com). When registering at Pearson VUE, you have the option to choose a testing center or to take the exam at home.

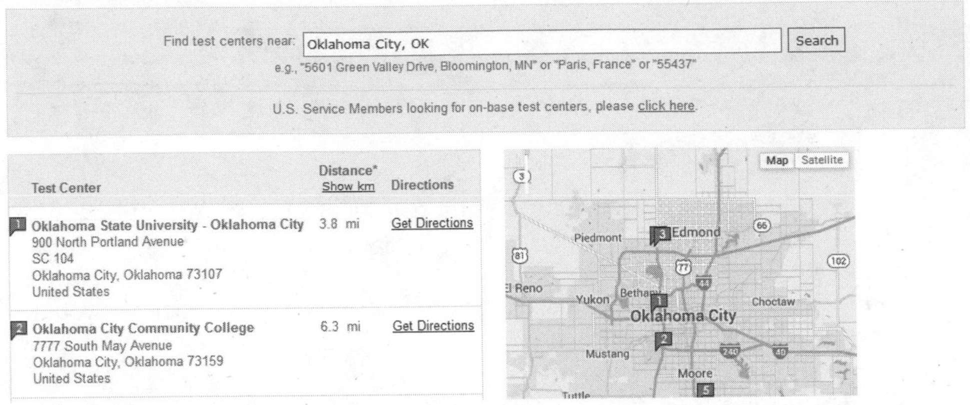

Figure 1 Locating a testing center near you

NOTE To take the exam at home, make sure you use a room that is very neat and free of books. No one can walk in the room while you are taking the exam; otherwise, the proctor will fail you, and no refunds. Learn more here: https://www.comptia.org/testing/testing-options/take-online-exam

To sign up for the CompTIA Linux+ exam, visit the CompTIA website https://store.comptia.org and purchase an exam voucher. You will find a promotional code for a 10 percent discount off the price of the exam voucher at the back of this book. Then visit the Pearson VUE website and locate a testing center near you. Just specify the exam you want to take and your local information. Unless you selected to take the exam at home, you will then be provided with a list of testing centers near you, as shown in Figure 1. Learn more here: https://www.comptia.org/testing.

Then use the Pearson VUE website to schedule the exam and submit the exam voucher. You can also call the test provider directly and schedule the exam over the phone. Be aware that they will need to verify your identity, so be prepared to share your Social Security or National ID number. The test provider will send you a confirmation e-mail listing the time and location of your exam.

On the day of the test, be sure to allow adequate travel time. You never know when you will run into a traffic jam or your car will break down. Try to show up early. If you are taking your exam at a community college, you may have to walk a very long distance to reach the exam.

When you check in at the testing center, you will be required to show *two* forms of original, unexpired identification, at least *one* of which must have your photo on it. The following are acceptable forms of ID:

- Driver's license
- Passport
- Social Security card or National ID card

- Signed credit card
- Common Access Card
- Personal identity verification card
- Military ID card
- NEXUS card
- State-issued ID card

When you check in, you must surrender your phone, tablet, keys, wallet, reference materials, and so on to the test proctor, who will place them in a locker. The center may inspect your eyeglasses for cameras. You are not allowed to take any materials into the exam room, including blank paper. Most testing centers will provide note-taking materials that remain in the room after the exam is completed.

Tips for Succeeding on the CompTIA Linux+ Certification Exam

Over the last decade, we have helped hundreds of candidates prepare for a variety of certification exams. As a result, we have learned several tips to help you pass the exam.

The most important things you can do are to thoroughly study and practice. No tip, trick, or strategy can compensate for a lack of study and practice. The goal is to move the information into your long-term memory. Here are some study tips to help you prepare.

Preparing for the Exam

- *Set a daily study appointment.* Start slow and build. Start with a half hour a day, and work up to an hour session twice a day if possible. (Studying two hours in a row is not productive.) Remember to keep this appointment just as you would any other important appointment. If you miss an appointment, don't worry; just don't miss the next one. Don't study more than two one-hour sessions per day.
- *If you are studying after work, give yourself a chance to wind down.* Try taking a shower and changing clothes. Maybe take a walk or spend some time listening to music. If you are hungry, eat light and healthy. Avoid watching video games or television before you study.
- *Ensure that your study environment is well lit and uncluttered.* Turn off the telephone. Have everything you need to study within your study environment. Once you sit down to study, stay there.
- *Use flashcards and mind maps.* These are great study tools. For more information on how flashcards can help, view the information found on the Mnemosyne Project website (https://mnemosyne-proj.org/).
- *Maintain study health.* Make time to get exercise and rest for best performance. Exercise facilitates study. We are not telling you to go to a gym; try walking after lunch and dinner. Television, video games, and cell phones interfere with study and sleep hours long after you have turned them off.

- *Study in manageable chunks.* After you have read a section, when possible, use the virtual machine image to validate what you studied. Make flashcards and mind maps to help retain that section's material, and use these tools for future study.
- *When you come to a quiz or chapter exam, don't blow through it.* Use the opportunity to learn how to evaluate a question. Make certain you understand why the correct answer or answers are correct and the other answers are incorrect.
- *When you do the exercises, understand what each command does and how and where to test the results.* Before you execute a command, determine what settings or configuration files will affect the command. Using this methodology will help you in real life and when breaking down questions. Get into the habit of executing a command and then testing the results.

Some people recommend setting a deadline by scheduling your exam in advance. We can't recommend that strategy for everyone. Scheduling the test can be productive or counterproductive. Setting a 30- or 60-day deadline may put unnecessary pressure on you, especially if you find a chapter that is giving you problems. We have seen success with the tortoise approach: slow and steady. If you are truly motivated to accomplish your goal, you will. Use your motivation to keep your study appointments. When you are ready to take the test, schedule the exam. If, however, you are the type of person who thrives under a deadline, go ahead and schedule the exam.

Close to the Exam Date

- Continue to use your flashcards and mind maps to review the material.
- Familiarize yourself with what 60 seconds of time passing feels like. During the test, the worst thing you can do is get stuck on a question. Use a timer to get used to 60-second intervals. When taking the test, if you can't answer a question within 60 seconds, mark the question to return to later.
- Practice evaluating questions. Write down key points or create a simple diagram.
- Pretend you are teaching the material. Try to explain the material in a section. If you can explain it, you know it.
- Use the virtual machine image and apply the knowledge you have learned.

The Night Before Your Exam

- Don't study.
- Place all the paperwork you will need for the exam in one place.
- Get a good night's rest.
- Set your alarm to allow plenty of time in the morning to get ready and go to the testing center.

Taking the Exam

- *Evaluate the question.* Determine what the question is asking. Break out the question into what information is pertinent and what is fluff. Determine how you would solve the problem. Here's an example:

  User `student1` wants to copy a file in the subdirectory `/public/test` to the directory `/data`. User `student1` does not own either of the parent directories, `/public` or `/data`, but is a member of the group that is the group owner for all directories. The group has read and execute permissions for all directories. What command will enable `student1` to copy the file from `/public/test` to `/data`?

  To answer the question, you must be familiar with which permissions are necessary to copy a file from one directory to another. To copy the file, you need execute permissions on the source directory and write and execute permissions on the target directory.

  The question tells you that `student1` is a member of the group that has group ownership of all directories and the group has read and execute permissions.

  What is missing? User `student1` cannot write the file to the target directory, `/data`, because the group that `student1` belongs to only has read and execute permissions.

  What is required? The group owners need write permissions on directory `/data`.

  Now you can look for the answer or answers that will apply write permissions to the directory `/data`.
- *Visually assess the question.* You can use the writing materials given to you to. As you had practiced earlier, write down key points or create a simple diagram. This might seem like a waste of time, but visual clues can help bring back memory. Your brain stores and relates to data in memory based on context.
- *Read each answer carefully.* Use the information from your assessment to determine if an answer satisfies the question's requirements. Eliminate the obviously incorrect answers first.
- *Make your best choice and move on.* From experience, we know that your first impression is usually the correct one.
- *Don't spend more than 60 seconds on a question.* If you pass 60 seconds, mark the question so you may return to it and move on.

NOTE Performance-based questions can take about 5 minutes to complete. Skip these and save them for the last 30 minutes of the exam. This will give you time to finish multiple-choice questions. Answer all questions. Don't leave any blank.

- *Your first answer is usually correct.* If you are concerned about a question, mark it for review and return to it later, but your first answer is usually correct.

After you finish the exam, your results will be automatically printed out for you. The report will be embossed with the CompTIA-certified examiner seal by your test proctor to certify the results. Don't lose this report; it is the only hard copy you will have until you receive your certification in the mail.

The report will display your performance on each section of the exam. The CompTIA Linux+ exam is pass/fail. Based on the information available upon publication of this book, if you score 720 or better, you pass!

If you don't pass, you can use the information on your report to identify the areas where you need to study. You can retake the exam immediately if you wish. However, there are two things to keep in mind:

- You have to pay full price for the retake exam (although you can find discount coupons via a quick online search).
- The retake exam probably will not be the same as your first exam.

If you don't pass the second exam, you must wait at least 14 days before taking the exam a third time.

If you fail with a score of 650 or higher, we suggest you study up on the items missed and schedule your retake within a day or two. If you wait any longer than that, your memory will probably go "cold," and you may need to go through the entire preparation process again.

EXAM TIP Avoid TNC failure! CompTIA provides you 28 minutes to read the "Terms and Conditions" (TNC) for the exam. If you do *not* select ACCEPT within that time period, *whether you have finished reading the terms or not,* the screen defaults to "Denied Acceptance of Terms," the exam shuts down, and your test voucher is "burned." No refunds. No voucher reuse. You must spend another $358 to schedule the exam again. Therefore, be sure to read the Candidate Agreement at the CompTIA website, before taking the exam: https://www.comptia.org/testing/testing-policies-procedures/test-policies.

CHAPTER 1

An Introduction to Linux and a Pre-Assessment Exam

In this chapter, you will learn about

- A brief history of Linux
- Linux operating system structure
- Linux distributions
- Common Linux implementations

The possibilities of our returning from this mission in one piece may have just doubled.

—Nichelle Nichols as Lt. Uhura, *Star Trek*

A Brief History of Linux

To understand Linux and its different distributions, you need to understand what was going on in the world of computing before Linus Torvalds began developing the Linux kernel. The 1950s saw the evolution of computers from single-user, single-task systems to batch processing systems.

The discussion starts from the mid-20th century and continues until the development of Linux, as follows:

- Batch processing
- MULTICS
- UNIX
- LINUX

Let's start with programming in the mid-1950s.

Batch Processing

Batch processing is the sequential execution of programs. A programmer would submit a program on punch cards or paper tape to a system operator. The system operator would later "run" the job and give the results back to the programmer.

Unfortunately, a programming error, typing error, damaged card (or tape), or card out of sequence would cause the program to fail. The programmer would have to repair the difficulty and resubmit the job.

ARPA/DARPA

On October 4, 1957, the Soviet Union launched Sputnik. The launch had many people wondering if the United States was falling behind technically. At that time, the U.S. Army, Navy, and Air Force had their own defense development projects. The rivalries between the services were unproductive and wasteful.

President Eisenhower asked members of his Science Advisory Committee to meet with newly appointed Secretary of Defense Neil McElroy to find a solution to the problem. The scientists' solution was to have a single civilian agency to control research and development and report to the Secretary of Defense.

Six months after the establishment of the Advanced Research Projects Agency (ARPA), NASA was created to separate civilian and military space travel. In 1972, ARPA's name was changed to DARPA (the Defense Advanced Research Projects Agency).

Compatible Time-Sharing System

Batch processing could not keep up with the increasing demand for computer resources. Massachusetts Institute of Technology (MIT) was one of several colleges that began to develop time-sharing systems, which allow multiple users to access system resources concurrently through remote terminals.

MIT developed an experimental time-sharing system, called Compatible Time Sharing System (CTSS), and produced the following applications that were later used in UNIX:

- **`RUNOFF`** A text formatting and printing utility that was the predecessor of `roff`, `groff`, `nroff`, and `troff`.
- **`RUNCOM` (run commands)** One of the first applications for running scripts. The `rc` directories in Linux's `/etc/init.d` directory are named after `RUNCOM` scripts.

MULTICS

In 1964, MIT, General Electric, and Bell Labs began development of the Multiplexed Information and Computing Service (MULTICS) operating system funded by DARPA. The goals for MULTICS were as follows:

- Remote terminal use
- Continuous operation
- A high reliability internal filesystem
- Support for a wide range of applications executing concurrently
- A system that can evolve with changes in technology and user requirements

Honeywell and MIT completed MULTICS and launched the first commercial version in October 1969. MULTICS remained a viable operating system for 25 years.

UNIX

Computer scientists Ken Thompson and Dennis Ritchie of Bell Labs worked on the MULTICS project. After Bell Labs withdrew, Ken Thompson decided he would develop his own operating system based on MULTICS operating principles. The initial version was released in 1970 and was called UNICS, for Uniplexed Information and Computing.

NOTE The UNIX development team consisted of Ken Thompson, Dennis Ritchie, Doug McIlroy, and Joe Ossanna.

The first two versions of UNICS were written in assembly language for a specific processor family. Applications written in assembly language for one processor family had to be rewritten for another processor family.

Dennis Ritchie developed the programing language C. Compiled languages convert source code to assembly language, which mitigated the need to rewrite the operating system for each new processor family. In 1973, UNICS was rewritten in C and renamed UNIX.

In 1974, AT&T held a monopoly on the U.S. telephone systems. As part of an agreement with the federal government, the company could keep its monopoly but was not allowed to sell software. Since it could not sell UNIX, AT&T licensed UNIX to educational institutions for a small distribution charge. This allowed colleges and universities to obtain the operating system and use it for teaching and development.

In 1982, AT&T was broken up into smaller phone companies, which permitted AT&T to sell software. Thus, UNIX was no longer "free" to educational institutions.

MINIX

When Andrew Tanenbaum heard AT&T UNIX Version 7 would no longer be made available for educational institutions, he began to work on MINIX, a microkernel-based, UNIX Version 7–compatible operating system. Initially, the operating system kept crashing, and Tanenbaum was about to terminate the project until one of his students informed him the crash was due to the Intel chip overheating, generating a thermal interrupt.

Tanenbaum fixed the problem, and MINIX was released freely to universities in 1987. Unfortunately, MINIX was copyrighted; therefore, no one was allowed to modify the source code. In 2000, MINIX licensing was changed to a permissive license called the Berkeley Software Distribution (BSD). Permissive licensing allows users to modify the source code but does not require modified source code to be made available.

The current version is MINIX 3 and is designed to be used in embedded systems. An embedded system contains an operating system and control program that is used to manage a specific device such as a FAX machine or digital camera.

GNU

On September 27, 1983, Richard Stallman announced the GNU project (GNU stands for GNU is Not UNIX). GNU was to be a free UNIX-like operating system that could be shared, studied, and modified by anyone. At that time, a free (as in cost) and open source version of UNIX did not exist. AT&T no longer provided free versions of UNIX to learning institutions, and Andrew Tanenbaum's MINIX was copyrighted.

In 1985, Stallman founded the Free Software Foundation and, with attorney David Wheeler, created the General Public License (GPL). GPL is also referred to as copyleft. The GPL license dictates that any software or work of art may be modified and distributed freely as long as the modified versions are also distributed without restrictions or cost.

Since no free UNIX kernel existed, the GNU project had to develop one.

Linux

Linus Torvalds entered the University of Helsinki in 1988. At that time, most universities used MINIX to teach UNIX to their students. Torvalds did not like the MINIX terminal emulator and decided to write a better one. As he added functionality to his emulator, he concluded it would be better to create an operating system from scratch.

On September 17, 1991, Torvalds released a development environment called Freax (Free UNIX) under a GPL license. Freax used many of the tools and utilities created by Richard Stallman's GNU project. One of the major design differences was that Torvalds decided to use a monolithic kernel rather than a microkernel. Six months later, the name of the operating system was changed to Linux. Linus then posted the source code and invited other programmers to review, modify, and contribute enhancements. This was the original Linux operating system.

Linus Torvalds holds a registered trademark for the Linux operating system and controls Linux kernel development. When most people talk about Linux, they're usually talking about an operating system with a Linux kernel.

Linux Operating System Structure

An operating system provides a means for users to execute programs on a computer. The Linux operating system consists of multiple functional layers (layered architecture), as detailed in the following list:

- **Hardware layer** Responsible for interacting with system hardware.
- **Kernel** The kernel layer is the core of the operating system. It provides the system with process, memory, and task management.
- **Shell** Application and user environment and interface.
- **Operating system software** Used to manage the operating system.
- **Application software** Editors and other user applications.

In this section you will learn the following details about the Linux operating system structure:

- Kernel
- Operating system software
- Application software

Let's first explore the Linux kernel.

Kernel

The kernel layer is the core of the operating system. Most Linux distributions use a monolithic kernel. Some (GNU) use a microkernel. The kernel also connects applications to system hardware. The kernel is divided into the following components:

- **System Call Interface (SCI)** Provides a connection between user space and kernel space
- **Process management** Responsible for creating, stopping, and communicating with system processes
- **Memory management** Responsible for memory allocation, virtual memory, and paging
- **Virtual filesystem** Provides an abstraction layer for multiple filesystem types
- **Network stack** Provides protocols used in network communications
- **Device drivers** Software used to communicate with hardware
- **Architecture-dependent code** System code specific to the type of processor

To understand the difference between a monolithic kernel and a microkernel, you must understand the terms *user space* and *kernel space.* Kernel processes execute in memory reserved for kernel processes (kernel space). User processes execute in memory reserved for user applications (user space). Separating user and kernel space protects kernel processes.

Monolithic Kernel

A monolithic kernel executes in kernel space. Monolithic kernels are made up of modules that perform specific functions. These modules may be dynamically loaded or unloaded.

Microkernel

A microkernel uses a small kernel executing in kernel space to manage memory, multitasking, and interprocess communication. Most other kernel functions are built in to "servers" that execute in user space.

Operating System Software

Operating system software is designed to manage system resources and provide a platform for application software. Most operating system software starts as part of the boot process and terminates when the system is shut down. (Details on operating system software are discussed in Chapter 11.)

After the system boots up, it's time to log in. Whether you are using a command-line interface (CLI) or graphical user interface (GUI), the system will prompt for your username and password, as shown here in a CLI:

```
localhost login: ted
Password:
Last login: Mon Apr 19 15:09:09 on tty2
ted $
```

When you type in your password, the cursor does not move and no ******** displays either, but the password is being read by Linux.

EXAM TIP The focus of the CompTIA Linux+ exam is use of the CLI, not the GUI.

Administrator Rights

The Linux+ certification exam proves you have the skillset to be a Linux administrator, not a Linux user, so you need to learn how to enable administrator rights on Linux systems. The two methods discussed here involve using the `su` and `sudo` commands.

`su` stands for *switch user* and allows you to become any user, but the default user is `root`. The `root` user can perform any function on Linux, such as kill any job, set up a network, or remove any file. Running `su` requires you to know the `root` password to become `root`, which is why many Linux administrators prefer `sudo`.

The `sudo` command allows you to run a single command with `root` privileges. Two advantages of `sudo` versus `su` is that you do *not* need to know the `root` password, and you don't stay in the `root` account. Instead, you immediately return to a standard account, as shown here:

```
ted $ passwd -S ted
Only root can do that.
ted $ sudo passwd -S ted
[sudo] password for ted: <enter ted's password>
ted PS 2024-08-06 1 99999 7 -1 (Password set, SHA512 crypt.)
ted $ su
Password: <enter root's password>
root # passwd -S ted
ted PS 2024-08-06 1 99999 7 -1 (Password set, SHA512 crypt.)
root # exit
ted $
```

The preceding example shows that using `su` converts you to the `root` user, as indicated by the `root #` prompt. To return to a standard user, run the `exit` command.

The `passwd` command is most commonly used to change your password. Running `passwd -S` displays user account status such as your login name, whether a password is set, date of the last password change, minimum password age, maximum password age, password warning period, inactivity period for the password, and the type of encryption used on the password.

NOTE If you are working in the GUI, to launch a command-line terminal click Activities and open the search bar, then search on **terminal**. Or, choose Applications | System Tools and choose Terminal.

Troubleshooting User Login and Password Issues

If you are having trouble logging in to a Linux system, first make sure you have an account on that system. After verifying this, make sure your settings in `/etc/passwd` are defined correctly. The `/etc/passwd` file is discussed in Chapter 4.

Once you are certain you have an account on the system and your password is not working, first make sure that the `Caps Lock` key is not engaged. Linux is a case-sensitive operating system, and that includes passwords. `Pass123!`, `PASS123!`, and `pass123!` are three distinct passwords on a Linux system. Strong passwords and security are discussed in Chapter 16.

Application Software

Application software is user-space software (for example, editors and spreadsheets) designed to perform specific tasks. Application software is not required to run the operating system. Application software only executes or terminates when requested by a user or another application.

Some important commands for CompTIA Linux+ certification include `ls`, `cd`, `pwd`, and `more`, as detailed in the following sections. (Feel free to try some of these commands on the virtual Linux system provided with this book.)

The `ls` Command

Type the `ls` command at the `ted $` prompt to list the files in your current directory, as shown here:

```
ted $ ls
Desktop    file1    file2    file.sh
```

The output shows that there are four files in the directory.

Like most commands on a Linux system, the `ls` command takes *options*. Everything on a Linux system is a type of file. Using the `-F` option, you can see what type a file is:

```
ted $ ls -F
Desktop/    file1    file2@    file.sh*
```

The preceding output shows that `Desktop` is a directory because the / follows the name. `file1` is a regular file, `file2` is a *shortcut* or symbolic link because the @ symbol follows the name (discussed in Chapter 3), and `file.sh` is an executable file because the * symbol follows the name (discussed in Chapter 6).

The cd and pwd Commands

Directories are like folders in a file cabinet and help you organize your files. To display your current working directory, use the pwd command as shown here:

```
ted $ pwd
/home/ted
ted $
```

The output shows you are currently in the /home/ted directory.

To change directories, use the cd command, as shown here:

```
ted $ cd Desktop
ted $ pwd
/home/ted/Desktop
ted $ ls
file4
ted $ cd ..
ted $ pwd
/home/ted
```

Running cd Desktop moves your working directory to /home/ted/Desktop. When you run the ls command here, you see there is one file in this directory, called file4.

To return to the original working directory enter cd ... This command moves you up one directory.

NOTE Like most books, periods are used to end a sentence in this book. But, periods are often used in Linux commands. If you try a command and it fails, it's possible you placed a period at the end of a command when you shouldn't, or vice versa. In the exercises in this book, when you are instructed to type a command, the command appears in bold, including any period in the command.

The history, who, and whoami Commands

To view a list of the commands that you just ran, use the history command, as shown here:

```
ted $ history
  1  ls
  2  ls -F
  3  pwd
  4  cd Desktop
  5  pwd
  6  ls
  7  cd ..
  8  pwd
  9  history
```

There are several ways to rerun a command listed in your command history. The first method is to use the arrow keys. Start with the Up Arrow key to view the most recently run command. The other arrow keys can be used to modify a command or view other commands.

The next method is to use the `!` (or bang) key. For example, to rerun the `pwd` command, enter `!8`. That reruns command number `8`, which is `pwd`.

The final method is to run `!` with the first few characters of the command to rerun. For example, `!p` will rerun `pwd` because it is the most recent command that starts with `p`, as shown here:

```
ted $ !8
pwd
/home/ted
ted $ !p
pwd
/home/ted
```

The `whoami` command displays who you are logged in as. The `who` command shows who is currently logged in to the system and which terminal they are using, as shown here:

```
ted $ whoami
ted
ted $ who
ted       tty0       2024-05-20  08:09 (tty0)
```

These tools and more are discussed in Chapters 4 and 5.

The echo, cat, and more Commands

The `echo` command is used for several purposes. It can be used to simply see how arguments will appear, to create a file, or to modify a file as shown here:

```
ted $ echo I am soon to be Linux+ certified
I am soon to be Linux+ certified
ted $ echo I am soon to be Linux+ certified > file3
ted $ cat file3
I am soon to be Linux+ certified
ted $ more file3
I am soon to be Linux+ certified
```

The `echo` command simply echoes the arguments provided.

To save the `echo` output to a file instead of displaying it on the screen, use the > as a redirect. In the preceding example, > redirects output to `file3` instead of the screen. To see the content saved within `file3`, use either the `cat` command or `more` command.

EXAM TIP In Chapter 2, you will learn how to modify files like `file3` with a text editor named `vi` or `nano`.

The `more` command is more useful than `cat` when viewing a large file like `/etc/passwd`. Running `cat /etc/passwd` scrolls through about 50 lines faster than you can read!

The `more` command dumps out a page at a time. When you run `more /etc/passwd`, press the `Enter` key to view the next line, or the `Spacebar` to scroll another page. To quit from `more`, press the `q` key. Details on the `cat`, `more`, and `less` commands are discussed in Chapter 5.

Command-Line Continuation Literalization is covered in Chapter 3, where you will learn how the backslash, \, makes the next character literal. This is also true for the `Enter` key, which on Linux means "carriage return, new line." To ignore the meaning of the `Enter` key, use the \ as shown here for command-line continuation:

```
ted $ echo this command string is going on and on and on and it is scrolling \
off onto a new line so I need to use the '\' key
this command string is going on and on and on and it is scrolling off onto a
new line so I need to use the \ key
ted $
```

This example is simple, but you can use this feature when you have so many arguments to a command that they start to scroll off the screen.

NOTE Running `echo # hi there` results in no output because the # key means "comment." Any text following the # is ignored in Linux.

The `man`, `whatis`, and `apropos` Commands

To learn more about command arguments and options, use the `man` command (`man` is short for manual). Following is partial output after running `man ls`:

```
LS(1)                        User Commands                        LS(1)
NAME
       ls - list directory contents
SYNOPSIS
       ls [OPTION]... [FILE]...
DESCRIPTION
       List information about the FILEs (the current directory by default).
```

`man` uses `more` command features so that you can use the `Enter` key to view one line at a time, the `Spacebar` to display an entire page, and finally `q` to quit from the manual page.

Manual pages are divided into eight sections. The `ls` manual page is in section `1`, as shown in the command-heading parentheses above `LS(1)`. The command header is shown in uppercase, *but Linux is a case-sensitive operating system.* Running the `LS` command results in a `command not found` error message. The command header is always shown in uppercase because of historical reasons. It hearkens back to the days when printers and screens only used uppercase characters. The following list details the manual page sections:

Section (1) – commands any user can run
Section (2) – system calls
Section (3) – library functions
Section (4) – special files
Section (5) – configuration file formats
Section (6) – games
Section (7) – miscellaneous
Section (8) – administrative user commands

For the rare circumstance that you are not able to access a search engine like Yahoo, Google, or Bing, Linux offers `whatis` and `apropos`. Both commands search the `man` pages. The `apropos` command searches both the command field and the short description field for any match. The `whatis` command searches only the command field for an exact match.

Another way to learn more about how to use a command is to use the `--help` option after the command. For example, `ls --help` displays the following partial output:

```
ted $ ls -help
Usage: ls [OPTION]... [FILE]...
List information about the FILEs (the current directory by default).
Sort entries alphabetically if none of -cftuvSUX nor --sort is specified.

Mandatory arguments to long options are mandatory for short options too.
  -a, --all                  do not ignore entries starting with .
```

If the output is long, you may want to send the output to the `more` command by using the pipe or | key. The | key shares the \ key on the keyboard. Just run `ls --help | more` to use the `more` paginator. Technically, the pipe or | sends output of the `ls --help` command to become the input of the `more` command. Try this on the virtual machine provided with the book.

NOTE In Chapter 13, you will learn another purpose of the | symbol, where it means "or." For example, `a | b` means option `a` or option `b`.

Linux Distributions

A Linux distribution is an operating system that contains the Linux kernel and a specific selection of operating system and application software. The selection of software is distribution dependent. In this section you will learn about

- Distribution differences
- Linux derivatives

Distribution Differences

Distributions may have technical or philosophical differences. Some distributions are designed to perform a specific function in a specific environment. Others are designed based on the publisher's interpretation and adherence to open source guidelines.

Technical Differences

Technical differences between distributions can include operating system and application software, configuration files, and command differences.

For instance, Red Hat and Debian distributions have the following differences:

- They use different package managers.
- They have different names for and locations of similar configuration files.
- They have differences in some command implementations.

For example, different versions of Linux use different methods to install software. Red Hat Enterprise Linux (RHEL) currently uses `rpm`, `yum`, and `dnf` as its package managers, whereas Debian uses `dpkg` and `apt`.

NOTE As of RHEL 8, Red Hat uses the DNF package manager.

Several configuration files are executed when you log in to a Linux system. The login configuration file in Red Hat is `/etc/bashrc`, and the login configuration file in Debian is `/etc/bash.bashrc`.

Creating new user accounts is done with the `useradd` command. The `useradd` command in Red Hat does not have the same functionality as the `useradd` command in Debian. The Red Hat version has the additional feature of adding a user to a different group. (More details in Chapter 4.)

Philosophical Differences

Most philosophical differences between distributions are based on their interpretation of open source licensing. For example, Fedora and Debian will only use free and open source software, whereas Red Hat allows proprietary (copyrighted) software.

Red Hat

In 1994, Marc Ewing developed his own Linux distribution called Red Hat Linux. In 1995, Bob Young purchased Red Hat and merged his UNIX software distribution company with Marc Ewing's Red Hat company. Red Hat is a commercial root distribution using the Linux kernel. Red Hat will provide its source code, but derivatives must remove any reference to Red Hat and components that are sold by Red Hat.

Fedora

Fedora is a root Linux distribution that has a large development community. Fedora uses faster release cycles to provide the latest technology to its users. Because the Fedora approach is largely experimental, it should *not* be used in a production environment.

The Fedora project is sponsored by Red Hat. Many of the advances developed in Fedora find their way to Red Hat Enterprise.

NOTE Red Hat Enterprise has a separate set of quality control tests from Fedora, and Red Hat provides support for up to 8 years versus 18 months for Fedora.

Debian

Debian is a root Linux distribution that was started by Ian Murdock in 1993. Debian's goal was to provide an operating system based on the principles of free software. Debian created the Debian Free Software Guidelines, which are used to determine what software may be included in Debian.

NOTE Initially, Debian provided two distributions: one distribution used the Linux kernel and the other distribution used the FreeBSD kernel. Debian discontinued development of the FreeBSD distribution and is now managed by the Free Software Foundation.

Linux Derivatives

Derivatives are operating systems derived from a distribution (root distribution) or another derivative. The derivative operating system may focus on a specific task by adding more or less software or a modified kernel.

NOTE A great deal of information on distributions and packages associated with distributions can be found at https://distrowatch.com.

The Linux kernel has several root distributions and many derivative distributions. Let's take a look at a few derivatives of both the Red Hat and Debian root distributions.

Red Hat Derivatives

SUSE and Oracle Unbreakable Linux are examples of Red Hat derivatives.

SUSE Software und System-Entwicklung (SUSE) developed by a German-based open source company, and the community version OpenSUSE, both use YaST rather than Anaconda as a setup program, `zypper` rather than `yum` as a package management application, and AppArmor (by default) over SELinux for enhanced security. Some of these products are covered in Chapters 11 and 16.

NOTE It is possible to disable AppArmor in SUSE and install SELinux.

Oracle Unbreakable Linux Oracle Linux is a binary-compatible derivative of Red Hat Enterprise Linux. Oracle customers have a choice of a compatible kernel or the Unbreakable Enterprise Kernel (UEK). The UEK is optimized to provide better performance. For details visit https://docs.oracle.com/en/operating-systems/uek/

Debian Derivatives

Although Debian has multiple derivatives, we are going to briefly look at two: Kali and Ubuntu.

Kali Kali is one of several Debian derivatives used for penetration testing. Kali is an example of creating a derivative for a specific task.

Ubuntu Ubuntu is one of the more popular Debian derivatives. Ubuntu, Linux for human beings, is an example where design philosophy takes precedence. The word *Ubuntu* is defined as a quality that includes the essential human virtues of compassion and humanity. Ubuntu's design philosophy was to make Linux more usable for human beings.

The Ubuntu Long-Term Support versions (Ubuntu LTS) are the only versions recommended for production environments because these offer at least 5 years of updates. Other versions are similar to Fedora in that they are experimental, and products introduced may disappear in future versions.

Linux Mint and Xubuntu are examples of Ubuntu derivatives.

EXAM TIP The exam focuses on Red Hat 7 derivatives and higher and Debian 10 derivatives and higher.

Common Linux Implementations

Because Linux is distributed under the GPL, software vendors can customize Linux to operate in a variety of roles, including the following:

- Using Linux on the desktop
- Using Linux on the server
- Using Linux on mobile devices
- Using Linux for virtualization
- Using Linux with cloud computing
- Using embedded Linux

Linux on the Desktop

Linux can be optimized to function extremely well as a desktop system. However, Linux has been somewhat slow to make inroads into this market. As of 2022, Linux had garnered only about 2 percent of the desktop market share, while Windows occupies over 90 percent.

There has been a historical lack of desktop productivity applications available for Linux. Fortunately, many productivity applications are available today that make Linux a viable option for the desktop (for example, LibreOffice).

Many vendors have been working on desktop-oriented Linux distributions that seek to simplify it. They have bundled application suites such as LibreOffice and added an easy-to-use graphical interface. Here are some of the more popular desktop Linux distributions:

- Ubuntu Desktop Edition
- openSUSE
- Fedora Desktop Edition

Linux on the Server

Linux works great as a server. In fact, Linux has experienced widespread acceptance in the server room, much more so than on the desktop. Depending on the services provided, Linux occupies between 40 and 97 percent of the server market share. This is because Linux can assume a variety of server roles, including the following, and perform them extremely well:

- **File and print server** Using the Network File System (NFS), the Common UNIX Printing System (CUPS), or Samba services, system administrators can configure Linux to provide network storage and printing of users' files.
- **Web and database server** Linux has been widely deployed as a web server. In fact, the most popular web service currently used on Linux is the Apache web server combined with MySQL, MariaDB, NoSQL, or PostgreSQL.
- **E-mail server** A variety of e-mail services are available for Linux that can turn your system into an enterprise-class mail server.
- **Supercomputer** Linux is the preferred operating system for deploying high-powered supercomputers.

The widespread popularity of Linux as a server is due to a number of reasons. These include stability, performance, and cost. Red Hat offers the Red Hat Enterprise Linux (RHEL) Server distribution, which has a proven track record as an enterprise-class server. SUSE Linux Enterprise Server (SLES) is also optimized for servers.

Mobile Linux

Linux has nearly taken over the mobile device market in the form of the Android operating system provided by Google, accounting for almost 50 percent of the smartphone market. Android is so popular for the following reasons:

- **Price** It is much cheaper than iOS.
- **Performance** Android performs extremely well on mobile devices.
- **App support** A plethora of apps are available for Android devices.

Linux and Virtualization

Virtualization is an aspect of information technology that is gaining a great deal of momentum in the industry.

Traditionally, one operating system (for example, Linux) is installed on a computer that has full rein over all the resources in the system, including the following:

- RAM
- Processor time
- Storage devices
- Network interfaces

Virtualization offers an alternative deployment model. Virtualization pools multiple operating system instances onto the same computer and allows them to run concurrently. To do this, virtualization uses a mediator called a *hypervisor* to manage access to system resources.

Each operating system instance is installed into a *virtual machine* and functions just like a physical host. This allows multiple platforms, including Windows and Linux, to run at the same time on the same hardware. This is a huge benefit for software developers and testers, making it much easier to test how an application in development performs on different platforms.

Several virtualization platforms are available for Linux, including the following:

- Xen (open source)
- VMware Workstation, Player, ESX, and ESXi (proprietary)
- VirtualBox (open source)
- KVM (open source)

These hypervisors turn the Linux system into a hypervisor that can run virtual machines.

Linux and Cloud Computing

Virtualization is a key component of cloud computing, where the hardware, software, and/or network resources are moved offsite and delivered over a network connection, and even over the Internet.

With cloud computing, a provider on the Internet deploys a new Linux virtual machine at its site. Customers pay fees to access this virtual server through their organization's network connection. The provider assumes all the responsibility of implementing, maintaining, and securing the server. This model is referred to *Infrastructure as a Service (IaaS)*.

In addition to IaaS, there are other cloud computing models, including the following:

- **Software as a Service (SaaS)** Provides access to software and data through the cloud. Examples of SaaS include Gmail, Outlook 365, and Salesforce.
- **Platform as a Service (PaaS)** Provides access to a full solution suite to accomplish a computing task, including networking and storage. An example of PaaS is HTML website hosting.

Many organizations set up Linux and virtualization using a private cloud, offering on-demand computing resources to other users in the organization.

Embedded Linux

One benefit of Linux is that it can be optimized down to a small footprint for IoT (Internet of Things) devices. Linux is ideal for embedding within intelligent devices such as the following:

- Network routers
- Video game systems
- Smart TVs
- Smartphones and tablets

Linux is customized to provide just essential functions, and unnecessary elements are removed. The operating system is finally embedded into flash memory chips within the device.

Chapter Review

This chapter provided you with an overview of the history of the Linux kernel and structure of Linux-based distributions. It also defined the differences between Linux distributions and derivatives and explained why the different distributions exist. Lastly, it described the various environments in which Linux-based distributions may be found. Here are some key takeaways from the chapter:

- Linux is an open source monolithic kernel.
- Linus Torvalds first developed the Linux kernel and Linux operating system in the early 1990s.
- Linux is licensed under the GPL.
- An operating system consists of kernel system software and application software.
- The kernel layer is the core of the operating system and provides process, memory, and task management.
- Running `passwd -S <username>` displays a user's account status.
- System software is used to manage system resources.
- Application software is used to perform user tasks.
- A Linux-based distribution contains the Linux kernel (possibly modified) and a selection of operating and application software.
- Linux-based distributions provide a stable environment for embedded systems and desktop, server, and cloud environments.

Pre-Assessment Test

Prior to reading the rest of the chapters of this book, first complete this pre-assessment test to identify key areas to focus on as you study for the CompTIA Linux+ exam.

In this activity, you will be presented with 90 assessment questions that mirror the type you are likely to see on the real exam. The weighting of objective domains used in the real exams is approximated in this activity.

To make this experience as realistic and accurate as possible, you should allocate 90 minutes of uninterrupted time to complete your practice exam. Turn off your phone, computer, TV, and music player and find a comfortable place to work. Set a timer for 90 minutes and then begin this activity. Allowing more than 90 minutes to complete this experience will yield inaccurate results. Be sure to work through all the questions in this activity before checking answers. Again, this pre-assessment should mimic a real testing environment as much as possible. Wait until you have answered every question before checking the answers.

Once the pre-assessment test is complete, use the "Quick Answer Key" along with the "In-Depth Answer Explanations" sections to evaluate the responses. Keep track of the number of questions answered correctly and compare this number with the table found in the "Analyzing Your Results" section. This table will give you valuable feedback based on the number of correct answers given. Finally, compare the questions missed with the domain maps at the end of this activity to identify areas to focus on as you study.

Ready? Set the timer for 90 minutes and begin!

Questions

1. Which bash configuration files are used for non-login bash shell sessions? (Choose two.)

A. `/etc/profile`

B. `/etc/bashrc`

C. `~/.bashrc`

D. `~/.profile`

E. `~/.bash_profile`

2. Which of the following commands can be used to schedule a job to run at 4 P.M.? (Choose two.)

A. `at 4PM`

B. `at noon+4`

C. `at 16`

D. `at teatime`

E. `at "4 o'clock"`

3. You've opened the `/var/opt/myapp/settings.txt` file in the `vi` editor. You need to enter new text into the file. Which key will switch a user into insert mode from normal or "command" mode?

   A. `i`

   B. `w`

   C. `z`

   D. `r`

   E. `x`

4. YAML files that are used to configure network cards to use DHCP or set up static IP addressing can be found where?

   A. `/etc/X11`

   B. `/etc/dnf`

   C. `/etc/yum.repos.d`

   D. `/etc/netplan`

5. To create a new directory in a user's home directory named `MyFiles`, which command would you use?

   A. `mkdir ~/myfiles`

   B. `mkdir ~/MyFiles`

   C. `md ~/myFiles`

   D. `mkdir ~ MyFiles`

   E. `md ~/MyFiles`

6. The `sealert` utility is used to determine that a user cannot access a file. Which command would aid in troubleshooting by showing access settings?

   A. `ls -s`

   B. `ls -Z`

   C. `ls -l`

   D. `restorecon`

   E. `aa-disable`

7. Which `vi` command-line mode commands can be used to save changes to the current file being edited and close the `vi` editor? (Choose three.)

   A. `ZZ`

   B. `:wq`

   C. `:q`

   D. `:q!`

   E. `:x`

8. Which command would you use to change the permissions of a file named `widgets.odt` such that the file owner can edit the file but no other users on the system will be allowed to view or modify it?

   A. `chmod 660 widgets.odt`

   B. `chmod 640 widgets.odt`

   C. `chmod 777 widgets.odt`

   D. `chmod 600 widgets.odt`

9. Which command would you use to change the permissions of a file named `projectx.odt` such that the file owner can edit the file, users who are members of the group that owns the file can view and edit it, and users who are not owners and don't belong to the owning group cannot view or modify it?

   A. `chmod 660 projectx.odt`

   B. `chmod 640 projectx.odt`

   C. `chmod 777 projectx.odt`

   D. `chmod 644 projectx.odt`

10. Which `usermod` command options must be used to add user accounts as members of a secondary group? (Choose two.)

    A. `-a`

    B. `-s`

    C. `-g`

    D. `-p`

    E. `-G`

11. Which control structure processes over and over as long as a specified condition evaluates to `false`?

    A. `while`

    B. `until`

    C. `for`

    D. `case`

12. For designing the implementation of a new Linux server in the company's network, the server will function as an internal file and print server for the organization. Employees will save their work-related files in shared storage locations on the server, and print jobs for shared printers will be managed by the server as well. What services should be included in the specifications? (Choose two.)

    A. Apache

    B. MySQL

    C. Samba

D. Telnet

E. Pure-FTP

F. CUPS

13. Which process takes over and kills processes that use too much memory because they score too high under this process's monitoring system?

A. `BOMB`

B. `BOM`

C. `KaBOOM`

D. `BOOM`

E. `OOM`

14. Which tools can be used to check for open network ports? (Choose two.)

A. `nmap`

B. `lsof`

C. `pwconv`

D. `ssh`

E. `cpio`

15. To insert a new kernel module into a Linux system that has no dependencies, which tool is best to use to utilize the module?

A. `dmesg`

B. `modinfo`

C. `insmod`

D. `depmod`

E. `lsmod`

16. Which of the following commands is used to find the domain's mail server?

A. `dig`

B. `ping`

C. `traceroute`

D. `route`

17. Which command updates every few seconds, displaying the routers that packets use to reach their destination?

A. `mtr`

B. `traceroute`

C. `tracert`

D. `iftop`

E. `top`

18. When using local authentication on a Linux system, which file contains the passwords for the user accounts?

    A. `/etc/passwd`

    B. `/etc/group`

    C. `/etc/gshadow`

    D. `/etc/shadow`

19. Consider the following entry from the `/etc/passwd` file:

    ```
    algreer:x:1001:100:Albert Greer:/home/algreer:/bin/bash
    ```

    What user ID (UID) has been assigned to this user account?

    A. `algreer`

    B. `1001`

    C. `100`

    D. `Albert Greer`

20. Consider the following entry from the `/etc/shadow` file:

    ```
    kmorgan:$2a$05$KL1DbTBqpSEMiL.2FoI3ue4bdyR.eL6GMKs7MU6
    .nZl5SCC7/REUS:15043:1:60:7:5::
    ```

    In how many days will this account be disabled after the user's password has expired?

    A. One day

    B. Seven days

    C. Five days

    D. Null value (never)

21. Which of the following contains files that populate new users' home directories when created with `useradd`?

    A. `/etc/login.defs`

    B. `/etc/default/useradd`

    C. `/etc/skel`

    D. `/etc/default/grub`

22. You need to create a new account for a user named Ian Mausi on a Linux system and specify a username of `imausi`, a full name of Ian Mausi, a default shell of `/bin/bash`, and that a home directory be created. Which command will do this?

    A. `useradd -c "Ian Mausi" -m -s "/bin/bash" imausi`

    B. `useradd -c "Ian Mausi" -m -s "/bin/bash" -u imausi`

    C. `usermod -c "Ian Mausi" -m -s "/bin/bash" imausi`

    D. `useradd -c "Ian Mausi" -s "/bin/bash" imausi`

23. Which file keeps a list of intentionally untracked files that `git` should ignore?
    A. `.gitnot`
    B. `gitnot`
    C. `.gitignore`
    D. `.git`

24. Command substitution, which allows a command to run within a command, is performed with which operators? (Choose two.)
    A. `` ` ` ``
    B. `$( )`
    C. `' '`
    D. `" "`
    E. `${ }`

25. An administrator runs `mount /dev/sdb2 /external` and realizes they have made a mistake because a filesystem was already mounted to `/external`. What happened to the files that were initially mounted onto `/external`?
    A. The files are destroyed and can only be recovered from backup tape.
    B. Linux does not allow for a filesystem to be mounted onto another.
    C. The files are temporarily merged with the new filesystem.
    D. Nothing. When the administrator runs `umount /dev/sdb2`, the files will reappear unharmed.

26. A script that requires the end user to enter the name of their supervisor will use which of the following lines to input the user's response into a variable named `SUP`?
    A. `read SUP`
    B. `input SUP`
    C. `prompt SUP`
    D. `query SUP`

27. When a new user attempts to run a script while in their home directory using the `./runme.sh` command from the shell prompt, they see the following error: `bash: ./runme.sh: Permission denied.`

    Which resolution will fix this issue?
    A. Copy the file to the `~/bin` directory.
    B. Add the home directory to the `PATH` environment variable.
    C. Enter `chmod u+x runme.sh` at the shell prompt.
    D. Change the sha-bang line of the script to `#!/bin/sh`.

28. Which of the following will make for the fastest restore, and fewest number of tapes to restore, assuming the system fails shortly after the Friday backup completes? (Key: F=Full, I=Incremental, D=Differential.)

A. Mon-F1, Tue-D1, Wed-I1, Thu-D2, Fri-F2

B. Mon-F1, Tue-D1, Wed-I1, Thu-D2, Fri-I2

C. Mon-F1, Tue-D1, Wed-D2, Thu-D3, Fri-D4

D. Mon-F1, Tue-I1, Wed-I2, Thu-I3, Fri-I4

29. Which of the following commands can convert a shell variable to an environment variable?

A. `env`

B. `export`

C. `set`

D. `chmod`

30. Which command would an administrator run to disable the loading of the unneeded kernel module `tg3`? (Choose two.)

A. `echo "blacklist tg3" > /etc/modprobe.d/network.conf`

B. `echo "blacklist tg3" >> /etc/modprobe.d/blacklist.conf`

C. `echo "blacklist tg3" >> /etc/modprobe.d/network.conf`

D. `echo "blacklist tg3" > /etc/modprobe.d/blacklist.conf`

E. `echo "blacklist tg3" << /etc/modprobe.d/blacklist.conf`

31. Which command can uncover a remote user's login name and password when they connect using Telnet or TFP?

A. `dig`

B. `nslookup`

C. `tcpdump`

D. `ip`

32. Which protocols encrypt the network traffic? (Choose two.)

A. SSH

B. FTP

C. Telnet

D. HTTPS

E. Finger

33. Which of the following is not a single sign-on system?

A. RADIUS

B. Kerberos

C. TACACS+

D. Circumference

E. LDAP

34. Consider the following IP address: 172.17.8.10/22. Which subnet mask is assigned to this address?

A. 255.255.252.0

B. 255.255.0.0

C. 255.255.255.0

D. 255.255.255.252

35. Which command would assign the `ens32` interface an IP address of 172.17.8.1 with a subnet mask of 255.255.0.0 and a broadcast address of 172.17.255.255?

A. `ip addr set ens32 172.17.8.1/255.255.0.0 bcast 172.17.255.255`

B. `ip addr 172.17.8.1/255.255.0.0 broadcast 172.17.255.255 dev ens32`

C. `ip addr set 172.17.8.1/255.255.0.0 broadcast 172.17.255.255 dev ens32`

D. `ip addr add 172.17.8.1/255.255.0.0 broadcast 172.17.255.255 dev ens32`

36. Which directive in `/etc/sysconfig/network/ifcfg-eth0` is used to specify whether the interface is automatically enabled when the system is booted?

A. `STARTMODE`

B. `BOOTPROTO`

C. `IPADDR`

D. `USERCONTROL`

37. Which system keeps one NIC sleeping and awakens when another NIC fails?

A. Active-passive

B. Active-active

C. Load balancing

D. Aggregation

38. For security reasons, a Linux system should resolve hostnames using the DNS server before trying to resolve them using the `/etc/hosts` file. Which file is reconfigured to change the name resolver order?

A. `/etc/resolv.conf`

B. `/etc/sysconfig/network/ifcfg-eth0`

C. `/etc/nsswitch.conf`

D. `/etc/sysconfig/services`

39. The `/etc/sudoers` file on your Linux system is configured by default such that users must supply their password when using `sudo` instead of the root password. Which commands are *best* used to modify the `/etc/sudoers` file? (Choose two.)

    A. `gedit`

    B. `vi`

    C. `notepad`

    D. `sudoedit`

    E. `visudo`

40. Which setting made in the proper file in the `/etc/pam.d/` directory tracks login attempts and locks out users after multiple attempts?

    A. `pam_access.so`

    B. `pam_loginuid.so`

    C. `pam_limits.so`

    D. `pam_tally2.so`

41. To secure the `sshd` service running on a Linux system from hackers, it is decided to configure it to listen for SSH requests on a port other than the default of `22`. Which directive in the `/etc/ssh/sshd_config` file can do this?

    A. `Port`

    B. `BindAddress`

    C. `Protocol`

    D. `Tunnel`

42. You want to write the `stdout` from the `ps` command to a file named `myprocesses` in the `/tmp` directory without overwriting the existing contents of that file. Which command will do this?

    A. `ps 3 < /tmp/myprocesses`

    B. `ps 1 > /tmp/myprocesses`

    C. `ps 2 <> /tmp/myprocesses`

    D. `ps 4 >> /tmp/myprocesses`

43. Which option to the `passwd` command is the same as `--status` that lists a user's password expiration parameters?

    A. `--STATUS`

    B. `-s`

    C. `-S`

    D. `--ss`

44. An administrator must configure the GRUB2 bootloader such that it will boot the first operating system in the boot menu by default unless an end user manually selects an operating system within the timeout period. Which file must the administrator modify to create this setting?

    A. `/etc/default/grub`

    B. `/boot/grub2/grub.cfg`

    C. `/boot/grub2`

    D. `/etc/grub.d/10_linux`

45. Which commands will switch a Linux system from a graphical environment to a multiuser text-based environment? (Choose two.)

    A. `systemctl isolate runlevel3.target`

    B. `systemctl isolate rescue.target`

    C. `systemctl isolate multi-user.target`

    D. `systemctl isolate runlevel5.target`

    E. `systemctl isolate graphical.target`

46. The system administrator just added a third SATA hard disk drive to the Linux system and needs to create a GPT partition on it. Which command should they use to do this?

    A. `fdisk /dev/sdb`

    B. `fdisk /dev/sdc`

    C. `fdisk /dev/sd2`

    D. `fdisk /dev/sd3`

47. On a Linux system with 16GB of RAM, two additional SATA hard disks (`/dev/sdb` and `/dev/sdc`) are added to the system and a partition is created on each one. The partitions are defined as LVM physical volumes. Which command is run to add both physical volumes to a new volume group named `DATA`?

    A. `lvscan -v`

    B. `vgcreate DATA /dev/sdb1 /dev/sdc1`

    C. `pvcreate /dev/sdb1`

    D. `lvcreate -L 700G -n research DATA`

    E. `pvcreate /dev/sdc1`

48. Which are true about logical volumes? (Choose three.)

    A. Can create and delete logical volumes

    B. Can adjust sound levels symmetrically

    C. Can create snapshots

    D. Can adjust sound levels asymmetrically

    E. Can change sizes of logical volumes

49. A new Linux system was installed about a week ago. Three days ago, an administrative user compiled and installed a new application from source code. Now, the Ethernet interface in the system sporadically goes offline. Which command does the administrator run to see the boot messages generated by the system when it was in a pristine state shortly after being installed?

    A. `journalctl -b 2`

    B. `logger -p 2`

    C. `journalctl -b`

    D. `journalctl -b -2`

50. The following content is listed in which file?

```
# Virtual consoles
tty1
tty2
tty3
```

    A. `/etc/securetty`

    B. `/dev/tty`

    C. `/etc/yum.conf`

    D. `/etc/ld.so.conf`

51. After installing GIT, which two configuration properties must be defined before issuing a commit?

    A. Username and e-mail address

    B. MAC address and project name

    C. IP address and MAC address

    D. Username and password

52. Which of the following is *not* a Linux desktop environment?

    A. Gnome

    B. VNC

    C. Unity

    D. Cinnamon

53. Which of the following modifies the `linux` parameter to override the default boot target so that an administrator can change a forgotten `root` password?

    A. `init=1`

    B. `systemd.unit=rescue.target`

    C. `systemd.unit=emergency.target`

    D. `init=S`

54. Which of the following allows the network administrator to add a default gateway of `10.5.3.1`? (Choose two.)

   A. `route add gateway 10.5.3.1`

   B. `ip route add default via 10.5.3.1`

   C. `ip route add default 10.5.3.1`

   D. `route add default gw 10.5.3.1`

   E. `route add default 10.5.3.1`

55. Consider the following routing table:

```
# netstat -rn
Kernel IP routing table
Destination    Gateway Genmask        Flags MSS Window irtt Iface
192.168.8.0    0.0.0.0 255.255.255.0 U      0   0       0    eth0
```

   Given this routing table, why does the following command fail?

```
route add default gw 10.5.3.1
```

   A. A default route is already defined.

   B. Default routes must be defined on static networks only.

   C. Because there is no route to 10.5.3.1.

   D. The genmask value must be 255.0.0.0.

56. The network administrator modified a configuration file to utilize a tier 1 timeserver. Since making the change, time updates via NTP are no longer occurring. What most likely has occurred?

   A. Port 123 is blocked on the firewall.

   B. The network administrator forgot to reboot the system.

   C. The network administrator improperly ran the `timedatectl` command.

   D. The feature is not available on Red Hat strains of Linux and must be converted to a Debian strain.

57. Amy attempts to update the file `/etc/apt/sources.list` and gets the error message "Operation not permitted." Which command does she need to run to write content to `/etc/apt/sources.list`?

   A. `chattr -i /etc/apt/sources.list`

   B. `chattr -I /etc/apt/sources.list`

   C. `chmod 755 /etc/apt/sources.list`

   D. `setfacl -m m:rw /etc/apt/sources.list`

58. Which of the following is *not* an initialization system used on Linux?
    A. systemd
    B. Upstart
    C. SysVinit
    D. sysinit
59. Which of the following describes the columns of the `/etc/fstab` file best?
    A. Device, mount point, filesystem type, options, fsck order, dump option
    B. Device, mount point, filesystem type, options, dump option, fsck order
    C. Device, mount point, options, filesystem type, dump option, fsck order
    D. Mount point, device, filesystem type, options, dump option, fsck order
60. Which are *not* journaled filesystems? (Choose two)
    A. ext2
    B. ext3
    C. isofs
    D. xfs
    E. ntfs
61. Which is *not* a method that results in an `ext3` type filesystem?
    A. `mke2fs -j /dev/sda2`
    B. `mkfs.ext3 /dev/sdb3`
    C. `tune2fs -t ext3 /dev/sdd4`
    D. `mkfs -t ext3 /dev/sdc7`
    E. `tune2fs -j /dev/sde8`
62. Which command shows who is logged in and which commands they are running?
    A. `whoami`
    B. `whom`
    C. `who`
    D. `w`
    E. `id`
63. Running the `df` command, the administrator sees they have 20 percent of disk space available, but running `df -i` they see there are no inodes left. Why cannot they not add new files?
    A. Remove files to free up file handles
    B. Run `mkfs.ext3` to change inode size

C. Increase the block size to > 4KiB blocks

D. Resize the filesystem

64. Which command deletes the user account *and* removes the user's files from their home directory plus their e-mail?

A. `usermod -r`

B. `useradd -d`

C. `userdel -d`

D. `userdel -r`

E. `usermod -d`

65. Which commands conduct password expiration for users? (Choose three.)

A. `usermod`

B. `chage`

C. `passwd`

D. `password`

E. `shadow`

66. Which of the following is the local system time zone configuration file?

A. `/etc/local/time`

B. `/lib/localtime`

C. `/usr/lib/localtime`

D. `/etc/localtime`

E. `/usr/bin/localtime`

67. Which option to the `localectl` command displays the current locale?

A. `list-locales`

B. `status`

C. `-l`

D. `-s`

68. Which environment variable will override all `LC_*` variables?

A. `LC_ALL`

B. `LC_NAME`

C. `LC_CTYPE`

D. `LANG`

69. Running `ls -l` displays the following output:

```
-rwsr-xr-x  1  todd   manf   55322  Mar  18  10:20   runme
```

When username `montrie` executes the `runme` command, what `EUID` will it run at?

A. `montrie`

B. `todd`

C. `root`

D. `manf`

70. So that new directories have a default permission of 750 and regular files have a default permission of 640, what must the `unmask`? (Choose two.)

A. `026`

B. `0026`

C. `027`

D. `0027`

E. `0036`

F. `036`

71. User Jeongeun gets an error message that she cannot create a new file because there is no more disk space; however, she is well below her `quota` use. What is the next command she runs to view total disk space utilization?

A. `quota`

B. `df -i`

C. `du -sh`

D. `df -h`

72. User Iohn notices that system performance is slowing and suspects that memory shortages are the issue. He cannot add additional memory, so as a quick fix decides to add a swapfile to use as additional swap space. After creating the swapfile and setting up the Linux swap area, he notices no change in performance. What command did he most likely forget to run?

A. `swapon`

B. `swapoff`

C. `mkswap`

D. `mount`

73. User Quiñonez discovers that she can get better disk drive performance by converting from `bfq` or `noop` to `mq-deadline`. What command should she run for proper conversion to `mq-deadline`?

A. `cat mq-deadline < /sys/block/sda/queue/scheduler`

B. `cat mq-deadlne > /sys/block/sda/queue/scheduler`

C. `echo mq-deadlinew > /sys/block/sda/queue/scheduler`

D. `echo mq-deadline < /sys/block/sda/queue/scheduler`

74. User Elimu is working on a bash script. The script contains this `case` statement:

```
case $fruit ________
  orange|tangerine)  echo taste like orange ;;
  *berry)   echo taste like berry ;;
  *)        echo Error: fruit not found ;;
esac
```

Which command should Elimu place into the blank?

A. `at`

B. `in`

C. `of`

D. `if`

75. User Wade is working on a bash script. The script contains this `for` statement:

```
for fruit in orange apple berry grape
do
    echo this fruit tastes like $fruit
_______
```

Which command should Wade place into the blank?

A. `end`

B. `rof`

C. `od`

D. `done`

76. A server administrator created 20 identical Linux instances. When testing network functionally of each instance, the admin notices the cloned devices have identical hostnames. What should the admin do on each device to change the hostnames of the devices permanently?

A. Run the `host` command

B. Edit the `/etc/dhcp/dhclient.conf` file

C. Run the `nslookup` command

D. Edit the `/etc/sysconfig/network` file

77. User Walter needs to examine the performance of his RAID array. He is learning how to use `mdadm` but is unsure as to which option to `mdadm` will show negative issues with the system (for example, disk failures). Which of the following are the best ways for Walter to accomplish this? (Choose three.)

A. `mdadm --build`

B. `mdadm --follow`

C. `mdadm -F`

D. `mdadm --monitor`

78. Users Landon and Lonnie monitor the virtual machines. One of the applications they use requires `telnet`, which unfortunately uses the same escape string `^]`. Which option to `virsh` allows them to change the escape string to `^[`?

    A. `--debug`

    B. `--chstr`

    C. `--esc`

    D. `--escape`

79. System administrators Laeia and Liara work side by side examining accounting results of disk drive performance. Laeia believes that poor performance is related to aging hard drives, and she consults with Liara as to the next steps. Liara knows that exact command to run to check for bad blocks. She recommends which of the following?

    A. `blockcheck`

    B. `badblocks`

    C. `kill`

    D. `bbcheck`

80. Sorana desires to display memory and swap utilization using the `free` command. Unlike `iostat`, `sar`, and others, `free` does *not* update periodically by default. Which command can she run with `free` to automatically display updates every two seconds, refreshing the screen every time?

    A. `period`

    B. `watch`

    C. `free`

    D. `twosec`

81. User Ugo decides that he wants new files and directories below the directory `work` to automatically have the same group permission as `work`. Which command can Ugo run to do this?

    A. `chmod g+s work`

    B. `chmod +a work`

    C. `chmod g=w work`

    D. `chmod g=rw work`

82. Zhang is a network administrator who needs to open the firewall to allow web access. Which of the following would do this for her?

    A. `firewall-cmd --zone=public --allow=http`

    B. `firewall-cmd --zone=public --add-service=http`

C. `firewall-cmd --zone=public --add-service=web`

D. `firewall-cmd --zone=public --add=http`

83. Henri is a network administrator who is required to open new ports for `NTP` and `HTTPd`. He needs to display the current firewall settings using `iptables`. Which of the following would do this for him?

A. `iptables -d`

B. `iptables -s`

C. `iptables -L`

D. `iptables -F`

84. Petra is a system administrator working on a Linux system running `SysVinit`. She runs the following as `root`:

```
# chkconfig --list | grep auditd
auditd 0:off 1:off 2:off 3:off 4:off 5:off 6:off
```

Which of the following would she run to enable `auditd` to start at runs state `3` or `5` upon reboot?

A. `chkconfig --level 35 auditd start`

B. `chkconfig --level 35 auditd on`

C. `chkconfig --level 35 start auditd`

D. `chkconfig --level 35 on auditd`

85. Milos is a storage administrator and notices disk space is running out on one of the logical volumes. Before using `lvextend` to enlarge the volume, what must he do first?

A. Know which volume group device to extend.

B. Reboot the system.

C. Restart the logical volume service.

D. Restart meta-device management.

86. Ushna is a cloud administrator who would like to orchestrate the setup of 500 Centos Linux servers. Of the tools listed, which is the one she would *not* choose as part of the configuration?

A. `Cloud-init`

B. Orchestrate

C. Anaconda

D. Kickstart

87. Thanasi, a cloud engineer, is updating files for orchestration. The following is some sample content that he is editing with `/bin/vi`:

```
yum_repos:
     epel-testing:
          baseurl: http://ftp.wheezy.com/pub/epel/$basesearch
          enable: false
          failovermethod: priority
```

This is most likely what type of file?

A. SAML

B. XML

C. JSON

D. YAML

88. Teliana, a cloud engineer, is updating files for orchestration. The following is some sample content that she is editing with `/bin/vi`:

```
{
     "firstName": "Maria",
     "lastName": "Bueno",
     "age": 25,
```

This is most likely what type of file?

A. SAML

B. XML

C. JSON

D. YAML

89. System administrator Juan has just enabled SELinux and is finding it very difficult to work with. He is just testing the system and does not require it to be fully functional. What should he run that will simply warn of any SELinux offenses?

A. `setenforce permissive`

B. `setenforce enforcing`

C. `setenforce disabled`

D. `setenforce warning`

90. System administrator Katerina is running a foreground job named `windsim` and she would like to stop it temporarily and have it continue later. What key sequence does she run to stop the job?

A. `Ctrl-C`

B. `Ctrl-Z`

C. `Ctrl-\`

D. `Ctrl-S`

Quick Answer Key

1. B, C
2. A, D
3. A
4. D
5. B
6. B
7. A, B, E
8. D
9. A
10. A, E
11. B
12. C, F
13. E
14. A, B
15. C
16. A
17. A
18. D
19. B
20. C
21. C
22. A
23. C
24. A, B
25. D
26. A
27. C
28. A
29. B
30. B, C
31. C
32. A, D
33. D
34. A
35. D
36. A
37. A
38. C
39. D, E
40. D
41. A
42. D
43. C
44. A
45. A, C
46. B
47. B
48. A, C, E
49. A
50. A
51. A
52. B
53. C
54. B, D
55. C
56. A
57. A
58. D
59. B
60. A, C
61. C
62. D
63. A
64. D
65. A, B, C
66. D
67. B
68. A
69. B
70. C, D
71. D
72. A
73. C
74. B
75. D
76. B
77. B, C, D
78. D
79. B
80. B
81. A
82. B
83. C
84. B
85. A
86. B
87. D
88. C
89. A
90. B

In-Depth Answer Explanations

1. ☑ **B** and **C** are correct. Both `/etc/bashrc` and `~/.bashrc` are used to configure non-login shell sessions, although other files may be used on some distributions.
   ☒ **A**, **D**, and **E** are incorrect. The `/etc/profile`, `~/.profile`, and `~/.bash_profile` files are used to configure login shell sessions. (Domain 1. System Management)

2. ☑ **A** and **D** are correct. Users can run `at 4PM`, `at 16:00`, or `at teatime` to schedule a job to run at 4 P.M.
   ☒ **B**, **C**, and **E** are incorrect. These other forms of running `at` will return a syntax error message. (Domain 3. Scripting, Containers, and Automation)

3. ☑ **A** is correct. Press the `Insert` or `i` key to enter insert mode in the `vi` editor.
   ☒ **B**, **C**, **D**, and **E** are incorrect. The `Esc` key is used to return to normal (command) mode from insert mode in the `vi` editor. The `a` key is used to append text after the cursor. The `o` key opens a new line below before allowing for text to be inserted. The `r` key is used to replace a single character, and the `x` key is used by the `vi` editor to delete a single character. The `w` and `z` keys are non-functional in normal mode. (Domain 1. System Management)

4. ☑ **D** is correct. Save a network configuration inside the `/etc/netplan/config.yaml` file to automate the configuration at boot time.
   ☒ **A**, **B**, and **C** are incorrect. The `/etc/X11` file is for the X-Window GUI setups, and the `/etc/dnf` and `/etc/yum.repos.d` files point to software installation repositories. (Domain 1. System Management)

5. ☑ **B** is correct. The `mkdir` command is used to create new directories in the filesystem, where ~ stands for the user's home directory (in this case, `/home/`*`user`*`/Myfiles` or `~/MyFiles`).
   ☒ **A** is incorrect because it uses the wrong case for the directory name. **C** and **E** are incorrect because they use the incorrect command for creating new directories (`md`). **D** is incorrect because it omits the / character after the tilde. (Domain 1. System Management)

6. ☑ **B** is correct. Running `ls -Z` will allow the user to see the current SELinux settings and determine whether or not they need to be changed.
   ☒ **A**, **C**, **D**, and **E** are incorrect. Neither the `ls -s` nor `ls -l` command will list any SELinux file information, instead only showing file sizes and a "long listing," respectively. The `restorecon` command fixes and repairs SELinux labels. The `aa-disable` command is used to disable AppArmor, not SELinux. (Domain 2. Security)

7. ☑ **A**, **B**, and **E** are correct. The `ZZ`, `:x`, and `:wq` commands will save any changes to the current file and then close the `vi` editor.
   ☒ **C** and **D** are incorrect. The `:q` command will close the current file and exit the editor without saving changes. The `:q!` command will discard any changes made to the current file, close it, and then exit the editor. (Domain 1. System Management)

8. ☑ **D** is correct. The `chmod 600 widgets.odt` command grants the owner `rw-` permissions but takes away permissions from all other users.
☒ **A**, **B**, and **C** are incorrect. **A** is incorrect because it allows the file owner to edit the file, but also grants read and write access to the group. **B** is incorrect because it grants the group the read (`r`) permission. **C** is incorrect because it grants the owner, group, and others all permissions to the file. (Domain 2. Security)

9. ☑ **A** is correct. The `chmod 660 projectx.odt` command grants the owner `rw-` permissions, the group `rw-` permissions, and others `---` permissions.
☒ **B**, **C**, and **D** are incorrect. **B** is incorrect because it fails to grant the group the write (`w`) permission. **C** is incorrect because it grants the owner, group, and others all permissions to the file. **D** is incorrect because it fails to grant the group the write (`w`) permission and it grants others read (`r--`) permission to the file. (Domain 2. Security)

10. ☑ **A** and **E** are correct. The `usermod -aG` command adds the users you specify as members of the specified group(s).
☒ **B**, **C**, and **D** are incorrect. The `-s` option is used by the `usermod` command to define the "login shell" that the user will run. The `-g` option assigns the user's *primary* group. The `-p` option changes the password assigned to the user. (Domain 1. System Management)

11. ☑ **B** is correct. An `until` loop runs over and over as long as the condition is `false`. As soon as the condition is `true`, it stops.
☒ **A**, **C**, and **D** are incorrect. A `while` loop executes over and over until a specified condition is no longer `true`. A `for` loop processes a specific number of times. A `case` statement is not a looping structure. (Domain 3. Scripting, Containers, and Automation)

12. ☑ **C** and **F** are correct. The Samba service provides file sharing. CUPS is used to manage printing.
☒ **A**, **B**, **D**, and **E** are incorrect. The Apache web server is frequently implemented on Linux in conjunction with the MySQL database server to develop web-based applications. Telnet is an older service that was formerly used for remote access. Pure-FTP provides an FTP service. (Domain 1. System Management)

13. ☑ **E** is correct. The Out of Memory Killer watches for processes that use too much memory and selects them for killing when the system has a serious memory shortage.
☒ **A**, **B**, **C**, and **D** are incorrect and are nonexistent Linux tools. (Domain 4. Troubleshooting)

14. ☑ **A** and **B** are correct. Either `nmap -sT -p 1-1024 10.0.0.*` is used to scan for open ports between 1 and 1024 or `lsof -i` is used to scan for open network ports.
☒ **C**, **D**, and **E** are incorrect. The `pwconv` command is used to create the `/etc/shadow` file from the `/etc/passwd` file. The `ssh` command is used to make secure remote login connections. The `cpio` command is used to create tape backups. (Domain 4. Troubleshooting)

15. ☑ **C** is correct. Use `insmod` to insert a module.

☒ **A**, **B**, **D**, and **E** are incorrect. The `dmesg` program shows hardware found during bootup. The `modinfo` command provides the user info about a module. The `depmod` command looks for module dependencies and updates the `modules.dep` file. The `lsmod` command shows a list of currently installed modules. (Domain 1. System Management)

16. ☑ **A** is correct. A system administrator could run `dig jordanteam.com MX` and list the location of the mail server.

☒ **B**, **C**, and **D** are incorrect. The `ping` command is used to test networks, and `traceroute` will list the routers used for a packet to reach its destination. The `route` command is used to define or display the default gateway. (Domain 1. System Management)

17. ☑ **A** is correct. Use the `mtr` command to visualize the routes a packet takes to reach its destination.

☒ **B**, **C**, **D**, and **E** are incorrect. The `traceroute` command is similar to `mtr`, but it is entered at the command line and does not operate periodically. The `tracert` command is the same as `traceroute` but works on the Windows operating system. The `iftop` command updates periodically and displays network traffic. The `top` command updates periodically and shows process activity. (Domain 4. Troubleshooting)

18. ☑ **D** is correct. The `/etc/shadow` file contains the encrypted passwords for user accounts.

☒ **A**, **B**, and **C** are incorrect. The `/etc/passwd` file contains the user accounts and user IDs. The `/etc/group` file is used for local group definitions. The `/etc/gshadow` file contains passwords for the groups. (Domain 2. Security)

19. ☑ **B** is correct. The third field in each user entry in `/etc/passwd` specifies the user's ID number (UID). In this case, it's `1001`.

☒ **A**, **C**, and **D** are incorrect. **A** is incorrect because it specifies the username. **C** is incorrect because it specifies the group ID (GID) of the user's primary group. **D** is incorrect because it specifies the user's full name. (Domain 1. System Management)

20. ☑ **C** is correct. The seventh field in each record in `/etc/shadow` specifies the number of days to wait after a password has expired to disable the account.

☒ **A**, **B**, and **D** are incorrect. **A** is incorrect because it specifies the minimum number of days (one) required before a password can be changed. **B** is incorrect because it specifies the number of days prior to password expiration before the user will be warned of the pending expiration. **D** is incorrect because it is assigned to the eighth field, which specifies the number of days since January 1, 1970, after which the account will be disabled. (Domain 2. Security)

21. ☑ **C** is correct. The `/etc/skel` directory contains files (usually startup scripts, like `.bashrc`) that populate a new user's home directory when created with `useradd`.

☒ **A**, **B**, and **D** are incorrect. The `/etc/login.defs` file defines the locations of a new user's mail directories, etc. The `/etc/default/useradd` file contains defaults used by the `useradd` utility (for example, user ID and default shell). The `/etc/default/grub` file contains booting defaults. (Domain 1. System Management)

22. ☑ **A** is correct. The `useradd -c "Ian Mausi" -m -s "/bin/bash" imausi` command creates a new user account for a user named Ian Mausi with a username of `imausi`, a full name of Ian Mausi, a default shell of `/bin/bash`, and a home directory.

☒ **B**, **C**, and **D** are incorrect. **B** is incorrect because it uses incorrect syntax for the `useradd` command, where `-u` is followed by a user ID number. **C** is incorrect because it uses an incorrect command (`usermod`). **D** is incorrect because it omits the `-m` option, which is required to create a home directory. (Domain 1. System Management)

23. ☑ **C** is correct. The `.gitignore` file keeps a list of files that should be ignored by the `git` command.

☒ **A**, **B**, and **D** are incorrect. **A** and **B** are incorrect because there are no such files as `.gitnot` or `gitnot`. **D** is incorrect because `.git` is a directory that contains the repository for the project. (Domain 3. Scripting, Containers, and Automation)

24. ☑ **A** and **B** are correct. Users can use the backticks (for example, `` echo Today is `date` ``) or a dollar sign and parentheses (for example, `echo Today is $(date)`). The output of the `date` command will be the input to the `echo` command.

☒ **C**, **D**, and **E** are incorrect. The single quotes make all characters literal. The double quotes make all characters literal except for the \, $, and ` (backtick), with some exceptions, such as !, @, and *, that are outside the scope of the exam. The dollar sign with curly braces, ${ }, are used to dereference a variable. (Domain 3. Scripting, Containers, and Automation)

25. ☑ **D** is correct. When the administrator runs `umount /dev/sdb2`, the files will reappear unharmed.

☒ **A**, **B**, and **C** are incorrect. The files are not destroyed, mounted to other filesystems, or temporarily merged. (Domain 1. System Management)

26. ☑ **A** is correct. The `read` command is used to pause the script and prompt the user to provide some type of input, which is assigned to the specified variable.

☒ **B**, **C**, and **D** are incorrect. The `input`, `prompt`, and `query` commands cannot be used to read user input, and are distractors. (Domain 3. Scripting, Containers, and Automation)

27. ☑ **C** is correct. The error shown is caused by not having the execute permission set for the user trying to run the script. The `chmod u+x runme.sh` command will allow the user who owns the file to run it.

    ☒ **A**, **B**, and **D** are incorrect. **A** and **B** are incorrect because they resolve path-related problems, which are not an issue in this scenario. **D** is incorrect because it changes the command interpreter to the `/bin/sh` (Bourne) shell, which is not necessary in this scenario. (Domain 3. Scripting, Containers, and Automation)

28. ☑ **A** is correct. If the system fails after the backup completes on Friday, the only tape required to fully restore would be F-2 (Full backup, Number 2 made on Friday).

    ☒ **B**, **C**, and **D** are incorrect. **B** would require three tapes to recover in this order: Full-1, Differential 2, and Incremental 2. **C** would require two tapes to recover in this order: Full 1 and Differential 4. **D** would require all tapes to recover in the order of F-1, I-1, I-2, I-3, and I-4. (Domain 2. Security)

29. ☑ **B** is correct. Running `export VAR1` will convert `VAR1` from a shell variable to an environment variable.

    ☒ **A**, **C**, and **D** are incorrect. The `env` command will display all the environment variables defined. The `set` command will display all of the shell variables defined. The `chmod` command can change read, write, and execute permissions on files. (Domain 3. Scripting, Containers, and Automation)

30. ☑ **B** and **C** are correct. When an administrator wants to safely disable a driver, they add it to the blacklist using >>.

    ☒ **A**, **D**, and **E** are incorrect. **A** and **D** are incorrect because they overwrite the file with the new content using >, which will disable other driver features unintentionally. **E** is incorrect because << is used for heredocs. (Domain 2. Security)

31. ☑ **C** is correct. The `tcpdump` command monitors network traffic and can display unencrypted login names and passwords.

    ☒ **A**, **B**, and **D** are incorrect. The `dig` and `nslookup` commands list the IP addresses that domain names belong to. The `ip` command is used to define and set up network devices. (Domain 4. Troubleshooting)

32. ☑ **A** and **D** are correct. SSH and HTTPS encrypt traffic traveling along the network.

    ☒ **B**, **C**, and **E** are incorrect. FTP, Telnet, and Finger communicate across the network using unencrypted data, and they should be disabled for best security. (Domain 2. Security)

33. ☑ **D** is correct. There is no single sign-on (SSO) system referred to as Circumference.

    ☒ **A**, **B**, **C**, and **E** are incorrect. All of these are single sign-on systems that allow a user to use a single digital identity across multiple domains. (Domain 2. Security)

34. ☑ **A** is correct. The /22 prefix length indicates the first two octets of the subnet mask (16 bits) are populated, plus 6 additional bits in the third octet.

☒ **B**, **C**, and **D** are incorrect. The prefix length for 255.255.0.0 would be /16. The prefix length for 255.255.255.0 would be /24. The prefix length for 255.255.255.252 would be /30. (Domain 4. Troubleshooting)

35. ☑ **D** is correct. This command will assign the `ens32` interface an IP address of 172.17.8.1, with a subnet mask of 255.255.0.0 and a broadcast address of 172.17.255.255.

☒ **A**, **B** and **C** are incorrect. They use incorrect parameters for setting the subnet mask and broadcast address. The `set` feature is used with `ip link set ens0 up`, for example. (Domain 4. Troubleshooting)

36. ☑ **A** is correct. `STARTMODE` determines whether the interface is started automatically at system boot or must be manually enabled.

☒ **B**, **C**, and **D** are incorrect. The `BOOTPROTO` parameter can be set to a value of `STATIC` to use static IP address assignments or to `DHCP` to configure dynamic IP addressing. `IPADDR` assigns an IP address to the interface but only works if `BOOTPROTO` is set to `STATIC`. `USERCONTROL` determines whether standard user accounts are allowed to manage the interface. (Domain 4. Troubleshooting)

37. ☑ **A** is correct. Active-passive clusters reserve a passive NIC that becomes active when another NIC fails.

☒ **B**, **C**, and **D** are incorrect. Active-active clusters keep all NICs active and running and are designed primarily for load balancing and load aggregation. Load balancing is used to configure the system's hostname. (Domain 1. System Management)

38. ☑ **C** is correct. Use `/etc/nsswitch.conf` (name service switch) to define the order in which services will be used for name resolution.

☒ **A**, **B**, and **D** are incorrect. **A** is incorrect because it is used to configure the IP address of the DNS server but does not configure the name service order. **B** is incorrect because it is used to configure IP addressing information but does not contain name resolution information. **D** is incorrect because it is used to configure how services will behave after they are updated. (Domain 1. System Management)

39. ☑ **D** and **E** are correct. Use `visudo` or `sudoedit /etc/sudoers` to modify the `/etc/sudoers` file securely.

☒ **A**, **B**, and **C** are incorrect. The `gedit` and `vi` commands could be used to edit `/etc/sudoers` as `root`, but using them is insecure because multiple users may be editing the file simultaneously, causing changes to be lost. The `notepad` command is an editor used with Microsoft Windows. (Domain 2. Security)

40. ☑ **D** is correct. Defining `pam_tally2.so` within proper files under `/etc/pam.d/` can lock an account after three improper login attempts, for example.

☒ **A**, **B**, and **C** are incorrect. Use `pam_access.so` for auditing and logging of access control. Use `pam_loginuid.so` to assist in login auditing as well. Use `pam_limits.so` to take advantage of `ulimit` features. (Domain 2. Security)

41. ☑ **A** is correct. The `Port` directive specifies the port on which the `sshd` daemon will listen for SSH requests.
☒ **B**, **C**, and **D** are incorrect. The `BindAddress` directive is used to specify the address on the local machine to be used as the source address of the connection. The `Protocol` directive specifies the protocol versions SSH should support. The `Tunnel` directive is used to set up forwarding between the SSH client and the SSH server. (Domain 2. Security)

42. ☑ **D** is correct. The `ps 4 >> /tmp/myprocesses` command appends the `stdout` from the `ps` command to a file named `myprocesses` in the `/tmp` directory.
☒ **A**, **B**, and **C** are incorrect. **A** is incorrect because < attempts to use `/tmp/myprocesses` as `stdin` to the `ps` command. **B** is incorrect because > will redirect `stdout` to the file `/tmp/myprocesses` and overwrite any data within the file. **C** is incorrect because, in some versions of bash, <> stands for read-write and would overwrite any data within `/tmp/myprocesses`. (Domain 1. System Management)

43. ☑ **C** is correct. Running `passwd -S` lists the user's name and fields related to password aging.
☒ **A**, **B**, and **D** are incorrect. Since Linux is a case-sensitive operating system, `--STATUS` is not the same as `--status`. `--ss` and `-s` are not options for the `passwd` command, and result in an error message if used. (Domain 1. System Management)

44. ☑ **A** is correct. The `GRUB_DEFAULT=0` directive is defined within `/etc/default/grub` and causes `GRUB2` to use the first menu entry by default, regardless of which operating system was selected on the last boot.
☒ **B**, **C**, and **D** are incorrect. The `/boot/grub2/grub.cfg` file is generated from `/etc/default/grub`. `/boot/grub2` is a directory, not a file. Users would modify `/etc/grub.d/40_custom` to add customizations. (Domain 1. System Management)

45. ☑ **A** and **C** are correct. Both `systemctl isolate runlevel3.target` and `systemctl isolate multi-user.target` are used to switch the system into a text-based, multiuser environment comparable to runlevel 3 on an init-based system.
☒ **B**, **D**, and **E** are incorrect. The `systemctl isolate rescue.target` command switches the system to a rescue environment equivalent to runlevel 1. To switch to the `systemd` equivalent of runlevel 5, enter either `systemctl isolate runlevel5.target` or `systemctl isolate graphical.target`. (Domain 1. System Management)

46. ☑ **B** is correct. To create a GPT partition on the third SATA hard disk in a Linux system, first switch to the root user and enter `fdisk /dev/sdc` at the shell prompt.
☒ **A**, **C**, and **D** are incorrect. **A** is incorrect because `fdisk /dev/sdb` represents the second SATA hard drive. **C** and **D** are incorrect because they are improper hard-drive representation syntax. (Domain 1. System Management)

47. ☑ **B** is correct. Use the `vgcreate` command to define a new volume group and assign physical partitions to it (`/dev/sdb1` and `/dev/sdc1` in this case). The `vgcreate` command is used after defining the physical volumes with `pvcreate /dev/sdb1 /dev/sdc1`.
☒ **A**, **C**, **D**, and **E** are incorrect. The `lvscan` command is used to view the logical volumes defined on the system. The `pvcreate` command is used to define a partition (or even an entire disk) as an LVM physical volume. The `lvcreate` command is used to define logical volumes on the system. (Domain 4. Troubleshooting)

48. ☑ **A**, **C**, and **E** are correct. Logical volumes can be used to create and delete logical volumes, take snapshots, and increase and decrease the sizes of logical volumes.
☒ **B** and **D** are incorrect. Logical volume management has nothing to do with Linux audio capabilities. (Domain 4. Troubleshooting)

49. ☑ **A** is correct. The `journalctl -b 2` command displays messages created during the second boot event found at the beginning of the journal. This should contain boot messages from the system's pristine state required by the scenario.
☒ **B**, **C**, and **D** are incorrect. The `logger` command is used to send test log events to the logging daemon. The `journalctl -b` command displays boot messages that were logged in the most recent boot event. The `journalctl -b -2` command displays system messages that were logged two boot events ago. (Domain 2. Security)

50. ☑ **A** is correct. The content shown is from the `/etc/securetty` file, which lists the terminals from which root *can* log in.
☒ **B**, **C**, and **D** are incorrect. **B** is incorrect because the `/dev/tty` file is a character device driver. **C** is incorrect because `/etc/yum.conf` is the configuration file for YUM repositories. **D** is incorrect because `/etc/ld.so.conf` is the configuration file for the location of dynamically linked libraries. (Domain 2. Security)

51. ☑ **A** is correct. For `GIT` to work properly, every commit must relate to some username and e-mail address so that all of the co-contributors can keep track of the changes.
☒ **B**, **C**, and **D** are incorrect. Co-contributor communications do not require a MAC address, IP address, project name, or password. (Domain 3. Scripting, Containers, and Automation)

52. ☑ **B** is correct. VNC (Virtual Network Computing) is not a Linux desktop environment; it is a utility for remote desktop computer access.
☒ **A**, **C**, and **D** are incorrect. Gnome, Unity, and Cinnamon are all Linux desktop environments, providing login screens and varied desktop appearances. Gnome is the default environment for several distributions, including openSUSE and Fedora. Unity is a popular desktop environment for Ubuntu Linux. Cinnamon is popular on Linux Mint. (Domain 3. Scripting, Containers, and Automation)

EXAM TIP Knowledge of default desktop environments is *not* a requirement for the CompTIA Linux+ exam

53. ☑ **C** is correct. While booting a system, the system administrator hits the `Esc` key when the `GRUB` menu appears, presses `E` to edit, scrolls down to the `linux` line and enters at the end of the line `systemd.unit=emergency.target`. The admin then presses the `F10` key to enter `emergency` mode and begins the process of removing and replacing the `root` password.
☒ **A**, **B**, and **D** are incorrect. **A** and **D** are incorrect for `systemd` systems, but would enter single-user mode on `SysVinit` systems when entered at the end of the `kernel` line. **B** is incorrect because it would enter single-user mode on a `systemd` system, requesting the `root` password, so the administrator would not be able to change the `root` password. (Domain 4. Troubleshooting)

54. ☑ **B** and **D** are correct. Either the `route` or `ip` command can be used to add a default gateway.
☒ **A**, **C**, and **E** are incorrect. They would result in syntax errors because of missing arguments within the commands. (Domain 1. System Management)

55. ☑ **C** is correct. In order for the gateway to exist, there must be some connection to the router, but the only connection shown is to the `192.168.8.0` network.
☒ **A**, **B**, and **D** are incorrect. In this case the issue is there is no connection to the `10.5.3.0` network. (Domain 4. Troubleshooting)

56. ☑ **A** is correct. When the network administrator converts to a tier 1 time server, that implies the system changes time updates from the intranet (LAN) to now from the Internet (WAN). NTP uses port 123, which now must be opened on the firewall.
☒ **B**, **C**, and **D** are incorrect. **B** is incorrect because the update can be made without a reboot. **C** is incorrect because there is no need to use the `timedatectl` command when modifying a configuration file. **D** is incorrect because NTP is available on all enterprise versions of Red Hat Linux. (Domain 4. Troubleshooting)

57. ☑ **A** is correct. To remove the immutable setting, Amy must run `chattr -i /etc/apt/sources.list`.
☒ **B**, **C**, and **D** are incorrect. There is no `-I` option for `chattr`. `chmod` and `setfacl` can add read/write privileges, but the error message is "Permission denied," not "Operation not permitted." (Domain 4. Troubleshooting)

58. ☑ **D** is correct. `sysinit` is *not* an initialization feature of Linux systems.
☒ **A**, **B**, and **C** are incorrect. `systemd`, `Upstart`, and `SysVinit` are all Linux initialization systems. (Domain 2. Security)

59. ☑ **B** is correct. The correct `/etc/fsck` column order is device, mount point, filesystem type, options, dump option, fsck order.
☒ **A**, **C**, and **D** are incorrect. None of these shows the correct column order. (Domain 1. System Management)

60. ☑ **A** and **C** are correct. EXT2 and ISOFS are not journaled filesystems.
☒ **B**, **D**, and **E** are incorrect. EXT3, XFS, and NTFS are journaled filesystems, which save changes in a buffer so that data loss is minimized in case of a system interruption. (Domain 1. System Management)

61. ☑ **C** is correct. The `tune2fs -t ext3 /dev/sdd4` command fails because there is no `-t` option for `tune2fs`.
☒ **A**, **B**, **D**, and **E** are incorrect. **A**, **B**, and **D** are incorrect because `mke2fs -j /dev/sda2`, `mkfs.ext3 /dev/sdb3`, and `mkfs -t ext3 /dev/sdc7` will create an `ext3` type filesystem on the partition. **E** is incorrect because the `tune2fs -j /dev/sde8` command will convert an `ext2` type filesystem to `ext3` by adding the journal. (Domain 1. System Management)

62. ☑ **D** is correct. The `w` command displays who is logged into the system and which processes they are running.
☒ **A**, **B**, **C**, and **E** are incorrect. **A** and **E** are incorrect because the `whoami` and `id` commands show who the user is currently logged in as, but not the processes they are running. **C** is incorrect because the `who` command will display all logged-in users, but not the processes they are running. **E** is incorrect because the `whom` command is a distractor and currently does not exist for Linux systems. (Domain 1. System Management)

63. ☑ **A** is correct. Files need to be removed to free up inodes (file handles).
☒ **B**, **C**, and **D** are incorrect. None of these options creates new file handles. (Domain 1. System Management)

64. ☑ **D** is correct. Running `userdel -r` will delete the user and the files from their `/home` directory and their mail spool. Files in other filesystems need to be deleted manually.
☒ **A**, **B**, **C**, and **E** are incorrect. **A**, **B**, and **E** are incorrect because the `usermod` and `useradd` commands are not capable of removing users. **C** is incorrect because the `-d` option is not available to `userdel`. (Domain 1. System Management)

65. ☑ **A**, **B**, and **C** are correct. Running `usermod -e` allows an administrator to add an expiration date. Running `passwd -e` will immediately expire a user's account. The `chage` command stands for "change age" and offers many password expiration features. One method is running `chage -E`.
☒ **D** and **E** are incorrect. The `password` command is a distractor and is not available in standard Linux. The `shadow` file is a database of password expiration details and *not* a command. (Domain 1. System Management)

66. ☑ **D** is correct. The time zone configuration file is called `/etc/localtime`.
☒ **A**, **B**, **C**, and **E** are incorrect. None of the files exist in standard Linux. (Domain 1. System Management)

67. ☑ **B** is correct. Running `localectl status` will display the current locale setting, keymap, keymap layout, and `X11` model.

☒ **A**, **C**, and **D** are incorrect. Running `localectl list-locales` will list available locales that can be set using `set-locale`. The `-s` and `-l` options are distractors and are currently not available within `localectl`. (Domain 1. System Management)

68. ☑ **A** is correct. Use `LC_ALL` to override the locality variables.

☒ **B**, **C**, and **D** are incorrect. The `LC_NAME` environment variable formats how first and last names appear in different countries. The `LC_CTYPE` environment variable formats the classification and conversion of characters. The `LANG` variable specifies locale when `LC_`*`var`* is not defined. (Domain 1. System Management)

69. ☑ **B** is correct. The `runme` program will run at the effective user ID (`EUID`) of `todd` because the `SUID` bit is set, as shown with the `s` in the permissions `-rwsr-xr-x`; therefore, the command is run at the `EUID` of the *owner* of the file, not the *user,* which is normally done.

☒ **A**, **C**, and **D** are incorrect. If the `SUID` bit were not set, `runme` would run with the `montrie` user's permissions. When logged in as a standard user, jobs do not normally run with an `EUID` of `root` or the group they belong to (in this case `manf`). (Domain 2. Security)

70. ☑ **C** and **D** are correct. The default file permissions are `666` and the default directory permissions are `777`. The purpose of `umask` is to make files more secure by removing permissions when files are created. `0027` or `027` removes `write` permission for the `group`, and `read`, `write`, and `execute` for `other`.

☒ **A**, **B**, **E**, and **F** are incorrect. `026` and `0026` would fail because the directory permission results to `751` instead of `750`. `0036` and `036` would fail because, although the file permission would result to `640`, directory permissions would result to `741`. (Domain 2. Security)

71. ☑ **D** is correct. When Jeongeun runs `df -h`, she will see that the hard drive is 100 percent full, and that is why she cannot create a new file.

☒ **A**, **B**, and **C** are incorrect. The question implies that Jeongeun has already run the `quota` command because of not getting any quota errors. The `df -i` command will show inode utilization, not disk space use. Running `du -sh` will only show disk space use in her home directory and below, not the entire system. (Domain 4. Troubleshooting)

72. ☑ **A** is correct. User Iohn forgot to run `swapon /d/swapfile` to enable the swap area.

☒ **B**, **C**, and **D** are incorrect. The `swapoff` command would disable the swap area. Iohn already ran `mkswap` since the swap area was already set up, as stated in the question. The `mount` command is used to access a filesystem, not swap space. (Domain 4. Troubleshooting)

73. ☑ **C** is correct. User Quiñonez would run `echo deadline > /sys/block/sda/queue/scheduler` to update the I/O scheduler from `cfq` or `noop` to `deadline`.

☒ **A**, **B**, and **D** are incorrect. The `cat` command in **A** and **B** would attempt to list a file called `deadline`, and the < in **A** and **D** means to read from standard input, instead of to write to standard output. (Domain 4. Troubleshooting)

74. ☑ **B** is correct. User Elimu completes the command as follows for proper completion of the case statement:

`case $fruit in`

☒ **A**, **C**, and **D** are incorrect. All would be syntax errors. The `at` command is used to schedule jobs. The `of` command is a distractor and not a part of standard Linux. The `if` command is a decision construct used within scripts. (Domain 3. Scripting, Containers, and Automation)

75. ☑ **D** is correct. User Wade would complete the statement with the `done` command.

☒ **A**, **B**, and **C** are incorrect. The `end` and `rof` commands are distractors and not a part of standard Linux. The `od` command provides an "octal dump" representation of a file. (Domain 3. Scripting, Containers, and Automation)

76. ☑ **B** is correct. The server administrator should modify `dhclient.conf` on each device to change the hostnames of the devices permanently.

☒ **A**, **C**, and **D** are incorrect. `/etc/sysconfig/network/` is a directory, not a file. `end` and `od` will give a syntax error. (Domain 3. Scripting, Containers, and Automation)

77. ☑ **B**, **C**, and **D** are correct. Walter can run either `mdadm --follow`, `mdadm -F`, or `mdadm --monitor` to "follow" or "monitor" the RAID array as a foreground or background job that notifies system administrators of any RAID issues.

☒ **A** is incorrect. The `mdadm --build` command creates a legacy RAID array that does not use superblocks (a type of filesystem database that tracks filesystem state and changes). (Domain 1. System Management)

78. ☑ **D** is correct. Lonnie and Landon run `virsh --escape ^[` to override the default escape sequence that `telnet` normally uses, `^]`.

☒ **A**, **B**, and **C** are incorrect. The `--debug` option performs up to five levels of logging and accounting for the `virsh` command. Neither `--esc` nor `--chstr` presently exists in Linux. (Domain 3. Scripting, Containers, and Automation)

79. ☑ **B** is correct. Laeia and Liara run the `badblocks` command to check for bad blocks on the hard drive.

☒ **A**, **C**, and **D** are incorrect. `blockcheck` and `bbcheck` are not presently Linux commands, and the `kill` command is used to control running processes. (Domain 4. Troubleshooting)

80. ☑ **B** is correct. Sorana can run the `watch` command with `free` to automatically display updates every two seconds, refreshing the screen every time.
☒ **A**, **C**, and **D** are incorrect. The `period` and `twosec` commands do not exist or are not available with standard Linux. Running `free --count 5 --seconds 2` would give similar results to what Sorana is hoping to achieve, but it does not refresh the screen during each update. (Domain 4. Troubleshooting)

81. ☑ **A** is correct. User Ugo can run `chmod g+s work` so that files and directories created below the `work` directory will belong to the same group as the `work` directory.
☒ **B**, **C**, and **D** are incorrect. `chmod +a work` will result in a syntax error. `chmod g=w work` and `chmod g=rw work` provide write and read/write privileges to the group, respectively, but new files and directories below the directory will belong to the `EGID` (effective group ID) of the creating user. (Domain 2. Security)

82. ☑ **B** is correct. Zhang can run the following to enable users to access her website: `firewall-cmd --zone=public --add-service=http`
☒ **A**, **C**, and **D** are incorrect. They all would give syntax errors because `--allow`, `=web`, and `--add` are improper arguments for `firewall-cmd`. (Domain 2. Security)

83. ☑ **C** is correct. Henri can run `iptables -L` to display the current firewall settings.
☒ **A**, **B**, and **D** are incorrect. `iptables -d` and `iptables -s` set up the source and destination port, respectively. Use `iptables -F` to flush (delete) the DNS tables. (Domain 2. Security)

84. ☑ **B** is correct. Petra would run `chkconfig -level 35 auditd on` to enable logging and accounting services for her Linux system.
☒ **A**, **C**, and **D** are incorrect. **A** would cause syntax errors because `start` is an improper argument. **C** and **D** are incorrect because the service cannot be the last argument. (Domain 1. System Management)

85. ☑ **A** is correct. Milos needs to know which volume group device to extend, so that he can then run `lvextend -L+20G /dev/myvg/myvol` to add another 20GB to the `/dev/myvg/myvol` volume.
☒ **B**, **C**, and **D** are incorrect. It is not necessary to reboot the system or restart services for extending or growing to take effect. (Domain 4. Troubleshooting)

86. ☑ **B** is correct. Ushna would not use a tool called Orchestrate because there is no such tool available to her on Centos Linux.
☒ **A**, **C**, and **D** are incorrect. They all are tools that Ushna could use to set up and orchestrate the installation of 500 servers. `Cloud-init` makes it easy to configure cloud images, Anaconda sets up cloud images, and Kickstart can perform automated operating system installation. (Domain 3. Scripting, Containers, and Automation)

87. ☑ **D** is correct. Thanasi is currently editing a YAML file.
☒ **A**, **B**, and **C** are incorrect. The file does not represent a SAML, XML, or JSON file. (Domain 3. Scripting, Containers, and Automation)

88. ☑ **C** is correct. Teliana is currently editing a JSON file.
☒ **A**, **B**, and D are incorrect. The file does not represent a SAML, XML, or YAML file. (Domain 3. Scripting, Containers, and Automation)

89. ☑ **A** is correct. Juan should run the `setenforce permissive` command as `root` to use SELinux in warning mode only.
☒ **B**, **C**, and **D** are incorrect. **B** is incorrect because `setenforce enforcing` is the current state Juan is in and has made the system mostly unfunctional. **C** is incorrect because running `setenforce disabled` would allow Juan to work but will not load any `SELinux` policies, so he will not be able to test it. **D** is incorrect because running `setenforce warning` would result in an error, as the `warning` option does not exist. (Domain 1. System Management)

90. ☑ **B** is correct. Katerina runs `Ctrl-Z` to stop the running the `windsim` job. If she runs `fg`, the job will wake and continue in the foreground. If instead she runs `bg`, the job will wake and continue in the background.
☒ **A**, **C**, and **D** are incorrect. `Ctrl-C` will cancel the job, `Ctrl-\` will cancel the job and "dump core" (a memory image of the job saved to the disk and named "core"), and `Ctrl-S` is ignored. If Katerina runs `cat really-long-file`, `Ctrl-S` and `Ctrl-Q` will stop and start the data stream as it displays on the screen. (Domain 1. System Management)

Analyzing Your Results

Now analyze the results! Use this information to identify two things:

- What resources to use to prepare for the exam
- Domains to spend some extra time studying

First, use the following table to determine what tools and resources to use to prepare for the exams:

Number of Answers Correct	Recommended Course of Study
0–53	If this had been the actual CompTIA Linux+ exam, you most likely would not have passed. Additional study is necessary before taking the real exam. At this level, it is recommended you review each chapter in detail. Set up the Linux virtual machine included with this book and practice completing the tasks covered in this book. Get real-world Linux experience at work by taking on more Linux assignments, or volunteer at a non-profit and assist them with their Linux projects. Plan on taking the exam about 180 days from now, assuming scores of 85%+ on "fresh" practice exams.

Number of Answers Correct	Recommended Course of Study
54–72	If this had been the actual CompTIA Linux+ exam, you likely would not have passed. Additional study and targeted review are recommended. At this level, list each item missed on paper and spend extra time studying the missed topics while going through this book. Set up the Linux virtual machine included with this book and practice completing the tasks covered in this book. You should be ready for the actual exam in 90 days or more, assuming you are scoring 85%+ on "fresh" practice exams.
73–90	Congratulations! If this had been the actual CompTIA Linux+ exam, there is a good chance you would have passed. I recommend scheduling the exam for about 14 days from now, to give you time to study and strengthen weaknesses, set up a test environment, and complete most of the Lab Projects in the book. The Linux+ exam is very difficult, so use the practice exam simulations and ensure scoring is consistently 85 percent or greater with "fresh" questions.

With the recommendations in the preceding table in mind, you can now use the following table to determine which domains to focus your study efforts on:

Official Exam Domain	Question Number
System Management (35)	1, 3, 4, 5, 7, 10, 12, 15, 16, 19, 21, 22, 25, 37, 38, 42, 43, 44, 45, 46, 54, 59, 60, 61, 62, 63, 64, 65, 66, 67, 68, 77, 84, 89, 90
Security (19)	6, 8, 9, 18, 20, 28, 32, 33, 39, 40, 41, 49, 50, 58, 69, 70, 81, 82, 83
Scripting, Containers, and Automation (17)	2, 11, 23, 24, 26, 27, 29, 30, 51, 52, 74, 75, 76, 78, 86, 87, 88
Troubleshooting (19)	13, 14, 17, 31, 34, 35, 36, 47, 48, 53, 55, 56, 57, 71, 72, 73, 79, 80, 85

CHAPTER 2

Using the vi Text Editor

In this chapter, you will learn about

- The role and function of the `vi` text editor
- Editing text files in `vi`
- Editing text files in `nano`

Every living thing is a masterpiece, written by nature and edited by evolution.

—Neil deGrasse Tyson, Hayden Planetarium

One of the important skills that you need when working with any Linux system is the ability to use a text editor effectively. Most system-configuration tasks in Linux are completed using an editor to modify a text file, whether you're rebuilding the operating system or configuring a service.

The Role and Function of the vi Text Editor

You may be familiar with text editors included with other operating systems, such as Notepad on Windows or TextEdit on macOS, but `vi` (pronounced *vee-eye*) is different. The `vi` utility was invented before computer mice and arrow keys. So, we devote time to `vi` because

- Knowing how to use a text editor is critical to managing a Linux system. If you cannot use a text editor, you will struggle with the rest of the topics presented in this book.
- Linux editors are difficult for most new users to learn.

There are two versions of `vi`. The classical version is called simply `vi`. The newer version is called `vim`, a `vi`-improved version that understands arrow keys. In newer versions of Linux, executing the command `vi` actually runs the `vim` command. Executing the command `vim` opens Vi IMproved (see Figure 2-1).

Each `vi` and `vim` installation contains a tutorial called `vimtutor`. Running `vimtutor` will teach you the basic `vi`-editing commands, such as maneuvering the cursor and saving your file changes.

With this in mind, let's discuss how to edit text files in `vi`.

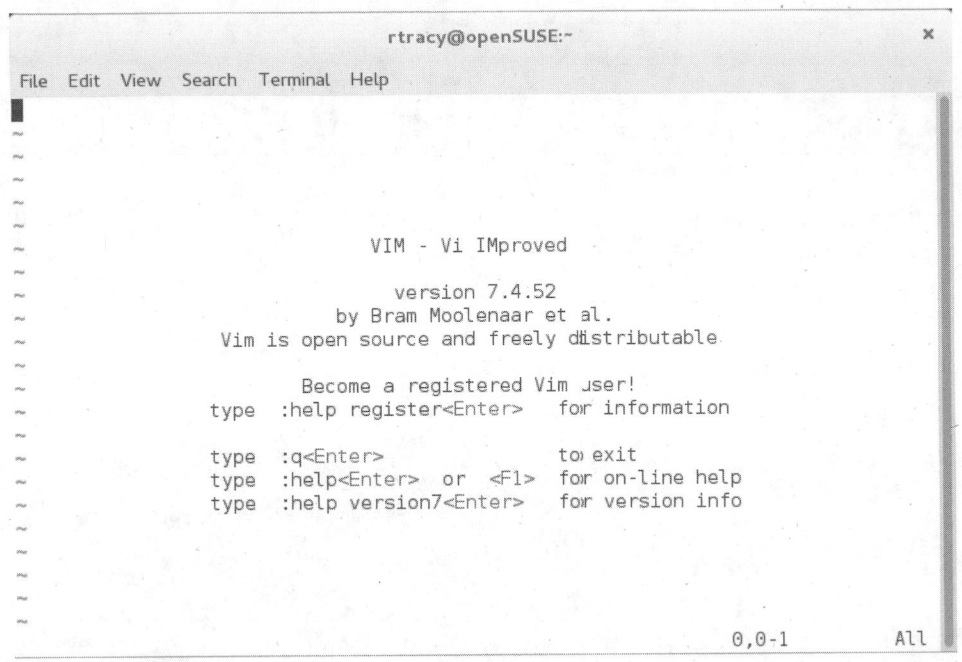
rtracy@openSUSE:~
File Edit View Search Terminal Help
VIM - Vi IMproved
version 7.4.52
by Bram Moolenaar et al.
Vim is open source and freely distributable
Become a registered Vim user!
type :help register<Enter> for information
type :q<Enter> to exit
type :help<Enter> or <F1> for on-line help
type :help version7<Enter> for version info
0,0-1 All

Figure 2-1 Using `vim`

Editing Text Files in `vi`

The first time you run `vi`, you will notice the user interface is very different from what you may have seen in other text editors. To help you become familiar with `vi`, we'll discuss the following topics:

- Opening files in `vi`
- The `vi` modes
- Working in normal mode
- Working in command-line mode

Opening Files in `vi`

To open a file from the shell prompt with `vi`, simply enter `vi <filename>`. You start within normal mode by default. For example, for a file named `myfile.txt`, simply enter `vi myfile.txt` at the shell prompt to load this file into the `vi` editor.

EXAM TIP Even though most Linux operating systems launch `vim` when a user runs `vi`, the Linux+ exam focuses on using `vi`, so knowledge of how to move the cursor *without arrow keys* is important. For the remainder of the chapter assume that `vi` and `vim` are the same command.

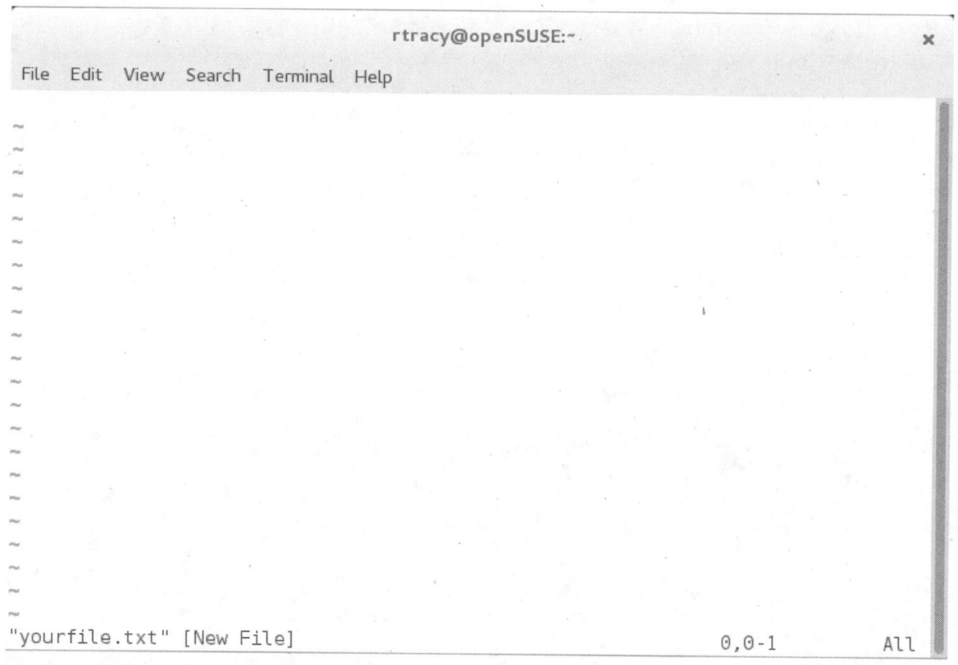

Figure 2-2 Creating a new file with `vi`

To create a new text file, simply enter `vi` followed by the name of the file to create at the shell prompt. For example, Figure 2-2 shows that the command `vi yourfile.txt` was entered at the shell prompt. Notice that when a blank file is opened in the `vi` editor interface, the "[New File]" indicator displays at the bottom of the screen. The file resides in the memory buffer until it is written or saved to the hard drive. If the file is not saved, it is lost!

Now, let's discuss `vi` modes.

The `vi` Modes

So far, so good, right? Most of the students I teach can handle opening or creating a file. However, once the file is open, things start to get a little tricky because, unlike other word processors such as Notepad or gedit, the mouse and arrow keys are disabled in `vi`. This is because `vi` was invented before mice and arrow keys were invented.

The `vi` command uses four different operating modes:

- Normal mode
- Command-line mode
- Insert mode
- Search mode

To switch between modes, press the `Esc` key. This will always return you to normal mode, from which you can access any other mode.

Normal Mode

Press the `Esc` key once to enter normal mode. Normal mode allows you to execute maneuvering commands, such as moving the cursor up, down, left, right, or scrolling up or down by a half or full page. The most common maneuvering commands are as follows:

- **`h`** Moves the cursor one character to the left
- **`l`** Moves the cursor one character to the right
- **`k`** Moves the cursor one character to the line above
- **`j`** Moves the cursor one character to the line below
- **`Ctrl-D`** Moves the cursor down half a page
- **`Ctrl-U`** Moves the cursor up half a page
- **`Ctrl-B`** Moves the cursor back a full page
- **`Ctrl-F`** Moves the cursor forward a full page

Also from normal mode, you can modify a character, change a word, execute a word search, and even enter command-line mode.

Command-Line Mode

Press `:` (the colon key) to move to command-line mode from normal mode. In command-line mode, you can execute commands that allow searching, replacing, saving, and quitting. Once you press `:`, the cursor moves to the bottom of the screen, where you can enter a command line. For example, to quit from `vi`, enter any of the following from normal mode:

- **`:x`** Writes the current file to disk and quits `vi`
- **`:wq`** Writes the current file to disk and quits `vi`
- **`:q`** Quits `vi` if the file has not been modified
- **`:q!`** Quits `vi` if the file has been modified, but any modifications will be lost

Note that the `:` places you into command-line mode, and `q!` runs the quit-without-saving command.

Insert Mode

There are at least six different insert options within `vi`. As with most commands in Linux, `vi` commands are case sensitive. You must first be in normal mode before entering insert mode. (If you are ever unsure of which mode you're in, press the `Esc` key.

That also switches to normal mode.) The following are the six basic insert options and what they enable you to do:

- **i** Insert text to the left of the cursor
- **I** Insert text at the beginning of the current line
- **a** Append text to the right of the cursor
- **A** Append text at the end of the current line
- **o** Open a newline below the current line and start inserting text
- **O** Open a newline above the current line and start inserting text

Search Mode

Use search mode to find a word, phrase, or string. Use the forward slash (/) to search forward, or use the question mark (?) to search in the reverse direction.

- **/<string>** Forward search. For example, `/test` forward searches for the string `test` from the current cursor position.
- **?<string>** Reverse search. For example, `?test` reverse searches for the string `test` from the current cursor position.
- **n** Continue the search in the same direction. Searches for the same string specified by `/<string>` or `?<string>` in the same direction.
- **N** Continue the search in the opposite direction. Searches for the same string specified by `/<string>` or `?<string>` in the opposite direction.

Search evaluates strings, so if you enter `/the` to find every occurrence of the string `the`, matches include `the`, `father`, `mother`, and any other word in which the `the` string appears.

Working in Normal Mode

When you open a file in `vi`, you are placed into normal mode. Note that on the left side of the screen, as shown in Figure 2-2, there are several lines of tildes (~). These characters simply indicate that the corresponding lines are empty. As you add lines to the file, the tildes begin to scroll away and disappear.

Cursor Movement

Unlike `vim`, `vi` does not support the use of the arrow keys or mouse to navigate the cursor, so the `vi` developers created alternate methods of navigation. Some of the most common methods of cursor navigation are listed here:

- **w** Moves the cursor right to the next word
- **b** Moves the cursor left to the previous word
- **^** Moves the cursor to the beginning of the line
- **$** Moves the cursor to the last character on the line

- `nG` Moves the cursor to line *n*
- `gg` Moves the cursor to the first line of the document
- `G` Moves the cursor to the last line of the document

Preceding a command by a number repeats the command that number of times. For example, `2h` moves the cursor two characters to the left and `5j` moves the cursor down five lines.

Deleting and Replacing Characters and Words

While in insert mode, you can remove recently added text by pressing the `Backspace` key. But in normal mode, use the following commands to delete a character, word, or line:

- `x` Deletes the character in the current cursor position
- `X` Deletes the character to the left of the cursor
- `u` Undoes the last edit
- `r` Replaces the character in the current cursor position
- `R` Replaces characters until return to normal mode
- `dw` Deletes a word from the current cursor position to the end of the word
- `D` Deletes the rest of the current line from the cursor position
- `dd` Deletes the current line

Changing a Word or Line

While in normal mode you can use the `C` or `c` prefix to change text in classic `vi` or in `vim`. The following list displays some of these features:

- `cw` Changes the current word
- `C` Changes from the current cursor position to the end of the line
- `cc` Changes the current line

Copying, Deleting, and Moving Lines

To copy or delete a line in normal mode, move the cursor to the line and copy (called *yanking*) or delete the lines as described here:

- `yy` Yanks (copies) the current line into the buffer
- `3yy` Copies the current line and the next two lines into the buffer
- `dd` Deletes the current line and places it into the buffer
- `5dd` Deletes the current line and the next four lines and places them into the buffer
- `p` Pastes the lines from the buffer in the line below the cursor
- `P` Pastes the lines from the buffer in the line above the cursor

Repeating a Command

To repeat the last command in normal mode, press the period (`.`) key.

Saving and Quitting in Normal Mode

From normal mode enter the `ZZ` command to write the current file to disk and quit.

Working in Command-Line Mode

The command line executes commands that are asserted against the entire document. To enter command-line mode, press `:` from normal mode. This places the cursor at the bottom of the current screen, as shown in Figure 2-3. Next, enter commands at the `:` prompt to accomplish file-related tasks, as discussed next.

NOTE Examples of commands written for command-line mode will always start with a leading `:` for clarification.

Deleting Lines

To delete lines in command-line mode, specify a line number or a range of line numbers followed by the `d` command:

- **`:nd`** Deletes line *n*
- **`:n,yd`** Deletes from line *n* to line *y*

Saving and Exiting from `vi`

To write the file to disk, from normal mode enter `:w <Enter>`. When complete, the prompt message at the bottom of the screen indicates the file has been written to disk, as shown in this example:

```
"file.txt" [New] 1L, 28C written                    1,26          All
```

Entering `w <filename>` or `save <filename>` at the command-line prompt writes the file to a different filename. These other commands also save and/or quit files from normal mode:

- **`:w!`** Overrides read-only file permission and forces write changes
- **`:e!`** Forgets changes since the last write and continues editing from where you left off without the recent changes

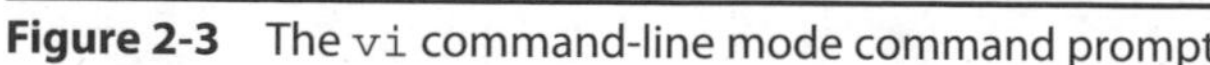

Figure 2-3 The `vi` command-line mode command prompt

Remember, the three ways to save and quit from `vi` are `:x`, `:wq`, and `ZZ` (with no colon).

Searching and Replacing Text

The following are command-line commands to search and replace strings within `vi`. By default, the search begins at the line the cursor is on.

- **`:s/<current_string>/<replacement_string>/`** Searches for a string *on the current line only* and replaces the first instance of the string. Given the line `breakfast is our morning break`, the command-line command `:s/break/old/` would produce the line `oldfast is our morning break`.
- **`:s/<current_string>/<replacement_string>g`** Searches for a string *on the current line* and replaces all instances of the string on the line. Given the line `breakfast is our morning break`, the command-line command `:s/break/old/g` would produce the line `oldfast is our morning old`.
- **`:%s/<current_string>/<replacement_string>/g`** Searches for all instances of the string in the document and replaces every instance.

Syntax Checker

Another reason to use `vim` over the `vi` editor is that it provides a very useful syntax checker. This feature can be a real lifesaver when you're writing scripts or editing configuration files.

The command-line command to enable and disable the syntax checker is `:syntax on | off` (the | or "pipe" symbol is commonly used for the word "or"). For example, to enable the syntax checker, enter the following within `vim`:

```
:syntax on
```

After doing so, different elements in the script or configuration file are denoted with different colors. If there is a syntax error, the syntax checker highlights the mistake with an alternate color to indicate that you need to correct it. An example of using the syntax checker within a configuration file is shown in Figure 2-4 (sans colors).

Configuration Files

The `vim` editor uses two configuration files: the system-wide configuration file `/etc/vimrc` and the user-specific file `~/.vimrc` in the user's home directory. The statement `set number` in either of these files will display line numbers in the `vi` files during editing.

After you've had a few months of experience working with `vi`, it becomes a simple yet powerful text editor to use. Let's flatten the learning curve a bit by spending some time practicing with `vi` in the following exercise.

```
root@openSUSE:/etc/xinetd.d
File Edit View Search Terminal Help
# default: off
# description: This serves out a VNC connection which starts at a KDM login \
#       prompt. This VNC connection has a resolution of 1024x768, 16bit depth.
service vnc1
{
        socket_type     = stream
        protocol        = tcp
        wait            = no
        user            = nobody
        server          = /usr/bin/Xvnc
        server_args     = -noreset -inetd -once -query localhost -geometry 1024x
768 -depth 16 -securitytypes none
        type            = UNLISTED
        port            = 5901
}
# default: off
# description: This serves out a VNC connection which starts at a KDM login \
#       prompt. This VNC connection has a resolution of 1280x1024, 16bit depth.
service vnc2
{
        type            = UNLISTED
        port            = 5902
        socket_type     = stream
"./vnc" 44L, 1306C                                        1,1           Top
```

Figure 2-4 Using the `vi` syntax checker

Exercise 2-1: Using the `vi` Editor

In this exercise, practice using the `vi` editor to create and manipulate text files.

VIDEO Watch the Exercise 2-1 video for a demonstration.

Log on to the virtual machine provided with this course as **`student1`** (password **`student1`**) and then follow these steps:

1. Open a terminal.
2. The current directory should be the user's home directory. Verify this by entering the command **`pwd`** at the shell prompt. (Typing the command `cd` will always return to the home directory.)
3. At the shell prompt, enter **`vi test.txt`**. The `vi` editor should run with `test.txt` open as a new file.
4. Press the **`I`** key to enter insert mode.
5. Enter the following text in the file:

```
Now is the time for all good men to come to the aid of their country.
```

6. Save the file by completing the following steps:
   a. Press **`Esc`** to return to normal mode.
   b. Enter **`:w <Enter>`**.
7. Exit `vi` by entering **`:wq <Enter>`**.
8. Reload test.txt in `vi` by entering **`vi test.txt`** at the shell prompt.
9. Display the status line by pressing **`Ctrl-G`** while in normal mode.
10. Use **`gg`** to move the cursor to the beginning of the first word in the first line of the file.
11. Search for all occurrences of the letter *a* by completing the following steps:
    a. While in normal mode, enter **`Esc /a <Enter>`**.
    b. Find the next instance of the letter *a* by pressing the **`n`** key.
12. Press **`Esc`** to enter normal mode. Use the **`h`**, **`j`**, **`k`**, and **`l`** keys to maneuver the cursor to the first letter of the word `time`.
    a. Delete the word `time` by using the **`dw`** command.
    b. Use the **`h`**, **`j`**, **`k`**, and **`l`** keys to move the cursor to the period at the end of the last line.
13. Exit the file without saving the changes by entering **`Esc :q!`**.
14. `vi` provides a user tutorial. Enter the command **`vimtutor`** to execute a self-paced tutorial for more practice with `vi`.

Editing Text Files in `nano`

GNU `nano` is a clone of Digital Equipment's `pico` editor. It is easier to use than `vim` because it does not contain command-line modes, understands arrow keys, and has a context-driven menu displayed at the bottom of the page (see Figure 2-5).

Command Keys

The `nano` editor uses both the `Ctrl` key (symbolized as ^ in the help menu) and the `Alt` key to issue commands. So, the command key sequence `^G` is actually entered as `Ctrl-G` and will open `nano`'s help screen. The command sequence `Alt-/` moves the cursor to the bottom of the document.

Table 2-1 illustrates some options for opening a file.

To move the cursor, use the key sequences specified in Table 2-2.

You can find additional `nano` documentation at https://www.nano-editor.org.

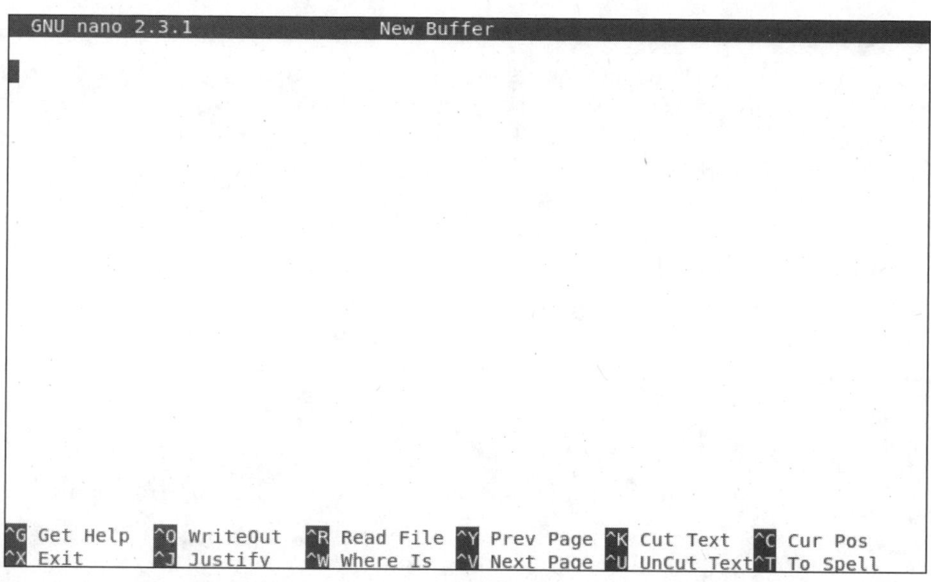

Figure 2-5 The nano editor screen

Option	Description
`<file_name>`	Opens a file with the name `<file_name>`. If the file does not exist, the file will be created once it is written.
`-v <file_name>`	Opens a file in view (read-only mode).
`-w`	Prevents line wrapping. This option (enabled by default in `/etc/nanorc`) is necessary when editing configuration files transferred from Windows to Linux.

Table 2-1 nano Open File Options

Key Sequence	Description
`Ctrl-F` or `Right Arrow`	Move the cursor one character to the right
`Ctrl-B` or `Left Arrow`	Move the cursor one character to the left
`Ctrl-P` or `Up Arrow`	Move the cursor up one line
`Ctrl-N` or `Down Arrow`	Move the cursor down one line
`Ctrl-Spacebar`	Move the cursor one word forward
`Alt-Spacebar`	Move the cursor one word back

Table 2-2 nano Key Sequences

Configuration Files

The nano editor uses two configuration files: the system-wide configuration file /etc/nanorc and the user-specific file ~/.nanorc in the user's home directory. The statement set nowrap in either of these files mitigates the need for the -w option, making it easier to work with files transferred from Windows computers.

Chapter Review

This chapter introduced some of the commands used to edit files using vi. As a CompTIA Linux+ candidate, you should be able to open a file, modify the contents of the file, and save the file. Use the built-in tutorial, vimtutor, to practice vi skills that are critical to passing the Linux+ exam.

In this chapter you learned the following:

- Linux uses text files to store operating system and application-configuration settings.
- The classic version of vi is called vi and the newest version is called vim (Vi IMproved).
- To open a file with vi, enter vi <filename>. If the file doesn't exist, a new file will be created.
- The vi editor opens into normal mode by default.
- To switch to insert mode, press i, I, a, A, o, or O.
- To switch back to normal mode, press the Esc key.
- dd Deletes the entire current line.
- p Pastes the lines from the buffer in the line below the cursor.
- P Pastes the lines from the buffer in the line above the cursor.
- u Undoes the last action.
- yy Yanks (copies) the current line into the buffer.
- ZZ Saves the current file and quits out of vi.
- h Moves the cursor left one character.
- j Moves the cursor down one line.
- k Moves the cursor up one line.
- l Moves the cursor right one character.
- From within normal mode, enter a colon (:) to switch to command-line mode.
- :w Writes the current file to disk.
- :x Writes the current file to disk and then exits vi.
- :wq Writes the current file to disk and exits vi.

- `:q` Closes `vi` without saving the current file.
- `:q!` Closes `vi` without saving changes, even if the file has been modified.
- `:e!` Forgets changes since the last write and continues editing from where you left off without the recent changes.
- Pressing `Ctrl-G` displays a status line at the bottom of the interface.
- Entering `/<string>` forward searches for the specified string.
- Entering `?<string>` reverse searches for the specified string.
- The `nano` editor is simpler than `vi` because the cursor can be maneuvered with arrow keys.
- To save and exit from `nano`, press `Ctrl-X`.

Questions

1. How are operating system and application configuration parameters stored on a Linux system?

A. In text files

B. In the Registry

C. In `.ini` files

D. In the system database

2. Beth is trying to quit a file *without* saving any new edits since the last time she wrote the file to disk. She receives the error message "No write since last change." Select the answer that correctly describes what has occurred and how to fix it.

A. The buffer has been modified without writing the change to disk. Execute `Esc :wq!`

B. The buffer has been modified without writing the change to disk. Execute `Esc :w!`

C. The buffer has been modified without writing the change to disk. Execute `Esc :w` and then `Esc :q`

D. The buffer has been modified without writing the change to disk. Execute `Esc :q!`

3. Your cursor is positioned at line 14 of the document. Which commands will bring the cursor to the top of the document? (Choose two.)

A. `Esc 1G`

B. `Esc :GG`

C. `Esc gg`

D. `Esc :gg`

4. Phillip has a terminal window open on his Linux system, and the current directory is `/tmp`. He needs to use `vi` to edit a text file named `vnc` in the `/etc/xinetd.d` directory. Which of the following commands should Phillip use to do this?

   A. `vi vnc`

   B. `vi /tmp/vnc`

   C. `vi /etc/xinetd.d/vnc`

   D. `vi /etc/xinetd.d`

5. Karrye has a terminal window open on her Linux system, and the current directory is `/home/karrye`. She needs to create a new file in her home directory named `resources.txt` using `vi`. Which of the following commands should Karrye use to do this?

   A. `vi resources.txt -new`

   B. `vi resources`

   C. `vi ~/resources`

   D. `vi resources.txt`

6. Which mode does `vi` open into by default?

   A. Command-line mode

   B. Insert mode

   C. Normal mode

   D. Replace mode

7. After opening a file, Ralph uses the `h`, `j`, `k`, and `l` keys to move the cursor to the line he wants to edit. He tries to type, but nothing happens. Why?

   A. The `vi` editor is in insert mode. He needs to switch to normal mode.

   B. The `vi` editor is in normal mode. He needs to switch to insert mode.

   C. The `vi` editor is in insert mode. He needs to switch to replace mode.

   D. The text file is corrupt.

8. Audrey uses `vi` to edit a text file in insert mode. Because of the nature of the changes she has made to the file, she needs to switch to replace mode. Which key or key combination should Audrey use to do this?

   A. `Esc R`

   B. `Ctrl-X Ctrl-R`

   C. `:`

   D. `I`

9. Roderick is using `vi` to edit a file in insert mode. He needs to switch back to normal mode. Which key should Roderick press to do this?
   A. `Insert`
   B. `:`
   C. `Esc`
   D. `Backspace`
10. Herman is using `vi` to edit a file in normal mode. He tries to use the `Backspace` key to delete a word, but nothing happens. What's wrong with the system?
    A. He needs to switch to normal mode.
    B. He needs to press `Ctrl-Backspace`.
    C. Nothing is wrong; `Backspace` doesn't work in normal mode.
    D. He needs to switch to command-line mode.
11. Pamela created a new file using `vi` and now needs to save the file without exiting the editor. Which command should Pamela use to do this?
    A. `:s`
    B. `:w`
    C. `:save`
    D. `:exit`
12. Ronald created a new file using `vi` and needs to save the file to disk and exit the program. Which commands should Ronald use to do this? (Choose three.)
    A. `:w`
    B. `:e!`
    C. `:wq`
    D. `:x`
    E. `Esc ZZ`
13. Sherry made several changes to a configuration file using `vi`. She has found a myriad of mistakes and wants to quit without saving the changes so that she can start over. Which command should Sherry use to do this?
    A. `:q!`
    B. `:exit`
    C. `:q`
    D. `:exit!`

14. Stephen is working with a file in `vi` normal mode. He locates a word in the file that needs to be deleted and places the cursor at the beginning of that word. Which command should Stephen use to delete this word without deleting the space that follows the word?

    A. `dw`

    B. `de`

    C. `d$`

    D. `dd`

15. Rene is using `vi` to edit a file. She is in normal mode. Which of the following commands should Rene use to forward search for the string "server" from the current cursor position?

    A. `/server`

    B. `search=server`

    C. `/"server"`

    D. `find "server"`

16. Referring to question 15, Rene would like to continue searching for the string "server" but wants to reverse the search direction. Which command should Rene use to do this?

    A. `n`

    B. N

    C. `?`

    D. `/`

Answers

1. **A.** Linux uses text files to store configuration parameters for both the operating system and applications or services running on the system.

2. **D.** `vi` requires users to write the contents of the buffer to disk before quitting. Users may override any errors by adding `!` to the end of the command. Therefore, the command-line command `:q!` will quit the file without writing new entries in the buffer to disk.

3. **A, C.** Both `Esc 1G` and `Esc gg` move the cursor to the first line (top) of the document.

4. **C.** Because the file to be loaded doesn't reside in the current directory, Phillip has to provide the full path to the file along with its filename when starting `vi`.

5. **D.** Because Karrye has not specified a path, `vi` will create the file in her current directory, which is what she wants.

6. **C.** By default, `vi` opens in normal mode.

7. **B.** The `vi` editor opens by default into normal mode. Ralph must press the `i`, `I`, `a`, `A`, `o`, or `O` key to switch to insert mode to start editing the file.
8. **A.** Pressing the key sequence `Esc R` places `vi` in replace mode.
9. **C.** Pressing `Esc` while in insert mode switches `vi` to normal mode.
10. **C.** The `Backspace` key doesn't work in normal mode. Herman must first switch to insert mode or replace mode.
11. **B.** Entering `:w` writes the current memory buffer to disk without exiting the editor.
12. **C, D, E.** Entering `:x` causes `vi` to save the current file and exit the program, as does entering `:wq` or `Esc ZZ`.
13. **A.** Entering `:q!` exits `vi` without saving changes to the current file.
14. **B.** Entering `de` in normal mode will cause `vi` to delete the word without deleting the space that follows the word.
15. **A.** Entering `/server` in normal mode will search forward for the expression "server" in the file.
16. **B.** The `N` command will reverse the current search direction.

CHAPTER 3

Working with the Linux Shell

In this chapter, you will learn about

- What a shell is
- Configuring the shell
- Setting a local environment
- Setting time
- Bash configuration files
- Redirection

It's really about how you collect the data, use the data, and turn it into action.

—Lisa P. Jackson, Apple, Inc.

Linux administrators generally work within a command-line environment called the shell, instead of a graphical environment like in operating systems such as macOS and Windows; because of this, understanding command-line utilities is critical in Linux. Linux allows for different shell environments which either secure or simplify the command-line experience. A majority of Linux administration work is done using a shell, and in this chapter, you will learn about the shell provided on all Linux versions known as `bash`.

You may find it helpful to log on to the virtual machine while reading this chapter.

What Is a Shell?

A *shell* is a program that functions as a user interface and command-line interpreter when using a command-line interface. It's called a shell because it provides an interface between the user and the hardware, so like a turtle's shell, it protects the hardware from the user. (Chapter 13 details another shell feature known as scripting.)

Users need a way to tell the operating system the tasks to complete, and the operating system needs a way to communicate results to users. A user interface allows a user to interact with the operating system. Linux provides two types of user interfaces:

- **Command-line interface (CLI)** The command-line interface allows users to communicate with the Linux operating system by typing a command and then pressing `Enter`. For example, you can type `ls` and press `Enter` to display the files available to you, or type `who` and press `Enter` to see who is currently using the computer.
- **Graphical user interface (GUI)** The easy-to-use graphical user interface allows users to interact with the Linux kernel using a mouse.

Configuring the Shell

In this section, we discuss different shell resources. The shell resources regulate the user environment and track how the shell operates.

In this section, you will learn about

- The life of a process
- Managing variables
- Configuring aliases

Let's start with shell processes.

The Life of a Process

A *process* is a single instance of a program that operates in its own memory space. The operating system assigns a unique process ID (PID) each time a program is started. This PID is used to control and track resources assigned to the program.

For example, when you execute the `vim` command, a `vim` process starts and is assigned a PID. If you execute `vim` again in another terminal, the new `vim` process starts with a different PID. Doing this a third time produces another instance of `vim` with a different PID. The result is three unique `vim` instances, as shown in Figure 3-1, where the `vim` PIDs are `7555`, `7567`, and `7568`, respectively.

Parent and Child Processes

After you log on to a system, you are presented with a default shell for passing commands to Linux. The default shell program is called `bash`.

Figure 3-1 Three instances of the `vim` process

```
student1  7555  3442  0 17:59 pts/1     00:00:00 vim
student1  7567  3336  0 17:59 pts/0     00:00:00 vim
student1  7568  3497  0 17:59 pts/2     00:00:00 vim
```

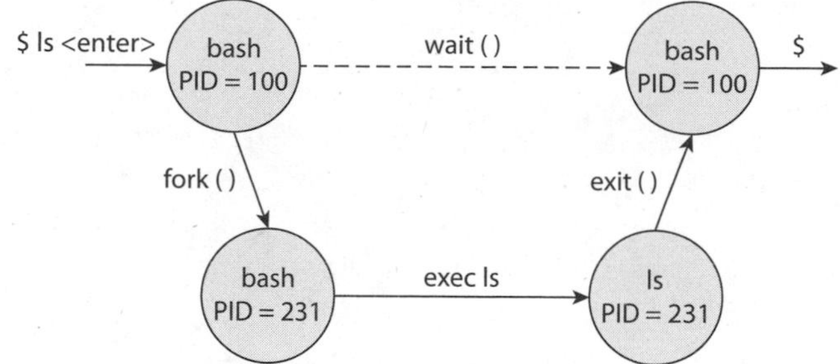

Figure 3-2 The life cycle of a process

When you execute a command such as `ls`, a subshell or child process is created to engage with the operating system. This new child process is initially a copy of the parent `bash` process, but using a new PID. The `exec` system call overwrites the new PID with the `ls` command. Once the `ls` command completes, it exits, and a prompt is displayed to run the next command. This process is detailed in Figure 3-2.

NOTE The term *spawn* is used to describe a parent process creating a child process.

Managing Variables

A *variable* is a memory location that is assigned a name and is used to store data. Variables are used to configure shell environments or to temporarily store program data. When a user logs off or the system is turned off, data stored in these memory locations are lost.

The two types of variables we'll discuss are shell variables and environment variables.

Shell Variables

A shell variable only exists in the memory space of the shell in which it was created. This means that when a shell variable is created within a parent process, the variable is available in that process but *not* in any child process.

The syntax for creating a shell variable is `<variable_name>=<value>`. The command `flower=rose` creates the shell variable `flower` and stores the word `rose`. Executing the command `flower=daisy` changes the contents of the shell variable `flower` to contain the word `daisy`.

To view the contents of a variable, execute the command `echo $<variable_name>`. The `echo` command displays a line of text. The dollar sign (`$`) preceding the variable name is a metacharacter that replaces the name of the variable with the value stored in the variable. Therefore, if the current value of the variable `flower` is `daisy`, the command `echo $flower` would display the output `daisy`.

The `set` command displays a list of all the shell variables and functions in the current process. Figure 3-3 displays partial output of the `set` command.

Figure 3-3 Partial output of the `set` command

```
BASH_ALIASES=()
BASH_ARGC=()
BASH_ARGV=()
BASH_CMDS=()
BASH_COMPLETION_COMPAT_DIR=/etc/bash_completion.d
BASH_LINENO=()
BASH_SOURCE=()
```

Environment Variables

Unlike shell variables, environment variables *are* visible to child processes. For example, the `EDITOR` variable contains the name of the system editor. If no assignment is made, `vi` becomes the user's default editor. If a user prefers the `nano` editor, they have to override `vi` being the default editor by changing the value of the `EDITOR` variable with the command `EDITOR=nano`. Since `EDITOR` is currently a shell variable, it will not be present when a child process is created.

To convert a shell variable to an environment variable, you need to assign an `export` attribute to the variable. When a parent spawns a child process, all variables with this attribute are visible to the child, as illustrated in Figure 3-4.

EXAM TIP The CompTIA Linux+ exam could show a *compound command* to set an environment variable using the `;` as follows: `<variable_name>=<value>;export <variable_name>`. Also, you can define an environment variable as follows: `export <variable_name>=<value>`.

To create the environment variable, execute the command `export <variable_name>=<value>`. For example, the command `export truck=chevy` creates the environment variable `truck` and assigns it the value of `chevy`, and this variable is now available in parent and child processes.

Convert existing shell variables to environment variables by running the command `export <variable_name>`; this assigns an `export` attribute to existing variables. The `unset` command deletes the variable and removes it from the environment. The `env` command displays a list of all environment variables in the current shell.

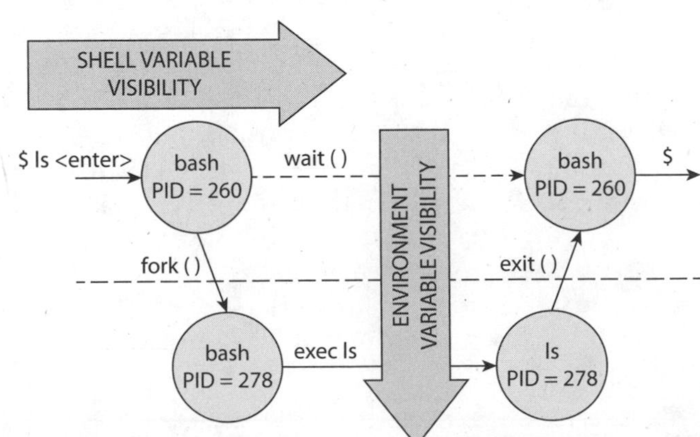

Figure 3-4 Shell versus environment variable visibility in parent and child processes

NOTE Running `declare -p <variable_name>` displays the variable's properties. The `-x` in the properties section of the output signifies that it is an environment variable.

Configuring Aliases

An *alias* is a command shortcut. By default, the `ls` command displays monochrome output. To colorize the output, execute `ls --color=auto`. To avoid typing the `--color=auto` option each time, create an alias using the following command syntax:

```
alias <alias_name>='<command>'
```

The command `alias ls='ls --color=auto'` creates an alias to replace the default `ls`. Aliases take precedence over all other commands, so every time the `ls` command is run, the command `ls --color=auto` executes.

NOTE An alias exists only in the shell in which it was created or loaded.

Line 1 of Figure 3-5 shows the results of creating the alias `ls='ls --color=auto'` (because the color is hard to discern in this black-and-white book, a color version of Figure 3-5 is available in the online resources). Executing the `alias` command (line 5) displays a list of aliases loaded into memory. Using the `grep` command and piping features (|) filters out desired aliases (the `grep` command, piping, and other features are detailed in Chapter 5).

```
1 # ls
2 anaconda-ks.cfg  Documents  initial-setup-ks.cfg  Pictures  Templates  vmware-tools-distrib
3 Desktop          Downloads  Music                 Public    Videos
4 #
5 # alias | grep ls=
6 alias ls='ls --color=auto'
7 #
8 # \ls
9 anaconda-ks.cfg  Documents  initial-setup-ks.cfg  Pictures  Templates  vmware-tools-distrib
10 Desktop         Downloads  Music                 Public    Videos
11 #
12 # ls
13 anaconda-ks.cfg  Documents  initial-setup-ks.cfg  Pictures  Templates  vmware-tools-distrib
14 Desktop          Downloads  Music                 Public    Videos
15 #
16 # unalias ls
17
18 #
19 # alias | grep ls=
20 #
21
22 # ls
23 anaconda-ks.cfg  Documents  initial-setup-ks.cfg  Pictures  Templates  vmware-tools-distrib
24 Desktop          Downloads  Music                 Public    Videos
```

Figure 3-5 Creating and removing an alias

On line 8, the backslash (\) that precedes the `ls` command temporarily negates the alias. Notice the output on line 9 (it is monochrome, although it may be hard to tell in this book).

On line 16, the command `unalias ls` removes the alias from memory. The output on line 23 is monochrome.

To permanently remove an alias, use the `unalias` command.

CAUTION Before creating an alias, make certain the alias name is not in use. Use the command `type -a <proposed_alias_name>` to display any commands, aliases, or functions currently using the proposed alias name.

The backslash (\) is a metacharacter that is used to negate the special significance of the following character or word and execute the command in its default configuration. Notice in the following example how the backslash before `$` negates the special significance of the metacharacter:

```
1. # echo $SHELL
2. /bin/bash
3. # echo \$SHELL
4. $SHELL
```

In line 1 of the example, the value of the `SHELL` environment variable is displayed on line 2. The \ is used in line 3 to negate the meaning of the `$`, so the result in line 4 is the literal $ and not the meaning of the `SHELL` variable.

Setting Up the Local Environment

Locale settings are used to set language- and country-specific settings such as date style, time style, and currency settings. Setting up the local environment means understanding the following:

- Locale settings
- Character encoding

Let's first cover what is tested on the CompTIA Linux+ exam.

Locale Settings

Locale settings are used to define output formats used by applications depending on the location of the Linux computer. Locale settings include address style, phone format, currency type, and more.

To set the locale, define the `LANG` variable, `LC` category variables, or the variable `LC_ALL` by using the `localectl` or `locale` command. Locale category variables are listed in Table 3-1.

Locale Category Variable	Definition
LC_ADDRESS	Address format
LC_COLLATE	How characters are compared and sorted
LC_IDENTIFICATION	Local code
LC_MEASUREMENT	Measure format
LC_MONETARY	Money format
LC_PAPER	Paper sizes
LC_TELEPHONE	Telephone number format

Table 3-1 Locale Categories

The command locale -k <locale_category> displays formatting information for that category. For example, the command locale -k LC_TELEPHONE displays the following output:

```
# locale -k LC_TELEPHONE
tel_int_fmt="+%c (%a) %l"
tel_dom_fmt="(%a) %l"
int_select="11"
int_prefix="1"
telephone-codeset="UTF-8"
```

Locale categories are associated with a locale name. The locale name defines formatting for a specific region. Locale names are formatted as follows:

```
<language>_<region>.<encoding_format>@<modifier>
```

An example of a locale name is en_US.UTF-8. An example of a modifier to specify use of euro currency is @euro.

Executing the command locale -a or localectl list-locales lists available locale names. The command localectl list-locales | grep en displays all locale names for the English language. Run locale to display the value of locale categories for the current session, as shown here:

```
#locale
LANG=en_US.UTF-8
LC_CTYPE="en_US.UTF-8"
LC_NUMERIC="en_US.UTF-8"
LC_TIME="en_US.UTF-8"
LC_COLLATE="en_US.UTF-8"
LC_MONETARY="en_US.UTF-8"
LC_MESSAGES="en_US.UTF-8"
LC_PAPER="en_US.UTF-8"
LC_NAME="en_US.UTF-8"
LC_ADDRESS="en_US.UTF-8"
LC_TELEPHONE="en_US.UTF-8"
LC_MEASUREMENT="en_US.UTF-8"
LC_IDENTIFICATION="en_US.UTF-8"
LC_ALL=
```

The variable LANG stores the locale name for the current login session. The following locale name shows that in this case, the current session uses the US English character set, which is encoded using UTF-8, and not some other encoding.

```
# echo $LANG
en_US.UTF-8
```

The variable LC_ALL overrides all locale category settings and the LANG variable.

The localectl Command

The command localectl is used to view and modify system locale and keyboard settings. For example, the command localectl set-locale LANG=<locale_name> sets the default system locale variable.

The command localectl set-locale LANG=en_CA.UTF-8 modifies the /etc/locale.conf file that stores the system locale and keyboard map settings. Use either localectl or localectl status to verify the change to the /etc/locale.conf file.

EXAM TIP Make sure you know how to verify changes within /etc/locale.conf using localectl status and how to list locality using localectl list-locales.

Character Encoding

This section on character encoding is written here for your reference; character encoding is *not* included in the CompTIA Linux+ exam objectives.

A character is a written symbol. A character set is a defined list of characters used for a specific purpose. The English alphabet is a character set that contains 26 letters, 10 digits, and 14 punctuation marks.

Characters are stored by assigning a numerical value to the character. The process of assigning a numerical value to a character is called *encoding*. The stored value is called a *code point*. An encoding format defines the number of bits used to store a character (code unit) and how the character is stored.

Let's take a brief look at the ASCII and UTF encoding formats.

An ASCII Primer

The American Standard Code for Information Interchange (ASCII) character set uses a 7-bit code unit. ASCII supports up to 128 characters (95 printable characters, 32 control codes, and 1 space character). Extended ASCII uses an 8-bit code unit and can support 256 characters.

A Unicode Primer

The code unit size of encoding formats such as ASCII and EBCDIC are unable to store all the different world characters. Unicode uses variable and fixed encoding formats to provide up to a 32-bit code unit and can store 1,114,112 different characters.

Unicode defines three encoding formats: UTF-8, UTF-16, and UTF-32 (see Table 3-2).

Table 3-2 Unicode Encoding Formats

Encoding Format	Description
UTF-8	Variable encoding. Uses 1, 2, 3, or 4 bytes to encode a character.
UTF-16	Variable encoding. Uses 2 or 4 bytes to encode a character.
UTF-32	Fixed encoding. Uses 4 bytes to encode a character.

UTF-8 and UTF-16 use up to 32 bits and variable encoding to store characters. Variable encoding uses the most significant bits of *code point*, or encoding value, to determine how to decode character information. UTF-32 uses *fixed encoding*, which means all 32 bits (4 bytes) are used to store a character.

Setting Time

The Linux operating system uses two clocks: the hardware clock, also known as the real-time clock (RTC), and the system clock. The RTC is a battery-powered circuit that maintains time even when system power is removed.

The system clock is the operating system clock. During the boot process, the system clock is set to the same value as the hardware clock. From that moment until the time the operating system is terminated, the system clock is maintained by the kernel. The system clock reports time using Coordinated Universal Time (UTC) and depends on individual processes to change UTC into local time.

NOTE UTC is a time standard and is also referred to as Zulu time.

The `date` Command

The `date` command is primarily used for reporting information from and managing the system clock. The `date` command displays the day, month, time (24-hour clock), time zone, and year.

```
# date
Thu Nov  6 23:02:00 EST 2014
```

With the `date` command's plus-percent feature, you can print just the minute, hour, or year by entering `date +%M` for the current minute, `date +%H` for the current hour, or `date +%Y` for the current year. Table 3-3 lists and defines additional percent codes, and the full listing is available from the `date` man page.

System administrators can set the date and time by using the `date -s` command using this format:

```
"Day Month Date Time Time-Zone Year"
```

Table 3-3 date Command Percent Codes

date **Percent Code**	**Definition**
%A	Full weekday name (e.g., Sunday)
%D	Date; same as %m/%d/%y
%F	Full date; same as %Y-%m-%d
%N	Nanosecond
%d	Day of the month
%j	Day of the year
%x	Date representation (e.g., 12/31/22)

The following illustration shows an example of using `date -s`:

```
# date
Wed Jun 22 14:56:06 EDT 2016
#
# date -s "Mon June 27 09:00:00 EDT 2016"
Mon Jun 27 09:00:00 EDT 2016
#
# date
Mon Jun 27 09:00:03 EDT 2016
```

The /usr/share/zoneinfo/ and /etc/localtime Files

The directory /usr/share/zoneinfo/ and the file /etc/localtime are used to configure the system's time zone. The directory contains binary data files for worldwide time zones and is used to set a default system-wide time zone by linking a file from zoneinfo to /etc/localtime.

The commands date, date +%Z, ls -l /etc/localtime, and timedatectl display the current system time zone.

EXAM TIP An ls option that hasn't been discussed yet is ls -d, which means do not descend into directories. The user will see the directory name but not the files listed in the directory. Run ls -ld to view directory permissions instead of file permissions; for example:

```
# ls -ld /usr/share/zoneinfo/
```

To reset the system-wide time zone, remove the current symbolic link to /etc/localtime by running unlink /etc/localtime or \rm /etc/localtime. (Symbolic links are covered in detail in Chapter 5.) Then, create another symbolic link, as in the following example to set Pacific Time:

```
ln -sf /usr/share/zoneinfo/America/Los_Angeles /etc/localtime
```

The `hwclock` Command

The `hwclock` command is used to manage the real-time clock, or RTC. The commands `hwclock`, `hwclock -r`, and `hwclock --show` display the current hardware clock time in local time, as shown here:

```
# hwclock
Tue 13 Aug 2019 10:39:04 AM EDT  -1.043752 seconds
#
#
# hwclock -r
Tue 13 Aug 2019 10:39:10 AM EDT  -1.042820 seconds
#
#
# hwclock --show
Tue 13 Aug 2019 10:39:19 AM EDT  -1.043072 seconds
```

The output to the right displays the time offset. Applying the offset to the displayed time produces the actual time.

The command `hwclock -s` or `hwclock --hctosys` (hardware clock to system clock) sets the system time using the RTC and sets the time zone to the current time zone. The command `hwclock -w` or `hwclock --systohc` sets the system clock to the same time as the hardware clock.

The `timedatectl` Command

The command `timedatectl` or `timedatectl status` can be used to view and manage system clocks. Executing the command `timedatectl` produces the output shown here:

```
1  # timedatectl
2        Local time: Sun 2019-08-18 20:17:49 PDT
3    Universal time: Mon 2019-08-19 03:17:49 UTC
4          RTC time: Mon 2019-08-19 03:17:49
5         Time zone: America/Los_Angeles (PDT, -0700)
6       NTP enabled: yes
7  NTP synchronized: yes
8   RTC in local TZ: no
9        DST active: yes
10  Last DST change: DST began at
11                   Sun 2019-03-10 01:59:59 PST
12                   Sun 2019-03-10 03:00:00 PDT
13  Next DST change: DST ends (the clock jumps one hour backwards) at
14                   Sun 2019-11-03 01:59:59 PDT
15                   Sun 2019-11-03 01:00:00 PST
```

Lines 6 and 7 confirm that the Network Time Protocol (NTP) is enabled and is being synchronized with an NTP server, which occurs every 11 minutes. Details on NTP are covered in Chapter 14.

The command `timedatectl list-timezones` displays a list of time zones. The command `timedatectl set-timezone "<time zone>"` immediately changes the system-wide time zone.

For example, the command `timedatectl set-timezone "America/New_York"` immediately changes the system-wide time zone to Eastern Time. Behind the scenes, this command updates the symbolic link between /etc/localtime and /usr/share/zoneinfo/America/New_York.

To change the RTC from local time to UTC, use the following command:

```
timedatectl set-timezone UTC
```

Setting System Time and Date

The command `timedatectl set-time 'HH:MM:SS'` sets the system time. To change the system date, execute the command `timedatectl set-time 'YYYY-MM-DD'`. The command `timedatectl set-time 'YYYY-MM_DD HH:MM'` changes both the system time and date.

If automatic time synchronization via NTP is enabled, setting the time with timedatectl commands will not work.

Bash Configuration Files

In the previous section, you learned how to manage variables, shell options, and aliases via the command line and how to change the system's locale and time settings. Variables, aliases, and shell option settings executed on the command line are stored in memory. These settings disappear when the user logs out of the system.

But when you create aliases and variables that make your job easier, you want to keep those settings. Configuration files define settings that remain persistent even after logging off or rebooting.

The bash configuration files are

- /etc/profile
- /etc/bashrc
- /home/<user_name>/.bash_profile
- /home/<user_name>/.bashrc
- /home/<user_name>/.bash_logout

The files /etc/profile and /etc/bashrc are system-wide configuration files applied to all applicable users when they log in. Files located in the user's home directory (/home/<user_name>) contain configuration information *only* for that user.

The configuration files /etc/profile and /home/<user_name>/.bash_profile contain a series of commands used to configure the user's working environment, such as environment variables. The configuration files /etc/bashrc and /home/<user_name>/.bashrc are used to configure Bash shell features, such as aliases. Use /home/<user_name>/.bash_logout to perform operations during logout, such as removing files older than 30 days from a wastebasket.

Concepts to understand for the CompTIA Linux+ exam include the following:

- Login script order
- The `source` command

Let's first discuss the login script order.

Login Script Order

When a user logs into a Linux system, customization scripts are read in the following order when using the Bash shell:

1. `/etc/profile`
2. `/home/<user_name>/.bash_profile`
3. `/home/<user_name>/.bashrc`
4. `/etc/bashrc`

The file `/etc/profile` is read once at login, and the user might find these environment variables:

- **`HOSTNAME`** The hostname of the computer or node
- **`MAIL`** The file where a user's receiving mail resides; for example, `MAIL=/var/spool/mail/<user_name>`

The file `/home/<user_name>/.bash_profile` is used to customize the bash environment for a user and is read once at login. The file contains variables used to configure the user's working environment, such as the default editor. The user might find these settings:

- **`EDITOR`** The default editor settings; for example, `EDITOR=/usr/bin/nano`
- **`PATH`** Search path of directories where executable programs can be found

The file `/home/<user_name>/.bashrc` is used to customize how the Bash shell runs and contains aliases, functions, or shell parameters. `/home/<user_name>/.bashrc` is executed each time a shell (pseudo-terminal) is started in a GUI environment. This file might contain aliases, such as these:

```
alias ls='ls --color=auto'
alias h=history
alias mroe=more
alias c=clear
```

EXAM TIP Linux uses the tilde (~) character to represent `/home/<user_name>/`, or a user's home directory. For example, `/home/<user_name>/.bashrc` can be represented as `~/.bashrc` for the currently logged-on user.

The file `/etc/bashrc` is also read when a pseudo-terminal starts and may contain these settings:

- **`SHELL`** The command shell for this login session; for example, `/bin/bash`
- **`PS1`** The command prompt configuration

NOTE Scripts in the directory `/etc/profile.d` contain configuration information for specific programs and are read or *sourced* automatically during the login process. Files ending in `.sh` are sourced when using the Bourne, Korn, or Bash shells. Files ending in `.csh` are sourced when using the C-shell.

The `source` Command

Configuration changes are not active until they are stored in memory, or *sourced*. To place changes in memory, the user must execute the commands in the configuration file. The command `source <filename>` or `. <filename>` (note the leading dot and space) executes the commands in a configuration file.

Once a user makes changes to a configuration file such as `~/.bash_profile`, they can run `source ~/.bash_profile` or `. ~/.bash_profile` to make the configuration changes available immediately.

Exercise 3-1: Working with Variables, Parameters, and Aliases

This exercise enables you to practice creating and removing variables, aliases, and shell options as well as editing shell configuration files. But first, I want to emphasize something useful for your career. When executing a command, be sure to test the results. For example, to open a child shell, use the following procedure:

1. Verify the process ID (PID) of the current shell using the **`ps`** or **`ps -f`** command.
2. Create the child process (`bash`).
3. Verify you are in a child shell by executing the **`ps -f`** command and then look for a PID whose parent process (PPID) is the same as you verified in step 1.

With that in mind, log on as user **`student1`** (password: **`student1`**) on the virtual machine provided with the book and then follow these steps:

VIDEO Watch the Exercise 3-1 video for a demonstration of this exercise.

1. Right-click the Desktop and select Open Terminal. This opens a text terminal (pseudo-terminal).

2. Execute the **ps** command to display a list of processes executing on the current terminal. Notice the process `bash`. Also notice the process ID associated with the command `bash` in the PID column. This is your current shell.
3. Execute the **bash** command.
4. Execute the command **ps -f**. Look at the second instance of `bash` and its PID. Now look at the parent process ID (PPID). The PPID is the process number of the shell that spawned the current shell (child). The second instance of `bash` is the child shell.
5. Type the **exit** command. This terminates the current shell and returns you to the parent shell.
6. Execute the **ps** command. Notice the PID.
7. Create the shell variable `flower` and assign it the value `rose` by executing the **flower=rose** command.
8. Execute the command **echo $flower** to see if the variable has been created. Execute the **set** command to see all shell variables and the **set | grep flower** command to view the shell variable `flower`.
9. Create the variable `nut` and assign it the value `almond` by executing the **nut=almond** command. Test to see if the variable has been created.
10. Open a child shell by executing the command **bash** and test to ensure you have created a child shell.
11. Determine if the variables `flower` and `nut` are present in the child shell.
12. Return to the parent shell.
13. Add an `export` attribute to the variable `flower` by executing the command **export flower**.
14. Open a child process by executing the command **bash**. Use the commands **echo $flower** and **echo $nut** to determine if either the variable `flower` or `nut` exists in the child process. Explain the results.
15. Return to the parent shell by executing the **exit** command.
16. Create an environment variable called `fruit` and assign it the value `apple` by executing the command **export fruit=apple**.

    Test to determine the following:

    - The variable has been created and is a shell variable in the current shell. To do this, type the command **echo $fruit** or **set | grep fruit**.
    - The variable has been assigned an export attribute. To do this, use the command **env | grep fruit**.
17. To view the status of all shell parameters, execute the command **set -o**.
18. Type the command **set -o | grep allexport** to view the status of the shell parameter `allexport`.

19. Type the command **`set -o allexport`**. This turns on the `bash` parameter, which automatically applies an `export` attribute to all newly created variables.
20. Verify the `allexport` parameter has been turned on by executing the command **`set -o | grep allexport`**.
21. Create the variable `truck` and assign it the value `chevy` by executing the **`truck=chevy`** command. Execute the command **`env | grep truck`** to determine if the variable has been assigned an `export` attribute.
22. Turn off `allexport` by executing the command **`set +o allexport`** and verify the shell parameter has been turned off.
23. Create the alias `ldetc`, which will execute the command `ls -ld /etc`, by executing the command **`alias ldetc='ls -ld /etc'`**.
24. Type the command **`alias`** to verify the alias `ldetc` has been created. You could also type the command `alias | grep ldetc`.
25. Type the command **`ldetc`**.
26. An alias only exists in the shell in which it is created. To test this, open a child shell and perform the following procedure:
    a. Execute the **`ps`** command to determine what the PID of the current shell is.
    b. Execute the **`bash`** command to open a new shell.
    c. Execute the command **`ps -f`** to verify a child shell has opened by making certain the PPID of the current shell is the PID discovered in step a.
    d. Determine if the alias created in step 23 exists by trying to execute **`ldetc`**.

       Alternatively, execute the command `alias`, `alias ldetc`, or `alias grep | ldetc` to list the aliases in memory.
27. Return to the parent shell by exiting the current process (**`exit`**).
28. Remove the alias `ldetc` by executing the command **`unalias ldetc`**. Use the command **`alias`**, **`alias ldetc`**, or **`alias | grep ldetc`** to verify the alias has been removed from memory.
29. Use `vi` to add **`set -o noclobber`** to the last line of the file `/home/student1/.bashrc` and then save the file. The shell option `noclobber` does not allow a user to redirect the standard output (>) to an existing file.
30. Execute the command **`set -o | grep noclobber`**.

    Is `noclobber` turned on or off? Why?
31. Start a child process by executing the command **`bash`**.
32. Determine if the shell option `noclobber` is turned on or off. Why?
33. Return to the parent process. Execute the command **`source /home/student1/.bashrc`**.

    Is `noclobber` turned on or off? Why?

Answers to Exercise 3-1

Answer to step 29 `vi /home/student1/.bashrc`

Answer to step 30 `noclobber` will be turned off. After you edit a configuration file, the changes must be read into memory.

Answer to step 32 `noclobber` is turned on. The file `/home/student1/.bashrc` is read each time a process is opened; therefore, changes were read into memory.

Answer to step 33 `.bashrc` is read when a child shell is created or a `source` command is issued. When you made the first change to `.bashrc` in the parent shell, you did not source `.bashrc`, so `noclobber` was off in the parent shell. When you opened a child shell (step 31), `.bashrc` was read; therefore, `noclobber` was turned on in the child shell. When you returned to the parent shell, `noclobber` is turned off. The command `source /home/student1/.bashrc` executes each line in `~/.bashrc` (including `set -o noclobber`). This command turns `noclobber` on in the current shell.

Redirection

When a user executes a command, user input is received via the standard input device (stdin), which is the keyboard by default. All output, except error messages, is sent to the standard output device (stdout), which is the monitor by default. Error messages are output to the standard error device (stderr), again the monitor by default. Figure 3-6 shows the default settings and their values, 0, 1, and 2, respectively.

Redirection permits a user to alter from the defaults for stdin, stdout, or stderr to a device or file using their file descriptors.

File Descriptors

A file descriptor is a reference, or *handle*, used by the kernel to access a file. A file descriptor table is created for every process. This table tracks all files opened by the process. A unique index number, or *file descriptor number*, is assigned to a file when it is opened by a process, as defined here:

- **`fd0`** Standard input device
- **`fd1`** Standard output device
- **`fd2`** Standard error device
- **`fd255`** The bash file descriptor 255 tracks controlling terminal information.

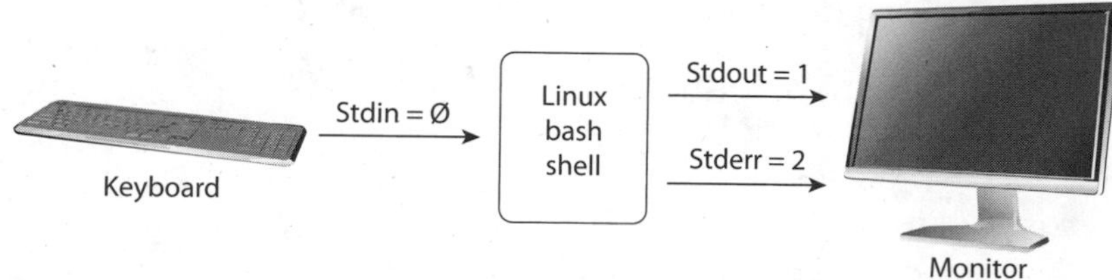

Figure 3-6 Standard input, standard output, and standard error defaults

Redirect stdin with <

Use the < operator to redirect standard input. For example, the `cat` command is used to list the contents of a file, as shown here:

```
$ cat /etc/hosts
127.0.0.1   localhost
10.0.0.1      pear  pear.funutation.com
10.0.0.2      orange  orange.funutation.com
```

To input from the `/etc/hosts` file directly instead of the keyboard, run

```
$ cat < /etc/hosts
127.0.0.1   localhost
10.0.0.1      pear  pear.funutation.com
10.0.0.2      orange  orange.funutation.com
```

The results appear the same in this case, and more uses of the < operator will be shown in future chapters.

Using Heredocs with <<

Another form of input redirection is the *heredoc*, or here document. The heredoc reads each input line from the current source until it reaches the limit word. Otherwise, all the lines read up to that point are used as the standard input for a command. For example:

```
$ cat << RNDI
> dummy
> CHAR
> EOF RNDI
> RNDI
dummy
CHAR
EOF RNDI
$
```

Notice that the keyword (in this case `RNDI`, but it could be most any set of characters) must match the characters in the last line. The `cat` command will print data up to, but not including, the keyword.

Although not tested on the current Linux+ exam, the here string, or <<< operator, allows a user to send a string to a command. For example,

```
$ cat <<< 'hello RNDI'
hello RNDI
$
```

sends the string `"hello RNDI"` to the `cat` command.

Redirect stdout with > and >>

Use the greater-than operator (>) to redirect standard output to a file. Use the double greater-than operator (>>) to append data to a file.

The who command lists all logged-on users on a system, as shown here:

```
$ who > whofile
$ cat whofile
nelson          tty2          2024-02-17 20:07


kwon            tty1          2024-03-05 14:27
$ pwd >> whofile
$ cat whofile
nelson     tty2          2024-02-17  20:07
kwon            tty1       2024-03-05 14:27
/home/kwon
$
```

The pwd command prints the user's current working directory /home/kwon and is appended to whofile with the >> operator in the preceding example.

The > operator will create a file if one does not exist and will overwrite the file if one does exist. The >> operator will also create the file if it does not exist, but it will append the standard output to it if it does exist.

NOTE The shell parameter noclobber does not allow the > redirection to overwrite an existing file. The command set -o | grep noclobber verifies if noclobber is set. The command set +o noclobber turns the parameter off.

Redirect stderr with 2>

The control operators 2> and 2>> are used to choose an alternate standard error file or device. The 2> operator will create a file if one does not exist and will overwrite the file if one does exist. The 2>> operator will create a file if one does not exist, but it will append the standard error to it if one does exist.

The command ls /etc /roses 2> errorfile attempts to list the properties of the directories /etc and /roses. The directory /roses does not exist. Since the /etc directory exists, its properties will be displayed on the standard output device, which is the screen.

Since the directory /roses does not exist, it produces an error message. The 2> control operator redirects the error message to the file errorfile.

NOTE As 2> redirects standard error messages, 1> redirects standard output messages. Most users use > to redirect stdout, but 1> also does the same as >.

Combining stdout and stderr

The control operators > and `2>` may be combined to send both outputs to the same file or device. The control operator `2>&1` redirects the standard error to the same location as the standard output. Here's how this works:

- The control operator `2>` designates altering the data stream for error messages.
- The `&` character is a Boolean AND.
- The `1` is the file descriptor number for the standard output device.

The command `ls -ld /etc /roses > errorfile 2>&1` writes the standard output and standard error to the file `errorfile`.

The control operator `1>&2` redirects the standard output to the same location as the standard error. Here's how it works:

- The `1>` control operator redirects the standard output.
- The `&` is a Boolean AND.
- The `2` is the file descriptor number for the standard error data stream.

The command `ls -ld /etc /roses 2> errorfile 1>&2` writes the standard output and standard error to the file `errorfile`.

Finally, the control operator `&>` also redirects both the standard error and standard output to the same file. The command `ls -ld /etc /roses &> errorfile` writes the properties of the `/etc` directory and the error message to the file `errorfile`.

Ignoring Error Messages with /dev/null

Often error messages from commands are warnings that can be ignored. Sometimes there are so many warnings, good stdout data is missed. Using the null device is one excellent solution. The `/dev/null` device is a zero-byte character device that is created each time the system boots. Data written to `/dev/null` is discarded immediately.

To recursively list all the files and directories in a filesystem, you can run `ls -R /`, but you will see several "permission denied" errors for files you are not allowed to view. To hide these error messages, run the command this way:

```
ls -R / 2> /dev/null
```

The good output (stdout) is displayed to the screen, and error messages are not saved, nor do they appear.

Send Data to a Command Using a Pipe

A pipe is a method of connecting the stdout of one process to the stdin of another process. There are two types of pipes: named and unnamed.

A named pipe is a file that facilitates interprocess communication. A named pipe takes output from one process and places it into a file. Another process removes the information from the file. The `mknod` and `mkfifo` commands create a named pipe file. Deleting the file removes the named pipe.

An unnamed pipe uses the output from the command to the left of the pipe symbol (|) as the input to the command to the right of the pipe symbol. To do this, a temporary file is created within Linux. When the command is completed, the temporary file is removed.

NOTE Press `Shift-|` on US keyboards to produce the pipe symbol. The | key (located above the `Enter` key) is the \ key if you don't press `Shift` simultaneously.

To understand how an unnamed pipe works, we will use a fictitious temporary file called `pipetemp`. The command `cat file1 | cat > filea` redirects the stdout of the command `cat file1` to be the input of the command `cat > filea`. The left part of the pipe executes `cat file1 > pipetemp` and then the right side of the pipe executes the command `cat pipetemp > filea`.

The `tee` command displays the output of a command to the console device *and* redirects the output to a file or device. The command `cat /etc/hosts | tee filea` displays the contents of `/etc/hosts` on the console device and writes the contents of the file to `filea`.

Exercise 3-2: Redirection Hands-on Project

In Exercise 3-2, you will perform the following tasks:

- Determine what your login shell is.
- Create local and environment values.
- Determine your process ID and parent process ID.
- Change shell options.
- Create aliases.

VIDEO Watch the Exercise 3-2 video for a demonstration.

Log on as user **`student1`** (password: **`student1`**) on the virtual machine provided with the book and then follow these steps:

1. Execute the **`cd`** command.
2. Type the **`pwd`** command. The output should display `/home/student1`.

3. Create the directory `redir` by executing the command **`mkdir redir`**.
4. Execute the command **`cd redir`**.
5. Execute the command **`pwd`**. The output should display `/home/student/redir`.
6. Use the command **`cat /etc/hosts > filea`** to read the contents of the file `/etc/hosts` and place the output in `filea`.
7. Read the contents of the file `/etc/default/useradd` and output the contents to `fileb`.
8. Use the **`cat`** command to view the contents of `filea` and `fileb`.
9. Redirect the output of the command `ls -ld /etc` to filea by executing the command **`ls -ld /etc > filea`**.

   What happened to the original contents of `filea`?
10. Append the output of the command `ls -ld /etc` to fileb by executing the following command:

    ```
    ls -ld /etc/ >> fileb.
    ```
11. Redirect the standard output of the command `ls -ld /etc /roses` to `filea` and the standard error to `fileb` by executing the following command:

    ```
    ls -ld /etc /roses > filea 2 >fileb
    ```
12. Execute the command **`ls -ld /etc /roses`**. Redirect the standard output to `fileb` and append the standard error to `filea`.
13. Execute the command **`ls -ld /etc /roses`** using three methods to redirect both the standard output and stderr to `file3`.

    Redirect the output of the command `cat /etc/hosts` to `file4` and display the contents on the console device using the command **`cat /etc/hosts | tee file4`**.
14. Execute the command **`cat < /etc/hosts > file5`**. What does it do?
15. Execute the command **`echo hello > /dev/tty2`**.
16. Switch to a text terminal by using the key sequence **`Ctrl-Alt-F2`**. Notice the output on the terminal.
17. Return to the graphical environment by using the key sequence **`Ctrl-Alt-F1`**.

NOTE This exercise omits some steps. This was intentional. I want you to troubleshoot issues. When an exercise step does not work, make certain no other conditions exist to prevent a command from executing properly. If there is difficulty, look at the answer section that follows, or watch the video.

Answers to Exercise 3-2

Answer to step 9 Upon executing the command `ls -ld /etc > filea`, you should receive the error `bash: filea: cannot overwrite existing file.` The shell parameter `noclobber` is preventing you from overwriting an existing file. Executing the command `set +o noclobber` turns off `noclobber` and allows you to redirect the output to an existing file.

Answer to step 12 Use the command `ls -ld /etc /roses >> fileb 2> filea.`

Answer to step 13 The three methods are `ls -ld /etc /roses &> file3`, `ls -ld /etc /roses > file3 2>&1`, and `ls -ld /etc /roses 2> file3 1>&2.`

Answer to step 15 The command `cat < /etc/hosts > file5` uses the file `/etc/hosts` as the input to the `cat` command and outputs the results to `file5`.

Chapter Review

This chapter introduced the Bash shell. We covered what a shell is and how to use various facilities to customize the user's environment and the shell's operating parameters. Here are some important points to note:

- The shell is a user interface, command-line interpreter, and scripting language.
- A process is a single instance of a program.
- A parent process can spawn child processes.
- Variables are used to store data.
- Shell variables only exist in the process in which they were created.
- Environment variables are copied from the parent process to the child process.
- Shell options are used to configure how a shell operates.
- When programs start, they may use configuration files to configure how they operate.
- The Bash shell has five configuration files: `/etc/profile`, `/etc/bashrc`, `/home/<user_name>/.bash_profile`, `/home/<user_name>/.bashrc`, and `/home/<user_name>/.logout`.
- `/etc/profile` and `/home/<user_name>/.bash_profile` are read when a user logs on or executes a command that requires a logon.
- `/etc/bashrc` and `/home/<user_name>/.bashrc` are read each time a new process is started.
- The source or "dot" (`.`) command is used to read changes in configuration files into memory.
- Redirection permits a user to alter the stdin, stdout, or stderr device or file.

Questions

1. Which of the following statements concerning a shell variable is true?
   - **A.** The variable will be copied when a new process is spawned.
   - **B.** The variable will not be copied when a new process is spawned.
   - **C.** The variable name must be in capital letters.
   - **D.** The variable name must be in lowercase letters.
2. What does the set command do?
   - **A.** Displays a list of shell options and their status
   - **B.** Displays a list of environment variables
   - **C.** Displays a list of shell variables
   - **D.** Prepares the system for a Linux installation
3. User student1 has logged on and discovered that a user-specific environment variable assignment is causing a problem. Select all actions student1 must complete to permanently resolve the problem. (Choose two.)
   - **A.** Remove the variable assignment from /home/student1/.bashrc.
   - **B.** Remove the variable assignment from /home/student1/.bash_profile.
   - **C.** Remove the variable from memory.
   - **D.** Remove the variable assignment from /etc/profile.
4. A user creates the environment variable test in their logon shell and then executes the command bash. Executing the command env | grep test verifies the variable is present in the child process. The user executes the command unset test. Which of the following statements is true?
   - **A.** The variable test is removed from the parent and child processes.
   - **B.** The variable test is removed from the child process and the child process is exited.
   - **C.** The variable test is removed from the child process.
   - **D.** The variable test is removed from the child process and becomes a shell variable in the parent process.
5. Select two commands that create an environment variable in the Bash shell. (Choose two.)
   - **A.** export <variable_name> = value
   - **B.** setenv <variable_name>
   - **C.** export <variable_name>=value
   - **D.** <variable_name>=<value>;export <variable_name>

6. Which commands are associated with shell variables? (Choose two.)

   A. `export <variable_name> = value`

   B. `<variable_name>=<value>`

   C. `env`

   D. `set`

7. Which commands are associated with environment variables? (Choose three.)

   A. `export <variable_name>=value`

   B. `export <variable_name>`

   C. `<variable_name>=<value>`

   D. `env`

   E. `set`

8. You execute the command `rm` but realize that it actually executes the alias `rm`, which is equal to `rm -i`. Without removing the alias from memory, what commands would offer a way around the issue? (Choose two.)

   A. `unalias rm`

   B. `/rm`

   C. `\rm`

   D. `/usr/bin/rm`

9. A user wants to redirect the standard output of a command to a file without overwriting the contents of the file. Which redirection operator should the user apply?

   A. `>`

   B. `2>`

   C. `>>`

   D. `2>>`

10. Which of the following will redirect the standard input and standard output to the same file? (Choose three.)

    A. `&>`

    B. `1>&2`

    C. `2>&1`

    D. `>`

    E. `2 <`

11. Assume the directory /fred does not exist and the files error1 and error2 contain content. What will the command ls -ld /etc /fred > error1 2>> error2 do? (Choose two.)
    - **A.** Overwrite the content of the file error1.
    - **B.** Overwrite the content of the file error2.
    - **C.** Append file error1.
    - **D.** Append file error2.
12. Refer to question 11. Which file will contain the error messages?
    - **A.** error1
    - **B.** error2
    - **C.** None of the above
    - **D.** Both error1 and error2
13. The file error1 exists in the current directory, but when a user attempts to redirect the output of a command to the file, they receive the message "Cannot overwrite an existing file." What is the cause of and fix to this problem?
    - **A.** noglob is turned on and it must be turned off using set -o noglob.
    - **B.** noglob is turned on and it must be turned off using set +o noglob.
    - **C.** noclobber is turned on and it must be turned off using set -o noclobber.
    - **D.** noclobber is turned on and it must be turned off using set +o noclobber.
14. Which locale variable will override all locale category settings?
    - **A.** LANG
    - **B.** LOCALE
    - **C.** LC
    - **D.** LC_ALL
15. What must you do if you modify settings in the file /etc/locale.conf using the localectl command?
    - **A.** Reboot the system
    - **B.** Execute the command . /etc/locale.conf
    - **C.** Reload systemd
    - **D.** Execute the command localectl
16. Which commands display system clock information? (Choose two.)
    - **A.** date
    - **B.** hwclock
    - **C.** timedatectl
    - **D.** localectl

17. Where are time zone data files stored?
    - A. /etc/locale
    - B. /etc/local
    - C. /usr/share/zoneinfo
    - D. /usr/lib/time
18. Which commands display the current system time zone? (Choose four.)
    - A. timedatectl
    - B. date
    - C. ls -l /etc/localtime
    - D. date +%Z
    - E. time

Answers

1. **B.** The variable will not be copied when a new process is spawned.
2. **C.** The set command displays a list of shell variables.
3. **B, C.** The question states that user student1 is logged on to the system Therefore, to remove the problem immediately, student1 must remove the variable from memory. /home/student1/.bash_profile contains user environment statements. To prevent the variable from being created the next time the user logs on, the variable assignment must be removed from /home/student1/.bash_profile.
4. **C.** Each process executes in its own memory space. Any actions in a child process do not affect the parent process. Therefore, removing a variable from a child process does not affect the variable in the parent process.
5. **C, D.** The command export <variable_name>=<value> creates an environment variable. The command <variable_name>=<value>;export <variable_name> uses a compound command to create and then export the variable. Answer A is incorrect because there are spaces around the equal sign; that is not allowed. (The ; is discussed in Chapter 13.)
6. **B, D.** The command <variable_name>=<value> creates a shell variable. The set command displays a list of all shell variables.
7. **A, B, D.** The command export <variable_name>=<value> creates an environment variable, and the command export <variable_name> assigns an export attribute to an existing variable. The env command displays a list of all variables in the current shell that have been assigned an export attribute.
8. **C, D.** The backslash (\) negates the special meeting of a character; when placed in front of an aliased command, it negates the alias. You could also supply the absolute path to the command. The absolute path to a command takes precedence over aliases, functions, and builtins.

9. **C.** The > and >> symbols redirect the stdout of a file. The >> symbol creates a file if one does not exist and appends to an existing file if it does exist, so it is the best choice for this scenario. The > symbol creates a file if it does not exist, but overwrites the file if it does exist. The `2>` operator redirects the standard error and would overwrite the file. `2>>` would redirect the standard error and append the file.

10. **A, B, C.** The operator `&>` redirects both the standard output and the standard error to the same file. The operator `1>&2` redirects the standard output and ANDs the standard error to the same file. The operator `2>&1` redirects the standard error and ANDs the standard output.

11. **A, D.** The `>` operator creates a file or overwrites the content of a file. The operator `>>` creates a file or appends the file.

12. **B.** The operator `2>` redirects the standard error. In question 11, the operator `2>>` appends error messages to file `error2`.

13. **D.** The bash option `noclobber` prevents redirecting the standard output to an existing file. The command `set +o noclobber` turns the option off.

14. **D.** The `LC_ALL` variable overrides all local category variables and the `LANG` variable.

15. **B.** Any time you modify `/etc/locale.conf`—either by the `localectl` command or manually—you must read the new configuration into memory by executing the command `. /etc/locale.conf` or the command `source /etc/locale.conf`.

16. **A, C.** The commands `date` and `timedatectl` display the system clock (operating system clock) information.

17. **C.** The directory `/usr/share/zoneinfo/` contains time zone data files.

18. **A, B, C, D.** The output of each of these commands will display the current system time zone.

CHAPTER 4

Managing Linux Users and Groups

In this chapter, you will learn about

- Linux users and groups
- Creating and managing Linux user accounts

It's all about data analytics for employee data.

—Ed Smith, Novell

Linux is a multiuser operating system, so it is necessary to restrict users' access to only those resources they should have permission to access. This chapter introduces Linux users and groups.

Understanding Linux Users and Groups

Linux uses a method called Discretionary Access Control (DAC) to permit or restrict access to files. On DAC-based systems the account owner decides who has permission to access, delete, or modify their files.

In this section you will learn details about

- Linux user accounts
- Displaying user and group IDs

NOTE Linux supports a more granular permission structure called Mandatory Access Control (MAC), which divides access into classified, secret, top secret, and so on. These rights are controlled by SELinux or AppArmor, as discussed in Chapter 16.

Linux User Accounts

A *user* is a person or service that requires access to system files or resources. A *user account* is a method of providing or restricting access to system resources.

Linux User IDs and Privileges

Linux implements user ID ranges to organize users. Depending on the user ID (`UID`), the individual will have few or many privileges. Most users are standard users and have limited access to system files, whereas the administrative account called `root` can perform any function on the computer. Details of these `UID`s and privileges are discussed next.

The Meaning of User IDs 0–99 Administrative users 0–99 are added to the operating system during the installation process. According to the Linux Standard Base (LSB) Core Specification, user accounts within this range are created by the operating system and may not be created by an application (such as LibreOffice).

The All-Powerful `root` Account The user `root` or `UID 0` (zero) is a privileged Linux account and the administrator of the system. The `root` user can do anything on the computer, such as

- Delete any file
- Kill any job
- Shut down the computer

The user `root` has access to all files and commands and has full control of the operating system, including the ability to bypass operating system or application restrictions. Any user assigned the user ID 0 has `root` privileges.

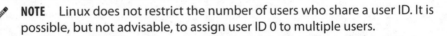

NOTE Linux does not restrict the number of users who share a user ID. It is possible, but not advisable, to assign user ID 0 to multiple users.

Since root activities could damage the system, it is important to limit access to `root` privileges. Most companies assign a system administrator with `root` privileges, and all other users work in standard user accounts with limited privileges (also known as "least privilege"—only enough privileges to do their job).

User and System Accounts A user account provides nonprivileged access to system resources. User account ID ranges are specified by the variables `UID_MIN` and `UID_MAX` in `/etc/login.defs`, the file that defines new user defaults, such as the location of the user's mailbox, their user ID, and their password aging defaults. The default minimum `UID` is 1000, and the default maximum `UID` is 60000, but it can be as high as 4.2 billion depending on the CPU model and Linux version.

A Linux service (an application that is running in the background, such as `abrt`) may be assigned a *user account*. The user account ID for a service is in the range 0–99 or between the values set by `SYS_UID_MIN` and `SYS_UID_MAX` in `/etc/login.defs`.

NOTE A system account is created by executing the command `useradd --system <system_account_name>`. There are many services that are not assigned a user account.

Service or system accounts are nonprivileged accounts created by a system administrator or application, and are sometimes used to restrict access to configuration or data files. Unlike user accounts, system accounts cannot log on to the system, do not require a password, do not have password aging applied, and do not have home directories.

Where Linux User Account Information Is Stored

For purposes of the CompTIA Linux+ exam, you will learn where Linux stores user configuration files on the local system. Information for users and groups is stored in the following configuration files:

- **`/etc/passwd`** Contains user account information
- **`/etc/shadow`** Contains user password and password aging information
- **`/etc/group`** Contains a list of groups and their members

Introducing the User Database File `/etc/passwd` The file `/etc/passwd` is an example of a flat-file database. Each line of the file contains a unique user record. Each record contains seven fields. A colon (`:`) is used as a delimiter to separate the fields.

The format for a record in the `/etc/passwd` file is as follows:

```
User_Name:Password:UID:GID:Comment:Home_Directory:Default_Shell
```

The following example illustrates the fields found in an `/etc/passwd` user record:

```
# egrep 'root:student' /etc/passwd
root:x:0:0:root:/root:/bin/bash
student1:x:0:0:Student1:/home/student1:/bin/bash
```

Here's what each of the fields contains:

- **`User_Name`** The username is a unique word used to identify a user who has access to the system. The username is supplied by the administrator. Oftentimes this follows a corporate policy–based convention of *firstname.lastname*, or first letter of first name and first seven letters of last name.
- **`Password`** When UNIX was first developed, the user's encrypted password was stored in this field. Unfortunately, the `/etc/passwd` file's permissions allowed everyone to read the file, making it easy to hijack and crack passwords. Passwords are now stored in the high-security `/etc/shadow` file, which only the `root` user can read.
- **`UID`** The Linux kernel identifies a user by their user ID, not their username. A user ID is a numerical identifier assigned to each user and mapped to their username. Each user ID should be unique. However, although it is not a secure practice, you can map multiple usernames to the same user ID.
- **`GID`** This field contains the group ID number of the user's *primary* group (a user is allowed to be a member of multiple groups). When a user creates a file, their primary group ID is assigned as the file's group owner. Secondary group memberships are found in `/etc/group`.

- **Comment** By default, this field contains the user's full name. You may change the information that appears in this field when adding or modifying the user account. (Traditionally this is known as the GECOS field, which stands for General Electric Comprehensive Operating Supervisor, a type of operating system for GE/Honeywell mainframes.)
- **Home_Directory** This field contains the absolute path to the user's home directory. When a user logs in, they automatically are placed at this directory.
- **Default_Shell** This field contains the absolute path of the shell interpreter to use, such as /bin/bash, or a command. Most Linux systems default to the Bourne-Again Shell or Bash (/bin/bash), but some users use the Korn shell (/bin/ksh), or C-Shell (/bin/csh). The CompTIA Linux+ exam covers only the Bash shell.

NOTE System accounts do not require a default shell. You will find these accounts have either /sbin/nologin or /bin/false in this field. Both prevent login. /bin/false immediately exits the login process. /sbin/nologin displays the message found in /etc/nologin and exits the login process.

Introducing the Protected User Password File /etc/shadow Encrypted passwords used to reside in the /etc/passwd file, which is readable by everyone. This left Linux systems vulnerable to hackers, who could download the passwords and crack them. Linux developers built the shadow utilities and moved the passwords to the file /etc/shadow. Now passwords are only visible by the root user.

The /etc/shadow file is a flat-file database that stores user passwords and password aging expirations. Each record in /etc/passwd should have a corresponding record in /etc/shadow. The format for a record in the /etc/shadow file is as follows:

```
Username:Password:Last_Modified:Min_Days:Max_Days:Warn_Days:Inactive:Expire
```

Here's an example using the grep command to search for the account student1 at the beginning of the line using the caret (^) symbol from the file /etc/shadow:

```
# grep ^student1 /etc/shadow
student1:$2a$05$KL1DbTBqpSEMiL.2FoI3ue4bdyR.eL6CC7REUS:15043:0:99999:7:::
```

Here's what each of the fields contains:

- **Username** This is the user's login name.
- **Password** This field stores the user's password in encrypted format. If this field only contains two exclamation points, as shown in Figure 4-1, an account password has never been assigned.
- **Last_Modified** This field displays the number of days since January 1, 1970, that the password was last changed. This number is used to calculate password aging dates.

```
# grep ^student2 /etc/shadow
student2:!!:17951:0:99999:7:::
```

Figure 4-1 User has no password assigned because of the !!

- **Min_Days** This field displays the minimum number of days required before a password can be changed. The default value is specified in /etc/login.defs.
- **Max_Days** This field displays the maximum number of days before a password expires. The default value is specified in /etc/login.defs.
- **Warn_Days** This field displays the number of days prior to password expiration the user will be warned of the pending expiration. The default value is specified in /etc/login.defs.
- **Inactive** This field displays the number of days after password expiration the user account will be disabled. The purpose of this field is to prevent open accounts that are not being used.

  During the period between password expiration and the number of inactive days exceeded, the user may still log on but will be forced to change their password. After the number of inactive days is exceeded, the account is disabled and requires an administrator to remediate the situation. The default INACTIVE value is specified in /etc/default/useradd.
- **Expire** This field displays the number of days since January 1, 1970, after which the account will be disabled.

Introducing the Group Database File /etc/group Assume you have a resource that all the company's tech writers need to access. By creating a group called tech_writers and making tech_writers the group owner of the resource, you can assign the necessary access permissions to the resource for the group.

Group information is stored in the /etc/group and /etc/gshadow files. The gshadow file maintains the list of encrypted group passwords.

The /etc/group file is a flat-file database that contains four fields:

```
Group:Password:GID:UserList
```

Here's an example using the egrep command to search for the groups root or users or tech_writers from the file /etc/group:

```
#egrep 'root|users|tech_writers' /etc/group
root:x:0:
users:x:1000:
tech_writers:x:1001:jin,ali,pradip,carol,joe
```

Here's what each of the fields contains:

- **Group** Specifies the name of the group, such as tech_writers.
- **Password** Specifies the group password. The x means the group password is stored in /etc/gshadow.
- **GID** Specifies the group ID (GID) number of the group.
- **UserList** Lists the members who are secondary members of the group.

With these new tools in mind, let's explore how to display your user and group IDs.

Displaying User and Group IDs

When a user logs on to a system, they are assigned the user ID and group ID stored in their /etc/passwd record. This user ID is called the UID, and the group ID is named the GID. To display the current UID and GID, use the id command. (There are real versus effective user and group IDs, which will be discussed in Chapter 6.)

Displaying All Logged-in Users with w and who

The w command displays the user ID (UID) of all logged-on users, what processes they are executing, and what devices the processes are executing from.

The who command is similar to the w command but does not display the processes that are executing.

Switching the User ID with su

The su or "switch user" command allows a user to assume the privileges of another user by switching their user ID (UID) and group ID (GID). Non-root users must know the password of the user they are switching to.

There are two formats for the su command:

- **su <username>** Changes the current user's UID, primary group ID, and home directory.
- **su - <username>** Does the same, but also reads the new user's profile (that is, reads all of the user's configuration files). In essence, the "su dash" allows you to become exactly like the new user.

Whenever the su command or su - command executes, your user ID (UID) and group ID (GID) change to the new user "switched" to. To view the current UID, execute the command id.

The id command displays the current user's user ID, group ID, and secondary groups. The command id <username> displays the user ID, primary group ID, and secondary groups for the user specified by the argument <username>.

Figure 4-2 demonstrates use of the `id`, `su`, `whoami`, `w`, and `tty` commands, and the steps are discussed as follows:

1. You are logged on as the user `root` (`UID 0`). The `tty` command on line 1 shows that you are displaying from window pseudo-terminal `/dev/pts/0`.
2. On line 4, execute the **w** command to display the username. Line 8 shows that user `root` is running the w process on pseudo-terminal `/dev/pts/0`, from X-Window display terminal `:0` (details on X-Window are provided in Chapter 20).
3. Verify the `UID` by executing the **`id`** command on line 10.
4. On line 13, execute the command **`su student1`**. This changes the user ID to user `student1` (`UID 1000`).
5. When executing the command w and reviewing line 15, you see that you are logged in as `root`, but when executing the commands `whoami` (line 21) and `id` (line 24), you see the effective user ID is `student1`, or `1000`, because of the previous `su` command (without the "dash").
6. Notice when trying to execute the command `useradd` on line 27 that you cannot. Even though you are logged on as `root` (who should be able to execute the command `useradd`), the effective user ID is `1000` (`student1`), and `student1` does not have permissions to execute the `useradd` command.

```
 1 # tty
 2 /dev/pts/0
 3 #
 4 # w
 5  00:49:25 up 3 min,  2 users,  load average: 0.83, 1.04, 0.48
 6 USER     TTY      FROM             LOGIN@   IDLE   JCPU   PCPU WHAT
 7 root     :0       :0               00:47   ?xdm?  31.02s  0.32s /usr/libexec/gnome-session-binary --session gnome-classic
 8 root     pts/0    :0               00:48    5.00s  0.09s  0.05s w
 9 #
10 # id
11 uid=0(root) gid=0(root) groups=0(root) context=unconfined_u:unconfined_r:unconfined_t:s0-s0:c0.c1023
12 #
13 # su student1
14 #
15 # w
16  00:51:15 up 5 min,  2 users,  load average: 0.13, 0.72, 0.43
17 USER     TTY      FROM             LOGIN@   IDLE   JCPU   PCPU WHAT
18 root     :0       :0               00:47   ?xdm?  34.22s  0.32s /usr/libexec/gnome-session-binary --session gnome-classic
19 root     pts/0    :0               00:48    3.00s  0.11s  0.00s w
20 #
21 # whoami
22 student1
23 #
24 # id
25 uid=1000(student1) gid=1000(student1) groups=1000(student1) context=unconfined_u:unconfined_r:unconfined_t:s0-s0:c0.c1023
26 #
27 # useradd fred
28 bash: /usr/sbin/useradd: Permission denied
```

Figure 4-2 Demo of the `id`, `su`, `whoami`, `w`, and `tty` commands

Creating and Managing User Accounts from the Command Line

System administrators create user accounts with the `useradd` command. Once a user's account is created, the user needs to set a password with the `passwd` command. Should a user's ID or group need to be changed, this is handled with `usermod`. Finally, for better security, administrators need to set password rules with `chage`. In this section, you will learn details about

- Provisioning new users with `useradd`
- Provisioning new workgroups with `groupadd`

Let's review how to create and manage user accounts.

Provisioning New Users with `useradd`

The `useradd` utility is used to add users to the Linux system. The `useradd` command obtains default values initially from `/etc/login.defs` and next from `/etc/default/useradd`. Entries within the directory `/etc/skel/` are used to populate the new user's home directory.

The Important `useradd` Options

Use the following `useradd` options to customize the user's home directory, their login shell, and more:

- **`-c`** User comment field. For security reasons, make certain the comment does not contain personal information.
- **`-e`** Specifies the date when the user account will be disabled (`-e YYYY-MM-DD`).
- **`-g`** Specifies the user's primary group.
- **`-G`** Specifies the user's secondary group memberships. Administrators may enter a comma-delimited list of group names or group IDs.
- **`-d`** Defines the location of the home directory.
- **`-m`** Creates (makes) the home directory. This option is not necessary if the variable `CREATE_HOME` in `/etc/login.defs` is `yes`.
- **`-r`** Specifies that the user being created is a system user. The system user ID will be in the range specified by `SYS_UID_MIN` and `SYS_UID_MAX` in `/etc/login.defs`.
- **`-s`** Specifies the absolute path to the default shell for the user.
- **`-u`** Allows an administrator to manually specify a user ID.

Any required settings not specified on the command line are supplied by `/etc/login.defs` and `/etc/default/useradd`.

Setting Defaults in /etc/default/useradd

The directory /etc/default/ is used to specify default variable settings. The file /etc/default/useradd contains default variables used by the command useradd, unless overridden by settings in /etc/login.defs. To view the values set in /etc/default/useradd, execute the following command:

```
# useradd -D
GROUP=100
HOME=/home
INACTIVE=-1
EXPIRE=
SHELL=/bin/bash
SKEL=/etc/skel
CREATE_MAIL_SPOOL=yes
```

To change the value of most of the variables in /etc/default/useradd, execute the command useradd -Dx. See Table 4-1 for available options.

Setting the Default Location of User Mail The following entries in /etc/login.defs specify where the user's mail will be stored. The value of the variable CREATE_MAIL_SPOOL in /etc/default/useradd determines if the file will be created when the user is added.

```
#QMAIL_DIR          Maildir
MAIL_DIR            /var/spool/mail
#MAIL_FILE          .mail
```

The following values in /etc/login.defs set the password aging defaults and the minimum password length unless overridden in the /etc/pam.d/passwd file:

```
PASS_MAX_DAYS      99999
PASS_MIN_DAYS      0
PASS_MIN_LENGTH    5
PASS_WARN_AGE      7
```

Option	Definition
-Dg <group_id>	Sets the default primary group.
-Db <directory>	Sets the default absolute path to the location of the home directory.
-Df <number_of_days>	Sets the default number of days after a password expires for the account to become inactive: -1 disables inactivity -0 sets the account to be inactive upon expiration Any other number sets that number of days after the password expires until the account is disabled.
-De <YYYY-MM-DD>	Sets the default expiration date.
-Ds <shell>	Sets the default absolute path to the default shell.

Table 4-1 Changing Default Entries in /etc/default/useradd

NOTE The default aging settings are a security risk. It is advisable to change `INACTIVE=30` in `/etc/default/useradd`. Also change the default minimum, maximum, and warning days in `/etc/login.defs`. The following settings would be more secure:

```
PASS_MAX_DAYS  90
PASS_MIN_DAYS  37
PASS_MIN_LENGTH  8
PASS_WARN_AGE  14
```

Building User Consistency with the /etc/skel/ Directory

The `/etc/skel/` directory is the default directory that contains the files and directories copied to a new user's home directory. You may modify the files in this directory if you want all new users to have specific files or settings.

You may also create a skeleton directory for users with similar needs. Let's assume you have a specific group that requires specific settings in `/home/<username>/.bash_profile` and `/home/<username>/.bashrc`, and you have certain scripts available. Create a directory named `/etc/skel_<group_name>/`. Next, copy all the files in `/etc/skel/` to that directory, edit the appropriate configuration files, and add any additional files desired into the new directory.

When adding a user for that group, use the option `-k <skel_directory>` (for example, `useradd -k /etc/skel_<group_name> <user_name>`).

Using passwd to Set a Password The `passwd` utility allows you or `root` to change your password and allows a system administrator to manage password aging.

As `root`, you can define how long a password may exist before it must be changed, specify the number of warning days before the password must be changed, and specify the minimum number of days a user must wait before changing their password again to prevent password reuse.

A user can change their own password by executing the command `passwd`. Unlike other operating systems where **** or .... might appear while entering the new password, nothing appears on the terminal in Linux.

```
# passwd kelly_morgan
New password:
Retype new password:
passwd: password updated successfully
```

User `root` can change a user's password by executing the command `passwd <username>`. Other `passwd` options that may be used by the system administrator include the following:

- **-l** Locks the user account but does not remove the current password. The encrypted password of an account locked using `passwd -l` will have two exclamation points (`!!`) preceding the password within `/etc/shadow`.
- **-u** Unlocks a user's account.

Figure 4-3
Disabled account

```
# grep ^student2 /etc/shadow
student2:*:17951:0:99999:7:::
```

- **-n** Sets the minimum number of days (MIN_DAYS) required before a password can be changed.
- **-x** Sets the maximum number of days (MAX_DAYS) before a password must be changed.
- **-w** Sets the number of days prior to password expiration (WARN_DAYS) when the user will be warned of the pending expiration.
- **-i** Sets the number of inactive days to wait after a password has expired before disabling the account.
- **-S** Displays password aging information. Password aging information may also be displayed by executing the chage -l <username> command, as discussed in the next section.

If a user account has an asterisk (*) in the Password field of /etc/shadow, the account is disabled, as shown in Figure 4-3. If a user account is disabled, the system administrator must remove the asterisk from the Password field in /etc/shadow to re-enable the account. User accounts in the ID range 1–99 that do not require a password will display an asterisk in this field.

You can force a user to change their password at their next logon by expiring the account using the command passwd -e <username> or setting the last change date to 0 using the command chage -d 0 <username>.

Changing Password Aging with the chage Command The chage (change aging) command allows you to view or change a user's password aging information.

The command chage -l displays the current user's aging information. As a system administrator, running the command chage -l <username> displays password aging for a specific user.

Let's look at some other system administrator chage options:

- **-d YYYY-MM-DD** Changes a user's last change date
- **-m** Sets the minimum number of days (MIN_DAYS) required before a password can be changed
- **-M** Sets the maximum number of days (MAX_DAYS) before a password must be changed
- **-W** Sets the number of days prior to password expiration (WARN_DAYS) when the user will be warned of the pending expiration
- **-I** Sets INACTIVE (the number of days to wait after a password has expired to disable the account)
- **-E YYYY-MM-DD** Sets the account expiration date

Figure 4-4 Using the `chage` text-based user interface

```
# chage student2
Changing the aging information for student2
Enter the new value, or press ENTER for the default

        Minimum Password Age [0]:
```

A system administrator may also use the command `chage <username>` to change a user's password aging information. This command opens a text-based user interface (TUI) that steps through each aging parameter, displays the current value, and allows the value to be changed, as shown in Figure 4-4.

Modifying User Settings with `usermod` The `usermod` command is used to modify an existing user account. The options for `usermod` are similar to those for `useradd`, with a few noted changes:

- **`-G <group_name>`** Removes all of the user's *secondary* groups and replaces them with a new secondary group or comma-delimited list of secondary groups.
- **`-aG <group_name>`** Adds a new secondary group.
- **`-l`** Changes the username (logon name).
- **`-d`** Changes the location of the user's home directory.
- **`-m`** Moves (renames) the current user's home directory to the new user's name. The following command renames user `student2` to `user2`:

  ```
  usermod -l user2 -d /home/user2 -m student2
  ```

Deprovisioning Users Using `userdel` The `userdel` command is used to remove a user account. The command `userdel <username>` removes a user's record from `/etc/passwd` and `/etc/shadow`, but their home directory and files remain to later be assigned to a new user and backed up for archives.

To remove the user's home directory and mail, execute the command `userdel -r <username>`. When deprovisioning a user this way, make sure to back up their files first!

EXAM TIP If you do not use the `-r` option with the `userdel` command, you must manually delete a user's home directory, `cron` jobs, `at` jobs, and mail.

Neither `userdel` nor `userdel -r` removes any groups from `/etc/group`.
You'll practice managing users in Exercise 4-1.

Exercise 4-1: Managing User Accounts from the Command Line

In this exercise, you will practice creating and modifying user accounts from the shell prompt of your Linux system. You can perform this exercise using the virtual machine that comes with this book.

VIDEO Please watch the Exercise 4-1 video for a demonstration on how to perform this task.

Complete the following steps:

1. Boot your Linux system and log in as the **`root`** user with a password of **`password`**.

NOTE In secure enterprises, administrators use a feature called `sudo` or must check out the `root` password from security for administrative rights. The `sudo` feature is discussed in Chapter 16.

2. Open a terminal session.
3. Execute the **`who`**, **`whoami`**, **`id`**, **`echo $HOME`**, and **`echo $PATH`** commands.
4. Open a second terminal and execute the command **`su student1`**.
5. Execute the **`who`**, **`whoami`**, **`id`**, **`echo $HOME`**, and **`echo $PATH`** commands. What has changed?
6. Open a third terminal and execute the command **`su - student1`**.
7. Execute the **`who`**, **`whoami`**, **`id`**, **`echo $HOME`**, and **`echo $PATH`** commands. Compare the difference in outputs in all three terminals. What are the differences? Why?

   Close the second and third terminals by typing the command **`exit`** twice. In the first terminal, type the **`clear`** command.
8. Create the user `student2` by executing the **`useradd student2`** command.
9. Use the following command to view the changes made to these files:

   ```
   grep ^student2 /etc/passwd /etc/shadow /etc/group /etc/gshadow
   ```

   Remember the settings in `/etc/default/useradd` and `/etc/login.defs`?

   Execute the command **`ls -l /var/spool/mail`** to determine if `user2`'s mail file was created.
10. Execute the **`passwd student2`** command. Use the password **`student2`**.
11. Execute the **`grep ^student2 /etc/shadow`** command. Look at the `Password` field. What has changed?
12. Press **`Ctrl-Alt-F2`** to open a text terminal. Log in as user **`student2`**.
13. To determine your real user ID, execute the **`who`** command.
14. Press **`Alt-F3`** to open another text terminal.
15. Log in as **`root`**, execute the **`passwd -l student2`** command, and then execute the **`grep ^student2 /etc/shadow`** command. What does the change in the `Password` field indicate?

16. Press **Alt-F2** to return to the previous text terminal. Execute the **clear** command. Notice that even though you have prevented `student2` from logging in, `student2` can still execute commands.
17. Type the **exit** command to log out and then try to log back in as **student2**. Notice you cannot log in because the account is locked.
18. Press **Alt-F3** to change to the terminal where you are logged in as `root`.
19. Execute the **su - student2** command.
20. Verify your effective user ID using the **whoami** command. Then execute **id** so you can see the difference in output between the two commands. If you execute the **who** command, you will see your real user ID is `root`.
21. Try to execute the **passwd -u student2** command. Why does the command fail?
22. Execute the **exit** and **whoami** commands. Now execute the **passwd -u student2** command.
23. Go back to the second text terminal (press **Alt-F2**) and try to log on as **student2**.
24. As student2, view your password aging by executing the `passwd -S` and `chage -l student2` commands. Notice only `root` can execute the `passwd` command.
25. Return to the GUI by pressing **Alt-F1**.
26. Type **chage student2**. The text user interface opens. Change `INACTIVE` to **0**. What does that do? Use the command **grep ^student2 /etc/shadow** to view the changes.
27. Use the command **chage -m 37 -M 45 -W 7 -I 14 student2** to change the `MIN_DAYS` (37), `MAX_DAYS` (45), `WARN_DAYS` (7), and `INACTIVE` (14) for user `student2`. Now view the changes by executing the **grep ^student2 /etc/shadow** command.
28. Create the user **student3**. This user's default group should be the group specified in `/etc/default/useradd` or `/etc/login.defs`. Use the command **id student3** to make certain `student3`'s primary group is `1003` because `/etc/login.defs` defines `USERGROUPS_ENAB=yes`.
29. Add the group `student1` as a secondary group for `student3` by executing the command **usermod -G student1 student3** and type the **groups student3** command. This will display which groups `student3` is a member of.
30. Add the group `100` (users) as a secondary group for `student3` using the command **usermod -G 100 student3** and then type the **groups student3** command. Notice that the group `student1` is no longer a secondary group. Using the `-G` option overwrote all the existing secondary groups. Execute the command **usermod -aG student1 student3** and then execute the **groups student3** command. The `-a` "appends" the group to the secondary group list.

31. Delete user student2 using the **userdel student2** command. Then execute

```
grep ^student2 /etc/passwd /etc/shadow;
ls -l /var/spool/mail/student2
```

Notice that student2's records in /etc/passwd and /etc/shadow have been removed, but student2's mail file remains.

32. Delete user student3 using the **userdel -r student3** command. Execute

```
grep ^student3 /etc/passwd /etc/shadow;
ls -l /var/spool/mail/student3
```

Notice student3's records in /etc/passwd and /etc/shadow have been removed as well as student3's mail file in /var/spool/mail.

Now that you know how to manage users, next we'll discuss how to manage groups.

Provisioning New Workgroups with groupadd

Linux uses groups to provide common access to a system resource for multiple users. In this section, we're going to discuss how Linux groups work and how to manage groups from the command line.

Managing Groups from the Command Line

As with users, groups can also be managed with either command-line or graphical tools. For example, the User Manager can be used to create, modify, and delete groups, as well as user accounts, on the Linux system. However, graphical tools are not listed in the CompTIA Linux+ exam objectives, so we will focus on managing groups from the command-line interface (CLI). We will review the following tools:

- groupadd
- gpasswd
- groupmod
- groupdel

Let's begin by looking at groupadd.

Provisioning a New Workgroup Using groupadd

As you can probably guess from its name, the groupadd utility is used to add groups to the Linux system. The syntax for using groupadd at the shell prompt is relatively simple. Just enter groupadd <options> <groupname>. For example, to add a group named dbusers, enter groupadd dbusers at the shell prompt.

When using groupadd, you can use the following options:

- **-g** Specifies a GID for the new group. As with users, it is not necessary to specify a group ID, as the system will automatically assign one.
- **-r** Specifies that the group being created is a system group.

Setting the Group Password with `gpasswd` The `gpasswd` command is used to manage the files `/etc/group` and `/etc/gshadow`. This command may be executed by a system administrator or a group administrator.

To assign a group administrator, a system administrator or group administrator should execute the `gpasswd -A <username>` command.

A system or group administrator may use any of the following `gpasswd` options:

- **`-a <username>`** Adds a user to the group
- **`-d <username>`** Deletes a user from the group
- **`-r`** Removes the group password

Changing Workgroup Settings with `groupmod` The `groupmod` command is used to modify group information using the following options:

- **`-g`** Changes the group's GID number
- **`-n`** Changes the group name

Deprovisioning the Workgroup with `groupdel` To delete an existing group from the system, use the `groupdel` command at the shell prompt. For example, to delete the `dbusers` group, enter the `groupdel dbusers` command.

Before deleting a group, make certain the users' access to files and directories is not compromised.

You'll practice managing groups in Exercise 4-2.

Exercise 4-2: Managing Groups from the Command Line

In this exercise, you will practice creating and modifying groups from the shell prompt of your Linux system. You can perform this exercise using the virtual machine that comes with this book.

VIDEO Please watch the Exercise 4-2 video for a demonstration on how to perform this task.

Suppose your company is putting together a new research and development team that will be using the Linux system. You need to create a new group for users who will be members of this team. To do this, complete the following steps:

1. Log on to the system as the user **`root`**.
2. Create a new group named `research` by executing the **`groupadd research`** command.
3. Add the group `research` as a secondary group of `student1` by executing the command **`usermod -aG research student1`**.

4. View the members of the `research` group by executing the command **`grep research /etc/group`**.
5. View all the secondary groups `student1` is a member of by executing the command **`grep student1 /etc/group`**.
6. View all the groups `student1` belongs to by executing the **`groups student1`** command.
7. Delete the group `research` by executing the **`groupdel research`** command. Verify the group has been removed by executing the **`grep research /etc/group`** command.

Chapter Review

In this chapter, we reviewed the user configuration files, how to use user and group management commands and configuration files, and how to temporarily change user and group IDs. Here are some key takeaways from this chapter:

- To authenticate to a system, a user must supply a username and password.
- User home directories are created in `/home` by default.
- The `root` user's home directory is `/root`.
- Every Linux user account should have a unique user ID (`UID`) number assigned to it.
- The `root` user's `UID` is `0`.
- The starting `UID` for standard users is `1000`.
- Use the `su` command to temporarily switch the user ID, primary group ID, and home directory.
- To temporarily log on as another user and use their profile, execute the `su - <username>` command.
- Use the `id` command to view a user's effective user ID.
- With local authentication, user accounts are stored in `/etc/passwd` and `/etc/shadow`.
- The `/etc/passwd` file stores user account information.
- The `/etc/shadow` file stores encrypted passwords and password aging information.
- You can use the `useradd` utility to provision users onto a Linux system.
- When used without any options, `useradd` uses system defaults defined in `/etc/login.defs` and `/etc/default/useradd` to create user accounts.
- Use the `passwd` utility to set a user's password.
- Use the `usermod` utility to modify an existing user account.
- Use the `userdel` utility to deprovision an existing user account.

- By default, `userdel` does not remove a user's home directory, `cron` and `at` jobs, and mail unless you specify the `-r` option with the command.
- Group accounts are stored in `/etc/group`.
- Use the `groupadd` utility to provision a new group to the system.
- Use the `usermod` utility to add or remove users to or from an existing group.
- Use the `groupdel` utility to deprovision an existing group.

Questions

1. Which files contain global user configuration settings for a user with `/bin/bash` as their default shell? (Choose two.)

   A. `/etc/passwd`

   B. `/etc/profile`

   C. `~/.bash_profile`

   D. `/etc/group`

   E. `/etc/bashrc`

   F. `~/.bashrc`

2. A user has a primary group and may be a member of more than one secondary group. Which file would you look in to find a user's secondary groups?

   A. `/etc/passwd`

   B. `/etc/profile`

   C. `~/.bash_profile`

   D. `/etc/group`

3. Which entries in an `/etc/passwd` record will prevent a user from logging on to the system? (Choose two.)

   A. `/bin/bash`

   B. `/bin/false`

   C. `/sbin/nologin`

   D. `/bin/nologin`

4. Which entry in an `/etc/shadow` record's `Password` field will indicate a user password has not been set for that user?

   A. `!!`

   B. `NP`

   C. `LK`

   D. `!`

5. A user cannot log on. Their `Password` field in `/etc/shadow` contains `!!<encrypted_password>`. What action would fix this problem? (Choose two.)

   A. The user should change their password.

   B. An administrator should execute the command `passwd -u <user_name>`.

   C. An administrator should execute the command `chage -u <user_name>`.

   D. An administrator should execute the command `usermod -U <user_name>`.

6. Which file contains the default password aging values used when adding a user?

   A. `/etc/default/useradd`

   B. `/etc/login.defs`

   C. `/etc/skel`

   D. `/etc/profile`

7. You are adding a user. The value stored in the variable `USERGROUPS_ENAB` in `/etc/login.defs` is `yes`. You do not wish to create a new group, but want the user's primary group to be the same as the value (`100`) stored in the `GROUP` variable in `/etc/default/useradd`. Which of the following commands would accomplish this? (Choose two.)

   A. Creating the user and then executing `usermod -g <username>`

   B. `useradd -n <username>`

   C. `useradd -G 100 <username>`

   D. `useradd -g 100 <username>`

8. A user cannot log on. You wish to view the password aging information for that user. What command would you execute? (Choose two.)

   A. `chage -S <username>`

   B. `passwd -S <username>`

   C. `chage -l <username>`

   D. `passwd -l <username>`

9. You want the default editor for all new users to be `nano`. Which file would you edit?

   A. `/etc/default/useradd`

   B. `/etc/login.defs`

   C. `/etc/profile`

   D. `/etc/skel/.bash_profile`

10. A user's password expired five days ago. The value of `INACTIVE` is `14`. What can the user do?

A. Nothing, the account has been disabled.

B. Log on normally.

C. Log on, but be ready to change their password.

D. Contact the system administrator to reset the account.

11. A user's password expired five days ago. The value of `INACTIVE` is `0`. What can the user do?

A. Nothing, the account has been disabled.

B. Log on normally.

C. Log on, but be ready to change their password.

D. Contact the system administrator to reset the account.

12. A user with a user ID of `3` has an asterisk in their `Password` field in `/etc/shadow`. What does this indicate?

A. The account has been disabled.

B. This is a system account and does not require a password.

C. This is a system application account and does not require a password.

D. This a system account that can only be called by `root` and does not require a password.

13. You are changing the logon name for user `student1` to `student3`. What is the *most* appropriate command?

A. `usermod -l student1 student3`

B. `usermod -l student3 student1`

C. `usermod -l student3 -d /home/student3 student1`

D. `usermod -l student3 -d /home/student3 -m student1`

14. What command will only delete the user record for `student3` in `/etc/passwd` and `/etc/shadow`?

A. `userdel -r student3`

B. `userdel student3`

C. `rm student3`

D. `rm -r student3`

15. You have removed the user records for `student3` in `/etc/passwd` and `/etc/shadow` but did not remove the home directory, `cron` jobs, `at` jobs, and mail associated with `student3`. What command will *best* do this?

    A. `userdel -r student3`

    B. `userdel -rf student2`

    C. None; the files must be removed manually.

    D. `\rm -r /home/student3`

16. You are logged in as `student1`. You execute the command `su student2`. What commands will display who you have logged on to the system as? (Choose two.)

    A. `id`

    B. `who`

    C. `w`

    D. `whoami`

Answers

1. **B, E.** `/etc/profile` and `/etc/bashrc` are generic (global) configuration files applied to all users whose default shell is the Bash shell. `/etc/profile` would also be read for users whose default shell is the Bourne or Korn shell.
2. **D.** The file `/etc/group` would contain a user's secondary group information. A user's primary group information would be stored in `/etc/passwd`.
3. **B, C.** The entries `/bin/false` and `/sbin/nologin` will prevent a user from logging on.
4. **A.** If the `Password` field of a user account in the file `/etc/shadow` only contains two exclamation points, a password has never been set.
5. **B, D.** The two exclamation points preceding the password indicate the account has been locked by the command `passwd -l`. Either command `passwd -u` or `usermod -U` will unlock the account.
6. **B.** The `/etc/login.defs` file contains the default password aging values.
7. **B, D.** The command `useradd -n` would negate the setting in `/etc/login.defs` and force the default in `/etc/default/useradd` to be used. The command `usermod -g 100` would set the primary group ID to 100. Although answer A would work, the question specifies that the administrator does not wish to create a new group. The command `useradd <username>` would create a new group.
8. **B, C.** The commands `passwd -S <username>` and `chage -l <username>` would display the password aging for a user.

9. **D.** Editing the file `/etc/skel/.bash_profile` would cause any changes to the file to be propagated to new users.
10. **C.** The user may log on, but will be forced to change their password.
11. **D.** An `INACTIVE` value of `0` automatically disables the account when the password expires, so there is nothing the user can do to fix the problem. A system administrator will have to manually remove the asterisk from the `Password` field in `/etc/shadow`.
12. **B.** The user ID indicates this is a system account that does not require a password.
13. **D.** When modifying a username, you must specify the location of the user's home directory (`-d <home_directory>`) and move the contents from the old username's directory to the new username's home directory (`-m`).
14. **B.** To remove a user record from `/etc/passwd` and `/etc/shadow`, use the `userdel <username>` command.
15. **C.** The files must be removed manually.
16. **B, C.** The commands `who` and `w` will display the user's real `UID` (`RUID`) or who they logged in as. The commands `id` (answer A) and `whoami` (answer D) will display their effective user ID (`EUID`) or who they `su`'d (switched user) as.

CHAPTER 5

Managing Linux Files and Directories

In this chapter, you will learn about

- The Filesystem Hierarchy Standard (FHS)
- Managing Linux files
- Finding files in the Linux filesystem
- Understanding commands and precedence
- Finding content within files

The datasets looked so good that we realized this will probably go into people's arms.

—Kizzmekia S. Corbett, National Institutes of Health

In this chapter, you get to know the Linux filesystem, including the hierarchical structure of the Linux filesystem and Linux file types. Then you will work with files and directories. Let's begin by discussing the role of the filesystem.

Understanding the Filesystem Hierarchy Standard

Linux stores data on physical hard disks, which in many cases are subdivided into partitions. Storing data on a partition requires a method for managing how the data is stored and retrieved. A filesystem controls how data is managed on a hard disk. Figure 5-1 shows one hard disk with three partitions. Each partition has a filesystem on which data is stored. What data is stored on a disk or partition and what filesystems are used to manage the data are determined as part of the system design process.

Figure 5-1 Filesystems and partitions

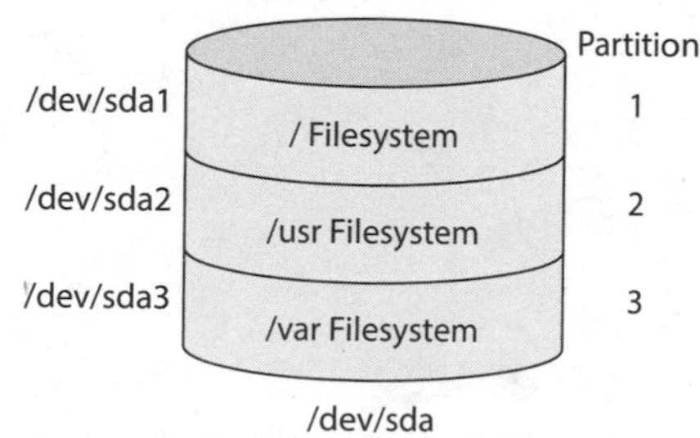

The logical location of a directory has no relationship to where the data is physically stored. A hierarchy is a method of organizing objects based on some classification. The Filesystem Hierarchy Standard (FHS) defines a suggested logical location of directories and files on Linux (and UNIX) distributions. These definitions include what should be contained in specific directories and files. Figure 5-2 shows an example of this structure. Currently, the Linux Foundation manages the FHS (https://refspecs.linuxfoundation.org/fhs.shtml).

Let's review the purpose of some of these directories:

- **/** The root directory, or top-level directory (pronounced *slash* directory, and the parent to all other files and directories)
- **/bin** Contains user commands, and can be linked to /usr/bin
- **/boot** Contains files required to boot the system
- **/dev** Contains special device driver files for hardware devices
- **/etc** Contains global configuration files
- **/lib** Contains system library files, also known as shared objects
- **/mnt** A mount point for temporarily mounted filesystems
- **/media** A mount point for removable media, such as DVD and USB drives
- **/opt** Directory intended for installation of third-party applications
- **/sbin** Contains system binaries used by root for booting or repairing the kernel; linked to `/usr/sbin`
- **/tmp** Directory for temporary files; known as a *pseudo-filesystem* because it resides in memory and, optionally, swap space
- **/usr** A suite of shareable, read-only UNIX system resources
- **/var** Contains files that vary in size (e.g., log files, e-mail files, and printing files)
- **/home** Contains home directories for user accounts
- **/root** The user `root`'s home directory (not to be confused with the / directory)
- **/run** Another pseudo-filesystem (resides on memory) and contains system information gathered from boot time forward; cleared at the start of the boot process
- **/srv** Contains data for services (e.g., HTTP and FTP) running on the server
- **/sys** Provides device, driver, and some kernel information
- **/proc** Another pseudo-filesystem that contains process and hardware information

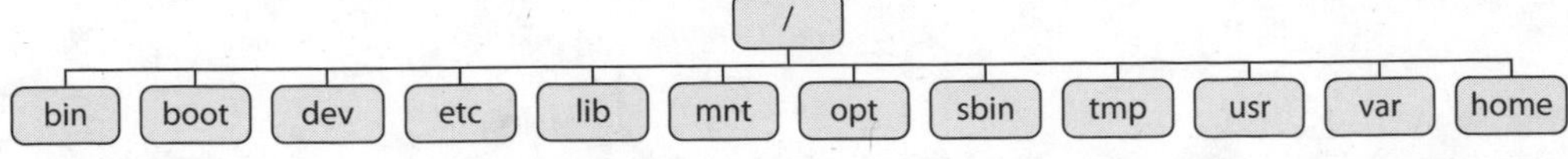

Figure 5-2 Directory structure

Frankly, files can be placed anywhere on a Linux system. Executable files can be placed in `/etc`, log files can be placed in `/usr/lib`, and so on, but as a Linux administrator, you do *not* want to do this. This makes it very difficult for other Linux administrators to manage the system in case you get promoted or change jobs. It is important to follow the FHS.

At this stage in your exam preparation studies, you must learn some Linux basics which include

- Navigating the Linux filesystem
- Viewing directory contents with `ls`

Let's first learn about maneuvering through the Linux filesystem.

Navigating the Linux Filesystem

As you work with the Linux filesystem from the shell prompt, one of the most common tasks to perform is maneuvering through the various directories on your storage devices. Your Linux system provides the following shell commands to do this:

- Print the current working directory with `pwd`
- Change directories using `cd`

Print the Current Working Directory with `pwd`

The `pwd` (print working directory) command displays the absolute path of the current directory on the terminal. The *absolute path* to a file is the path from the root (/) directory. Figure 5-3 displays the absolute path to `file2` as `/dir1/file2`. An absolute path always begins with `/`.

To display the absolute path of the current directory, execute the command `pwd`. Here's an example:

```
$ pwd
/home/student1
```

Figure 5-3
Absolute path

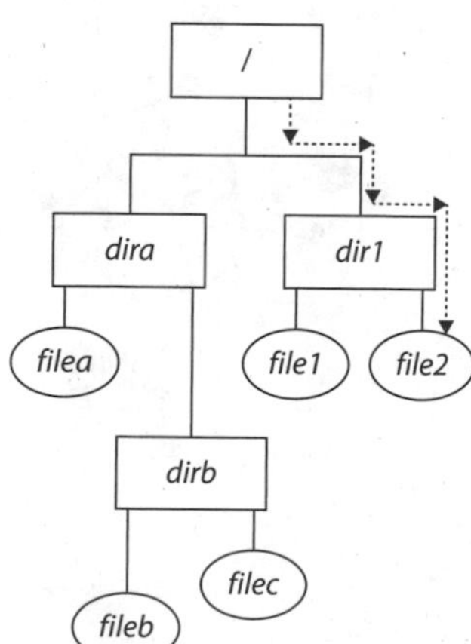

Change Directories with cd

The cd (change directory) command is used to change from your current working directory to another directory. When specifying a directory, use the absolute or *relative* path. The relative path specifies the path to a directory from the current directory and never starts with a leading /. In Figure 5-4, the current working directory is dira. The relative path to fileb is dirb/fileb.

The absolute path to fileb is /dira/dirb/fileb. To change the directory to the directory that contains fileb (dirb), you could execute the command using the relative method, cd dirb, or the absolute method, cd /dira/dirb.

NOTE Remember ~ represents a user's home directory. For example, cd ~ takes the user Paul to his home directory /home/paul. Because ~ always starts with a leading /, it is also considered an absolute path name.

Executing the command cd without an argument changes the current working directory to your home directory. Executing the command cd ~ also moves you to your home directory.

Executing the command cd ~<username> changes your current working directory to the home directory of the user specified by the argument <username> as long as there is permission to enter the home directory. The command cd ~student1 changes the current working directory to user student1's home directory, /home/student1.

Finally, executing the command cd .. ("cd dot dot") changes your current working directory to the parent directory, because .. means parent directory. The . or "dot" means the current directory, so cd . keeps you in the directory that you are currently in. This is not very useful, but uses of "dot" will be discussed in Chapter 10.

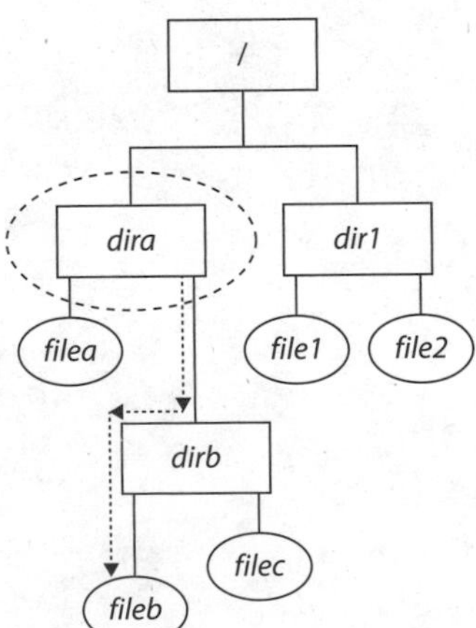

Figure 5-4 Relative path

Viewing Directory Contents with `ls`

The `ls` command (lowercase letters *l* and *s*) shows a list of filenames and directories stored in the current directory. Here's an example:

```
# ls
bin      Documents Music    Public      Templates test.txt words
Desktop  Downloads Pictures public_html test2.txt Videos   yourfile.txt
```

If you provide an absolute path to a directory, `ls` displays the contents of the directory, as shown here:

```
# ls /var/log
acpid      cups          mail           ntp                Xorg.0.log.old
apparmor   faillog       mail.err       pk_backend_zypp    YaST2
audit      firewall      mail.info      pm-powersave.log   zypp
boot.log   gdm           mail.warn      samba              zypper.log
boot.msg   krb5          messages       warn
boot.omsg  lastlog       NetworkManager wtmp
ConsoleKit localmessages news           Xorg.0.log
```

When working with `ls`, you can use a variety of options to customize how it works. Here are some of these options:

- **`-a`** Displays all files, *including hidden files*. Hidden filenames are prefixed with a period or "dot." Many configuration files are hidden files. The thinking of the Linux developers was that if nonprivileged users could not easily see these files, they would not change them.

  In the following example, the `ls -a` command has been issued in the `/home/student1` directory:

  ```
  $ ls -a
  .              .esd_auth        .inputrc              test2.txt
  ..             .fontconfig      .local                test.txt
  .bash_history  .fonts           .mozilla              .themes
  .bashrc        .gconf           Music                 .thumbnails
  bin            .gconfd          .nautilus             Videos
  .cache         .gnome2          Pictures              .viminfo
  .config        .gnome2_private  .profile              .vimrc
  .dbus          .gstreamer-0.10  Public                words
  Desktop        .gtk-bookmarks   public_html           .xim.template
  .dmrc          .gvfs            .pulse                .xinitrc.template
  Documents      .hplip           .pulse-cookie         .xsession-errors
  Downloads      .ICEauthority    .recently-used.xbel   .xsession-errors.old
  .emacs         .icons           Templates             yourfile.txt
  ```

  If you provide the filename of a hidden file (for example, `ls -l .exrc`), the `-a` option is not necessary.

- **`-l`** Displays a long listing of the directory contents. The first line shows total space, in blocks, used in the directory. The other lines display file properties showing the permissions, number of links, file owner, group owner, file size in bytes, modification date, and filename. An example is shown here:

  ```
  $ ls -l
  total 56
  drwxr-xr-x 2 student1 users 4096 2023-01-19 10:41 bin
  ```

```
drwxr-xr-x 2 student1 users 4096 2023-01-19 10:42 Desktop
drwxr-xr-x 2 student1 users 4096 2023-01-19 10:42 Documents
drwxr-xr-x 2 student1 users 4096 2023-01-19 10:42 Downloads
drwxr-xr-x 2 student1 users 4096 2023-01-19 10:42 Music
drwxr-xr-x 2 student1 users 4096 2023-01-19 10:42 Pictures
drwxr-xr-x 2 student1 users 4096 2023-01-19 10:42 Public
drwxr-xr-x 2 student1 users 4096 2023-01-19 10:41 public_html
drwxr-xr-x 2 student1 users 4096 2023-01-19 10:42 Templates
-rw-r--r-- 1 student1 users   37 2023-01-20 11:04 test2.txt
-rw-r--r-- 1 student1 users  182 2023-01-21 11:48 test.txt
drwxr-xr-x 2 student1 users 4096 2023-01-19 10:42 Videos
-rw-r--r-- 1 student1 users   23 2023-01-20 11:32 words
-rw-r--r-- 1 student1 users  121 2023-01-21 11:46 yourfile.txt
```

- **-R** Displays directory contents recursively; that is, it displays the contents of the current directory as well as the contents of all subdirectories. Depending on the number of entries in the directory, you may want to append `| more` after using this option, by running `ls -R /etc | more`. This causes the `more` utility to pause and display one page of output at a time. Press the `Spacebar` to see the next page, and press `q` to quit.
- **-i** Displays the inode a filename belongs to. This is demonstrated a bit later in the "Soft and Hard Links" section.

EXAM TIP Knowledge of `ls` options `-l`, `-i`, `-R`, and `-a` is vital to passing the CompTIA Linux+ exam. Make sure you know that the `-l` option lists the permissions, number of links, user and group owners, file size, modification time, and filename.

Let's practice navigating the filesystem in Exercise 5-1.

Exercise 5-1: Navigating the Filesystem

In this exercise, practice using shell commands to navigate the Linux filesystem.

VIDEO Please watch the Exercise 5-1 video for a demonstration on how to perform this task.

For this exercise, log on to the virtual machine provided with the book as user **root** (password **password**) and follow these steps:

1. Open a terminal session.
2. Assuming you have just logged on, what should be your current working directory? Use the **pwd** command to verify your current working directory. If you are not in your current working directory, execute the **cd** command to return to your home directory. Test the results with the **pwd** command.

3. Change your current working directory to user `student1`'s home directory by using one of the following commands:
   - `cd ~student1`
   - `cd /home/student1`
4. Execute the command **`ls`** and then the command **`ls -a`**. What is the difference in the output? Why?
5. Execute the commands in step 4 again, but this time display the file's properties by using the command **`-l`**.
6. Use an absolute path to change your current working directory to the `pam.d` subdirectory in `/etc` by executing the command **`cd /etc/pam.d`**. Verify you are in the correct directory.
7. Move up to the parent directory by executing the command **`cd ..`** and verify you are in the `/etc/` directory.
8. Return to your home directory and again verify you are in the correct directory.

Answer to Exercise 5-1

Step 4 Executing the command `cd` returns you to your home directory, which contains many configuration files and directories that you will not see if you execute the command `ls`; they become visible if you execute the command `ls -a`.

Managing Linux Files

Everything in Linux is referenced by a file. Even a directory is a file. We now investigate the types of Linux files and how to manage them by discussing

- Files, filenames, and inodes
- Creating and validating files with `touch` and `stat`
- Soft and hard links
- Creating new directories with `mkdir`
- Determining the file type
- Viewing file contents
- Deleting files
- Copying and moving files

Files, Filenames, and Inodes

Linux files consist of a filename, inode, and data block(s). When a file is created, it is given a name by the user or application and assigned a unique inode number (index number) by the filesystem. The operating system uses the inode number, not the filename, to access the file and its information.

Figure 5-5 Example contents of a directory file

/home/aria/files	
inode	filename
103	.
102	..
14870	Funutation.odp
14890	BusinessPlan.odt
61583	zbest.txt

Filenames and inode numbers are kept in directory files. *If* the contents of a directory file could be displayed, for example, by running `cat /home/aria/files`, it would appear as shown in Figure 5-5; in this example, files `Funutation.odp`, `BusinessPlan.odt`, and `zbest.txt` are in the `/home/aria/files` directory.

A Linux filename may contain up to 255 characters, and must not contain a forward slash or null character. A filename may contain metacharacters (for example, `file1*`), but this is not advisable. Also, `file1`, `File1`, and `FILE1` are three *different* files because Linux is case sensitive.

The Linux operating system ignores extensions but allows applications to recognize them. For example, `mfc70.txt` indicates a text file for the `gedit` utility. By default, LibreOffice, the free and open source office suite, stores files using Open Document Format and uses Open Document filenames to distinguish its files. For example, the suffix `.odt` indicates a word processor file, `.ods` a spreadsheet, and `.odp` a presentation document.

You can append multiple suffixes to filenames to make searching for files easier. The filename `fstab.12232024.abc` could indicate that this is a copy of the file `/etc/fstab` made on December 23, 2024, by a user with the initials abc.

If you intend to share files among multiple operating systems, make sure that your filenames follow the rules for all operating systems. For example, if you create the files `version1.txt` and `Version1.txt` on a Linux system in the same directory, Linux will treat them as separate files. But, if those two files are shared with a Windows system, one of the files will be overwritten because Windows is not case sensitive.

Creating and Validating Files with `touch` and `stat`

Creating a new file can be accomplished by executing the `touch` command. Assuming the file `filea` does not exist, the command `touch filea` will create an empty file (0 bytes) named `filea`:

```
$ touch filea
$ ls -l filea
-rw-r--r-- 1 student1 users 0 2023-05-23 11:36 filea
```

Three file timestamps—access, modification, and change—are part of a file's metadata. The access timestamp is updated, by default, each time the file contents are read. The modification timestamp is updated each time the contents are changed.

The change timestamp is updated whenever the file's metadata (for example, ownership or permissions) is changed. The `touch` command may be used to modify timestamps. If a file exists, you can change its modification time by executing the command `touch <filename>`.

To view the timestamps and inode numbers of the file, use the `stat` command, as shown here:

```
$ stat filea
  File: filea
  Size: 0               Blocks: 0          IO Block: 4096   regular empty file
Device: fd02h/64770d    Inode: 3221235654  Links: 1
Access: (0644/-rw-r--r--)  Uid: ( 1002/ student1)   Gid: (  100/   users)
Context: unconfined_u:object_r:user_home_t:s0
Access: 2023-05-23 11:41:44.838544287 -0500
Modify: 2023-05-23 11:41:44.838544287 -0500
Change: 2023-05-23 11:41:44.838544287 -0500
 Birth: 2023-05-23 11:36:23.442872832 -0500
```

The `stat` command also lists the file's birth, permissions, number of links, device, user ID, group ID, file size, and SELinux settings. SELinux is discussed in Chapter 16.

EXAM TIP On `ext`-based filesystems such as `ext3` and `ext4`, all inodes are created when the filesystem is built, so it is possible to run out of inodes even though there is plenty of disk space available! XFS filesystems support dynamic inode allocation, building inodes as needed, so they do not suffer from inode exhaustion issues.

Soft and Hard Links

A link is a method of referring to data stored in an inode or another file. This allows us to change the data in one file and have that change reflected in other filenames.

Prior to discussing links, however, let's look at how files are stored on most filesystems. A file's metadata is stored in an inode. Inodes contain all the information about a file, such as the permissions, number of links, user and group owners, file size, timestamps, and data pointers, *but not the filename*, as shown in Figure 5-6.

Figure 5-6 Structure of an inode

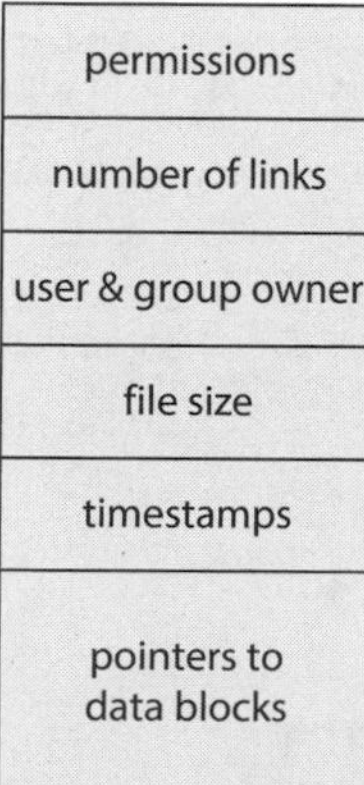

When a file is created, it is assigned an inode number from a list of available inode numbers in the filesystem. When a user enters a filename, the operating system finds the inode number associated with that filename from a directory file. Then the data is accessed from the file's inode.

For our discussion, the term *source* indicates the original file and the term *destination* indicates the file being created.

Creating and Manipulating Hard Links with `ln`

A hard link associates the file's name with the file's inode. To create additional hard links, use the `ln` command (lowercase letters *l* and *n*). Hard links only work when used within the same filesystem. Assume that `zbest.txt` is linked to inode number `61583` inside the `/home/aria/files` directory. After running the command `ln zbest.txt zlink.txt`, inode number `61583` now has two links, `zbest.txt` and `zlink.txt`, as shown in Figure 5-7.

In Figure 5-8, running `ls -il z*` displays the inode number `61583` and other properties of the files `zbest.txt` and `zlink.txt`. Notice the circled number; this indicates the number of filenames referencing this file's inode number. It incremented from `1` to `2` because inode `61583` has two filenames, `zbest.txt` and `zlink.txt`.

Figure 5-7 An inode with two links

/home/aria/files	
inode	filename
103	.
102	..
14870	Funutation.odp
14890	BusinessPlan.odt
61583	zbest.txt zlink.txt

```
$ ls -il                          # List the files in /home/aria/files
total 12
14890 -rw-r--r--. 1 aria users 1106 May 23 13:53 BusinessPlan.odt
14870 -rw-r--r--. 1 aria users  206 May 23 13:52 Funutation.odp
61583 -rw-r--r--. 1 aria users   43 May 23 13:37 zbest.txt
$
$ ls -il z*                       # List files that start with the letter 'z'
61583 -rw-r--r--.(1)aria users 43 May 23 13:37 zbest.txt
$
$ ln zbest.txt zlink.txt          # Hard link zlink.txt to inode 61583
$
$ ls -il z*                       # List files that start with the letter 'z'
61583 -rw-r--r--.(2)aria users 43 May 23 13:37 zbest.txt
61583 -rw-r--r--.(2)aria users 43 May 23 13:37 zlink.txt
$
$ \rm zbest.txt                   # Unlink zbest.txt from inode 61583
$
$ ls -il z*                       # List files that start with the letter 'z'
61583 -rw-r--r--.(1)aria users 43 May 23 13:37 zlink.txt
$
$ ▮
```

Figure 5-8 Creating hard links

In the last command, the file `zbest.txt` is removed using the `\rm zbest.txt` command. The file `zlink.txt` can still access its data because its filename is still associated with inode `61583`. No disk space is reclaimed due to the removal of `zbest.txt` because there is still one link to the inode, filename `zlink.txt`. Once `zlink.txt` is deleted, then 43 bytes of data will be reclaimed by the operating system.

EXAM TIP You could also use the `unlink zbest.txt` command to remove `zbest.txt`.

Creating and Manipulating Soft Links

A symbolic link, also called a soft link, can reference a file in the same filesystem, another filesystem, directories, or even across the network! Unlike the hard link, each symbolic link file has its own inode. The data within the "symlink" contains the *filename* it is linked to, similar to a shortcut in macOS or Windows computers (see Figure 5-9).

To create a soft link, run `ln` with the `-s` option as follows:

```
ln -s <source_file> <destination_file>
```

Notice the output of the `ls -il` command in Figure 5-10. The files `zbest.txt` and `zlink.txt` are hard linked because they are linked to the same inode, and the link count is `2`.

Next, a soft link is created, named `symlink.txt`, by running the following command:

```
ln -s zbest.txt symlink.txt
```

Figure 5-9 Contents of a soft link

```
$ ls -il                          # List the files in /home/aria/files
total 16
14890 -rw-r--r--. 1 aria users 4066 May 23 16:13 BusinessPlan.odt
14870 -rw-r--r--. 1 aria users 2136 May 23 16:13 Funutation.odp
61583 -rw-r--r--. 2 aria users   43 May 23 13:37 zbest.txt
61583 -rw-r--r--. 2 aria users   43 May 23 13:37 zlink.txt
$
$ ln -s zbest.txt symlink.txt     # Create the symbolic link file, symlink.txt
$
$ ls -il                          # List the files in /home/aria/files
total 16
14890 -rw-r--r--. 1 aria users 4066 May 23 16:13 BusinessPlan.odt
14870 -rw-r--r--. 1 aria users 2136 May 23 16:13 Funutation.odp
 8552 lrwxrwxrwx. 1 aria users    9 May 23 16:17 symlink.txt -> zbest.txt
61583 -rw-r--r--. 2 aria users   43 May 23 13:37 zbest.txt
61583 -rw-r--r--. 2 aria users   43 May 23 13:37 zlink.txt
$
$ ▌
```

Figure 5-10 Soft linking a file

Notice the file type and properties of `symlink.txt` shown as `lrwxrwxrwx`. The lowercase *l* indicates the file is a *soft link*, and the permissions `rwxrwxrwx` grant *all* permissions to all users when accessing the file. The permissions to a soft link are based on the file it is linked to, so these are overridden and become `rw-r–r--`, the `zbest.txt` permissions.

Also notice that the filename has an arrow (`->`) pointing to the file it is linked to, `zbest.txt`. The contents of the soft link contain the name of the file it is referencing. Since `zbest.txt` is nine characters, the file size is 9 bytes, not the size of `zbest.txt`.

Finally, notice that the link count remains `2` and does not change to `3`. This is because a soft link creates its own inode instead of adding another filename to the current inode. The key difference is that hard links point to an inode number and soft links point to a filename.

NOTE You can also use the `readlink` command to determine what file a symbolic link is linked to, as follows: `readlink symlink.txt`

To remove a symbolic link, run either `rm <destination_link_file_name>` or `unlink <destination_link_file_name>`. Removing `symlink.txt` with `rm symlink.txt` (or `unlink symlink.txt`) has no effect other than losing the symbolic link. But if you remove the source file with `rm zbest.txt`, the system prints `cat: symlink.txt: No such file or directory` after you run `cat symlink.txt`, as shown in Figure 5-11, because `zbest.txt` no longer exists.

The link works again after re-creating `zbest.txt`. The data is not the same because a new `zbest.txt` file was created, but `zbest.txt` could have been relinked to `zlink.txt`. As far as the file `symlink.txt` goes, it points to `zbest.txt` no matter what data it contains, as shown in the last five lines of Figure 5-11.

```
$ ls -il                        # List the files in /home/aria/files
total 16
14890 -rw-r--r--. 1 aria users 4066 May 23 16:13 BusinessPlan.odt
14870 -rw-r--r--. 1 aria users 2136 May 23 16:13 Funutation.odp
 8552 lrwxrwxrwx. 1 aria users    9 May 23 16:17 symlink.txt -> zbest.txt
61583 -rw-r--r--. 2 aria users   43 May 23 13:37 zbest.txt
61583 -rw-r--r--. 2 aria users   43 May 23 13:37 zlink.txt
$
$ rm zbest.txt                  # Remove symlink.txt's destination file zbest.txt
$
$ cat symlink.txt               # Error message follows because zbest.txt is deleted
cat: symlink.txt: No such file or directory
$
$ cat zlink.txt                 # But the contents of inode 61583 still exist
--this data is within inode number 61583--
$
$ echo 'not same' > zbest.txt   # Create a new inode/file for zbest.txt
$
$ cat symlink.txt               # zbest.txt is back, but with different data
not same
$
$ █
```

Figure 5-11 Removing and adding destination to soft link

Using Soft Links Is More Common than Hard Links

Hard links are easier to find on a filesystem compared to soft (symbolic) links. The `find` command with the `-inum` option searches for files by inode number, as discussed in the "Finding Files in the Linux Filesystem" section later in this chapter. But symbolic links are used more frequently on Linux systems because they can link to anything, including directories and network files. Hard links work properly only if the files share the same filesystem.

Creating New Directories with `mkdir`

The `mkdir` (make directory) command is used to create a directory. In the following example, the command `mkdir MyDir` has been executed in `student1`'s home directory:

```
$ cd
$ mkdir MyDir
$ ls
bin          Downloads  Pictures     Templates  Videos
Desktop      Music      Public       test2.txt  words
Documents    MyDir      public_html  test.txt   yourfile.txt
```

You can use an absolute or relative path to create a directory somewhere other than the current directory. For example, to create a new directory named `backup` in the `/tmp` directory, enter `mkdir /tmp/backup` at the shell prompt.

The `mkdir -p` command creates a directory tree. For example, running the command `mkdir -p ~/temp/backups/daily` creates the `temp` directory, then creates the subdirectory `backup`, and finally creates the subdirectory `daily`.

NOTE Use the `tree` command to list contents of directory paths. This will display the parent directories and their children.

Determining the File Type

The first character of the output of the `ls -l` command is a code that indicates the file type, as shown in Table 5-1.

Table 5-1 File Type Codes

File Type Code	Description
-	Plain text
L	Symbolic link
D	Directory
P	Named pipe
C	Character device
B	Block device
S	Socket

Figure 5-12 Plain text file type

```
1 -ro-r--r--. 1 root root  2316 Jan 25 17:25 /etc/passwd
2 -rw-r--r-- root 8018 Mar 12 10:38 testfile1.odt
3 -rwsr-xr-x. 1 root root 27832 Jun 10  2014 /usr/bin/passwd
```

Looking at lines 1 through 3 in Figure 5-12, you can see each file is a plain text file. This information tells nothing about the detailed contents of the files.

When most files are created, the first several bytes of the file contain the file signature, or *magic number*, which indicates the type of content stored in the file.

The `file` command compares the file's magic number with databases of file signatures contained in `/usr/share/misc/magic`, `/usr/share/misc/magic.mgc`, and `/etc/magic` to determine the file type.

Figure 5-13 displays sample outputs of the `file` command. Notice how the `file` command provides a description of the content of the file because it uses the magic number to determine the type of content stored in the file.

Viewing File Contents

You may find that you often want to quickly view a text file onscreen without loading the `vi` text editor. Linux provides a variety of command-line tools to do this, including the following:

- **`cat`** The `cat` command is used to display plain text. The command `cat` <filename> displays the specified text file onscreen. For example, to view the contents of `/etc/passwd`, execute the command `cat /etc/passwd`.
- **`less`** The `less` command is called a pager. It may be used to manage how text is displayed and how the cursor is moved with a file. The `less` command automatically pauses a long text file one page at a time. You can use the `Spacebar`, `Page Up`, `Page Down`, `Left Arrow`, and `Right Arrow` keys to navigate around the output.
- **`more`** Like the `less` command, the `more` command also paginates through a file. Use the same keyboard keys to navigate around the output. Use the `q` key to quit.
- **`head`** By default, the `head` command displays the first 10 lines of a file. The command `head -n` displays the first *n* number of lines of a file.

```
# file /etc/passwd
/etc/passwd: ASCII text
#
# file testfile1.odt
testfile1.odt: OpenDocument Text
#
# file /usr/bin/passwd
/usr/bin/passwd: setuid ELF 64-bit LSB shared object, x86-64, version 1 (SYSV), dy
namically linked (uses shared libs), for GNU/Linux 2.6.32, BuildID[sha1]=1e5735bf7
b317e60bcb907f1989951f6abd50e8d, stripped
```

Figure 5-13 The `file` command

- **`tail`** The `tail` command is used to display the last 10 lines of a text file onscreen. The command `tail -n` displays the last *n* lines of a file. The `tail` command is particularly useful when displaying a log file onscreen. When viewing a log file, you usually need to see the end of the file only and don't care about log entries made several days or weeks ago. Use `tail` to see just the last few log entries added to the end of the file.

  The `tail` command also includes the `-f` option, which is very useful to *follow,* or monitor, a file. As new content is updated to the file, new lines are displayed onscreen. System administrators often run the command `tail -f /var/log/messages` to monitor the file for new entries.

Deleting Files

There will be times when you need to delete an existing file from the Linux filesystem. To delete a file, you must have write and execute permissions on the directory the file is located in and execute permissions on any parent directories.

To delete a file, simply enter `rm <filename>`. In the following example, the `myfile.txt` file is deleted using the `rm` command:

```
$ rm myfile.txt
$
```

In many distributions, the `rm` command is aliased to `rm -i`. The `-i` option means *interactive,* which requires user confirmation prior to deleting a file. To override the `rm -i` alias, put a \ (backslash) in front of `rm`; for example, `\rm <filename>`.

The recursive option, `-R` or `-r`, is used to recursively remove the directory tree until all directories, subdirectories, and files are deleted. Execute `rm -R Directory` to delete the directory, subdirectories, and files.

EXAM TIP You can also use the `rmdir` command to delete a directory, but this only works when the directory is already empty. `rm -r` works whether the directory is empty or not.

Copying and Moving Files

In addition to creating and deleting files in the Linux filesystem, you can also copy and move them. To copy or move a file, you must have read permissions to the file, execute permissions to the directory the file is located in, execute permissions to any parent directories, and write and execute permissions to the destination directory.

Copying Files with the `cp` Command

The `cp` (copy) command makes a duplicate of a file or directory in the Linux filesystem. The command `cp <source> <destination>` is used to copy a file. For example, running the command `cp file1 file2` would make a duplicate of `file1` named `file2`. The ownership of a copied file is changed to the user who copied the file.

Figure 5-14 The mv command

```
# ls -il mvtest1
1072491 -rw-r--r--. 1 root root 0 Mar 13 11:48 mvtest1
#
# mv mvtest1 mvtest2
#
# ls -il mvtest[12]
1072491 -rw-r--r--. 1 root root 0 Mar 13 11:48 mvtest2
```

For example, if user `root` copied a file owned by `student1`, the copied file would be owned by user `root`.

Multiple files may be copied as long as the destination is a directory (for example, `cp file1 file2 directory-a`).

The `cp` option `-i` prevents a user from copying a file to an existing file. In many systems, the command `cp -i` is a default alias to the `cp` command so that users don't accidently overwrite important files.

The recursive option, `-R` or `-r`, is used to recursively copy the directory tree until all directories, subdirectories, and files are copied to the destination directory. For example, execute `cp -R DirectoryA DirectoryB` to copy `DirectoryA` to `DirectoryB`.

Renaming Files with the `mv` Command

The `mv` command is used to move or rename a file or directory. For example, to rename `mvtest1` to `mvtest2`, execute the command `mv mvtest1 mvtest2`. Notice the inode numbers in Figure 5-14; the new name linked to inode `1072491` is now `mvtest2`.

If the source and destination files are not in the same filesystem, the `mv` command copies the source to the new location and then deletes the original.

The recursive option, `-R` or `-r`, is used to recursively move the directory tree until all directories, subdirectories, and files are copied to the destination directory. For example, execute `mv -R DirectoryA DirectoryB` to move `DirectoryA` to `DirectoryB`.

Exercise 5-2: Managing Files and Directories

In this exercise, practice creating and viewing the properties of files and directories and moving between directories.

VIDEO Please watch the Exercise 5-2 video for a demonstration on how to perform this task.

For this exercise, log on to the virtual machine provided with the book as user **`student1`** (password **`student1`**) and then follow these steps:

1. Open a terminal session.
2. Verify that you are in `student1`'s home directory. If not, change your current working directory to user `student1`'s home directory by executing the **`cd ~`** command.

3. Execute the **touch touchtest; alias rm='rm -i'** command.
4. Create the subdirectory `cars` relative to your home directory by executing the **mkdir cars** command.
5. Verify the directory has been created by executing the **ls -ld cars** command.
6. Execute the **ls -lR cars** command. Notice there are no subdirectories.
7. Execute the **rmdir cars** command.
8. Execute the **ls -ld cars** command. Notice the directory has been removed.
9. Create the subdirectory `pastry` relative to your home directory by executing the **mkdir pastry** command.
10. Verify the directory has been created by executing the **ls -ld pastry** command.
11. Execute the **ls -lR pastry** command. Notice there are no subdirectories.
12. Execute the **mkdir -p pastry/pies/cakes** command.
13. Execute the command **ls -lR pastry** to view the new subdirectories.
14. Try to use the **rmdir pastry** command to remove the `pastry` directory. Why did this command not work?
15. Execute the **\rm -r pastry** command. Did the directories delete?
16. Using `vi`, create the file `filea` with the content `This is filea`.
    a. Start `vi` by executing the **vi filea** command.
    b. Place `vi` in insert mode by pressing the **i** key.
    c. Type **This is filea**.
    d. Save the file and exit `vi` by pressing **Esc ZZ**.
    e. Type the command **ls filea** to verify the file has been created.
    f. Type **cat filea** to verify the contents of the file.
17. Create a symbolic link where the source file is `filea` and the destination file is `fileb` by executing the **ln -s filea fileb** command.
18. Test the results of the preceding command by executing the **ls -il file[ab]** command. Notice the file types: `filea` is an ASCII file and `fileb` is a symbolic link. Look at the inode numbers of the files. Are they the same or different? Why?
19. Execute the command **cat filea; cat fileb** to view the content of the files. Was the output what you expected?
20. Create a hard link where `filea` is the source and `filec` is the destination by executing the **ln filea filec** command.
21. Execute the command **cat filea; cat fileb; cat filec** to view the contents of the files.
22. Test the results of the command executed in step 20 by executing the **ls -il file[a-c]** command. Look at the properties of `filea` and `filec`. Notice the files have the same inode and the number of links sharing the inode is `2`. Why?

23. Remove filea by executing the **`\rm filea`** command.
24. Execute the command **`ls -l file[a-c]`** and examine the output. Notice the number of files sharing the inode in `filec` and notice the broken link of `fileb`.
25. Use the **`vi`** command to create a new **`filea`** with the content **`This is new filea`**.
26. Execute the **`ls -il file[a-c]`** command. Notice the symbolic link is no longer broken. Why?
27. Execute the **`cat filea; cat fileb; cat filec`** command. Is the output what you expected?
28. Execute the **`ls -l fileb`** and **`file fileb`** commands.
29. Execute the **`ls /var/lib/mlocate/mlocate.db`** and **`file /var/lib/mlocate/mlocate.db`** commands.
30. Execute the **`ls -il touchtest`** command. Notice the timestamp. Execute the command **`touch touchtest`** and view the timestamp again.
31. Use the **`touch cpytest`** command to create the file `cpytest`.
32. Execute the **`ls -l cpytest`** command. Notice the file is owned by the user `student1`.
33. Execute the command **`su -`** and press the **`Enter`** key. When asked for `root`'s password, enter **`password`**.
34. Execute the **`id`** or **`whoami`** command to ensure your effective user ID is `0`.
35. Execute the command **`cp ~student1/cpytest .`** (the period after the filename `cpytest` means "current directory"). This command copies the file `cpytest` from `student1`'s home directory to `root`'s home directory.
36. Execute the **`ls -l cpytest`** command. Notice that `root` owns the file.
37. Execute the **`exit`** command.
38. Execute the command **`touch cpytest2`** and verify the file was created.
39. Execute the **`alias | grep cp`** command. You should see `alias cp='cp -i'`. If it is not there, execute the **`alias cp='cp -i'`** command.
40. Execute the **`cp cpytest2 cpytest`** command. You should receive an error because the `-i` option will not allow you to overwrite an existing file. Try the command again by negating the alias using the backslash as follows: **`\cp cpytest2 cpytest`**
41. Execute the **`ls -il cpytest2`** command. Notice and *write down* the inode number using pen/pencil and paper.
42. Execute the **`mv cpytest2 mvtest1`** command.
43. Execute the command **`ls -il cpytest2 mvtest1`** to verify the name of `cpytest2` has been changed to `mvtest1`. Notice the inode has stayed the same because it matches the one you wrote down with pen/pencil and paper.

44. Change your effective user ID to user `root` by executing the **`su`** command and entering the appropriate password.
45. Execute the **`mv ~student1/mvtest1 /etc`** command.
46. Execute the **`ls -il ~student1/mvtest1`** and **`ls -il /etc/mvtest1`** commands. Notice the file no longer exists in `student1`'s home directory, and the inode number has changed. In the virtual machine supplied with this book, `/etc` is on a different filesystem than `/home`, so the `mv` command copied the file to the new filesystem and deleted the file in `/home/student1`.

Finding Files in the Linux Filesystem

Linux includes utilities to search for files in the filesystem. In this part of the chapter, you'll learn about

- Using `find` to search for files
- Using `xargs` to run commands from standard input
- Using `locate` to find files

Using `find` to Search for Files

The `find` utility is a fantastic tool that can be used to search for files by *brute force* instead of searching through a pre-allocated database. The `find` command's searches by default are recursive through directories, but can be limited by using the `-mindepth` and `-maxdepth` options (both options are beyond the scope of this text).

To use `find`, simply enter `find <start_directory> <expression>` at the shell prompt. The `<start_directory>` argument defines the search start point. You can specify multiple start directories. If you do not enter a start directory, the current working directory is the starting point.

The `<expression>` defines what to search for. To use metacharacters in the expressions—for example, `*` for any character—the expression must be enclosed in quote marks. For example, to find all files named `core1`, `core2`, and `core3` on the filesystem, run the `find / -name 'core[123]'` command.

EXAM TIP To find files and display them on the screen once they are found, use the `-print` option. The `-print` option is the default (it didn't used to be), so executing `find / -name 'core[123]'` is the same as executing `find / -name 'core[123]' -print`.

Table 5-2 illustrates some of the single-word `find` expressions, but there are many others. (Refer to the `find` man pages for more information.)

The `-size` expression searches for a file based on its size. For example, run the command `find -size 5M` to find files that are exactly 5MB. Run the command `find -size +5M` to find files larger than 5MB. You may also use the command `find -size +5M -size -10M` to find a file that is smaller than 10MB but greater than 5MB.

Expression	Description
`-name`	Matches name of file, for example, `-name filea`
`-size`	Matches file size. Use `b` for blocks, `c` for bytes, `w` for word, `k` for kilobytes, `M` for megabytes, or `G` for gigabytes.
`-type`	Matches file type: `-f` Regular text file `-d` Directory `-l` Symbolic link `-p` Named pipe
`-inum <number>`	Matches file with a specific inode number, for example, `-inum 10977`
`-user`	Matches owner of file, for example, `-user student1`
`-group`	Matches group owner, for example, `-group admin`
`-perm`	Matches the file permission, for example `-perm 644` finds files with the permissions `644`.
`-readable`	Matches files that are readable.
`-writeable`	Matches files that are writeable.
`-executable`	Matches files that are executable.

Table 5-2 `find` Expressions

Boolean operators combine expressions using `-a` for "and," `-not` for "not," or `-o` for "or." For example, execute either the `find -name test -user student1` command or the `find -name test -a -user student1` command to find all files with the name of `test` owned by `student1`.

You may also execute a command on the results of the `find` command. The two expressions `-exec` and `-ok` take the standard output from the `find` expression and make it the standard input to the specified command.

- **`-exec`** Executes the command without asking for confirmation
- **`-ok`** Executes the command but requires user confirmation

The command `find /var/log -name "*.log -exec ls l {} \;` finds all the files in `/var/log` with the name `<name>.log` and then automatically executes the command `ls -l`. The command `find /var/log -name "*.log -ok ls l {} \;` finds all the files in `/var/log` with the name `<name>.log` and then requires user confirmation before executing the command `ls -l`.

NOTE The curly braces, `{ }`, are used as a placeholder for the standard output of the `find` command. This standard output becomes the standard input of the command executed by `-exec` or `-ok`. The `\;` defines the command's end.

Using `xargs` to Run Commands from Standard Input

The `xargs` command is used to read whitespace-delimited input and execute a command on each input. A whitespace delimiter is a space, tab, or newline. The `xargs` command is easier to explain by demonstrating its operation.

In the example shown in Figure 5-15, we take the space-delimited output of the `echo` command and use it to create files. Remember from Chapter 3 that the pipe (|) takes the standard output of the command on the left and makes it the standard input of the command on the right. By default, the unnamed pipe cannot process multiple arguments. In Figure 5-15, the `echo` command on the right side of the unnamed `pipe` produces the following:

```
filea
fileb
filec
```

The pipe passes this output to `xargs`, and `xargs` passes to the `touch` command one whitespace-delimited argument at a time as input.

In Figure 5-16, we expand our usage of the `xargs` command. The `-I` option in the command is a string replacement option and the curly braces are a placeholder for the standard input.

The output of the command `ls file*` provides the whitespace-delimited arguments `filea`, `fileb`, and `filec` to `xargs`. The `xargs` command places the current argument in the placeholder (`-I {}`). It then executes the `mv` command to rename the current filename to `test.<filename>`. In our example, when `xargs` processes the argument `filea`, it executes the command `mv filea test.filea`.

The `xargs` command is normally used with the `find` command. In the example shown in Figure 5-17, we pipe to the `xargs` command to run the `rm` command and remove a list of commands.

Figure 5-15
`xargs` example

```
# echo file{a,b,c}
filea fileb filec
#
# ls -il file[a-c]
ls: cannot access file[a-c]: No such file or directory
#
# echo file{a,b,c} | xargs touch
#
# ls -l file[a-c]
-rw-r--r--. 1 root root 0 Mar 14 07:09 filea
-rw-r--r--. 1 root root 0 Mar 14 07:09 fileb
-rw-r--r--. 1 root root 0 Mar 14 07:09 filec
```

Figure 5-16
Example using `xargs` and `mv`

```
# ls file*
filea  fileb  filec
#
# ls file* | xargs -I {} mv {} test.{}
# ls test.*
test.filea  test.fileb  test.filec
```

```
# ls -il file[a-c]
1076996 -rw-r--r--. 1 root root 0 Mar 20 13:05 filea
1076997 -rw-r--r--. 1 root root 0 Mar 20 13:05 fileb
1076998 -rw-r--r--. 1 root root 0 Mar 20 13:05 filec
#
# find . -name "file[a-c]" | xargs rm
#
# ls -il file[a-c]
ls: cannot access file[a-c]: No such file or directory
```

Figure 5-17 Example using `xargs` and `find`

```
# find . -name "file[a-c]" | xargs -p \rm
rm ./filea ./fileb ./filec ?...
```

Figure 5-18 Example using `find` and `xargs -p`

In the example shown in Figure 5-18, we pipe to the `xargs` command and print the command before it executes, using the `-p` flag. You must confirm the command execution (`y`) or stop the command execution (`n` or `Ctrl-c`).

Review the `find` man page to learn more about the `find` command and its numerous options. Additional options include finding files by creation date, modification date, change date, and more.

Using `locate` to Find Files

Even though the `locate` command is *not* included in the CompTIA Linux+ exam objectives, it is worth discussing. The `locate` command finds files by looking for the filename in a pre-allocated database. The database (by default, `/var/lib/mlocate/mlocate.db`) is updated daily. The output of the `locate` command lists the absolute path to the file.

Manually Updating the Locate Database with `updatedb`

The `updatedb` command may be used to update the `mlocate.db` file. The configuration file `/etc/updatedb.conf` is used to configure the `updatedb` command.

The file `/etc/updated.conf` contains variables that determine how the `updatedb` command operates (see Table 5-3).

Variable	Description
PRUNEFS	A space-delimited list of filesystem types (such as `ext2` and `ext3`) that should be skipped when executing `updatedb`. For example: `PRUNEFS = "sysfs iso9660"`
PRUNEPATHS	A space-delimited list of directories that should be skipped when executing `updatedb`. For example: `PRUNEPATHS = "/tmp /mnt"`
PRUNENAMES	A space-delimited list of filenames that should be skipped when executing `updatedb`. For example: `PRUNENAMES = "/.bak .old"`

Table 5-3 `/etc/updatedb.conf` Options

Understanding Commands and Precedence

Even though functions and the `alias`, `which`, `whereis`, `hash`, and `type` commands are *not* included in the CompTIA Linux+ exam objectives, they are worth discussing because Linux administrators commonly use them. Linux contains four types of commands and we will learn about

- Creating aliases
- Creating and using functions
- Using builtin commands
- Using external commands

Both *aliases* and *functions* are loaded into and executed from memory. *Builtin* and *external* commands are executed from a file.

Let's take a look at the different command types.

Creating Aliases

An *alias* is described as a command shortcut. As an example, rather than type the `ls --color=auto` command each time you want a color output, you can create an alias so each time you execute the command `ls` the command `ls -l --color=auto` is executed.

To create an alias, execute the command `alias <alias_name>='<command>'`. In the previous example, the command `alias ls='ls --color=auto'` creates an alias to `ls` so that when `ls` is run, it produces a color output. To determine if the alias has been created, execute the command `alias` or `alias <alias_name>`. Figure 5-19 shows how the `alias` and `unalias` commands work.

NOTE To make aliases available every time you log in, define them inside of the file `~/.bashrc`.

Figure 5-19 Using `alias` and `unalias`

```
# alias | grep ls
alias l.='ls -d .* --color=auto'
alias ll='ls -l --color=auto'
alias ls='ls --color=auto'
#
# ls
anaconda-ks.cfg  Documents  initial-setup-ks.cfg  Pictures  Templates
Desktop          Downloads  Music                 Public    Videos
#
# unalias ls
#
# alias | grep ls
alias l.='ls -d .* --color=auto'
alias ll='ls -l --color=auto'
#
# ls
anaconda-ks.cfg  Documents  initial-setup-ks.cfg  Pictures  Templates
Desktop          Downloads  Music                 Public    Videos
#
```

```
# pwd()
> {
> uname -r
> date +%m/%d%y
> }
#
```

Figure 5-20 Creating a function

To override the alias, precede the alias name with a backslash (\). The backslash tells the shell to ignore the alias and use the literal command. So, running `\ls` would result in a file listing without color.

Creating and Using Functions

A *function* is a list of commands performed as a group that can be called from other programs. To create a Bash function on the command line, type the function name followed by opening and closing parentheses, `( )`. Enclose the function commands between left and right curly braces, { }, and then complete the function by using the key sequence `Ctrl-D`. This sequence saves the function to memory and exits the process creating the function. You can view this procedure in Figure 5-20.

A function only exists in the shell it is created in. Therefore, if you want a function to be available at login time, make certain you define the function in `~/.bashrc`.

To view all functions loaded into memory, use the `typeset -f` or `declare -f` command. To remove a function from memory, use the `unset <function_name>` command.

Using Builtin Commands

Builtin commands are commands that are built into the shell and execute as part of the shell process. To see a list of bash builtin commands, execute `help`, `compgen -b`, or `enable`, or view the `bash(1)` man page.

In some cases, a keyword represents multiple command types. For example, the command `pwd` is both a builtin command and an external command. In this situation, execute the command `/usr/bin/pwd` for the external command, or create an alias to the external command since aliases have precedence over builtin commands.

If an alias or function exists with the same name as the builtin, the command `builtin <builtin_command_name>`, `\builtin_command_name`, or `'<builtin_command_name>'` will force a builtin command to run. To receive help for builtin commands, execute the `help <builtin_command_name>` command.

Using External Commands

External commands are file-based commands. Once the shell has looked through the aliases, functions, and builtin commands, it will use the variable `PATH` to determine where to search for commands (see Figure 5-21). The shell looks through each directory in the `PATH` variable in the order in which it has been presented until it finds the command.

```
[student1]$ echo $PATH
/usr/local/bin:/bin:/usr/bin:/usr/local/sbin:/usr/sbin:/home/student1/.local/bin:/home/student1/bin
```

Figure 5-21 A `PATH` variable setting

Based on Figure 5-21, the first directory searched will be /usr/local/bin, followed by /bin, and so on. Linux does not search the local directory for commands by default.

Hashed Commands

When you execute a command, the absolute path to the command is stored in a hash table. Before the shell looks for external commands, it views the hash table to see if the command has executed before.

The hash table contains the absolute path to commands and the number of times the commands have been executed (hits). The command hash displays those commands stored in the hash table. The command hash -r clears the hash table.

Using the type Command

The type command evaluates a keyword and displays how the keyword will be interpreted as a command. The type command evaluates shell keywords, aliases, functions, builtins, and external commands.

The command type <keyword> displays the type of command that will execute when the command is entered on the command line. Executing type -a displays executable keywords in order of precedence.

Using the which Command

The which -a <keyword> command lists aliases and external commands associated with a keyword in order of precedence. The command which <keyword> displays (based on precedence) whether an alias or external command will be executed.

Figure 5-22 shows an example of creating an alias and function for the keyword pwd. Notice the difference in the output between the which -a pwd command and type -a pwd command.

NOTE The whereis command is similar to the which command in that it displays the full path to a command, but whereis also displays the full path to the man page of the command.

Figure 5-22 Comparing the which and type commands

```
1 # which -a pwd
  alias pwd='ls -ld /etc'
          /usr/bin/ls
          /bin/ls
  /usr/bin/pwd
  /bin/pwd
  #
2 # type -a pwd
  pwd is aliased to `ls -ld /etc'
  pwd is a function
  pwd ()
  {
      date
  }
  pwd is a shell builtin
  pwd is /usr/bin/pwd
  pwd is /bin/pwd
```

Exercise 5-3: Finding Files

In this exercise, practice using shell commands to navigate the Linux filesystem. For this exercise, log on to the virtual machine provided with the book as user **student1** (password **student1**). Here are the steps to follow:

VIDEO Please watch the Exercise 5-3 video for a demonstration on how to perform this task.

1. Open a terminal session.
2. Verify you are in user `student1`'s home directory (**pwd**). If not there, execute the **cd ~** command.
3. Create the directory `finddir` as a subdirectory of your home directory using the **mkdir finddir** command.
4. Use the command **ls -ld finddir** to verify the directory has been created.
5. Create the files `file1`, `file2`, and `file3` by using the **touch file{1,2,3}** command.
6. Verify the files are created.
7. Execute the following commands:
   - `find -name file1`
   - `find -name file"[12]"`
   - `find -name "file*"`
   - `find -name "file[1-3]" ! -user student1`
8. Execute the **locate file*** command. Remember, the locate database (`mlocate.db`) is updated only once per day.
9. Change your effective user ID to `0` by executing the command **su** and pressing **Enter**. When asked for a password, enter the user `root`'s password (`password`). Verify the change by executing the command **whoami** or **id**.
10. Create a locate database of user `student1`'s home directory by executing the **updatedb -U ~student1 -o file.db** command. Verify the file exists by typing the **file ~student1/file.db** command.
11. Type **exit** to return to user `student1`.
12. Use the database created in user `student1`'s home directory to locate `file1` by executing the **locate -d ~student1/file.db file1** command.
13. Execute the following commands:
    - `find -name "file[1-3]" -exec ls -l {} \;`
    - `find -name "file[1-3]" -ok ls -l {} \;`

- `find -name "file[1-3]" | xargs ls -l`
- `find -name "file[1-3]" | xargs -p ls -l`

14. Determine what man pages exist for the keyword `passwd` by executing the **`whereis -m passwd`** command.
15. Use the command **`whereis -b passwd`** to see which binary files are associated with the keyword `passwd`.
16. Have the keyword `pwd` execute the `date` command by creating an alias (**`alias pwd='date'`**). Execute the following commands and notice and explain any differences in the outputs:
    - `which pwd`
    - `type pwd`
    - `which -a pwd`
    - `type -a pwd`
17. Execute the **`unalias pwd`** command.

Finding Content Within Files

Earlier in this chapter, we discussed shell commands that can be used to search for files in the filesystem. Linux also provides several utilities to search for content within a file. Here we will learn about

- Using `grep` to search within files
- Using `egrep` to search within files

Using `grep` to Search Within Files

The `grep` utility may be used to search for specific content *within* a file. By default, `grep` displays the line on which the string is found.

The command `grep <option> <string>` may be used to search for a string in a file. For example, the command `grep student1 /etc/passwd`, shown in Figure 5-23, searches for the string "`student1`" in the file `/etc/passwd`. If the string is found, by default, `grep` will print the line the string is on.

The `grep` utility can also search for a text string across multiple files. The command `grep student1 /etc/passwd /etc/shadow /etc/group` searches for the string "`student1`" in `/etc/passwd`, `/etc/shadow`, and `/etc/group`.

Figure 5-23 The output of `grep /etc/passwd`

```
# grep student1 /etc/passwd
student1:x:1000:1000:Student1:/home/student1:/bin/bash
```

Metacharacter	Function	Example
*	Matches preceding character zero or more times	grep ro* matches roo, root
\	Makes the next metacharacter literal	grep ro* matches ro*
?	Matches preceding character zero or one time	grep ca?t matches cat or ct
^<string>	Matches string at the beginning of a line	grep ^<root> matches the string "root" at the beginning of a line
<string>$	Matches string at the end of a line	grep bash$ matches the string "bash" at the end of a line
.	Matches any single character	grep r..t matches root, art truck, r{}t
+	Matches one or more of the previous characters	grep b9+ matches b9, b99, b999, b99999999
[abc]	Matches any character in the current range	grep fog[123] matches fog1, fog2, and fog3
[^abc]	Matches any character not within the range	grep fog[^123] matches foga, fog5, and fog_
[a-z]	Matches any single character in the range	grep fog[1-5] matches fog1, fog2, fog3, fog4, fog5

Table 5-4 grep Metacharacters

Adding the -n option to the grep command will display the number of the line on which the string was found. Other options to grep include

- **-i** Ignores case when searching for the text
- **-l** Only displays the filename in which a string occurs
- **-n** Displays matching line numbers
- **-r** Searches recursively through subdirectories of the path specified
- **-v** Displays all lines that *do not* contain the search string

The grep command uses regular expressions to extend its capabilities, as detailed in Table 5-4.

Using egrep to Search Within Files

The command egrep extends the capabilities of the grep command. The egrep command has been deprecated but is still functional. The replacement command is grep -E and uses additional metacharacters not available with standard grep.

Table 5-5 illustrates *additional* metacharacters available in extended regular expressions.

Metacharacter	Function	Example
{*n*}	Matches *n* occurrences of the previous character.	`egrep fog1{2}` matches fog11
{*n*,*m*}	Matches minimum of *n* and maximum of *m* occurrences of previous character.	`egrep fog1{2,3}` matches fog11 and fog111
{*n*,}	Matches *n* or more occurrences of previous character.	`egrep fog1{2,}` matches fog11, fog111, fog11111111
{,*m*}	Matches *m* or fewer occurrences of previous character.	`egrep fog1{,2}` matches fog11, fog1, fog
|	OR. Matches the string on left or right; multiple ORs may be placed together.	`egrep 'fog1|fog2'` matches fog1 or fog2

Table 5-5 The Additional `egrep` Metacharacters

NOTE There was a fast version of grep called `fgrep` designed for better performance. *Fast grep* got its speed by reducing features. The `fgrep` command is not programmed to use metacharacters like `*` or `?`, so those are seen as literals. To compare functionality, run the **`grep -F`** command.

Exercise 5-4: Using `grep`

In this exercise, practice using Linux search tools. Log on to the virtual machine provided with the book as **`student1`** (password **`student1`**) and then follow these steps:

VIDEO Please watch the Exercise 5-4 video for a demonstration on how to perform this task.

1. To view any entries that contain the string `student1` in the files `/etc/passwd`, `/etc/shadow`, and `/etc/group`, execute the following command:
   ```
   grep student1 /etc/passwd /etc/shadow /etc/group
   ```
2. Add the **`-n`** option to the command in step 1 by executing:
   ```
   grep -n student1 /etc/passwd /etc/shadow /etc/group
   ```
   Notice that this added line numbers to the output.
3. Execute **`grep root /etc/passwd`** to display the string `root` line in the file `/etc/passwd`.
4. The first field of a record in `/etc/passwd` is the username. Use the command **`grep ^root /etc/passwd`** to display the user record for user `root`.

5. The last field for user accounts in the file `/etc/passwd` contains the absolute path to their default shell. Use the command **`grep bash$ /etc/passwd`** to display all users whose default shell is `bash`.
6. Execute the **`grep roo* /etc/passwd`** and **`grep ro\.`** commands. Explain the differences in the output.
7. Display any string that has two lowercase *o*'s together using either the command **`egrep o{2} /etc/passwd`** or the command **`grep -E o{2} /etc/passwd`**.
8. Use the command **`egrep 'root|Root'`** to display the user record for user `root` or `Root` in `/etc/passwd`.

Chapter Review

In this chapter, we discussed the role of the Linux filesystem and the role of the various standard directories used in a typical Linux system as specified in the Filesystem Hierarchy Standard (FHS). We also discussed various commands used to manage files. The role of the filesystem is to store and organize data such that it can be easily located and retrieved.

- The `file` command displays the type of content stored in a file.
- Linux uses a hierarchical filesystem.
- The Linux filesystem hierarchy is based on the Filesystem Hierarchy Standard (FHS).
- The topmost directory is / (pronounced *slash*).
- Other standard directories are created beneath / and serve functions defined in the FHS:
  - `/bin`
  - `/boot`
  - `/dev`
  - `/etc`
  - `/home`
  - `/lib`
  - `/sbin`
  - `/tmp`
  - `/usr`
  - `/var`
- The `pwd` command is used to display the current working directory.
- The `cd` command is used to change directories.
- The `ls` command is used to display directory contents.

- Using `ls` with the `-l` option displays the properties of files and directories.
- Using `ls` with the `-R` option displays directory contents recursively.
- The `touch` command is used to create new files or change the modification timestamp of an existing file.
- The `mkdir` command is used to create new directories.
- Use `cat` to view a text file onscreen.
- Use `less` or `more` to view a text file onscreen.
- The `less` or `more` command pauses the display one line at a time.
- The `head` command can be used to display the first few lines of a text file.
- The `tail` command can be used to display the last few lines of a text file.
- The `tail` command can be used with the `-f` option to monitor a text file for changes.
- You can use `rmdir` to delete an empty directory.
- You can use `rm -r` to delete a populated directory.
- You can use `rm` to delete files.
- The `cp` command is used to copy files.
- The `mv` command is used to move or rename files.
- The `ln` command allows you to create link files that point to other files or directories in the filesystem.
- Hard links are made with `ln` and point directly to the inode of another file.
- Soft links are made with `ln -s`, have their own inode, and point to a filename.
- The `find` utility manually walks the filesystem hierarchy to search for files.
- The `locate` utility maintains a database of all files.
- The `which` command displays aliases and external commands associated with a keyword.
- The `whereis` command displays the location of source files, external commands, and man pages associated with a keyword.
- Use `grep` to search for text within a file.

Questions

1. Which directory would contain boot configuration files?

A. `/bin`

B. `/dev`

C. `/etc`

D. `/boot`

2. What command would create a file that shares the same inode as the file `filea`?
   A. `cat < filea > fileb`
   B. `ln -s filea fileb`
   C. `ln filea fileb`
   D. `ln -s fileb filea`
3. What command would display how many files share the same inode as `filea`?
   A. `cat < filea > fileb`
   B. `ln -l filea`
   C. `ls -l filea`
   D. `ln -sl filea`
4. The inode number for `filea` is `1234`. What command would display a list of files that share the same inode as `filea`?
   A. `find / -name filea`
   B. `find / -name filea -a -inum 1234`
   C. `find / -inum 1234`
   D. `find / -name filea -o inum 1234`
5. The command `find /etc -name useradd` will begin searching for the file `useradd` in which directory?
   A. `/`
   B. `/etc`
   C. `/passwd`
   D. `/usr`
6. A user would like to create a link between two files located in different filesystems. What command should the user use?
   A. `ln`
   B. `ln -s`
   C. `ls -l filea`
   D. `ln -sl filea`
7. The command `pwd` is both a builtin and external command. Which command would display this information?
   A. `type -a pwd`
   B. `which -a pwd`
   C. `type pwd`
   D. `which pwd`

8. Which commands will display the location of the man pages for the keyword `passwd`? (Choose two.)
   - A. `find / passwd`
   - B. `locate passwd`
   - C. `whereis -m passwd`
   - D. `whereis passwd`
9. Which commands will change your current working directory to your home directory? (Choose two.)
   - A. `cd`
   - B. `echo $HOME`
   - C. `cd ~`
   - D. `$HOME`
10. A user has executed the command `mkdir -p cars/chevy/impala`. They immediately decide to remove the directories they just created. Which command would they use?
    - A. `rmdir cars`
    - B. `rm -r cars`
    - C. `rmdir etc`
    - D. `rmdir usr`
11. Which commands would display the first 10 lines of the file `/etc/passwd`? (Choose two.)
    - A. `head +10 /etc/passwd`
    - B. `head /etc/passwd`
    - C. `head -10 /etc/passwd`
    - D. `head 10 /etc/passwd`
12. A user has created a symbolic link using the command `ln -s filea fileb`. Which command will display the permissions granted to a user accessing `fileb`?
    - A. `ls -l fileb`
    - B. `ls -l filea`
    - C. `ls -lL filea`
    - D. `ls -lL fileb`
13. Which of the following is *not* a valid Linux filename?
    - A. `Filea`
    - B. `filea`
    - C. `r*`
    - D. `user/one`

14. What command would display the content type of a file?

  A. file

  B. ls -l

  C. cat <filename>

  D. less <filename>

15. What command other than alias may be used to determine if an alias is associated with a keyword?

  A. file <keyword>

  B. which -a <keyword>

  C. ls -l<keyword>

  D. type -a <keyword>

16. What commands would find files filea, fileb, and filec in student1's home directory and remove them, but require confirmation before removing them? (Choose two.)

  A. find /student1 -name "file[a-c] -exec rm {} \;

  B. find /student1 -name "file[a-c] -ok rm {} \;

  C. find /student1 -name "file[a-c] | xargs rm

  D. find /student1 -name "file[a-c] | xargs -p rm

17. What command will create the directory tree cars/chevy/vega?

  A. mkdir cars/chevy/vega

  B. mkdir -p cars/chevy/vega

  C. mkdir /cars/chevy/vega

  D. mkdir cars;mkdir chevy;mkdir vega

18. You have just created the directory tree fruit/apples/types relative to the current working directory. What commands could you execute to delete the directory types? (Choose two.)

  A. rmdir fruit

  B. cd fruit/apples ; rmdir types

  C. rmdir fruit/apples/types

  D. rm -r fruit

19. You want to copy file1 to an existing file, file2. You execute the command cp file1 file2 and receive the message "cp: overwrite file2." What commands would you execute to troubleshoot the problem and prevent this message from occurring?

  A. which -a ; \cp file1 file2

  B. which -a ; /cp file1 file2

C. `type -a cp ; cp file1 file2`

D. `type -a cp ; \cp file1 file2`

20. Which commands will display all strings with two occurrences of a lowercase *o* (oo)? (Choose three.)

A. `grep 'o{2}'`

B. `grep 'o\{2\}'`

C. `egrep o{2}`

D. `grep -E 'o{2}'`

21. Which commands will display the user record for `student1` or `root` from the file `/etc/passwd`? (Choose three.)

A. `grep 'root \| student1' /etc/passwd`

B. `grep -E '^student1|^root' /etc/passwd`

C. `egrep '^student1|^root' /etc/passwd`

D. `grep '^student1\|^root' /etc/passwd`

22. Which expression will search for the string `student1a` through to the string `student9z`?

A. `grep student[1a-9z]`

B. `grep student[0-9][a-z]`

C. `grep student[1-9][A-Z]`

D. `grep student[1-9][a-z]`

Answers

1. **D.** The `/boot` directory contains boot configuration files.
2. **C.** The command `ln filea fileb` would create the file `fileb`, which would share the same inode as `filea`.
3. **C.** The command `ls -l filea` would display the number of links (i.e., number of files) sharing the same inode.
4. **C.** The command `find / -inum 1234` would display a list of files with the same inode number. The command `find / -name filea -o inum 1234` (answer D) would fail because there is no – in front of `-inum`. If there were a "dash" it would work, but it is possible to have multiple files named `filea` that would not have the inode number `1234`, so this answer is incorrect.
5. **B.** The first argument of the `find` command specifies the start location of the search. If a start location is not specified, the search begins in the current working directory.
6. **B.** Linking files in different filesystems requires use of a symbolic link; therefore, the user should execute the command `ln -s`.

7. **A.** The command `type -a` displays builtins, external commands, aliases, and functions. The command `which -a` only displays external commands and aliases.

8. **C, D.** The `whereis -m passwd` command only displays the location of man pages associated with the keyword `passwd`. The command `whereis passwd` displays the location of the source code, binary, and man page files associated with the keyword `passwd`.

9. **A, C.** The commands `cd` and `cd ~` change the current working directory to the user's home directory.

10. **B.** The command `rmdir` only removes empty directories. Since the directory `cars` contains a subdirectory of `chevy`, the command would generate an error. Therefore, the command `rm -r cars` must be used.

11. **B, C.** The command `head <filename>` displays the first 10 lines of a file. The command `head -n <filename>` displays the first *n* lines of a file.

12. **D.** The `ls -l fileb` command (answer A) displays the properties of `fileb`. The command `ls -lL fileb` displays the properties of the file it is linked to.

13. **D.** Linux does not allow use of a whitespace character in a filename, nor the use of a forward slash (/) or null character. (Note that although `r*` is a legal filename, it is not a good choice.)

14. **A.** The `file` command uses the magic number to determine the type of content stored in the file. The `ls -l` command (answer B) displays the code that represents the type of file (directory, ASCII, and so on).

15. **B.** The `which -a <keyword>` command lists aliases and external commands associated with a keyword, in order of precedence.

16. **B, D.** Since the question states the command requires user confirmation prior to executing the command, you would need to use `-ok` with the `find` command and `-p` with the `xargs` command. Answers A and C would not require user intervention.

17. **B.** The command `mkdir -p` creates a directory tree. It is important to note that the directory tree must be created relative to the current working directory.

18. **B, C.** The `rmdir` command only removes empty directories. Answer B uses `cd` to change the directory to the parent of directory types, and the `rmdir` command removes the directory types. Answer C uses a relative path to remove the directory types. Answer D could work, but it would strip too much, so it is not the best answer.

19. **D.** To troubleshoot the error, you must determine what command is executing by executing the command `type -a cp` (or `which -a cp`). The output tells you the `cp` command is aliased to `cp -i`, which is preventing the command from overwriting an existing file. To negate the alias, execute the command `\cp file1 file2`.

20. **B, C, D.** Remember that `grep` and `egrep` use two different regular expression engines, so the formatting of the expression is different, and `grep` requires a backslash before some of the expression metacharacters, which is why A is incorrect. It is also important to remember the command `grep -E` is the same as executing the command `egrep`.
21. **B, C, D.** The question asks for the commands that will display the records for the user `root` or `student1`. Since a user record in `/etc/passwd` begins with the username, you are looking for the username string at the beginning of the line (^).
22. **D.** Each character position requires its own range specification. The question states that you need to look for the string `student1a` through to string `string9z`. The first character range position (after the *t*) would be `[1-9]` and the second character range position would be `[a-z]`.

CHAPTER 6

Managing Ownership and Permissions

In this chapter, you will learn about

- Managing file ownership
- Managing file and directory permissions
- Configuring file attributes and access control lists

The system and the group are intimately interacting entities.

—Clarence "Skip" Ellis, University of Colorado, Boulder

There are two tasks to accomplish when managing user access to a Linux system:

- Control who can access the system.
- Define what users can do after they have logged in to the system.

Access control is implemented by defining users and groups and then defining what those users and groups are authorized to do after they log into the system. Let's begin by discussing file and directory ownership.

Managing File Ownership

To effectively control who can do what in the filesystem, system administrators need to first consider who "owns" files and directories. A user's file and directory settings default to predefined Linux settings, but these can be modified to better suit a user's purpose. You will learn about the following:

- Viewing default file permissions and ownerships
- Managing ownership from the command line

Let's start by looking at a file's default settings.

Viewing Default File Permissions and Ownership

Any time a user creates a new file or directory, their user account is assigned as that file's or directory's "owner." By default, the owner of a directory on a Linux system receives read, write, and execute permissions to the directory. In essence, the owner can do whatever they want with that directory. Likewise, the owner of a file on a Linux system receives read and write permissions to that file by default. For example, suppose the `tcboony` user logs in to her Linux system and creates a file named `contacts.odt` using LibreOffice.org in her home directory. Because she created this file, `tcboony` is automatically assigned ownership of `contacts.odt`. Figure 6-1 shows the user and group settings of a file.

Notice in Figure 6-1 that there are two settings to discuss for `contacts.odt`. The first is the name of the user who owns the file. In this case, it is `tcboony`. In addition, the file belongs to the `staff` group. That's because `staff` is the primary group `tcboony` belongs to.

You can also view file ownership from the command line using the `ls -l` command. This has been done in `tcboony`'s home directory in this example:

NOTE In this example, both instances of `l` are the lowercase letter *l*, not the number one.

```
tcboony@openSUSE:~> ls -l
total 40
drwxr-xr-x 2 tcboony staff 4096 2024-03-10 16:43 bin
-rw-r--r-- 1 tcboony staff  304 2024-03-18 08:02 contacts.odt
drwxr-xr-x 2 tcboony staff 4096 2024-03-10 16:44 Desktop
drwxr-xr-x 2 tcboony staff 4096 2024-03-10 16:44 Documents
drwxr-xr-x 2 tcboony staff 4096 2024-03-10 16:44 Downloads
drwxr-xr-x 2 tcboony staff 4096 2024-03-10 16:44 Music
drwxr-xr-x 2 tcboony staff 4096 2024-03-10 16:44 Pictures
drwxr-xr-x 2 tcboony staff 4096 2024-03-10 16:44 Public
drwxr-xr-x 2 tcboony staff 4096 2024-03-10 16:43 public_html
drwxr-xr-x 2 tcboony staff 4096 2024-03-10 16:44 Templates
drwxr-xr-x 2 tcboony staff 4096 2024-03-10 16:44 Videos
```

Notice that the third column in the output displays the name of the file or directory's user (`tcboony`), while the fourth column displays the name of the group that owns it (`staff`). Even though file and directory ownership is automatically assigned at creation, it can be modified, as explained in the following section.

```
[tcboony@localhost ~]$ ls -l contacts.odt
-rw-r--r--. 1 tcboony staff 15 Aug 23 18:08 contacts.odt
```

user group

Figure 6-1 Viewing the owner and group of a file

Managing Ownership from the Command Line

File and directory ownership is not a fixed entity. Even though ownership is automatically assigned at creation, it can be modified. Only root can change the user who owns a file or directory. To change the group of a file or directory, become root, or as a user, already belong to the group that the file is changing to.

Modifying file or directory ownership can be done with either graphical or command-line tools. Staying true to the form of the CompTIA Linux+ exam, this discussion focuses on two command-line utilities, chown and chgrp, and not the graphical utilities.

Using chown to Change Ownership

The chown utility changes the user or group that owns a file or directory. The syntax for using chown is chown <user>:<group> <file or directory>. For example, if there is a file named myfile.txt in /tmp that is owned by root, to change the file's owner to the tcboony user, as root enter chown tcboony /tmp/myfile.txt, as shown here:

```
root@openSUSE:~ # ls -l /tmp/myfile.txt
-rw-r--r-- 1 root root 90 Mar 18 09:38 /tmp/myfile.txt
root@openSUSE:~ # chown tcboony /tmp/myfile.txt
root@openSUSE:~ # ls -l /tmp/myfile.txt
-rw-r--r-- 1 tcboony root 90 Mar 18 09:38 /tmp/myfile.txt
```

The root user can also change both the user and the group all at once with a single chown command by entering chown tcboony:staff /tmp/myfile.txt, for example. This tells chown that the user to change ownership to is tcboony and the group to change ownership to is staff.

TIP Use the -R option with chown to change ownership on many files at once in the current directory and below. This is also known as changing ownership "recursively."

Using chgrp to Change Group

In addition to using chown, root can also use chgrp to change the group that owns a file or directory. Simply enter chgrp <group> <file or directory>. For example, to change the group ownership of the /tmp/myfile.txt file (discussed in the previous examples) from root to staff, enter chgrp staff /tmp/myfile .txt, as shown here:

```
root@openSUSE:~ # ls -l /tmp/myfile.txt
-rw-r--r-- 1 tcboony root 90 Mar 18 09:38 /tmp/myfile.txt
root@openSUSE:~ # chgrp staff /tmp/myfile.txt
root@openSUSE:~ # ls -l /tmp/myfile.txt
-rw-r--r-- 1 tcboony staff 90 Mar 18 09:38 /tmp/myfile.txt
```

Exercise 6-1: Managing Ownership

In this exercise, practice modifying file and directory ownership from the shell prompt of the Linux system. Perform this exercise using the virtual machine that comes with this book.

VIDEO Please watch the Exercise 6-1 video for a demonstration on how to perform this task.

Complete the following steps:

1. Log in to the system using the login name **`student1`** and password **`student1`**.
2. Open a terminal session by clicking Applications | Favorites | Terminal.
3. Switch to the `root` user account with the **`su -`** command using a password of **`password`**.
4. Verify the `student1` user account is a member of the `research` group by doing the following:

NOTE The `research` group was configured in Exercise 4-2 of Chapter 4.

   a. At the shell prompt, enter **`cat /etc/group`**.
   b. Verify that the `student1` user is a member of the `research` group.
   c. If the `student1` user is not a member of the `research` group, add `student1` to the group using the `usermod` command as follows: **`usermod -aG research student1`**
5. Change to the / directory by entering **`cd /`** at the shell prompt.
6. Create a new directory named `RandD` by entering **`mkdir RandD`** at the shell prompt.
7. At the shell prompt, enter **`ls -l`**. Notice that the `root` user account and the `root` group are the owners of the new directory.
8. Change ownership of the directory to the `student1` user account and the `research` group by entering **`chown student1:research RandD`** at the shell prompt.
9. Enter **`ls -l`** again at the shell prompt. Verify that ownership of the `RandD` directory has changed to the `student1` user account and the `research` group, as shown here:

```
[root@cent71-5t /# ls -l
total 104
drwxr-xr-x   2 student1 research  4096 Nov 25 17:34 RandD
```

Managing File and Directory Permissions

Managing ownership represents only a part of what needs to be done to control access to files and directories in the Linux filesystem. Ownership only specifies who *owns* what, not *what* one can or cannot do with files and directories. This section covers

- How permissions work
- Managing permissions from the command line
- Working with default permissions
- Working with special permissions

To start, you will have to understand how *permissions* work, which is discussed next.

How Permissions Work

Unlike ownership, permissions are used to specify exactly what an end user may do with files and directories in the filesystem. Permissions may allow an end user to view a file but not modify it, for example, or allow an end user to open and modify a file. Permissions may even allow an end user to run an executable file. Permissions can be configured to prevent an end user from even seeing a file within a directory.

Each file or directory in the Linux filesystem stores the specific permissions assigned to it. These permissions together constitute the *mode* of the file. Any file or directory can have the permissions shown in Table 6-1 as their mode.

These permissions are assigned to each of three different entities for each file and directory in the filesystem:

- **owner/user (`u`)** This is the end user that has been assigned to be the file's or directory's owner. Permissions assigned to the owner or user apply only to that end user's account.

Permission	Symbol	Effect on Files	Effect on Directories
Read	`r`	Allows a user to open and view a file. Does not allow a file to be modified or saved. Allows use of less, more, cat, and so on.	Allows a user to list the contents of a directory; for example, by executing the `ls` command.
Write	`w`	Allows a user to modify a file; for example, with the `vi`, `nano`, `gedit`, `emacs`, and so on.	Allows a user to add or delete files from the directory. Good for commands such as `touch`, `rm`, `cp`, and so on.
Execute	`x`	Allows a user to run an executable file; for example, LibreOffice is a program, so it has the execute bit set.	Allows a user to enter a directory; for example, using the `cd` command.

Table 6-1 Linux Permissions and Their Effects

- **group (`g`)** This is the group that has been assigned to the file or directory. Permissions assigned to the group apply to all accounts that are members of that group.
- **world/other (`o`)** This entity, also known as world or other, refers to all other users who have successfully authenticated to the system but are neither the owner nor belong to the group. Permissions assigned to this entity apply to these user accounts.

Linux first checks if the end user is the *owner/user*; if so, they are assigned the *owner/user* permission. If the end user is not the user but belongs to the *group*, they get the *group* permission. Finally, if the end user is neither the user nor a member of the group, they get the *other* permission. For example, suppose the user permissions are read-only and the group and other permissions are read/write; then the end user will have the weakest permissions of anyone since *user* is set to read-only.

Users run the `ls -l` command to view the permissions assigned to files or directories in the filesystem. Consider the example shown here:

```
tcboony@openSUSE:~> ls -l          # Remember, ls dash "el"
total 48
drwxr-xr-x 2 tcboony staff 4096 Nov 25 17:30 bin
drwxr-xr-x 2 tcboony staff 4096 Nov 25 18:33 Desktop
drwxr-xr-x 2 tcboony staff 4096 Nov 25 18:33 Documents
drwxr-xr-x 2 tcboony staff 4096 Nov 25 18:33 Downloads
drwxr-xr-x 2 tcboony staff 4096 Nov 25 18:33 Music
drwxr-xr-x 2 tcboony staff 4096 Nov 25 18:33 Pictures
-rw-r--r-- 1 tcboony staff  123 Nov 25 18:36 Project_design.odt
-rw-r--r-- 1 tcboony staff  104 Nov 25 18:36 Project_schedule.odt
drwxr-xr-x 2 tcboony staff 4096 Nov 25 18:33 Public
drwxr-xr-x 2 tcboony staff 4096 Nov 25 17:30 public_html
drwxr-xr-x 2 tcboony staff 4096 Nov 25 18:33 Templates
drwxr-xr-x 2 tcboony staff 4096 Nov 25 18:33 Videos
```

The first column displayed is the mode for each file and directory. The first character of the mode denotes the file type, which can be a regular file (`-`), a directory (`d`), a symbolic link (`l`), a block device (`b`), or character device (`c`). As you can see, `Project_design.odt` and `Project_schedule.odt` are regular files, whereas `Desktop` is a directory.

A *block device* is a driver for some type of hardware, such as a hard disk drive, that transfers data in "blocks" from the hard disk to memory. A *character device* is a driver for hardware, such as a keyboard or a mouse, that transfers data one bit or byte at a time. A *symbolic link* is like a shortcut that gets redirected to the file it is "linked" to, as discussed in Chapter 5.

The next three characters are the permissions assigned to the entry's owner: the *user*. For example, `Project_schedule.odt` has `rw-` assigned to its user (`tcboony`). This means `tcboony` has read and write permissions to the file, but not execute. Because the file isn't a program or script, no executable permission needs to be set. If the file were a program or script and the execute permission were assigned, the permission would show as `rwx`. Because the user has read and write permissions, `tcboony` can open, edit, and save the file changes.

The next three characters are the permissions assigned to the group. In this case, it is the `staff` group. Any user on the system who is a member of the `staff` group is

Table 6-2 Numeric Values Assigned to Permissions

Permission	Value
Read	4
Write	2
Execute	1

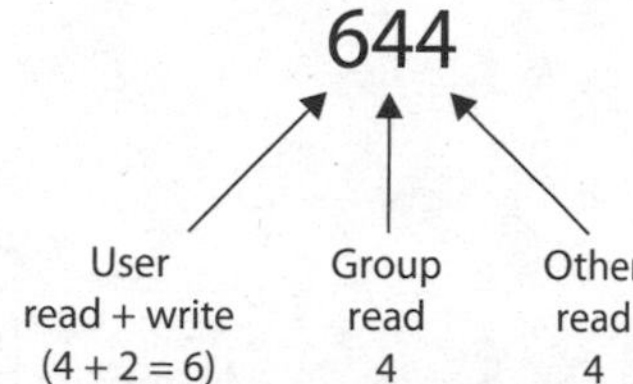

Figure 6-2 Representing permissions numerically

granted `r--` access to the `Project_schedule.odt` file. This means they have the read privilege, allowing them to open the file and view its contents, but they are not allowed to save any changes to the file.

Before we progress any further, permissions for each entity can also be represented numerically. This is done by assigning a value to each permission, as shown in Table 6-2.

Using these values, the permissions assigned to user (`u`), group (`g`), or other (`o`) can be represented with a single digit. Simply add up the value of each permission. For example, suppose *user* is assigned read and write permissions to a file. To determine the numeric value of this assignment, simply add the values of read and write together (4 + 2 = 6). Often a file's or directory's mode is represented by three numbers that define owner, group, and other. Consider the example shown in Figure 6-2.

In this example, the associated file's user has read and write permissions (6), the group has the read permission (4), and other also has read permission (4). Using the `ls -l` command, this mode would be represented as `-rw-r--r--`, as shown here for the file `myfile.txt`:

```
root@openSUSE:~ # ls -l /tmp/myfile.txt
-rw-r--r-- 1 tcboony root 90 Mar 18 09:38 /tmp/myfile.txt
```

So, what if these permissions aren't correct? Use the `chmod` utility to modify them! Let's discuss how this is done next.

Managing Permissions from the Command Line

Although using the GUI is not covered on the CompTIA Linux+ exam, Linux administrators can modify permissions graphically. For example, using the file browser in the GNOME desktop environment, you can right-click any file or directory and then select Properties | Permissions to change the file permissions. The screen shown in Figure 6-3 is displayed.

However, for the Linux+ exam, you must be able to accomplish the task with command-line tools using `chmod` to modify permissions. To use `chmod`, you must either own the file or be logged in as `root`.

Figure 6-3 Setting permissions in file browser

Several different syntaxes can be used with `chmod`. The first is to enter the command `chmod <entity=permissions> <filename>` at the shell prompt. Substitute `u` for owner, `g` for group, and `o` for other in the `entity` portion of the command. Also substitute `r`, `w`, and/or `x` for the `permissions` portion of the command. For example, to change the mode of the `contacts.odt` file to `-rw-rw-r--` (giving *user* and *group* read and write permissions while giving *other* only read access), enter `chmod u=rw,g=rw,o=r contacts.odt` *or* `chmod ug=rw,o=r contacts.odt` at the shell prompt (assuming the file resides in the current directory). The permissions are adjusted as shown here:

```
root@openSUSE:/home/tcboony # chmod u=rw,g=rw,o=r contacts.odt
root@openSUSE:/home/tcboony # ls -l contacts.odt
-rw-rw-r-- 1 tcboony staff 304 Mar 18 08:02 contacts.odt
```

Also use `chmod` to toggle a particular permission on or off using the + or – sign. For example, to turn off the write permission given to group for `contacts.odt` file, enter `chmod g-w contacts.odt` at the shell prompt. Once executed, the specified permission is turned off, as shown here:

```
root@openSUSE:/home/tcboony # chmod g-w contacts.odt
root@openSUSE:/home/tcboony # ls -l contacts.odt
-rw-r--r-- 1 tcboony staff 304 Mar 18 08:02 contacts.odt
```

To turn the permission back on, enter `chmod g+w contacts.odt`. Or, substitute `u` or `o` to modify the permission to the file or directory for *owner* or *other,* respectively.

Feature for Teams Working on a Project

There is a special setting for directories when working as a team on a project. When setting the special permission bit on the group of the directory with `chmod g+s <directory>`, any files created in that directory thereafter will inherit the group of the directory instead of the primary group of the user who creates the file. See the example of a subdirectory called `temp` shown here:

```
openSUSE:/home/tcboony/temp # chgrp wheel .          # change temp to wheel group
openSUSE:/home/tcboony/temp # chmod g+s .            # set special bit on temp dir
openSUSE:/home/tcboony/temp # touch apple            # create the apple file
openSUSE:/home/tcboony/temp # ls -l apple
-rw-r--r-- 1 tcboony wheel 0 Mar 18 08:02 apple     # apple inherits group of temp
```

`root` Privileges Through the `wheel` Group

Historically, the `wheel` group is a special group for system administrators. Members of this group can execute restricted commands within a standard user account. *Be cautious* assigning members to the `wheel` group and adding files, directories, and commands to the `wheel` group, because this is a security risk.

A better feature to assign administrative controls is `sudo`, because it logs administrative activity. Today, members added to the `wheel` group on RHEL-based systems or the `sudo` group on Debian-based systems are granted `sudo` access. Further details are provided in Chapter 16.

Changing Permissions Numerically

Finally, you can also use numeric permissions with `chmod`, which system administrators use most often. Just modify all three entities at once. To do this, enter `chmod <numeric_permission> <filename>`.

Going back to the earlier example, suppose an end user wants to grant read and write permissions to user and group but remove all permissions from other. That would mean the permissions of user and group would be represented numerically as 6. And, because other gets no permissions, it would be represented by 0. Implement this by entering `chmod 660 contacts.odt` at the shell prompt. When done, the appropriate changes are made, as shown in the following example:

```
openSUSE:/home/tcboony # chmod 660 contacts.odt
openSUSE:/home/tcboony # ls -l contacts.odt
-rw-rw---- 1 tcboony staff 304 Mar 18 08:02 contacts.odt
```

TIP Use the `-R` option with `chmod` to change permissions on many files at once, recursively.

Troubleshooting Tips for user and group Permissions

When a user attempts to read a file they do not have access to, they will get a cryptic error message, as shown here:

```
openSUSE:/home/patbijou # cat file.txt
cat: file.txt: Permission denied
```

Yes, the error printed could be better, such as `cat: file.txt: read permission denied`, but Linux is slowly improving and becoming more user friendly.

So, after viewing a `Permission denied` error message, run `ls -l <filename>` to find which user or group permission is missing on the file, and run `ls -ld .` to discover which user or group permission is missing on the directory. After determining the problem, the permission can be changed by the file owner or a system administrator.

Let's practice managing permissions in the following exercise.

Exercise 6-2: Managing Permissions

In this exercise, you practice modifying permissions from the shell prompt of the Linux system. You also create a design document for a hypothetical Research and Design team and modify its permissions to control access. Perform this exercise using the virtual machine that comes with this book.

VIDEO Please watch the Exercise 6-2 video for a demonstration on how to perform this task.

Complete the following steps:

1. Log in to the system using the login name **student1** and password **student1**. Start a terminal by clicking Applications | Terminal.
2. Switch to the `root` user account with the **su -** command, and enter the password.
3. Change to the `/RandD` directory by entering **cd /RandD** at the shell prompt.
4. Create a design document for the team and restrict access to it by doing the following:
   a. Create a new file named `design_doc.odt` by entering **touch design_doc.odt** at the shell prompt.
   b. At the shell prompt, enter the **ls -l** command. Notice that the `root` user account and the `root` group are the owners of the new file.
   c. Change ownership of the file to the `student1` user account and the `research` group using the following command:
      chown student1:research design_doc.odt
   d. Enter **ls -l** again at the shell prompt. Verify that ownership of the file directory has changed to the `student1` user account and the `research` group. Notice that user has `rw-` permissions to the file, but group only has `r--` permission.
   e. Grant `Group rw-` permissions by entering **chmod g+w design_doc.odt** at the shell prompt.
   f. Enter **ls -l** again at the shell prompt. Notice that *user* and *group* now both have read/write access to the file.

g. Notice that *other* has read access to the file. To keep this document confidential, remove this access by entering **`chmod 660 design_doc.odt`** at the shell prompt.

h. Enter **`ls -l`** again. Verify that *other* has no permissions to this file.

5. Next, control access to the research directory itself using permissions. Do the following:

   a. Enter **`ls -ld`** at the shell prompt. Notice that *user* has full access to the `RandD` directory, but *group* is missing the write permission to the directory. Also notice that *other* can read the directory contents (`r`) and can enter the directory (`x`).

   b. Grant *group* full access to the directory and remove *other* access to the directory completely by entering **`chmod 770 RandD`** at the shell prompt.

   c. Enter **`ls -ld`** at the shell prompt. Verify that *user* and *group* have full access and that *other* has no access.

Working with Default Permissions

Whenever a new file or directory is created in the filesystem, a default set of permissions is automatically assigned.

By default, Linux assigns `rw-rw-rw-` (`666`) permissions to every file whenever it is created in the filesystem. It also assigns `rwxrwxrwx` (`777`) permissions to every directory created in the filesystem. However, these are not the permissions the files or directories actually end up with because of a security feature called `umask`. Let's look at an example.

Suppose `tcboony` was to create a new directory named `revenue` in her home directory and a file named `projections.odt` in the revenue directory. Based on what we just discussed, the `revenue` directory should have a mode of `rwxrwxrwx` and the `projections.odt` file should have a mode of `rw-rw-rw-`. However, this is not the case, as shown here:

```
tcboony@openSUSE:~> ls -ld revenue rev*/projectors.odt
drwxr-xr-x 2 tcboony staff 4096 2024-03-18 11:06 revenue
-rw-r--r-- 1 tcboony staff 5128 2024-03-18 11:06 revenue/projections.odt
```

Notice that the `revenue` directory has a mode of `drwxr-xr-x` (`755`). This means the directory's user has read, write, and execute permissions to the directory. group and other have read and execute permissions to the directory. Likewise, notice that the `projections.odt` file has a mode of `-rw-r--r--` (`644`). `Owner` has read and write permissions, whereas group and other have only the read permission.

These are not the default permissions Linux is supposed to assign! Why did this happen? Because the default permissions are not secure. Think about it. The default directory mode would allow anyone on the system to enter any directory and delete any files they wanted to. Likewise, the default file mode would allow any user on the system to modify a file you created. What a nightmare!

Using `umask` to Secure Files and Directories

To increase the overall security of the system, Linux uses `umask` to automatically remove permissions from the default mode whenever a file or directory is created in the filesystem. The value of `umask` is a three- or four-digit number, as shown here:

```
openSUSE:~ # umask
0022
```

For most Linux distributions, the default value of `umask` is `0022` or `022`. Each digit represents a permission value to be *removed*. For a `umask` of `022`, the first digit (`0`) references—you guessed it—*user*. The middle digit (`2`) references *group*, and the last digit (`2`) references *other*. Because `0` (zero) is listed for *user*, no permissions are removed from the default mode for a file or directory user.

However, because `2` is listed for group and other, the write permission is removed from the default mode whenever a file or directory is created in the filesystem for group and other. The function of `umask` is shown in Figure 6-4. (For a `umask` of `0022`, the first `0` is discussed in the upcoming section "Working with Special Permissions.")

The default value of `umask` works for most Linux administrators. However, there may be situations where you need to tighten or loosen the permissions assigned when a file or directory is created in the filesystem. To do this, change the value assigned to `umask`.

You can do this by making a temporary change to `umask`, by entering `umask <value>` at the shell prompt. For example, to remove the execute permission that is automatically assigned to other whenever a new directory is created, enter `umask 023`. This would cause the write permission (`2`) to be removed from *group* upon creation, as well as write (`2`) and execute (`1`) from *other*. This will effectively disallow anyone from entering the new directory except for the directory's *user* or members of *group*. This is shown here:

```
openSUSE:~ # umask 023
openSUSE:~ # umask
0023
openSUSE:~ # mkdir /home/tcboony/temp
openSUSE:~ # ls -ld /home/tcboony/temp   # -d option will not descend a directory
drwxr-xr-- 2 root  root  4096 Mar 18 11:14 temp/
```

Notice that, because the value of `umask` was changed, the execute permission (`x`) was removed from *other* in the mode when the `temp` directory was created.

Figure 6-4 How `umask` works

```
                          Files
        Default Mode : rw-rw-rw-
Subtracted by umask : ----w--w-

             Result:  rw-r-r--

                    Directories
        Default Mode:  rwxrwxrwx
Subtracted by umask:  ----w--w-

             Result:  rwxr-xr-x
```

EXAM TIP Because regular files have a permission of `-rw-rw-rw-`, no *execute* permission bit is set by default. A `umask` value of `0111` would have no effect on a regular file.

Setting a Permanent `umask` Value

The method for modifying `umask` discussed in the prior section works great, but it is not *persistent*. If the system restarted, the `umask` would revert to its original value. That is because the value of `umask` is automatically set each time the system boots using the `umask` parameter in the configuration files `/etc/profile`, `/etc/bashrc`, `/etc/login.defs`, or `~/.bashrc`, depending on the distribution (where ~ means the end user's home directory).

To make the change to `umask` permanent, simply edit the appropriate configuration file in a text editor and set the value of `umask` to the desired value.

Next, let's look at special permissions.

Working with Special Permissions

As previously mentioned, the value of `umask` is a four-digit number, as shown here:

```
openSUSE:~ # umask
0022
```

Let's discuss the leading `0` here, which is called a *special permission* bit.

Most tasks completed with permissions will be with the read, write, and execute permissions. However, there are three other special permissions to assign to files and directories in the filesystem. These are shown in Table 6-3.

Permission	Description	Effect on Files	Effect on Directories
SUID (`s`)	Set User ID. Can only be applied to binary executable files (not shell scripts).	When an executable file set with SUID is run, the end user temporarily runs the file at the `User` (owner) privilege of the file.	None.
SGID (`s`)	Set Group ID. Can be applied to binary executable files (not shell scripts).	When an executable file with SGID set is run, the end user temporarily runs the file at the `Group` privilege of the file.	When the end user creates a file in a directory that has SGID set, the group assigned to the new file is set to the group of the SGID-defined directory.
Sticky Bit (`t`)	Can be applied to directories.	None.	When the Sticky Bit is set, users can only delete files within the directory for which they are the `User` (owner). If the Sticky Bit is *not* set, anyone can delete anyone's files.

Table 6-3 Special Permissions

These special permissions are referenced as an extra digit added to the *beginning* of the file's or directory's mode. As with regular permissions, each of these special permissions has a numerical value assigned to it, as shown here:

- SUID: 4
- SGID: 2
- Sticky Bit: 1

Assign these special permissions to files or directories using `chmod`. Just add an extra number to the beginning of the mode that references the special permissions to associate with the file or directory. For example, to apply the SUID and SGID permissions to a file named `runme` that should be readable and executable by user and group, enter `chmod 6554 runme` at the shell prompt. This specifies that the file has SUID (`4`) and SGID (`2`) permissions assigned (for a total of `6` in the first digit). user and group both have read and execute permissions (5), and other has read-only permissions.

To set the special bits mnemonically, execute

```
chmod ug=srx,o=r runme
```

This is equivalent to `chmod 6554 runme`.

To remove the sticky bit for the file user and group, run

```
chmod u-s,g-s runme
```

This is equivalent to `chmod ug-s runme`.

Overriding the real userid (RUID) and real groupid (RGID)

Assuming the SUID and SGID bits are set for the `runme` command, what does that mean when the command is executed? Let's say you are logged in as the user `ian`, and `ian`'s default group is `users`. Normally when `ian` runs a command, it runs at the effective userid (EUID) of `ian`'s real userid (RUID) `ian` and the effective groupid (EGID) of `ian`'s real groupid (RGID) `users`.

But, when the SUID and SGID bits are set, the RUID and/or RGID are overridden and *take the command's permission*. Now whenever `ian` runs `runme`, the EUID becomes the owner of the command and the EGID becomes the group of the command. In the following example, the SUID and SGID are set because an `s` is shown for the user (owner) and group of the command:

```
openSUSE:~ # ls -l runme
-rwsr-sr-- 1 tcboony wheel 0 Mar 18 09:38 runme
```

Whenever `ian` or any user runs the `runme` command, their EUID will be `tcboony` and their EGID will be `wheel`. Their real userid (RUID) and real groupid (RGID) are overridden because of the special permission bit settings.

Two commands that use special permission bits include `/usr/bin/passwd`, the command you use to change your password, and `/usr/bin/locate`, the command you use to locate files on a Linux filesystem, as shown here:

```
openSUSE:~ # ls -l /usr/bin/passwd /usr/bin/locate
-rwsr-xr-- 1 root  bin     33424 Mar 18 09:38 /usr/bin/passwd
-rwxr-sr-- 1 root  slocate 21104 Mar 18 09:38 /usr/bin/locate
```

When a user runs the `passwd` command, they temporarily obtain `root` *user* privileges for the purpose of that command. In this case, only the `root` user can modify the file that contains passwords, `/etc/shadow`.

When a user runs the `locate` command, they temporarily obtain `slocate` *group* privileges to access databases critical for the `locate` command to function.

Using Special Permissions to Reduce Abuse of Shared Directories

Initially when a shared directory is created, any user can remove anyone else's files. The reason is that, to allow shared directories to work, everyone, including `other`, needs write permission to the directory, which appears as `drwxrwsrwx`.

To rid the abuse of users removing files that do not belong to them, enable the sticky bit on the shared directory. Again, use `chmod` by one of these two methods so that only file `users` (and `root`) can remove their files from within the shared directory and not anyone else:

```
chmod ugo=rwx,o=trwx dira
```

```
chmod 1777 dira
```

One directory that uses the sticky bit is `/tmp`. Notice the `t` setting for other, which means the sticky bit setting is enabled:

```
openSUSE:~ # ls -ld /tmp
drwxrwxrwt 1 root root  4096 Mar 18 09:38 /tmp
```

Now only file owners (and `root`) can remove their files within the shared directory.

Practice managing default and special permissions in the following exercise.

Exercise 6-3: Managing Default and Special Permissions

In this exercise, practice modifying default permissions with `umask` and start creating files. Also practice adding special permissions to directories. Perform this exercise using the virtual machine that comes with this book.

VIDEO Please watch the Exercise 6-3 video for a demonstration on how to perform this task.

Complete the following steps:

1. Log in to the system using login name **student1** and password **student1**. Start a terminal by clicking Applications | Terminal.
2. If necessary, switch to the `root` user account with the **su -** command and a password of **password**.
3. Change to the `/RandD` directory by entering **cd /RandD** at the shell prompt.
4. Create several Research and Development documents in the `RandD` directory. However, make sure these documents are secure from prying eyes. Recall from the previous exercise that `Other` is automatically granted read access to files when created. You don't want this to happen. You need `Other` to have no access at all to any documents created. Do the following:
   a. Change the default permissions by entering **umask 027** at the shell prompt.
   b. Verify the value of `umask` by entering **umask** at the shell prompt. It should display `0027`.
   c. Create a new file named `schedule.odt` by entering **touch schedule.odt** at the shell prompt.
   d. Enter **ls -l** at the shell prompt. Verify that user has `rw-`, group has `r--`, and other has `---` permissions.
5. Having the write permission to a directory allows anyone in the `research` group to delete any file in the directory. We want to configure the directory so that users in the `research` group can only delete files they actually own. Do the following:
   a. At the shell prompt, enter the **cd /** command.
   b. At the shell prompt, add the Sticky Bit permission to the `RandD` directory by entering **chmod 1771 RandD**.
   c. At the shell prompt, enter **ls -l RandD** and notice that a `t` has been added to the last digit of the other portion of the mode of the `RandD` directory. This indicates that the sticky bit has been set:

```
openSUSE:/ # ls -l
total 105
drwxrwx--t   2 tux  research  4096 Mar 18 11:25 RandD
...
```

Configuring File Attributes and Access Control Lists

Linux offers advanced features to provide more security for files and directories. Linux administrators can set even tighter access controls on files by using features of the following:

- File attributes
- File access control lists

File Attributes

File attributes allow an operator to provide additional capabilities to files. For example, a file can be made to be append-only or immutable. An administrator can use the `chattr` command to change attributes and use the `lsattr` command to list attributes, as shown here:

```
root@openSUSE:/home/tcboony # chattr +i contacts.odt
root@openSUSE:/home/tcboony # lsattr contacts.odt
----i--------e- contacts.odt
root@openSUSE:/home/tcboony # chattr -i contacts.odt
root@openSUSE:/home/tcboony # lsattr contacts.odt
-------------e- contacts.odt
```

The preceding example shows the immutable bit being set using the command `chattr +i contacts.odt`, and then the immutable feature being removed with `chattr -i contacts.odt`. The `e` setting means extent format, which is always the case on `ext4` filesystems and allows files to be saved properly.

Other modifiable file attributes include the following:

- `c` Compressed
- `j` Data journaling
- `S` Synchronous updates

Visit the `chattr(1)` and `lsattr(1)` man pages to learn about other modifiable attributes.

Troubleshooting Tips for Attributes

Users might find that even though they have permission to remove a file, they cannot remove it. They will see that running `ls -ld .` shows they have write permission on the directory, but yet cannot remove the file. Their next step is to run `lsattr` to see if an attribute is set, then contact an administrator to remove the attribute with `chattr`, because changing attributes requires `root` privilege.

EXAM TIP Once file immutability is set, no one can remove the file, including `root`!

File Access Control Lists

Users can extend their file security settings by implementing a feature called access control lists (ACLs). This feature allows users to assign specific, more granular privileges to their files and directories. For example, in the `staff` group directory, user `nathand` has read and write access to the files because he is a member of the `staff` group. However, an administrator determines `nathand` only needs read access to contacts.odt, which is also part of the `staff` group. ACLs can reduce his privilege to read-only without removing the file's `staff` group membership.

To view the current ACL settings, use the `getfacl` command:

```
tcboony@openSUSE:~> getfacl contacts.odt
# file: contacts.odt
# owner: tcboony
# group: staff
user::rw-
group::rw-
other::r--
```

Since `nathand` is a member of the group `staff`, he has read-write privileges. To give `nathand` read-only privileges on the file but still allow him read-write privileges on other files that belong to the `staff` group, set an ACL using `setfacl`.

In this example, we run `setfacl` with the `-m` option to modify the file's ACL value:

```
tcboony@openSUSE:~> setfacl -m u:nathand:r contacts.odt
tcboony@openSUSE:~> getfacl contacts.odt
# file: contacts.odt
# owner: tcboony
# group: staff
user::rw-
user:nathand:r--
group::rw-
mask::rw-
other::r--
```

User `nathand` now only has read access to the file `contacts.odt` even though he belongs to the group `staff`, which has a higher privilege of read-write.

The mask value that appears is a security mechanism to automatically limit privileges to a maximum value. For example, if the mask is set to `r--` by using the command `setfacl -m mask:r contacts.odt`, all users would only have read access even if their user or group membership is higher.

Troubleshooting Tips for Groups and ACLs

A user might belong to the `staff` group yet find they do not have the read privilege they are supposed to have. Running `ls -l <filename>` shows they have read privilege. But then the user notices a + sign at the end of the permissions. This means that an ACL is defined on the file, as shown here:

```
root@openSUSE:/ # ls -l contacts.odt
-rw-r-----+  1 matia  staff  3096 Mar 18 11:25 contacts.odt
```

Now, when the user runs `getfacl <filename>`, they see that an ACL was set that limits their permission to read-only. To raise the privilege, they need to request the change from the owner of the file or the system administrator.

Chapter Review

In this chapter, we discussed ownership and permissions. Assigning users and groups can only control who accesses the filesystem, but not what they can do with files or directories in the filesystem. To do this, we need to implement ownership and permissions.

Whenever a user creates a file or directory, that user is automatically assigned to be its owner. In addition, the group the user belongs to becomes the file's or directory's group owner. These defaults can be changed; however, only `root` can change a file or directory's owner. The owner can change its group.

To modify ownership, use the `chown` command. This command can change both the `user` and/or the `group` that owns a file or directory. To only change the `group`, use the `chgrp` command. The permissions assigned to user, group, and other together constitute a file or directory's mode.

The `chmod` tool is used to manage permissions from the shell prompt, using any of the following syntaxes to assign permissions to `user`, `group`, and/or `other`:

- `chmod u=rw,g=rw,o=r <file_or_directory>`
- `chmod ug=rw,o=r <file_or_directory>`
- `chmod 664 <file_or_directory>`

By default, Linux automatically assigns new files with `-rw-rw-rw-` permissions and new directories with `drwxrwxrwx` permissions upon creation. However, to increase security, the `umask` variable is used to automatically remove some privileges.

We also briefly discussed the special permissions that can be assigned. Assign these permissions numerically with `chmod` by adding an extra digit before the user digit in the command using the values just shown. For example, `chmod 6755 <command>` will set the SUID and SGID bits for the command. Now the program will run at the privilege of the user (owner) and group permissions of the command, not the end-user permissions.

Finally, additional file security settings can be created with ACLs and file attributes. Use the `setfacl` command to set granular permissions beyond `chmod`. Use the `chattr` command to secure a file by making it immutable. This keeps a file from being accidentally deleted by every user, including `root`!

- Use the `ls -l` command to view ownership (note that this command uses a lowercase *l*, not a number one).
- Use the `chown` utility to configure user and group ownership of a file or directory.
- You must be logged in as `root` to change user ownership.
- You must be logged in as `root` or as the file/directory owner to change group ownership.
- Permissions are used to define what users may or may not do with files or directories in the filesystem.
- Linux uses the read, write, and execute permissions for files and directories.
- Linux permissions are assigned to user (`u`), group (`g`), and other (`o`).
- Permissions can be represented numerically: read = 4, write = 2, and execute = 1.
- These permissions are too insecure for most situations, so the `umask` variable is used to subtract specific permissions from the defaults.
- The default value of `umask` is `022`, which subtracts the write permission (`2`) from group and other.

- Modify the value of `umask` to change the default permissions assigned upon creation.
- Linux also includes three default special permissions: Sticky, SUID, and SGID.
- Assign special permissions with `chmod` by adding an additional digit before the user digit in the command.

Questions

1. You need to change the owner of a file named `/var/opt/runme` from `mireland`, who is a member of the `staff` group, to `dnelson`, who is a member of the `editors` group. Assuming you want to change both user and group owners, which command will do this?
   A. `chown mireland dnelson /var/opt/runme`
   B. `chown -u "dnelson" -g "editors" /var/opt/runme`
   C. `chown dnelson /var/opt/runme`
   D. `chown dnelson:editors /var/opt/runme`
2. Which permission, when applied to a directory in the filesystem, will allow a user to enter the directory?
   A. Read
   B. Write
   C. Execute
   D. Access Control
3. A user needs to open a file, edit it, and then save the changes. What permissions does the user need in order to do this? (Choose two.)
   A. Read
   B. Write
   C. Execute
   D. Modify
4. A file named `employees.odt` has a mode of `-rw-r--r--`. If `mhuffman` is not the file's owner but is a member of the group that owns it, what can he do with it?
   A. He can open the file and view its contents, but he can't save any changes.
   B. He can open the file, make changes, and save the file.
   C. He can change ownership of the file.
   D. He can run the file as an executable program.

5. A file named `myapp` has a mode of `755`. If `dnelson` does not own this file and is not a member of the group that owns the file, what can she do with it?

   A. She can change the group that owns the file.

   B. She can open the file, make changes, and save the file.

   C. She can change ownership of the file.

   D. She can run the file as an executable program.

6. You need to change the permissions of a file named `schedule.odt` so that the file owner can edit the file, users who are members of the group that owns the file can edit it, and users who are not owners and don't belong to the owning group can view it but not modify it. Which command will do this?

   A. `chmod 664 schedule.odt`

   B. `chmod 555 schedule.odt`

   C. `chmod 777 schedule.odt`

   D. `chmod 644 schedule.odt`

7. The Linux system's `umask` variable is currently set to a value of `077`. A user named `jcarr` (who is a member of the `staff` group) creates a file named `mythoughts.odt`. What can users who are members of the `staff` group do with this file?

   A. They can view the file, but they can't modify or save it.

   B. They can open, modify, and save the file.

   C. They can open, modify, and save the file. They can also execute the file if it is an executable.

   D. They have no access to the file at all.

8. An executable file has the SUID permission set, and it is owned by `root`. If this file is run on the system by a `guest` user, which privilege will the program run at?

   A. The user who created the file remains the owner.

   B. The user who ran the file becomes the file's permanent owner.

   C. The program will run at `root` privilege.

   D. The `root` user becomes the file's owner.

9. Which command lists the file ACL?

   A. `setfacl --get`

   B. `getfacl`

   C. `getfacl --list`

   D. `setfacl -g`

10. Which of the following commands is used to make a file immutable?
    A. `chattr +i <filename>`
    B. `chattr -i <filename>`
    C. `chattr --immutable <filename>`
    D. `chattr ++immutable <filename>`

Answers

1. **D.** Entering `chown dnelson:editors /var/opt/runme` will change the user and group owners of the `runme` file to `dnelson` and `editors`.
2. **C.** The execute permission allows a user to enter a directory in the filesystem.
3. **A, B.** The user must have read and write permissions to open and modify a file.
4. **A.** In the mode shown, `Group` is given the read permission only. Because `mhuffman` is a member of the group, he can only open and view file contents. He cannot modify and save the file.
5. **D.** Because `dnelson` isn't the owner and isn't a member of the owning group, she is granted the rights assigned to `Other`, which are read (`4`) and execute (`1`). This allows her to run the file.
6. **A.** Entering `chmod 664 schedule.odt` will grant `User` and `Group` read (`4`) and write (`2`) permissions. It will also grant `Other` read (`4`) permission.
7. **D.** Because `umask` is set to `077`, all permissions (read = `4`, write = `2`, execute = `1`) are removed from `Group` and `Other`. Therefore, members of the owning group have no access to the file, so `mythoughts.odt`'s final permission will be `600`.
8. **C.** The `SUID` permission causes the file's `User` (owner) to temporarily become the command's owner.
9. **B.** To list a file's ACL, use the `getfacl` command.
10. **A.** `chattr +i <filename>` will set the immutable bit on the file, making it unremovable, even by `root`.

CHAPTER 7

Managing Storage

In this chapter, you will learn about

- An overview of storage
- Creating partitions
- Creating filesystems
- Managing Linux filesystems
- Managing quotas

You can't make the leap from fish to mammal, but it's an important first step in the puzzle.

—Ralph Etienne-Cummings, John Hopkins University

This chapter introduces the elements used to construct and manage storage. Storage concepts are the foundations for file, block, and object storage systems. You will also learn how to create encrypted filesystems and quotas for users and groups.

An Overview of Storage

A new disk is a large storage space. Partitions are used to allocate the whole or portions of the drive into logical storage spaces (see Figure 7-1).

The partition type available, MBR or GUID, is dictated by the bootstrap method.

You need to understand a few fundamentals about storage devices so that they can be configured correctly to save data. These fundamentals include an understanding of the following topics:

- The master boot record
- The GUID partition table
- The device naming conventions
- Viewing disk partitions

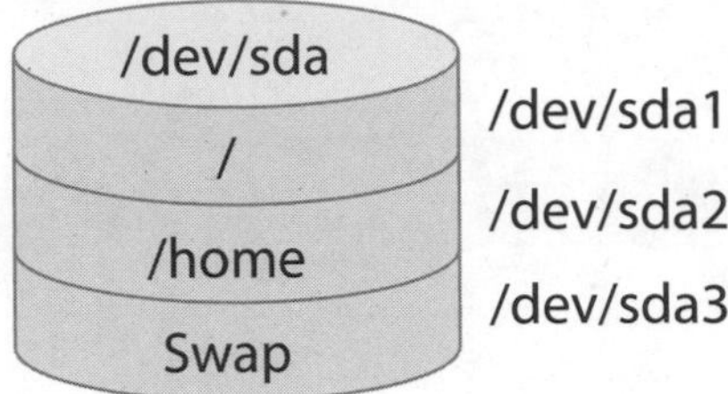

Figure 7-1 Hard disk divided into partitions

The Master Boot Record

The master boot record (MBR) is found on the first sector of a hard drive on systems that use the basic input/output system (BIOS).

NOTE A sector is the smallest storage unit for a hard disk device. Traditionally this size was 512 bytes, but new hard drives using Advanced Format (AF) can increase the sector size to 4,096 bytes. AF-capable hard drives can emulate a 512-byte sector.

The MBR was designed to fit in one 512-byte sector (see Figure 7-2). The first 446 bytes are allocated to boot code and error messages, the next 64 bytes contain the partition table, and the last 2 bytes store the disk signature. The disk signature points to the bootloader's root directory.

The MBR's partition table was designed to contain four 16-bit partition table entries. This limitation precluded BIOS-based systems from supporting more than four primary partitions. The four-partition limitation was overcome by using an *extended partition*. An extended partition is a primary partition that may be divided into logical partitions. The extended partition tracks the logical partitions using an extended master boot record (EMBR). A logical partition is a partition that resides in an extended partition. Logical partition numbering starts at five. A sample partitioning scheme is shown in Figure 7-3.

NOTE BIOS supports 24-bit cylinder, head, sector (CHS) addressing and 32-bit logical block addressing. Thirty-two-bit addressing limits the maximum disk size to 2TB.

Figure 7-2 Master boot record layout

Master boot record

Boot loader (bootstrap) 446 bytes	Partition table 64 bytes	Disk signature 2 bytes

Figure 7-3 BIOS partitioning schema

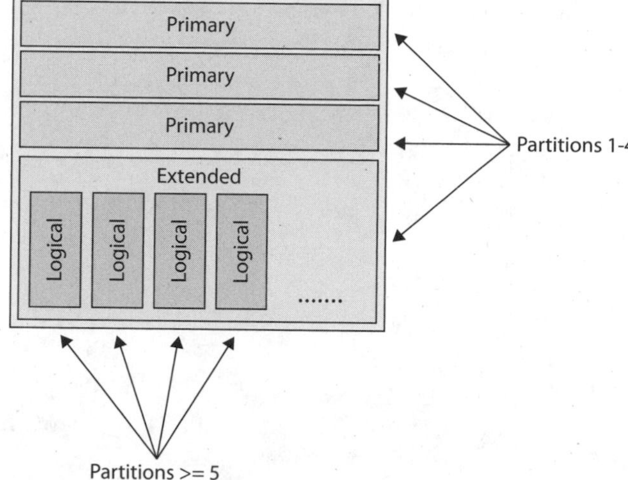

The GUID Partition Table

The GUID Partition Table (GPT) was designed to overcome some of BIOS's limitations and provide more security by adding redundancy. The name GUID Partition Table refers to the assignment of a globally unique identifier (GUID) to each partition. This concept is similar to the function of a universally unique identifier (UUID), which provides a unique identification number for filesystem and system devices.

GPT Partition Table Scheme

GPT is a single partition that extends across an entire disk device. Components of the partition are accessed via a logical block address (LBA). When viewing LBA numbers associated with the GPT partition scheme, you will see positive LBA numbers, which denote block locations offset from the beginning of the drive, and negative LBA numbers, which denote block locations offset from the end of the disk device (see Figure 7-4).

Figure 7-4 GPT logical block address numbering

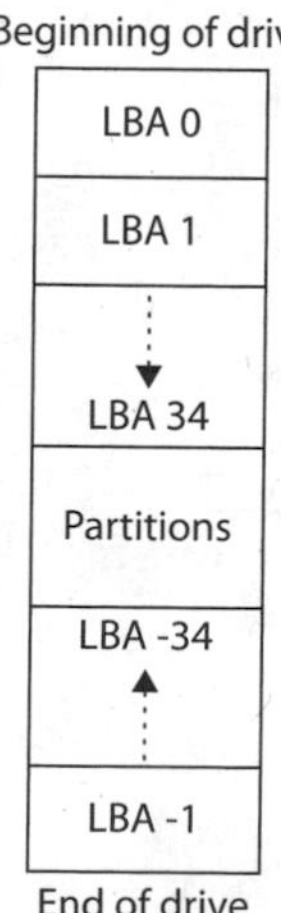

The information stored in the positive number blocks are primary entries, and the information stored in negative number blocks are secondary (backup) entries.

EXAM TIP Detailed features of the GUID Partition Table (GPT) are listed here for reference only. They are not part of the Linux+ exam objectives and will not appear on the exam. Chapter 20 provides more details on GPT partition structures.

GPT Benefits

Some of the benefits of a GPT partition include the following:

- 4KB sectors
- Disk size capabilities from 2.2 terabytes (TB) to approximately 8 zettabytes (ZB) due to support of 64-bit addressing
- Redundancy, because the partition header and table details are stored at the beginning and end of the drive
- Human-readable partition names

The Device Naming Conventions

A device name format is *xxyz*, where

- *xx* is the device type.
- *y* indicates the device's logical unit number.
- *z* indicates the partition number.

Device Type (`xx`)

Some examples of device types include storage devices, such as `sd` (SCSI/SATA devices) and `hd` (IDE hard drives). Other devices include terminals, such as `tty` (text terminals) and `pts` (pseudo-terminals).

Logical Unit Number (`y`)

Next, the device name contains the device's *logical unit number*, a unique identifier for a device within a group of devices. For example, a system may have multiple SCSI devices (device type `sd`). To distinguish one SCSI device from another, each SCSI device is assigned a unique identifier. Logical unit `sda` refers to the first SCSI device. The second SCSI device would be `sdb`. Also,

- `tty1` refers to the first text terminal.
- `pts/0` refers to the first pseudo-terminal.

- `lp0` refers to the first printer.
- `st0` refers to the first SCSI tape drive.
- `sr0` refers to the first optical (CD/DVD) drive.

Partition Number (*z*)

A block device may be split into numbered partitions. The device name for the first partition of the first SCSI device is `sda1`, as previously shown in Figure 7-1.

EXAM TIP `/dev/sda1` is the driver for the first partition of the first hard drive. `/dev/sdb3` is the driver for the third partition of the second hard drive.

Viewing Disk Partitions

There are times when you need to view how a disk device is partitioned. You can do so with the commands `lsblk`, `fdisk -l`, and `parted -l`.

`lsblk` Command

The `lsblk` command, shown in Figure 7-5, displays a list of block devices and their partitions. To see a list of USB devices, their model, and manufacturer information run the `lsusb` command.

`fdisk -l` Command

The command `fdisk -l`, shown in Figure 7-6, displays the partition table of all block devices.

The command `fdisk -l /dev/<device_name>`, shown in Figure 7-7, displays the partition information of the physical block device supplied in the argument `/dev/<device_name>`.

Figure 7-5 `lsblk` output

```
# lsblk
NAME        MAJ:MIN RM  SIZE RO TYPE MOUNTPOINT
sda           8:0    0    4G  0 disk
sdb           8:16   0   18G  0 disk
├─sdb1        8:17   0  500M  0 part /boot
├─sdb2        8:18   0  7.5G  0 part
│ └─USR-usr 253:0    0  7.5G  0 lvm  /usr
├─sdb3        8:19   0    3G  0 part
│ └─VAR-var 253:1    0    3G  0 lvm  /var
├─sdb4        8:20   0    1K  0 part
├─sdb5        8:21   0    1G  0 part /
├─sdb6        8:22   0    1G  0 part /home
├─sdb7        8:23   0    1G  0 part /tmp
└─sdb8        8:24   0    1G  0 part [SWAP]
sdc           8:32   0    4G  0 disk
sr0          11:0    1 1024M  0 rom
```

```
Disk /dev/sda: 4294 MB, 4294967296 bytes, 8388608 sectors
Units = sectors of 1 * 512 = 512 bytes
Sector size (logical/physical): 512 bytes / 512 bytes
I/O size (minimum/optimal): 512 bytes / 512 bytes
Disk label type: dos
Disk identifier: 0x102e2452

   Device Boot      Start         End      Blocks   Id  System

Disk /dev/sdb: 19.3 GB, 19327352832 bytes, 37748736 sectors
Units = sectors of 1 * 512 = 512 bytes
Sector size (logical/physical): 512 bytes / 512 bytes
I/O size (minimum/optimal): 512 bytes / 512 bytes
Disk label type: dos
Disk identifier: 0x000b5f25

   Device Boot      Start         End      Blocks   Id  System
/dev/sdb1   *        2048     1026047      512000   83  Linux
/dev/sdb2         1026048    16664575     7819264   8e  Linux LVM
/dev/sdb3        16664576    22964223     3149824   8e  Linux LVM
/dev/sdb4        22964224    37748735     7392256    5  Extended
/dev/sdb5        22966272    25063423     1048576   83  Linux
/dev/sdb6        25065472    27162623     1048576   83  Linux
/dev/sdb7        27164672    29261823     1048576   83  Linux
/dev/sdb8        29263872    31361023     1048576   82  Linux swap / Solaris


Disk /dev/mapper/USR-usr: 8002 MB, 8002732032 bytes, 15630336 sectors
Units = sectors of 1 * 512 = 512 bytes
Sector size (logical/physical): 512 bytes / 512 bytes
I/O size (minimum/optimal): 512 bytes / 512 bytes


Disk /dev/mapper/VAR-var: 3221 MB, 3221225472 bytes, 6291456 sectors
Units = sectors of 1 * 512 = 512 bytes
Sector size (logical/physical): 512 bytes / 512 bytes
I/O size (minimum/optimal): 512 bytes / 512 bytes
```

Figure 7-6 `fdisk -l` output

```
# fdisk -l /dev/sdb

Disk /dev/sdb: 19.3 GB, 19327352832 bytes, 37748736 sectors
Units = sectors of 1 * 512 = 512 bytes
Sector size (logical/physical): 512 bytes / 512 bytes
I/O size (minimum/optimal): 512 bytes / 512 bytes
Disk label type: dos
Disk identifier: 0x000b5f25

   Device Boot      Start         End      Blocks   Id  System
/dev/sdb1   *        2048     1026047      512000   83  Linux
/dev/sdb2         1026048    16664575     7819264   8e  Linux LVM
/dev/sdb3        16664576    22964223     3149824   8e  Linux LVM
/dev/sdb4        22964224    37748735     7392256    5  Extended
/dev/sdb5        22966272    25063423     1048576   83  Linux
/dev/sdb6        25065472    27162623     1048576   83  Linux
/dev/sdb7        27164672    29261823     1048576   83  Linux
/dev/sdb8        29263872    31361023     1048576   82  Linux swap / Solaris
#
```

Figure 7-7 `fdisk -l /dev/sdb` output

`parted -l` Command

The commands `parted -l <device_name>`, shown in Figure 7-8, and `fdisk -l` will both display disk partition information. The `parted` command will print some detailed logical volume information.

To view an individual device using `parted`, execute the `parted` command (line 1 in Figure 7-9). Once you view the `parted` prompt, use `select` to choose the device to review (line 7). Once you have selected the device, execute the command `print` (line 10) to print the device's partition table. Notice this method does not print meta-device information.

```
# parted -l
Model: VBOX HARDDISK (scsi)
Disk /dev/sda: 4295MB
Sector size (logical/physical): 512B/512B
Partition Table: msdos
Disk Flags:

Number  Start  End  Size  Type  File system  Flags


Model: ATA VBOX HARDDISK (scsi)
Disk /dev/sdb: 19.3GB
Sector size (logical/physical): 512B/512B
Partition Table: msdos
Disk Flags:

Number  Start   End     Size    Type      File system     Flags
 1      1049kB  525MB   524MB   primary   ext4            boot
 2      525MB   8532MB  8007MB  primary                   lvm
 3      8532MB  11.8GB  3225MB  primary                   lvm
 4      11.8GB  19.3GB  7570MB  extended
 5      11.8GB  12.8GB  1074MB  logical   xfs
 6      12.8GB  13.9GB  1074MB  logical   xfs
 7      13.9GB  15.0GB  1074MB  logical   xfs
 8      15.0GB  16.1GB  1074MB  logical   linux-swap(v1)


Model: Linux device-mapper (linear) (dm)
Disk /dev/mapper/VAR-var: 3221MB
Sector size (logical/physical): 512B/512B
Partition Table: loop
Disk Flags:

Number  Start  End     Size    File system  Flags
 1      0.00B  3221MB  3221MB  xfs


Model: Linux device-mapper (linear) (dm)
Disk /dev/mapper/USR-usr: 8003MB
Sector size (logical/physical): 512B/512B
Partition Table: loop
Disk Flags:

Number  Start  End     Size    File system  Flags
 1      0.00B  8003MB  8003MB  xfs
```

Figure 7-8 `parted -l /dev/<device_name>` output

Figure 7-9 `parted select` command output

```
# parted

GNU Parted 3.1
Using /dev/sda
Welcome to GNU Parted! Type 'help' to view a list of commands.

(parted) select /dev/sdb
Using /dev/sdb

(parted) print
Model: ATA VBOX HARDDISK (scsi)
Disk /dev/sdb: 19.3GB
Sector size (logical/physical): 512B/512B
Partition Table: msdos
Disk Flags:

Number  Start   End     Size    Type      File system     Flags
 1      1049kB  525MB   524MB   primary   ext4            boot
 2      525MB   8532MB  8007MB  primary                   lvm
 3      8532MB  11.8GB  3225MB  primary                   lvm
 4      11.8GB  19.3GB  7570MB  extended
 5      11.8GB  12.8GB  1074MB  logical   xfs
 6      12.8GB  13.9GB  1074MB  logical   xfs
 7      13.9GB  15.0GB  1074MB  logical   xfs
 8      15.0GB  16.1GB  1074MB  logical   linux-swap(v1)
```

Creating Partitions

A partition is a section of a physical disk device treated as a logical block device. The commands `fdisk`, `parted`, and `gdisk` are applications used to create partitions on a disk device. `gdisk` is used specifically for devices with a GPT partition.

This section discusses the planning and execution of creating partitions. In this section we discuss

- Partition considerations
- `fdisk` partitioning utility
- `parted` partitioning utility
- `gdisk` partitioning utility
- Block device encryption

Partition Considerations

You must consider several factors when adding a partition, including partition availability, disk space availability, partition size, and swap partition size.

Partition Availability

A SCSI device can have up to 15 partitions, and an IDE device can have 63 partitions. In the example shown in Figure 7-10, I have used eight partitions on a SCSI device, so I can add up to seven more partitions.

```
1 # fdisk /dev/sdb
2 Welcome to fdisk (util-linux 2.23.2).
3
4 Changes will remain in memory only, until you decide to write them.
5 Be careful before using the write command.
6
7
8 Command (m for help): p
9
10 Disk /dev/sdb: 19.3 GB, 19327352832 bytes, 37748736 sectors
11 Units = sectors of 1 * 512 = 512 bytes
12 Sector size (logical/physical): 512 bytes / 512 bytes
13 I/O size (minimum/optimal): 512 bytes / 512 bytes
14 Disk label type: dos
15 Disk identifier: 0x000b5f25
16
17    Device Boot      Start         End      Blocks   Id  System
18 /dev/sdb1   *        2048     1026047      512000   83  Linux
19 /dev/sdb2         1026048    16664575     7819264   8e  Linux LVM
20 /dev/sdb3        16664576    22964223     3149824   8e  Linux LVM
21 /dev/sdb4        22964224    37748735     7392256    5  Extended
22 /dev/sdb5        22966272    25063423     1048576   83  Linux
23 /dev/sdb6        25065472    27162623     1048576   83  Linux
24 /dev/sdb7        27164672    29261823     1048576   83  Linux
25 /dev/sdb8        29263872    31361023     1048576   82  Linux swap / Solaris
26
27 Command (m for help):
```

Figure 7-10 `fdisk -l /dev/sdb` command output

Disk Space Availability

You can determine if space is available to add additional partitions by determining the difference between the total number of sectors on the device (line 10 in Figure 7-10) and the ending sector of the last partition.

Partition Size

Most operating systems and applications have documentation that indicates the amount of disk space they require. Many third-party applications specify requirements based on the type of application, number of users accessing the application, and the projected amount of data. Also consider using logical volume management (LVM), covered in Chapter 8, which enables administrators to dynamically increase the size of a partition and filesystem.

Swap Partition Size

Swap space is virtual memory space created on a swap filesystem. The swap filesystem may be created on a partition or in a file. When active processes require more memory than is available, the operating system uses swap space by moving (swapping) inactive pages of memory to the block device. Swap space should be larger than the amount of memory installed on the system, because when a system crashes, it dumps its memory into swap for later analysis.

`fdisk` Partitioning Utility

The `fdisk` utility is used to modify a partition table of a disk device. Any changes made while working within the application are stored in memory until the changes are written to the disk's partition table.

Field	Description
`Device`	The device path
`Boot`	An asterisk (*) in this column indicates this partition is the boot partition.
`Start`	Partition's start sector.
`End`	Partition's end sector.
`Blocks`	Number of blocks occupied by the partition.
`Id`	Also called a partition code; `83` = Linux, `8e` = Linux LVM, `82` = Linux swap.
`System`	Text description of the `Id` column.

Table 7-1 `fdisk` Partition Columns

The command `fdisk <device_path>` is used to manage partitions for a specific device. For example, the command `fdisk /dev/sda` allows us to modify the partition tables of `/dev/sda`.

EXAM TIP The Linux+ certification exam focuses on `fdisk` because it is the most often used command-line utility to partition hard drives.

Prior to making changes to a device, know its current configuration. For our purposes, we will use the command `fdisk -l /dev/sdb` as shown earlier in Figure 7-7.

Table 7-1 provides a summary of the columns used to describe a partition.

Reviewing the information, we find that this disk device contains four primary partitions. One of the primary partitions is an extended partition that contains three logical partitions.

NOTE When partitioning a disk device, the extended partition should be the last primary partition and should take up the remaining available space on the drive.

With `fdisk` running, we now have a command prompt we can use to enter `fdisk` commands. You can enter `m` to view a help menu of available commands, as shown here:

```
Command (m for help): m
Command action
  a   toggle a bootable flag
  b   edit bsd disklabel
  c   toggle the dos compatibility flag
  d   delete a partition
  g   create a new empty GPT partition table
  G   create an IRIX (SGI) partition table
  l   list known partition types
  m   print this menu
  n   add a new partition
  o   create a new empty DOS partition table
  p   print the partition table
  q   quit without saving changes
  s   create a new empty Sun disklabel
  t   change a partition's system id
```

```
  u   change display/entry units
  v   verify the partition table
  w   write table to disk and exit
  x   extra functionality (experts only)

Command (m for help):
```

Creating a Partition

If you want to create a new partition, enter n and then specify whether you want to create a primary (p), extended (e), or logical (l) partition.

NOTE You can create logical partitions only in an extended partition. If an extended partition does not exist, you will not be offered the choice to create a logical partition.

To create a primary partition, enter p when prompted. To create an extended partition, enter e. You are then prompted to specify a partition number:

```
Command (m for help): n
Partition type:
  p   primary (0 primary, 0 extended, 4 free)
  e   extended
Select (default p): p
Partition number (1-4, default 1): 1
```

Pressing the Enter key will apply the default partition number. The default partition number will be the next available partition. You can specify any number between 1 and 4. However, you cannot use a partition number that has been allocated.

The next entry is the starting sector. Usually you'll want to accept the default. Although you can change the starting sector, you must be mindful of the following: If you choose a sector in an existing partition, you will receive a "value out of range" error. You can also choose a starting sector number greater than the default, but this wastes disk space. Many years ago, data was placed on the most efficient parts of the drive to improve efficiency and speed, thus causing a gap. This practice is no longer necessary.

You can specify the size of the partition by entering the number of sectors, or the size in kilobytes, megabytes, or gigabytes.

After specifying the size, you should verify your new partition by entering p. This displays all partitions for the disk, as shown in the next example:

```
Command (m for help): p

Disk /dev/sdb: 1073 MB, 1073741824 bytes, 2097152 sectors
Units = sectors of 1 * 512 = 512 bytes
Sector size (logical/physical): 512 bytes / 512 bytes
I/O size (minimum/optimal): 512 bytes / 512 bytes
Disk label type: dos
Disk identifier: 0xd489eb71

   Device Boot      Start         End      Blocks   Id  System
/dev/sdb1            2048     2097151     1047552   83  Linux

Command (m for help):
```

You can verify the size by multiplying the number of blocks by the current block size or determine the number of sectors used and multiply by the sector size.

The `ID` column contains a filesystem code. By default, partitions are assigned a partition code of `83`. If you are creating a partition that will contain a different filesystem type, you must change the filesystem code. This is done by entering `t` and then entering the number of the partition you want to change. If you don't know the partition code, enter a lowercase `l` to list all valid partition codes (`ID`) and their descriptions.

For example, the partition code for a Linux swap partition is `82`. To change the type of the partition, you could enter `t`, specify a partition number to change, and then type `82` for the partition code to change the partition to a swap partition.

Deleting a Partition

To delete partitions using `fdisk`, enter `d` at the command prompt and specify the partition number to delete. Any data that resides on the partition will be lost once you commit the change to disk.

Writing Changes to the Partition Table

Once you have finished editing the partition table in memory, you must write the new partition table to disk using the write (`w`) command, like so:

```
Command (m for help): w

The partition table has been altered!
Calling ioctl() to re-read partition table.
Syncing disks.
```

Once the partition table is written, the write command will attempt to update the kernel with the new information, but if any of the disk partitions are mounted, the kernel update will fail with `error:ioctl device busy`.

To force the kernel to read the new partition table into memory, execute the command `partprobe` or `partprobe <device_path>`.

`parted` Partitioning Utility

To use the `parted` command, enter `parted` at the shell prompt and then use the `select` command to specify which disk to manage. Be very careful, though, because `parted` will automatically select the first hard disk, the one with your system and home partitions on it. Accidentally deleting a partition on this disk could be bad because you will lose all your data! If you intend to work on a disk other than `/dev/sda`, be sure you use the `select` subcommand.

CAUTION The `parted` utility writes partition changes immediately to the disk. Be absolutely certain of the changes you want to make when using `parted`!

After selecting the appropriate hard disk, create a new partition using the `mkpart` subcommand at the `parted` prompt. You need to specify the following:

- **The type of partition to be created** For example, to create a standard Linux partition, you would specify a value of `linux`.
- **The starting point on the disk for the partition (in megabytes)** For example, to create a partition that starts at the 1GB point on the disk, you would specify a value of `1024`.
- **The ending point on the disk for the partition (in megabytes)** For example, to create a partition that ends at the 11GB point on the disk, you would specify a value of `11264`.

To view the partitions that have been created on the disk, you can use the `print` subcommand at the `parted` prompt. In the following example, a 10GB partition is created on the second hard disk in the system (`/dev/sdb`):

```
# parted
GNU Parted 2.4
Using /dev/sda
Welcome to GNU Parted! Type 'help' to view a list of commands.
(parted) select /dev/sdb
Using /dev/sdb
(parted) mkpart linux 1024 11264
(parted) print
Model: VMware Virtual disk (scsi)
Disk /dev/sdb: 17.2GB
Sector size (logical/physical): 512B/512B
Partition Table: gpt

Number  Start   End     Size    File system  Name   Flags
1       1024MB  11.3GB  10.2GB               linux

(parted)
```

You can also use the following commands at the `parted` prompt to manage disk partitions:

- To rename a partition, enter `name <partition_name>`.
- To move a partition to a different location on the disk (which is a very handy thing to be able to do), enter `move <partition> <start_point> <end_point>`.
- To resize a partition on the disk (another very handy thing to be able to do), enter `resize <partition> <start_point> <end_point>`.
- To delete a partition from the disk, enter `rm <partition>`.

gdisk Partitioning Utility

To manage GPT partitions, use the gdisk utility. gdisk understands extensible firmware interface (EFI) hard drive structure. The utility can be used to perform the following tasks:

- Convert an MBR partition table to a GPT partition table.
- Verify a hard disk
- Create and delete GPT partitions
- Display information about a partition
- Change the name and type of a partition
- Back up and restore a disk's partition table

For example, to add a GPT partition to a second disk, first switch to the root user and enter gdisk /dev/sdb at the shell prompt. gdisk uses many of the same command options that are available for the fdisk's command. Enter ? to view a list of gdisk subcommands, as shown here:

```
# gdisk /dev/sdb
GPT fdisk (gdisk) version 0.8.7

Partition table scan:
 MBR: not present
 BSD: not present
 APM: not present
 GPT: not present

Creating new GPT entries.

Command (? for help): ?
b       back up GPT data to a file
c       change a partition's name
d       delete a partition
i       show detailed information on a partition
l       list known partition types
n       add a new partition
o       create a new empty GUID partition table (GPT)
p       print the partition table
q       quit without saving changes
r       recovery and transformation options (experts only)
s       sort partitions
t       change a partition's type code
v       verify disk
w       write table to disk and exit
x       extra functionality (experts only)
?       print this menu

Command (? for help):
```

To add a new partition to the disk, enter `n` at the `gdisk` prompt. You are then prompted to specify the following:

- **The partition number** Partition numbers are sequential. `EFI` permits partition numbers from `1` to `128`. You may supply a unique partition number or accept the suggested partition number.
- **The size of the partition** You can either specify the beginning and ending sectors of the partition or specify where on the disk you want the partition to start and end (such as at the 10GB and 20GB points on the disk).
- **The type of partition** The partition type numbers with `gdisk` are different from those used with MBR partitions. For example, to create a Linux partition, use a partition type of `8300`. Press either uppercase `L` or lowercase `l` at the `gdisk` prompt to view a list of all possible partition types and their codes.

This process is shown in the following example:

```
Command (? for help): p
Disk /dev/sdb: 33554432 sectors, 16.0 GiB
Logical sector size: 512 bytes
Disk identifier (GUID): 1D3E9F48-D822-4DDF-AB94-C59B7A4E12C8
Partition table holds up to 128 entries
First usable sector is 34, last usable sector is 33554398
Partitions will be aligned on 2048-sector boundaries
Total free space is 12582845 sectors (6.0 GiB)

Number  Start (sector)    End (sector)  Size       Code  Name
   1            2048        20973567   10.0 GiB    8300  Linux filesystem

Command (? for help): w

Final checks complete. About to write GPT data. THIS WILL OVERWRITE EXISTING
PARTITIONS!!

Do you want to proceed? (Y/N): y
OK; writing new GUID partition table (GPT) to /dev/sdb.
The operation has completed successfully.
```

Once this is done, enter `p` at the `gdisk` prompt to view a list of the partitions on the disk. As with `fdisk`, the changes you make with `gdisk` are not actually committed to disk until you write them. To accept the changes made to the disk partitioning, press `w` at the `gdisk` prompt. To delete a partition, enter `d`. To change a partition's type, enter `t` and then enter the partition type code to use. To quit and start over without saving any changes, enter `q` instead.

Block Device Encryption

Block device encryption protects data confidentiality on the block device, even if the device is removed from the system, by encrypting data as it is written and decrypting data as it is read. To access the device, you must enter a passphrase during system startup to activate the decryption key.

```
[root@localhost ~]# cryptsetup luksFormat /dev/sda9

WARNING!
========
This will overwrite data on /dev/sda9 irrevocably.

Are you sure? (Type uppercase yes): YES
Enter passphrase for /dev/sda9:
Verify passphrase:
```

Figure 7-11 Encrypting a block device

```
1 # cryptsetup luksUUID /dev/sda9
2 bfa7c906-b366-4232-9d11-d71f2d702d02
3
4 # cryptsetup luksOpen /dev/sda9 luks-bfa7c906-b366-4232-9d11-d71f2d702d02
5 Enter passphrase for /dev/sda9:
```

Figure 7-12 Naming the encrypted device

Creating an Encrypted Block Device

Linux Unified Key Setup (LUKS) supports physical volumes, logical volumes, RAID, and, of course, physical block devices.

Use the command dd if=/dev/urandom of=<device_name> to place random data on the block device. Placing random data on a hard drive makes it difficult for an attacker to distinguish between real and random data.

Use the command cryptsetup luksFormat <device> (see Figure 7-11) to format the device as an encrypted device. After you've entered the command, you are asked to verify that you know all data will be destroyed, and you must respond YES to proceed. After you enter the passphrase twice, the device will be formatted.

Each encrypted block device is assigned a UUID, which is used to give the encrypted device a device mapper name that's used to access the contents of the device.

The command cryptsetup luksUUID /dev/<device_name> (line 1 in Figure 7-12) illustrates how to obtain an encrypted block device's UUID and display it. The command crypsetup luksOpen <device> <device_name> (line 4 in Figure 7-12) creates a device mapper name. Notice that luks-<UUID> is used as a device name. This example uses the same UUID as the encrypted block device. This is certain to provide a unique device mapper name. You can use the command ls -l /dev/mapper to verify the device name has been created.

Creating Filesystems

A filesystem manages the storage and retrieval of data. Linux supports multiple filesystems via kernel modules and an abstraction layer called the virtual filesystem (VFS).

In this section you will learn the following about filesystems:

- Available filesystems
- Building a filesystem
- Mounting a filesystem
- Mounting a filesystem automatically at boot
- Unmounting a partition with umount

Available Filesystems

To use a specific filesystem type, the appropriate kernel module must be available. To determine which filesystem modules are available, execute the following command (see Figure 7-13):

```
ls -l /lib/modules/$(uname -r)/kernel/fs
```

To determine which kernel filesystem modules are currently loaded, execute the command `cat /proc/filesystems`. The term `nodev` (no device) in Figure 7-14 indicates the filesystem is not located on a block device but is loaded in memory.

The command `blkid`, shown in Figure 7-15, displays the UUID and filesystem type of a partition.

Figure 7-13 Displaying the available filesystems

```
# ls -l /lib/modules/$(uname -r)/kernel/fs

drwxr-xr-x. 2 root root   25 Jan 25 17:09 btrfs
drwxr-xr-x. 2 root root   24 Jan 25 17:09 ext4
drwxr-xr-x. 2 root root   60 Jan 25 17:09 fat
drwxr-xr-x. 2 root root   42 Jan 25 17:09 fuse
drwxr-xr-x. 2 root root   24 Jan 25 17:09 gfs2
drwxr-xr-x. 2 root root   25 Jan 25 17:09 isofs
drwxr-xr-x. 2 root root   24 Jan 25 17:09 jbd2
drwxr-xr-x. 2 root root   25 Jan 25 17:09 lockd
drwxr-xr-x. 6 root root  137 Jan 25 17:09 nfs
drwxr-xr-x. 2 root root   46 Jan 25 17:09 nfs_common
drwxr-xr-x. 2 root root   24 Jan 25 17:09 nfsd
drwxr-xr-x. 2 root root 4096 Jan 25 17:09 nls
drwxr-xr-x. 2 root root   23 Jan 25 17:09 udf
drwxr-xr-x. 2 root root   23 Jan 25 17:09 xfs
```

Figure 7-14 `cat /proc/filesystems` command output

```
# cat /proc/filesystems
nodev   sysfs
nodev   rootfs
nodev   proc
nodev   tmpfs
nodev   devtmpfs
nodev   debugfs
nodev   selinuxfs
        xfs
        ext3
        ext2
        ext4
```

Figure 7-15 `blkid` command output

```
# blkid /dev/sdb1
/dev/sdb1: UUID="a05ba7d2-1136-42e7-ad26-95daf6087a18" TYPE="ext4"
```

Filesystem Type	Description
ext3	Third extended filesystem. Successor to ext2, ext3 is a journaled filesystem. Journaling improves filesystem reliability and recovery. ext3 supports volumes of 16 terabytes with maximum file sizes of 2 terabytes.
ext4	Fourth extended filesystem. Successor to ext3 and supports larger volumes of up to 1 exabytes and file sizes of up to 16 terabytes.
xfs	High-performance journaling filesystem that uses parallel I/O. It supports a maximum filesystem size of 1 petabyte and a maximum file size of 8 exabytes.
btrfs	Journaled filesystem and lately the default filesystem for SUSE. Often pronounced "butter FS" with builtin capabilities for copy-on-write, snapshots, pooling, and logical volumes.
reiserfs	Had been a popular journaling filesystem for SUSE and other Linux operating systems. Lost popularity for several reasons including that Dr. Reiser was imprisoned.
nfs	Network File System (NFS) is a filesystem protocol that allows a user to access files over a network
smb	Server Message Block (SMB) is used to provide shared access to files, printers, and serial ports.
cifs	Common Internet File System (CIFS) a version of SMB.
ntfs	Microsoft's New Technology File System (NTFS). Features include journaling, file compression, volume shadow copy, encryption, and quotas.
FUSE	Filesystem in Userspace (FUSE), which allows standard users to mount filesystems without root privileges.

Table 7-2 Filesystem Types

Building a Filesystem

Once you create a partition, prepare it for storing data. To do this, create a filesystem on the partition. This is accomplished using one of several commands. In this part of the chapter, we look at mkfs, xfs, btrfs, and mkswap.

Table 7-2 describes a few filesystem types.

Using mkfs to Create a Filesystem

The mkfs utility is used to make an ext2, ext3, or ext4 filesystem on a partition. Specify which filesystem to use with the -t option and the type of filesystem. For example, to create an ext4 filesystem on the first partition of the second hard drive, enter mkfs -t ext4 /dev/sdb1. Here is an example:

```
# mkfs -t ext4 /dev/sdb1
mke2fs 1.42.8 (20-Jun-2013)
Filesystem label=
OS type: Linux
Block size=4096 (log=2)
Fragment size=4096 (log=2)
Stride=0 blocks, Stripe width=0 blocks
524288 inodes, 2096474 blocks
104823 blocks (5.00%) reserved for the super user
```

```
First data block=0
Maximum filesystem blocks=2147483648
64 block groups
32768 blocks per group, 32768 fragments per group
8192 inodes per group
Superblock backups stored on blocks:
    32768, 98304, 163840, 229376, 294912, 819200, 884736, 1605632

Allocating group tables: done
Writing inode tables: done
Creating journal (32768 blocks): done
Writing superblocks and filesystem accounting information: done
```

Here are some items to note in the preceding output:

- **`Block size=4096`** This specifies that the block size is 4KB. This value was determined to be optimal for the small 8GB partition that the filesystem was created on in this example. Smaller partitions will have small block sizes.
- **`524288 inodes, 2096474 blocks`** The filesystem has a maximum of 524,288 inodes and 2,096,474 blocks. This means it can hold a maximum of 524,288 files on the partition. Once 524,288 files are created, no more files can be added, even if there's free disk space available. If you multiply the total number of blocks (2,086,474) by the block size (4,096), you can calculate the total size of the partition (in this case, about 8GB).
- **`Superblock backups stored on blocks: 32768, 98304, 163840, 229376, 294912, 819200, 884736, 1605632`** A superblock lists filesystem metadata and is the roadmap into the entire filesystem. If the superblock is damaged, the filesystem becomes inaccessible. The superblock may be restored from copies found in each block group.

  Filesystems are divided into block groups (originally called cylinder groups). Block groups manage smaller sections of the filesystem. Each block group contains data blocks, a copy of the superblock, block group metadata such as inode tables, and maps to data blocks.

Modify a Filesystem Using `tune2fs`

The command `tune2fs` is used to adjust various filesystem parameters on `ext2, ext3, and ext4` filesystems. Table 7-3 details some options to use.

The command `tune2fs -L` places a label on the filesystem:

```
# tune2fs -L NewVol /dev/sdb1
tune2fs 1.45.6 (20-Mar-2020)
```

Creating an XFS Filesystem

The Extents File System (XFS) was created by Silicon Graphics (SGI) for its IRIX operating system. It's a very fast, flexible filesystem. It has been ported over to run on Linux as well, although in my opinion it doesn't function under Linux as well as it does under IRIX.

Option	Argument	Description
-L	<fs label>	Add or change the filesystem label. A label is a human-readable name for the filesystem.
-j		Add a journal to an ext2 filesystem.
-c	n	Set the number of mounts (n) after which the filesystem will automatically be checked by fsck. This check is made at boot and by default is disabled.
-m	*n*	Set the reserved block percentage. When storage displays 100 percent full, that's true for all users except root, which has 5 percent reserved by default to help clean up full disk drives.
-i		Set the filesystem check (fsck) interval:
	d	Number in days
	w	Number in weeks
	m	Number in months

Table 7-3 tune2fs Command Options

Creating an XFS filesystem is very easy. It is done in the same manner as creating ext*x* filesystems using the mkfs command. First, create a standard Linux partition (type 83) using fdisk. Then, at the shell prompt, enter mkfs.xfs <device> or mkfs -t xfs <device>.

Use the xfs_admin command to change parameters and administer XFS filesystems. Running xfs_admin -L <label> <device> sets the filesystem label.

Creating a BTRFS Filesystem

The B-tree File System (BTRFS) provides copy-on-write (COW) and logical volume features. It's a very fast, flexible filesystem designed to scale to storage that is required and is the current default filesystem on SUSE Linux.

Creating a BTRFS filesystem is straightforward. First, create a standard Linux partition using fdisk, parted, or gdisk. Then, at the shell prompt, enter mkfs.btrfs <device>.

To administer a BTRFS filesystem, use the btrfs command. Running btrfs filesystem show displays information about the btrfs filesystem on the computer.

Managing Swap Space

System memory may be physical RAM (random access memory) or virtual memory. Running applications are stored in RAM. Swap space is virtual memory created on block devices.

When RAM becomes full, some memory must be released to make room to execute additional programs. To do this, memory management software will take pages of data stored in RAM that are not currently being used and swap them to virtual memory.

Creating a Swap Partition To create a swap partition, you must first add a partition of type 82. Executing the mkswap command creates a swap area on a partition.

Column	Description
Total (memory)	Total installed memory
Total (swap)	Total amount of swap memory
Free (memory or swap)	Unused memory or allocated swap memory
Buffer	Used by kernel buffers
Cache	Memory used by page cache
Used (memory)	Used memory = Total – free – buffers – cache
Used (swap)	Swap memory being used
Available (memory)	How much memory is available for a process without swapping

Table 7-4 free Command Output

The syntax for this command is mkswap <device_path>. For example, mkswap /dev/sdb2 produces the following output:

```
# mkswap /dev/sdb2
Setting up swapspace version 1, size = 1959924 KiB
no label, UUID=1f51a8d7-ac55-4572-b68a-7a3f179aac61
```

Even though you have created a swap partition, the swap space is not available to the operating system until enabled. Before enabling the newly created swap space, execute the command free, which displays the total amount of memory and swap space available and used (see Table 7-4).

Next, you can execute the command swapon -s to determine swap partitions currently in use. Execute the command swapon </device_path> to turn on the newly created swap space and then execute the free and swapon -s commands to verify the swap space is working.

The priority of a swap filesystem determines when it will be used. Higher-priority swap filesystems are used first. If the user does not specify a priority when creating the swap filesystem, the kernel will assign a negative priority number.

To set a priority for a swap space, add the option -p <priority_number>. For example, the command mkswap /dev/sdb2 -p 60 would assign a priority of 60 to the swap filesystem on /dev/sdb2.

Swap partitions with the same priority are accessed in a round-robin fashion. To increase the efficiency, consider creating multiple swap partitions with the same priority and using the highest priority number.

To disable an existing swap partition, enter swapoff <device> at the shell prompt (for example, swapoff /dev/sdb2).

Creating a Swap File

If you do not want to create a new swap partition but require additional swap space, you can create a swap file. To do so, use the dd, chmod, mkswap, and swapon commands. Use the dd command to create the file by copying input from the file /dev/zero and writing it to another file.

Table 7-5 dd Command Options

Option	Description
if	Input file
of	Output file
bs	Block size
count	Number of blocks of block size bs to copy

CAUTION One euphemism of the disk-to-disk copy tool dd is *disk destroyer*. Be careful using this command!

For our purposes we will use the dd options displayed in Table 7-5.

The following command creates a 500MB file called swapfile in the directory /root:

```
dd if=/dev/zero of=/root/swapfile bs=1024 count=500000
```

EXAM TIP The dd tool lacks a standard progress bar. To view progress of the dd session, send the kill signal -SIGUSR1 or -10 to the running dd process. The kill and killall commands are discussed in Chapter 9.

Next, change the permissions of the file to 600 so that it's readable and writeable only by root. These permissions do not limit user access to the file as swap space; they just prevent users from modifying swapfile using an editor such as vi.

```
chmod 600 /root/swapfile
```

Place a swap filesystem on the file /root/swapfile by executing the mkswap command:

```
mkswap /root/swapfile
```

To make the new swap space available, execute the following command:

```
swapon /root/swapfile
```

Now you have added swap space in a way that is much simpler than making swap space available on the hard drive you are currently using. Should you no longer need the swapfile, disable it with the swapoff command, and delete the swapfile.

Troubleshooting Journaled Filesystems

One benefit of journaled filesystems like ext4 and xfs is that they have fast bootup recovery times after server interruption. If boot recovery is taking hours and days after an accidental unplug of the server, verify the system is not running an ext2 filesystem by running df -hT to display the filesystem type:

```
# df -hT
Filesystem      Type      Size  Used Avail Use% Mounted on
/dev/sdb1       ext2      6.0G  4.4G  1.3G  78% /Chadbourne
```

This example displays that `/dev/sdb1` is an `ext2` filesystem. This can be converted to the journaled `ext3` type filesystem by running `tune2fs -j /dev/sdb1` as `root`.

Mounting a Filesystem

A mount point is a logical connection between a directory and a filesystem, and the connection is made using the `mount` command. This allows users to access a filesystem on a storage device.

Prior to mounting a partition, create a new directory, which will become the mount point. For example, you might create the directory `/public` and have that directory point to partition `/dev/sdb1`.

The directories `/mnt` and `/media` serve as temporary mount points. The `/mnt` directory holds mount points for temporarily automounted filesystems from a network filesystem, and `/media` would be the mount point for temporarily mounted media such as optical or USB flash drives.

Using the `mount` command requires root access. Run the following command syntax to create a temporary mount point:

```
mount -t <filesystem_type> <device> <mount_point>
```

The following command would create a link from the directory `/public` to the `ext4` filesystem on the first partition on the second hard disk in the system:

```
# mount -t ext4 /dev/sdb1 /public
```

Now, whenever you execute the command `cd /public`, you will access the data stored on `/dev/sdb1`.

`mount` Command Options

The `-o` option with the `mount` command includes a variety of mounting suboptions. For example, use `-o ro` to mount the partition as read-only. See the `mount` man page for a complete listing of all the available options. Table 7-6 describes the `mount` command options.

The `mount` command with no switches displays mounted filesystems. You can look through the output to verify that a device is mounted. The following line from the output of the `mount` command indicates that `/dev/sdb1` is mounted on `/public` and uses the `ext4` filesystem:

```
/dev/sdb1 on /public type ext4 (rw,relatime,data=ordered)
```

The command `cat /proc/mounts` displays a list of mounted filesystems. To view a specific mount point, execute either `cat /proc/mounts | grep < mount_point>` or `mount | grep <mount_point>`.

To remount a filesystem with new options, execute the following command as the `root` user:

```
mount -o remount,<new_mount_options> <mount_point>
```

Then, running the command `mount -o remount,ro /public` will remount the device associated with the `/public` mount point as read-only.

Option	Description
`defaults`	Implements the default options of `rw`, `suid`, `dev`, `exec`, `auto`, `nousers`, and `async`.
`rw`	Mounts a filesystem in read/write mode (default).
`ro`	Mounts a read-only filesystem.
`async`	Enables asynchronous I/O. Changes are cached and then written when the system isn't busy. Generally used for hard drives.
`auto`	Indicates to automatically mount the filesystem at boot when the `mountall` command is executed.
`exec`	Allows executable binaries to execute.
`suid`	Allows suid, which means you can set the setuid bit on commands (details in Chapter 6).
`nousers`	The device may only be mounted and unmounted by `root`.
`dev`	Interprets a block device as a block and character device.

Table 7-6 Mount Options

Mounting Removable Media

All Linux distributions support external storage devices. When a removable device is plugged in and enumerated via `uevent`, an entry is made into `/var/log/messages`.

If a `udev` rule or automatic mount information is available for the device, the device name and filesystem mount point will be automatically applied. If the device needs to be enumerated, you can view device name details by executing the command `dmesg`. To avoid looking through the entire log, you can use the command `dmesg | tail -30` to view the last device enumerated. Other commands such as `lsblk` and `lsusb` may be helpful.

Once you have determined the device name, create a partition and mount the device onto an empty directory (ideally). Mounting devices this way is great until reboot. You will have to mount the devices again. To ensure that they are available at boot time, you will need to update a configuration file, as discussed next.

Mounting Filesystems Automatically at Boot

Devices can be automatically mounted by creating an entry in the filesystem table named `/etc/fstab` or by creating a mount system unit.

Adding a Mount Point in `/etc/fstab`

The file `/etc/fstab` contains the mount parameters for a device.

EXAM TIP Prior to making changes in `/etc/fstab`, make a backup. Errors in `/etc/fstab` can prevent your system from booting, but you can recover a backup version of `/etc/fstab` by booting in rescue mode, as will be discussed in Chapter 9.

Field	Function
1	Specifies the device and partition to be mounted (for example, /dev/sda3).
2	Specifies the directory (mount point) where the partition is to be mounted.
3	Specifies the filesystem type of the partition.
4	Lists the mount options.
5	Specifies whether the filesystem should be backed up using the dump command: 0 means don't dump, whereas 1 means dump.
6	Specifies the order in which fsck should check the filesystem at reboot. The root partition should be set to a value of 1. Other partitions should have a value of 2.

Table 7-7 Fields in the /etc/fstab File

Run the command cat /etc/fstab to view the contents of /etc/fstb, as shown in the following example:

```
# cat /etc/fstab
/dev/sda1       /          ext4        defaults,acl,user_xattr        1 1
/dev/sda2       /home      ext4        defaults,acl,user_xattr       1 2
/dev/sda3       swap                   defaults                       0 0
```

To specify a swap priority, add pri=# after specifying swap as the filesystem, as shown here:

```
/dev/sda3       swap       pri=60      defaults                       0 0
```

Table 7-7 describes the fields in /etc/fstab.

If a device has either the auto or defaults option, that device will be mounted at boot or whenever the command mount -a is executed.

If a device record exists in /etc/fstab, it may be mounted by executing the command mount <device> or mount <mount point> or unmounted by executing the command umount <device> or umount <mount_point>.

Adding a Mount Point as a Mount Unit

You may also automatically mount a device by creating a systemd mount unit (see Figure 7-16). User-defined units are placed in /etc/systemd/system. After making these changes, execute the systemctl daemon-reload command. More on managing system features with systemd and systemctl is provided in Chapter 9.

The filename for the unit must be the same as the mount point. In Figure 7-16, the filename for the mount point LabExercises is LabExercises.mount.service.

Figure 7-16 Mount by systemd unit file

```
[Unit]
Description=Exercises_mount

[Mount]
What=LabExercises
Where=/Exercises
Type=vboxsf
Options=defaults

[Install]
WantedBy=multi-user.target
```

Field	Description
1	Device name Example: /dev/mapper/<name>
2	Device Device path (/dev/sda4), UUID (UUID=<uuid_number>)
3	Absolute path to passphrase file (/etc/keyfile) If a path is not present or is set to none, the user will enter a passphrase at boot

Table 7-8 Fields in the /etc/crypttab File

Mounting an Encrypted Device

In order to automatically mount an encrypted device, an entry for the device must be made in the file /etc/crypttab. If it does not exist, as user root, create the file with 744 permissions.

Each record is divided into three space- or tab-delimited fields, as detailed in Table 7-8.

Once you have made an entry in /etc/crypttab, create an entry in /etc/fstab using the encrypted block device's device name.

Unmounting a Partition with umount

The umount command (notice, not *un*mount) writes whatever device information is in memory to the device and then removes the mount point. You cannot unmount a filesystem if any user is using the filesystem.

The command fuser -vm <mount_point> displays users and processes accessing a filesystem. The command fuser -vm /home displays the user and process accessing the filesystem mounted on the directory /home.

To unmount a partition, simply enter umount followed by the device or the mount directory for the partition. To unmount /dev/sdb1 from the mount point /public, for example, enter umount /dev/sdb1 or umount /public. Here is an example:

```
# umount /dev/sdb1
```

Troubleshooting Mounts

Mounting options can affect how a filesystem responds to users. If after mounting the filesystem a user cannot save their work, it could be that the filesystem was mounted read-only. Verify mounting options by running the mount command, as shown in the following example. If the filesystem was mounted read-only, remount the filesystem as read-write.

```
# mount | grep lee-st
/dev/sdd1 on /lee-st  type ext4   (ro,nosuid,nodev,relatime,attr2)
```

The preceding example shows that the /dev/sdd1 filesystem is mounted onto /lee-st as read-only. To resolve the issue, as root run mount -o remount,rw /dev/sdd1 /lee-st to convert the mount to read-write.

Troubleshooting Corruptions and Mismatches

Running `fsck` will repair most filesystem corruptions. If you see an error message such as `Corrupt group descriptor`, answer `YES` to all of the `fsck` questions. The filesystem will mount afterward in most cases before having to go to backup tapes.

Another reason filesystems may not mount is a mismatch of settings in `/etc/fstab`. If you are mounting an `ext4` type filesystem but have it defined as `ext3` in `/etc/fstab`, it will not mount correctly. In the following example, `/dev/sdd2` was created as an `ext4` filesystem:

```
# grep '/dev/sdd2' /etc/fstab
/dev/sdd2       /renfrew    ext3  defaults    0   0
```

Change the `ext3` setting to `ext4` in `/etc/fstab` to resolve the mismatch issue.

Managing Linux Filesystems

Just as with any other operating system, you need to monitor, maintain, and sometimes troubleshoot your Linux filesystems. In this section, we cover the following topics:

- Using `df` to verify free disk space
- Using du to verify directory usage
- Reporting filesystem status using `dumpe2fs`
- Verifying XFS filesystems using `xfs_admin`
- Checking the filesystem integrity

Using `df` to Verify Free Disk Space

In order to add files to a filesystem, you must have disk space and available inodes. The `df` ("disk free") utility will display available space information for mounted filesystems, as shown here:

```
# df
Filesystem     1K-blocks    Used Available Use% Mounted on
/dev/sda1        6194480 4528228   1328540  78% /
devtmpfs          760928      32    760896   1% /dev
tmpfs             772004      96    771908   1% /dev/shm
tmpfs             772004    3832    768172   1% /run
tmpfs             772004       0    772004   0% /sys/fs/cgroup
tmpfs             772004    3832    768172   1% /var/lock
tmpfs             772004    3832    768172   1% /var/run
/dev/sda2        7985600   21380   7535524   1% /home
/dev/sdb1        5029504   10232   4740744   1% /mnt/extraspace
```

The command `df <filename>` displays information about the partition on which the specified file resides, as in this example:

```
# df /mnt/extraspace/myfile.txt
Filesystem     1K-blocks  Used Available Use% Mounted on
/dev/sdb1        5029504 10232   4740744   1% /mnt/extraspace
```

The default output displays size in blocks. The -h option displays space statistics in human-readable format:

```
# df -h
Filesystem        Size  Used Avail Use% Mounted on
/dev/sda1         6.0G  4.4G  1.3G  78% /
devtmpfs          744M   32K  744M   1% /dev
tmpfs             754M   96K  754M   1% /dev/shm
tmpfs             754M  3.8M  751M   1% /run
tmpfs             754M     0  754M   0% /sys/fs/cgroup
tmpfs             754M  3.8M  751M   1% /var/lock
tmpfs             754M  3.8M  751M   1% /var/run
/dev/sda2         7.7G   21M  7.2G   1% /home
/dev/sdb1         4.8G   10M  4.6G   1% /mnt/extraspace
```

Adding the -T option will display the filesystem type, as shown here:

```
# df -hT
Filesystem     Type      Size  Used Avail Use% Mounted on
/dev/sda1      ext4      6.0G  4.4G  1.3G  78% /
devtmpfs       devtmpfs  744M   32K  744M   1% /dev
tmpfs          tmpfs     754M   96K  754M   1% /dev/shm
tmpfs          tmpfs     754M  3.9M  751M   1% /run
tmpfs          tmpfs     754M     0  754M   0% /sys/fs/cgroup
tmpfs          tmpfs     754M  3.9M  751M   1% /var/lock
tmpfs          tmpfs     754M  3.9M  751M   1% /var/run
/dev/sda2      ext4      7.7G   43M  7.2G   1% /home
/dev/sdb1      ext4      4.8G   10M  4.6G   1% /mnt/extraspace
```

When a file is created, it is assigned an inode number. If a filesystem runs out of inodes, files can no longer be created, even if space exists. The df -i command lists inode usage of mounted filesystems:

```
# df -i
Filesystem     Inodes  IUsed  IFree IUse% Mounted on
/dev/sda1      402400 168063 234337   42% /
devtmpfs       190232    376 189856    1% /dev
tmpfs          193001      9 192992    1% /dev/shm
tmpfs          193001    503 192498    1% /run
tmpfs          193001     13 192988    1% /sys/fs/cgroup
tmpfs          193001    503 192498    1% /var/lock
tmpfs          193001    503 192498    1% /var/run
/dev/sda2      516096    516 515580    1% /home
/dev/sdb1      327680     12 327668    1% /mnt/extraspace
```

Using du to Verify Directory Usage

Another utility you can use to monitor disk space usage is the du ("directory usage") utility. Its function is to provide you with a summary of disk space usage of each file, recursively, for a specified directory. The syntax is du <filename or directory>. Some useful options with du include the following:

- **-c** Used to calculate a grand total
- **-s** Used to calculate a summary for each argument
- **-h** Used to display output in human-readable format

The -h option is the most useful. Here is an example of viewing the space used by files in the /tmp directory in human-readable format:

```
# du -h /tmp
4.0K    /tmp/.esd-485
4.0K    /tmp/.X11-unix
4.0K    /tmp/.XIM-unix
4.0K    /tmp/.Test-unix
4.0K    /tmp/.esd-1000
4.0K    /tmp/.font-unix
4.0K    /tmp/systemd-private-otNWQw/tmp
8.0K    /tmp/systemd-private-otNWQw
4.0K    /tmp/VMwareDnD
4.0K    /tmp/.ICE-unix
4.0K    /tmp/vmware-root
4.0K    /tmp/systemd-private-OSAy3Q/tmp
8.0K    /tmp/systemd-private-OSAy3Q
4.0K    /tmp/orbit-student
64K     /tmp
```

Troubleshooting Low Disk Space Issues

When running low on disk space, use the df and du commands together to find files that can be deleted. Running df shows how much free disk space you have. Next, run du -sh * on all the directories to see a summary of which directories are using the most space. In the following example, /home/ted would be a great place to look to recover disk space.

```
# du -sh /home/*
96M     /home/aria
16K     /home/lisa
170M    /home/ted
37M     /home/theo
12K     /home/thom
```

An ideal area to recover disk space is under /var/log. Log files can grow and grow. If not properly rotated, they can eventually fill the hard drive and cause system failure. Make sure to enable log rotation using the logrotate command to mitigate this issue.

Reporting Filesystem Status Using dumpe2fs

A filesystem uses a superblock and cylinder groups to manage the filesystem's metadata. The output of the dumpe2fs command shows the statistics stored in both the superblock and block groups. The -h option, dumpe2fs -h <device_path>, limits the output to the information stored in the filesystem's superblock.

Verifying XFS Filesystems Using xfs_admin

XFS has several administrative tools, including the df command.

xfs_admin modifies various parameters (detailed in Table 7-9) of an unmounted XFS filesystem.

Table 7-9 Sample of `xfs_admin` Options

Option	Argument	Description
-L	<label>	Assigns a label to the filesystem
-l		Prints the filesystem label
-U	<generate> <nil>	Generates a new UUID for the filesystem Sets a null UUID
-u		Displays the filesystem's UUID

```
# xfs_info /dev/sdb5
meta-data=/dev/sdb5              isize=512    agcount=4, agsize=65536 blks
         =                       sectsz=512   attr=2, projid32bit=1
         =                       crc=1        finobt=0 spinodes=0
data     =                       bsize=4096   blocks=262144, imaxpct=25'
         =                       sunit=0      swidth=0 blks
naming   =version 2              bsize=4096   ascii-ci=0 ftype=1
log      =internal               bsize=4096   blocks=2560, version=2
         =                       sectsz=512   sunit=0 blks, lazy-count=1
realtime =none                   extsz=4096   blocks=0, rtextents=0
```

Figure 7-17 `xfs_info` command output

The command `xfs_info`, shown in Figure 7-17, displays filesystem geometry, such as the inode size (`isize`) and block size (`bsize`).

Checking the Filesystem Integrity

The Filesystem Check utility, `fsck`, checks the integrity of a filesystem. To use this utility, you must first `umount` the filesystem to check. Then enter `fsck <device>` at the shell prompt. For example, to check the filesystem on the first partition of the second hard drive in your system, you would enter `fsck /dev/sdb1`. The `fsck` utility then checks the filesystem and displays a report, as shown here:

```
# umount /dev/sdb1
# fsck /dev/sdb1fsck from util-linux 2.23.2
e2fsck 1.42.8(20-Jun-2013)/dev/sdb1:clean,12/402192 files,61153/1605632 blocks
```

Notice in this example that `e2fsck` was run. That's because `fsck` is a front end to several error-checking utilities. `fsck` chooses the correct utility based on the type of filesystem. If the utility encounters errors, it displays a code that represents the sum of the errors encountered.

After the check is complete, remount the partition using the `mount` command.

Troubleshooting Input/Output and Device Issues

Poor performance can be improved on storage devices such as NVMe, SSD, SCSI, and SATA devices by adjusting I/O scheduling values. You can configure settings in `/sys/block/sda/queue/scheduler` to improve performance on storage devices, as shown here:

```
# cat /sys/block/sda/queue/scheduler
[mq-deadline] kyber bfq none
```

The none value implements a first-in, first-out (FIFO) scheduling algorithm and is good for enterprise applications. The mq-deadline scheduler sorts I/O requests in batches and is best for virtualized guests. The bfq scheduler uses a fair-queuing mechanism and is best for desktop systems. The kyber scheduler tunes itself for best latency results and is best for fast devices such as NVMe and SSD devices.

To change the setting to bfq, for example, run the following:

```
# echo kyber > /sys/block/sda/queue/scheduler
# cat /sys/block/sda/queue/scheduler
mq-deadline [kyber] bfq none
```

Analyze performance and compare scheduler settings by running ioping and iostat. While running your most important applications, analyze iostat output, as follows:

```
# iostat 3 4
avg-cpu:  %user  %nice  %system  %iowait  %steal  %idle
           0.07   0.00    0.18     0.01     0.00   99.7
Device             tps   kB_read/s  kB_wrtn/s  kB_read  kB_wrtn
                   0.99    18.87       6.93    1698456  652389
# ioping /dev/sda
4 KiB <<< /dev/sda (block device 2.00 TiB): request=1 time=100.7 us
4 KiB <<< /dev/sda (block device 2.00 TiB): request=2 time=108.2 us
--- /dev/sda (block device 2.00 TiB) ioping statistics ---
2 requests completed in 233.2 us, 8 KiB read, 8.57 k iops, 33.5 MiB/s
generated 2 requests in 2.36 s, 12 KiB, 1 iops, 5.08 KiB/s
min/avg/max/mdev = 108.2 us / 116.6 us / 125.1 us / 8.44 us
```

Improve latency, I/O waits, low throughput, and low IOPS by changing from bfq to kyber, mq-deadline, and none. Compare results and select the scheduler that provides the best overall performance for your applications.

Managing Quotas

Quotas are a method of limiting the number of files or the amount of disk space a user or group may use. Quotas are applied to filesystems. In this section you will learn the steps for setting up quotas, which include the following:

- Editing /etc/fstab to set up quotas
- Creating quota database files
- Assigning a quota to users and groups

For our discussion we will create quotas on the /home filesystem.

Editing /etc/fstab to Set Up Quotas

You must enable quotas by filesystem. To do this, add the filesystem option usrquota to monitor user quotas and/or grpquota to manage group quotas. The entry will look like this within /etc/fstab:

```
/dev/sda2     /home    ext4     defaults,usrquota,grpquota    1 2
```

Once you make the changes, you must remount the filesystem. You can do this by executing the command `mount -o remount <filesystem_name>`. If the filesystem is busy, you can use the command `mount -f -o remount < filesystem_name>`. In our example the command would be `mount -f -o remount /home`. *Be aware you may be kicking someone out of a file.*

Another method of working with a busy filesystem is to execute a command that lists open files, like `lsof | grep <filesystem_name>`, to determine the process IDs and users who are using the filesystem. In our example the command would be `lsof | grep home`. At that point you can contact the users and ask them to close their files and then remount the filesystem.

Creating Quota Database Files

Once the filesystem is repaired, you must create the quota database files in the top directory of the filesystem.

For users we will use the `quotacheck` command to create the user database file `aquota.user` and/or the group database file `aquota.group`. The `quotacheck` command uses the options listed in Table 7-10.

The command `quotacheck -cug /<filesystem_name>` will create the user and group database files in the top directory of a filesystem. To create the files in `/home`, you would execute the command `quotacheck -cug /home`.

Assigning a Quota to Users and Groups

Assigning a quota uses three elements: hard limit, soft limit, and grace period. The number of files is specified in the number of inodes (an inode is created for each file), and the size is specified in blocks, as shown here using the `edquota` command:

```
# edquota -g robot_group
Disk quotas for group robot_group (gid 1010):
  Filesystem    blocks     soft     hard     inodes     soft     hard
  /dev/sdb1          0     1000     2000          0        5       10
```

The *hard limit* specifies an exact limit. For our example we will assign a hard file limit of ten files and a hard limit size of 20MB. The *soft limit* specifies a limit that may be exceeded for the number of days specified by the grace period. The *grace period* is the number of days after the soft limit is reached that the user or group has to go below the soft limit. After the grace period, the soft limit becomes the new hard limit, requiring the user or group to remove some files before new ones can be created.

Table 7-10 `quotacheck` Command Options

Option	Description
`-c`	Create
`-u`	User
`-g`	Group

Setting a Quota for a User or Group

The command `edquota -u <user_name>` is used to set a quota for a user, and the command `edquota -g <group_name>` is used to specify a quota for a group. Or, you can create a quota for a user by using an existing user as a prototype. For example, to copy and paste the quota settings for `user1` to `user2`, execute the command `edquota -p user1 user2`.

To change the grace period, execute the command `edquota -t`. You can specify the time in days, hours, minutes, or seconds.

Reporting on Quotas

There are two commands to gather quota reports:

- **`repquota`** Produces quota reports for a filesystem
- **`repquota -a`** Prints a quota report for all users and groups on all filesystems

Use the option `-u` (users) or `-g` (groups) to isolate the report to users or groups, respectively. The command `repquota <filesystem_name>` reports on both user and group quotas for a filesystem.

The `quota` command displays quota information for a specific user or group. Users can only display their own quota information by executing the command `quota`. The user `root`, however, can display any user's quota information.

Troubleshooting Quotas

Users may find that they cannot create any more files. This could mean they ran out of disk space or inodes. They can check this by running the `df -h` command or `df -i` command, respectively. But, after learning disk space and inodes are not the problem, they should run the `quota` command to list their quota limits:

```
# quota
User quotas for user ianmausi (uid 1210):
  Filesystem    blocks    soft    hard    inodes    soft    hard
  /home           1500    1000    2000        10       5      10
```

In this example, user `ianmausi` has exceeded the soft limit on blocks. With just this information the user can create more files; but the inodes have reached the hard limit, and this is the reason why the user cannot create more files.

Exercise 7-1: Managing Linux Partitions

In this exercise, you practice working with Linux partitions.

VIDEO Please watch the Exercise 7-1 video for a demonstration on how to perform this task.

You can perform this exercise using the virtual machine that comes with this book. You must be logged on as user **`root`** (password **`password`**). Follow these steps:

CAUTION Be sure to create a snapshot before proceeding.

1. View the partition table of /dev/sda using the **fdisk -l /dev/sda** command.
2. View the partition table of /dev/sda using parted:
   a. Execute the **parted** command.
   b. Type **select /dev/sda**.
   c. Type **print**.
   d. Type **quit** to exit parted.
3. Create a Linux swap partition on /dev/sda:
   a. Type **fdisk /dev/sda**.
   b. Enter **n** to create a new partition.
   c. Accept the default partition type.
   d. Accept the starting sector.
   e. Specify the size as **500MB**.
   f. Use the **t** command to change the partition code:
      i. Enter the partition number to change.
      ii. Enter **82** for the partition code.
   g. Use the **p** command to verify the partition is created and has the correct partition code.
   h. Use the **w** command to write the changes to the partition table.
   i. Notice the kernel was not updated. *Do not run* partprobe.
4. Create a swap partition by executing the **mkswap <device_name>** command. The device name should be /dev/sda8.
   a. Notice the error message.
   b. Execute the **partprobe** command.
   c. Execute the **mkswap <device_name>** command.
5. Type the command **swapon -s** to determine existing swap spaces.
6. Type the command **free** to determine the total amount of swap space and how much swap space is free.
7. Execute the command **swapon /dev/sda8** and then use the **swapon -s** command to test that the swap space has been enabled.
8. Execute the command **free** to see the difference in swap space.
9. Disable /dev/sda8 swap space by executing the command **swapoff /dev/sda8** (verify the results of this command).

10. Using the steps in step 3, create the following partitions (size 500MB) in the order specified:
    a. Create one Linux partition (partition code **83**; device name should be **/dev/sda9**).
    b. Create two LVM physical volumes (partition code **8e**; device names should be **/dev/sda10** and **/dev/sda11**).
    c. Create two software RAID partitions (partition code **fd**; device names should be **/dev/sda12** and **/dev/sda13**).
    d. Write the partition table.
11. Create an ext4 filesystem on /dev/sda9 by running **mkfs.ext4 /dev/sda9**.
12. Use the command **dumpe2fs -h /dev/sda9** to display the filesystem superblock.
13. Create the directory /public by running **mkdir /public**.
14. Mount the filesystem on /dev/sda9 to the directory /public by executing the **mount -t ext4 /public** command.
15. Use the command **mount** or **mount | grep public** to ensure the filesystem is mounted.
16. Change the directory to /public and execute the **touch file{1,2,3}** command.
17. Verify the files have been created by executing the **ls -l /public** command.
18. Make your current working directory /public by running **cd /public**.
19. Unmount the filesystem by typing the **umount /public** command.
20. Determine which user or process is accessing the filesystem attached to /public by executing the **fuser -vm /public** command.
21. Execute the **cd** command and verify with the **pwd** command you are no longer in /public.
22. Unmount /public and verify it is no longer mounted by running **umount /public**.
23. Execute the **fsck /dev/sda9** command.
24. Use the command **tune2fs -L public /dev/sda9** to add the label public to the filesystem on /dev/sda9.
25. Execute the **blkid /dev/sda9** command.
26. Execute the **findfs LABEL-public** command.
27. Mount the filesystem on /dev/sda9 by executing the **mount -L public /public** command.
28. Test that the filesystem has been mounted by running **ls /public**.
29. Unmount /dev/sda9.

30. Create a copy of `/etc/fstab` by executing the **`cp /etc/fstab /etc/fstab.lab`** command.
31. Execute the command **`vi /etc/fstab`** and go to the last line by using the key sequence **`Esc-G`**. Enter **`o`** to insert text into a newline:
    a. Enter several hash marks (**####**) and press **`Enter`**. The hash marks are a visual reminder of where you have entered new configuration information. Enter the following line:
    `/dev/sda9 /public defaults 0 0`
    b. Save the file by using the **`Esc :wq`** sequence.
    c. Type the **`mount -a`** command.
    d. Test to see that the filesystem in `/dev/sda9` has been mounted.
32. Unmount `/dev/sda9` and enter **`vi /etc/fstab`**.
    a. Place your cursor on the line configuring `/dev/sda9`.
    b. Use the key sequence **`Esc i`** to place `vi` in insert mode.
    c. Place a hash mark (**#**) at the beginning of the line so the line will be ignored.
    d. Use the key sequence **`Esc o`** to open a line below.
    e. Type **`LABEL=public /public defaults 0 0`**.
    f. Exit `vi` by executing the **`Esc :wq`** command.
    g. Use the **`mount -a`** command to remount `/dev/sda9` using its label.

Chapter Review

In this chapter we discussed what a partition is and the differences between MBR and GPT partitioning. From there, we talked about the different partition types and how to manage partitions. After creating the filesystem, you learned how to create a logical relationship between a directory and a filesystem placed on a partition as well as how to manually and automatically mount filesystems.

Here are some key takeaways from this chapter:

- You must partition and format a disk before you can mount it in the Linux filesystem.
- The `fdisk` utility is used to create an MBR partition on hard disks.
- You must set the partition type when partitioning disks.
- Partition changes are only saved in memory until you commit them to disk.
- Newer Linux distributions support GPT partitions, which are designed to address many of the shortcomings of the older MBR-type partitions.
- To manage GPT partitions, use the `gdisk` utility or the `parted` utility.
- After partitioning a disk, you need to format it with `mkfs`.

- After formatting a disk, you can mount it using the `mount` command.
- You can also use `cat /proc/mounts` to view mounted filesystems.
- You can unmount a mounted filesystem using the `umount` command.
- All filesystems must be unmounted before Linux is shut down.
- Mounted filesystems won't be remounted on reboot unless they have an entry in the `/etc/fstab` file.
- The `/etc/fstab` file specifies mount points and other options for specific devices.
- You can monitor disk space and inode usage using the `df` and `du` utilities.
- The `fsck` utility is used to check and repair filesystems.
- The `tune2fs` utility is used to adjust various filesystem parameters on `ext2`, `ext3`, and `ext4` filesystems.
- The `dumpe2fs` utility can display superblock and block group information for `ext` filesystems.
- The `xfs_admin` utility is the XFS equivalent of `tune2fs`.
- The `xfs_info` utility displays useful information about XFS filesystems.
- Removable devices must be mounted in the Linux filesystem before they can be accessed.
- `/etc/fstab` is used to automatically mount devices when the `mountall` or `mount -a` command is executed.

Questions

1. You need to use `fdisk` to create an MBR partition for the fourth SATA hard drive in your system. Which is the correct command to do this?

   A. `fdisk /dev/hdd`

   B. `fdisk /dev/sdd`

   C. `fdisk /dev/sda4`

   D. `fdisk /dev/sdb2`

2. You've used `fdisk` to create a new MBR partition on the second hard drive in your Linux system. You want to use the partition as a second swap partition for your system. Which partition type do you need to change it to?

   A. `83`

   B. `82`

   C. `85`

   D. `1`

3. You need to format the first partition on the fourth SATA hard disk using the `ext3` filesystem. Which is the correct command to do this?

   A. `mkext3fs /dev/sdd1`

   B. `mkfs -t ext3 /dev/sdd1`

   C. `mkfs -t ext3 /dev/sda4`

   D. `mkreiserfs -t ext3 /dev/sdd1`

4. You've created a new swap partition (`/dev/sdb1`) using the `fdisk` utility. You need to format and enable this partition. Which commands should you use to do this? (Choose two.)

   A. `mkswap /dev/sdb1`

   B. `mkfs -t swap /dev/sdb1`

   C. `swapon /dev/sdb1`

   D. `swapon -a`

   E. `mkfs -t vfat /dev/sdb1`

5. You've created an `ext4` filesystem on the first partition on the second SCSI hard disk in your system and now need to mount it in `/mnt/extraspace` in read-write mode. Which commands will do this? (Choose two.)

   A. `mount -t ext4 /dev/sda1 /mnt/extraspace/`

   B. `mount -t ext4 /dev/sdb1 /mnt/extraspace/`

   C. `mount -a /dev/sdb1 /mnt/extraspace/`

   D. `mount -t ext /dev/sdb1 /mnt/extraspace/`

   E. `mount -t ext4 -o ro /dev/sdb1 /mnt/extraspace/`

6. You have an ISO image file named `discimage.iso` in your home directory and you want to mount it in the `/mnt` directory in your Linux filesystem so that you can extract several files from it. Which command will do this?

   A. `mount ~/discimage.iso /mnt`

   B. `mount -a ~/discimage.iso /mnt`

   C. `mount -t iso9660 ~/discimage.iso /mnt`

   D. `mount -o loop ~/discimage.iso /mnt`

7. You have mounted the `/dev/sdb1` partition in the `/mnt` directory and now need to unmount it. Which commands will do this? (Choose two.)

   A. `umount /mnt`

   B. `unmount /mnt`

   C. `umount /dev/sdb1`

   D. `mount --unmount /dev/sdb1`

   E. `unmount /dev/sdb1`

8. Which file is used to automatically mount filesystems when the system initially boots?
    A. `/etc/mtab`
    B. `/proc/mounts`
    C. `/etc/inittab`
    D. `/etc/fstab`
9. Which `fstab` mount option causes pending disk writes to be committed immediately?
    A. `async`
    B. `sync`
    C. `rw`
    D. `auto`
10. Which command will provide you with a summary of inode consumption on your `/dev/sda2` partition?
    A. `df -i`
    B. `df -h`
    C. `df -hT`
    D. `du -inode`
11. The `/dev/sda1` partition on your Linux system currently has no volume label. Given that it is an `ext4` partition, which command will set the label to `DATA`?
    A. `dumpe2fs -L DATA /dev/sda1`
    B. `tune2fs -L DATA /dev/sda1`
    C. `lsof /dev/sda1 --label "DATA"`
    D. `mkfs -t ext4 -L "DATA" /dev/sda1`
12. You are concerned about the condition of a hard drive containing a heavily used `ext3` disk partition (`/dev/sda2`). To ensure data integrity, you want to increase the frequency of automatic `fsck` checks. Which utility should you use to configure this?
    A. `dumpe2fs`
    B. `e2fsck`
    C. `fsck`
    D. `tune2fs`
13. You need to mount an optical disc in `/media/dvd`. Which command will do this?
    A. `mount -t iso9660 /dev/cdrom /media/dvd`
    B. `mount -t dvd /dev/cdrom /media/dvd`
    C. `dvdmount -t iso9660 /dev/cdrom /media/dvd`
    D. `mount -t iso9660 /dev/cdrom ~/dvd`

14. You need to mount a USB flash drive on your Linux system. Given that your Linux system currently has one SATA hard drive (/dev/sda), what should be the flash drive's device name?

    A. /dev/hdb

    B. /dev/usb0

    C. /dev/sdb

    D. /dev/sda

15. A performance-tuning engineer runs the following command:
    ```
    # cat /sys/block/sda/queue/scheduler
    mq-deadline [kyber] bfq none
    ```
    What command should the engineer run to change the scheduler setting to bfq?

    A. sed s/kyber/bfq/ /sys/block/sda/queue/scheduler

    B. echo bfq < /sys/block/sda/queue/scheduler

    C. cat bfq > /sys/block/sda/queue/scheduler

    D. echo bfq > /sys/block/sda/queue/scheduler

Answers

1. **B.** The fdisk /dev/sdd command uses the correct syntax to create an MBR partition for the fourth SATA hard drive in your system. Answer C is incorrect because /dev/sda4 represents the fourth partition of the first hard drive.
2. **B.** Type 82 defines a Linux swap partition. Type 83 represents a Linux partition.
3. **B.** The mkfs -t ext3 /dev/sdd1 command uses the correct syntax to format the first partition on the fourth SATA drive using the ext3 filesystem.
4. **A, C.** The mkswap /dev/sdb1 command is used to create the swap filesystem, and the swapon /dev/sdb1 command enables it as a swap partition.
5. **B, C.** Either the mount -t ext4 /dev/sdb1 /mnt/extraspace/ command or the mount -a /dev/sdb1 /mnt/extraspace/ command will mount the /dev/sdb1 partition in /mnt/extraspace/.
6. **D.** The mount -o loop ~/discimage.iso /mnt command mounts the image file in the /mnt directory.
7. **A, C.** Either the umount /mnt command or the umount /dev/sdb1 command will unmount the partition from the filesystem.
8. **D.** The /etc/fstab file is used to automatically mount filesystems at boot.
9. **B.** The sync option causes pending disk writes to be written immediately.
10. **A.** The df -i command displays a summary of inode consumption for all mounted filesystems.

11. **B.** The `tune2fs -L DATA /dev/sda1` command will set the volume label to DATA.
12. **D.** The `tune2fs` command with the `-c` option can be used to customize the frequency of automatic `fsck` checks.
13. **A.** The `mount -t iso9660 /dev/cdrom /media/dvd` command uses the correct syntax on most distributions, assuming a symbolic link named `/dev/cdrom` has been created that points to `/dev/sr0`.
14. **C.** The device will be referenced by `/dev/sdb` because there is one other drive in the system.
15. **D.** Running `echo bfq > /sys/block/sda/queue/scheduler` will properly set the CPU scheduler to `bfq` from `kyber`.

CHAPTER 8

Configuring Volume Management

In this chapter, you will learn about

- Implementing logical volume management (LVM)
- Creating archives and performing compression
- Enabling redundant array of independent disks (RAID)

The digital footprint per person is expected to grow to over 15 terabytes.

—Curtis Tearte, IBM

As filesystems grow and become larger, systems must be designed to make disk volumes manageable. Logical volumes allow administrators to create disk space without downtime, and RAID speeds data throughput and nullifies downtime by cutting the impact of disk failures. But it is still important to protect data by making backups.

Data compression improves data speeds through networks and reduces disk space use, thus cutting costs for organizations. And encrypted backups make your data more secure.

In this chapter you will learn how to create, extend, and make instant backups called *snapshots* in logical volumes. Next, you will discover how to make backups more efficient and secure using compression and encryption. Finally, you will configure software RAID solutions for Linux to build resiliency into your organization.

Implementing Logical Volume Management

Logical volume management (LVM) is an option to use when partitioning Linux hard disk drives. It provides an alternative to the traditional process of creating disk partitions. Instead, volume groups are created from storage devices in the system. From the volume group, space is allocated to specific logical volumes that are managed by the LVM. Instead of mounting partitions, administrators mount logical volumes at mount points in the filesystem. This provides administrators with a great deal of flexibility when allocating space on the system. For example, when a volume at `/home` begins to run out of space, it is easy to reallocate space from a spare volume group and "grow" it onto `/home`. That is very difficult to do with traditional disk partitions!

LVM allows adding space with no downtime. For example, to add capacity, simply install a new hard drive and then allocate its space to `/home`. The size of the volume is increased on a live system without backing up and restoring data as would be done with traditional partitions.

In this part of this chapter, we're going to look at the following LVM topics:

- LVM components
- LVM configuration
- LVM snapshots
- Extending LVMs

LVM Components

LVM creates a virtual pool of memory space, called a *volume group*, from which logical volumes can be created. Linux uses logical volumes just like standard disk partitions created with `fdisk`. However, the way logical volumes are defined is quite a bit more complex. The basic structure of LVM consists of the following components:

- **Physical volumes** A physical volume can be either a partition or an entire hard disk.
- **Volume groups** A volume group consists of one or more physical volumes grouped together to form data pools. This means additional hard disks or partitions can be added to the volume group whenever more storage space is needed.
- **Logical volumes** A logical volume is defined from the volume group pool. Logical volumes can be formatted with a Linux filesystem and mounted just like physical partitions.

The way these components work together to provide storage for the Linux system is shown in Figure 8-1.

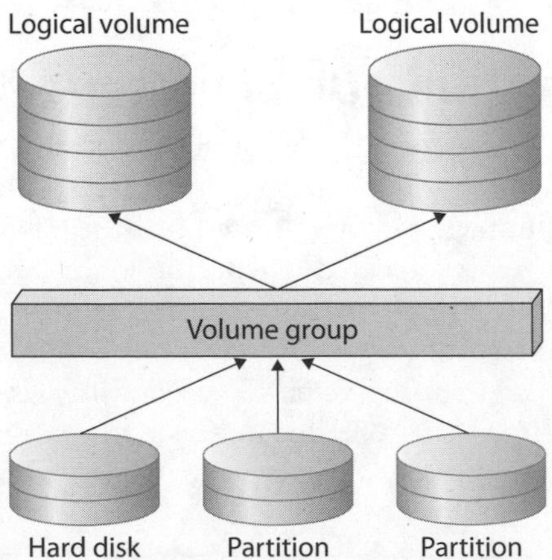

Figure 8-1 LVM components

LVM Configuration

To create and mount logical volumes, first create physical volumes, then volume groups, and finally logical volumes.

Creating LVM Physical Volumes

Disk partitions or even entire disks are physical LVM volumes. To use an existing partition, set the partition type to `Linux LVM (8e)` with `fdisk`, as shown here:

```
Command (m for help): t
Partition number (1,2, default 2): 1
Hex code (type L to list all codes): 8e
Changed type of partition 'Linux' to 'Linux LVM'
```

Once you have determined which disks and partitions to use, run the `pvcreate` command at the shell prompt to define them as LVM physical volumes. The syntax is `pvcreate <device>`. In the following example, the first two partitions on `/dev/sdb` are defined as physical volumes, as well as the entire `/dev/sdc` hard disk:

```
openSUSE:~ # pvcreate /dev/sdb1
openSUSE:~ # pvcreate /dev/sdb2
openSUSE:~ # pvcreate /dev/sdc
```

Next, use the `pvscan -v` command to view all physical volumes on the system along with their size, as shown here:

```
openSUSE:~ # pvscan -v
   Volume Groups with the clustered attribute will be inaccessible.
   Wiping cache of LVM-capable devices
   Wiping internal VG cache
   Walking through all physical volumes
   PV /dev/sdc                            lvm2 [5.00 GiB]
   PV /dev/sdb1                           lvm2 [4.66 GiB]
   PV /dev/sdb2                           lvm2 [6.52 GiB]
   Total: 3 [16.18 GiB] / in use: 0 [0   ] / in no VG: 3 [16.18 GiB]
```

NOTE If later a hard disk drive fails, use the `pvmove` utility to move the data from the physical volume to be removed to another physical volume defined in the system.

Next, use the `pvs` (or `pvdisplay`) command to display the physical volumes:

```
openSUSE:~ # pvs
   PV        VG   Fmt  Attr  Psize  Pfree
   /dev/sdb1 DATA lvm2 a--   4.6g   0
   /dev/sdb2 DATA lmv2 a--   6.5g   0
```

Once the physical volumes are defined, you can create volume groups.

Creating LVM Volume Groups

The `vgcreate` utility is used to create volume groups on the system. The syntax is `vgcreate<volume_group_name><physical_volume1><physical_volume2>` (and so on). In the following example, a volume group named `DATA` is created using the `sdb1`, `sdb2`, and `sdc` physical volumes:

```
openSUSE:~ # vgcreate DATA /dev/sdb1 /dev/sdb2 /dev/sdc
openSUSE:~ # pvscan -v
   Volume Groups with the clustered attribute will be inaccessible.
   Wiping cache of LVM-capable devices
   Wiping internal VG cache
   Walking through all physical volumes
   PV /dev/sdb1    VG DATA    lvm2 [4.65 GiB / 4.65 GiB free]
   PV /dev/sdb2    VG DATA    lvm2 [6.52 GiB / 6.52 GiB free]
   PV /dev/sdc     VG DATA    lvm2 [5.00 GiB / 5.00 GiB free]
   Total: 3 [16.16 GiB] / in use: 3 [16.16 GiB] / in no VG: 0 [0    ]
```

Notice in the output of the `pvscan` command that the three physical volumes are now members of the `DATA` volume group. Use the `vgs` (or `vgdisplay`) command to display the volume group:

```
openSUSE:~ # vgs
   VG   #PV  #LV #SN Attr    Vsize  Vfree
   DATA  1    2    0 wz-n-  16.0g    0
```

After initially creating a volume group, use the following commands to manage it:

- `vgextend`
- `vgreduce`
- `vgremove`

Once the volume group has been defined, you can create logical volumes.

NOTE Users can still use the `ln` command to hard link files across the volumes because a single filesystem is created with LVM. Use either the `rm` command or the `unlink` command to remove a hard link. The `unlink` command can only remove one file at a time, so globbing characters such as `*`, `?`, and `[ ]` will not work.

Creating LVM Logical Volumes

Use the `lvcreate` command to create logical volumes within a volume group. The syntax is as follows:

```
lvcreate -L <volume_size> -n <volume_name> <volume_group_name>
```

In the following example, two 7GB volumes (named `research` and `development`, respectively) are defined from the `DATA` volume group:

```
openSUSE:~ # lvcreate -L 7G -n research DATA
openSUSE:~ # lvcreate -L 7G -n development DATA
openSUSE:~ # lvscan -v
   Volume Groups with the clustered attribute will be inaccessible.
   Finding all logical volumes
   ACTIVE            '/dev/DATA/research' [7.00 GiB] inherit
   ACTIVE            '/dev/DATA/development' [7.00 GiB] inherit
```

Use the `lvscan` command to view the logical volumes defined, as shown in the preceding example. Also notice that the two defined logical volumes are from the volume group, which itself is created by pooling together all the storage space from two disk partitions and one entire hard disk drive. Pretty cool!

Use the `lvs` (or `vgdisplay`) command to display the logical volumes:

```
openSUSE:~ # lvs
  LV   VG   Attr   Lsize Pool Origin Data% Meta% Move Log Cpy%Sync
  data DATA -wi-ao---- 16.00g
```

To manage the logical volumes, use the following commands:

- `lvreduce` Reduces the size of a logical volume
- `lvremove` Removes a logical volume from the system

CAUTION Use extreme caution when working with `lvreduce` and `lvremove`! If the filesystem is larger than the size specified with `lvreduce`, there is a risk of chopping off chunks of data. The administrator should migrate any critical data to a different logical volume before using `lvremove`.

Once the logical volumes are complete, you can create filesystems on them and then mount them. Create a filesystem with `mkfs`, just as with traditional partitions, using the following syntax:

```
mkfs -t <filesystem> /dev/<volume_group>/<logical_volume>
```

Next, mount the logical volume using the `mount` command, just like mounting filesystems on traditional partitions. Use the following syntax:

```
mount -t <filesystem> /dev/<volume_group>/<logical_volume> /<mount_point>
```

LVM Snapshots

Linux systems run 24 hours a day, 7 days a week, making it hard to find a time in which to boot a system into single-user mode and get a clean backup. LVM snapshots allow administrators to create consistent backups on live systems, as well as allow systems to quickly revert to a clean state if corrupted after a snapshot is made.

A snapshot represents the state of a volume at the time the snapshot was taken, and it holds changes of the filesystem that occur over the life of the snapshot.

Making Snapshot Volumes

From the 2GB that are left from the DATA volume group, you can allocate snapshot space into a logical volume. Make sure to allow enough space to hold anticipated data changes; otherwise, if it gets full, the data will be lost. Use the -s or --snapshot flag with lvcreate to build the snapshot:

```
openSUSE:~ # lvcreate -L 1G -s -n snapshot DATA
lvcreate - WARNING: the snapshot must be disabled if it gets full
lvcreate - INFO: using default snapshot chunk size of 64 K for /dev/DATA
lvcreate - doing automatic backup of "DATA"
lvcreate - logical volume "/dev/DATA/snapshot" successfully created
```

To start using the snapshot, create a mount point to access the volume and then mount the device using the mount command:

```
openSUSE:~ # mkdir /mnt/snapshot
openSUSE:~ # mount /dev/DATA/snapshot /mnt/snapshot
mount: block device /dev/DATA/snapshot is write-protected, mounting read-only
```

To remove snapshots, use the umount and lvremove commands:

```
openSUSE:~ # umount /mnt/snapshot
openSUSE:~ # lvremove /dev/DATA/snapshot
lvremove - do you really want to remove /dev/DATA/snapshot? [y/n]: y
lvremove - doing automatic backup of volume group "DATA"
lvremove - logical volume "/dev/DATA/snapshot" successfully removed
```

This will make the filesystem unavailable and remove any saved data in the snapshot.

Checking for Open Files

Although it is not necessary, some administrators feel more comfortable stopping certain jobs, like databases or mail servers, before engaging their snapshots. To observe which files are open for specific processes, use the lsof (list open files) command.

One useful option is -p. Follow this option with the PID of the process being monitored, and it will submit a listing of the files the process has open:

```
openSUSE:~ # lsof -p 5
COMMAND    PID USER   FD      TYPE DEVICE SIZE/OFF NODE NAME
kworker/0    5 root  cwd       DIR    8,5      260   64 /
kworker/0    5 root  rtd       DIR    8,5      260   64 /
kworker/0    5 root  txt   unknown                      /proc/5/exe
```

Extending LVMs

As disk space is utilized, there becomes less and less space for users to work. Increasing disk space in the past involved backing up the current drive, installing a larger drive, and then restoring the system—a risky process that could take an entire workday to accomplish if nothing goes wrong.

Time and risk are reduced with logical volume management. Continuing with our current example, use `lvextend` to extend the current filesystem by 1GB and then use `resize2fs` to resize the filesystem to match, as shown here:

```
openSUSE:~ # lvextend -L +1G /dev/DATA/development
   Extending logical volume development to 8.0 GiB
   Logical volume development successfully resized
openSUSE:~ # resize2fs /dev/DATA/development
```

LVM Troubleshooting

Logical volumes are activated by the kernel by default, but this can fail in certain circumstances. In these rare cases, activate the logical volume using the `lvchange` command using the `-ay` option to "activate" and answer "yes" to the only question asked, "`Do you really want to activate the volume?`" as follows:

```
openSUSE:~ # lvchange -ay /dev/DATA/development
```

Creating Archives and Performing Compression

One of the key roles administrators must perform is data backups. When an organization puts thousands of hours of human effort into creating data, securing that data is critical. One of the best ways to do this is to back up the data to tape, disk, or cloud.

Hard drives have motors and other moving parts that slowly wear out over time. In fact, hard drives have a mean time between failure (MTBF) value assigned by the manufacturer. This value provides an estimate of how long a drive will last before it fails. Basically, it's not a matter of *if* a hard drive will fail; it's a matter of *when*.

There are several components to a backup plan. In this section, we're going to discuss the following topics:

- Selecting a backup medium
- Selecting a backup strategy
- Linux backup and compression utilities

Let's begin by discussing how to select a backup medium.

Selecting a Backup Medium

Today, administrators use tape drives, hard drives, and the cloud to back up their data. Tape drives use magnetic tape to store data. They store a lot of data and are very reliable. However, magnetic tape does wear out after years of use and is slower than backing up to disk.

Most businesses back up to disk or cloud. Hard drives are cheap. An external 10TB hard drive costs less than US$300. Using external hard drives for backups has the advantage of being much faster than tape drives. Enterprises use a type of backup called *virtual tape libraries (VTLs)*, which is a disk-based backup but the software "thinks" it's tape.

Of course, backing up to the cloud provides the benefits of high reliability and distance from the worksite, the latter of which is highly useful in disaster recovery. For example, if an earthquake occurs around corporate headquarters, the data is protected because the cloud backups are stored in a different geographical region (assuming proper disaster recovery planning).

EXAM TIP The `rsync` utility provides a hot-backup solution over standard backups. The tool can be set up to synchronize locally or remotely at defined periods set up within `cron` (every hour, for example). If the main system goes down, simply switch over to the backup system.

Once the backup medium is selected, purchase the appropriate equipment, and then connect and install it onto the system. Once everything is in place, define a backup strategy.

Selecting a Backup Strategy

When creating a backup plan, select a backup type and determine what to back up. First choose the backup type.

Selecting a Backup Type

Depending on the backup utility chosen, the system administrator can implement at least three different types of backups:

- **Full** A full backup backs up all specified files, regardless of whether or not they have been modified since the last backup. After being backed up, each file is flagged as having been backed up. A full backup generally takes the longest time to complete.
- **Incremental** An incremental backup backs up only the files that have been modified since the last backup (full or incremental). After being backed up, each file is flagged as having been backed up. This is generally the fastest backup type.
- **Differential** A differential backup backs up only the files that have been modified since the last full backup. Even though they have been backed up during a differential backup, the files involved are not flagged as having been backed up.

Running a full backup every time is thorough but exhaustive. However, a full backup is the fastest to restore. Running daily incremental backups is the fastest way to back up but the longest to restore.

Many administrators mix full with incremental or differential backups to take advantage of the speed benefits. The restore order is important, so wise administrators label their backups with the date, order, and type of backup.

Finally, make sure to verify backups. Most backup utilities provide the option of checking backups after completion.

Determining What to Back Up

One option is to back up the entire system. This is safe but slow due to the sheer amount of data involved. Instead, prioritize backing up only critical data, such as user data and configuration files. The theory behind this strategy is that in the event of a disaster, administrators can simply reinstall a new system and then restore the critical data. Consider backing up these important directories:

- `/etc`
- `/home`
- `/root`
- `/var`

Notice that this strategy doesn't back up Linux or its utilities. Instead, it only backs up configuration files, user data, log files, and web/FTP files.

Linux Backup and Compression Utilities

When working with Linux, there are a host of different utilities for conducting backups. Many come with the operating system; others can be obtained from third parties. For the CompTIA Linux+ exam, you should be familiar with the tools that are common to most distributions and know how to run them from the shell prompt. The following topics are covered in this section:

- Using `gzip`, `bzip2`, `zip`, and `xz` for compression
- Using `tar` and `cpio` for backups
- Using `dd` for disk cloning

Using `gzip`, `bzip2`, `zip`, and `xz` for Compression

Compression is used to help save space on hard drives and speed traffic through a network. In both cases, a minimized representation of the real data is saved or sent and then converted back to real data for processing.

The `gzip`, `bzip2`, `zip`, and `xz` utilities are installed by default on most Linux versions, with `gzip` being the most popular compression tool because it has been available the longest. The `bzip2` tool provides even better compression than `gzip`, but requires more memory to perform the task. The `xz` program provides even better compression but is not as widely used. The following display compression example uses `gzip`, `bzip2`, and `xz`. Note how the suffixes differ depending on the type of compression:

```
openSUSE:~ # ls a.txt b.txt c.txt
a.txt        b.txt        c.txt
openSUSE:~ # gzip a.txt ; bzip2 b.txt ; xz c.txt
openSUSE:~ # ls a.txt.* b.txt.* c.txt.*
a.txt.gz     b.txt.bz2    c.txt.xz
```

Users can use the `gunzip`, `bunzip`, and `unxz` utilities to uncompress their compressed files. The `zip` application provides the best support to compress and uncompress to and from Microsoft Windows systems. Use the `-r` flag with `zip` and follow it with the name of the file to compress, as shown here to compress the `d.txt` file:

```
openSUSE:~ # zip -r d d.txt
openSUSE:~ # ls d.*
d.txt       d.zip
```

Use the `unzip` utility to uncompress the `zip` file back to the normal state.

Using `tar` and `cpio` for Backup

The `tar` (tape archive) utility has been around for a very long time and is a commonly used backup tool. The `tar` utility takes a list of specified files and copies them into a single archive file (`.tar`). The `.tar` file can then be compressed with the `gzip` utility on the Linux system, resulting in a file with a `.tar,.gz`, or `.tgz` extension. This is called a *tarball*.

The `tar` utility can be used to send backup jobs to a variety of backup media, including tape drives and removable hard disk drives. The syntax for using `tar` to create backups is as follows:

```
tar -cvf <filename> <directory>
```

The `-c` option tells `tar` to create a new archive. The `-v` option tells `tar` to work in verbose mode, displaying each file being backed up onscreen. The `-f` option specifies the name of the `tar` archive to be created.

For example, to create a backup of the `/home` directory and name it `backup.tar` on an external USB hard drive mounted in `/media/usb`, enter the following `tar` command:

```
openSUSE:/ # tar -cvf /media/usb/backup.tar /home
tar: Removing leading '/' from member names
/home/
/home/tux/
/home/tux/.gftp/
/home/tux/.gftp/gftp.log
/home/tux/.gftp/bookmarks
/home/tux/.gftp/gftprc
/home/tux/.nautilus/
/home/tux/.local/
/home/tux/.local/share/...
```

Notice in this example that the message `tar: Removing leading '/' from member names` is displayed. When a `tar` archive is created, absolute paths are converted to relative paths by default to simplify restores (for example, restoring to a different location). As a result, the leading / is removed.

NOTE The `tar` utility was created before subscripts became popular, so when making a `tarfile`, the user must add `.tar` in order for the file to be recognized as a `tarfile`.

Option	Function
`-c` `--create`	Create a new archive file.
`-J` `--xz`	Do one of two things. During archive creation, these options compress the new `tar` archive by running it through the `xz` utility. During extraction, they first decompress the `tar` archive using the `xz` utility.
`-t` `--list`	List the contents of an archive file.
`-x` `--extract`	Extract files from an archive.

`-z`
`--gzip`
`--gunzip`
	Do one of two things. During archive creation, these options compress the new `tar` archive by running it through the `gzip` utility. During extraction, they first decompress the `tar` archive using the `gunzip` utility.

`-j`
`--bzip2`
`--bunzip`
	Do one of two things. During archive creation, these options compress the new `tar` archive by running it through the `bzip2` utility. During extraction, they first decompresses the `tar` archive using the `bunzip2` utility.

Table 8-1 The `tar` Command Options

Other `tar` options are shown in Table 8-1.

To back up to a tape drive, replace the `<filename>` parameter with the device name for the tape drive. On most distributions, the first SCSI or SATA tape drive in the system is referenced as `/dev/st0` (that's the digit zero, not an uppercase *O*). Therefore, enter `tar -cvf /dev/st0 /home` to run the same backup as in the previous example, but send it to a tape drive instead.

To restore a `tar` archive, simply enter `tar -xvf <filename>`. For example, to extract the archive created, enter `tar -xvf /media/usb/backup.tar`. This will extract the archive into the current working directory.

The `cpio` utility can also be used to make archive files like `tar`. For example, to back up multiple files in the current directory, use the `-o` option to write the data "out" to a file:

```
openSUSE:/ # ls z.txt y.txt x.txt | cpio -ov > /media/usb/backup.cpio
```

To restore files from a `cpio` archive, run `cpio` from the shell prompt using the `-i` option to read files "in." For example, to extract the archive just created, enter the following:

```
openSUSE:/tmp # cpio -iv < /media/usb/backup.cpio
x.txt
y.txt
z.txt
341 blocks
```

Like `tar`, `cpio` does not compress the archive by default. Use `zip`, `gzip`, `bzip2`, or `xz` to compress the archive after it has been created with `cpio`.

NOTE The previous examples were done on a USB drive, but high-security organizations typically prohibit USB drives because they make it easier for an insider threat to exfiltrate confidential data.

Using dd for Disk Cloning

The dd command is a great command for copying files, the master boot record (MBR), filesystems, and entire disk drives.

To copy a file with dd, use the syntax dd if=<input_file> of=<output_file>. Here's an example:

```
openSUSE:/ # dd if=./e.txt of=./e.bak
29+1 records in
29+1 records out
15112 bytes (15 kB) copied, 0.000263331 s, 57.4 MB/s
```

The dd command allows administrators to perform drive cloning. To copy an entire partition or drive, enter dd if=<device_file> of=<output_file> at the shell prompt. The device file of the partition is used as the input file. All the contents of the partition are written to the output file specified.

In the example that follows, the dd command is used to copy the entire hard drive, /dev/sda, to an identical or larger hard drive:

```
openSUSE:/ # dd if=/dev/sda of=/dev/sdb bs=1024
dd: writing to '/dev/sdb':
7500249+0 records in
7500248+0 records out
3840126976 bytes (3.8 GB) copied, 108.441 s, 35.4 MB/s
```

The dd command can even create an image file of an entire hard disk. Again, the syntax is dd if=<device_file> of=<output_file>. The difference is that an administrator can simply specify the device file of the hard disk itself instead of a partition. In the next example, the entire /dev/sdb hard drive is archived into the drivebackup file:

```
openSUSE:~ # dd if=/dev/sdc of=/mnt/bigdrive/drivebackup
16777216+0 records in
16777216+0 records out
8589934592 bytes (8.6 GB) copied, 157.931 s, 54.4 MB/s
```

Another useful feature of dd is that it can create a backup copy of the hard drive's MBR and partition table. The syntax is as follows:

```
dd if=<device_file> of=<output_file> bs=512 count=1
```

This tells dd to grab just the first 512-byte block of the hard drive, which is where the MBR and partition table reside. This is shown in the following example:

```
openSUSE:/tmp # dd if=/dev/sda of=/root/mbrbackup bs=512 count=1
1+0 records in
1+0 records out
512 bytes (512 B) copied, 0.0123686 s, 41.4 kB/s
```

EXAM TIP The MBR is the first 512 bytes of the hard drive, which bootstraps the GRUB bootloader, which in turn bootstraps the kernel. The partition table, which defines the hard drive layout, is part of the MBR and starts at byte 440. To back up the MBR without the partition table, run the following command:

```
dd if=/dev/sda of=/dev/sdb bs=440 count=1
```

Exercise 8-1: Backing Up Data

In this exercise, practice data backups. Perform this exercise using the virtual machine provided online.

VIDEO Please watch the Exercise 8-1 video for a demonstration on how to perform this task.

Complete the following steps:

1. With the system up and running, open a terminal session.
2. Change to the root user account by entering the **`su -`** command.
3. Enter **`tar -cvf ./backup.tar /home`** at the shell prompt.
4. Enter **`ls`** and then verify that the backup file exists.
5. Change to the `/tmp` directory by entering **`cd /tmp`** at the shell prompt.
6. Enter **`tar -xvf /root/backup.tar`** to extract the `.tar` file to the current directory.
7. Use the **`ls`** command to verify that the files from the `tar` archive were extracted to the current directory.
8. Enter **`exit`** to switch back to the standard user account.

Enabling Redundant Array of Independent Disks

Enabling redundant array of independent (or inexpensive) disks, commonly called RAID, allows administrators to create filesystems over multiple hard drives. For example, an administrator can combine five 10TB hard drives and make them appear to users as a single 50TB hard drive. This is called RAID 0 (zero) or *striping*. RAID 0 provides superior data performance, as these drives can read and write striped data at the same time. The best applications include streaming media. The downside is that if a hard drive fails, the entire system fails and needs to be recovered from backup archives. See Figure 8-2 for the RAID 0 setup.

Other RAID concepts provide superior reliability. RAID 1 (one), also known as mirroring, offers the best in reliability because it clones devices. On a hot-backup system, if

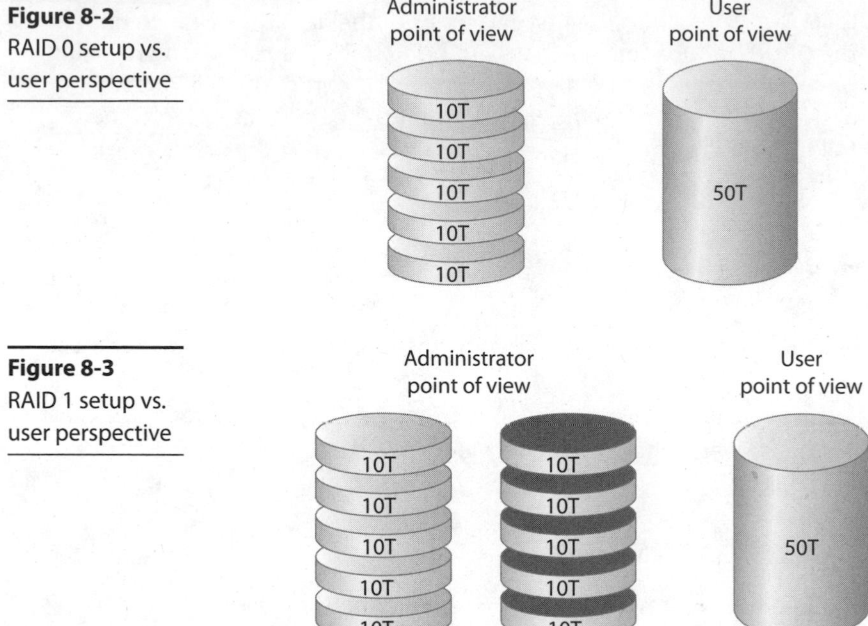

Figure 8-2 RAID 0 setup vs. user perspective

Figure 8-3 RAID 1 setup vs. user perspective

a hard drive fails, it can be swapped with a good hard drive while the system is operating, thus allowing systems to run 24/7. The "insurance" is expensive because every hard drive requires a backup, so five 10TB hard drives will have a duplicate of five 10TB hard drives. See Figure 8-3 for the RAID 1 setup.

RAID 5 offers reliability at a much lower cost than RAID 1. Instead of duplicating all the hard drives, RAID 5 adds a single hard drive that mathematically calculates data records; this is known as *parity*.

When a drive dies on a hot-backup system, the administrator swaps it out with a good hard drive, RAID 5 restores the data by reversing the parity calculations, and the system continues to operate. Unlike RAID 1, if two drives fail at the same time, the parity calculations fail and therefore need to be recovered with backups from tapes or the cloud. See Figure 8-4 for the RAID 5 setup.

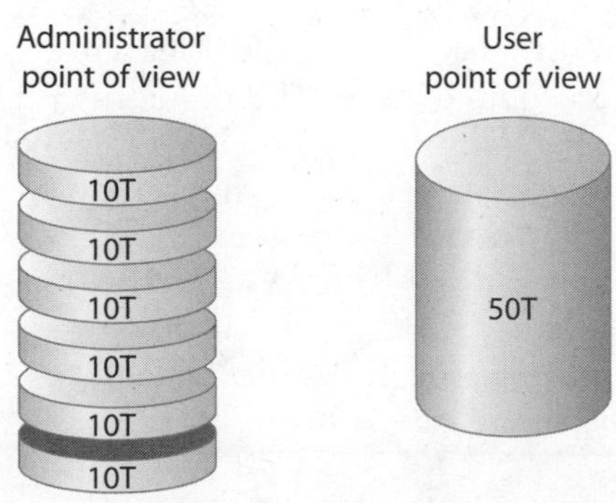

Figure 8-4 RAID 5 setup vs. user perspective

Figure 8-5 RAID 6 setup vs. user perspective

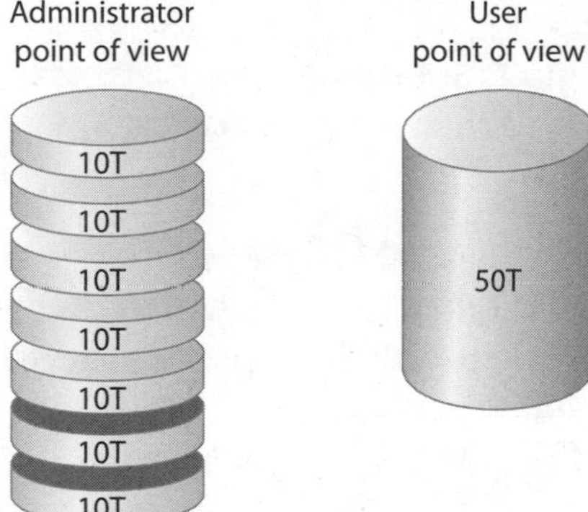

RAID 6 improves reliability over RAID 5 by providing an additional parity drive so that if two hard drives fail at the same time, the system can quickly recover by swapping in two good hard drives. The downside of RAID 5 and RAID 6 is performance. Performance is lost because the systems must calculate parity. See Figure 8-5 for the RAID 6 setup.

RAID 1+0 (or RAID 10) provides administrators a balance between the reliability of RAID 1 and the performance of RAID 0. Figure 8-6 displays this setup, which combines the RAID 1 technique of mirroring each set of data with the RAID 0 technique of striping the data. RAID 10 requires much more hardware, but the uptime is tremendous.

Next, we look at the following RAID topics:

- Configuring software RAID
- Verifying RAID status

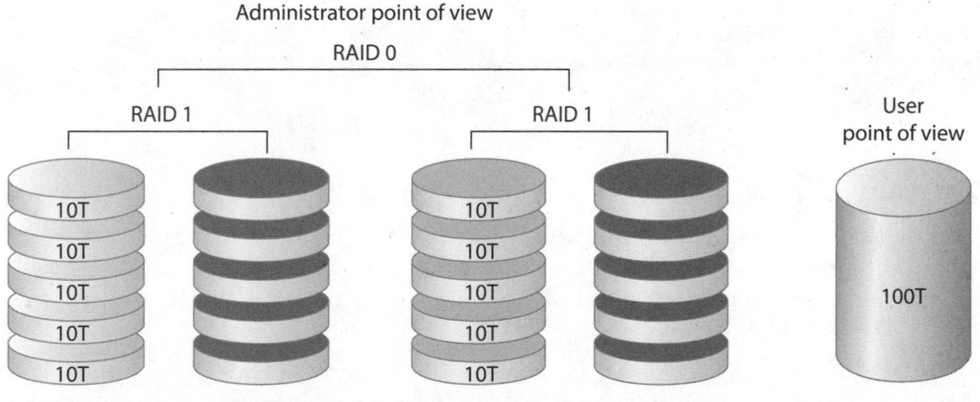

Figure 8-6 RAID 10 setup vs. user perspective

EXAM TIP Other RAID systems weigh differently on reliability and performance, such as RAID 3 and RAID 4, but RAID 0, 1, 5, 6, and 10 are the only versions mentioned on the CompTIA Linux+ exam.

Configuring Software RAID

Of course, there are hardware RAID solutions, but to create any RAID system using the Linux Meta-device Administrator tool starts with selecting the hard drives that will form the solution and then using the `mdadm` command to create the RAID device, as shown here:

```
openSUSE:~ # mdadm -C /dev/md0 --level=1 --raid-disks=2 /dev/sdb /dev/sdc
```

The preceding meta-device administration command uses `-C` to create a new meta-device called `/dev/md0` at a RAID 1 level, which is disk mirroring. This system will use only two hard drives, `/dev/sdb` and `/dev/sdc`, as defined by `--raid-disks`.

Once the RAID 1 meta-device is created, treat it like any other filesystem. That is, create the filesystem and then mount it onto an empty directory. To make the filesystem permanent at boot time, update the `/etc/fstab` file:

```
openSUSE:~ # mkfs.ext4 /dev/md0
mke2fs 1.42.9 (28-Dec-2013)
Filesystem label=
OS type: Linux
Block size=1024 (log=0)
Fragment size=1024 (log=0)
Stride=0 blocks, Stripe width=0 blocks
62744 inodes, 250880 blocks
12544 blocks (5.00%) reserved for the super user
First data block=1
Maximum filesystem blocks=33816576
31 block groups
8192 blocks per group, 8192 fragments per group
2024 inodes per group
...
openSUSE:~ # mkdir /raidone
openSUSE:~ # mount /dev/md0 /raidone
```

Verifying RAID Status

To verify the status of the running RAID system, again use the `mdadm` command. The `mdmonitor` service provides RAID monitoring and management. To get details of the current setup, including the devices and description of the array, use the `--detail` option with `mdadm` or view the `/proc/mdstat` file:

```
openSUSE:~ # mdadm --detail /dev/md0
/dev/md0:
          Version : 1.2
    Creation Time : Wed Mar 27 10:48:01 2025
       Raid Level : raid1
       Array Size : 250880 (245.00 MiB 256.90 MB)
```

```
    Used Dev Size : 250880 (245.00 MiB 256.90 MB)
     Raid Devices : 2
    Total Devices : 2
      Persistence : Superblock is persistent
      Update Time : Wed Mar 27 10:48:04 2025
            State : clean
   Active Devices : 2
  Working Devices : 2
   Failed Devices : 0
    Spare Devices : 0
...
openSUSE:~ # less /proc/mdstat
Personalities : [raid1]
md0 : active raid1 sdc[1] sdb[0]
250880 blocks super 1.2 [2/2] [UU]
unused devices: <none>
openSUSE:~ # mdadm --detail /dev/md0 --scan » /etc/mdadm.conf
```

The `/etc/mdadm.conf` configuration file created assembles RAID arrays properly after reboots and simplifies the description of the devices and arrays.

Use the `mdadm` command to manage hot spares; for example, `mdadm --fail` marks the drive as faulty and prepares it for removal with the `mdadm --remove` command. After the hard drive has been physically removed and replaced, reenable it using `mdadm --add`. If the new device is part of the failed array, it will be used as part of RAID; otherwise, the drive will be seen as an available hot spare.

RAID Troubleshooting

Poorly performing RAID systems using SSD drives may need to be tuned to run at normal performance. SSDs are used with RAID systems because they perform so much better than IDE or SCSI drives.

The first step is to assure that the RAID system is composed entirely of SSD drives. Use the `lsscsi` command to list SCSI devices, and assure those drives are not part of the RAID system. Next, investigate if the RAID system is using the SSD TRIM capabilities. To do this, run the `fstrim` command using the `-av` options. The `-a` option trims all of the SSD with TRIM features, and `-v` lists the output verbosely.

For RAID systems that are not failing over properly, assure that the `multipathd` daemon is running properly. The `multipathd` daemon checks for failed paths to enforce proper redundancy. For example, there may be several failover disk drives connected via Fibre Channel. Review and verify these drives by running `fcstat`.

Exercise 8-2: Configuring RAID and Logical Volumes

In this exercise, practice using RAID and LVM. In Part I you will create the hard drives for the exercise. In Part II you will build your RAID and LVM systems. Perform this exercise using the virtual machine provided online.

Part I: Create additional hard drives

To conduct this exercise, create four additional virtual hard drives within the hypervisor. To do this with VirtualBox, shut down the virtual Linux system, click Details in the upper right, and then click Storage (about halfway down in the Oracle VM VirtualBox Manager). See the following illustration.

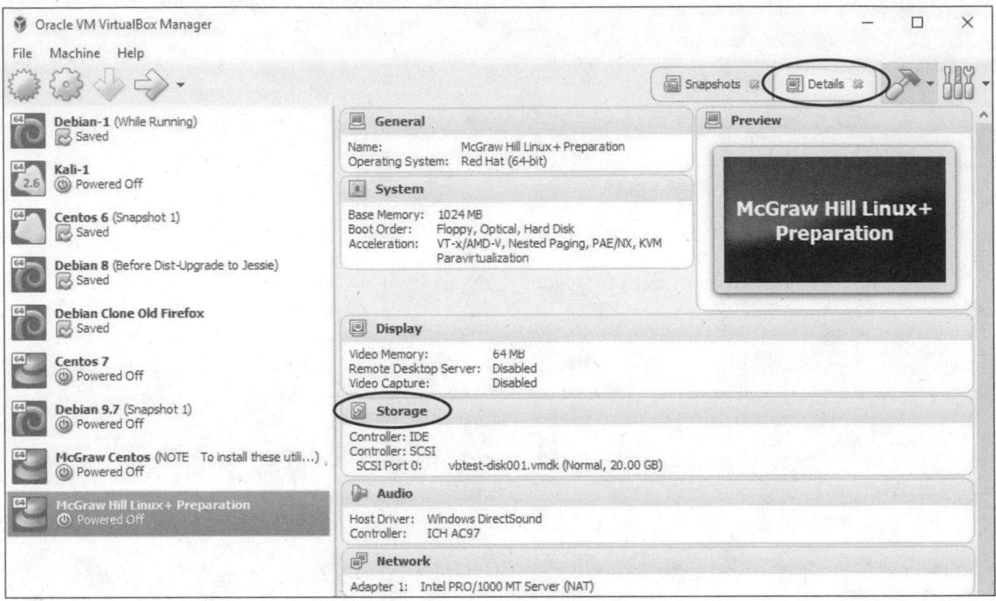

Click Controller: SCSI and then click the square icon just to the right with the green plus sign, as shown here.

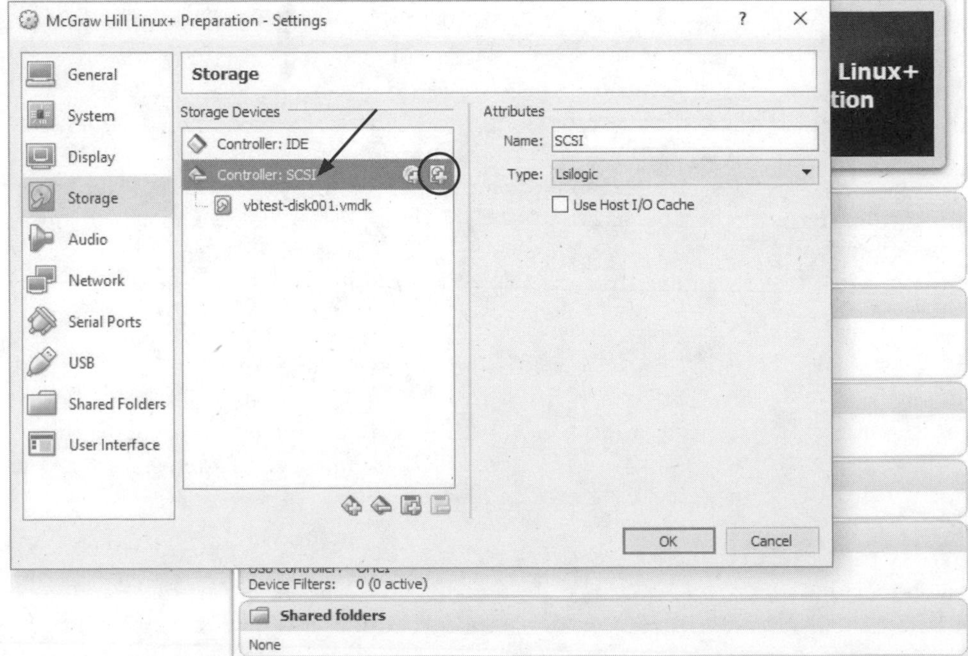

In the VirtualBox Question dialog box that appears, choose Create New Disk, as shown next.

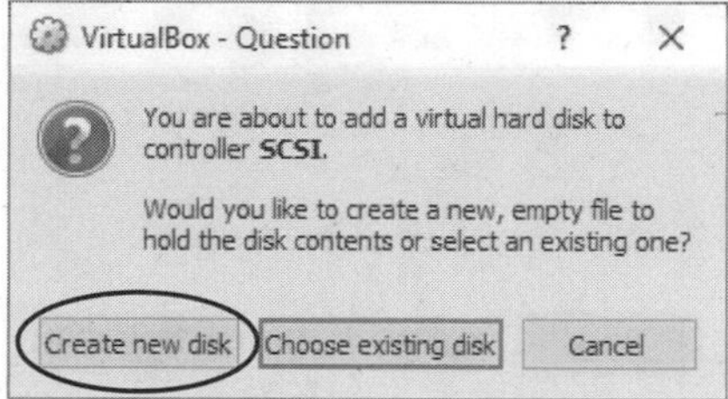

The next window asks you which type of file you'd like to use for the new virtual hard disk. Choose VDI (VirtualBox Disk Image), as shown next, and then choose Dynamically Allocated in the next window.

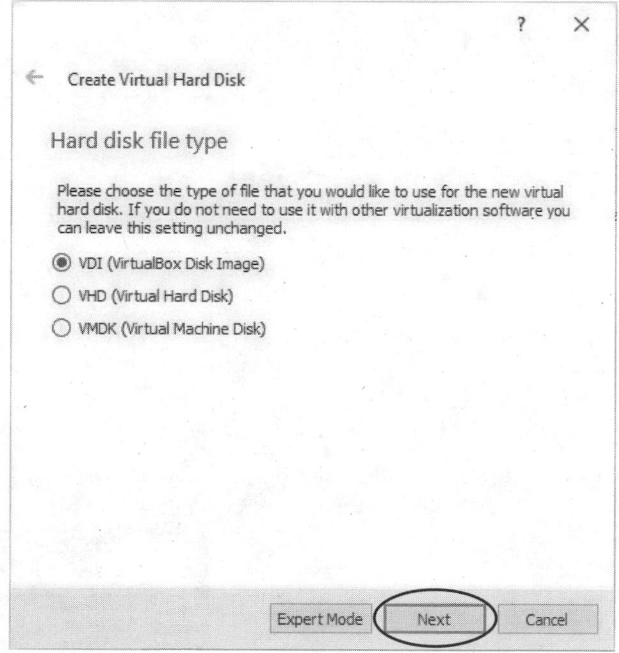

Change the name of the hard drive. For example, in the following illustration, I named the first hard drive NewVirtualDisk10. The next hard drive I create will be named NewVirtualDisk11, and so on, up to 13. Set the size of the virtual hard disk to 256.0MB and click Create.

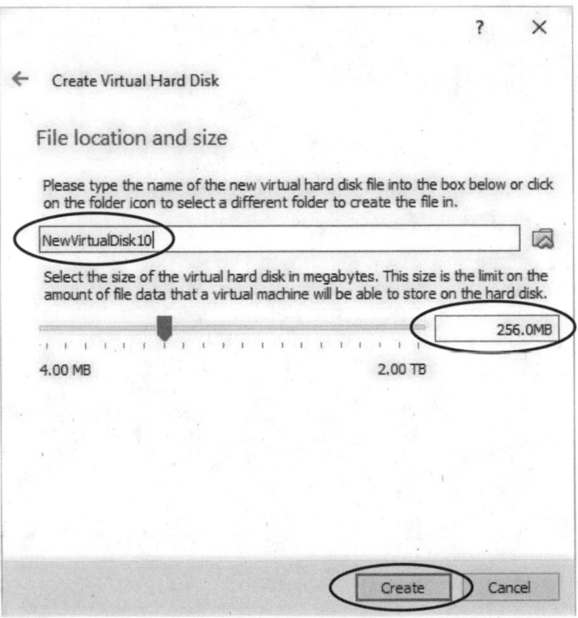

Repeat the steps to create a new disk until you have a total of *four additional 256MB virtual hard drives.* Click OK in the Storage Settings to finalize creation of the hard drive. The following illustration displays the final results; you should see your new hard drive added to the virtual machine. Power on the system to complete the next lab.

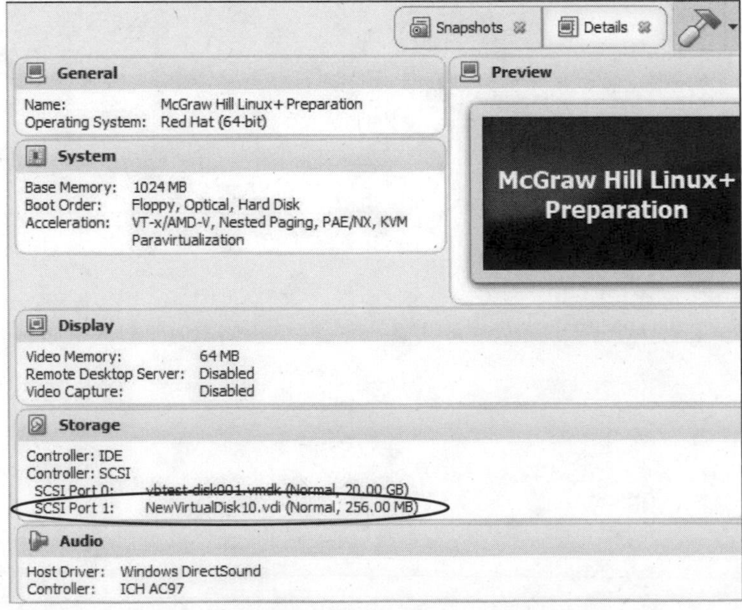

If you get an error during this process, it likely has to do with a naming conflict. Make sure the new hard drive name is different from earlier names. *Remember to take a snapshot of the virtual machine before starting the lab.*

VIDEO Please watch the Exercise 8-2 video for a demonstration on how to perform this task.

Part II: Configure RAID and LVM systems

Once you have your four additional virtual hard drives using the virtual machine provided online, complete the following steps to practice using RAID and LVM:

1. With the system up and running, open a terminal session.
2. Change to the root user account by entering the **`su -`** command.
3. Convert two of the hard drives into physical volumes for LVM by running the following command:
   ```
   pvcreate /dev/sda10 ; pvcreate /dev/sda11 ; pvdisplay; pvs
   ```
4. Create the volume group called `labvg` using the default extent size:
   ```
   vgcreate labvg /dev/sda10 /dev/sda11 ; vgdisplay; vgs
   ```
5. Create a 200MB logical volume called `lablvm` from the new volume group:
   ```
   lvcreate -L 200M -n lablvm ; lvdisplay; lvs
   ```
6. Create the filesystem and mount it onto a new empty directory. Display the new logical volume settings using `lvs` and `lvdisplay`:
   ```
   mkfs.ext4 /dev/labvg/lablvm ; mkdir /lablvm
   mount /dev/labvg/lablvm /lablvm
   lvdisplay
   lvs
   ```
7. Observe how much disk space is available using the `df -h` command and resize the logical volume to 300MB:
   ```
   df -h
   lvresize -r -L 300M /dev/labvg/lablvm
   df -h
   ```
8. There is still not enough space. Add another 100MB:
   ```
   lvresize -r -L +100M /dev/labvg/lablvm
   df -h
   ```
9. Create a RAID 1 mirror using `mdadm`:
   ```
   mdadm -C /dev/md0 --level=1 --raid-disks=2 /dev/sda12 /dev/sda13
   ```
10. Create a filesystem on the RAID device and mount the filesystem:
    ```
    mkfs.ext4 /dev/md0 ; mkdir /labraid ; mount /dev/md0 /labraid
    ```
11. Save the meta-device settings into `/etc/mdadm.conf` to be observed at boot time and then review the status of the RAID device:
    ```
    mdadm --detail --scan » /etc/mdadm.conf
    mdadm --detail
    cat /proc/mdstat
    ```

12. To mount the new LVM and RAID devices at boot time, add the following entries to /etc/fstab:

```
echo /dev/md0  /labraid ext4  defaults    0 0 » /etc/fstab
echo /dev/labvg/lablvm  /lablvm  ext4 defaults  0 0 » /etc/fstab
```

13. Enter **exit** to switch back to the standard user account.

Chapter Review

Logical volume management provides a solution to easily grow a filesystem while in use, and it eases archiving because of its snapshot capability. Physical volumes such as partitions are pooled together into volume groups. This data pool, or "volume group," can be divided into logical volumes. The logical volumes are formatted into filesystems. Instead of mounting partitions, logical volumes are mounted onto directories in the filesystem.

Administrators must conduct backups on a regular schedule. This requires selecting a backup medium and backup strategy and then implementing the strategy with backup and compression utilities.

Software RAID systems are a feature of logical volume management. RAID systems can be designed for performance (for example, RAID 0) or for data reliability (for example, RAID 1). To balance cost, reliability, and performance, implement RAID 5 or RAID 6. For the best in reliability and performance, implement RAID 10.

Here are some key facts to remember about volume management:

- LVM enables administrators to dynamically add space to the system.
- To create LVM storage, use the following process:
  - Create physical volumes with the pvcreate command.
  - Create a volume group using the vgcreate command.
  - Create logical volumes using the lvcreate command.
- Use the lsof command at the shell prompt to display a list of open files.
- Backup medium choices include tape drives, removable hard drives, and/or the cloud.
- Administrators must select a backup strategy, such as full, incremental, or differential backups. Administrators combine them to design a backup strategy.
- Full backups back up everything and flag the files as having been backed up.
- Incremental backups back up everything that has been modified since the last full or incremental backup and flag the files as having been backed up.
- Differential backups back up everything that has been backed up since the last full backup. However, they don't flag the files as having been backed up.
- Commonly backed-up filesystems include /etc, /home, /root, and /var.
- The tar and cpio utilities work with most backup media.
- The dd utility can copy an entire partition or even clone an entire hard drive.

- RAID 0, also known as striping, is designed for performance and not reliability.
- RAID 1 is known as mirroring and is designed for reliability.
- RAID 5 offers reliability by maintaining a single-parity drive.
- RAID 6 offers reliability by maintaining a dual-parity drive system.
- Use the `mdadm` command to configure, maintain, and monitor RAID. Use the `--fail`, `--remove`, and `--add` options to mark devices as faulty, removed, or added, respectively.

Questions

1. Which type of backup backs up all files modified since the last full backup and does not flag the files as having been backed up?
   A. Full
   B. Incremental
   C. Differential
   D. Partial
2. A system administrator creates a backup of `/etc` to a removable hard disk drive mounted at `/mnt/USB`. Which `tar` command will do this?
   A. `tar -cvf /mnt/USB/backup.tar /etc`
   B. `tar -xvf ~/backup.tar /etc`
   C. `tar -xzf /mnt/USB/backup.tar /etc`
   D. `tar -cvf /mnt/USB/backup.tar ~/etc`
3. Which command will create a compressed `cpio` archive of all the files in the `Projects` directory within the user's home directory to `/mnt/usbdrive/Projectsbackup.cpio.gz`?
   A. `cpio -ov ~/Projects | gzip > /mnt/usbdrive/Projectsbackup.cpio.gz`
   B. `ls ~/Projects | cpio -ovz | > /mnt/usbdrive/Projectsbackup.cpio.gz`
   C. `ls ~/Projects | cpio -ov | gzip > /mnt/usbdrive/Projectsbackup.cpio.gz`
   D. `cpio -ovz ~/Projects > /mnt/usbdrive/Projectsbackup.cpio.gz`
4. Which command can be used to create an image of the `/dev/sda2` partition in the `/mnt/usb/volback` file?
   A. `dd if=/dev/sda2 of=/mnt/usb/volback`
   B. `cp /dev/sda2 /mnt/usb/volback`
   C. `dd if=/mnt/usb/volback of=/dev/sda2`
   D. `dd if=/dev/sda of=/mnt/usb/volback`

5. Create a new GPT partition on the `/dev/sdc` hard disk drive. After running `gdisk /dev/sdc` at the shell prompt, which subcommand will create a new partition that is 100GB in size?

   A. `n`

   B. `p`

   C. `new -size=100G`

   D. `t`

6. After adding a third 1TB solid state drive (SSD) to a Linux server, it needs to be added as storage space to an LVM volume group named `DATA` on the system. Which command should be entered first to do this?

   A. `vgextend DATA /dev/sdc`

   B. `pvscan /dev/sdc DATA`

   C. `pvcreate /dev/sdc`

   D. `lvextend -L 1T -n DATA`

7. Fill in the blank with the option to create a snapshot. (Choose two.)
   `lvcreate -L 1G ____ -n snapshot DATA`

   A. `--clone`

   B. `-s`

   C. `--snapshot`

   D. `--snap`

8. Which RAID system has two additional hard drives for parity?

   A. RAID 0

   B. RAID 1

   C. RAID 5

   D. RAID 6

9. Which commands will extend a logical volume filesystem from 500MB to 1000MB? (Choose two.)

   A. `lvextend -L +500 /dev/lvm1`

   B. `lvextend -L +500M /dev/lvm1`

   C. `lvextend -L 1000 /dev/lvm1`

   D. `lvextend -L 1000M /dev/lvm1`

10. Which command will compress files by default?

    A. `tar`

    B. `cpio`

    C. `dd`

    D. `xz`

11. Which command is run to verify RAID status?
    - **A.** `mdadm --detail /dev/md0`
    - **B.** `lvdisplay`
    - **C.** `lvs`
    - **D.** `mkfs.ext4 /dev/md0`
12. Place the steps in the proper order to grow a filesystem.
    - **A.** `resize2fs`
    - **B.** `pvcreate`
    - **C.** `lvextend`
    - **D.** `vgextend`

Answers

1. **C.** A differential backup backs up all files modified since the last full backup and does not flag the files as having been backed up.
2. **A.** The `tar -cvf /mnt/USB/backup.tar /etc` command uses the correct syntax.
3. **C.** The `ls ~/Projects | cpio -ov | gzip > /mnt/usbdrive /Projectsbackup.cpio.gz` command will generate a listing of files in the `Projects` directory, send the list to the `cpio` command to create an archive, and send the archive to `gzip` for compression.
4. **A.** The `dd if=/dev/sda2 of=/mnt/usb/volback` command creates an image of the `/dev/sda2` partition in the `/mnt/usb/volback` file.
5. **A.** Within `gdisk`, type `n` to create a new partition. After doing so, the user is prompted to specify its size.
6. **C.** Before allocating space from a storage device to a volume group, first define it as an LVM physical volume. In this scenario, use the `pvcreate /dev/sdc` command.
7. **B, C.** The `-s` and `--snapshot` options create a snapshot with the `lvcreate` command.
8. **D.** RAID 6 has two additional hard drives for parity. (RAID 0 provides striping. RAID 1 provides mirroring. RAID 5 uses a single drive for parity.)
9. **B, D.** Both `lvextend -L +500M /dev/lvm1` and `lvextend -L 1000M /dev/lvm1` will extend a logical volume filesystem from 500MB to 1000MB.

10. D. The `xz` command compresses files by default. The other options only archive data by default.

11. A. The `mdadm` command displays the status of the RAID array. The `lvdisplay` and `lvs` commands display logical volume details. The `mkfs.ext4` command creates an `ext4` filesystem.

12. B, D, C, A. The correct order of the steps is `pvcreate`, `vgextend`, `lvextend`, `resize2fs`.

CHAPTER 9

Managing Linux Processes

In this chapter, you will learn about

- Understanding Linux processes
- Managing processes
- Scheduling jobs

When I corrected his mistake and ran the code again, he didn't laugh anymore.

—Christine Darden, NASA

In this chapter, you will learn how the Linux operating system handles executable programs and running scripts. Also, you will discover how to manage executables while they run on the system.

EXAM TIP Be very familiar with how Linux handles running processes. Know how to use shell commands to view running processes and how to run processes in the foreground and background. Also, understand how to kill a process from the command line and automate jobs using the `at` and `cron` utilities.

Understanding Linux Processes

The key to being able to effectively manage Linux processes is to first understand how processes function within the operating system. So, what exactly is a process? For our purposes, a *process* is a program that has been loaded from a storage drive into system RAM and is currently being processed by the CPU on the motherboard. This section covers the following topics:

- Types of Linux programs
- User processes versus system processes
- How Linux processes are loaded

Type of Program	Description
Binary executables	Programs originally created as a text file using a programming language such as C or Java. The text file is run through a compiler, which converts the program into machine language. This final binary file is processed by the CPU.
Internal shell commands	Commands that are rolled into a shell program itself, like the Bash shell. For example, when entering `cd`, `history`, or `exit` at a shell prompt, it actually runs an internal shell command. Learn more by reading the `bash` man page.
Shell scripts	Text files that are interpreted through the Bash shell itself. They include commands that run binary executables and internal shell commands within the shell script. More details on shell scripts are provided in Chapter 13.

Table 9-1 Linux Programs That Can Create Processes

Types of Linux Programs

Many different types of programs can be executed to create a process. On the Linux system, the types of programs listed in Table 9-1 can be loaded into RAM and executed by the CPU.

Remember that the Linux operating system can run many processes "concurrently" on a single CPU. Depending on how the Linux system is being used, it may have only a few processes or hundreds of processes running concurrently. The term *concurrently* is qualified in quotes because single-core CPUs cannot run multiple processes at the same time. Instead, Linux quickly switches between various processes running on the CPU, making it appear as if multiple processes run concurrently. However, the CPU actually only executes a single process at a time. All other processes currently "running" wait in the background for their turn. Linux maintains a schedule that determines when each process is allowed access to the CPU, called *multitasking*.

For true concurrency, consider either a multicore or hyperthreading CPU. Multicore CPUs can actually execute more than one process at a time because each core in the processor package is a separate CPU. Hyperthreading CPUs are designed such that a single processor can run more than one process at a time.

User Processes Versus System Processes

The Linux operating system uses several types of processes. Some processes are created by the end user when they execute a command from the shell prompt or through the graphical interface. These processes are called *user processes*. User processes are usually associated with some kind of end-user program running on the system.

To view processes, simply run the `ps` (process status) command, as shown here:

```
cgreer@openSUSE:~> ps -a
 PID  TTY          TIME CMD
28041 pts/0    00:00:00 ps
```

The `ps` command lists process IDs (`PID` column), the terminal they are running within (`TTY`), how long each process has been running in CPU time (`TIME`), and the process command (`CMD`). In this example, you see one process: the `ps` user process, which is process ID `28041`, running in pseudo-terminal `0`, and it ran very quickly in system time at `00:00:00`.

The key point to remember about user processes is that they are called from within a shell and are associated with that shell session.

However, not all processes running on the system are user processes. In fact, most processes executing on a given Linux system will probably be of a different type, called *system processes* or *daemons*. Unlike a user process, a system process (usually) does not provide an application or an interface for an end user to use. Instead, a system process is used to provide a system service, such as a web server, an FTP server, a file service such as Samba, a print service such as CUPS, or a logging service. Such processes run in the background and usually don't provide any kind of user interface.

For example, consider the processes shown in Figure 9-1 after executing the `ps -e` command. The figure shows only a few lines of the output, but the `-e` option displays every process running on the system, not only your processes.

NOTE Most system processes are noted with a letter `d` at the end of the name, which stands for daemon. The system has many system processes running, and these are loaded after the kernel is booted so they are not associated with a shell. User processes are tied to the shell instance they were called from.

rtracy@openSUSE:~

File Edit View Search Terminal Help

```
27290 ?        00:00:00 evolution-sourc
27309 ?        00:00:00 evolution-alarm
27310 ?        00:00:05 tracker-store
27312 ?        00:00:00 deja-dup-monito
27331 ?        00:00:00 tracker-miner-f
27340 ?        00:00:00 evolution-calen
27347 ?        00:00:02 vmtoolsd
27373 ?        00:00:02 libsocialweb-co
27376 ?        00:00:00 obexd
27413 ?        00:00:00 gvfsd-burn
27437 ?        00:00:00 gvfsd-metadata
27501 ?        00:00:02 kworker/u4:2
27649 ?        00:00:00 kworker/1:0
27756 ?        00:00:02 gnome-terminal-
27766 ?        00:00:00 gnome-pty-helpe
27767 pts/0    00:00:00 bash
27913 pts/0    00:00:00 oosplash
27935 pts/0    00:00:05 soffice.bin
27995 ?        00:00:00 sshd
27998 ?        00:00:00 sshd
27999 pts/2    00:00:00 bash
28042 ?        00:00:00 kworker/1:1
28071 pts/0    00:00:00 ps
rtracy@openSUSE:~>
```

Figure 9-1 System processes

By default, most Linux distributions boot with many daemons configured to automatically start at boot. Some of these daemons are critical to the overall function of the system.

When implementing a new Linux system, whether as a server or as a workstation, it is wise to turn off all the daemons that are not needed. Running unnecessary daemons consumes system resources, such as memory and CPU time. More seriously, unnecessary daemons can also open up gaping security holes. Be aware of which system services are running. If the service is needed, keep it. If not, get rid of it!

How Linux Processes Are Loaded

All Linux processes are loaded by one single process—either the legacy `SysVinit` (`init`) or the newer `systemd`, depending on the distribution—that is started by the Linux kernel when the system boots. Understand that any process running on a Linux system can launch additional processes. The process that launched the new process is called the *parent process*. The new process itself is called the *child process*. (For purposes of this discussion, `systemd` also means `init`.) This parent/child relationship constitutes the *heredity* of Linux processes, as shown in Figure 9-2.

In Figure 9-2, the grandparent process spawned three child processes. Each of these three child processes then spawned child processes of their own.

For any process on a Linux system, you need to be able to uniquely identify it as well as its heredity. Whenever a process is created on a Linux system, it is assigned two resources:

- **Process ID (`PID`) number** This is a number assigned to each process that uniquely identifies it on the system.
- **Parent process ID (`PPID`) number** This is the `PID` of the process's parent process (that is, the process that spawned it).

By assigning these two numbers to each process, you can track the heredity of any process through the system. The Linux kernel uses the process table to keep track of the processes running on the system. The process table is maintained in memory by

Figure 9-2 Generations of processes

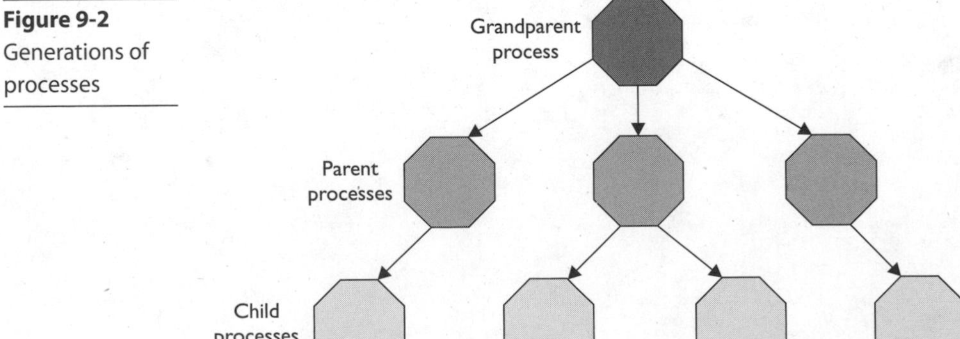

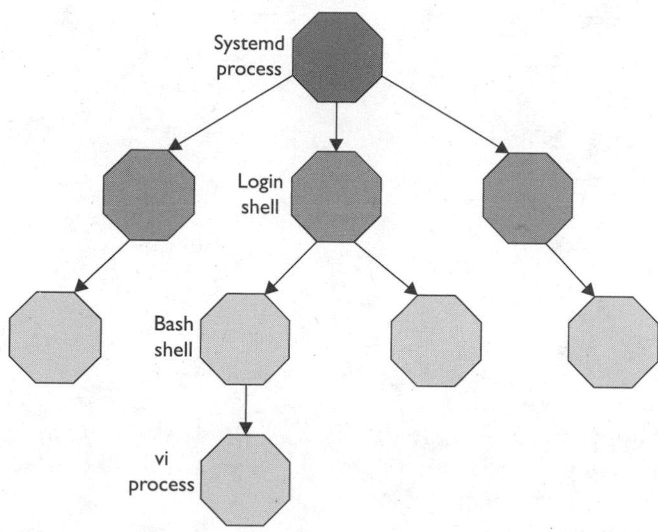

Figure 9-3 The `systemd` process as the grandparent of all other processes

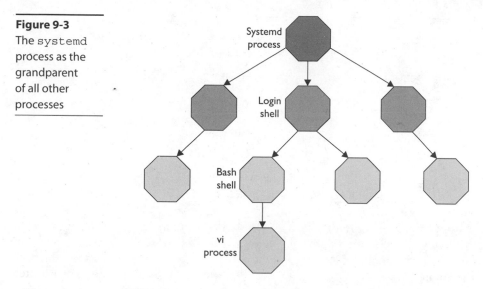

the operating system to facilitate switching between processes, scheduling processes, and prioritizing processes. Each entry in the table contains information about one specific running process, such as the process name, the state of the process, the priority of the process, and the memory addresses used by the process.

NOTE Older distributions still use `SysVinit` or `init`. Modern Linux releases have migrated to `systemd`, which is the recommended choice today for security and performance.

The kernel loads the `systemd` process automatically during bootup. The `systemd` process then launches child processes, such as a login shell, that in turn launch other processes, such as that used by the `vi` utility, as shown in Figure 9-3.

New processes are assigned the next highest available `PID` numbers, and `systemd` is always assigned a `PID` of `1`. This brings up an interesting point. If `systemd` is the first process from which all other processes descend, what then is its `PPID`? Does it even have one? Actually, it does. Because the `systemd` process is launched directly by the Linux kernel (which always has a `PID` of `0`), the `PPID` of the `systemd` process is always `0`. This is shown in Figure 9-4.

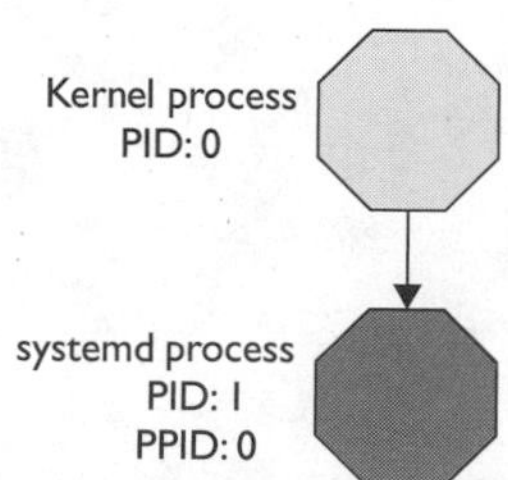

Figure 9-4 The `PPID` of the `systemd` process

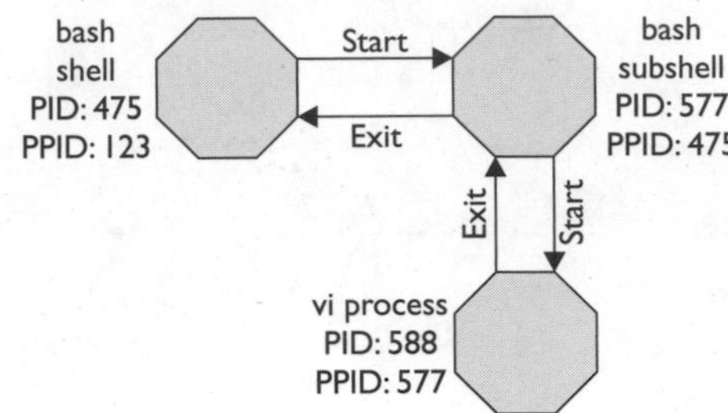

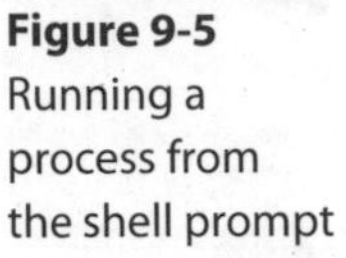
Figure 9-5 Running a process from the shell prompt

The `systemd` process is responsible for launching all system processes that are configured to automatically start on bootup. It also creates a login shell that is used for login.

This brings up an important point. Notice back in Figure 9-3 a second Bash shell beneath the login shell. One might ask, "Couldn't I just run `vi` from within the login shell? Do I have to launch a second Bash shell?" Actually, in this figure, `vi` was launched from the login shell. Why, then, does the figure show a second shell between the `vi` process and the login shell? Because any time a user runs a command from within any shell, a *subshell* is created that the process runs within. The subshell is a separate process in and of itself and has its own `PID` assigned. The `PPID` of the subshell is the `PID` of the shell where the command was entered.

The subshell process remains active for as long as the command is in use. The process for the command runs within the subshell and is assigned its own `PID`. The `PPID` of the command's process is, of course, the `PID` of the subshell it is running within. When the command process is complete and has exited, the subshell is terminated and control is returned to the original shell session. This process of creating a new subshell and running the command process within it is called *forking*.

For example, in Figure 9-5, the user has issued the `vi` command at the shell prompt of a Bash shell. A new subshell is created and the `vi` process is run within it. When the user exits `vi`, the subshell is destroyed and control is returned to the original shell instance.

Managing Processes

Managing running processes is one of the key tasks performed on Linux systems. This section covers the following topics:

- Starting system processes
- Viewing running processes
- Prioritizing processes
- Managing foreground and background processes
- Ending a running process
- Keeping a process running after logout

Starting System Processes

There are two basic ways to start a process on a Linux system. For a user process, simply enter the command or script name at the shell prompt. For example, to run the vi program, simply enter vi at the shell prompt. When done, the vi process is created, as shown here:

```
cgreer@openSUSE:~> ps -a
 PID TTY          TIME CMD
3719 pts/1    00:00:00 vi
3729 pts/0    00:00:00 ps
```

For system processes, however, use either an `init` *script* or a service *file*, depending on whether the distribution uses `init` or `systemd`. System services manage processes that start the web server (HTTPD), File Transfer Protocol (FTP) server, Secure Shell (SSH) server, Domain Name System (DNS) server, and so on.

These scripts are stored in a specific directory, and the location depends on the Linux distribution (the details of which are discussed in Chapter 11). For example, for an `init`-based system, the actual scripts reside in the `/etc/init.d/` directory. Whenever a service is installed on a system, a corresponding `init` script is automatically installed into the directory. Once there, an administrator can execute any script by simply running it from the command prompt. The syntax is as follows:

```
/etc/init.d/<script_name> start | stop | restart
```

For example, to enable file and print services with Microsoft Windows systems, start Samba by entering `/etc/init.d/smb start` at the shell prompt. To stop it, enter `/etc/init.d/smb stop`. To restart it, enter `/etc/init.d/smb restart`.

If the Linux distribution uses `systemd` instead of `init`, then the system services are managed using service files, which have a `.service` extension. Use the `systemctl` command at the shell prompt to start, stop, restart, or check the status of services on the system:

- To start a service, enter `systemctl start <service_name>`
- To stop a service, enter `systemctl stop <service_name>`
- To restart a service, enter `systemctl restart <service_name>`
- To view the status of a service, enter `systemctl status <service_name>`

For example, to enable the `sshd` daemon on a distribution that uses `systemd`, enter `systemctl start sshd` at the shell prompt.

Linux administrators must become more familiar with `systemd` and the `systemctl` commands. The `systemd` utility is superior to `SysVinit` or `init` because it efficiently handles dependencies and performs parallel booting, thus getting systems up and running significantly faster.

EXAM TIP It is important to know a few `systemd` commands like `systemctl` and their subcommands for the exam.

Viewing Running Processes

This section covers how to view running processes on the system and details the following tools:

- Using `top` and `htop`
- Using `ps`
- Using `pgrep` and `pidof`

Using top and htop

Linux provides a wide variety of tools to view running processes on the system. Two popular utilities include the `top` and `htop` programs. These list processes, and update process status every three seconds, ranking by CPU utilization. Run `top` by simply entering `top` at the shell prompt. When done, the interface shown in Figure 9-6 is displayed.

In Figure 9-6, notice that `top` displays some of the running processes, one on each line. The `top` report is helpful for detecting high CPU utilization and high run queues. The following columns are used to display information about each process:

- **PID** The process ID of the process.
- **USER** The name of the user who owns the process.

```
root@openSUSE:~
File  Edit  View  Search  Terminal  Help
top - 17:52:43 up 11 min,  3 users,  load average: 0.74, 0.72, 0.43
Tasks: 144 total,   2 running, 142 sleeping,   0 stopped,   0 zombie
%Cpu(s):  4.7 us,  1.7 sy,  0.0 ni, 93.7 id,  0.0 wa,  0.0 hi,  0.0 si,  0.0 st
KiB Mem:   1544012 total,   613836 used,   930176 free,    27880 buffers
KiB Swap:  2103292 total,        0 used,  2103292 free,   248316 cached

  PID USER      PR  NI    VIRT    RES    SHR S  %CPU  %MEM     TIME+ COMMAND
  634 root      20   0   68800  17724   7120 S 6.960 1.148   0:26.67 Xorg
 3476 rtracy    20   0  614076 147864  38720 S 4.308 9.577   0:28.47 gnome-she+
 3734 rtracy    20   0  246640  16812  12596 S 0.663 1.089   0:01.25 gnome-ter+
   31 root      20   0       0      0      0 S 0.331 0.000   0:03.49 kworker/1+
 3593 rtracy    20   0   34452  13248  11044 S 0.331 0.858   0:01.04 vmtoolsd
 3886 root      20   0    3636   1236    892 R 0.331 0.080   0:00.33 top
    1 root      20   0    5928   3236   2208 S 0.000 0.210   0:05.99 systemd
    2 root      20   0       0      0      0 S 0.000 0.000   0:00.01 kthreadd
    3 root      20   0       0      0      0 S 0.000 0.000   0:00.05 ksoftirqd+
    5 root       0 -20       0      0      0 S 0.000 0.000   0:00.00 kworker/0+
    6 root      20   0       0      0      0 S 0.000 0.000   0:00.85 kworker/u+
    7 root      rt   0       0      0      0 S 0.000 0.000   0:00.05 migration+
    8 root      -2   0       0      0      0 S 0.000 0.000   0:00.41 rcuc/0
    9 root      -2   0       0      0      0 S 0.000 0.000   0:00.00 rcub/0
   10 root      20   0       0      0      0 S 0.000 0.000   0:01.23 rcu_preem+
   11 root      20   0       0      0      0 S 0.000 0.000   0:00.00 rcu_bh
   12 root      20   0       0      0      0 S 0.000 0.000   0:00.00 rcu_sched
   13 root      rt   0       0      0      0 S 0.000 0.000   0:00.01 watchdog/0
   14 root      rt   0       0      0      0 S 0.000 0.000   0:00.02 watchdog/1
   15 root      -2   0       0      0      0 S 0.000 0.000   0:00.38 rcuc/1
```

Figure 9-6 Using `top` to view running processes

- **PR** The priority assigned to the process.
- **NI** The `nice` value of the process (`nice` is discussed later in the chapter).
- **VIRT** The amount of virtual memory used by the process.
- **RES** The amount of physical RAM the process is using (its resident size) in kilobytes.
- **SHR** The amount of shared memory used by the process.
- **S** The status of the process. Possible values include the following:
  - **D** Uninterruptible sleep
  - **R** Running
  - **S** Sleeping
  - **T** Traced or stopped
  - **Z** Zombie

NOTE A zombie process has completed execution, but *after* its parent has died, thus being unable to cleanly exit. The zombie eventually clears up on its own, as `systemd` becomes the new parent. If that fails, you can attempt to kill the zombie or wait until the next scheduled reboot. The name sounds scary, but zombies are harmless to the system, only tying up a process slot.

- **%CPU** The percentage of CPU time used by the process.
- **%MEM** The percentage of available physical RAM used by the process.
- **TIME+** The total amount of CPU time the process has consumed since being started.
- **COMMAND** The name of the command that was entered to start the process.

You can sort `top` and `htop` output not only by the default CPU utilization, but also by memory utilization (by pressing the `M` key), by `PID` (by pressing the `N` key), or back to %CPU (by pressing the `P` key). Also, to see more processes, press the `Up Arrow` and `Down Arrow` keys to scroll through the many processes. The `Left Arrow` and `Right Arrow` keys display more details about the running processes, such as their full path.

The `htop` command has additional features such as color coding, mouse scrolling to maneuver through process output, and function keys that provide help, search, and other sorting features. Figure 9-7 shows a sample of `htop` output.

Pressing the **?** key while `top` or `htop` is running displays the help screen, which outputs the keystrokes required to sort by a particular category. The `top` help screen is shown in Figure 9-8. To learn more about `top` and `htop`, review their man pages.

Using `ps`

The `ps` utility displays running processes on the system. Unlike `top`, which displays processes dynamically, `ps` displays a *snapshot* of the current processes running.

```
  CPU[||                         1.4%]   Tasks: 106, 279 thr; 1 running
  Mem[|||||||||||||||||||||620M/1.94G]   Load average: 0.00 0.00 0.00
  Swp[                         0K/976M]  Uptime: 00:43:00

    PID△USER      PRI  NI  VIRT   RES   SHR S CPU% MEM%   TIME+  Command
      1 root       20   0  176M 12684  7808 S  0.0  0.6  0:01.32 /sbin/init
    235 root       20   0 48780 19864 18216 S  0.0  1.0  0:00.24 /lib/systemd/sys
    259 root       20   0 23400  6560  4096 S  0.0  0.3  0:00.06 /lib/systemd/sys
    452 systemd-t  20   0 88512  6204  5476 S  0.0  0.3  0:00.04 /lib/systemd/sys
    456 systemd-t  20   0 88512  6204  5476 S  0.0  0.3  0:00.00 /lib/systemd/sys
    464 root       20   0  230M  7208  6480 S  0.0  0.4  0:00.04 /usr/libexec/acc
    466 avahi      20   0  7272  3488  3140 S  0.0  0.2  0:00.04 avahi-daemon: ru
    467 root       20   0  6684  2724  2516 S  0.0  0.1  0:00.00 /usr/sbin/cron -
    468 messagebu  20   0  9828  6016  3976 S  0.0  0.3  0:00.42 /usr/bin/dbus-da
    469 root       20   0  248M 16504 14220 S  0.0  0.8  0:00.26 /usr/sbin/Networ
    472 root       20   0  230M  9796  6644 S  0.0  0.5  0:00.65 /usr/libexec/pol
    473 root       20   0  215M  4308  3344 S  0.0  0.2  0:00.04 /usr/sbin/rsyslo
    475 root       20   0  230M  7208  6480 S  0.0  0.4  0:00.01 /usr/libexec/acc
    477 root       20   0  230M  9796  6644 S  0.0  0.5  0:00.00 /usr/libexec/pol
    481 root       20   0  227M  6160  5612 S  0.0  0.3  0:00.00 /usr/libexec/swi
    483 root       20   0  215M  4308  3344 S  0.0  0.2  0:00.01 /usr/sbin/rsyslo
    484 root       20   0  215M  4308  3344 S  0.0  0.2  0:00.00 /usr/sbin/rsyslo
    485 root       20   0 22132  7384  6448 S  0.0  0.4  0:00.09 /lib/systemd/sys
    486 root       20   0  215M  4308  3344 S  0.0  0.2  0:00.01 /usr/sbin/rsyslo
    488 root       20   0  384M 14524 10372 S  0.0  0.7  0:00.10 /usr/libexec/udi
F1Help  F2Setup  F3SearchF4FilterF5Tree  F6SortByF7Nice -F8Nice +F9Kill  F10Quit
```

Figure 9-7 Using `htop` to view running processes

```
root@openSUSE:~
File  Edit  View  Search  Terminal  Help
Help for Interactive Commands - procps-ng version 3.3.8
Window 1:Def: Cumulative mode Off.  System: Delay 3.0 secs; Secure mode Off.

  Z,B,E,e   Global: 'Z' colors; 'B' bold; 'E'/'e' summary/task memory scale
  l,t,m     Toggle Summary: 'l' load avg; 't' task/cpu stats; 'm' memory info
  0,1,2,3,I Toggle: '0' zeros; '1/2/3' cpus or numa node views; 'I' Irix mode
  f,F,X     Fields: 'f'/'F' add/remove/order/sort; 'X' increase fixed-width

  L,&,<,> . Locate: 'L'/'&' find/again; Move sort column: '<'/'>' left/right
  R,H,V,J . Toggle: 'R' Sort; 'H' Threads; 'V' Forest view; 'J' Num justify
  c,i,S,j . Toggle: 'c' Cmd name/line; 'i' Idle; 'S' Time; 'j' Str justify
  x,y     . Toggle highlights: 'x' sort field; 'y' running tasks
  z,b     . Toggle: 'z' color/mono; 'b' bold/reverse (only if 'x' or 'y')
  u,U,o,O . Filter by: 'u'/'U' effective/any user; 'o'/'O' other criteria
  n,#,^O  . Set: 'n'/'#' max tasks displayed; Show: Ctrl+'O' other filter(s)
  C,...   . Toggle scroll coordinates msg for: up,down,left,right,home,end

  k,r       Manipulate tasks: 'k' kill; 'r' renice
  d or s    Set update interval
  W,Y       Write configuration file 'W'; Inspect other output 'Y'
  q         Quit
          ( commands shown with '.' require a visible task display window )
Press 'h' or '?' for help with Windows,
Type 'q' or <Esc> to continue
```

Figure 9-8 Viewing the `top` help screen

Entering ps displays the processes associated with the current shell, as shown here:

```
openSUSE:~ $ ps
 PID TTY          TIME CMD
3947 pts/0    00:00:00 bash
3994 pts/0    00:00:00 ps
```

In this example, the following processes are displayed by ps:

- **bash** The current Bash shell session.
- **ps** Because ps is in use to list current processes, its process is also listed.

Notice that the following information is displayed by default:

- **PID** The process ID of the process
- **TTY** The name of the terminal session (shell) that the process is running within
- **TIME** The amount of CPU time used by the process
- **CMD** The name of the command that was entered to create the process

To see all processes running on the system, use the -e option with ps. Here is an example:

```
openSUSE:~ $ ps -e
 PID TTY          TIME CMD
   1 ?        00:00:06 systemd
   2 ?        00:00:00 kthreadd
   3 ?        00:00:00 ksoftirqd/0
   5 ?        00:00:00 kworker/0:0H
   7 ?        00:00:00 migration/0
   8 ?        00:00:00 rcuc/0
   9 ?        00:00:00 rcub/0
  10 ?        00:00:01 rcu_preempt
  11 ?        00:00:00 rcu_bh
  12 ?        00:00:00 rcu_sched
  13 ?        00:00:00 watchdog/0
  14 ?        00:00:00 watchdog/1...
```

As shown in this example, the -e option results in many more processes being displayed by the ps command. Also notice that most of the processes shown have a question mark (?) in the TTY column. This indicates the process is a system process. Remember that system processes (daemons) are loaded by the systemd process at startup and therefore are not associated with any shell. Because of this, a ? is displayed in the TTY column in the output of ps.

The ps command has other options displayed within the ps(1) man page. For example, the -f option will provide "full" detail. Combined with -e, as shown here, it will result in a "full" listing of every process running on the system:

```
openSUSE:~ $ ps -ef
UID          PID  PPID  C STIME TTY          TIME CMD
root           1     0  0 17:41 ?        00:00:06 /sbin/init showopts
root           2     0  0 17:41 ?        00:00:00 [kthreadd]
root           3     2  0 17:41 ?        00:00:00 [ksoftirqd/0]
```

```
root          5     2  0 17:41 ?           00:00:00 [kworker/0:0H]
root          7     2  0 17:41 ?           00:00:00 [migration/0]
root          8     2  0 17:41 ?           00:00:00 [rcuc/0]
root          9     2  0 17:41 ?           00:00:00 [rcub/0]
root         10     2  0 17:41 ?           00:00:01 [rcu_preempt]
root         11     2  0 17:41 ?           00:00:00 [rcu_bh]
root         12     2  0 17:41 ?           00:00:00 [rcu_sched]
root         13     2  0 17:41 ?           00:00:00 [watchdog/0]
root         14     2  0 17:41 ?           00:00:00 [watchdog/1]...
```

The `-f` option displays additional information, including the following:

- **UID** The user ID of the process's owner
- **PPID** The `PID` of the process's parent process
- **C** The amount of processor time utilized by the process
- **STIME** The time that the process started

For further detail, use the `-l` option with the `ps` command. The `-l` option displays the long format of the `ps` output. Here is an example combined with `-e` and `-f`:

```
openSUSE:~ $ ps -efl
F S UID         PID  PPID  C PRI  NI ADDR SZ WCHAN  STIME TTY          TIME CMD
1 S root          2     0  0  80   0 -     0 kthrea 11:09 ?        00:00:00 [kth]
1 S root          3     2  0 -40   - -     0 migrat 11:09 ?        00:00:00 [mig]
1 S root          4     2  0  80   0 -     0 run_ks 11:09 ?        00:00:00 [kso]
5 S root          5     2  0 -40   - -     0 watchd 11:09 ?        00:00:00 [wat]
1 S root          6     2  0 -40   - -     0 migrat 11:09 ?        00:00:00 [mig]
1 S root          7     2  0  80   0 -     0 run_ks 11:09 ?        00:00:00 [kso]
5 S root          8     2  0 -40   - -     0 watchd 11:09 ?        00:00:00 [wat]
1 S root          9     2  0  80   0 -     0 worker 11:09 ?        00:00:00 [eve]
1 S root         10     2  0  80   0 -     0 worker 11:09 ?        00:00:00 [eve]
1 S root         11     2  0  80   0 -     0 worker 11:09 ?        00:00:00 [net]
...
```

With the `-l` option, the user can view the following information about processes running on the system:

- **F** The flags associated with the process. This column uses the following codes:
  - **1** Forked, but didn't execute
  - **4** Used root privileges
- **S** The state of the process. This column uses the following codes:
  - **D** Uninterruptible sleep
  - **R** Running
  - **S** Interruptible sleep
  - **T** Stopped or traced
  - **Z** Zombie
- **PRI** The priority of the process.
- **NI** The `nice` value of the process.

- **ADDR** The memory address of the process.
- **SZ** The size of the process.
- **WCHAN** The name of the kernel function in which the process is sleeping. A dash (–) in this column means the process is currently running.

EXAM TIP Knowledge of various column outputs for `ps` is not critical for the CompTIA Linux+ exam. For example, you don't need to know that `-l` will list process states and `-f` will not. Just know that `ps` lists `PIDs` and process names, and `-e` lists every process.

The `ps` command has two flavors: `System V` and `BSD`. We have demonstrated `System V` examples. `BSD` examples do not use a leading dash (`-`). For example, to list all processes in `BSD` style, use the command `ps aux` instead of `ps -elf`. Running `ps aux` displays additional details such as %CPU and %MEM utilization, which is helpful for performance tuning and troubleshooting, as shown in this snippet:

```
openSUSE:~ $ ps aux
USER    PID %CPU %MEM     VSZ  RSS TTY    STAT START   TIME COMMAND
ian    1823  0.0  0.2 208644 5920 tty2   Ssl+ 17:47   0:00 /usr/lib/gdm/gdm-x
ian    1825  0.1  5.4 715688 1480 tty2   Sl+  17:47   0:11 /usr/bin/X vt2
ian    1835  0.0  0.7 420420 1496 tty2   Sl+  17:47   0:00 /usr/lib/gnome
```

Now let's explore how to find the process ID if we know the process name.

Using `pgrep` and `pidof`

The `ps` command is very useful for viewing process information. However, sometimes the output of `ps` can be overwhelming, especially when just looking for a specific process. For example, to view just the `bash` processes running, run the following:

```
openSUSE:~ $ ps -e | grep bash
3947 pts/0    00:00:00 bash
3998 pts/1    00:00:00 bash
```

Another option to do the same is to use either the `pgrep` command or `pidof` command. As its name implies, `pgrep` combines the functionality of `ps` and `grep` into a single utility. When you run `pgrep` or `pidof`, you specify certain selection criteria to view. Then the command searches through all the currently running processes and outputs a list of process IDs that match the criteria specified, as shown here:

```
openSUSE:~ $ pgrep bash
3947
3998
openSUSE:~ $ pidof bash
3947 3998
```

Use the following options with `pgrep` to display more details of processes:

- **-l** Lists the process name and process ID
- **-u <user_name>** Matches on the specified process owner

The pgrep command lists only the PID of the matching processes by default. To view the name of the process as well as its PID, use the -l option. For example, to view a list of all processes owned by the cgreer user, use the following command:

```
openSUSE:~ $ pgrep -l -u cgreer
3947 bash
3998 bash
```

Now that you have learned how to view which processes are running on a system with top/htop, ps, and pgrep/pidof, next you'll learn how to prioritize processes to help improve system performance.

Prioritizing Processes

Recall from the first part of this chapter that Linux is a multitasking operating system. It rotates CPU time between each process running on the system, creating the illusion that all of the processes are running concurrently.

To improve Linux system performance, you can specify a priority level for each process. Doing so determines how much CPU time a given process gets in relation to other processes on the system.

By default, Linux tries to equalize the amount of CPU time given to all processes on the system. However, sometimes you may want to adjust the priority assigned to a process. Depending on how the system is deployed, a particular process may be set to have a higher priority than other processes. This can be done using several Linux utilities. In this section, we review the following topics:

- Setting priorities with nice
- Changing priorities with renice

Setting Priorities with nice

The nice utility can be used on Linux to launch a program with a different priority level. Recall from our previous discussion of top and ps that each process running on the system has a PR value and NI value associated with it, as shown in Figure 9-9.

The PR value is the process's kernel priority. The *higher* the number, the *lower* the priority of the process. The lower the number, the higher the priority of the process. The NI value is the nice value of the process, from the adage "nice guys finish last." The nice value is factored into the kernel calculations that determine the priority of the process. The nice value for any Linux process ranges between -20 and +19. The *lower* the nice value, the *higher* the priority of the process.

You cannot directly manipulate the priority of a process, but you can manipulate the process's nice value. The easiest way to do this is to set the nice value when starting the command using the nice command. Any time a program starts, the default "niceness" is 0 (zero). But the default for starting a program with nice is 10. To set higher priorities (that is, negative niceness), you must be root. The syntax is nice -n <nice_level> <command>.

```
root@openSUSE:~
File  Edit  View  Search  Terminal  Help
top - 19:45:24 up  2:03,  4 users,  load average: 0.12, 0.04, 0.05
Tasks: 149 total,   2 running, 147 sleeping,   0 stopped,   0 zombie
%Cpu(s):  3.5 us,  1.3 sy,  0.0 ni, 95.2 id,  0.0 wa,  0.0 hi,  0.0 si,  0.0 st
KiB Mem:   1544012 total,   788312 used,   755700 free,    37736 buffers
KiB Swap:  2103292 total,        0 used,  2103292 free,   387936 cached

  PID USER      PR  NI    VIRT    RES    SHR S  %CPU  %MEM     TIME+ COMMAND
  634 root      20   0   68800  17724   7120 S 4.631 1.148   0:49.28 Xorg
 3476 rtracy    20   0  620012 154720  38864 S 3.639 10.02   1:32.26 gnome-she+
 3593 rtracy    20   0   34452  13248  11044 S 0.662 0.858   0:16.79 vmtoolsd
 4341 root      20   0    3636   1244    892 R 0.662 0.081   0:00.12 top
 3734 rtracy    20   0  246824  17044  12620 S 0.331 1.104   0:02.06 gnome-ter+
    1 root      20   0    5928   3236   2208 S 0.000 0.210   0:06.18 systemd
    2 root      20   0       0      0      0 S 0.000 0.000   0:00.01 kthreadd
    3 root      20   0       0      0      0 S 0.000 0.000   0:00.06 ksoftirqd+
    5 root       0 -20       0      0      0 S 0.000 0.000   0:00.00 kworker/0+
    7 root      rt   0       0      0      0 S 0.000 0.000   0:00.06 migration+
    8 root      -2   0       0      0      0 S 0.000 0.000   0:00.48 rcuc/0
    9 root      -2   0       0      0      0 S 0.000 0.000   0:00.00 rcub/0
   10 root      20   0       0      0      0 R 0.000 0.000   0:01.42 rcu_preem+
   11 root      20   0       0      0      0 S 0.000 0.000   0:00.00 rcu_bh
   12 root      20   0       0      0      0 S 0.000 0.000   0:00.00 rcu_sched
   13 root      rt   0       0      0      0 S 0.000 0.000   0:00.07 watchdog/0
   14 root      rt   0       0      0      0 S 0.000 0.000   0:00.09 watchdog/1
   15 root      -2   0       0      0      0 S 0.000 0.000   0:00.43 rcuc/1
   16 root      rt   0       0      0      0 S 0.000 0.000   0:00.09 migration+
   17 root      20   0       0      0      0 S 0.000 0.000   0:00.04 ksoftirqd+
```

Figure 9-9 Viewing `PR` and `NI` values

The following example shows launching various subshells with different priorities using `nice`:

```
openSUSE:~ $ nice bash
openSUSE:~ $ nice -n 19 bash
openSUSE:~ $ ps -o pid,pri,ni,cmd
 PID PRI   NI CMD
8279  19    0 bash
8389   9   10 bash
8470   0   19 bash
8511   0   19 ps -o pid,pri,ni,cmd
```

The `ps -o` option allows us to list the columns to view from `ps`. Notice that `PID 8389` runs at the default `nice` value of `10`, and `PID 8470` runs at `19`.

The `nice` command works great for modifying the `nice` value when running a command to start a process. But to change the `nice` value of a running command, you will use the `renice` command.

Changing Priorities with `renice`

Instead of having to kill a process and restart it with `nice` to set its `nice` value, use the `renice` command to adjust the `nice` value of a process that is currently running on the system. The syntax for using this command is `renice <nice_value> <PID>`.

For example, in the example in the previous section, the `PID` of a `bash` process is `8389` with a `nice` value of `10`. To adjust the priority of the `bash` process to a lower level without unloading the program, enter `renice 15 8389` at the shell prompt, as shown in this example:

```
openSUSE:~ $ renice 15 8389
8389: old priority 10, new priority 15
openSUSE:~ $ ps -o pid,pri,ni,cmd
 PID PRI   NI CMD
8279  19    0 bash
8389   4   15 bash
8470   0   19 bash
8511   0   19 ps -o pid,pri,ni,cmd
```

As this example shows, the `nice` value of the `PID 8389` process was increased from `10` to `15`. This caused the overall priority of the process to go from `9` to `4`, thus decreasing the process's overall priority level.

Only `root` can *decrease* `nice` values (that is, *raise* priority) with `renice`. For example, if you attempt to return the niceness of `PID 8470` back to `10`, you will not be allowed. But when you run with `root` privileges using `sudo` you then will be allowed, as shown here:

```
openSUSE:~ $ renice 10 8389
renice: failed to set priority for 8389 (process ID): Permission denied
openSUSE:~ $ sudo renice 10 8389
8389: old priority 15, new priority 10
```

Troubleshooting CPU Priorities with `nice` and `renice`

On a multiuser system, you may have one user that has a job that slows down the Linux system for all the other users because the user's job uses significant resources. Ask the user to start the job using the `nice` command to lower the priority. By *default* the niceness is set to `10`.

Over time you may find that the priority needs to be even lower. Use `renice` to adjust the job's `nice` value to `15`. It will take a little longer for the user to get their results, but you will have fewer complaining users because now they all can get their work done.

Let's now shift gears and talk about foreground and background processes.

EXAM TIP Make sure to understand `nice` and `renice` basics, such as how to use them, their defaults, and minimum and maximum settings.

Managing Foreground and Background Processes

In this section, we discuss running processes in the foreground and background. We'll address the following topics:

- Running processes in the background
- Switching processes between background and foreground

Running Processes in the Background

Recall from our earlier discussion of processes that when entering any command at the shell prompt, a subshell is created, and the process runs within it. As soon as the process exits, the subshell is destroyed. While the process is running, the `$` shell prompt is unavailable, so the user is unable to run another command until the current process completes. For example, the `sleep` command simply "sleeps" in the foreground for several seconds. Here's an example:

```
openSUSE:~ $ sleep 20     # wait 20 seconds before returning prompt
                        < waits for 20 seconds >
openSUSE:~ $
```

Programs by default run in the foreground, whether they are text-based shell programs or graphical programs. However, it is possible to run a program in the background. These programs launch normally, but control is immediately returned to the shell. Then you can use the shell to launch other programs.

To run a program in the background, simply append an ampersand (`&`) character to the command. This tells the shell to run the program in the background. So, let's use `sleep` again, but for a much longer period this time. The following command will still run, but the end user is allowed to continue working:

```
openSUSE:~ $ sleep 216000 &                # sleep for 60 hours
[1]  9148
          < prompt returns immediately >
openSUSE:~ $
```

Notice that two values are displayed on the screen after the process was run in the background. The first value, `[1]`, is the job ID (JID) assigned to the background job, and the second value, `9148`, is the process ID (`PID`) of the process. The JID is unique to the shell it runs in; the `PID` is unique to the computer. To view all background jobs running on the system, enter `jobs` at the shell prompt:

```
cgreer@openSUSE:~> jobs
[1]+  Running                              sleep 216000 &
```

In this example, the output of the `jobs` command displays the status of the job as well as the name of the command that created the background job. To see the process ID, use the `ps` command:

```
cgreer@openSUSE:~> ps
 PID TTY          TIME CMD
3947 pts/0    00:00:00 bash
9148 pts/0    00:00:00 sleep
9149 pts/0    00:00:00 ps
```

Switching Processes Between Background and Foreground

Just because a process was started in the background does not mean it has to stay there. To switch processes between foreground and background, use the following commands:

- **`fg`** Moves a background process to the foreground
- **`bg`** Moves a foreground process to the background

To use the `bg` utility, first put the foreground job to sleep by pressing CTRL-Z. This pauses the process and then assigns a job ID to it. Next, enter `bg` to move the process to the background, where it will continue running from where it left off.

In the following example, the `sleep` program is loaded into the foreground and then stopped by using CTRL-Z, where it is assigned a job ID of `1`. It is then sent to the background using the `bg` command. Finally, the job is returned to the foreground with the `fg` command.

```
cgreer@openSUSE:~> sleep 10000
CTRL-Z
[1]+  Stopped                 sleep 10000
cgreer@openSUSE:~> bg
[1]+ sleep 10000 &
cgreer@openSUSE:~> fg
sleep 10000
```

The `bg` and `fg` commands are shell commands; to learn more about these, read the `bash(1)` man page.

NOTE `Ctrl-z` is often shown as `^Z`. Control characters are not case sensitive, unlike most every other commands in Linux. There are other control characters; for example, `^C` will "cancel" a job, causing it to stop and quit, and `^D` means "done" or "end of input," to notify Linux that there is no further input.

Ending a Running Process

Up to now we have run, viewed, prioritized, and moved processes from background to foreground. The final topic we need to cover is how to end a process that is running on the system.

Normally, entering CTRL-C ends a running process. But if the job is running in the background, CTRL-C will not work. Also, processes sometimes hang and become difficult to close properly. In this section, we discuss how to kill such processes in the following ways:

- Using `kill` and `killall`
- Using `pkill`

Using `kill` and `killall`

The `kill` command is used to terminate a process using the process ID or job ID. The syntax for using `kill` is `kill -<signal> <PID>` or `kill -<signal> %<JID>`. The command `kill` is a misnomer because end users can also pause and resume jobs using `kill` by sending a specific kill signal to the process. There are 64 kill signals an end user can send to a process, but the CompTIA Linux+ exam focuses only on the following ones:

- **`SIGHUP`** This is `kill` signal 1. This signal restarts the process while keeping the same `PID`. This is useful for restarting a website after making changes to a configuration file.

- **`SIGINT`** This is `kill` signal 2. This signal sends a CTRL-C key sequence to the process.
- **`SIGKILL`** This is `kill` signal 9. This is a brute-force `kill` and should be used only as a last resort. If the process is hung badly, this option forces it to stop, but its child processes orphan and become zombies because the parent process isn't there to clean them up. If these are not removed, you can wait until the next scheduled reboot. Avoid using `SIGKILL` on databases, mail servers, and print servers because this could corrupt them.
- **`SIGTERM`** This is `kill` signal `15`, and the *default* signal. This signal tells the process to terminate gracefully, gently killing the child processes, and then the parent.

When using `kill`, you can use the signal name, such as `SIGTERM`, or the signal value, such as `15`. You can use `ps` to first identify the `PID` of the process before using `kill` to stop it. Here, the `sleep` process is running with a `PID` of `8312`:

```
openSUSE:~ # ps
 PID TTY          TIME CMD
8278 pts/0    00:00:00 su
8279 pts/0    00:00:00 bash
8312 pts/0    00:00:00 sleep
8313 pts/0    00:00:00 ps
openSUSE:~ # kill -SIGTERM 8312
openSUSE:~ #
```

Also, any of the following could be used to `kill`, or specifically terminate, our sleep process:

- `kill 8312`
- `kill -15 8312`
- `kill -TERM 8312`
- `kill -s TERM 8312`
- `kill -s 15 8312`
- `kill -s SIGTERM 8312`

The CompTIA Linux+ exam may show any of these forms, so they are listed here for your preparation. Again, using `SIGKILL` will work, but it is best to try gentler signals first. Only if these signals fail should you use the harsher `SIGKILL` signal. When experiencing a hung process that needs to be killed, use the following sequence:

1. Send a `SIGTERM`. Usually, this will fix the problem and allow the process to exit cleanly. If it doesn't, then go on to step 2.
2. Send a `SIGKILL`.

In addition to `kill`, you can also use `killall` to kill processes by name, which is more convenient than running `ps` or `pgrep` to determine the `PID` first and then running the `kill` command.

The `killall` command syntax is similar to the `kill` command syntax. For example, to kill the `sleep` process in the preceding example with `killall` instead of `kill`, simply run `killall -15 sleep`. This command sends the SIGTERM signal to the process named `sleep`. Again, `-15` is the default kill signal for `killall`, so `killall sleep` would also work.

NOTE If the end user is running multiple `sleep` processes, the `killall` command will terminate all of them.

To learn more about `kill(1)` and `killall(1)`, review the `kill(1)` and `killall(1)` man pages. These tools are very useful, such as using the `-u` option with `killall` to end processes owned by a specific user.

EXAM TIP If you use the `dd` command, sending kill signal `SIGUSR1` reports the `dd` progress status. Simply run `killall -10 dd` while `dd` is running and the user will be informed of how much data `dd` has transferred.

Using `pkill`

Like `killall`, the `pkill` command can also stop a running process by name. The `pkill` command is a cousin of the `pgrep` command reviewed earlier. In fact, they use exactly the same options and even share the same man page!

Again like `killall`, `pkill` will kill all processes that match the argument name. For example, to kill all running processes named `sleep` with the `SIGTERM` signal, execute `pkill -SIGTERM sleep` at the shell prompt. Again, since `SIGTERM` is the default, `pkill sleep` terminates the process in the same manner.

EXAM TIP For the Linux+ exam, make sure to know that the `top` utility may also be used to kill processes using the `k` key!

Keeping a Process Running After Logout

The last topic to address regarding process management is how to keep a process running after logging out from the system. As discussed, signals are sent to running processes to indicate that a system event has occurred and that the process needs to respond.

A commonly used signal is the hang-up signal, `SIGHUP`. When a user logs out of a terminal session, Linux sends a `SIGHUP` signal to all the programs associated with that terminal.

However, a process can also be told to ignore `SIGHUP` signals, which allows it to remain running even after the end user logs out! This is done by using the `nohup` utility to run the program. This causes the process created by the command to ignore all `SIGHUP` signals.

For example, suppose you are about to leave the office for the day and start a shell script called `updatemydb`, which runs for six hours. If you leave for home without logging out, an attacker could compromise your account; but, if you log out, `updatemydb` gets killed. What is the solution?

To allow the script to run and have the security of logging out, you can start the script with the `nohup` command. Just enter `nohup updatemydb &` at the shell prompt and then log out. If the command generates output that is usually sent to the stdout, `nohup` will redirect the output to the `~/nohup.out` file.

It is important to note that a command run under `nohup` is only immune to `SIGHUP` signals. All other kill signals still work. For example, terminating the program using the `SIGTERM` signal using the `kill` command will be successful.

You can practice working with Linux processes in Exercise 9-1.

Exercise 9-1: Working with Linux Processes

In this exercise, practice using shell commands to manage processes running on the system. Perform this exercise using the virtual machine provided online.

VIDEO Please watch the Exercise 9-1 video for a demonstration on how to perform this task.

Complete the following steps:

1. Boot the Linux system and log in as a standard user.
2. Open a terminal session.
3. Switch to the root user account by entering **`su -`** and provide the password.
4. Practice starting system processes by doing the following:
   a. At the shell prompt, enter the **`systemctl status atd`** command. What's the status of the `at` daemon? (For most distributions, the `atd` daemon is not configured to run by default.)
   b. Start the `atd` daemon by entering **`systemctl start atd`** at the shell prompt.
   c. Enter **`systemctl status atd`** again at the shell prompt. The `atd` service should now be shown as running.
5. Practice using the `top` utility by following these steps:
   a. Enter **`top`** at the shell prompt.
   b. View the running processes.
   c. Press **`h`** to access the `top` help screen. Which keystroke will sort the display by CPU stats?
   d. Press **`p`** to sort the display by CPU stats. Which processes are using the most CPU time on the system?

e. Press **m** to sort the display by memory usage. Which processes are using the most memory?
f. Add columns by pressing **f**.
g. Add the PPID column to the display by pressing **b** and then the **Spacebar**. Note that the PPID of each process is added to the display.
h. Exit top by pressing **q**.

6. Practice using the ps utility to view processes by doing the following procedure:
   a. Enter **ps** at the shell prompt. What processes are associated with the current shell session?
   b. View all running processes on the system by entering **ps -ef | more** at the shell prompt.
   c. Press the **Spacebar** until the atd service comes into view. What username does atd run under? (On most distributions, it should run under the at user.)
   d. Enter **ps -el | less** at the shell prompt.
   e. Locate the Status (S) column.
   f. Press the **Spacebar** and look for the atd service. What is the status of the service? (Because it isn't being used at the moment, it's probably sleeping.)
7. Practice managing process priorities by completing the following steps:
   a. Enter **top** at the shell prompt.
   b. What are the priority (PR) and nice (NI) values associated with the top process? (For most distributions, these values should be 16 and 0, respectively.)
   c. Press **q** to stop the top process.
   d. Enter **nice -n -20 top** at the shell prompt.
   Now what are the PR and NI values for the top process?
   e. Note the PID for the top process.
   f. Open a new terminal window and use **su** to switch to the root user.
   g. Adjust the nice value of the top process while it's running by entering **renice 1 <top_PID>** at the shell prompt.
   h. Switch back to the first terminal session where top is running. What are its PR and NI values now?
   i. Press **q** to exit top.
8. Practice switching processes between the foreground and the background by performing the following procedure:
   a. Load top again by entering **top** at the shell prompt.
   b. In the terminal where top is running, press CTRL-Z.
   c. Note the background job ID number assigned to the process.

d. Enter **bg %<background_job_ID>** at the shell prompt.
   The output from top disappears while the process runs in the background.

e. Press CTRL-C.

f. Enter **fg %<background_job_ID>** at the shell prompt.
   The output from top reappears as the process now runs in the foreground.

9. Practice killing processes by completing the following steps:

   a. Ensure that top is still running.

   b. Switch to the other terminal session where logged in as root.

   c. Enter **ps -e | grep top** at the shell prompt.

   d. Note the PID of the top process.

   e. Enter **kill -SIGTERM <top_PID>** at the shell prompt.

   f. Switch back to the terminal session where top was running. Verify that top has exited.

   g. Load **top** again at the shell prompt.

   h. Switch back to the other terminal session where logged in as root.

   i. Kill the top process by entering the **killall -15 top** command.

   j. Switch back to the first terminal window and verify that top has exited.

10. Exit out of top by pressing **Esc** and then exit out of the screen by entering **exit**.

Scheduling Jobs

There are many occasions when a process needs to run automatically without your intervention. Backups are a good example. One key problem with backups is that people forget to do them! One of the worst things you can do in the backup strategy is to rely on yourself to remember to run them.

Instead, configure the Linux system to run programs automatically. This removes the human element from the equation and ensures that the specified programs execute regularly and on time. Three key utilities are used to schedule processes to run in the future. We'll discuss the following topics in this section:

- Using the at daemon
- Using the cron daemon
- Using systemd timers

Using the at Daemon

Using the at utility is a great way to schedule a process. The at service uses the atd system daemon, which runs in the background and monitors the time and when to run at jobs. Most Linux distributions install this service during the basic installation of the system. If not, it may need to be installed manually with a package manager like `rpm`, `dpkg`, `yum`, `apt-get`, and so on.

To check the status of `at`, run the following command:

```
Phx:bigphil # systemctl status atd.service
```

To start that `atd` daemon, run the following as `root`:

```
Phx:bigphil # systemctl start atd.service
```

To ensure that `atd` starts at boot time, run the following as `root`:

```
Phx:bigphil # systemctl enable atd.service
```

Next, you need to specify which users can and cannot create `at` jobs. You can do so by editing the following files:

- **`/etc/at.allow`** Users listed in this file are allowed to create `at` jobs.
- **`/etc/at.deny`** Users listed in this file are not allowed to create `at` jobs.

NOTE Because the `atd` service checks the `/etc/at.allow` file first, if an end user is listed in both `/etc/at.allow` and `/etc/at.deny`, they will be allowed to use `at`!

To use `at` to schedule jobs, complete the following steps:

1. At the shell prompt, enter the following:

   ```
   Phx:tallphil # at time
   ```

   The `at` daemon is very flexible as to how to specify the *`time`* value for the command. Observe the syntax shown in Table 9-2.

   After running the at command, the `at>` prompt is displayed, as shown here:

   ```
   Phx:tallphil # at now +10 minutes
   warning: commands will be executed using /bin/sh
   at>
   ```

2. At the `at>` prompt, you then enter the command(s) to run at the scheduled time. If the commands normally display output on the screen, an e-mail of the output is sent to your account.

   Alternatively, you can also redirect output to a file using > or >>. Here's an example:

   ```
   Phx:tallphil # at now +10 minutes
   warning: commands will be executed using /bin/sh
   at> updatedb_script > $HOME/outfile
   ```

3. Press ENTER to add additional commands. To run multiple commands within the same job, each command should be on its own line.

Type of Reference	Syntax	Description
Fixed	`HH:MM`	Specifies the exact hour and minute when the commands should run. The `at` daemon assumes that the hour/minute specified is today unless that time has already passed; then it assumes tomorrow. Add `am` or `pm` to the value to specify morning or afternoon, respectively.
	`noon`	Specifies that a command run at 12:00 P.M.
	`midnight`	Specifies that a command run at 12:00 A.M.
	`teatime`	Specifies that a command run at 4:00 P.M.
	`MMDDYY` or `MM/DD/YY` or `MM.DD.YY`	Specifies the exact month, date, and year when a command is to run.
	`HH:MM MMDDYY`	Specifies the exact month, date, year, and time when a command is to run.
Relative	`now`	Specifies that the command run immediately.

	`now + value`	Specifies that the command run at a certain time in the future. For example:
		`now +5 minutes`
		`now +3 days`

	`today`	Specifies that the command run today. For example: `2 pm today`
	`tomorrow`	Specifies that the command be run tomorrow. For example: `2 pm tomorrow`

Table 9-2 The `at` Command Time Syntax Options

4. When done entering commands, press CTRL-D to see `<EOT>`, and the `at>` prompt will disappear, the job will be scheduled, and a job number will be assigned, as shown here:

```
Phx:tallphil # at now +10 minutes
warning: commands will be executed using /bin/sh
at> updatedb_script > $HOME/outfile
at> <EOT>
job 3 at 2025-04-02 08:57
Phx:tallphil #
```

Once you have configured the schedule, you can use the `atq` command to view a list of pending `at` jobs. Output similar to the following is shown:

```
Phx:tallphil # atq
3       2025-04-02 08:57 a root
```

As a regular user, the `atq` command displays only the jobs associated with the current user account. As root, `atq` displays all pending jobs for all users. To remove a pending job from the list, use the `atrm <job_number>` command.

NOTE Another utility related to `at` is `batch`. The `batch` command is not tested on the CompTIA Linux+ exam but is a nice way to schedule a job. Instead of scheduling a specific time, the `batch` utility waits for low system load and then starts the job.

In addition to using the `at` daemon, you can use the `cron` daemon to schedule *repeatable* jobs (such as nightly backups or database updates), as discussed next.

Using the `cron` Daemon

The `at` daemon is great, but it can only schedule a job to run once in the future. Jobs often require running on a regular schedule. For example, backups may need to run daily or weekly, and Linux provides a tool for this.

The `cron` daemon, `crond`, can handle repetitious schedules. Unlike `at`, `cron` runs commands on a schedule you specify. For example, you can set up `cron` jobs to run nightly or weekly backups. That way, backups occur automatically on a regular schedule.

The discussion continues with these following topics:

- How `cron` works
- Using `cron` to manage scheduled system jobs
- Using `cron` to manage scheduled user jobs

How `cron` Works

The `crond` daemon is a service that runs continuously in the background and checks a special file called `crontab` once every minute to see if there is a scheduled job it should run. Use the `systemctl` command to manage the `crond` daemon.

By default, `crond` is configured to run automatically every time the system boots on most Linux distributions. If it is not, to start it manually, you need to do the following as `root`:

```
TableMove:dave #  systemctl start crond.service
```

To check the `crond` daemon status, run the following:

```
TableMove:dave #  systemctl status crond.service
```

To ensure that `crond` starts at boot time, run the following as `root`:

```
TableMove:dave #  systemctl enable crond.service
```

You can configure `cron` to run system jobs or user-specific jobs, which is covered next.

NOTE Extensions, or what Linux calls *suffixes* (such as `.service`, `.c`, `.doc`, and `.txt`), are ignored by Linux but are important to applications such as `systemctl`, `gcc`, LibreOffice, `gedit`, and so on. Learn more from the `suffixes(7)` man page.

Using `cron` to Manage Scheduled System Jobs

Using `cron` to schedule system jobs is extremely useful for a Linux system administrator. You can configure systems to perform a wide variety of tasks on a regular schedule automatically; for example, system backups or rotating and compressing log files.

To schedule system jobs, use `crond` and the `/etc/crontab` file to configure which jobs to run and when:

```
openSUSE:/etc #  head -5 /etc/crontab
SHELL=/bin/sh
PATH=/usr/bin:/usr/sbin:/sbin:/bin:/usr/lib/news/bin
MAILTO=root
#
# check scripts in cron.hourly, cron.daily, cron.weekly, and cron.monthly
#
```

In this example, the `/etc/crontab` file contains commands that are used to run scripts found in four different directories:

- **`/etc/cron.hourly/`** Contains `cron` scripts that are run every hour
- **`/etc/cron.daily/`** Contains `cron` scripts that are run every day
- **`/etc/cron.weekly/`** Contains `cron` scripts that are run weekly
- **`/etc/cron.monthly/`** Contains `cron` scripts that are run once a month

All scripts found in any of these directories are automatically run by `cron` according to the specified schedule at `root` privilege. For example, the `/etc/cron.daily/` directory contains a variety of scripts that are used to clean up the system and rotate the logs once each day. These scripts are shown here:

```
openSUSE:/etc/cron.daily # ls
logrotate                    suse-clean_catman          suse.de-backup-rpmdb
mdadm                        suse-do_mandb              suse.de-check-battery
packagekit-background.cron   suse.de-backup-rc.config   suse.de-cron-local
```

If you have a system task that needs to be run on one of these four schedules, simply create a script file and copy it into the appropriate `cron` directory in `/etc/`.

Using `cron` to Manage Scheduled User Jobs

You can create your own scheduled jobs using a `crontab` file associated with your user account. Depending on the Linux version, your `crontab` file is saved in either `/var/spool/cron/crontabs/<username>`, `/var/spool/cron/tabs/<username>`, or `/var/spool/cron/<username>`.

A `crontab` file is simply a text file that uses one line per job. Each line has six fields, separated by tabs, as detailed in Table 9-3. The `crontab` file also accepts characters such as the asterisk (`*`), comma (`,`) , and hyphen (`-`) to fine-tune the schedule for various domains and ranges. Also, you can use the forward slash (`/`) for *step values.*

Field	Description
Minute	Specifies the minute the command should run and ranges from 0 to 59.
Hour	Specifies the hour the command should run and ranges from 0 to 23.
Day of Month	Specifies the day of the month on which the command should run and ranges from 1 to 31.
Month	Specifies the month the command should run and ranges from 1 to 12.
Day of Week	Specifies the day of the week the command should run. Saturday is 6, Sunday is 0, and Monday through Friday are 1 through 5, respectively.
Command	Specifies the full path to the name of the command or script to run.

Table 9-3 The crontab File Fields

For example, */2 in the Hour field means every two hours, instead of showing 0,2,4,6,8,10,12,14,16,18,20,22. You create and edit your crontab file by running the following from the command prompt:

```
actionshots:~ # crontab -e
```

This opens the default editor to enable you to create or modify the crontab file.

NOTE To change the default editor to gedit, for example, you can enter the following:

```
actionshots:~ # EDITOR=/usr/bin/gedit ; export EDITOR
```

To schedule a backup job that runs at 5:10 P.M. every day, after running crontab -e, enter the following:

```
# min   hr    dom    mon    dow     command
  10    17     *      *      *     /bin/tar -cvf ~/homebak.tar ~
```

After editing the file, save and quit. A new or modified crontab file is completed in /var/spool/cron. In addition, the cron service is reloaded so the new configuration can be applied.

To display the crontab file updates, run the following:

```
actionshots:~ # crontab -l
```

Finally, crontab -r removes the crontab file.

If you incorrectly configure a cron job, you can cause system failure; therefore, many system administrators restrict end users from using cron. This is done by utilizing the /etc/cron.allow and /etc/cron.deny files.

By default, only the /etc/cron.deny file is created automatically, and it contains only one restriction by default for the guest user account. All other users are allowed to create crontab files to schedule jobs. If the administrator creates the /etc/cron.allow file, then only the users in that file will be allowed to create crontab files; all others will be denied. Because the crond service checks the /etc/cron.allow file first, if an end user is listed in both /etc/cron.allow and /etc/cron.deny, they will be *allowed* to use cron!

NOTE cron assumes computers run 24 hours a day. Laptops or desktops are likely to be off or asleep during certain periods, so cron won't run. The anacron service works around this issue; if a job is scheduled but the system is off, the missed job will automatically run when the system comes back up.

Now practice working with Linux processes in Exercise 9-2.

Exercise 9-2: Scheduling Linux Processes

In this exercise, practice using the cron and at commands to schedule processes to run in the future on the system. Perform this exercise using the virtual machine provided online.

VIDEO Please watch the Exercise 9-2 video for a demonstration on how to perform this task.

Complete the following steps:

1. Boot the Linux system and log in as a standard user.
2. Open a terminal session.
3. Switch to the root user account by entering **su -** followed by the root password.
4. Practice using the at daemon by doing the following:
   a. At the shell prompt, enter the **systemctl status atd** command.
   b. Verify that the at daemon is running. If it isn't, enter **systemctl start atd** at the shell prompt.
   c. Enter **at now +5 minutes** at the shell prompt.
   d. Enter **ps -ef > ~/psoutput.txt** at the at> prompt.
   e. Press CTRL-D.
   f. Generate a listing of pending at jobs by entering the **atq** command. The job just created will be displayed.
   g. Wait for the pending at job to complete.
   h. Use the **cat** command to check the ~/psoutput.txt file and verify that the output from the ps command was generated correctly.

i. Enter **at 2 pm tomorrow** at the shell prompt.

j. Enter **ps -ef > ~/psoutput.txt** at the at> prompt.

k. Press ENTER.

l. Press CTRL-D.

m. Generate a listing of pending at jobs by entering **atq** and notice the job just created. Note its job number.

n. Remove the pending job by entering the **atrm <job_number>** command.

o. Enter **atq** again. The pending job should be gone.

5. Practice using cron by completing the following steps:

a. Log out of the root user account by entering **exit**.

b. Enter **crontab -e** at the shell prompt.

c. Press **Insert**.

d. Configure the system to create a backup of the user's home directory every day at 5:05 P.M. by entering the following:

```
05    17    *    *    *    /bin/tar -cvf ~/mybackup.tar ~/
```

If waiting until 5:05 P.M. is inconvenient, specify a time value that is only two or three minutes in the future.

e. Press **Esc**.

f. Enter **:x** and notice the message on the screen indicating that a new crontab file has been installed.

g. Enter **crontab -l** and verify that the job was created correctly.

h. Wait until the time specified in the crontab file and then check the user's home directory and verify that the mybackup.tar file was created.

i. Remove the user's crontab file by entering **crontab -r** at the shell prompt.

Using systemd timers

The cron daemon is great when you want to automate tasks down to the minute, but what if you want certain tasks to start at a specific second, or 60 minutes after booting? This is where systemd timers come in.

To schedule automated backups with systemd timers, you must first create a system .service file, and then a .timer file. In this section, you will learn how to

- Create a systemd .service file
- Create a systemd .timer file
- Launch the systemd timer

Creating a `systemd .service` File

You can create your own `systemd service` by creating a `.service` file and placing it in the `/usr/lib/systemd/system/` directory. As `root`, create a new `.service` file to automate backups:

```
openSUSE:/ #  cat > /usr/lib/systemd/system/autobackup.service
[Unit]
Description=Automated backup tool
WantedBy=multi-user.target

[Service]
Type=simple
ExecStart=/usr/bin/bash /usr/local/bin/autobackup.sh
Restart=always
User=backup
Group=backup
<Ctrl>D
```

The `.service` file is divided into two stanzas:

- **`[Unit]`** Contains components shared by every `systemd` unit file
- **`[Service]`** Configures settings for the new service

For the `[Unit]` stanza, `Description` simply states what the service does, and is displayed in the service list when running `systemctl list-units`. `WantedBy` tells `systemd` that when `multi-user.target` starts, make sure to start the new `autobackup.service` too. Other options for `WantedBy` include `graphical.target`, `network.target`, and more.

The `[Service]` stanza lists which application or script to start when the new `autobackup.service` is called; this is listed in `ExecStart`, and in the previous example `bash` starts the `autobackup.sh` script. Always use the full path when setting the application. `ExecStop` and `ExecReload` also exist to cleanly stop or restart a service, respectively.

The `Type` setting can be set to `simple` or `forking` and determines how `systemd` knows when a service is running. The `simple` setting considers the application launched as the one running the service. If the application stops, the service has stopped as well. The `forking` setting is used for applications that fork another application. The fork is the process tracked and is managed by the `PID` of the fork. You would need to save the `PID` of the forked process to a file in order to track it.

The `Restart` setting tells the service when it should be restarted. The `Restart` options are `always`, `no`, `on-abnormal`, and `on-failure` and are explained in Table 9-4.

The `User` and `Group` settings allow you to define which user and group the process will run under. Launching all services as `root` could cause security issues, so only set `User` and `Group` to `root` when absolutely necessary.

`Restart` **Setting**	**Description**
`always`	When the process crashes, `systemd` will restart it. Good for servers and keeps you from manually restarting the service.
`no`	When the process crashes, `systemd` will not restart it.
`on-abnormal`	If the process crashes, restart it *unless* it exited normally, then do not restart it.
`on-failure`	If the process crashes, restart it. Also, if it exited normally but with a non-zero exit code, restart it. Do not restart if it exited with a zero exit code.

Table 9-4 `Restart` Settings for `.service` Files

To inform `systemd` of the new service, execute `systemctl`'s daemon-reload feature as shown here:

```
OpenSUSE:/ #  systemctl daemon-reload
OpenSUSE:/ #  systemctl start autobackup.service
OpenSUSE:/ #  systemctl enable autobackup.service
OpenSUSE:/ #  systemctl status autobackup.service
```

Running `systemctl start`, `enable`, and `status` as shown in this example will immediately start the service, enable the service to start at boot time, and print the status of the service.

Creating a systemd `.timer` File

A systemd `.timer` file offers the benefit of assuring a job runs only once, whereas with `cron` a job can run over itself if it takes too long to complete. For example, a `cron` job that starts every hour can conflict with itself if it takes two hours to complete the job. Multiple instances will start. This is an issue `.timer` mitigates; if the job is already running, it won't start the new job.

Your first step is to remove the `WantedBy` setting from the `autobackup.service` so that you can specify a time for the `autobackup` service to start. You can use the `sed` command and its `in-place` feature to update the file, as shown next. (`sed` is known as a *stream editor* and is detailed in Chapter 13.)

```
OpenSUSE# cd /usr/lib/systemd/system
OpenSUSE# sed -i s/WantedBy=multi-user.target// autobackup.service
```

Next, you can create the timer by building the `autobackup.timer` file. Notice the suffix is now `.timer`, *not* `.service`. Create this file as `root`, as follows:

```
openSUSE:/ #  cat > /usr/lib/systemd/system/autobackup.timer
[Unit]
Description=Automated backup tool

[Timer]
OnCalendar=* *-*-* 20:00:00
RandomizedDelaySec=3600
Persistent=true

[Install]
WantedBy=timers.target
<Ctrl>D
```

Similar to a .service file, the .timer file is divided into stanzas. OnCalendar sets the time the job will trigger, and its syntax is Day Year-Month-Date Hour:Minute:Second. In our example, autobackup will start at 8 P.M. every day. If the job is already running, it will be skipped until the next day.

Unlike cron, OnCalendar understands shortcuts. For example, 8 P.M. everyday can be listed as follows:

```
Sun..Sat *-*-* 20:00:00
*-*-* 20:00:00
20:00:00
20:00
```

OnCalendar supports other values, such as daily if you want the job to run once per day. Other settings include minutely, hourly, monthly, weekly, yearly, quarterly, and semiannually.

RandomizedDelaySec starts a job later than requested if the system load is too high at the trigger time. Provide the maximum number of seconds that you're comfortable with delaying the job. In our example, the job can be delayed up to one hour because it is set to 3600 seconds.

Persistent assures a job runs if the computer was powered off at the job's scheduled time. Once the system boots up, it will see that your job didn't run as scheduled and start it right away.

To configure a job to start after booting, use the OnBootSec option instead of the OnCalendar option within the [Timer] stanza. If you want a job to start 10 minutes after booting, set OnBootSec to 600 seconds as follows:

```
OnBootSec=600
```

or

```
OnBootSec=10 minutes
```

Timers start at boot through systemd. So that your new timer triggers, make sure to set WantedBy to the timers.target.

NOTE Use the systemd-analyze tool to test when your jobs will actually start, like so:

```
# systemd-analyze calendar '*-*-* 20:00:00'
```

Launching the systemd timer

You can start the new timer within the system by reloading the systemd daemon as follows:

```
OpenSUSE:/ #  systemctl daemon-reload
```

Now, systemd has a way to manage and monitor your new timer.

Next you need to enable your new timer as follows:

```
OpenSUSE:/ #  systemctl enable --now autobackup.timer
OpenSUSE:/ #  systemctl status autobackup.timer
```

Running `systemctl status autobackup.timer` informs you of the last time the timer ran and when it is expected to run again if defined with `OnCalendar`.

If you no longer need the timer, you can disable it as follows:

```
OpenSUSE:/ #  systemctl disable -now automated.timer
```

To track how your timers and services are running, use the `journalctl` command to view system logs as follows:

```
OpenSUSE:/ #  journalctl --catalog --lines=1000 --pager-end
```

The `--catalog` option provides more details to log messages where possible, `--lines` displays the last 1,000 lines of the log file, and `--pager-end` jumps you to the last page of the output instead of the first page. You can use the `Right Arrow`, `Left Arrow`, `PageUp`, and `PageDown` keys to maneuver through the output.

Finally, to get a listing of available services and timers, run the following commands:

```
openSUSE# systemctl list-units --type=service
openSUSE# systemctl list-units --type=timer
```

To track error messages on your system, use the `journalctl` search feature to learn more about specific services, as follows:

```
OpenSUSE:/ #  journalctl --catalog --lines=1000 --pager-end --grep='dhcp'
```

The `--grep` option searches for just DHCP-related issues in this example. To view messages from a specific time, use the `--since` argument:

```
OpenSUSE:/ #  journalctl --catalog --since='2023-08-08 10:00:00'
```

EXAM TIP Make sure you are familiar with several `OnCalendar` formats within your timers.

Chapter Review

In this chapter, you learned that Linux is a multitasking operating system and appears to run processes simultaneously, but only runs one job at a time on a single CPU system. The jobs run so quickly, they appear to run at the same time.

When a daemon is loaded, a system process is created. When you enter a command at the shell prompt, a user process is created. User processes are associated with a shell session; system processes are not. Managing running processes is one of the key tasks performed on Linux systems. Configuring the Linux system to run specified programs automatically ensures that the programs execute regularly and on time.

You can schedule jobs using `cron`, `at`, or `systemd timers`. Using `systemd timers` has the advantage of not restarting a job if `systemd` sees the job is already running. This reduces conflicts within the Linux system.

Here are some key facts to remember about Linux processes:

- When the systemd process loads a daemon, a system process is created.
- A process that spawns another process is called the *parent*.
- The new process that was created by the parent is called the *child*.
- All Linux processes can trace their heredity back to the systemd process (depending on the distribution), which is the first process loaded by the kernel on system boot.
- For distributions that use systemd, use the systemctl command to start and stop system services.
- Use the top utility to view system processes.
- By default, the ps command only displays running processes in the current shell.
- nice values range from -20 to +19.
- The lower the nice value, the higher the priority of the process.
- The syntax for using renice is renice <nice_value> <PID>.
- Only root can assign a nice value less than 0 and use renice to set a lower nice value than the current one.
- By default, processes launched from the shell prompt run in the foreground, and the shell prompt is locked until the process is complete.
- To run a process in the background, append an & character to the end of the command.
- When executed, the background process is assigned a job ID number.
- To move a process running in the background to the foreground, enter fg <job_ID> at the shell prompt.
- To move a foreground process into the background, press CTRL-Z to stop the process and then enter bg <job_ID> to move the process to the background.
- Use the kill, pkill, top, or killall command to terminate a job.
- Common kill signals used with kill or killall include
  - SIGHUP (1)
  - SIGINT (2)
  - SIGKILL (9)
  - SIGTERM (15), the default
- To kill a process with kill, enter kill -<signal> <PID> at the shell prompt.
- To kill a process with killall, enter killall -<signal> <process_name>.

- Load a program using the `nohup` command to allow the process to continue running after logging out.
- To schedule a process to run once in the future, use the `at` command.
- The `at` time value can be a fixed time, such as the following:
    - `HH:MM`
    - `noon`
    - `midnight`
    - `teatime`
- Use the `atq` command to view a list of pending `at` jobs.
- Use the `atrm` command to remove a pending `at` job.
- A `crontab` file contains one line for each command to run; each line contains six fields:
    - `1 Minutes`
    - `2 Hour`
    - `3 Day`
    - `4 Month`
    - `5 Day of the week`
    - `6 Command to execute`
- A user can create a `crontab` file by entering `crontab -e` at the shell prompt.
- The `OnCalendar` syntax is `Day Year-Month-Date Hour:Minute:Second`.
- `OnCalendar` understands shortcuts. 6 P.M. everyday can be listed as
    - `Sun..Sat *-*-* 18:00:00`
    - `*-*-* 18:00:00`
    - `18:00:00`
    - `18:00`

Questions

1. Which two commands below output the process ID (`PID`) of a program? (Choose two.)

   A. `pidof`

   B. `pgrep`

   C. `pname`

   D. `proc`

2. Which process could be the grandparent of all processes running on a Linux system?
   A. `bash`
   B. `sh`
   C. `ps`
   D. `systemd`
3. Which of the two following are valid `OnCalendar` date settings? (Choose two.)
   A. `15 * * * 1-5 /usr/local/bin/job.sh`
   B. `15:34`
   C. `teatime`
   D. `* *-*-* 15:34:00`
4. Which `ps` command will display extended information about only the processes associated with the current terminal session?
   A. `ps`
   B. `ps -e`
   C. `ps -f`
   D. `ps -ef`
5. What is a zombie process?
   A. A process that has finished executing but whose parent process has not released the child process's `PID`
   B. A process that has stopped executing while waiting for user input
   C. A process that is being traced by another process
   D. A process that has gone to sleep and cannot be interrupted
6. Which `ps` option can be used to display all currently running processes?
   A. `-c`
   B. `-e`
   C. `-f`
   D. `-l`
7. The `myapp` process has a `nice` value of `1`. Which of the two following `nice` values would increase the priority of the `myapp` process? (Choose two.)
   A. `-15`
   B. `5`
   C. `19`
   D. `0`
   E. `2`

8. Which of the following two shell commands will load the `myapp` program with a `nice` value of `-5`? (Choose two.)
   - **A.** `myapp -n -5`
   - **B.** `nice -5 myapp`
   - **C.** `renice -5 myapp`
   - **D.** `nice -n -5 myapp`
   - **E.** `nice -5 myapp`
9. The `myapp` process (`PID 2345`) is currently running on the system. Which of the following two commands will reset its `nice` value to `-5` without unloading the process? (Choose two.)
   - **A.** `myapp -n -5 -p 2345`
   - **B.** `renice -n -5 2345`
   - **C.** `renice -5 2345`
   - **D.** `nice -n -5 2345`
10. Which command will load the `myapp` program from the shell prompt and run it in the background?
    - **A.** `myapp -b`
    - **B.** `myapp &`
    - **C.** `myapp -bg`
    - **D.** `myapp`
11. Which kill signal sends a CTRL-C key sequence to a running process?
    - **A.** `SIGHUP`
    - **B.** `SIGINT`
    - **C.** `SIGKILL`
    - **D.** `SIGTERM`
12. A user needs to kill a hung process by its process name, not its `PID`. Which two utilities could best be used? (Choose two.)
    - **A.** `killall`
    - **B.** `kill`
    - **C.** `hangup`
    - **D.** `SIGKILL`
    - **E.** `pkill`

13. You want to run the rsync command to synchronize the home directory with another server on the network, but you know this command will take several hours to complete and you don't want to leave the system logged in during this time. Which command will leave rsync running after logout?

    A. SIGHUP

    B. `nohup`

    C. `stayalive`

    D. `kill -NOHUP`

14. It's currently 1:00 in the afternoon. To schedule the myapp program to run automatically tomorrow at noon (12:00), which two of the following at commands is best to use? (Choose two.)

    A. `at 12 pm tomorrow`

    B. `at tomorrow -1 hour`

    C. `at now +1 day`

    D. `at today +23 hours`

    E. `at now +23 hours`

15. Which of the following crontab lines will cause the /usr/bin/myappcleanup process to run at 4:15 A.M. on the first of every month?

    A. `15 4 1 * * /usr/bin/myappcleanup`

    B. `15 4 * 1 * /usr/bin/myappcleanup`

    C. `1 4 15 * * /usr/bin/myappcleanup`

    D. `4 1 * * 15 /usr/bin/myappcleanup`

Answers

1. **A, B.** Running `pidof <process_name>` or `pgrep <process_name>` will output the PID of the running process.
2. **D.** All processes can trace their heredity to systemd.
3. **B, D.** OnCalendar will run a job every day at 3:34 in the afternoon with either of these two settings.
4. **C.** The `ps -f` command will display extended information about processes associated with the current shell session.
5. **A.** A zombie process is one that has finished executing but whose parent process wasn't notified and, therefore, hasn't released the child process's PID.
6. **B.** The `ps -e` command can be used to display a list of all running processes on the system.

7. **A, D.** The lower the `nice` value, the higher the priority of the process. Therefore, `nice` values of `-15` and `0` will increase the priority of the `myapp` process.
8. **D, E.** The `nice -n -5 myapp` and `nice --5 myapp` commands will load `myapp` with a `nice` value of `-5`.
9. **B, C.** The `renice -n -5 2345` and `renice -5 2345` commands will reset the `nice` value of the `myapp` process while it's running.
10. **B.** The `myapp &` command will cause `myapp` to run in the background.
11. **B.** The `SIGINT` kill signal sends a CTRL-C key sequence to the specified process.
12. **A, E.** The `killall` utility uses the process name in the command line and can be used to kill the process in this scenario. The `pkill` command can be used to search for and kill a hung process by its name.
13. **B.** The `nohup` command can be used to load a program so that it will ignore the SIGHUP signal that is sent when the user logs out, thus allowing the process to remain running.
14. **A, E.** Enter `at 12 pm tomorrow` or `at now +23 hours` to cause the `atd` daemon to run the specified command at 12:00 P.M. on the following day.
15. **A.** The `15 4 1 * * /usr/bin/myappcleanup` crontab line will cause the `myappcleanup` process to be run at 4:15 A.M. on the first day of every month no matter what day of the week it is.

CHAPTER 10

Managing Linux Applications

In this chapter, you will learn about

- Using a package manager to install applications
- Installing applications on Red Hat with RPM
- Installing RPMs with YUM, DNF, and ZYpp
- Installing applications on Debian with `dpkg`
- Installing applications on Debian with APT
- Using universal Linux app stores
- Installing applications from source code
- Managing shared libraries

What I liked about computers is that they were pure logic…thinking things through.

—Roy L. Clay, HP Computer

As a Linux system administrator, you must know how to install and manage software on a Linux system. The CompTIA Linux+ exam includes questions testing your knowledge of the RPM, `dpkg`, YUM, DNF, APT, and ZYpp package management tools. Also, make sure you are familiar with compiling and installing applications from source code.

Using a Package Manager to Install Applications

Regardless of which package manager your distribution uses, it will perform tasks similar to all package managers, including the following:

- Installing applications
- Updating applications that have already been installed
- Uninstalling applications
- Querying installed applications
- Verifying the integrity of installed applications

Term	Definition
Package	A package is a group of files (for example, documentation, library files, or scripts) used by a package manager to install an application or applications.
Package group	A package group is a group of individual packages that have a similar purpose. For example, the Gnome Desktop package group contains all packages or groups of packages required.
Version number	A version number defines the edition of a package. A version number format is `Edition.Major-Change.Minor-Change`. (`Minor-Change` may be a feature addition or bug fix.)
Release number	A release number identifies a version released to the public.
Architecture	Architecture refers to the processor (for example, `x86_64`) the package will be able to run on. Some packages will run on multiple architectures, and others are not architecture dependent.
Source code	Source code consists of a text file or files made up of instructions written in a programming language (for example, C, C++, Visual Basic), which are later translated into object code by a compiler. Having source code to an application enables a programmer to modify the application to their specific needs.
Repository	A software repository is a location used by package managers to retrieve stored packages.

Table 10-1 Package Management Terms

Two key aspects of package managers are that they install files according to the Linux Filesystem Hierarchy Standard (discussed in Chapter 5), putting files where they belong. The other job is handling application dependencies. For example, if you install the application `A.PKG`, the man pages will be placed in `/usr/man`, the libraries in `/usr/lib`, and the application in `/usr/bin`.

If `A.PKG` is dependent on `B.PKG`, then `B.PKG` must be installed first. During software installation, you can get into a situation where package `B.PKG` requires `C.PKG` to be installed first, `C.PKG` requires `D.PKG` to be installed first, and so on until you get to `ZZZ.PKG` needs to be installed. System administrators call this *dependency hell*, and what you thought was a five-minute job becomes an all-day job because you must search for dependencies just so you can successfully install `A.PKG`.

This is resolved with repository-aware package managers like YUM, ZYpp, and DNF, which automatically find, download, and install dependencies. Now, a five-minute installation is only five minutes! These will be discussed after you learn about installing with RPM.

Table 10-1 lists some package manager terms you should know.

Installing Applications on Red Hat with RPM

The Red Hat Package Manager, RPM, was originally developed in 1997 to install and upgrade software applications in Red Hat Linux distributions. RPM also contains facilities to query the package database and verify the integrity of installed packages.

RPM applications are used on Red Hat Enterprise Linux (RHEL), CentOS, SUSE Linux Enterprise Server (SLES), OpenSUSE, Oracle Linux, Rocky Linux, and Fedora-based systems. In this section, we will discuss

- RPM package naming conventions
- RPM command options
- RPM application installation
- RPM application upgrades
- RPM application removal
- RPM application verification
- RPM database querying
- RPM conversion to CPIO

To install, update, and remove RPM applications, you'll use the `rpm` command. The command `rpm --help` displays RPM help information. Let's begin by exploring RPM naming conventions.

RPM Package Naming Conventions

The syntax of an RPM package name is as follows:

```
<package_name>-<version_num>-<release_num>.<distribution>.<arch>.rpm
```

The following list explains these elements, using an example of a package named `bash-3.2-32.el5.x86_64`:

- **`package_name`** This part of the filename simply identifies the name of the package. In this example, the name of the package is `bash`.
- **`version_num`** This part of the package name specifies the version of the software in the package. In our example, the version number `3.2` indicates the third edition of the software and that it has had two major changes since the third edition was released.
- **`release_num`** This part of the package name indicates the current release of the software version. In our example, the software release is `32`.
- **`distribution`** The distribution designator indicates that the package has been compiled for a specific Linux distribution. In our example, the distribution designator is `el5` (Red Hat Enterprise Linux 5).
- **`arch`** This part of the package name specifies the CPU architecture that the software inside the package will run on. In our example, the architecture is specified as `x86_64`, which means the software will run on 64-bit x86 CPUs. You may also see the following architectures specified in a package's filename:
    - **`i386`** Specifies that the software will run on an Intel 80386 or later CPU
    - **`i586`** Specifies that the software will run on an Intel Pentium or later CPU

- **i686** Specifies that the software will run on Intel Pentium 4 or later CPUs
- **x86_64** Specifies that the software will run on 64-bit x86 CPUs
- **athlon** Specifies that the software is intended to run on an AMD Athlon CPU
- **ppc** Specifies that the software is intended to run on the PowerPC CPU
- **noarch** Specifies that the package is not architecture dependent

RPM Command Options

The command syntax for managing rpm packages is as follows:

```
rpm <mode> <mode_options> <package_name(s) | <package_filename>
```

The rpm command may require either the application name or application filename as an argument. The application name is used when referencing the databases in /var/lib/rpm. The application filename is the path to the storage location of the application.

RPM uses multiple modes to manage packages, as detailed in Table 10-2.

RPM Application Installation

To install, erase, update, or freshen a package, you must have root privileges. The command rpm -i <package_name> will install an application on your system. Use the command rpm -i ftp://<ftp_address> <package_name> to install a package from an FTP server.

Table 10-3 contains a partial list of RPM installation options.

Mode	Option	Description
Install	-i --install	Installs a package file.
Freshen	-F --freshen	Upgrades only (freshens) installed packages. If the package is not already installed, then no upgrade or installation is performed.
Upgrade	-U --upgrade	Upgrades the operating system. This option upgrades current packages and installs new operating system packages as necessary. The freshen option -F upgrades only installed packages.
Erase	-e --erase	Removes a package.
Query	-q --query	Retrieves package information from the RPM database.
Verify	-V --verify	Compares information from the package database with installed files.

Table 10-2 RPM Modes

Option	Description
`--test`	Checks for possible installation issues (for example, dependency) without installing the package.
`--force`	Forces the installation of a package, even if the package is installed on the system. Forces the installation of an older package over a newer package.
`--nodeps`	Indicates to not check package dependencies.
`-K` `--checksig`	Verifies the package is not corrupted by checking the MD5 checksum. You may check the signature of an existing package by executing the following command: `rpm -K --nosignature <package_name>`
`--prefix <path>`	Installs the package in the directory specified by the argument `<path>`.
`-v`	Verbose. Prints progress information.
`-vv`	Prints debugging information.

Table 10-3 RPM Installation Options

RPM Application Upgrades

The RPM upgrade option, `-U` or `--upgrade`, will upgrade current applications *or* install new applications if not already installed.

When RPM upgrades an application, it retains the configuration files. When the upgrade changes default configuration files, instead of overwriting it, it saves the new configuration files as `.rpmnew`. You should review this file to determine if you should modify or replace the current configuration file.

Sometimes the new configuration file must replace the current one. In this case, your old file is saved as `.rpmsave` in case there are settings you need to add to the new configuration file.

Some `--upgrade` options are displayed in Table 10-4.

EXAM TIP Key exam concepts are to understand that the `-i` option only installs a package, the `-F` option updates only existing packages, and the `-U` option upgrades existing packages or installs packages if not already installed.

Option	Description
`--oldpackage`	Permits a newer version package to be upgraded with an older version package
`--force`	Has the same effect as `--oldpackage`

Table 10-4 RPM Upgrade Options

RPM Application Removal

The `--erase` option removes a package. For example, the command `rpm -e <pkg_name>` removes a package. During the package removal, `rpm -e`

- Checks to make certain no other package depends on the package to be erased.
- Determines whether any of the package configuration files have been modified and saves a copy of any modified files.
- Determines if a file that's part of the package is required by another package. If it's not, the file is erased.
- Removes all traces of the package and associated files from the RPM database.

Finally, note that a package may contain pre-uninstall and post-uninstall scripts. These scripts would be executed as part of the erase process. The `--erase` option will not erase a package if there are dependencies, unless the `--nodeps` option is specified. Also, consider using the `--test` option prior to erasing a package to check for any potential conflicts.

RPM Application Verification

RPM tracks changes to packages and files. The `--verify` option compares files and packages installed on the system with the RPM database and also verifies whether package dependencies are met. The output of the `--verify` option is a series of codes that may be used to determine if the system configuration has changed or the RPM database is corrupt. The changes are usually benign, but could also mean the files were tampered with, *possibly by a hacker*!

The `--verify` option compares the following install information with the RPM database:

- File ownership
- File group ownership
- File permissions
- File checksum
- File size
- Validity of symbolic links
- File major and minor numbers (used only for block and character device files)
- File modification time

To verify a package, execute the command `rpm -V <package_name>` or `rpm --verify <package_name>`. Adding an additional `-v` will display files associated with the package, even if there are no errors. To verify all packages, execute the command `rpm -Va`.

The output of the command is a series of code designators as follows:

```
SM5DLUGT   <attribute marker>  <filename>
```

Table 10-5 RPM Verify Codes

Code Designator	Definition
`S`	Indicates a size difference
`M`	Indicates a mode (permissions) difference
`5`	Indicates a signature difference
`D`	Indicates a difference in major and minor numbers
`L`	Indicates a difference in symbolic links
`U`	Indicates a difference in file ownership
`G`	Indicates a difference in file group ownership
`T`	Indicates a difference in modification time
`.`	Indicates no difference

Table 10-6 RPM Verify Attribute Codes

Attribute Code	Definition
`c`	Configuration file
`d`	Documentation file
`g`	Ghost file (that is, a file not included in the package)
`l`	License file
`r`	Readme file

If the code designator appears, then the condition exists. For example, if the number `5` appears, then the current checksum differs from the original checksum, which means the file has been modified.

Table 10-5 defines the different verify code designators.

Table 10-6 defines the RPM verify attribute codes. Attribute codes appear only if the attribute is applied to the file.

Figure 10-1 contains the edited output of the `rpm -Va` command:

- Line 2 indicates the configuration file `/var/lib/unbound/root.key` has a different size, file signature, and modification time.
- Line 3 states that the file `/var/run/pulse` is missing.
- Line 4 shows that the permissions have changed in the ghost file `/var/lib/setroubleshoot/email_alert_recipients`.
- Line 6 indicates that the owner and group owner of the ghost file `/var/run/avahi-daemon` have changed.

Figure 10-1 Error codes for `rpm -Va`

```
1 [root@localhost ~]# rpm -Va
2 S.5....T.  c /var/lib/unbound/root.key
3 missing      /var/run/pulse
4 .M.......  g /var/lib/setroubleshoot/email_alert_recipients
5 ....L....  c /etc/pam.d/fingerprint-auth
6 .....UG..  g /var/run/avahi-daemon
```

Option	Description
`-q <package_name>` `--query`	Displays the package name and version if the package is installed.
`-qa` `--query --all`	Displays all packages installed on the system. You can combine this with `grep` to find specific packages (for example, `rpm -qa | grep kernel`).
`-qf <absolute_path_filename>` `rpm -q --whatprovides <filename>`	Determines which package a file came from. The file cannot be a symbolic link.
`-qi <package_name>`	Displays package information. This information includes version, vendor, architecture, installation date, and other package information.
`-ql <package_name>`	Lists files in a package.
`-qR` `-q --requires`	Lists package dependencies.
`-q --whatrequires <package_name>`	Lists packages dependent on this package.
`-qd <package_name>`	Lists package documentation.
`-qp <package_name>.rpm`	Queries the uninstalled package.

Table 10-7 RPM Query Options

RPM Database Querying

The `--query` mode allows a user to search for package data in the RPM database. Several `--query` options are shown in Table 10-7.

The command `rpm -qcf /usr/bin/passwd` displays the configuration files for the `passwd` command. Consider using the command `rpm -qif /usr/bin/passwd` to find out package information for the package that contains the `passwd` command.

RPM Conversion to CPIO

The command `rpm2cpio` produces a `cpio` archive from an RPM package. This allows you to extract the application without installing it, in case you want to do further investigation before using it. The syntax is as follows:

```
rpm2cpio <package_name> | cpio <cpio_options>
```

Table 10-8 lists some `cpio` options.

Table 10-8 `cpio` Options

Option	Description
`-t`	List contents
`-i`	Extract
`-d`	Create subdirectories
`-v`	Verbose output

To list the contents of a package, execute the command

```
rpm2cpio <package_filename> | cpio -t
```

To extract an entire package, execute the command

```
rpm2cpio <package_filename> | cpio -idv
```

Extract a file from an RPM package with

```
rpm2cpio <package_filename> | cpio -idv <filename>
```

NOTE The extraction will occur in the current working directory. It is advisable that you use an empty directory.

Next apply some of what you learned in this section by completing Exercise 10-1.

Exercise 10-1: Practicing Package Manipulation with RPM

In this exercise, you'll practice using some of the RPM commands you have just learned. Be sure to use the CentOS image provided and log in as user **`root`** with a password of **`password`**. Follow these steps:

VIDEO Please watch the Exercise 10-1 video for a demonstration on how to perform this task.

1. Create a snapshot.
2. Determine the installation date of the `bash` package by executing the **`rpm -qi bash`** or **`rpm -qif /usr/bin/bash`** command.
3. Look at the package that installed the command `/usr/bin/bash` by executing the command **`rpm -qf /usr/bin/bash`**, and then review the output of the command in step 2 to see the package the `/usr/bin/bash` file came from.
4. What other packages are required (package dependencies) by the `bash` package? Execute the **`rpm -qR bash`** or **`rpm -q --requires bash`** command for the answer.
5. Determine what packages are required by the `lsscsi` package and then try to remove the `lsscsi` package by executing the command **`rpm -e --test lsscsi`** (this will simulate removing the package). Compare the output of the `rpm -q --whatrequires "lsscsi"` command with the output of the `rpm -e --test lsscsi` command.
6. Use the **`rpm -qc bash`** command to determine which configuration files are provided with the `bash` package.

7. Determine what configuration files are affecting a command. Use the command **rpm -qcf /usr/bin/passwd** to determine the configuration files used by the `passwd` command.
8. Verify the package that provides the command `lsscsi` by executing the following commands:

```
rpm -V lsscsi; sleep 5; rpm -qvf /usr/bin/lsscsi; sleep 5; \
rpm -Vv lsscsi
```

9. Execute the `sudo rpm -qVf /etc/at.deny` command and review its output. The output displays what has changed since the file was installed.
10. View the list of files in the `bash` package. Execute the command **cd /run/media/root/"CentOS 7 x85_64"/Packages**
    Next, execute the **rpm2cpio $(rpm -qf /usr/bin.bash).rpm | cpio -t** command.

    The `rpm2cpio` command requires a package filename. The command `rpm -qf` will provide a package name but not a package filename. `$(rpm -qf /usr/bin/bash)` will output the package name, and `.rpm` adds the suffix `.rpm` to the end of the package name.

Installing RPMs with YUM, DNF, and ZYpp

In this section you will learn the following package managers for Red Hat–class systems:

- The YUM package manager
- The DNF package manager
- The ZYpp package manager

YUM, DNF, and ZYpp all make use of package repositories to download, install, or update applications. Unlike RPM, repository-aware applications search for dependencies and download those automatically.

The YUM Package Manager

YUM, or Yellowdog Updater, Modified, is a package manager that is a command-line front end to RPM. YUM allows users with root privileges to add, remove, and search for available packages and their dependencies.

YUM's main configuration file is `/etc/yum.conf`, discussed next.

The `/etc/yum.conf` File

The file `/etc/yum.conf` is a global YUM configuration file that contains a list of directives assigned a value (see Figure 10-2). If the directive's value is `0`, the directive is not asserted; if the directive value is `1`, the directive is asserted.

Figure 10-2 A sample /etc/yum.conf file

```
[main]
cachedir=/var/cache/yum/$basearch/$releasever
keepcache=0
debuglevel=2
logfile=/var/log/yum.log
exactarch=1
obsoletes=1
gpgcheck=1
plugins=1
installonly_limit=5
bugtracker_url=http://bugs.centos.org/set_project.php?project_id=23&ref=\
http://bugs.centos.org/bug_report_page.php?category=yum

distroverpkg=centos-release


#  This is the default, if you make this bigger yum won't see if the metadata
# is newer on the remote and so you'll "gain" the bandwidth of not having to
# download the new metadata and "pay" for it by yum not having correct
# information.
#  It is esp. important, to have correct metadata, for distributions like
# Fedora which don't keep old packages around. If you don't like this checking
# interupting your command line usage, it's much better to have something
# manually check the metadata once an hour (yum-updatesd will do this).
# metadata_expire=90m

# PUT YOUR REPOS HERE OR IN separate files named file.repo
# in /etc/yum.repos.d
```

Directives configured in /etc/yum.repos.d take precedence over directives configured in /etc/yum.conf. Table 10-9 reviews some directives found in /etc/yum.conf.

The /etc/yum.repos.d Directory

As stated earlier, packages are stored in repositories. For yum to install a package, it must know how to locate the repositories. The location of repositories is defined in /etc/yum.conf or files inside of the /etc/yum.repos.d directory.

Directive	Description
[main]	The main configuration section of /etc/yum.conf.
cachedir	Specifies the location where downloads are saved.
keepcache	YUM, by default, stores package files in the directive specified by cachedir. The keepcache directive determines if the packages are retained after install.
gpgcheck=	Specifies whether GNU Privacy Guard (GPG) is enabled. A value of 1 enables GPG checking for all packages in all repositories. A value of 0 disables GPG checking.
installonly_limit=	Specifies the maximum number of versions of any single package that may be installed. The default value is 3 but should not be less than 2.
distroverpkg	Used by yum to determine the distribution version. If the line distroverpkg is not available, the value is obtained from the file /etc/redhat-release.

Table 10-9 yum.conf Directives

```
[base]
name=CentOS-$releasever - Base
mirrorlist=http://mirrorlist.centos.org/?release=$releasever&arch=$basearch&repo=os&infra=$infra
#baseurl=http://mirror.centos.org/centos/$releasever/os/$basearch/
gpgcheck=1
gpgkey=file:///etc/pki/rpm-gpg/RPM-GPG-KEY-CentOS-7

#released updates
[updates]
name=CentOS-$releasever - Updates
mirrorlist=http://mirrorlist.centos.org/?release=$releasever&arch=$basearch&repo=updates&infra=$infra
#baseurl=http://mirror.centos.org/centos/$releasever/updates/$basearch/
gpgcheck=1
gpgkey=file:///etc/pki/rpm-gpg/RPM-GPG-KEY-CentOS-7
```

Figure 10-3 A sample repo configuration file

Repository Definition Files

Repository definition files contain information on how to access a specific repository. Figure 10-3 shows edited output of the file CentOS-Base.repo. We examine some of the directives in this section.

Section Name Each repository definition starts with a repository name enclosed in left and right brackets, called a *stanza*. In Figure 10-3, we find two repositories: [base] and [updates].

name= The name directive is a description of the repository definition file.

mirrorlist= The mirrorlist directive defines a location that contains a list of base URLs.

baseurl= This directive is a URL to the directory where repository data is located. The directive has several formats:

- If the repository is located on the local machine, use file:///<path_to_repository>
- If the repository is on an FTP server or is sent over HTTP, use ftp://<path_to_repository> or http://<path_to_repository>
- To add a username or password, you use ftp://<username>:<password>@<path_to_repository> or http://<username>:<password>@<path_to_repository>

gpg There are two directives associated with gpg:

- The directive gpgcheck= takes a value of 0 or 1. A value of 1 tells yum to check GPG signatures.
- gpgkey= defines the location yum will use to import the GPG key.

enable= The enable= directive also takes a value of 0 or 1. If the value is 0, yum will not use the repository defined in the section as a data source.

EXAM TIP Understand that /etc/yum.conf and /etc/yum.repos.d manage package repositories, but the content and syntax of these files are not tested on the exam.

YUM Commands

The YUM utility will search for packages from repositories listed in /etc/yum.conf and /etc/yum.repos.d/ and install, update, list, and remove them and their dependencies. Common YUM commands for listing installed and available packages are described in Table 10-10.

Command	Description
yum list available	Displays a list of all available packages in enabled repositories. This command may be used with the grep command. For example, yum list available | grep kernel
yum list installed	Lists all packages installed on your system.
yum list all	Displays a list of installed packages and packages available on enabled repositories.
yum list installed <pkg>	Lists installed packages with a specific package name. For example, yum list installed kernel
yum list <pkg>	Lists installed and available packages with a specific package name. For example, yum list kernel
yum list update <pkg>	Checks for updates for the specified package.
yum info <pkg>	Displays information about the specified package, including its version and dependencies.
yum deplist <pkg>	Displays a list of package dependencies.
yum provides <file> yum whatprovides <file>	Identifies the RPM package that provides the specified <file>. You must use the absolute path to the file.
yum search <string>	Searches the package names and descriptions of packages on enabled repositories.
yum grouplist	Displays a list of installed and available package groups.
yum groupinfo <group>	Displays the description and contents of a package group. For example, yum groupinfo "Gnome Desktop"
yum repolist	Displays a list of enabled repositories.
yum clean packages	Removes cached package data.
yum clean all	Removes cached packages and metadata.

Table 10-10 Basic yum Listing Commands

NOTE One repository that you might like is the EPEL repository, which provides Extra Packages for Enterprise Linux. For example, the extra packages include Python modules and popular browsers. Run `yum install -y epel-release` to access the new features.

Using YUM to Install, Remove, and Update Packages

In this section, we review commands and options used to install, remove, and update packages using the YUM package manager. Table 10-11 displays the commands used to install, update, and remove packages.

EXAM TIP Note that some packages have different names than expected, such as the `httpd` package for `apache2`, or the `bind` package for the DNS nameserver. For example, the command to install the DNS server is `yum install bind`, *not* `yum install dnsd`.

There may be cases where you want to download an application before installing it. To do this, either run

```
yum install <package_name> --downloadonly --downloaddir=<directory>
```

or use the `yumdownloader` utility and run `yumdownloader <pkg>`.

Command	Description
`yum install <pkg>`	Installs the specified package
`yum groupinstall <pkg_group>`	Installs a package group
`yum install <file>`	Installs the package associated with a file
`yum install <pkg> --enablerepo=<repo>`	Installs a package from a specific repository
`yum check-update`	Searches enabled repositories for package updates
`yum list updates`	Generates a list of updates for all installed packages
`yum update`	Updates packages to the current version
`yum update <pkg>`	Updates a package to the current version
`yum upgrade`	Updates packages to the current version and deletes obsolete packages
`yum remove <pkg>` `yum erase <pkg>`	Uninstalls the specified package
`yum clean packages`	Removes cached package data
`yum autoremove <pkg>`	Removes a specified package, packages that depend on the package, and related dependencies
`yum clean all`	Removes cached packages and metadata

Table 10-11 `yum` Install, Erase, and Update Commands

Exercise 10-2: Practicing Package Manipulation with YUM

In this exercise, practice using some of the yum commands you have just learned. Be sure to use the CentOS image provided and log in as user **root** with a password of **root**. Follow these steps:

VIDEO Please watch the Exercise 10-2 video for a demonstration on how to perform this task.

1. Create a snapshot.
2. Look at the package that installed the command /bin/bash by executing the **yum provides /bin/bash** command.
3. Execute the **yum deplist bash** command to see what other packages are required (package dependencies) by the bash package.
4. Execute the command **yum repolist** to display a list of enabled repositories.
5. Use the command **yum list installed** to list the packages installed on your system.
6. Execute the command **yum list kernel** to list installed kernel packages.
7. Execute the command **yum list available kernel*** to list available kernel packages.
8. Use the command **yum check-update** to check the enabled repositories for available package updates.
9. Select one of the packages on the list and execute the **yum update <package>** command.
10. Execute the command **yum update** to update all the packages on your system. *Warning*: This may take a long time.

The DNF Package Manager

DNF, or Dandified YUM, is the package manager that has replaced YUM on Red Hat–class systems and SUSE. Major improvements of DNF over YUM are improved dependency resolution, better memory usage, and higher performance. The subcommands are the same as for YUM, as shown in Tables 10-10 and 10-11. In fact, you can redo Exercise 10-2 by replacing all instances of yum with dnf.

One subcommand available in DNF but not YUM is system-upgrade. Use this option with the dnf command to perform a kernel update and upgrade to the latest Red Hat version.

File	Description
/etc/dnf/	Contains DNF configuration files and directories
/etc/dnf/dnf.conf	Global configuration file
/var/cache/dnf/	Contains DNF cache files
/etc/yum.repos.d/	Contains repository configuration files

Table 10-12 dnf Configuration Files

DNF uses a few new configuration files and directories to manage repositories. Table 10-12 lists and describes DNF configuration files.

Again, most of the yum commands may be executed with dnf by changing yum to dnf. For example, the command `dnf install vim` will install the vi-improved application. Refer to the preceding section on YUM, as we will not duplicate other command examples here.

The ZYpp Package Manager

ZYpp is the SUSE repository-aware package manager that is the front end to the RPM package manager.

NOTE SUSE also offers a GUI-based, all-purpose systems administration tool called YaST that manages packages, users, security, networking, and so on.

ZYpp uses configuration files and directories to manage repositories. Table 10-13 lists and describes ZYpp configuration files.

Installing, Updating, and Removing Packages with ZYpp

The command `zypper install <package_name>` or `zypper in <package_name>` is used to install a package. You may also use the install subcommand to remove one package while adding another by using the + or - character. For example, the command `zypper install nano -vim` or `zypper remove vi +nano` will install nano and remove vim.

File	Description
/etc/zypp/	Contains the zypper configuration files and directories
/etc/zypp/zypp.conf	Global configuration file
/var/cache/zypp/	Contains ZYpp cache files
/etc/zypp/repos.d/	Contains repository configuration files

Table 10-13 zypper Configuration Files

Option	Description
--provides	Displays packages that provide a file
--requires	Displays a list of package dependencies
-t	Displays the type of package: package RPM package patch Released patch product Group of packages used to install an application pattern Group of packages used to provide a function

Table 10-14 Package Info Options

Updating Packages with zypper

ZYpp is capable of patching existing packages and updating the system. The command zypper list-patches displays a list of required patches. The command zypper patch installs existing patches.

System-wide package updates may be applied using the command zypper update. To apply updates to a specific package, execute the command zypper update <package>.

Removing Packages with zypper

To remove a package, execute the command zypper remove <package_name> or zypper rm <package_name>.

Using zypper to Dump Package Info

The zypper info command may be used to obtain package information. The syntax is zypper info <option> <package_name> or zypper if <option> <pkg_name>.

Table 10-14 lists and describes some package info options.

Working with ZYpp Repositories

Every zypper repository has a unique identification number (see Figure 10-4), alias name, and repository name and priority. The command zypper repos or zypper lr will display a list of repositories and their alias names. The output also indicates whether the repository is enabled and if it has been refreshed.

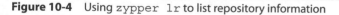

```
#  | Alias                      | Name                                   | Enabled | GPG Check | Refresh | Type
---+----------------------------+----------------------------------------+---------+-----------+---------+-----
1  | repo-debug                 | Debug Repository                       | No      | ----      | ----    | NONE
2  | repo-debug-non-oss         | Debug Repository (Non-OSS)             | No      | ----      | ----    | NONE
3  | repo-debug-update          | Update Repository (Debug)              | No      | ----      | ----    | NONE
4  | repo-debug-update-non-oss  | Update Repository (Debug, Non-OSS)     | No      | ----      | ----    | NONE
5  | repo-non-oss               | Non-OSS Repository                     | Yes     | ( p) Yes  | No      | NONE
6  | repo-oss                   | Main Repository                        | Yes     | ( p) Yes  | No      | NONE
7  | repo-source                | Source Repository                      | No      | ----      | ----    | NONE
8  | repo-source-non-oss        | Source Repository (Non-OSS)            | No      | ----      | ----    | NONE
9  | repo-update                | Main Update Repository                 | Yes     | ( p) Yes  | No      | NONE
10 | repo-update-non-oss        | Update Repository (Non-Oss)            | Yes     | ( p) Yes  | No      | NONE
```

Figure 10-4 Using zypper lr to list repository information

Command	Description
zypper ref zypper refresh	Downloads package metadata
zypper ref -f	Forces download of metadata even if the metadata has not expired

Table 10-15 zypper Refresh Repository Commands

Table 10-15 displays commands used to refresh repository information.

Repository configuration information may be found by executing the command `zypper repos -d`.

Adding a Repository with zypper

The command `zypper ar <url>` or `zypper addrepo <url>` will add a repository. Once the repository is added, you can add an alias name. First, use `zypper lr` to find the new repository's ID number. Then use the command `zypper nr <id_number> <repo_name>` or `zypper namerepo <id_number> <repo_name>`.

Removing a Repository with zypper

The command `zypper rr <repo_name>` or `zypper removerepo <repo_name>` will remove a repository.

Enabling and Disabling Repositories with zypper

A repository may be modified by using the command `zypper mr` or `zypper modifyrepo`. Referring again to Figure 10-4, you will see the repository ID 6, `rep-oss`, is enabled. To disable the repository, execute `zypper mr -d 6` or `zypper modifyrepo -d 6`. To enable a repository, change the `-d` to `-e`.

Installing Applications on Debian with dpkg

Distributions based on the Debian distribution use the Debian Package Manager (`dpkg`) instead of RPM, YUM, DNF, or ZYpp. Popular distributions include Ubuntu, Mint, Parrot, Knoppix, and Kali. In this section, we discuss how to manage Debian software packages. The following topics are addressed:

- Debian package naming conventions
- Managing applications with `dpkg`
- Viewing application information with `apt-cache`

Debian Package Naming Conventions

Debian packages use a naming convention similar to RPM packages. The syntax is `<package_name>_<version>_<architecture>.deb`. For example, for `3dchess` the format is `3dchess_0.8.1-16_i386.deb`. The convention is detailed here:

- **`package_name`** Like with RPM, this is simply the name of the package. In the example, the name of the application in the package is `3dchess`.

- **version** Specifies the version number of the package. In this example, it is 0.8.1-16.
- **architecture** Specifies the hardware the package will run on. In the example, i386 indicates the package will run on Intel 80386 or later CPUs.

Managing Applications with dpkg

The key command-line utility used to install, remove, and upgrade Debian packages is dpkg. The syntax for using dpkg is dpkg <action> [<options>] <package_name> (or <package_filename>).

You can use the actions and options listed in Tables 10-16 and 10-17 with the dpkg command to install an application *but* ignore dependencies, or remove a package *and* the configuration files.

For example, to do a dry-run install of the hoichess application, combine the -i action with the --dry-run option as shown here:

```
dpkg -i --dry-run hoichess_0.22.0-2_amd64.deb
```

This assumes that the hoichess_0.22.0-2_amd64.deb file is in the current directory.

The dpkg configuration files are located in /etc/dpkg and /var/lib/dpkg. For example, the /etc/dpkg/dpkg.cfg file contains the dpkg default options, and the /var/lib/dpkg/status file contains the status of the available packages.

NOTE There is a package available called alien that converts .deb packages to .rpm, and vice versa. Run apt install alien on Debian-class systems, or dnf install alien on Red Hat–class systems if the EPEL repository is configured.

Action	Description
-i	Installs or upgrades the specified package.
-r	Uninstalls the specified package but does not delete configuration files.
-P	Uninstalls the specified package and deletes all its configuration files.
--configure	Reconfigures the specified package (can also be done using the command dpkg-reconfigure).
-p	Displays information about the specified package. The package must already be installed.
-I	Displays information about a package that isn't currently installed on the system.
-l	Lists all installed packages on the system.
-L	Lists all files that were installed by the specified package on the system.
-S <filename>	Identifies the package that installed the specified file.

Table 10-16 dpkg Command Actions

Use This Option	With Action	Description
-B	-r	When you're uninstalling a package that other packages are dependent on, this option disables those packages.
-G	-i	This option tells dpkg to not install the specified package if a newer version of the same package is already installed.
-E	-i	This option tells dpkg to not install the specified package if the same version of that package is already installed.
--ignore-depends=<pkg>	-i or -r	This option causes dpkg to ignore dependency checking for <pkg> when installing or removing a package.
--no-act	-i or -r	This option tells dpkg to check for problems (such as unresolved dependencies) when installing or removing a package.
--recursive	-i	This option allows you to install multiple packages at once using * in the package filename part of the command. All matching packages in the current directory as well as subdirectories will be installed.

Table 10-17 dpkg Command Options

Viewing Application Information with apt-cache

In addition to dpkg, you can also use several APT (Advanced Package Tool) tools to manage packages on Debian-class systems. The apt-cache command is used to query package information from the Debian package repository database which includes /etc/apt/apt.conf and /etc/apt/sources.list files or the /etc/apt/apt.conf.d/ or /etc/apt/sources.list.d/ directories. These files and directories contain the locations as to where to search and find devices and applications. Common apt-cache commands are shown in Table 10-18.

Common apt-cache Command	Description
apt-cache showpkg <package> or apt-cache show <package>	Displays information about the package.
apt-cache stats	Displays the number of packages installed, dependency information, and other package cache statistics.
apt-cache unmet	Reports any missing dependencies in the package cache.
apt-cache depends <package>	Displays all the package's dependencies.
apt-cache pkgnames [<package>]	Checks whether a package is installed on the system. Leaving out the package name displays a list of all the packages installed on the system.
apt-cache search <keyword>	Searches package descriptions for the specified keyword.

Table 10-18 Common apt-cache Commands

Installing Applications on Debian with APT

In addition to apt-cache, the APT suite of tools also includes a repository-aware installer called apt-get or apt. This is the equivalent to the yum repository-aware utility on an RPM system.

The /etc/apt/sources.list file and the /etc/apt/sources.list.d/ directory define the repositories from which apt can install packages. As with yum, these repositories can reside on a local optical disc, a local hard drive, or a server on the Internet. A sample sources.list file is shown here:

```
root@debian11:/etc/apt# cat sources.list
#deb cdrom:[Debian 11.3 _Bullseye_ - Release amd64 (20221028.5)]/
bullseye contrib main
deb http://security.debian.org/debian-security/ bullseye-security main contrib
deb-src http://security.debian.org/debian-security/ bullseye-security main contrib
```

Package repositories are identified in this file with the prefix deb, whereas source file repositories are identified with deb-src. After the prefix, the URL to the repository is specified.

The syntax for using apt is pretty straightforward:

```
apt action [options] <package_name>
```

Commonly used apt actions and options are listed in Tables 10-19 and 10-20, respectively.

Troubleshooting an Application Crash

When installing applications with APT, DNF, or ZYpp, you must be certain that you're installing the latest software. Differences in software versions, because a version is too old, for example, could cause applications to crash.

On Red Hat–class systems run dnf update or dnf upgrade (or zypper refresh and then zypper update on SUSE systems) to make sure you're pulling applications from the most recently updated repositories; otherwise, you could download old applications that can cause system downtime.

apt Action	Description
install	Installs the latest version of a specified package
remove	Removes the specified package
update	Displays updated information about all packages available in your configured package repositories
upgrade	Upgrades all installed packages to the newest version
dist-upgrade	Upgrades all installed packages to the newest version and performs a kernel update
full-upgrade	Upgrades all installed packages to the newest version, but avoids upgrading packages if the upgrade would break a dependency
autoremove	Removes outdated dependencies that are no longer needed

Table 10-19 Common apt Actions

apt Option	Associated Action	Description
-d	upgrade or install	Downloads the specified package but doesn't install it
-s	All commands	Simulates the actions associated with the specified command but does not perform them
-f	install or remove	Checks for unmet dependencies and fixes them, if possible
-q	All commands	Suppresses progress information
-y	All commands	Sends a default "yes" answer to any prompts displayed in the action
--no-upgrade	install	Tells apt not to upgrade a package if an older version of the package has already been installed

Table 10-20 Common apt Options

On Debian-class systems, run `apt update` first, then `app upgrade`. On Red Hat `update` and/or `upgrade` both connect to the latest repositories and upgrade applications. But on Debian systems, `update` verifies that you're connected to the most updated repositories, then `upgrade` performs the software upgrade. So when performing an upgrade on Debian, run `apt update`, then `apt upgrade`.

EXAM TIP To manipulate software on an Arch Linux distribution, use the `pacman` command. Run `pacman -S <pkgname>` to install, and `pacman -R <pkgname>` to remove an application.

Using Universal Linux App Stores

As you have seen, each Linux version has its own method to install applications. Wouldn't it be nice to have a package manager that works on all versions of Linux? What comes closest to this are universal packaging systems.

Universal packaging allows you to run a mixed Linux environment of Oracle Linux, Ubuntu, and SUSE and not have to bother with knowing when to use DNF, APT, or ZYpp. In this section, we'll discuss the three most popular sandboxed applications:

- Snap fundamentals
- Flatpak fundamentals
- AppImage fundamentals

Snap Fundamentals

Snap is managed by Canonical, the same organization that releases Ubuntu Linux. Canonical maintains the Snap package manager and the Snap Store. A snap is a bundle of an app and its dependencies that works without modification across Linux distributions.

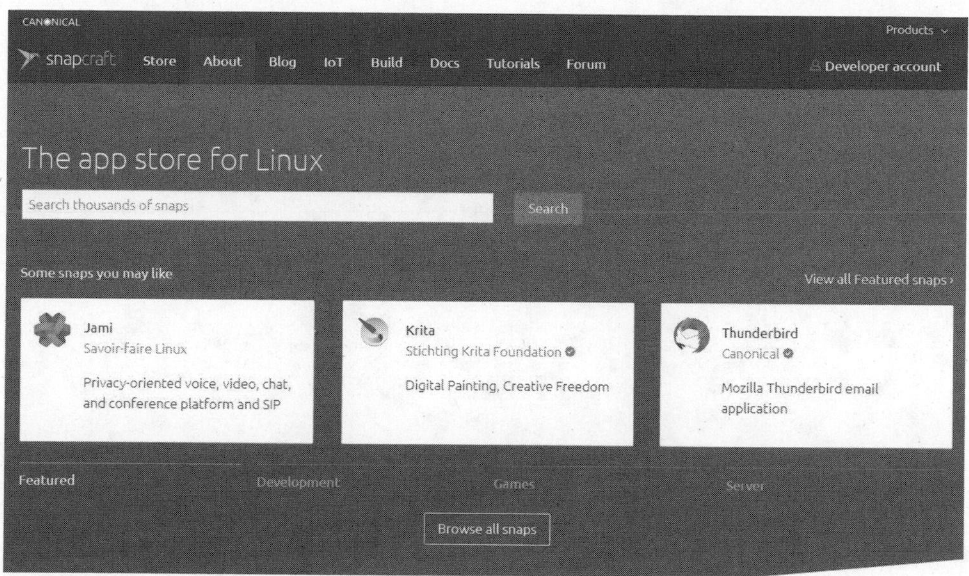

Figure 10-5 The `snapcraft.io` app store

From the Snap Store, you can download development apps, games, social networking apps, productivity apps, photo and video production apps, and more. Plus, the Snap Store has snaps to manage and update your Internet of Things (IoT) devices. The `snapd` demon runs in the background to keep your applications running while using Snap. Visit the Snap store at `https://snapcraft.io`, shown in Figure 10-5, to get started using snaps.

Flatpak Fundamentals

Like Snap, Flatpak (`https://flatpak.org/`) offers a universal package manager for many Linux distributions. Flatpak works together with the Flathub app store as its package repository, which offers the latest stable packages. Flatpak's app library is primarily composed of desktop applications. Visit the Flathub app store at `https://flatpak.org` or `https://flathub.org`, shown in Figure 10-6, to get started using Flatpak.

AppImage Fundamentals

Of the three universal package managers, AppImage is the most popular, storing more than 1,000 applications in the AppImages store. A huge benefit is that dependencies are handled internally, so you will not have to handle any dependency issues. Visit the AppImages app store at `https://appimage.github.io`, shown in Figure 10-7, to get started using AppImage. AppImage uses their app image hub to store their AppImage package manager.

The key idea of the AppImage format is one app = one file. Learn more at `https://appimage.org`.

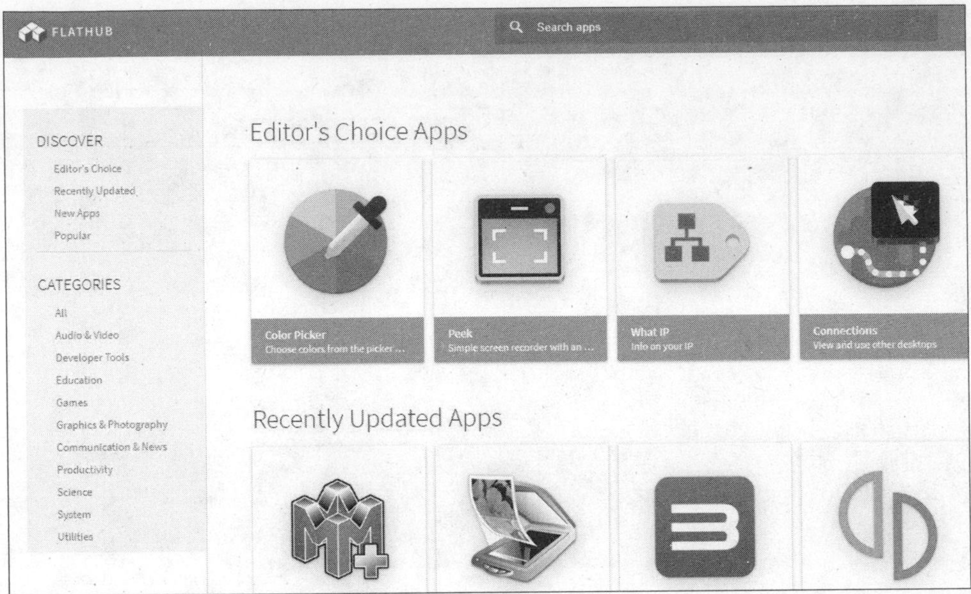

Figure 10-6 The `flathub.org` app store

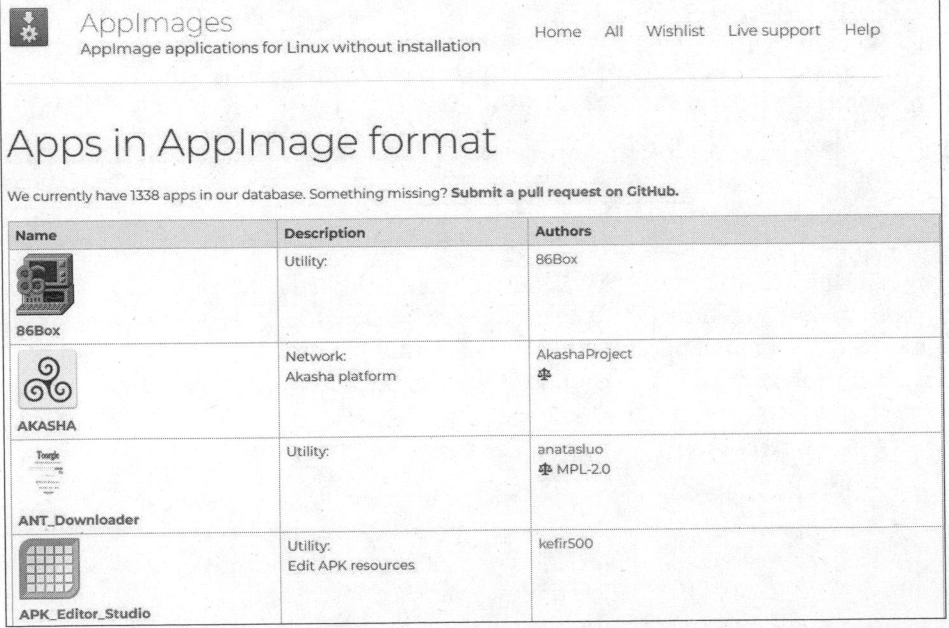

Figure 10-7 The `appimage.github.io` app store

Installing Applications from Source Code

In addition to installing software using a package manager, you can install software on Linux from source code. In fact, many of the applications and services you will install on a Linux system will be delivered as source code, not as a binary executable. When you install the software on your local system, you actually compile the source code from the installation files into a binary executable that can be run.

Distributing software in this manner has many advantages. Key among these is the fact that you don't have to create a separate executable and installation package for each delivery architecture and platform. You can have the installation process detect the type of system the software is being installed on and compile the software appropriately.

The key disadvantage to this approach is the fact that it makes the installation process much more complex. Users must have a compiler installed on their system; otherwise, they won't be able to compile the source code into a binary executable. In addition, the user must know the proper procedure for compiling the source code and installing the resulting executable.

Fortunately, a standard process for completing this task has been adopted by most developers. This process is composed of

1. Preparing the installation files
2. Compiling the executable
3. Installing the executable

Finally, you will learn how to uninstall software compiled from source code.

Preparing the Installation Files

The first step in installing an application from source code is to download the appropriate installation files from the Internet. For example, if you wanted to install the `pure-ftpd` service, an FTP server, you would navigate to the website `https://www.pureftpd.org/project/pure-ftpd/` and download the installation files.

Using `wget` and `curl` to Download Source Code

The `wget` and `curl` commands are utilities available for downloading software and source code when a web browser such as Firefox cannot be used; for example, from a server with only a command-line interface (CLI).

As an example of using `wget`, running the following command downloads the `gnuchess` source code:

```
wget https://ftp.gnu.org/gnu/chess/gnuchess-6.2.9.tar.bz2
```

To use `curl` to download the source code of the `emacs` editor to replace the `vi` editor, run

```
curl -o emacs.tgz https://ftp.gnu.org/gnu/emacs-28.1.tar.gz
```

EXAM TIP The wget and curl commands are common utilities used on Linux servers for downloading source code on command-line interfaces. For a command-line web browser, use links.

One thing you'll notice about installation files used to install from source code is that they are usually distributed as a tarball file. Tarball files usually have a .tar.gz or .tgz extension. Because these applications are distributed as tarballs, you must first use the command gunzip to decompress the archive and the tar command to extract the archive. For example, running gunzip pureftpd.tar.gz would create the file pureftpd.tar.

Next, execute the command tar -xvf <tar_filename> to *untar* the file. The tar command is used to create and extract archive files. To *untar* pureftpd.tar, you would run the command tar xvf pureftpd.tar (the dash for the tar command is optional).

TIP tar stands for tape archiver, because it was originally designed for making backups to magnetic tape.

You don't have to uncompress the file with gunzip first; tar has built compression into the application. After downloading the tarball, create a directory to extract the file to and then move the file to that directory. Change to that directory, and then run tar -zxvf <filename> to decompress and extract the archive to the current directory.

NOTE You can also run tar xvf file.tar.gz. The tar command automatically recognizes when a file is compressed and extracts it properly.

For example, to extract pureftpd you can enter tar zxvf pureftpd.tar.gz at the shell prompt. The z option performs the gzip or gunzip compression operations depending on if you are creating or extracting an archive. The source files are extracted to the current directory and are used to create the executable application, as well as a variety of utilities needed to help create the executable. Here is a sample list of files:

```
openSUSE:/root/work# ls
AUTHORS                         README.Donations        depcomp
CONTACT                         README.LDAP             gui
COPYING                         README.MacOS-X          install-sh
ChangeLog                       README.MySQL            m4
FAQ                             README.PGSQL            man
HISTORY                         README.TLS              missing
INSTALL                         README.Virtual-Users    pam
Makefile.am                     README.Windows          pure-ftpd.png
Makefile.gui                    THANKS                  pure-ftpd.spec
Makefile.in                     aclocal.m4              pure-ftpd.spec.in
NEWS                            compile                 puredb
README                          config.h.in             pureftpd-ldap.conf
README.Authentication-Modules   configuration-file      pureftpd-mysql.conf
README.Configuration-File       configure               pureftpd-pgsql.conf
README.Contrib                  configure.ac            pureftpd.schema
README.Debian                   contrib                 src
```

With the files extracted, you next need to prepare the installation files to be compiled. You do so by using the `configure` script. To run this script, first verify that you're in the directory created when the tarball was extracted; then enter `./configure` at the shell prompt, as shown here:

```
openSUSE:/root/work # ./configure
checking for a BSD-compatible install... /usr/bin/install -c
checking whether build environment is sane... yes
checking for a thread-safe mkdir -p... /bin/mkdir -p
checking for gawk... gawk
checking whether make sets $(MAKE)... yes
checking for ranlib... ranlib
checking for gcc... gcc
checking whether the C compiler works... yes
checking for C compiler default output file name... a.out
...
```

Placing `./` in front of `configure` tells Linux to look in the current directory for the file named `configure`, because `.` means current directory.

The `configure` file is a script that does two things when it is run. First, it checks your system to make sure all the necessary components required to compile the program are available. One of the most important tools it checks for is the existence of a C compiler. If you don't have a C compiler, such as the GNU C Compiler (`gcc`) or the GNU C++ Compiler (`gcc-c++`), the `configure` script will display an error on the screen instructing you to install a compiler and then run `configure` again. It also verifies that your overall system environment is compatible with the program you're going to install.

Second, the `configure` file also creates a very important file called `Makefile`. Because most source code applications are designed to be deployed on a variety of distributions and architectures, the installation program needs to know how to customize the source code files such that the resulting executable will run on your specific system.

One of the last steps the `configure` script takes is to create a `Makefile` file. The `Makefile` file contains specific instructions for how the executable should be compiled to run on your platform.

Once `configure` has been run and the `Makefile` created, the next step in the process is to compile the executable. Let's discuss how this is done next.

Compiling the Executable

At this point, the program to install still exists only as source code. Before you can run it, you must convert the text-based source code into a binary executable file. You do so by using the `make` command.

The `make` command calls the C compiler and directs it to read the source code files, using the specifications and options listed in the `Makefile` file, and then generates a compiled executable file. Simply enter `make` at the shell prompt without any options. Here is an example:

```
openSUSE:/root/work # make
make  all-recursive
make[1]: Entering directory '/home/tux/Downloads/pure-ftpd-1.0.29'
Making all in puredb
make[2]: Entering directory '/home/tux/Downloads/pure-ftpd-1.0.29/puredb'
Making all in src
```

```
make[3]: Entering directory '/home/tux/Downloads/pure-ftpd-1.0.29/puredb/src'
gcc -DHAVE_CONFIG_H -I. -I../..    -I/usr/local/include -DCONFDIR=\"/etc\" -
DSTATEDIR=\"/var\"  -g -O2 -MT puredb_read.o -MD -MP -MF .deps/puredb_read.Tpo -c
-o puredb_read.o puredb_read.c
mv -f .deps/puredb_read.Tpo .deps/puredb_read.Po
rm -f libpuredb_read.a
ar cru libpuredb_read.a puredb_read.o
...
```

Understand that make only creates the executable. Before you can use your new program, it needs to be installed according to the Filesystem Hierarchy Standard (FHS). make can copy the executable, startup scripts, and documentation files to the appropriate directories in your filesystem. Let's discuss how this is done next.

Installing the Executable

To install the new executable on your system, run `make install`. This tells make to place the executable program into /usr/bin/, the program libraries into /usr/lib/, and the program's man pages into /usr/man/, following the instructions in the INSTALL portion of the Makefile file. The make utility will then install the application, as shown here:

```
openSUSE:/root/work # make install
Making install in puredb
make[1]: Entering directory '/home/tux/Downloads/pure-ftpd-1.0.29/puredb'
Making install in src
make[2]: Entering directory '/home/tux/Downloads/pure-ftpd-1.0.29/puredb/src'
make[3]: Entering directory '/home/tux/Downloads/pure-ftpd-1.0.29/puredb/src'
make[3]: Nothing to be done for 'install-exec-am'.
make[3]: Nothing to be done for 'install-data-am'.
...
```

At this point, the application or service is ready to run. Simply enter the appropriate commands at the shell prompt.

Exercise 10-3: Building Software from Source Code

In this exercise, you will practice installing the Pure-FTPd software from a tarball.

You can perform this exercise using the virtual machine that comes with this book. Make certain you are logged in as user **root** with a password of **root**. Follow these steps:

VIDEO Please watch the Exercise 10-3 video for a demonstration on how to perform this task.

1. Use the **cd /LABS/Chapter_10/work** command. Use the **ls** command to verify the file pure-ftpd-1.0.29.tar.gz exists in the directory.

NOTE There are two copies of the compressed file. One is in /LABS/Chapter_10/work and the other in /LABS/Chapter_10/source. Make certain you use the file in /LABS/Chapter_10/work. The file in /LABS/Chapter_10/source is a backup copy.

2. Enter **`tar -zxvf pure-ftpd-1.0.29.tar.gz`** at the shell prompt.
3. Use the **`cd`** command to change to the directory created by `tar`. This should be `pure-ftpd-1.0.29`.
4. Enter **`ls`** to view the files extracted from the tarball.
5. Enter **`./configure`** at the shell prompt. The `configure` script will check your system and verify that the software can be installed. You must have a C compiler installed on your system. If `configure` reports that you're missing a compiler, use the **`yum -y install gcc`** command or **`yum -y groupinstall "Development Tools"`** to download all the tools needed for proper software builds.
6. When the `configure` script is done, compile the executable by entering **`make`** at the shell prompt.
7. When the compilation is complete, install the executable by entering **`make install`** at the shell prompt.
8. Start the service by entering **`/usr/local/sbin/pure-ftpd &`** at the shell prompt.
9. Test the system by entering **`ftp localhost`** at the shell prompt.
10. When prompted, enter **`anonymous`** for a username. You should be logged in to the FTP server at this point.
11. Enter **`quit`** to close the connection.

    At this point, you have a functioning FTP server running on your Linux system!

Uninstalling Software Compiled from Source Code

Uninstalling software compiled from source code is very similar to the installation process.

For most applications or services that are installed using the standard build process we discussed earlier, you must (in most cases) have access to your installation files to uninstall the associated software. The issue here is that many Linux administrators delete the installation source files once the installation process is complete to save disk space. If you do this, you've just deleted the files you'll need if you ever decide to uninstall the software. I recommend that you create a protected directory in your filesystem somewhere that only `root` can access and keep your source installation files there. Yes, it does take up a little bit of disk space, but you'll have the files you need if uninstalling ever becomes necessary.

The uninstall process can vary slightly from product to product. Some applications may include an uninstall script. If this is the case, execute this script to uninstall the application from your system.

Other products may include an `UNINSTALL` target in their `Makefile` file. If this is the case, first run ./`configure` from the original directory created when extracting the tarfile, just as you did when you first installed the software. Then, instead of running `make install`, run `make uninstall`. This causes the `make` utility to follow the instructions in the `UNINSTALL` portion of the `Makefile` to remove the software from your system. (As an extra project, try running `make uninstall` to remove the Pure-FTPd service from your system that you installed in Exercise 10-3.)

How do you know which method to use? The tarball you downloaded should include a `README` file that documents both the install and uninstall processes for the software. Check this file first. If the information isn't available, then check the FAQ or knowledge base on the website of the organization that produced the software. One of these resources should provide you with the steps you need to follow to uninstall the software.

Managing Shared Libraries

In addition to checking for software package dependencies, you may also need to verify that your system is configured properly to access the libraries for an application to run. In this section, you will learn how to do this. The following topics are addressed:

- How shared libraries work
- Managing shared library dependencies

Let's begin by discussing how shared libraries work.

How Shared Libraries Work

On Linux, applications running on the system can share code elements called *shared libraries.* This is very useful. Shared libraries make it such that software developers don't have to reinvent the wheel each time they write a new program.

If you think about it, many functions are commonly used across many programs. For example, the process for opening a file, saving a file, and closing an open file are the same no matter which application is being used. Without shared libraries, programmers would have to include the code for completing these basic tasks in every application they write. What a waste of time and resources!

Instead, with shared libraries, software developers can focus on the code elements that are unique to the individual application. For common elements that are shared across applications, they can simply link to the prewritten code in a shared library and not worry about rewriting the code.

NOTE Shared libraries in Linux work in much the same manner as dynamic link libraries (DLLs) on Windows systems.

Using shared libraries has many benefits. Obviously, it dramatically speeds up development time. It also makes the programs being written smaller and leaner.

There are two types of shared libraries on Linux:

- **Dynamic** Dynamic shared libraries exist as files in the Linux filesystem. Programmers simply insert links to these functions in their program code.

The functions are called from dynamic libraries when the program runs. Using dynamic shared libraries decreases the overall size of the executable; however, they do create a dependency issue. If the program calls a function from a library that isn't installed or is unavailable, the application will fail.

- **Static** In contrast to dynamic shared libraries, static shared libraries are linked statically into the program when it's compiled. In essence, with static libraries, the actual code elements for the functions called are integrated directly into the application. Obviously, this results in larger applications. However, it has the advantage of making the application independent of having the library installed, unlike with dynamic libraries.

Which type is best? It depends on the application. Most applications use dynamic libraries. This allows them to provide a lot of functionality with a relatively small footprint on the hard drive. However, there are applications that use static libraries, especially applications that are designed to help you rescue a malfunctioning system. Instead of linking to dynamic shared libraries, which may not be available in a system rescue scenario, applications that use static libraries are completely self-contained and can run in a minimal Linux environment.

Shared library files use a special naming format to help you identify the type of shared library it is. This syntax is `libname.type.version`.

Notice that the filename of all shared libraries starts with `lib`. It is followed by the name of the shared library. The *`type`* part of the filename identifies the type of shared library: `so` indicates the file is a dynamic shared library, whereas `a` indicates the file is a static library. The *`version`* part of the filename specifies the version number of the library. For example, `libfreetype.so.6.4.0` is a dynamic shared library.

With this in mind, let's discuss how you manage shared library dependencies.

Managing Shared Library Dependencies

Linux uses a configuration file to tell applications running on the system where they can find the dynamic shared library files on the system. Using this type of configuration provides application developers with a degree of independence. They don't have to worry about where the shared libraries will reside when their programs are run. They let the configuration file tell the program where they are, wherever that happens to be on a particular Linux system.

The dynamic shared library configuration file is `/etc/ld.so.conf`. Here is a sample file:

```
openSUSE:/etc # cat ld.so.conf
/usr/X11R6/lib64/Xaw3d
/usr/X11R6/lib64
/usr/local/lib
/lib64
/lib
/usr/lib64
/usr/lib
/usr/local/lib64
include /etc/ld.so.conf.d/*.conf
```

As you can see in this example, the file simply contains a list of paths in the filesystem where shared library files are stored. Applications that are linked to functions in these files will search through these paths to locate the appropriate libraries.

To view a list of all shared libraries available on your Linux system, enter `ldconfig -p` at the shell prompt. Here is an example:

```
openSUSE:~ # ldconfig -p
1423 libs found in cache '/etc/ld.so.cache'
      libzypp.so.706 (libc6,x86-64) => /usr/lib64/libzypp.so.706
      libzio.so.0 (libc6,x86-64) => /usr/lib64/libzio.so.0
      libz.so.1 (libc6,x86-64) => /lib64/libz.so.1
      libz.so.1 (libc6) => /lib/libz.so.1
...
```

You can also view the shared libraries required by a specific application using the `ldd` command. The syntax is `ldd -v <executable_filename>`. For example, if you wanted to see what shared libraries are required by the `ip` command, to manage network connections, you would enter `ldd -v /sbin/ip` at the shell prompt:

```
openSUSE:~ # ldd -v /sbin/ip
      linux-vdso.so.1 =>  (0x00007fffe4ab2000)
      libdl.so.2 => /lib64/libdl.so.2 (0x00007f7c07e7d000)
      libc.so.6 => /lib64/libc.so.6 (0x00007f7c07b1d000)
      /lib64/ld-linux-x86-64.so.2 (0x00007f7c08081000)
```

NOTE You need to specify the full path to the executable along with the executable's filename with the `ldd` command.

One of the key uses for the `ldd` command is to check for shared library dependencies. It determines whether all of the libraries required by the application have been installed. If they have, you won't see any error messages, as shown in the preceding example. If a library file is missing, an error message will be displayed. You can then locate and install the missing library and all will be well with the world.

So, how does an application know which directories to look in when trying to locate a shared library? The applications don't actually check the `/etc/ld.so.conf` file. Instead, they check the library cache and the `LD_LIBRARY_PATH` environment variable. The library cache is `/etc/ld.so.cache`. This file contains a list of all the system libraries and is refreshed when the system is initially booted.

This is key. If you add a new dynamic library directory to the `/etc/ld.so.conf` file, you'll be very frustrated when you try to run the applications that are linked to the libraries in this directory. That's because the library cache hasn't been updated with the new information. To fix this, you have two options:

- **Use `ldconfig`** The `ldconfig` command is used to rebuild the library cache manually.

- **Set `LD_LIBRARY_PATH`** You can also add the path to the `LD_LIBRARY_PATH` environment variable. You probably want to add the new path to the end of the list of directories that may already exist in the variable, so you should use the following commands:

```
LD_LIBRARY_PATH=$LD_LIBRARY_PATH:new_path
export LD_LIBRARY_PATH
```

Generally speaking, using `ldconfig` is the preferred option. This ensures the shared libraries are always available to the applications that need them, even if the system is rebooted. I usually set the value of `LD_LIBRARY_PATH` only in situations where I don't have the `root` password, or I have two versions of the same shared library installed in different directories and I want to use one version over the other.

Exercise 10-4: Working with Shared Libraries

In this exercise, you will practice managing shared libraries. You can perform this exercise using the virtual machine that comes with this book.

VIDEO Please watch the Exercise 10-4 video for a demonstration on how to perform this task.

Complete the following:

1. With your system running, open a terminal session.
2. If necessary, change to your `root` user account by entering **`su -`** followed by your root user's password.
3. View the shared libraries used by the `ping` executable on your system by entering **`ldd -v /bin/ping`** at the shell prompt. You should see that `ping` requires the `libc.so.6` shared library.
4. Find the location of the `libc.so.6` library file on your system by entering **`find / -name libc.so.6`** at the shell prompt. You should see that the file resides in `/lib64`.
5. View your system's library cache by entering **`ldconfig -p`** at the shell prompt.
6. Rebuild your library cache by entering **`ldconfig -v`** at the shell prompt.

Chapter Review

The chapter began with a definition of terms used in package management. Also you learned multiple methods of installing packages.

We first reviewed Red Hat Package Manager and went over RPM commands to add, erase, and upgrade packages. You also learned to query the RPM database to retrieve package information. Next, we reviewed the capabilities of the YUM package manager.

YUM is also able to add, remove, and upgrade packages as well as search for and report package information. You learned that YUM is being deprecated and is being replaced by DNF. You saw that DNF uses different configuration files than YUM, with the exception of `/etc/yum.repos.d/`. You also learned that many of the commands in YUM are duplicated in the DNF package. You then learned that ZYpp is SUSE's package manager and investigated some of its command syntax.

To this point, all the package managers we investigated were front ends to RPM. We then reviewed `dpkg`, the Debian Package Manager.

Tarfiles provide a method of installing and uninstalling files. We reviewed how to create tarfiles, extract source code and applications from tarfiles, and install a package from a tarfile. You can download tarfiles from the Internet using `wget` or `curl` and add additional library search paths to the `LD_LIBRARY_PATH` variable.

Finally, you learned about shared libraries and modules.

Here are some key facts to remember about managing Linux software:

- RPM packages are installed using the Red Hat Package Manager.
- RPM packages are compiled for a specific architecture and sometimes a specific Linux distribution.
- You can enter `rpm --checksig` to verify the digital signature of an RPM package before you install it.
- You can enter `rpm -i` to install a package file on your system.
- To uninstall an RPM package, use the `rpm -e` command.
- You can install or update a package using the `rpm -U` command.
- You can upgrade an existing package to a newer version using the `rpm -F` command. If the older package doesn't exist, no upgrade is performed.
- To query a package, use the `-q` option with `rpm`.
- To verify a package, use the `-V` option with `rpm`.
- The `yum` utility allows you to download and then install a package and all its dependencies.
- The `yum install <packagename>` command installs a package on Red Hat.
- The `yum remove <packagename>` command uninstalls a package.
- Repository information can be stored in the repository section of `/etc/yum.conf` or in the directory `/etc/yum.repos.d/`.
- DNF is an upgrade and eventual replacement of YUM.
- The `dnf install <packagename>` command installs a package on Red Hat.
- The `dnf remove <packagename>` command uninstalls a package.
- The `zypper install <packagename>` command installs a package on SUSE.

- The `zypper remove <packagename>` command uninstalls a package.
- The `pacman -S <packagename>` installs a package on Arch Linux.
- The `pacman -R <packagename>` removes a package.
- Flatpak, Snap, and AppImage are universal packaging systems for Linux.
- To install from source code, first download and extract a tarball file; for example, with `wget` or `curl`.
- To download `gnuchess` using `wget`, run `wget https://ftp.gnu.org/gnu/chess/gnuchess-6.2.9.tar.bz2`
- To download the `emacs` editor using `curl`, run `curl -o emacs.tgz https://ftp.gnu.org/gnu/emacs-28.1.tar.gz`
- In the installation directory, run `configure`, `make`, and `make install`.
- The `configure` command checks your system to verify compatibility and creates the `Makefile` file.
- The `make` command compiles a binary executable from the source code text using the specifications in the `Makefile` file.
- The `make install` command installs files to `/usr/bin/`, `/usr/lib/`, and `/usr/man/`.
- The `make uninstall` command is typically used to uninstall an executable installed from source.
- Distributions based on the Debian distribution use `dpkg`, the Debian Package Manager.
- Debian packages include dependency information.
- You use the `dpkg` command to install, uninstall, query, and verify Debian packages.
- The `apt-cache` command is used to query package information from the Debian package database.
- The `apt` command automatically downloads and installs packages (along with all dependent packages) for you.
- Run `apt update` before running `apt upgrade` to assure you're getting the latest software on a Debian system.
- Run `zypper refresh` then `zypper update` to install the latest applications on a SUSE-based system.
- Applications running on a Linux system can share code elements called shared libraries.
- Linux applications can use either dynamic or static shared libraries.
- The dynamic shared library configuration file is `/etc/ld.so.conf`.

- The `/etc/ld.so.conf` file contains a list of paths in the filesystem where shared library files are stored.
- To view a list of the shared libraries available on a Linux system, enter `ldconfig -p` at the shell prompt.
- You can view libraries required by a specific application with `ldd -v <command>`.
- The library cache is `/etc/ld.so.cache`.
- The `ld.so.cache` file contains a list of all the system libraries and is refreshed when the system is initially booted.
- If you add library files to a directory not listed in the `/etc/ld.so.conf` file, you must use the `ldconfig` command to rebuild the library cache manually.
- You can also add a new library file path to the `LD_LIBRARY_PATH` environment variable.

Questions

1. You've just downloaded a file named `FC-6-i386-DVD.iso` to the `/home/tux/` directory on your Linux system. Which two commands were most likely used to download this file? (Choose two.)

   A. `wget`

   B. `upload`

   C. `curl`

   D. `download`

2. After running `apt upgrade` on Ubuntu, you get an error. Which command or commands should you run next?

   A. `dpkg update`, then `dpkg upgrade`

   B. `./configure update`

   C. `apt update`, then `apt upgrade` again

   D. `zypper update`, then `apt upgrade` again

3. You've just downloaded a file named `BitTorrent-7.10.1.tar.gz` to your home directory. Assuming the current directory is ~, what command would you enter at the shell prompt to extract all the files from this archive?

   A. `gzip -d ./BitTorrent-7.10.1.tar.gz`

   B. `tar -axvf ./BitTorrent-7.10.1.tar.gz`

   C. `tar -xvf ./BitTorrent-7.10.1.tar.gz`

   D. `tar -zxvf ./BitTorrent-7.10.1.tar.gz`

4. Where does RPM store its database of installed packages?
   A. `/var/lib/rpm`
   B. `/etc/rpm`
   C. `/var/rpmdb`
   D. `/tmp/rpm`
5. You've just downloaded an RPM package file named `evolution-2.6.0-41.i586.rpm` to your home directory. Assuming the current directory is ~, what command could you use to check the digital signature of the downloaded file to verify that it hasn't been tampered with?
   A. `rpm --checksig evolution-2.6.0-41.i586.rpm`
   B. `rpm --verify evolution-2.6.0-41.i586.rpm`
   C. `rpm -tamperproof evolution-2.6.0-41.i586.rpm`
   D. `rpm --signature evolution-2.6.0-41.i586.rpm`
6. You've just downloaded an RPM package file named `evolution-2.6.0-41.i586.rpm` to your home directory. Assuming the current directory is ~, what command could you use to install the package on your system, displaying a progress indicator as the installation is completed? (Choose two.)
   A. `rpm -i evolution-2.6.0-41.i586.rpm`
   B. `rpm -ihv evolution-2.6.0-41.i586.rpm`
   C. `rpm -U evolution-2.6.0-41.i586.rpm`
   D. `rpm -install --progress evolution-2.6.0-41.i586.rpm`
   E. `rpm --Uhv evolution-2.6.0-41.i586.rpm`
7. You need to uninstall the `pure-ftpd` service from your Linux system. You've switched to the directory where the original installation files are located. What's the first command to enter to uninstall this package?
   A. `./configure`
   B. `make`
   C. `make remove`
   D. `make uninstall`
8. You've installed an RPM package file named `evolution-2.6.0-41.i586.rpm` on your Linux system. What command would you use to uninstall this package?
   A. `rpm -U evolution`
   B. `rpm -U --remove evolution`
   C. `rpm -i --remove evolution`
   D. `rpm -e evolution`

9. You currently have an RPM package file named `evolution-2.2.0-2.i586.rpm` installed on your Linux system. You've recently downloaded the `evolution-2.6.0-41.i586.rpm` package from www.sourceforge.net. What command would you use to install the newer version of this package? (Choose two.)

   A. `rpm -U evolution-2.6.0-41.i586.rpm`

   B. `rpm -i evolution-2.6.0-41.i586.rpm`

   C. `rpm -i --upgrade evolution-2.6.0-41.i586.rpm`

   D. `rpm -e evolution-2.2.0-2.i586.rpm`

   E. `rpm -F evolution-2.6.0-41.i586.rpm`

10. You currently have an RPM package file named `evolution-2.6.0-41.i586.rpm` installed on your Linux system. What command would you enter to display summary information about the package?

    A. `rpm -s evolution`

    B. `rpm -qs evolution`

    C. `rpm -qi evolution`

    D. `rpm -V --summary evolution`

11. You've used the `rpm` command with the `-q --requires` option to determine the components required by the RPM package. One of the required components is `/usr/bin/perl`. What command would you enter to find out which RPM package provides this component?

    A. `rpm -q --whatprovides /usr/bin/perl`

    B. `rpm -qs --requires /usr/bin/perl`

    C. `rpm -qi --requires /usr/bin/perl`

    D. `rpm -q --provides perl`

12. You've used the `rpm` command with the `-V` option to verify an RPM package installed on your system. The output from the command listed the following error code:

    ```
    S.5....T     c     /opt/kde3/share/config/kdm/kdmrc
    ```

    What does this error code indicate? (Choose three.)

    A. There's a problem with the size of the file.

    B. There's a problem with the mode of the file.

    C. There's a problem with the timestamp of the file.

    D. There's a problem with the checksum.

    E. There's a problem with a file's ownership.

13. You need to extract a single file out of an RPM package. Which utility can be used to do this?

    A. `tar`

    B. `rpm`

    C. `dpkg`

    D. `rpm2cpio`

14. You need to install the GNU C Compiler (`gcc`) package on your system. Which command will do this? (Choose two.)

    A. `yum gcc`

    B. `yum install gcc`

    C. `dnf install gcc`

    D. `dnf installpkg gcc`

15. Which command generates a list of available updates for all installed packages on a Linux system?

    A. `yum list updates`

    B. `yum info`

    C. `dnf list available`

    D. `dnf list all`

16. What does the `configure` script do in an application's installation directory? (Choose two.)

    A. It compiles the source code into a binary executable.

    B. It checks the local system to verify that the necessary components are available.

    C. It copies the binary executable and other files, such as documentation, to the appropriate directories in the filesystem.

    D. It creates the `Makefile` file.

    E. It verifies that the installation files haven't been corrupted or tampered with.

17. What does the `make` command do when installing an application from source code?

    A. It compiles the source code into a binary executable.

    B. It checks the local system to verify that the necessary components are available.

    C. It copies the binary executable and other files, such as documentation, to the appropriate directories in the filesystem.

    D. It creates the `Makefile` file.

18. What does the `make install` command do when installing an application from source code?

A. It compiles the source code into a binary executable.

B. It checks the local system to verify that the necessary components are available.

C. It copies the binary executable and other files, such as documentation, to the appropriate directories in the filesystem.

D. It creates the `Makefile` file.

19. Which action, when used with the `dpkg` command, uninstalls a specified package and deletes all its configuration files?

A. `-r`

B. `-p`

C. `-P`

D. `-U`

20. You want to use `apt` to download and install the `3dchess` package on your Linux system. Which command can you use to do this?

A. `apt install 3dchess`

B. `apt -d install 3dchess`

C. `apt upgrade 3dchess`

D. `apt -s install 3dchess`

21. Which type of shared library is integrated directly into an executable file when it is initially compiled?

A. Dynamic

B. Shared

C. Static

D. Linked

22. Which file is checked by applications on startup for the location of shared libraries on the Linux system?

A. `/etc/ld.so.conf`

B. `/etc/ld.so.cache`

C. `/lib/ld.so`

D. `/usr/lib/ld.so`

23. Which variable is updated to supply additional shared libraries for a standard user?

A. `LIBRARY_PATH`

B. `LD_LIBRARY_PATH`

C. `LDD_LIBRARY_PATH`

D. `ld_library_path`

Answers

1. **A, C.** The `upload` and `download` commands are not Linux commands.
2. **C.** The error occurred because the latest repositories were not being used on this Debian-class system, so run `apt update`, then `apt upgrade`. You would use `dpkg -i` to upgrade a package on Debian. Running `./configure` is used to prepare a source code installation. The `zypper` command only works on SUSE-class systems.
3. **D.** To extract the file, you would enter `tar -zxvf ./BitTorrent-7.10.1.tar.gz`. Using `gzip` would just uncompress the file. The `-a` option is used to determine the compression program. Running `tar -xvf` would unsuccessfully attempt to untar a compressed file.
4. **A.** The RPM database is stored in `/var/lib/rpm`.
5. **A.** The `rpm --checksig evolution-2.6.0-41.i586.rpm` command would be used to check the file's digital signature.
6. **B, E.** Either the `rpm -ihv evolution-2.6.0-41.i586.rpm` command or the `rpm -Uhv evolution-2.6.0-41.i586.rpm` command will install the file and display a progress indicator composed of hash marks on the screen as the installation progresses.
7. **A.** The `./configure` command would be used first to generate the `Makefile` file. The `configure` file contains the `UNINSTALL` target that can then be used with the `make` utility to uninstall the software.
8. **D.** To erase `rpm` from the system, you would enter `rpm -e evolution`.
9. **A, E.** The `rpm -U evolution-2.6.0-41.i586.rpm` command will upgrade the existing RPM to the newer version, or install it if the older version is not installed. The `rpm -F evolution-2.6.0-41.i586.rpm` command will also upgrade the existing RPM to the newer version because the older version is installed. If the older version were not installed, no upgrade would occur using `-F`.
10. **C.** The `rpm -qi evolution-2.6.0-41.i586.rpm` command will query the package and display summary information on the screen.
11. **A.** The `rpm -q --whatprovides /usr/bin/perl` command displays the name of the package that provides this component.
12. **A, C, D.** The `S`, `5`, and `T` in the error code indicate that there is a problem with the file's size, MD5 checksum, and timestamp. The `c` indicates that the file is a configuration file, so these errors may or may not be significant.
13. **D.** The `rpm2cpio` utility can be used to create a `cpio` archive file from the RPM package. You can then extract individual files from the archive using the `cpio` utility.

14. **B, C.** The `yum install gcc` command or `dnf install gcc` command can be used to download and install the `gcc` package on your Linux system, including all packages it is dependent on.
15. **A.** The `yum list updates` command can be used to generate a list of available updates for all installed packages on a Linux system.
16. **B, D.** The `configure` script is used to check the local system to make sure it has the components required to install and run the software. It also creates the `Makefile` file.
17. **A.** The `make` command compiles the text-based source code into a binary executable that can be run on the system.
18. **C.** The `make install` command installs the program and its associated support files (such as documentation and configuration files) into the appropriate directories in the filesystem.
19. **C.** The `-P` option, when used with the `dpkg` command, uninstalls a specified package and deletes all its configuration files.
20. **A.** The `apt install 3dchess` command can be used to download and install the `3dchess` package on your Linux system, along with all other packages it is dependent on.
21. **C.** Static shared libraries are integrated directly into an executable file when it is initially compiled.
22. **B.** The `/etc/ld.so.cache` file is checked by applications on startup for the location of shared libraries on the Linux system.
23. **B.** The `LD_LIBRARY_PATH` file is used to update the supply of additional shared libraries for a standard user.

CHAPTER 11

Managing the Linux Boot Process

In this chapter, you will learn about

- The BIOS power-on self-test phase
- The GRUB2 bootloader phase
- The kernel initialization phase
- The System V initialization phase
- The `systemd` initialization phase

You can't be a leader if you turn around and there's no one there.

—April Walker, Microsoft

When you power on your Linux system, it goes through four major steps to start processes and display the login screen:

- The BIOS power-on self-test (POST) phase
- The GRUB2 bootloader phase
- The kernel initialization phase
- The `systemd` initialization phase (formerly System V initialization)

Figure 11-1 illustrates the boot process after powering on the Linux system. Boot-specific messages are written to `/var/log/boot.log`. The `systemd` command `journalctl -b` will display boot messages from your last boot, but may also be configured to store boot logs from previous boots by creating the `/var/log/journal/` directory as `root`.

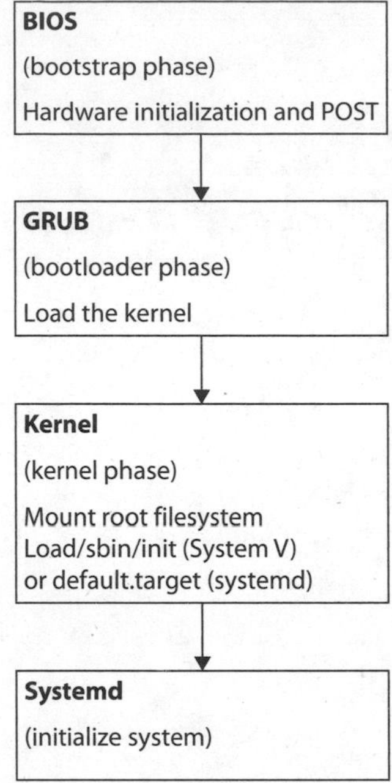

Figure 11-1 System boot process

The BIOS POST Phase

After turning on the computer, the system firmware initializes. The system first runs the power-on self-test (POST) to ensure that the memory is good and that there is enough to load the kernel. The system also verifies that the keyboard, graphics, and other components are available and initialized. Next, the system searches for the location of instructions responsible for loading the operating system, whether it is from a hard drive, network, or even USB thumb drive.

You should be familiar with the following bootstrap methods:

- The classic BIOS
- The modern UEFI

The Classic BIOS

The BIOS, or basic input/output system, is the traditional bootstrap program stored on a flash memory chip on the system motherboard. Once power has been applied, the BIOS initializes the motherboard POST. If the POST encounters any problems, it either displays an error message onscreen or plays a series of beeps. The website http://www.bioscentral.com has a listing for most motherboard POST error codes.

Once the POST is complete, the BIOS looks through the list of devices for bootloader code. You can manipulate the order in which this list is searched by entering the BIOS. Figure 11-2 shows a system configured to search for removable devices and then a list of hard drives. Figure 11-3 shows the same system configured to search the network for a bootable image and then look at local removable drives, followed by local hard drives.

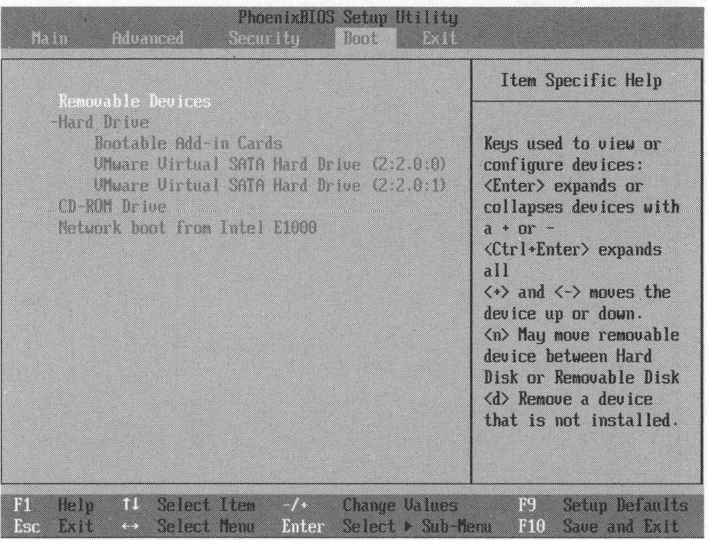

Figure 11-2 Selecting a boot device

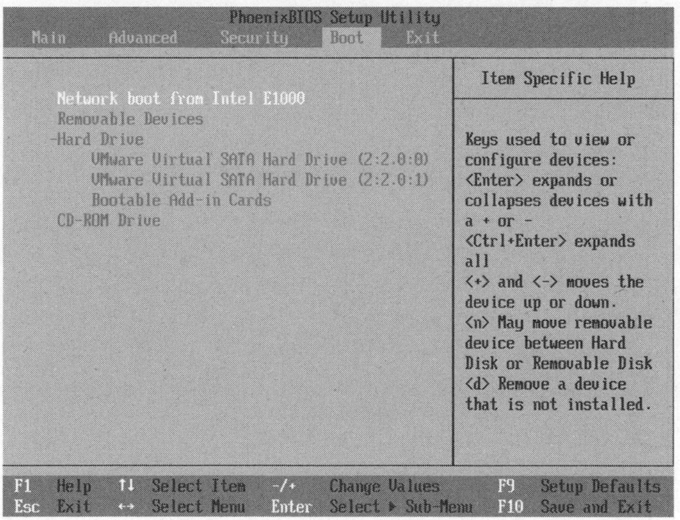

Figure 11-3 Selecting a removeable or network boot device

When searching these devices, the BIOS searches for the master boot record (MBR). For example, when booting from a hard drive, the BIOS looks in the first sector of the disk device, also known as the boot sector, or MBR, illustrated in Figure 11-4.

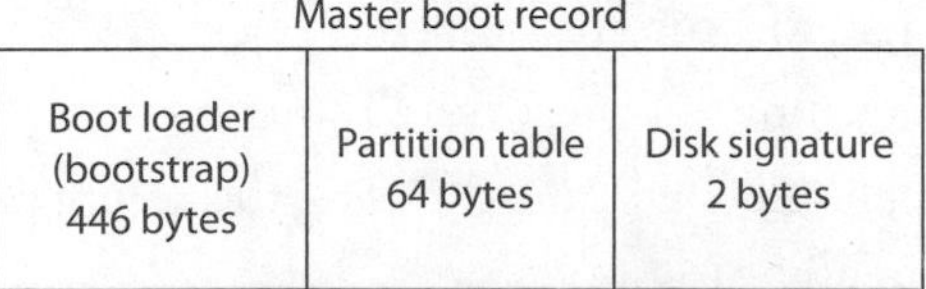

Figure 11-4 The master boot record (MBR) details

The MBR is divided into three sections. The first 446 bytes of the MBR contain the first stage of the master boot code. The master boot code contains error messages (such as "missing operating system") and the code required for loading the second stage of the bootloader, called GRUB2. The next 64 bytes contain the drive's partition table, and the last 2 bytes contain a disk signature. The disk signature identifies the device that contains the `/boot` directory, which contains files required by the boot process.

Once the BIOS has begun loading the bootloader, control of the boot process is turned over to the GRUB2 bootloader.

PXE

PXE (pronounced *pixie*), or Preboot Execution Environment, is an OS-neutral client/server facility that can be used to remotely boot operating systems or provision computer systems from a network server. PXE requires the client system have a network card that supports PXE and has PXE enabled as a boot device in flash memory.

When power is applied to a PXE client, the enabled NIC card "looks" for a DHCP server by broadcasting a series of DHCP discover packets, which are requests from the client to obtain an IP address from a DHCP server. The Dynamic Host Configuration Protocol (DHCP) server is used to automatically assign an IP address to the client and provide the client with the location of one or more Trivial File Transfer Protocol (TFTP) servers.

The Modern UEFI

The BIOS did not keep pace with advancements in technology. It was limited to 16-bit addressing, could only access 1MB of memory, could not boot from drives larger than 2.1TB, and could manage only a limited number of devices.

The Unified Extensible Firmware Interface (UEFI) is an OS-neutral, architecture-independent software interface between firmware and the operating system designed to overcome the limitations of the BIOS. One of the UEFI's most important features is its ability to execute applications prior to the operating system loading.

Some features of UEFI include the following:

- It provides a user interface prior to the operating system being available.
- It operates in 32- or 64-bit mode.
- It has access to all system memory and devices.
- It can mount partitions and read some filesystems (FAT12, FAT16, FAT32, and VFAT).
- It has network capabilities without the OS being loaded.
- It can boot drives larger than 2.1TB.
- It enables you to add applications that can be executed as part of the boot process or from the UEFI command shell.
- It supports remote diagnostics and storage backup.
- It can be configured via the OS using the command `efibootmgr`.

NOTE If UEFI is implemented, the directory `/sys/firmware/efi/` will exist and the command `efibootmgr` should be available.

The UEFI controls the boot process using UEFI boot services. While the operating system is running, the UEFI provides a connection between the OS and firmware.

After hardware initialization, the UEFI looks for a storage device with an EFI system partition (ESP). This partition is a FAT32 partition that contains the bootloader code, applications, and device drivers. The partition is normally mounted on `/boot/efi/`. Applications contained here can be part of the boot process or utilities that can be chosen by the user at boot time.

Vendor-specific applications or EFI utilities are stored in the `/boot/efi/` directory. For example, Red Hat EFI files are stored in `/boot/efi/EFI/redhat/`, and CentOS stores its bootloader information in `/boot/efi/EFI/centos/`. If multiple operating systems are available, each has its own directory in `/boot/efi/`.

Depending on the contents of the ESP, several things could happen. You could be prompted to execute a UEFI application or load a specific operating system, or the UEFI could automatically load another bootloader, such as GRUB2.

The GRUB2 Bootloader Phase

Once the BIOS POST phase has completed, the bootloader is used to load the Linux kernel. Although multiple bootloaders are available, we will confine our discussion to what is tested on the CompTIA Linux+ exam, the *Grand Unified Bootloader version 2 (GRUB2)*. In this section you will learn how to

- Modify the GRUB2 bootloader
- Change a forgotten root password

Modify the GRUB2 Bootloader

As its name indicates, GRUB2 is a newer version of the original GRUB bootloader. GRUB2 works in a completely different manner than the original GRUB Legacy bootloader. GRUB version 1.98 or later is considered "GRUB2." Any version of GRUB earlier than 1.98 is considered "GRUB Legacy." You can run one of two commands, as `root`, at the shell prompt to see which version of GRUB your Linux system is using:

- `grub-install -V`
- `grub2-install -V`

An example is shown here:

```
# grub2-install -V
grub2-install (GRUB2) 2.00
```

File or Directory	Description
/boot/grub2/grub.cfg	This file replaces /boot/grub/menu.lst as GRUB2's main configuration file. This file is created using the grub2-mkconfig command and may not be edited.
/etc/default/grub	This file contains default variables used when configuring GRUB2.
/etc/grub.d/	This directory contains GRUB2 scripts.

Table 11-1 GRUB2 Configuration Files

One important difference between Legacy GRUB and GRUB2 is device names. Whereas Legacy GRUB started device numbering at 0, GRUB2 starts numbering at 1.

Table 11-1 lists the configuration files and directory used by GRUB2.

EXAM TIP Running grub2-install /dev/sda reinstalls GRUB2 configuration files into /boot/grub2/ onto the first hard drive.

Variables in /etc/default/grub

The file /etc/default/grub contains GRUB configuration variables, as detailed in Table 11-2. The settings in this file are used to build the /boot/grub2/grub.cfg file when built with grub2-mkconfig.

Variable	Description
GRUB_TIMEOUT	Boots the default entry in *n* number of seconds if no user action takes place.
GRUB_HIDDEN_TIMEOUT	Displays a blank screen (or a splash image if you configure it to do so) for a specified number of seconds. After the end of the timeout period, the system will boot. While the screen is blank, the user can press Shift to display the menu.
GRUB_DEFAULT	Indicates the default operating system to boot after the number of seconds in GRUB_TIMEOUT is reached. This entry may be a number or a menu entry title.
GRUB_SAVED_DEFAULT	If set to true, GRUB2 automatically selects the last selected operating system from the menu as the default operating system to be used on the next boot. This parameter could potentially conflict with the GRUB_DEFAULT parameter. Therefore, you can use either one, but not both.
GRUB_DISTRIBUTOR	Used when creating menu titles. Sets the operating system's name.
GRUB_CMDLINE_LINUX	Linux kernel parameters.

Table 11-2 GRUB2 /etc/default/grub Variables

```
[root@localhost grub.d]# ls -l
total 72
-rwxr-xr-x. 1 root root  8702 Jan 30 08:58 00_header
-rwxr-xr-x. 1 root root  1043 Jul  4  2018 00_tuned
-rwxr-xr-x. 1 root root   232 Jan 30 08:58 01_users
-rwxr-xr-x. 1 root root 10781 Jan 30 08:58 10_linux
-rwxr-xr-x. 1 root root 10275 Jan 30 08:58 20_linux_xen
-rwxr-xr-x. 1 root root  2559 Jan 30 08:58 20_ppc_terminfo
-rwxr-xr-x. 1 root root 11169 Jan 30 08:58 30_os-prober
-rwxr-xr-x. 1 root root   214 Jan 30 08:58 40_custom
-rwxr-xr-x. 1 root root   216 Jan 30 08:58 41_custom
-rw-r--r--. 1 root root   483 Jan 30 08:58 README
```

Figure 11-5 Files in /etc/grub.d/

Files in the /etc/grub.d/ Directory

The directory /etc/grub.d/ contains scripts used to build the /boot/grub2/grub.cfg file when built with grub2-mkconfig (see Figure 11-5). Scripts are processed in order of their script number. Table 11-3 describes some of those scripts.

Interactive Booting Options

You can press Esc to interrupt the boot process. This allows you to boot a different operating system, or even enter emergency mode for troubleshooting, using the keys detailed in Table 11-4.

grub.d Script File	Description
00_header	Loads GRUB2 settings from /etc/default/grub.
10_linux	Identifies Linux kernels and places them in the menu.
30_os_prober	Searches for non-Linux operating systems and puts the results in memory.
40_custom	Template for adding custom menu entries.

Table 11-3 Grub Script Files in /etc/grub.d/

Key	Description
e	Edit the current menu entry.
Ctrl-X	Boot the system. You must be editing a menu entry to use this key sequence.
Tab	List available GRUB commands. The command help <grub_command> will display help documentation. You must be editing a menu entry to use this key sequence.
Ctrl-C	Enter a GRUB2 shell. When finished executing GRUB2 shell commands, you can exit the shell using the command normal_exit. You must be editing a menu entry to use this key sequence.
Esc	Discard edits and return to the previous screen.

Table 11-4 Interactive Boot Control Keys

Changing GRUB2 Boot Operations

To make changes to GRUB2's configuration, you can modify the file /etc/default/grub or change the 40_custom script in /etc/grub.d/. If you make changes to these files, you must execute the command grub2-mkconfig -o <config_filename>. After making a backup of /boot/grub2/grub.cfg, to update grub.cfg run the command grub2-mkconfig -o /boot/grub2/grub.cfg, or update-grub2.

To change update-grub2 to grub2-update, use the ln command as follows:

```
root@kermit# ln /usr/sbin/update-grub2 /usr/sbin/grub2-update
```

This allows a consistent method of running GRU2 commands, since most of them start with grub2-.

Change a Forgotten root Password

Occasionally, you might forget the root password, or one of your co-workers might depart your organization unexpectedly and not leave the password. To recover a forgotten or lost password, perform the following steps on Red Hat Linux:

1. Power on the computer and press **Esc** when the GRUB2 menu appears as shown in Figure 11-6.
2. Press **e** to edit the default Linux option, as shown in Figure 11-6. This allows you to access the GRUB2 boot script.
3. Find the ro option (read-only) in the linux or linux16 line and change that to **rw init=/sysroot/bin/sh**, as shown in Figure 11-7.
4. Press **Ctrl-x** to start the system into *shell* mode, which is similar to *emergency* mode but will not ask you for the root password.

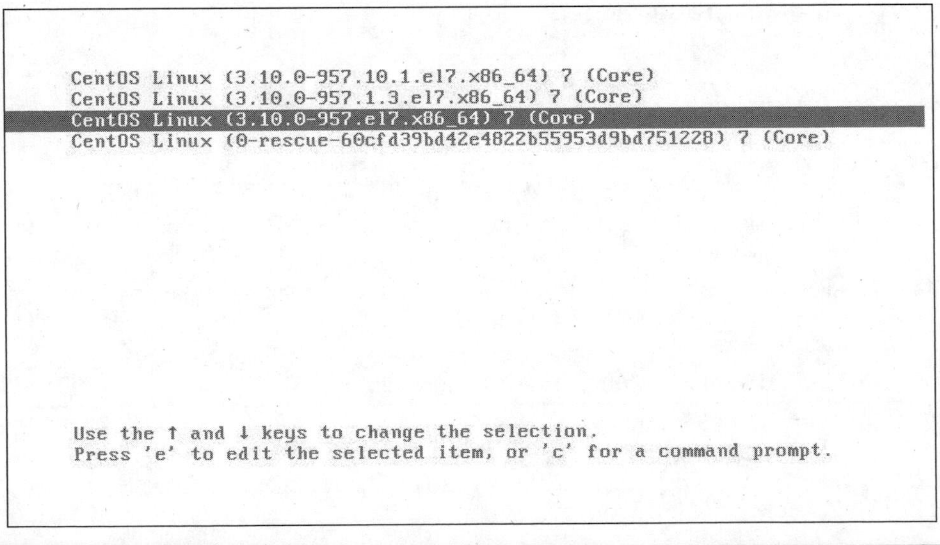

```
CentOS Linux (3.10.0-957.10.1.el7.x86_64) 7 (Core)
CentOS Linux (3.10.0-957.1.3.el7.x86_64) 7 (Core)
CentOS Linux (3.10.0-957.el7.x86_64) 7 (Core)
CentOS Linux (0-rescue-60cfd39bd42e4822b55953d9bd751228) 7 (Core)

Use the ↑ and ↓ keys to change the selection.
Press 'e' to edit the selected item, or 'c' for a command prompt.
```

Figure 11-6 GRUB2 boot menu

```
        insmod ext2
        set root='hd0,msdos1'
        if [ x$feature_platform_search_hint = xy ]; then
          search --no-floppy --fs-uuid --set=root --hint-bios=hd0,msdos1 --hin\
t-efi=hd0,msdos1 --hint-baremetal=ahci0,msdos1 --hint='hd0,msdos1'  87bcb08d-e\
8b2-4380-99a5-eaa23472c956
        else
          search --no-floppy --fs-uuid --set=root 87bcb08d-e8b2-4380-99a5-eaa2\
3472c956
        fi
        linux16 /vmlinuz-3.10.0-957.el7.x86_64 root=UUID=eb37c67d-25c0-4f24-bd\
d0-a8e0c9ed4870 rw init=/sysroot/bin/sh rd.lvm.lv=USR/usr rhgb quiet LANG=en_U\
S.UTF-8
        initrd16 /initramfs-3.10.0-957.el7.x86_64.img


      Press Ctrl-x to start, Ctrl-c for a command prompt or Escape to
      discard edits and return to the menu. Pressing Tab lists
      possible completions.
```

Figure 11-7 Altering GRUB boot script to access shell mode

5. Run the following sequence of commands to change the root password, as shown in Figure 11-8:

```
chroot /sysroot           # Running cd / will now take you to /sysroot
passwd root               # Allows you to set the new password for root
touch /.autorelabel       # Informs SELinux to update its settings on reboot
exit
logout
```

6. Reboot the system.

After rebooting you will be able to log in as `root` with your new password. My students are always surprised to discover how simple this is. For better security, also set a BIOS/UEFI password or a GRUB2 password (discussed later in this chapter). Finally, physical security, such as keeping the system in a secure environment, mitigates password attacks.

```
Type "journalctl" to view system logs.
You might want to save "/run/initramfs/rdsosreport.txt" to a USB stick or /boot
after mounting them and attach it to a bug report.


:/# chroot /sysroot
:/# passwd root
Changing password for user root.
New password:
Retype new password:
passwd: all authentication tokens updated successfully.
:/# touch /.autorelabel
:/# exit
:/# logout
```

Figure 11-8 Changing the `root` user password

EXAM TIP Another way to boot into single-user mode is to modify the `linux64` or `linux` GRUB2 setting by adding `systemd.boot=rescue .target`.

Exercise 11-1: Working with GRUB2

In this exercise, practice customizing your GRUB2 menu. You can perform this exercise using the virtual machine.

VIDEO Please watch the Exercise 11-1 video for a demonstration on how to perform this task.

Complete the following steps:

1. Boot your Linux system and log in as user **`root`** using the password **`root`**.
2. Create a snapshot.
3. Enter **`vi /etc/default/grub`** at the shell prompt.
4. Change the `GRUB_TIMEOUT` value to **`15`** seconds.
5. Change the `GRUB_DEFAULT` parameter to automatically load the first menu entry if the user makes no selection within the timeout period.
6. Save your changes and exit the `vi` editor.
7. Make a copy of `/boot/grub2/grub.cfg` using the following command:
   ```
   cp  boot/grub2/grub.cfg  /boot/grub2/grub.cfg.$(date +%m%d).old
   ```
8. Execute the following command to create a new configuration file:
   ```
   grub2-mkconfig -o /boot/grub2/grub.cfg.$(date +%m%d).new
   ```
9. Copy the new file to `/boot/grub.cfg` using the following command:
   ```
   cp  /boot/grub2/grub.cfg.$(date +%m%d).new  /boot/grub2.cfg
   ```
10. Reboot your system and verify the changes have been applied to the bootloader.

The Kernel Initiation Phase

The purpose of the bootloader is to load the system kernel, `vmlinux`, and start the initial RAM disk, `initrd`, or the initial RAM filesystem, `initramfs`. GRUB2 loads the compressed Linux kernel named `vmlinuz`, then the kernel decompresses and mounts `initrd` or `initramfs`.

This RAM disk is a temporary filesystem that contains kernel modules and applications necessary to access the devices and filesystems required to boot the operating system. For example, the `mount` command is included so that the system hard drive can be mounted.

NOTE The `initrd.img` and `initramfs.img` files are created from `mkinitrd`, which uses `dracut` to generate the RAM disk files. The `initrd.img` and `initrd` files are the same file, just different names.

The kernel first initializes memory and then configures the attached hardware by using drivers found in `initrd`. When all device drivers are loaded, the kernel mounts the root filesystem in read-write mode and begins operating system initialization.

System V Initialization

System V was fine in its day, but `systemd` provides performance and security features that render System V relatively obsolete. System V is still discussed here for purposes of understanding certain `systemd` concepts.

Once the kernel is running, `initrd` is unmounted and the `init` process starts the system scheduler with a process ID (PID) of zero (`0`). The `init` process is the last step of the boot process.

The `init` process executes the command `/sbin/init`, which becomes the grandparent of all other processes running on the system. Its process ID is always one (`1`). `/sbin/init` reads a file called `/etc/inittab`. This configuration file brings the operating system to a predefined runlevel.

In this section you will learn about

- The Linux runlevels
- The `inittab` startup file
- Shutting down the system

The Linux Runlevels

A runlevel defines what services and resources are available at different boot runlevels. Most user environments run a secured version of runlevel 5 so that users can work and do research with a web browser.

Many security operation centers (SOCs) run a secured version of runlevel 3, which is a command-line–only server. Table 11-5 describes the seven runlevels.

The `inittab` Startup File

The command `/sbin/init` uses the configuration file `/etc/inittab` to initialize the system. Configuration lines in `/etc/inittab` have the following format:

```
<line_id>:<applicable_run_level>:<action>:<command>
```

On line 21 in Figure 11-9, you can see the line ID is `si`. Since no runlevel numbers are assigned, this line will be executed for all runlevels. The action is `sysinit`, and the command will execute the script `/etc/rc.d/rc.sysinit`.

Runlevel	Mode	Description
0	Halt	Halts the system.
1	Single User	Single user only. Also known as maintenance mode. (Text mode.)
2	Multiuser Client	Multiuser access and acts as network client. (Text mode.)
3	Multiuser Server	Multiuser access and can be a server, such as a web server, DNS server, SSH server, etc. (Text mode.)
4	Not Used	User customizable.
5	Graphics Mode	Full multiuser server mode. (Graphics mode.)
6	Reboot	Brings the system to runlevel 0 and then back to the default runlevel.

Table 11-5 System V Runlevels

Figure 11-9 An excerpt from `/etc/inittab` showing the default runlevel

```
18 id:5:initdefault:
19
20 # System initialization.
21 si::sysinit:/etc/rc.d/rc.sysinit
```

Line 18 of Figure 11-9 specifies the default runlevel. In this example, the operating system will boot to runlevel `5`. To change the default runlevel, change the number in this line with an editor when running System V.

NOTE Use the `init` command or `telinit` command to change runlevels. For example, `init 2` switches the system to runlevel 2. The `runlevel` command shows the previous and current runlevels.

```
# runlevel
3 5
```

Shutting Down the System

As with any other operating system, you need to shut down a Linux system properly. This ensures any pending disk write operations are committed to disk before the system is powered off.

You can use several commands to properly shut down a Linux system, including the following:

- **`init 0`** Switches the system to runlevel `0`, which halts the system
- **`init 6`** Switches the system to runlevel `6`, which reboots the system

- **halt** Shuts down the system
- **reboot** Reboots the system

In addition to these commands, you can also use the shutdown command to either shut down or reboot the system. It has several key advantages over the preceding commands:

- You can specify that the system go down after a specified period of time. This gives your users time to save their work and log out before the system goes down. It also allows you to shut down the system at a specified time even if you're not there to do it.
- It allows you to send a message to all logged-in users warning them that a shutdown is pending.
- It does not allow other users to log in before the pending shutdown.

The syntax for using shutdown is shutdown +*m* -h|-r <message>. The +*m* option specifies the amount of time (in minutes) before shutting down the system. You can also use the now option instead of +*m* to specify that the system go down immediately. If you need the system to go down at a specific time, you can replace +*m* with the time (entered as *hh*:*mm*) when the shutdown should occur. The -h option specifies that the system be halted, whereas the -r option specifies that the system be rebooted. Some examples of using shutdown are shown here:

```
shutdown +10 -h Please save your work and log out.
```

When you enter this command, all other logged-in users see the following message:

```
Please save your work and log out.
The system is going DOWN for system halt in 10 minutes!
```

If you've scheduled a shutdown using the shutdown command and later need to cancel that shutdown, enter shutdown -c at the shell prompt.

You can also use the wall command to send messages to users to inform them of system events, such as a system reboot or a runlevel change. To use wall, you must send the message to the stdin of the wall command. An example is shown here:

```
# echo "The system is going down for a reboot." | wall
Broadcast Message from deguzman
       (/dev/pts/1) at 16:26 ...
The system is going down for a reboot.
```

The systemd Initialization Phase

The traditional init process starts services one at a time in sequential fashion. systemd is a system and service manager created by Red Hat developers Lennart Poettering and Kay Sievers. systemd uses compiled startup programs instead of scripts, so it boots up much faster than System V–based systems. Also, systemd takes advantage of security features such as universally unique identifiers (UUIDs) and trusted platform modules (TPMs) for improved integrity and confidentiality.

systemd Unit Files

The main configuration file for systemd services is called a *unit*. Default units are found in /usr/lib/systemd/system/. Modified and custom units are contained in /etc/systemd/system/. Unit files in /etc/systemd/system/ override the entries in /usr/lib/systemd/system/.

The command systemctl -t help, shown here, displays a list of available units.

```
[root@localhost boot]# systemctl -t help
Available unit types:
service
socket
busname
target
snapshot
device
mount
automount
swap
timer
path
slice
scope
```

The command systemctl list-units --type=<unit_type> displays all active units of a specific type. The edited output in the following illustration shows the results of the command systemctl list-units --type=mount, which displays all active units of type mount. Adding the --all option, systemctl list-units --type=mount --all displays both active and available units of type mount.

```
[root@localhost boot]# systemctl list-units --type=mount
UNIT                          LOAD   ACTIVE SUB     DESCRIPTION
-.mount                       loaded active mounted /
boot.mount                    loaded active mounted /boot
```

A unit file consists of stanzas that contain configuration directives. The contents of the vsftpd.service unit file are shown next. The [Unit] stanza summarizes the service and specifies which stage is called next. The [Service] stanza describes how the service should start and which application to initiate. The [Install] stanza describes which run state makes the unit begin.

```
[Unit]
Description=Vsftpd ftp daemon
After=network.target

[Service]
Type=forking
ExecStart=/usr/sbin/vsftpd /etc/vsftpd/vsftpd.conf

[Install]
WantedBy=multi-user.target
```

NOTE Daemon names usually end in the letter d. The unit type for daemons is service.

Option	Description
Description	Describes the service.
Documentation	Identifies the location of documentation for this unit.
After	Defines the service that must be started before this service.
Before	Defines services that must be started after this service.
Requires	Specifies units that this unit requires to operate. If any required units do not start, the unit is not activated.
Wants	Specifies units that, if not started, will not prevent the unit from starting.
Conflicts	Specifies units that conflict with this unit.

Table 11-6 [Unit] Stanza Directives

Option	Description
Type	systemd contains multiple unit categories called types. systemd types are target, service, device, mount, slice, timer, socket, and scope.
ExecStart	Contains the absolute path and arguments for the command used to start the service.
ExecStartPre	Commands to be executed before ExecStart.
ExecStartPost	Commands to be executed after ExecStart.
ExecStop	Commands required to stop the service. If this directive does not exist, the process will be killed when the service is stopped.
ExecStopPost	Commands executed after ExecStop.
User	Which user privilege to run the service as.

Table 11-7 [Service] Stanza Directives

The [Unit] stanza is found in all unit configuration files. It contains a description of the unit and generic unit options. Some [Unit] stanza options are explained in Table 11-6.

The [Service] stanza contains configuration information only found in units of type service. Other unit types may have different sections. For example, a mount unit contains a mount section. Table 11-7 contains a few [Service] stanza directives.

Operating parameters for a specific unit may be viewed by executing the command systemctl show <unit_name>.

The [Install] stanza, detailed in Table 11-8, contains directives associated with the activation of the unit. Since you are starting the vsftpd networking service, you need to boot in at least multi-user.target. This target will start networking services.

Option	Description
Alias	Space-delimited list of additional names for this unit. Alias names may be used for most systemctl commands, except for systemctl enable.
RequiredBy	List of units that require this unit.
WantedBy	List of units that depend on but do not require this unit.
Also	Contains a list of units that will be installed when the unit is started and uninstalled when the unit is removed.

Table 11-8 [Install] Stanza Directives

Option	Description
What	The absolute path of the device to mount.
Where	The absolute path of the mount point.
Type	An optional setting for the filesystem type.
Options	Comma-separated list of mounting options.

Table 11-9 [Mount] Stanza Directives

Mount Unit Naming Conventions

Mount points controlled by `systemd` are configured under the `systemd.mount` protocol. The `[Mount]` stanza, detailed in Table 11-9, contains directives associated with the activation of the unit. Mount units may also be configured via `/etc/fstab`, or can be converted to mount units. Mount units can include `[Unit]` and `[Install]` stanzas.

Bootup Dependencies

To display a list of units that a unit is dependent on, execute the command `systemctl list-dependencies <unit_name>`. To display a list of units that are dependent on a unit, execute the command `systemctl list-dependencies --reverse <unit_name>`.

The output of these commands will be a tree-like structure that lists the units that apply. The left margin will contain a green dot if the unit is active and a red dot if inactive.

Viewing Unit Status

The command `systemctl status <unit_name>` displays the operational status of a unit. Figure 11-10 shows the output of the command `systemctl status cups.service`.

```
● cups.service - CUPS Printing Service
   Loaded: loaded (/usr/lib/systemd/system/cups.service; enabled; vendor preset: enabled)
   Active: active (running) since Mon 2019-05-06 11:28:31 EDT; 11h ago
 Main PID: 7510 (cupsd)
    Tasks: 1
   CGroup: /system.slice/cups.service
           └─7510 /usr/sbin/cupsd -f

May 06 11:28:31 localhost.localdomain systemd[1]: Started CUPS Printing Service.
```

Figure 11-10 The results of the `systemctl status cups.service` command

Option	Description
loaded	Loaded into memory
inactive (dead)	Unit not running
active (running)	Running with one or more active processes
active (exited)	Completed configuration
active (waiting)	Running and listening for a request
enabled	Will start when system boots
disabled	Will not start when system boots
static	Must be started by another service (cannot be enabled)

Table 11-10 Unit Status Definitions

Table 11-10 defines some terms provided in the output.

Failed Units

To list all failed units, execute the command `systemctl --failed`. To list all failed units of a specific type, execute the command `systemctl --failed --type=<unit_type>`.

Service Procedures

You may control services using the syntax `systemctl <command> <unit>`. For example, to start the Apache web server on a Red Hat–class Linux system, run `systemctl httpd start`. To shut down the SSH server, run `systemctl stop sshd`. Table 11-11 provides a list of control commands.

Command	Description
systemctl enable <unit>	Turns on service at boot
systemctl disable <unit>	Does not turn on service at boot
systemctl start <unit>	Starts service immediately
systemctl stop <unit>	Stops service immediately
systemctl restart <unit>	Stops and then starts unit specified on the command line
systemctl reload <unit>	Rereads the configuration file and continues running
systemctl mask <unit>	Makes a unit unavailable by creating a symbolic link to /dev/null
systemctl unmask <unit>	Removes mask

Table 11-11 Controlling Services

Runlevel (System V)	Target (systemd)	Description
0	runlevel0.target poweroff.target	Shut down and power off.
1	runlevel1.target rescue.target	Rescue mode.
2	runlevel2.target multi-user.target	Text-based multiuser mode.
3	runlevel3.target multi-user.target	Text-based multiuser mode.
4	runlevel4.target multi-user.target	Text-based multiuser mode. Runlevel 4 is not used in Linux systems using System V initialization.
5	runlevel5.target graphical.target	Graphics multiuser mode.
6	runlevel6.target reboot.target	System reboot.

Table 11-12 The `systemd` Runlevels

Targets

A unit defines a specific service. A *target* is a grouping of units and/or other targets to provide a specific function. For example, the target `network-online.target` waits for a network to be "up" before network-related services start. A target name is suffixed by `.target`. The command `systemctl --type=target` lists all active targets. The command `systemctl --type=target -all` lists all available targets.

The first target for `systemd` is `default.target`. The file `/etc/systemd/system/default.target` is linked to the default runlevel target file. You may also execute the command `systemctl get-default` to display the default runlevel. Table 11-12 displays the `systemd` runlevels and their System V equivalents.

To view the current runlevel, execute the command `systemctl get-default`. To change the default runlevel, type `systemctl set-default <runlevel_target>`. To change the current runlevel, type the command `systemctl isolate <runlevel_target>`. Note that `isolate` is used when switching runlevels to stop anything that is not part of the new runlevel.

Troubleshooting Services Not Starting on Time

Understanding the boot process is very important if you have boot issues with a system. Error messages can give you some idea of where the fault occurs. Review Table 11-13 for a list of errors and where to start looking for the fault.

Error Message	Problem
`Can't find hard drive`	The hard drive is missing or BIOS/UEFI is misconfigured.
`Can't find bootloader`	GRUB2 is incorrectly configured, or misconfigured.
`Can't load kernel`	GRUB2 could be misconfigured, or the kernel could be misconfigured.
`Web service failed to start`	System booted successfully, but some applications may be misconfigured.

Table 11-13 Booting Troubleshooting

Kernel Panic

A *kernel panic,* also called a *kernel oops,* is a protective measure generated by the kernel to prevent the risk of data loss or corruption when the kernel detects an unrecoverable error. Panics occur due to configuration or software problems; missing, misconfigured, or failed hardware or hardware drivers; or system resource problems. System utilities `kexec`, `kdump`, and `crash` are used to store and troubleshoot a kernel panic. These tools may be installed during system installation or at a later time.

When a kernel panic occurs, the `kdump` utility, by default, saves the crash dump to memory. `kdump` may store the dump data on a remote machine.

`kdump` requires system memory reserved specifically for storing kernel crash information. The memory is reserved during the boot process via the `crashkernel` directive on the GRUB command line. The amount of memory reserved is dependent on the type of hardware and the total amount of system memory. You may also adjust this setting to allocate the correct amount of memory automatically.

The `kexec` utility boots the kernel from another kernel but does not use the BIOS. This preserves the current system state so you may analyze the crash dump data using the `crash` command.

Chapter Review

In this chapter, you learned about the boot process. The bootstrap phase is used to initialize system hardware, and we explored the difference between the BIOS, UEFI, and PXE bootstraps. We then explored the configuration of the GRUB2 bootloader. You learned how to configure the bootloader and use it in interactive mode. We continued the boot process by discussing how the kernel and root filesystem are loaded. Finally, we reviewed both the System V and `systemd` initialization processes as well as how to control services.

- In the bootstrap phase, the computer's BIOS chip has control of the system.
- The BIOS tests the system hardware using the power-on self-test (POST) routine and then locates a storage device with boot files on it.

- The BIOS turns over control of the system to a bootloader.
- The bootloader points to and loads a temporary kernel.
- The first stage of a BIOS bootloader resides in the master boot record (MBR) of the boot device or in the boot partition on the drive.
- The Linux kernel is located in `/boot` and is named `vmlinuz-version.gz` or `vmlinux`.
- `/boot` is the root directory for GRUB2.
- You can add an encrypted password to your GRUB2 menu to restrict access.
- The configuration files used by GRUB2 are as follows:
  - The `/boot/grub/grub.cfg` file
  - The files in the `/etc/grub.d` directory
  - The `/etc/default/grub` file
- With GRUB2, the `menu.lst` file has been replaced by the `/boot/grub2/grub.cfg` file.
- The GRUB2 configuration is stored in several script files in the `/etc/grub.d` directory.
- After making a change to the GRUB2 configuration, you must run the command `grub2-mkconfig -o <output_file>`.
- Linux defines seven runlevels (0–6):
  - **0** Halts the system.
  - **1** Runs Linux in single-user mode.
  - **2** Runs Linux in multiuser mode as a networked client in command-line interface only.
  - **3** Runs Linux in multiuser mode as a network server in command-line only.
  - **4** Unused.
  - **5** Runs Linux in multiuser mode as a network server. The graphical user interface is used.
  - **6** Reboots the system.
- Most Linux distributions today have migrated away from `init` to `systemd`.
- The `systemd` daemon uses the concept of targets, which function in a way similar to runlevels.
- The traditional `init` runlevels are shown here with their equivalent `systemd` boot target files:
  - runlevel 3 = `multi-user.target` or `runlevel3.target`
  - runlevel 5 = `graphical.target` or `runlevel5.target`
- On a system that uses `systemd`, you use the `systemctl` command to manage services and boot targets.

Questions

1. What is the role of the BIOS during system boot? (Choose two.)
   - **A.** It tests system hardware.
   - **B.** It creates an `initrd` image in a RAM disk.
   - **C.** It locates a bootable storage device.
   - **D.** It provides a menu that lets you choose which operating system to boot.
   - **E.** It points to your operating system kernel.
2. Where can your Linux bootloader reside? (Choose two.)
   - **A.** In the BIOS
   - **B.** In an `initrd` image
   - **C.** In the MBR of a storage device
   - **D.** In the bootable partition
   - **E.** In the system chipset
3. Where does the Linux kernel reside?
   - **A.** In `/boot`
   - **B.** In the MBR
   - **C.** In `/proc`
   - **D.** In `/kernel`
4. You want to install GRUB2 into the first partition on the first SATA hard disk drive of your system. Which shell command will do this?
   - **A.** `grub /dev/sda1`
   - **B.** `grub2-install /dev/sda1`
   - **C.** `grub-install /dev/sda`
   - **D.** `grub /dev/hda1`
5. Which command will start the Apache web server on a Red Hat–class Linux system?
   - **A.** `systemctl start httpd`
   - **B.** `systemctl start apache`
   - **C.** `systemctl start apache2`
   - **D.** `systemctl start apachev2`
6. Which of the following configuration files is *not* used by the GRUB2 bootloader?
   - **A.** `/boot/grub/grub.cfg`
   - **B.** `/etc/grub.d`
   - **C.** `/etc/default/grub`
   - **D.** `/boot/grub/menu.lst`

7. Which GRUB2 configuration script file can detect a Windows installation on the same hard disk as Linux?
   - **A.** `00_header`
   - **B.** `10_linux`
   - **C.** `30_os_prober`
   - **D.** `40_custom`
8. Which configuration parameter in `/etc/default/grub` specifies how long the user has to make a menu selection from the GRUB menu before the default operating system is booted?
   - **A.** `GRUB_TIMEOUT`
   - **B.** `GRUB_DEFAULT`
   - **C.** `GRUB_SAVED DEFAULT`
   - **D.** `GRUB_HIDDEN_TIMEOUT`
9. Which runlevel uses a graphical user interface by default?
   - **A.** 2
   - **B.** 3
   - **C.** 4
   - **D.** 5
10. Which runlevels use a command-line user interface by default? (Choose two.)
    - **A.** 0
    - **B.** 2
    - **C.** 3
    - **D.** 5
    - **E.** 4
11. Which file is used to set the default runlevel of a Linux system that uses the `init` daemon?
    - **A.** `/etc/inittab`
    - **B.** `/etc/runlevel.conf`
    - **C.** `/etc/init.conf`
    - **D.** `/etc/sysconfig/init`
12. Which command can be used to switch runlevels while the system is running?
    - **A.** `runlevel`
    - **B.** `chrun`
    - **C.** `mode`
    - **D.** `init`

13. Your Linux system uses `systemd` instead of `init`. You need to switch the system into runlevel 3. Which command should you use?
    A. `systemctl isolate graphical.target`
    B. `systemctl isolate multi-user.target`
    C. `systemctl isolate runlevel5.target`
    D. `systemctl isolate nongraphical.target`

Answers

1. **A, C.** The BIOS tests your system hardware during the POST routine and then locates a bootable storage device.
2. **C, D.** The Linux bootloader can be stored in the MBR of the storage device and in the bootable partition on the disk.
3. **A.** The Linux kernel resides in `/boot` in the filesystem.
4. **B.** The `grub2-install /dev/sda1` command will install GRUB2 into the first partition on the first hard disk drive.
5. **A.** To start the Apache web server on a Red Hat–class system, run `systemctl start httpd`. On Debian-class systems, run `systemctl start apache2`.
6. **D.** The `/boot/grub/menu.lst` file is used by GRUB Legacy. It's not used by GRUB2.
7. **C.** The `30_os_prober` GRUB2 script can detect other operating systems, such as Windows, installed on the same system as Linux. It can use the information it finds to add menu items to the GRUB menu that will launch those operating systems.
8. **A.** The `GRUB_TIMEOUT` parameter is used by GRUB2 to specify how long the user has to make a menu selection from the GRUB menu before the default operating system is booted.
9. **D.** Runlevel 5 uses a graphical user interface by default.
10. **B, C.** Runlevels 2 and 3 use a command-line interface by default.
11. **A.** The `/etc/inittab` file is used to set the default runlevel of a Linux system.
12. **D.** The `init` command can be used to switch runlevels while the system is running.
13. **B.** The `systemctl isolate multi-user.target` command will switch the system into the `systemd` equivalent of `init` runlevel 3.

CHAPTER 12

Managing Hardware Under Linux

In this chapter, you will learn about

- Discovering devices
- Managing kernel modules
- Referencing kernel and user space
- Configuring hardware devices
- Configuring Bluetooth
- Configuring Wi-Fi
- Configuring storage devices
- Printing in Linux

Consumer products actually have to be stronger than military.

—Jerry Lawson, Fairchild

In this chapter we are going to explore how system devices are discovered and made available to system applications as well as some of the commands you may use to obtain information concerning system hardware. Only the first two topics, "Discovering Devices" and "Managing Kernel Modules," are covered on the Linux+ exam. The other material is provided as reference for the Linux+ administrator.

NOTE All of the figures and examples in this chapter were created using the same virtual machine image you have access to. Remember that even though we are using the same image device, when you execute the commands in this chapter, the information may not be the same. You will learn why in this chapter.

Discovering Devices

Part of the system boot process is discovering hardware devices. The discovery process starts with searching through system busses for devices. When a device is found, its properties are discovered and then named (enumerated) so applications may access the device.

Table 12-1
Device Terms

Term	**Definition**
Bus	A system device used to transfer data between devices
Port	A physical connection to a bus
Device	A system component capable of receiving or providing data
Driver	A file or group of files used to control a hardware device

In this section, you will learn how to discover the hardware installed on Linux systems using the following:

- Displaying the kernel ring buffer with `dmesg`
- Detecting USB devices with `lsusb`
- Detecting PCI devices with `lspci`

Table 12-1 contains a list of device terms we will use in our discussion.

Displaying the Kernel Ring Buffer with `dmesg`

The `dmesg` command is used to read, display, and control the kernel ring buffer. The ring buffer is a cyclical storage space of specific size that contains kernel log messages. Once a ring buffer's space has been used, data will be overwritten (starting from the beginning of the buffer). In many cases, log information found in the ring buffer will be handled by the `syslog` facility kernel.

To search the `dmesg` ring buffer use the `syslog` facility and priority names (see Table 12-2). The `syslog` logging utility is discussed in detail in Chapter 16.

NOTE `dmesg` uses the term "level" to describe a `syslog` priority.

Table 12-2
Syslog Facilities and Priorities

`syslog` **Facilities**	`syslog` **Priorities**
`kern`	`emerg`
`user`	`alert`
`mail`	`crit`
`daemon`	`err`
`auth`	`warn`
`syslog`	`notice`
`lpr`	`info`
`news`	`debug`

```
#dmesg -T -f kern -l notice | grep sdb
[Tue Jun  4 11:44:02 2019] sd 3:0:0:0: [sdb] 15240576 512-byte logical blocks: (7.80 GB/7.26 GiB)
[Tue Jun  4 11:44:02 2019] sd 3:0:0:0: [sdb] Write Protect is off
[Tue Jun  4 11:44:02 2019] sd 3:0:0:0: [sdb] Attached SCSI removable disk
```

Figure 12-1 Adding a timestamp to `dmesg` output

```
[  315.048403] usb 1-1: new high-speed USB device number 2 using ehci-pci
[  315.283444] usb 1-1: New USB device found, idVendor=0930, idProduct=6545
[  315.283451] usb 1-1: New USB device strings: Mfr=1, Product=2, SerialNumber=3
[  315.283479] usb 1-1: Product: DataTraveler 2.0
[  315.283484] usb 1-1: Manufacturer: Kingston
[  315.283489] usb 1-1: SerialNumber: C860008862E4ED606A1C00A0
[  315.473822] usb-storage 1-1:1.0: USB Mass Storage device detected
[  315.476678] scsi host3: usb-storage 1-1:1.0
[  315.476751] usbcore: registered new interface driver usb-storage
[  315.479338] usbcore: registered new interface driver uas
[  316.564135] scsi 3:0:0:0: Direct-Access     Kingston DataTraveler 2.0 PMAP PQ: 0 ANSI: 4
[  316.565705] sd 3:0:0:0: Attached scsi generic sg2 type 0
[  317.997706] sd 3:0:0:0: [sdb] 15240576 512-byte logical blocks: (7.80 GB/7.26 GiB)
```

Figure 12-2 `dmesg` kernel events

The command `dmesg -T -f kern -l notice | grep sdb` (shown in Figure 12-1) displays all messages in the ring buffer that have a kernel message (`-f` or `--facility`) of level notice (`-l` or `--level`) and contain the string `sdb`. The `-T` option displays the message timestamp.

Figure 12-2 illustrates kernel log entries during the discovery process of the USB flash drive.

Table 12-3 displays three `dmesg` command options.

Line 1 of Figure 12-3 illustrates how you may search for specific objects by adding the `grep` command by running `dmesg | grep usb`.

Table 12-3 Options Used with the `dmesg` Command

Option	Description
`-L`	Adds color to the output
`-T`	Displays timestamp
-H	Enables human-readable output

```
[ 5790.274589] usb 1-1: Manufacturer: Kingston
[ 5790.274591] usb 1-1: SerialNumber: C860008862E4ED606A1C00A0
[ 5790.442630] usb-storage 1-1:1.0: USB Mass Storage device detected
[ 5790.458073] scsi host3: usb-storage 1-1:1.0
[ 5790.458407] usbcore: registered new interface driver usb-storage
[ 5790.461915] usbcore: registered new interface driver uas
```

Figure 12-3 Using `dmesg` to look for USB events

```
1 # lsusb -t
2 /:  Bus 02.Port 1: Dev 1, Class=root_hub, Driver=uhci_hcd/2p, 12M
3     |__ Port 1: Dev 2, If 0, Class=Human Interface Device, Driver=usbhid, 12M
4     |__ Port 2: Dev 3, If 0, Class=Hub, Driver=hub/7p, 12M
5 /:  Bus 01.Port 1: Dev 1, Class=root_hub, Driver=ehci-pci/6p, 480M
6     |__ Port 1: Dev 2, If 0, Class=Mass Storage, Driver=usb-storage, 480M
```

Figure 12-4 Displaying a USB device tree

Detecting USB Devices with `lsusb`

The command `lsusb -t` produces a hierarchical view of USB hubs and devices attached to the hubs. Lines 1 and 5 of Figure 12-4 display the USB hub, driver, and transfer speed. `12M` indicates 12 megabits per second (USB 1.0) and `480M` indicates 480 megabits per second (USB 2.0). Lines 3, 4, and 6 shows the devices that are attached.

Figure 12-5 displays a list of USB devices detected using `lsusb`. Looking at line 3, you can see information concerning the flash storage device. Notice this device is connected to `Bus 001`. `Device 002` indicates this is the second device on the bus.

The USB Root Hub

Line 4 in Figure 12-5 refers to the first device as a *root hub*. The root hub is responsible for communicating with devices attached to hub ports and the hub controller. The hub controller performs the following tasks:

- It monitors devices being placed on or removed from the hub.
- It manages power for devices on the host's ports.
- It manages communications on the controller's bus.

The ID numbers in the `lsusb` output are contained in two fields: `<manufacturer>:<device_id>`. If you look at the table found at the website www.linux-usb.org/usb.ids (shown in Figure 12-6), you will see 930 is the manufacturer ID for Toshiba Corp. and the device ID 6545 is a Kingston DataTraveler flash drive.

You can find out additional information by executing the following command syntax:

```
lsusb -D /dev/bus/usb/<bus_number><device_number>
```

```
1 #lsusb
2
3 Bus 001 Device 002: ID 0930:6545 Toshiba Corp. Kingston DataTraveler 102/2.0 / HEMA Flash Drive 2 GB / PNY Attache 4GB Stick
4 Bus 001 Device 001: ID 1d6b:0002 Linux Foundation 2.0 root hub
5 Bus 002 Device 003: ID 0e0f:0002 VMware, Inc. Virtual USB Hub
6 Bus 002 Device 002: ID 0e0f:0003 VMware, Inc. Virtual Mouse
7 Bus 002 Device 001: ID 1d6b:0001 Linux Foundation 1.1 root hub
```

Figure 12-5 List of USB devices detected using `lsusb`

Figure 12-6 Sample of USB device IDs

```
092f  Northern Embedded Science/CAVNEX
      0004  JTAG-4
      0005  JTAG-5
0930  Toshiba Corp.
      653c  Kingston DataTraveler 2.0 Stick (512M)
      653d  Kingston DataTraveler 2.0 Stick (1GB)
      653e  Flash Memory
      6540  TransMemory Flash Memory
      6544  TransMemory-Mini / Kingston DataTraveler 2.0 Stick
      6545  Kingston DataTraveler 102/2.0 / HEMA Flash Drive 2 GB / PNY Attache 4GB Stick
```

```
#lsusb -D /dev/bus/usb/001/002
Device: ID 0930:6545 Toshiba Corp. Kingston DataTraveler 102/2.0 / HEMA Flash Drive 2 GB / PNY Attache 4GB Stick
Device Descriptor:
  bLength                18
  bDescriptorType         1
  bcdUSB               2.00
  bDeviceClass            0 (Defined at Interface level)
  bDeviceSubClass         0
  bDeviceProtocol         0
  bMaxPacketSize0        64
  idVendor           0x0930 Toshiba Corp.
  idProduct          0x6545 Kingston DataTraveler 102/2.0 / HEMA Flash Drive 2 GB / PNY Attache 4GB Stick
  bcdDevice            1.00
  iManufacturer           1 Kingston
  iProduct                2 DataTraveler 2.0
  iSerial                 3 C860008862E4ED606A1C00A0
```

Figure 12-7 `lsusb -D` output (edited for brevity)

For example, the output of the command `lsusb -D /dev/bus/usb/001/002` displays additional information concerning the flash drive (see Figure 12-7).

Detecting PCI Devices with `lspci`

Peripheral Component Interconnect (PCI) is a system specification that defines the implementation of the PCI bus. The bus supports 32- or 64-bit addressing and Ultra DMA burst mode, and it can auto-detect PCI peripheral boards. Multiple PCI busses may be joined using a bridge.

PCI limits the number of busses to 256 per system. Each bus can host up to 32 devices. Larger systems may require additional PCI busses. This is accomplished by using domains.

The PCI bus is a hierarchical structure (shown in Figure 12-8) that starts at the top bus (0).

The format of the `lspci` command's output is `Bus:Device:Function Class Vendor Name`.

NOTE The `-D` option displays the domain number, `Domain:Bus:Device:Function`, when executing the `lspci` command. If the `-D` option is not used, the domain is assumed to be `0000`.

Figure 12-9 shows edited output of the `lspci` command. Line 1 shows the first device (`00`) located on bus `02`. The device is a USB controller manufactured by VMware and its name is USB1.1 UHCI Controller. Lines 2–4 show three other devices located on bus `02`.

Figure 12-8 PCI hierarchical structure

```
#lspci -t
[0000:00]-+-00.0
          +-01.0-[01]--
          +-07.0
          +-07.1
          +-07.3
          +-07.7
          +-0f.0
          +-10.0
          +-11.0-[02]--+-00.0
          |            +-01.0
          |            +-02.0
          |            \-03.0
```

```
02:00.0 USB controller: VMware USB1.1 UHCI Controller
02:01.0 Ethernet controller: Intel Corporation 82545EM Gigabit Ethernet Controller (Copper) (rev 01)
02:02.0 Multimedia audio controller: Ensoniq ES1371/ES1373 / Creative Labs CT2518 (rev 02)
02:03.0 USB controller: VMware USB2 EHCI Controller
```

Figure 12-9 Output of the `lspci` command

The class of device, manufacturer, and device name are stored as a numeric value. This information may be found in `/usr/share/hwdata/pci.ids`. Device classes are stored at the end of the file.

Notice in line 3 of Figure 12-10 that the class ID for the USB controller is `0c03`, and the vendor information for the device (`<vendor:device>`) is `15ad` (VMware)`: 0770` (USB2 EHCI Controller).

The `-v` and `-vv` options display additional bus information, as shown in Figure 12-11.

In Figure 12-12, we combine the `-t` and `-v` options. The `-t` option displays a tree structure and the `-v` option prints more detailed information.

```
1 02:01.0 Ethernet controller [0200]: Intel Corporation 82545EM Gigabit Ethernet Controller (Copper) [8086:100f] (rev 01)
2 02:02.0 Multimedia audio controller [0401]: Ensoniq ES1371/ES1373 / Creative Labs CT2518 [1274:1371] (rev 02)
3 02:03.0 USB controller [0c03]: VMware USB2 EHCI Controller [15ad:0770]
```

Figure 12-10 Using `lspci` to view vendor and class ID

```
 #lspci -v | grep -A8  USB2
02:03.0 USB controller: VMware USB2 EHCI Controller (prog-if 20 [EHCI])
        Subsystem: VMware USB2 EHCI Controller
        Physical Slot: 35
        Flags: bus master, fast devsel, latency 64, IRQ 17
        Memory at fd5ef000 (32-bit, non-prefetchable) [size=4K]
        Capabilities: [40] PCI Advanced Features
        Kernel driver in use: ehci-pci

 #lspci -vv | grep -A8  USB2
02:03.0 USB controller: VMware USB2 EHCI Controller (prog-if 20 [EHCI])
        Subsystem: VMware USB2 EHCI Controller
        Physical Slot: 35
        Control: I/O- Mem+ BusMaster+ SpecCycle- MemWINV- VGASnoop- ParErr- Stepping- SERR- FastB2B- DisINTx-
        Status: Cap+ 66MHz- UDF- FastB2B- ParErr- DEVSEL=fast >TAbort- <TAbort- <MAbort- >SERR- <PERR- INTx-
        Latency: 64 (1500ns min, 63750ns max)
        Interrupt: pin A routed to IRQ 17
        Region 0: Memory at fd5ef000 (32-bit, non-prefetchable) [size=4K]
        Capabilities: [40] PCI Advanced Features
                AFCap: TP+ FLR+
```

Figure 12-11 The `-v` and `-vv` options of `lspci`

```
 #lspci -t
          +-11.0-[02]--+-00.0
          |            +-01.0
          |            +-02.0
          |            \-03.0


#lspci -tv
          +-11.0-[02]--+-00.0  VMware USB1.1 UHCI Controller
          |            +-01.0  Intel Corporation 82545EM Gigabit Ethernet Controller (Copper)
          |            +-02.0  Ensoniq ES1371/ES1373 / Creative Labs CT2518
          |            \-03.0  VMware USB2 EHCI Controller
```

Figure 12-12 The `-t` and `-v` options of `lspci`

Host Bus Adapter

A host bus adapter (HBA), also called a host adapter or host controller, is an expansion card used to connect multiple devices, using a single controller, with a computer system. Here are some examples of host adapters:

- IDE, SCSI, and SATA controllers
- iSCSI and Fiber Channel controllers
- Network controllers

To view HBA adapters, execute the command `lspci -nn | grep -i hba` or the command `systool -c <adapter_class>`. You could also look for information in `/sys/class`.

Managing Kernel Modules

As with most other operating systems, you can manually list, load, or unload Linux kernel modules. To view all currently loaded kernel modules, use the `lsmod` command. This command pulls data from the `/proc/modules` file and reformats into a human-readable table. To use this command, simply enter `lsmod` at the shell prompt, as shown in the following example:

```
openSUSE:~ # lsmod
Module                  Size  Used by
lp                     10913  0
parport_pc             37547  1
af_packet              23229  0
joydev                 11942  0
st                     41564  0
fuse                   75897  3
...
```

The `lsmod` output displays the size and dependents of the module. The `Size` field is a relic of the 20th century when 64MB RAM was a lot of memory. System administrators were always looking for ways to save memory, and if removing an unimportant module would help, it would be blacklisted.

EXAM TIP To blacklist a module, such as `joydev`, add it to a `/etc/modprobe.d/` configuration file. Also, to keep the `joydev` module from being installed as a dependency for another device, set the module to `/bin/false`, as follows:

```
# echo "blacklist joydev" >> /etc/modprobe.d
/blacklist.conf
# echo "install joydev /bin/false" >> /etc
/modprobe.d/blacklist.conf
```

To view more information about a loaded module, use the `modinfo` command. You can first use `lsmod` to find the module, and then enter `modinfo <module_name>` at the shell prompt. In the preceding example, one of the modules displayed by `lsmod` is joydev, which is the system's joystick kernel module. To view more information about this module, enter modinfo joydev at the shell prompt, as shown in this example:

```
openSUSE:~ # modinfo joydev
filename:       /lib/modules/2.6.34.7-0.7-desktop/kernel/drivers/input/joydev.ko
license:        GPL
description:    Joystick device interfaces
author:         Vojtech Pavlik vojtech@ucw.cz
srcversion:     B57DA6AAEE9B8102A061E91
alias:          input:b*v*p*e*-e*1,*k*2C0,*r*a*m*l*s*f*w*
alias:          input:b*v*p*e*-e*1,*k*130,*r*a*m*l*s*f*w*
alias:          input:b*v*p*e*-e*1,*k*120,*r*a*m*l*s*f*w*
alias:          input:b*v*p*e*-e*3,*k*r*a*6,*m*l*s*f*w*
alias:          input:b*v*p*e*-e*3,*k*r*a*8,*m*l*s*f*w*
alias:          input:b*v*p*e*-e*3,*k*r*a*0,*m*l*s*f*w*
depends:
vermagic:       2.6.34.7-0.7-desktop SMP preempt mod_unload modversions
```

To load a kernel module, you first need to run the depmod command from the shell prompt. This command is used to build a file named modules.dep that is stored in /lib/modules/*kernel_version*/, as shown here:

```
openSUSE:/usr/lib/modules/modules/3.11.10-21-desktop # ls
kernel              modules.builtin.bin modules.order       systemtap
modules.alias       modules.dep         modules.softdep     vdso
modules.alias.bin   modules.dep.bin     modules.symbols     weak-updates
modules.builtin     modules.devname     modules.symbols.bin
```

Within this file, depmod lists the dependencies between modules. This helps other kernel module management utilities ensure that dependent modules are loaded whenever you load a module. (The depmod command is a good utility to understand, but it is not included in the CompTIA Linux+ exam objectives.)

With the modules.dep file created, you can now go ahead and load kernel modules. You can use one of two different commands to do this. The first is the insmod command. The syntax for insmod is insmod <module_filename>. The module filename is usually a kernel module located in a subdirectory of /lib/modules/*kernel_version*/kernel/. For example, if you wanted to load the driver for a standard PC parallel port, you would enter the following at the shell prompt, after uncompressing the module using unxz:

```
insmod /lib/modules/$(uname -r)/kernel/drivers/parport/parport_pc.ko
```

NOTE If you accidentally keep typing imsmod instead of insmod because you're using a DVORAK keyboard, for example, create a link by running: sudo ln /usr/sbin/insmod /usr/sbin/imsmod

In addition to insmod, you can also use the modprobe command. Most Linux admins prefer modprobe to insmod because insmod doesn't install module dependencies identified by depmod, but modprobe does.

The syntax for using modprobe is modprobe <module_name>. As with insmod, the module loaded with modprobe is in a subdirectory of /lib/modules /*kernel_version*/kernel/. For example, the /lib/modules/3.11.10-21-desktop/kernel/drivers/net/ethernet directory contains kernel modules for a variety of network devices, as shown here:

```
ws1:/lib/modules/modules/3.11.10-21-desktop/kernel/drivers/net/ethernet # ls
3c59x.ko      chelsio      hamachi.ko    myri10ge      qlcnic      sunhme.ko
8139cp.ko     cnic.ko      hamradio      natsemi.ko    qlge        tehuti.ko
8139too.ko    cxgb3        hp100.ko      ne2k-pci.ko   r6040.ko    tg3.ko
...
```

To load the kernel module for the 3c590 network card, enter modprobe 3c590 at the shell prompt. You're probably wondering at this point if the module will be persistent across system restarts after it has been loaded with modprobe. The answer is no.

To automatically detect devices during boot, modprobe is now automatically run every time the kernel loads. It reads the information contained in /etc/modprobe.d/*.conf files to determine what kernel modules should load during startup.

The /etc/modprobe.d/*.conf files use the following directives:

- **install <module_name>** Tells modprobe to load the specified module. It can also be used to run any valid shell command, providing flexibility when loading modules.
- **alias <alias_name> <module_name>** Gives a kernel module an alias name that can be used to reference it from the shell prompt.
- **options module_name options** Gives modprobe a list of options, such as irq= and io=, that should be used when a particular kernel module loads.

If you need to unload a currently loaded kernel module, use rmmod <module_name> at the shell prompt. Be warned that this command won't work if the device serviced by the module is in use. Like insmod, rmmod does not take module dependencies into account, so they are ignored. To remove a module and take dependencies into account, use modprobe by running modprobe -r <module_name>.

Next, practice working with kernel modules in Exercise 12-1.

Exercise 12-1: Working with Kernel Modules

In this exercise, you will practice viewing information about kernel modules. You can perform this exercise using the virtual machine that comes with this book. Run **snapshot 12-1** for the correctly configured environment.

VIDEO Please watch the Exercise 12-1 video for a demonstration on how to perform this task.

Complete the following:

1. Boot your Linux system and log in as the **student** user.
2. Open a terminal session.
3. Switch to your `root` user account by entering the **su -** command.
4. View the status of your system's kernel modules by entering **lsmod | less** at the shell prompt.
5. Page through the list of kernel modules. When finished, press **q**.
6. View information about the `parport` kernel module by entering **modinfo parport** at the shell prompt.
7. Create a list of module dependencies by entering **depmod** at the shell prompt.
8. Use the **less** or **more** utility to review the dependency file, `modules.dep`, you just built in `/lib/modules/$(uname -r)/`. The string `$(uname -r)` lists the kernel version, and is explained more in Chapter 13.
9. Enter **lsmod | grep joydev** at the shell prompt. You should see a `0` on the output line, indicating the module is loaded but the hardware is not in use.
10. Remove the `joydev` module by entering **rmmod joydev** at the shell prompt.
11. Verify that the `joydev` kernel module was unloaded by entering **lsmod | grep joydev** again at the shell prompt. You should see no output listed, indicating the module isn't loaded.
12. Reload the joystick module by entering **modprobe joydev** at the shell prompt.
13. Enter **lsmod | grep joydev** at the shell prompt again. You should again see a `0` on the output line, indicating the module is loaded but the hardware is not in use, as shown here:

```
openSUSE:/etc/modprobe.d # lsmod | grep joydev
joydev                 11942  0
```

Referencing Kernel and User Space

To protect kernel information from users, system memory is divided into kernel space and user space. The kernel memory is only accessible to the kernel, and the user memory is accessible to users and applications. Some kernel data is made available to users via directories such as `/proc` and `/sys`, and USB devices can be customized through `udev`.

/sys and sysfs

The `sysfs` filesystem is a memory-based filesystem mounted on the directory `/sys`. The `sysfs` filesystem provides user space with the properties and dynamic operational statistics of system hardware and filesystems.

Subdirectory	Description
block	Contains block device (disk and partition) information.
bus	Lists system devices used to connect components. A data bus transfers information. An address bus contains the memory location where data should be read from or written to. A control bus carries device control information between the CPU and system devices.
device	Presents a hierarchical list of devices.
firmware	Displays system firmware.
fs	Shows mounted filesystems and devices using the filesystem type.
kernel	Displays kernel status.
modules	Prints loaded modules.
power	Displays information about power management.

Table 12-4 /sys (sysfs) Directories

Directory	Device Attributes
dev	Lists major and minor number (used to create entry in /dev)
device	Displays operation statistics
driver	Shows symbolic link to device driver (/sys/bus<bus_type> /drivers/<device>)

Table 12-5 sys Device Attribute Directories

NOTE Do not confuse /sys with /proc/sys. /proc/sys contains kernel operating parameters, which may be manipulated by changing entries in the /proc/sys directory (temporary changes) or /etc/sysctl.conf file (permanent changes).

On boot, the Linux kernel modules detect and initialize devices by scanning each system bus. Device manufacturers assign to each device a vendor name and device ID. The Linux kernel assigns to the device a major number and minor number based on the vendor name and device ID.

Next, the kernel creates a directory in /sys. Each directory contains subdirectories (see Table 12-4) that contain device attributes. Table 12-5 lists some device attribute directories.

block

The block directory contains an entry for each system block device. This information is used by the lsblk command (see Figure 12-13).

The entries in the block directory are symbolic links to directories in /sys/devices (lines 1–9 in Figure 12-14). The block device directory contains operational information for the devices (lines 11–15 in Figure 12-14).

Figure 12-13 Output of the `lsblk` command

```
# lsblk
NAME          MAJ:MIN RM  SIZE RO TYPE MOUNTPOINT
sda             8:0    0    4G  0 disk
sdb             8:16   0   18G  0 disk
├─sdb1          8:17   0  500M  0 part /boot
├─sdb2          8:18   0  7.5G  0 part
│ └─USR-usr   253:0    0  7.5G  0 lvm  /usr
├─sdb3          8:19   0    3G  0 part
│ └─VAR-var   253:1    0    3G  0 lvm  /var
├─sdb4          8:20   0    1K  0 part
├─sdb5          8:21   0    1G  0 part /
├─sdb6          8:22   0    1G  0 part /home
├─sdb7          8:23   0    1G  0 part /tmp
└─sdb8          8:24   0    1G  0 part [SWAP]
sdc             8:32   0    4G  0 disk
sr0            11:0    1 1024M  0 rom
```

```
# cd /sys/block
#
# ls -l
total 0
lrwxrwxrwx. 1 root root 0 May 27 09:30 dm-0 -> ../devices/virtual/block/dm-0
lrwxrwxrwx. 1 root root 0 May 27 09:30 dm-1 -> ../devices/virtual/block/dm-1
lrwxrwxrwx. 1 root root 0 May 27 09:30 sda -> ../devices/pci0000:00/0000:00:10.0/host2/target2:0:0/2:0:0:0/block/sda
lrwxrwxrwx. 1 root root 0 May 27 09:26 sdb -> ../devices/pci0000:00/0000:00:11.0/0000:02:03.0/usb1/1-1/1-1:1.0/host3/target3:0:0/
3:0:0:0/block/sdb
lrwxrwxrwx. 1 root root 0 May 27 09:30 sr0 -> ../devices/pci0000:00/0000:00:07.1/ata2/host1/target1:0:0/1:0:0:0/block/sr0
#
# cd /sys/block/sda
# ls
alignment_offset  dev                events              ext_range  power  removable  sda2  sda5  sda8  slaves     trace
bdi               device             events_async        holders    queue  ro         sda3  sda6  sda9  stat       uevent
capability        discard_alignment  events_poll_msecs   inflight   range  sda1       sda4  sda7  size  subsystem
```

Figure 12-14 View of `/sys/block`

NOTE For a closer view of Figure 12-14 and other selected images from this chapter, download the full-resolution images from the online content for this book.

You can also use the `systool` command to examine system busses. The `systool` command is part of the `sysfsutil` package, which is not installed by default. Executing the command `systool` displays a list of supported busses, classes, devices, and modules. This package is installed on your system. Figure 12-15 illustrates the use of the command `systool -c block` to display block devices. The `-p` option displays the path to the block devices.

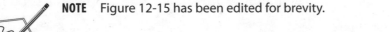

NOTE Figure 12-15 has been edited for brevity.

```
#systool -pc block
Class = "block"

  Class Device = "dm-0"
  Class Device path = "/sys/devices/virtual/block/dm-0"

  Class Device = "dm-1"
  Class Device path = "/sys/devices/virtual/block/dm-1"

  Class Device = "sda"
  Class Device path = "/sys/devices/pci0000:00/0000:00:10.0/host2/target2:0:0/2:0:0:0/block/sda"
    Device = "2:0:0:0"
    Device path = "/sys/devices/pci0000:00/0000:00:10.0/host2/target2:0:0/2:0:0:0"


  Class Device = "sr0"
  Class Device path = "/sys/devices/pci0000:00/0000:00:07.1/ata2/host1/target1:0:0/1:0:0:0/block/sr0"
    Device = "1:0:0:0"
    Device path = "/sys/devices/pci0000:00/0000:00:07.1/ata2/host1/target1:0:0/1:0:0:0"
```

Figure 12-15 `systool -c` block

bus

A bus is a system device used to transfer data between devices. The `/sys/bus` directory contains operational statistics for all system busses. Lines 1–6 in Figure 12-16 display different bus types. On lines 12–14 in Figure 12-16, you can see the files found in the `/sys//bus/usb` directory.

Each directory in `/sys/bus/` contains device and driver directories. The device directory (lines 21–25 in Figure 12-16) contains entries for devices discovered on the bus. Most of these files are symbolic links to the directory `/sys/devices/`.

The `drivers` directory (lines 30–36 in Figure 12-16) contains device driver information for all discovered devices on the bus.

```
 1 # cd /sys/bus
 2 #
 3 # ls
 4 ac97         clocksource  edac          i2c    machinecheck  mipi-dsi  nvmem        platform  serio    thunderbolt  workqueue
 5 acpi         container    event_source  iio    mdio_bus      nd        pci          pnp       snd_seq  usb          xen
 6 clockevents  cpu          hid           ishtp  memory        node      pci_express  scsi      spi      usb-serial
 7 #
 8 # cd /sys/bus/usb
 9 #
10 # ls -l
11 total 0
12 drwxr-xr-x. 2 root root    0 May 27 09:21 devices
13 drwxr-xr-x. 9 root root    0 May 27 09:26 drivers
14 -rw-r--r--. 1 root root 4096 May 28 08:23 drivers_autoprobe
15 --w-------. 1 root root 4096 May 28 08:23 drivers_probe
16 --w-------. 1 root root 4096 May 28 08:23 uevent
17 #
18 # cd devices
19 # ls -l
20 total 0
21 lrwxrwxrwx. 1 root root 0 May 27 09:22 1-0:1.0 -> ../../../devices/pci0000:00/0000:00:11.0/0000:02:03.0/usb1/1-0:1.0
22 lrwxrwxrwx. 1 root root 0 May 27 09:26 1-1 -> ../../../devices/pci0000:00/0000:00:11.0/0000:02:03.0/usb1/1-1
23 lrwxrwxrwx. 1 root root 0 May 27 09:26 1-1:1.0 -> ../../../devices/pci0000:00/0000:00:11.0/0000:02:03.0/usb1/1-1/1-1:1.0
24 lrwxrwxrwx. 1 root root 0 May 27 09:22 usb1 -> ../../../devices/pci0000:00/0000:00:11.0/0000:02:03.0/usb1
25 lrwxrwxrwx. 1 root root 0 May 27 09:22 usb2 -> ../../../devices/pci0000:00/0000:00:11.0/0000:02:00.0/usb2
26
27 # cd /sys/bus/usb/drivers
28 [root@localhost drivers]# ls -l
29 total 0
30 drwxr-xr-x. 2 root root 0 May 28 08:25 hub
31 drwxr-xr-x. 2 root root 0 May 27 09:26 uas
32 drwxr-xr-x. 2 root root 0 May 28 08:24 usb
33 drwxr-xr-x. 2 root root 0 May 28 13:57 usbfs
34 drwxr-xr-x. 2 root root 0 May 28 13:57 usbhid
35 drwxr-xr-x. 2 root root 0 May 28 13:57 usbserial_generic
36 drwxr-xr-x. 2 root root 0 May 27 09:26 usb-storage
```

Figure 12-16 View of `/sys/bus`

```
 #systool -pb scsi
Bus = "scsi"

  Device = "1:0:0:0"
  Device path = "/sys/devices/pci0000:00/0000:00:07.1/ata2/host1/target1:0:0/1:0:0:0"

  Device = "2:0:0:0"
  Device path = "/sys/devices/pci0000:00/0000:00:10.0/host2/target2:0:0/2:0:0:0"

  Device = "host0"
  Device path = "/sys/devices/pci0000:00/0000:00:07.1/ata1/host0"

  Device = "host1"
  Device path = "/sys/devices/pci0000:00/0000:00:07.1/ata2/host1"

  Device = "host2"
  Device path = "/sys/devices/pci0000:00/0000:00:10.0/host2"

  Device = "target1:0:0"
  Device path = "/sys/devices/pci0000:00/0000:00:07.1/ata2/host1/target1:0:0"

  Device = "target2:0:0"
  Device path = "/sys/devices/pci0000:00/0000:00:10.0/host2/target2:0:0"
```

Figure 12-17 Using `systool` to display bus devices

You can also use the command `systool -pb scsi` to display SCSI bus information. Figure 12-17 displays the instances of a SCSI bus (`-b scsi`) and paths (`-p`).

`class`

A device class contains devices that perform similar operations, such as block (block device). Figure 12-18 illustrates listings found in `/sys/class`.

`udev`

`udev` stands for `userspace /dev/`. The `/dev/` directory provides access to system devices. After the kernel module detects a device and has made the appropriate entries in `/sys/`, it generates a `uevent`. The `udev` service, `systemd-udevd.service`, responds to the `uevent` and matches the attributes of the device specified in `/sys/` to a `udev` configuration rule, which ensures a device's configuration is persistent across system reboots.

Location of `udev` Rules

`udev` rules are located in `/lib/udev/rules.d` (system default rules) and `/etc/udev/rules.d` (custom rules). In Figure 12-19, you can see that each rule begins with a number and then a short name. The `udev` daemon searches for rules in

```
# ls /sys/class

ata_device  bsg          drm_dp_aux_dev  i2c-adapter  misc           powercap      scsi_device   spi_master     typec
ata_link    cpuid        gpio            input        msr            power_supply  scsi_disk     spi_transport  usbmon
ata_port    devcoredump  graphics        iommu        nd             ppdev         scsi_generic  thermal        vc
backlight   dma          hidraw          leds         net            pwm           scsi_host     tpm            vtconsole
bdi         dmi          hmm_device      mdio_bus     pci_bus        raw           sound         tpmrm          watchdog
block       drm          hwmon           mem          pcmcia_socket  rtc           spi_host      tty
```

Figure 12-18 View of `/sys/class`

Figure 12-19 /lib/udev/rules.d directory (edited for brevity)

```
1 #pwd
2 /lib/udev/rules.d
3  #ls --format=single-column
4 01-md-raid-creating.rules
5 10-dm.rules
6 11-dm-lvm.rules
7 11-dm-mpath.rules
8 13-dm-disk.rules
9 60-cdrom_id.rules
10 60-keyboard.rules
11 60-net.rules
12 60-persistent-storage.rules
13 99-vmware-scsi-udev.rules
```

```
# by-label/by-uuid links (filesystem metadata)
ENV{ID_FS_USAGE}=="filesystem|other|crypto", ENV{ID_FS_UUID_ENC}=="?*", SYMLINK+="disk/by-uuid/$env{ID_FS_UUID_ENC}"
ENV{ID_FS_USAGE}=="filesystem|other", ENV{ID_FS_LABEL_ENC}=="?*", SYMLINK+="disk/by-label/$env{ID_FS_LABEL_ENC}"

# by-id (World Wide Name)
ENV{DEVTYPE}=="disk", ENV{ID_WWN_WITH_EXTENSION}=="?*", SYMLINK+="disk/by-id/wwn-$env{ID_WWN_WITH_EXTENSION}"
ENV{DEVTYPE}=="partition", ENV{ID_WWN_WITH_EXTENSION}=="?*", SYMLINK+="disk/by-id/wwn-$env{ID_WWN_WITH_EXTENSION}-part%n"

# by-partlabel/by-partuuid links (partition metadata)
ENV{ID_PART_ENTRY_SCHEME}=="gpt", ENV{ID_PART_ENTRY_UUID}=="?*", SYMLINK+="disk/by-partuuid/$env{ID_PART_ENTRY_UUID}"
ENV{ID_PART_ENTRY_SCHEME}=="gpt", ENV{ID_PART_ENTRY_NAME}=="?*", SYMLINK+="disk/by-partlabel/$env{ID_PART_ENTRY_NAME}"
```

Figure 12-20 Persistent storage rules example

Figure 12-21 /etc/udev/rules.d

```
1  #pwd
2 /etc/udev/rules.d
3  #ls --format=single-column
4 70-persistent-ipoib.rules
5 99-vmware-scsi-udev.rules
```

dictionary order (numbers first, then short name). Later rules (higher number) can override earlier rules.

Figure 12-20 displays a section of the rule `60-persistent-storage.rules`, which creates the entries `by-label`, `by-uuid`, `by-id`, `by-partlabel`, and `by-partuuid` in `/dev/` for a disk device.

Notice the entry `99-vmware-scsi-udev.rules` in both `/lib/udev/rules.d` (line 13 in Figure 12-19) and `/etc/udev/rules.d` (line 5 in Figure 12-21). This tells us that the default rule in `/lib/udev/rules.d` has been customized and `udev` will use the rule `/etc/udev/rules.d` rather than the rule in `/lib/udev/rules.d`.

udevadm

`udevadm` is a utility that can manage and obtain information about a system device.

udevadm info

The command `udevadm info` (see Figure 12-22) searches the `udev` database for device information. The format of the command is as follows:

```
udevadm info --query=<query_type> | -q <type> --path=<device_path> |  -p
<device_path>
```

or

```
udevadm info --query=<query_type> | -q <type> --name=<device_name> |  -n
<device_name>
```

```
#udevadm info -q property -n /dev/sdb
DEVLINKS=/dev/disk/by-id/usb-Kingston_DataTraveler_2.0_C860008862E4ED606A1C00A0-0:0 /dev/disk/by-path/pci-0000:02:03.0-usb-0:1:1.0
-scsi-0:0:0:0
DEVNAME=/dev/sdb
DEVPATH=/devices/pci0000:00/0000:00:11.0/0000:02:03.0/usb1/1-1/1-1:1.0/host6/target6:0:0/6:0:0:0/block/sdb
DEVTYPE=disk
ID_BUS=usb
ID_DRIVE_THUMB=1
ID_INSTANCE=0:0
ID_MODEL=DataTraveler_2.0
ID_MODEL_ENC=DataTraveler\x202.0
ID_MODEL_ID=6545
ID_PART_TABLE_TYPE=dos
ID_PATH=pci-0000:02:03.0-usb-0:1:1.0-scsi-0:0:0:0
ID_PATH_TAG=pci-0000_02_03_0-usb-0_1_1_0-scsi-0_0_0_0
ID_REVISION=PMAP
ID_SERIAL=Kingston_DataTraveler_2.0_C860008862E4ED606A1C00A0-0:0
ID_SERIAL_SHORT=C860008862E4ED606A1C00A0
ID_TYPE=disk
ID_USB_DRIVER=usb-storage
ID_USB_INTERFACES=:080650:
ID_USB_INTERFACE_NUM=00
ID_VENDOR=Kingston
ID_VENDOR_ENC=Kingston
ID_VENDOR_ID=0930
MAJOR=8
MINOR=16
MPATH_SBIN_PATH=/sbin
SUBSYSTEM=block
TAGS=:systemd:
USEC_INITIALIZED=80555195
```

Figure 12-22 Sample `udevadm info` command

Table 12-6 `udevadm` Info Query Types

Query Type	Description
`name`	Displays the device name
`symlink`	Displays the symbolic link attached to a device
`path`	Displays the physical path to the device
`property`	Displays the device properties
`all`	Displays the properties of parent devices

Table 12-6 lists the query types for `udevadm` info.

The attribute walk option (`-a`) of `udevadm info` may assist you in troubleshooting. Its output will display a device and its attributes as well as the attributes of all its parent devices. An example of the command is `udevadm -a --name=/dev/sda`.

`udevadm` monitor

The command `udevadm monitor` listens for `uevents` and displays them on the console. By default, `udevadm monitor` will display the kernel `uevent` and the `udev` process.

You can restrict the output to kernel `uevents` (`-k` or `--kernel`) or to `udev` events (`-u` or `--udev`). In addition, the option `-p` will display the properties of devices associated with the event.

`udevadm control`

The command `udevadm control` is used to control `systemd-udevd.service`.

Creating `udev` Rules

A `udev` rule is used to match a `uevent` with some action. You create rules by using a comma-delimited set of key/value entries. These keys can be either match keys or assign keys.

Table 12-7 udev Built-in Substitutions

String	Definition
`$$`	`$`
`%%`	`%`
`%r` or `$root`	`/dev/`
`%p` or `$devpath`	Value of `DEVPATH`
`%k` or `$kernel`	Kernel device name (for example, `/dev/sdb`)
`%n` or `$number`	Device number
`%M` or `$major`	Device's major number
`%m` or `$minor`	Device's minor number
`%E{variable}` `$attr{variable}`	Value of an environment variable
`%s` `$attr{attribute}`	Value of a `sysfs` attribute
`%c` or `$result`	Output of an executed `PROGRAM`

It is important to remember that udev rules are read in order of priority (lower number to higher number). When you're initially creating rules, use the command line. Once a rule has been completed, test the rule before adding it to /etc/udev/rules.d.

udev rules support the following globbing characters:

```
*
?
[ ]
```

udev supports substitutions, such as $(pwd), and also maintains a built-in list of substitution strings, listed in Table 12-7.

Prior to creating rules for a device, you must know its properties. Executing the udevadm info command enables you to display device properties. In Figure 12-22, I executed the command udevadm info -q property -n /dev/sdb to view the properties of the drive.

NOTE The examples in this chapter use a DataTraveler flash drive enumerated as /dev/sdb.

Match Keys

Match keys are used to match conditions that must exist for the rule to apply. Table 12-8 reviews some of the match keys.

When matching a key with a value, you use one of the operators in Table 12-9. The value must be enclosed in double quotes (" ").

The following key/value pairs would match our device, the DataTraveler flash drive:

Table 12-8 udev Rule Match Keys

Key	Description
ACTION	The name of the event (that is, add or remove)
add	Adds a rule
remove	Removes a rule
DEVPATH	The device path
KERNEL	Kernel name for the device
BUS	Bus type (for example, scsi or usb)
SUBSYSTEM	Subsystem of the device (for example, usb)
ATTR{filename}	Matches a device attribute
DRIVER	Matches a device driver name
ENV{key}	Matches an environment variable

Match Operator	Description
==	Double equal sign search to find a match between the match key and value.
!=	Not equal to. The key and value are not a match.

Table 12-9 udev Match Operators

NOTE udev requires one rule per line. If a rule will exceed a single line, use a \ to join multiple lines, known as command-line extension (as discussed in Chapter 1).

```
SUBSYSTEM=="block", ENV{ID_SERIAL_SHORT}==\
"C860008862E4ED606A1C00A0-0:0"
```

This could also have been written as follows:

```
SUBSYSTEM=="block",  %E{ID_SERIAL_SHORT}=="C860008862E4ED606A1C00A0-0:0"
```

Or it may have been written like this:

```
SUBSYSTEM=="block", $attr{ID_SERIAL_SHORT}==\
"C860008862E4ED606A1C00A0-0:0"
```

Assign Keys

Once you have matched the device, you can assign values using the assign operators in Table 12-10 and the assign keys in Table 12-11.

Assign Operator	Description
=	Assigns a value to a key. If the key had any values assigned to it, they all would be replaced by this assignment.
+=	Adds a value to an existing key.

Table 12-10 udev Assign Operators

Assign Key	Description
ACTION== add remove	The name of the event (add or remove). Adds a device. Removes a device.
NAME	Assigns a name to the device node. This will overwrite the existing name. Any rules assigned to the previous name will be ignored. The following rule will assign the node name MYUSB to our flash drive: SUBSYSTEM=="block", ENV{ID_SERIAL_SHORT}==\ "C860008862E4ED606A1C00A0-0:0", NAME="MYUSB"
SYMLINK	A symlink is established when the device is first enumerated; therefore, you can add a symlink to a device. This is especially useful if you have two devices of the same type because you can assign them different symlinks. The + before the = indicates to add a symlink to existing symlinks: SYMLINK+="8GUSB"
OWNER, GROUP, MODE	Assigns a device owner, group owner, and permissions: OWNER="<user_name>" GROUP="<group_name>" MODE="0655"
ATTR{key}	Assigns an attribute to a device. If double equal signs (==) are used, this key is used to match rather than to assign: ATTR{<attribute_name>}=="<value>"
ENV{key}	Creates an environment variable. If double equal signs (==) are used, this key is used to match rather than to assign.
RUN	Executes a program. The following line will execute the script found in test.sh: RUN+="test.sh"
GOTO <label>	Skips rules until after the LABEL.
LABEL	Creates a label (see GOTO).
IMPORT{type} program file	Loads variables into the environment. Executes a program and imports the output. Imports a text file.
OPTIONS last_rule ignore_device ignore_remove all_partitions	Ignores any additional rules set for the defined device. Here's an example: KERNEL="/dev/sda",OPTIONS="last-rule" Ignores a device. The following rule effectively disables USB devices: BUS=="usb", KERNEL="sd*", SUBSYSTEM="block" \ OPTIONS+="ignore-device Adds a udev rule for all partitions found on the device.

Table 12-11 udev Assign Keys

Assign keys are used to add an action or value to a device.

Once you have completed your rule, you need to test it. The command `udevadm test --action <udev_rule>` will test the rule without implementing it. If no error messages are displayed, the rule has no functional errors.

`udev` automatically detects changes to rules files when a rule is added or changed. Therefore, most changes will take place immediately. Existing devices may require the command `udevadm control --reload` for rule changes to be applied.

Configuring Hardware Devices

In this section, you will learn general elements and commands that are used to configure hardware devices. The following is for your reference.

lsdev

The `lsdev` command displays information about installed hardware. `lsdev` retrieves information from `/proc/interrupts`, `/proc/ioports`, and `/proc/dma` and displays the following columns:

- `Device`
- `DMA`
- `IRQ`
- `I/O Ports`

Figure 12-23 shows output of the `lsdev` command. The `lsdev` command lists data on DMA, IRQ, programmable interrupts, and more as discussed in the following subsections.

DMA

Direct memory access (DMA) enables devices to transfer data directly without the need of the CPU controlling the transfer.

DMA is implemented on the motherboard using the DMA controller chip (DCC). The DCC has four leads that connect it to the memory controller chip (MCC).

```
Device              DMA   IRQ  I/O Ports
ACPI                           1000-1003 1004-1005 1008-100b 100c-100f 1010-1015
ata_piix              14 15    0170-0177 01f0-01f7 0376-0376 03f6-03f6 1060-106f
cascade              4
dma                            0080-008f
dma1                           0000-001f
dma2                           00c0-00df
e1000                          2000-203f
ehci_hcd:usb2            17
keyboard                       0060-0060 0064-0064
uhci_hcd:usb1            18
```

Figure 12-23 `lsdev` (output edited for brevity)

Figure 12-24
DMA controller

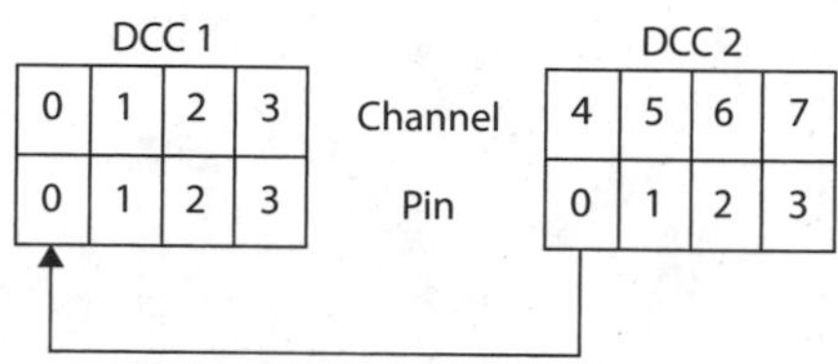

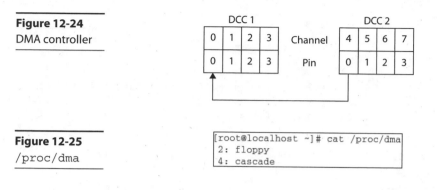

Figure 12-25
`/proc/dma`

```
[root@localhost ~]# cat /proc/dma
2: floppy
4: cascade
```

Each of these leads is referred to as a *DMA channel.* Two DCC chips may be connected together via channel 0 on the first chip and channel 4 on the second chip (cascade), as shown in Figure 12-24. Only one device may be assigned per channel. By default, channels 1 and 2 are reserved.

Ultra DMA is a method that allows devices to bypass the DMA controller and transmit data in bursts of either 33 or 66 Mbps. (Normal DMA transfer speeds are approximately 7.2 Mbps.)

The file `/proc/dma` (shown in Figure 12-25) displays active DMA channels. (The `cascade` entry shown is simply a placeholder, noting that channel 4 is unavailable to drivers.)

Interrupts

Every device is assigned an interrupt. Each interrupt is assigned a priority (interrupt request level) based on the importance of the device it is associated with.

Programmable Interrupt Controller A programmable interrupt controller (PIC) can manage eight interrupts per controller. The interrupt request line of a device is electrically attached to an interrupt line on the PIC.

Systems using PIC chips have one PIC chip (master) managing interrupts 0–7 and a second PIC chip (slave) managing interrupts 8–15.

Devices configured to use interrupt 2 use interrupt 9. Interrupt 9 is used for peripherals or the SCSI host adapter. Interrupt 2 is used by the slave PIC to signal the master PIC. The master PIC is connected to the CPU.

Advanced Programmable Interrupt Controller The Advanced Programmable Interrupt Controller (APIC) has eight additional interrupts to manage PCI interrupts and can support 255 physical interrupt request lines. This system consists of a Local APIC (LAPIC) and an I/O APIC.

NOTE It is easy to confuse APIC (Advanced Programmable Interrupt Controller) with ACPI, which stands for Advanced Configuration and Power Interface.

The LAPIC is built into the CPU and is used to accept and generate interrupts. The I/O APIC contains a table that directs interrupt requests to one or more LAPICs.

Figure 12-26 /proc/interrupts (edited for brevity)

```
# cat /proc/interrupts
           CPU0
  0:        131     XT-PIC-XT         timer
  1:        754     XT-PIC-XT         i8042
  2:          0     XT-PIC-XT         cascade
  5:      22126     XT-PIC-XT         ahci, Intel 82801AA-ICH
  8:          0     XT-PIC-XT         rtc0
  9:          0     XT-PIC-XT         acpi
 10:      13953     XT-PIC-XT         eth0
 11:          0     XT-PIC-XT         ohci_hcd:usb1
 12:      12240     XT-PIC-XT         i8042
 14:          0     XT-PIC-XT         ata_piix
 15:          0     XT-PIC-XT         ata_piix
```

If a system has APIC capabilities, but `grub.conf` contains the entry `noapic`, the system will use PIC.

/proc/interrupts Figure 12-26 displays edited output of the file `/proc/interrupts`, which contains the following information:

- The interrupt number.
- Number of times the interrupt has been requested (per CPU). If the system contains multiple CPUs, there would be a column for each CPU.
- Type of interrupt.
- Interrupt name.

Interrupt Request Channels The first system resource you need to be familiar with is the interrupt request channel. Interrupt request channels are also referred to as *IRQs* or just *interrupts*.

When a device is installed in a PC system, it needs some means of letting the CPU know when it needs attention. Many devices in your PC need lots of CPU time; other devices need the CPU only on occasion. We need a way to make sure the busy devices get the attention they need without wasting time on devices that don't need as much. This is done through interrupts.

The CPU in your system has one wire on it called the interrupt (INT) wire. If current is applied to this wire, the CPU will stop what it is doing and service the device that placed current on the wire. If no current is present on the wire, the CPU will continue working on whatever processing task has been assigned to it.

The interrupt system in a PC is very similar to a typical classroom. In a classroom setting, the instructor usually presents the material she has prepared to the students. If a student has a question, he can raise his hand and interrupt the instructor's presentation. After the question is answered, the instructor resumes the presentation.

PC interrupts work in much the same manner. Like the instructor, the CPU goes about its business until it is interrupted. Once interrupted, the CPU diverts its attention to the device that raised the interrupt. Once the device's request has been satisfied, the CPU goes back to what it was doing before.

The advantage to using interrupts is that the CPU services system devices only when they need it. It doesn't waste processing time on devices that are idle.

The PIC chip is connected to the INT wire on the CPU as well as the interrupt wires in your motherboard's expansion bus. When a device needs attention, it applies current to its interrupt wire. The PIC is alerted by this event and applies current to the CPU's INT wire. The CPU acknowledges the interrupt, and the PIC then tells the CPU which interrupt number was activated. The CPU can then service the device.

Early PCs had only eight interrupts and a single PIC, as just related. However, a modern PC has many more interrupts. Newer systems use an Advanced Programmable Interrupt Controller (APIC) chip that supports up to 255 IRQ lines.

When working with interrupts, you should keep in mind the following important facts:

- Every device in the PC must be assigned an interrupt.
- Two PCI devices can share interrupts.
- Some system devices have interrupts assigned to them by default. Some of these can be changed or disabled, but many cannot:
  - IRQ 0: System timer
  - IRQ 1: Keyboard
  - IRQ 3: COM 2
  - IRQ 4: COM 1
  - IRQ 5: LPT 2
  - IRQ 6: Floppy drive
  - IRQ 7: LPT 1
  - IRQ 8: Real-time clock
- Interrupts 0, 1, and 8 are hardwired. Under no circumstances can you use these interrupts for any other device in the system.
- If a device with a default interrupt assignment isn't installed in the system or is disabled, you can use its interrupt for another device.

In addition to interrupts, devices also require an I/O address to function in a PC system. Let's talk about I/O addresses next.

Input/Output Addresses

Input/output (I/O) addresses go by a variety of names in a PC system. You may hear them referred to as *I/O ports*, *port addresses*, or simply *ports*. An I/O port is a memory address used to communicate with a hardware device. The file `/proc/ioports` will contain a list of I/O ports being used (see Figure 12-27).

I/O addresses allow communications between the devices in the PC and the operating system. I/O addresses are very similar to mailboxes. To send a letter to someone, you must know their mailing address. You write their address on the letter, and the mail carrier delivers it to the box with that address. Likewise, the person you wrote to can respond to your letter and leave it in their mailbox for the mail carrier to pick up.

Figure 12-27 /proc/ioports (edited for brevity)

```
# cat /proc/ioports
0000-001f : dma1
0020-0021 : pic1
0040-0043 : timer0
0050-0053 : timer1
0060-0060 : keyboard
0064-0064 : keyboard
0070-0071 : rtc_cmos
  0070-0071 : rtc0
0080-008f : dma page reg
00a0-00a1 : pic2
00c0-00df : dma2
00f0-00ff : fpu
0170-0177 : 0000:00:01.1
  0170-0177 : ata_piix
01f0-01f7 : 0000:00:01.1
  01f0-01f7 : ata_piix
0376-0376 : 0000:00:01.1
  0376-0376 : ata_piix
03c0-03df : vga+
```

I/O addresses work in much the same manner. They serve as mailboxes for the devices installed in the system. Data can be left for a device in its I/O address. Data from the device can be left in the I/O address for the operating system to pick up.

On a personal computer, there are 65,535 port addresses for devices to use.

NOTE I/O addresses are written using hexadecimal notation. Because hex and decimal numbers can sometimes be easily mistaken, administrators often put an *h* either before or after any hex number.

When working with I/O addresses, keep the following important facts in mind:

- All devices must have an I/O address assigned.
- Most devices will use a range of I/O addresses.
- Devices must use unique I/O ports.
- Default I/O port assignments include the following:
  - 0000h: DMA controller
  - 0020h: PIC 1
  - 0030h: PIC 2
  - 0040h: System timer
  - 0060h: Keyboard
  - 0070h: CMOS clock

- 00C0h: DMA controller
- 00F0h: Math co-processor
- 0170h: Secondary IDE hard disk controller
- 01F0h: Primary IDE hard disk controller
- 0200h: Joystick
- 0278h: LPT2
- 02E8h: COM4
- 02F8h: COM2
- 0378h: LPT1
- 03E8h: COM3
- 03F0h: Floppy disk drive controller
- 03F8h: COM1

lshw

The `lshw` (list hardware) command may be used to display detailed hardware configuration information. `lshw` is a replacement for the deprecated `hwinfo` command and should be executed by a user with `root` privileges.

The syntax for `lshw` is `lshw -<format> <options>`. The output of the command `lshw` is a detailed description of system hardware, starting at the top of the device tree.

In Figure 12-28, I have used the short format option (`lshw -short`). This option displays the hardware path (bus address), device name, class of device, and storage path.

```
#lshw -short
H/W path                Device      Class        Description
/0/100/10               scsi0       storage      53c1030 PCI-X Fusion-MPT Dual Ultra320 SCSI
/0/100/10/0.0.0         /dev/sda    disk         21GB VMware Virtual S
/0/100/10/0.0.0/1       /dev/sda1   volume       500MiB EXT4 volume
/0/100/10/0.0.0/2       /dev/sda2   volume       8196MiB Linux LVM Physical Volume partition
/0/100/10/0.0.0/3       /dev/sda3   volume       3076MiB Linux LVM Physical Volume partition
/0/100/10/0.0.0/4       /dev/sda4   volume       8707MiB Extended partition
/0/100/10/0.0.0/4/5                 volume       1GiB Linux filesystem partition
/0/100/10/0.0.0/4/6     /dev/sda6   volume       500MiB EXT4 volume
/0/100/10/0.0.0/4/7     /dev/sda7   volume       500MiB EXT4 volume
/0/100/10/0.0.0/4/8     /dev/sda8   volume       1GiB Linux swap volume
/0/100/10/0.0.0/4/9     /dev/sda9   volume       500MiB Linux filesystem partition
/0/100/11                           bridge       PCI bridge
/0/100/11/0                         bus          USB1.1 UHCI Controller
/0/100/11/0/1           usb2        bus          UHCI Host Controller
/0/100/11/0/1/1                     input        VMware Virtual USB Mouse
/0/100/11/0/1/2                     bus          VMware Virtual USB Hub
/0/100/11/1             ens33       network      82545EM Gigabit Ethernet Controller (Copper)
/0/100/11/2                         multimedia   ES1371/ES1373 / Creative Labs CT2518
/0/100/11/3                         bus          USB2 EHCI Controller
/0/100/11/3/1           usb1        bus          EHCI Host Controller
```

Figure 12-28 Command `lshw` using `-short` output format (edited for brevity)

NOTE The command `lshw` requires the format option `-businfo` to display the bus address.

Additional format options are `-html` and `-xml`. When either of these format options is used, the output must be redirected to a file.

We can focus our output on a specific class or multiple classes of devices by adding the option `-class <class_name>`. Here are the available classes:

```
address          generic        printer
bridge           input          processor
bus              memory         storage
communication    multimedia     system
disk             network        tape
display          power          volume
```

The commands `lshw -short -class storage`, `lshw -short -class disk`, and `lshw -short -class volume` (shown in Figure 12-29) display hardware information on devices of class `storage`, `disk`, and `volume`, respectively.

```
 #lshw -short -class storage
H/W path               Device       Class          Description
==============================================================
/0/100/7.1             scsi2        storage        82371AB/EB/MB PIIX4 IDE
/0/100/10              scsi0        storage        53c1030 PCI-X Fusion-MPT Dual Ultra320 SCSI
 #

 #lshw -short -class disk
H/W path               Device       Class          Description
==============================================================
/0/100/7.1/0.0.0       /dev/cdrom   disk           VMware IDE CDR10
/0/100/7.1/0.0.0/0     /dev/cdrom   disk
/0/100/10/0.0.0        /dev/sda     disk           21GB VMware Virtual S
 #


 #lshw -short -class volume
H/W path               Device       Class          Description
==============================================================
/0/100/7.1/0.0.0/0/2                volume         15EiB Windows FAT volume
/0/100/10/0.0.0/1      /dev/sda1    volume         500MiB EXT4 volume
/0/100/10/0.0.0/2      /dev/sda2    volume         8196MiB Linux LVM Physical Volume partition
/0/100/10/0.0.0/3      /dev/sda3    volume         3076MiB Linux LVM Physical Volume partition
/0/100/10/0.0.0/4      /dev/sda4    volume         8707MiB Extended partition
/0/100/10/0.0.0/4/5                 volume         1GiB Linux filesystem partition
/0/100/10/0.0.0/4/6    /dev/sda6    volume         500MiB EXT4 volume
/0/100/10/0.0.0/4/7    /dev/sda7    volume         500MiB EXT4 volume
/0/100/10/0.0.0/4/8    /dev/sda8    volume         1GiB Linux swap volume
/0/100/10/0.0.0/4/9    /dev/sda9    volume         500MiB Linux filesystem partition
```

Figure 12-29 Displaying device details using `lshw`

/root/lshw_html_out

file:///root/lshw_html_out

H/W path	Device	Class	Description
/0/100/7.1/0.0.0/0/2		volume	15EiB Windows FAT volume
/0/100/10/0.0.0/1	/dev/sda1	volume	500MiB EXT4 volume
/0/100/10/0.0.0/2	/dev/sda2	volume	8196MiB Linux LVM Physical Volume partition
/0/100/10/0.0.0/3	/dev/sda3	volume	3076MiB Linux LVM Physical Volume partition
/0/100/10/0.0.0/4	/dev/sda4	volume	8707MiB Extended partition
/0/100/10/0.0.0/4/5		volume	1GiB Linux filesystem partition
/0/100/10/0.0.0/4/6	/dev/sda6	volume	500MiB EXT4 volume
/0/100/10/0.0.0/4/7	/dev/sda7	volume	500MiB EXT4 volume
/0/100/10/0.0.0/4/8	/dev/sda8	volume	1GiB Linux swap volume
/0/100/10/0.0.0/4/9	/dev/sda9	volume	500MiB Linux filesystem partition

Figure 12-30 `lshw` formatted as HTML output

The command `lshw -html -short -class volume > lshw_html_out` will produce a file in HTML format. In Figure 12-30, I have used Firefox to display the output.

Exercise 12-2: Discovering Devices

This exercise reviews some of the tools you have learned to view block devices.

VIDEO Please watch the Exercise 12-2 video for a demonstration on how to perform this task.

1. View the block devices on your system by executing the **`lsblk`** command.
2. Now view the block device entries in `/sys` by executing the **`ls -l /sys /block`** command.
3. You can also view system block devices using the **`systool -c block`** command.
4. You know that a bus is a device. View SCSI bus devices by executing the **`ls /sys/bus/scsi/devices`** or **`systool -b scsi`** command.
5. The command `lspci -t | more` will display the PCI bus hierarchy. Adding the `-v` option (`lspci -tv | more`) will add information about devices.
6. Prior to creating a `udev` rule, you'll want to view the properties of the device. To display the properties of the device `/dev/sda`, for example, you could execute this command: **`udevadm info -q property -n /dev/sda`**.
7. Display active DMA channels by executing the **`cat /proc/dma`** command.
8. To see interrupt request statistics, view the file `/proc/interrupts`.
9. The command `less /proc/ioports` will display the memory address ranges used to communicate with hardware devices.

10. The `lshw` command will list hardware devices. To display types of storage devices, execute the **`lshw -class storage`** command.
11. The `lsblk` command will display block storage devices by devices and partitions. The command `lshw -class volume` will display more detailed partition information.

Configuring Bluetooth

Bluetooth is a device interconnect designed to replace RS232 with wireless communication operating between 2.4 GHz and 2.485 GHz. The following is information for your reference.

A Bluetooth master (transmitter) can connect up to seven devices (receivers) via a *piconet*, also called a *personal area network (PAN)*. Although the technology is not currently refined, multiple piconets may be connected. Multiple networked piconets are called a *scatternet*.

Classes

Bluetooth classes determine the transmission range of the Bluetooth device. Table 12-12 details the Bluetooth classes and their transmission ranges.

Bluetooth Commands

Bluetooth commands are provided by the `bluez` package. To see if Bluetooth is active, execute the command `systemctl status bluetooth`.

The command `bluetoothctl list` displays a list of available Bluetooth controllers. The command `bluetoothctl show` displays a list of controllers and their status.

The command `bluetoothctl scan on` displays a list of available controllers that have not been paired.

To configure a Bluetooth device, you need to know the device's MAC address. The command `hcitool scan` provides a controller's MAC address and name.

Once you know the controller's address, execute the command `bluetoothctl select <controller_MAC_address>` to apply any `bluetoothctl` commands issued in the next three minutes to that controller.

Table 12-13 outlines some additional `bluetoothctl` options. Notice that some commands are applicable to the controller, whereas others are applicable to the device.

Table 12-12 Bluetooth Class Transmission Ranges

Class	Maximum Distance
1	300 feet
2	30 feet
3	3 feet
4	1.5 feet
5	500 feet

Argument	Description
Controller Arguments	
`agent on`	Turns on Bluetooth support. If the controller is a USB adapter, it will remain on as long as it is plugged in.
`discoverable on`	Makes the controller visible to other Bluetooth devices.
`discoverable off`	Hides the controller from other Bluetooth devices.
`pairable on`	Makes the controller ready for pairing.
Device Arguments	
`info <device_MAC_address>`	Displays device information.
`connect <device_MAC_address>`	Makes the device ready for pairing.
`pair <device_MAC_address>`	Pairs the device with the controller.

Table 12-13 `bluetoothctl` Options

Configuring Wi-Fi

Wi-Fi is a generic name for a wireless technology that uses radio waves to access a network via wireless access points. You can determine if a Wi-Fi network device is installed by using the tools discussed next.

Scanning for Network Devices

The following commands may be used to scan for network interfaces:

- `ip link show`
- `ifconfig -a`
- `ncmli connection show`
- `ncmli device status`
- `netstat -i`

Table 12-14 contains a partial list of interface names.

Configuring a Wi-Fi Network

Next we will explore configuring a Wi-Fi connection using the `iw` command.

Table 12-14 Network Interface Names

Interface Name	Description
`lo`	Loopback.
`eth` or `ens`	Ethernet interface.
`wlan`	Wireless network interface. Most wireless interface names begin with the letter `w`.

NOTE The `iwconfig` command has been deprecated and replaced by the `iw` command.

The following are some Wi-Fi terms that are helpful to know:

- **Frequency** A frequency is the speed with which data is transmitted and received. Most Wi-Fi adapters provide a frequency of 2.4 GHz or both 2.4- and 5-GHz frequencies. The frequencies may be modulated using direct sequence spread specrum (DSSS) or orthogonal frequency division multiplexing (OFDM). Frequencies may be divided into channels.
- **Channel** A channel is like a pipe set inside a frequency as a path for data. Each channel has an upper and lower frequency and is separated from other channels by 5 MHz. Overlapping channels share bandwidth. If you look at Channel 1 on 2.4 GHz, you'll notice it has a lower frequency of 2,401 MHz and an upper frequency of 2,423 MHz (20-MHz bandwidth). Channel 2 has a lower frequency of 2,406 MHz and an upper frequency of 2,428 MHz.
- **ESSID** Extended Service Set Identification (ESSID) is the identifier (name) used by a wireless device to connect to a router or access point.
- **Router** A router is a device that routes data between two or more networks.
- **Access point** An access point is a device that connects wireless devices to a network. Most access points have routers built in.

iw

The `iw` command is used to set up a wireless interface. Executed without any options or arguments, `iw` lists a help menu. To view the status of wireless interfaces, execute the command `iw list`.

Most wireless interfaces begin with the letter *w*, for example, `wlan0`. To view the status of interface `wlan0`, you would execute the command `iw wlan0 info`.

You may need to know what access points can be seen by a wireless interface. The command `iw <interface_name> scan` searches for available access points.

The command `iw <interface_name> essid <essid_name>` connects you to a wireless access point. Assuming an ESSID name of `network_one`, the following command connects `wlan0` to `network_one`:

```
iw wlan0 essid network_one
```

You can use a specific channel by adding the `channel` option:

```
iw wlan0 channel 11
```

Once the changes are made, execute the command `iw wlan0 commit` to ensure that all changes are applied to the interface.

Configuring Storage Devices

This section introduces the various types of storage devices and the commands associated with them.

IDE

Integrated Drive Electronics (IDE) refers to a technology in which the disk controller is integrated into the drive. The controller on one drive can control two devices (master and slave). IDE I/O cards or motherboards that support IDE contain two IDE channels (primary and secondary).

A single motherboard can support four devices:

- Primary master
- Primary slave
- Secondary master
- Secondary slave

If a system contains multiple IDE drives, the primary master drive is the default boot drive. Newer versions of IDE drives (ATA-4 forward) support Ultra DMA. ATA-6, which is also called Parallel ATA (PATA), can reach data transfer speeds of 133 Mbps.

SCSI

Small Computer System Interface (SCSI) is a parallel interface used to connect peripheral devices. SCSI devices are connected in a chain through an internal ribbon or external cable. It is important that the last SCSI device has a terminator installed.

SCSI devices are defined by the number of bits they transfer at a time and speed per second. Some SCSI device types are listed in Table 12-15.

Table 12-15
SCSI Device Types

Device	Description
Narrow SCSI	Supports eight devices (0–7) Data transfer: 8 bits Speed: 10 MBps
Wide SCSI	Supports 16 devices (0–15) Data transfer: 16 bits Speed: 20 MBps
Ultra SCSI	Data transfer: 8 bits Speed: 20 MBps
Ultra2 SCSI	Data transfer: 16 bits Speed: 40 MBps
Wide Ultra 2SCSI	Data transfer: 16 bits Speed: 80 MBps
Ultra3 SCSI	Data transfer: 16 bits Speed: 160 MBps

SCSI Device ID and Priorities

Each SCSI device is assigned an ID. The device ID may be set using a thumb wheel, jumper, or firmware. The device ID determines the priority of the device. Here are some points to keep in mind:

- The host bus adapter (HBA) is always assigned the highest priority (7).
- Narrow SCSI device priority order is 7, 6, 5, 4, 3, 2, 1, 0.
- Wide SCSI device priority order is 7, 6, 5, 4, 3, 2, 1, 0, 15, 14, 13, 12, 11, 10, 9, 8.

SATA

A Serial AT Attachment (SATA) drive communicates bit by bit (serial communications) to a dedicated hard disk channel via a high-speed serial cable. The cable contains seven pins (two data pair and three ground wires). One pair of wires is used to receive data, and the other pair is used to transmit acknowledgements. This wiring scheme is much simpler than the 40-pin or 80-pin ribbon connector required by IDE and removes many of the electrical limitations imposed by the IDE cable. SATA data transfer rates range from 150 MBps to 600 MBps.

eSATA

An eSATA port is used to connect external SATA devices to a system. Power for the device is supplied by an external power supply.

eSATAp

An eSATAp (powered eSATA) port is capable of supplying power to the external SATA device. An eSATAp port can also support USB.

Optical Drives

Optical drives have the ability to store large amounts of data. Data is written on a photo-conductive surface using a high-intensity laser. Data is represented by pits and lands. Pits represent a binary 0, and lands represent a binary 1. A lower intensity laser is used to read the data. There are three major types of optical media:

- CD
- DVD
- Blue-ray

Solid State Drives

Solid state drives (SSDs) use flash memory circuitry to store data. Information stored in flash memory is retained when system power is removed. Data is stored as if the device was an actual hard drive (cylinder/head/sector, or CHS). In most cases, SSD drives use the same interface as SATA, but they can implement other interfaces.

Since data is accessed electronically rather than mechanically, SSD data is accessed faster than on a traditional hard drive. However, an SSD's performance may degrade over time.

USB

USB is a high-speed Plug and Play (PnP) interface that allows multiple devices to connect via a single bus. A USB bus can support 127 devices in a star topology. The speed of the bus is limited to the speed of the slowest device on the bus. Standard bus speeds are as follows:

- USB 1.0: 12 Mbps
- USB 2.0: 480 Mbps
- USB 3.0: 800 Mbps
- USB 4.0: 40 Gbps

NOTE USB 3.0 is capable of 800 Mbps, but multiple USB devices may be connected to the USB interface via a USB hub, which could slow down the connection.

Make sure you are familiar with the following terms for our discussion of USB devices:

- **USB** A bus type used for data transfer
- **Port** A physical connection to a bus
- **Flash drive** A storage device that contains a USB interface and flash memory; also known as a thumb drive because of its physical size

USB devices may draw power from the USB connection or require an external power supply.

NOTE For the following examples, I have attached a Kingston 4G DataTraveler flash drive to a virtual machine.

Connecting a USB Device

When a flash drive is connected, the kernel creates a `uevent`, `udev` configures the device, and `dbus` informs user applications the device is available. We can view some of this activity using the `dmesg` command.

`hdparm`

`hdparm` is another utility used to query hard disk statistics and can change drive operating parameters. Use extreme caution when changing drive parameters. Table 12-16 shows options for the `hdparm` command.

Table 12-16
hdparm Options

Option	Description
-v <device>	Displays disk settings
-I <device>	Displays detailed disk statistics

```
# lsscsi
[1:0:0:0]    cd/dvd  NECVMWar VMware IDE CDR10 1.00  /dev/sr0
[2:0:0:0]    disk    VMware,  VMware Virtual S 1.0   /dev/sda
```

Figure 12-31
lsscsi

Table 12-17
lsscsi Options

Option	Description
<no option>	Lists SCSI devices
-H --hosts	Lists SCSI host adapters
-l --long	Lists SCSI device information
-d	Displays major and minor numbers

lsscsi

The lsscsi command is used to get SCSI device and host information. The lsscsi command displays a list of SCSI devices and hosts, as shown in Figure 12-31. The output on the left represents [host:channel:target_number:lun]. Here's a breakdown of the output:

- The host number indicates the number assigned to the adapter card.
- The channel indicates the bus number.
- The target number is the device number.
- The LUN is the logical unit number.

In larger systems, there may be an additional number at the beginning: [domain:host:channel:target_number:lun].

Table 12-17 shows options for the lsscsi command.

Printing in Linux

The following is good reference information about Linux printing. I created file-based printers to demonstrate the commands in this section. To do this, I removed the comment symbol (#) before the directive FileDevice in the file /etc/cups/cup-files.conf and changed the value to Yes (that is, FileDevice Yes).

To specify a printer device name, use the syntax file:///dev/tty[2-5]. A printer named tty2printer has been configured as a raw printer on /dev/tty2 (file:///dev/tty2).

To view printer output on these terminals from the GUI environment, use the key sequence CTRL-ALT-F[2-4] (F2 would be function key 2). To move between the text terminals, use the key sequence ALT-F[2-5]. To return to the GUI, use the key sequence ALT-F1.

The Common UNIX Printing System provides tools that manage printing. The directory that contains CUPS configuration files is /etc/cups/.

The CUPS daemon executes in the background, waiting for print requests. The CUPS daemon may be configured in the file /etc/cups/cupsd.conf.

Adding Printers

You can add printers via the command line, the GUI, or web access. Use the lpadmin command to add and configure printers and printer classes. Printer configuration information is stored in /etc/printers.conf. Printer class information is stored in /etc/cups/classes.conf.

A printer class is a group of printers associated with a single print queue. As print jobs are submitted to the queue, they are sent to the next available printer in the queue.

Prior to creating a printer, execute lpinfo -v (shown in Figure 12-32) to determine available devices.

The lpinfo -m command determines what drivers are available. The command lpinfo -m | grep -i <printer_name> lists all the driver files. Find the appropriate model and write down the provider printer description (PPD) filename so that you can download the correct PPD file from the printer manufacturer's website.

Table 12-18 displays some lpadmin options.

The following command creates printer tty3printer on /dev/tty3 using raw printing:

```
lpadmin -p tty3printer -v file:///dev/tty3 -m raw
```

Raw printing bypasses a printer driver and sends characters directly to the printer. The command lpstat -p tty3printer (line 1 in Figure 12-33) shows the printer is disabled. To start the printer and allow the printer's print queue to accept print jobs, issue the command lpadmin -p tty3printer -E (see line 5). Line 8 shows that the printer is enabled. You could execute the following command to create and enable the printer:

```
lpadmin -p tty3printer -v file:///dev/tty3 -m raw -E
```

Figure 12-32
lpinfo -v

```
#lpinfo -v
network ipp
network ipps
network http
network https
network socket
network lpd
serial serial:/dev/ttyS0?baud=115200
network beh
direct parallel:/dev/lp0
network smb
```

Option	Description
-E	Enables (starts) a printer and allows the print queue to accept print jobs.
-p	Printer name used when adding a printer or changing printer attributes.
-v	Device name (local).
-s	Server name.
-m	Printer driver.
-d	Makes the printer the default printer.
-c <class_name>	Adds a printer to a class. If the class does not exist, creates it.
-r <class_name>	Removes a printer from a class.
-x <class|printer_name>	Removes a printer or class.
-u allow:<user>	Comma-delimited list of users allowed to use the printer. @<group_name> specifies a group.
-u deny:<user>	Comma-delimited list of users not allowed to use the printer. @<group_name> specifies a group.

Table 12-18 lpadmin Options

```
#lpstat -p tty3printer
printer tty3printer disabled since Tue 04 Jun 2019 10:45:12 AM EDT -
        reason unknown

 #lpadmin -p tty3printer -E

 #lpstat -p tty3printer
printer tty3printer is idle.  enabled since Tue 04 Jun 2019 11:03:29 AM EDT
```

Figure 12-33 Determining the status of tty3printer

The command `lpadmin -d` sets the default system printer.

A printer class groups two or more printers. Instead of printing to a specific printer, you may print to the printer class. If one printer in the class is busy, the print job will be serviced by another printer in the class. The command `lpadmin -p tty3printer -c testclass` adds printer `tty3printer` to the printer class `testclass`. If the class does not exist, it will be created.

NOTE You cannot assign a printer as a default printer or assign a printer to a class until it has been created.

To remove a printer from a class, use the following command:

```
lpadmin -p <printer_name> -r <class_name>
```

If you are removing the last printer in the class, the class will be deleted.

Figure 12-34 Using `lpstat -c` to view printer classes

```
1  #lpstat -c
2  members of class testclass:
3          tty3printer
4
5  #lpstat -c testclass
6  members of class testclass:
7          tty3printer
8
9  #lpadmin -p tty2printer -c testclass
10
11 #lpadmin -p tty2printer -c testclass2
12 #
13 #lpstat -c
14 members of class testclass:
15         tty3printer
16         tty2printer
17 members of class testclass2:
18         tty2printer
```

The command `lpstat -c` displays a list of all printer classes and printers that are members of that class (see line 1 of Figure 12-34). To view members of a specific printer class, use the command `lpstat -c <printer_class>` (see line 5). Lines 9 and 11 add `tty2printer` to the classes `testclass` and `testclass2`.

To remove a printer from a class, execute the following command:

```
lpadmin -p <printer_name> -r <printer_class_name>
```

Web Interface

You can administer a printer via a web browser. Open a browser and enter `http://localhost:631` (see Figure 12-35). This is the port for the CUPS web interface. From this interface, you can manage all printer functions.

Selecting the Printers tab displays the available printers. Selecting a printer opens a management window for that printer (see Figure 12-36).

Printing to a Printer

You can use the commands `lpr` and `lp` to print to a printer. If no printer is specified, the default printer will be used. To determine the default printer, execute the command `lpstat -d`.

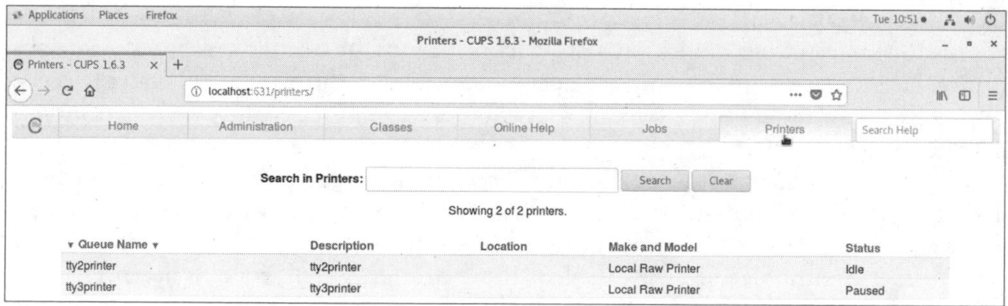

Figure 12-35 The CUPS web interface

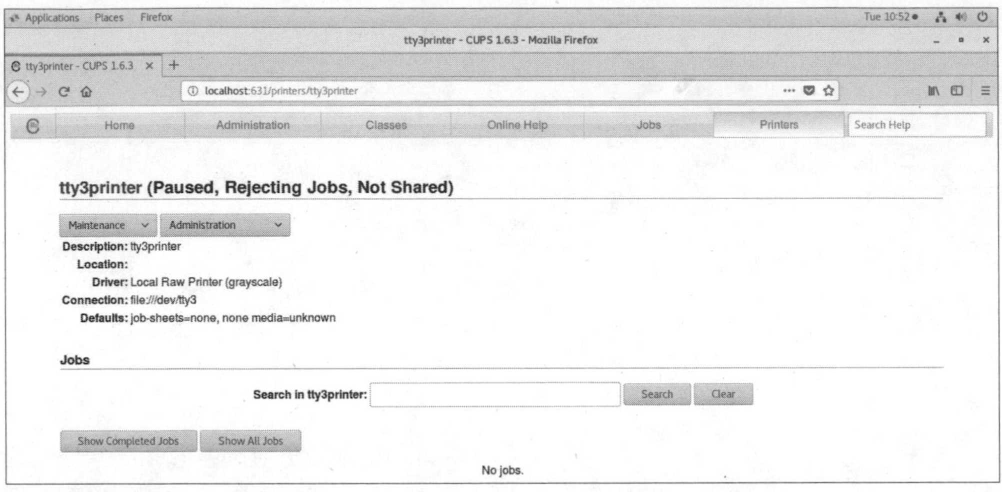

Figure 12-36 Web interface for managing a printer

Figure 12-37 Output of the print job

```
#lp -d tty2printer /etc/hosts
request id is tty2printer-5 (1 file(s))
```

The command `lp -d tty2printer /etc/hosts` will print the file `/etc/hosts` to `tty2printer`. When the job is submitted, a job ID will be displayed. The job ID consists of `<printer_queue_name>-<job_id>` (see Figure 12-37).

To print to a printer class, use the following command:

```
lp -d <printer_class_name> <filename>
```

Managing Printers and Print Queues

A printer queue is created each time a printer or printer class is added. The queue name is the same as the printer or printer class added.

cupsaccept, cupsreject, cupsenable, cupsdisable

A print queue can accept print jobs or reject print jobs. When it's accepting print jobs, print requests may be entered into the queue and passed to the printer. When it's rejecting print jobs, a submitted print job receives an error message. A reason for rejecting print jobs may be a broken printer.

To reject jobs for a print queue, execute the command `cupsreject <queue_name>`. To accept jobs for a print queue, execute the command `cupsaccept <queue_name>`. Once a job has been spooled to the queue, it is sent to the printer.

A printer is either enabled or disabled. If the printer is enabled, it is accepting print jobs from the print queue. A disabled printer is not accepting jobs from the print queue.

```
1  #lpstat -o
2 tty3printer-6          root                1024   Tue 04 Jun 2019 12:37:42 PM EDT
3 tty2printer-7          root                1024   Tue 04 Jun 2019 12:54:01 PM EDT
4
5  #lpstat -o tty3printer
6 tty3printer-6          root                1024   Tue 04 Jun 2019 12:37:42 PM EDT
7
8  #lpstat -o tty2printer
9 tty2printer-7          root                1024   Tue 04 Jun 2019 12:54:01 PM EDT
10
11  #lpq -P tty2printer
12 tty2printer is not ready
13 Rank     Owner   Job     File(s)                         Total Size
14 1st      root    7       hosts                           1024 bytes
15
16  #lpq -P tty3printer
17 tty3printer is not ready
18 Rank     Owner   Job     File(s)                         Total Size
19 1st      root    6       hosts                           1024 bytes
```

Figure 12-38 Using lpstat and lpq to view print queues

In this case, print jobs are stored in the queue until the printer is enabled or the print jobs are moved to another queue.

To disable a printer, execute the command cupsdisable <printer_name>. To enable a printer, execute the command cupsenable <printer_name>.

The command lpstat -p <printer_name> prints the printer status. The command lpq -P <queue_name> prints the status of a print queue. The status includes any print jobs held in the queue. The command lpstat -o displays all print jobs, and the command lpstat -o <queue_name> displays print jobs for a specific queue.

The following conditions were applied prior to executing the commands shown in Figure 12-38:

- The commands cupsdisable tty2printer and cupsdisable tty3printer were executed to disable printers tty2printer and tty3printer.
- The commands lp -d tty2printer /etc/hosts and lp -d tty3printer /etc/hosts were executed.

The lpstat -o command on line 1 of Figure 12-38 displays all print jobs in all queues. You can look at jobs in specific queues by executing the command lpstat -o <queue_name> (lines 5–9). The lpq command (lpq -P <queue_name>) on lines 11 and 16 displays the status and jobs queued for the respective queue names.

Canceling Print Jobs

The cancel command is used to cancel print jobs. The command cancel <job_id> (Figure 12-39, line 5) cancels a specific print job.

The command cancel <queue_name> (line 10) cancels all jobs in the queue. The command cancel -a removes all jobs from all queues.

```
#lpstat -o
tty3printer-6          root          1024   Tue 04 Jun 2019 12:37:42 PM EDT
tty3printer-7          root          1024   Tue 04 Jun 2019 12:54:01 PM EDT

#cancel 7

#lpstat -o
tty3printer-6          root          1024   Tue 04 Jun 2019 12:37:42 PM EDT

#cancel tty3printer

#lpstat -o
```

Figure 12-39 Canceling print jobs

```
1  #lpstat -o
2 tty3printer-6          root          1024   Tue 04 Jun 2019 12:37:42 PM EDT
3 tty2printer-7          root          1024   Tue 04 Jun 2019 12:54:01 PM EDT
4
5  #lpmove 6 tty2printer
6
7  #lpstat -o
8 tty2printer-6          root          1024   Tue 04 Jun 2019 12:37:42 PM EDT
9 tty2printer-7          root          1024   Tue 04 Jun 2019 12:54:01 PM EDT
10
11  #lpmove tty2printer  tty3printer
12
13  #lpstat -o
14 tty3printer-6          root          1024   Tue 04 Jun 2019 12:37:42 PM EDT
15 tty3printer-7          root          1024   Tue 04 Jun 2019 12:54:01 PM EDT
```

Figure 12-40 Moving printer jobs

`lpmove`

The `lpmove` command moves print jobs from one queue to another. In line 2 of Figure 12-40, you can see that job 6 is in the print queue `tty3printer`. The command `lpmove <job_id> <printer_queue>` moves a print job from one queue to another.

The output of the `lpstat` command on lines 8 and 9 of Figure 12-40 indicates both print jobs are in the queue of `tty2printer`. Run `lpmove <old_print_queue> <new_print_queue>` to move all jobs from the old print queue to another. Run `lpmove tty2printer tty3printer` (line 11) to move all the print jobs in `tty2printer` to `tty3printer` (lines 13–15).

Removing a Printer or Printer Class

Prior to removing a printer, you need to disable the printer by running the command `cupsdisable <printer_name>`. Then stop the queue from accepting any additional print jobs by executing the command `cupsreject <queue_name>`. Next, use the `cancel` or `lpmove` command to remove all jobs from the current queue. Verify there are no jobs left in the queue by running `lpstat -o <queue_name>`. Delete the printer or class by executing the command `lpadmin -x <printer_name>|<class_name>`.

Exercise 12-3: Printing

For this exercise, log in as user **`root`** (password **`root`**). Remove all printer classes and all printers except `tty2printer` by following these steps:

VIDEO Please watch the Exercise 12-3 video for a demonstration on how to perform this task.

1. Determine what printers and print classes are currently on your system by executing the **`lpstat -p`** command. You should have the printer `tty2printer`.
2. Determine if there are any print jobs in the print queues by executing the command **`lpstat -o`** or **`lpstat <queue_name>`**.
3. Create the class `labclass` and add `tty2printer` to it by executing the **`lpadmin -p tty2printer -c labclass`** command.
4. Verify your command by executing the command **`lpstat -c -p tty2printer`**.
5. Create a raw printer (`tty3printer`) using device `/dev/tty3`; the printer should be a member of the printer class `labclass` and be the default printer:

```
lpadmin -E -p tty3printer -v file:///dev/tty3 -m raw && \
lpadmin -p tty3printer -c labclass && lpadmin -d tty3printer
```

6. Verify the printer was created correctly using the **`lpstat -p`**, **`lpstat -c`**, and **`lpstat -d`** commands.
7. Disable printers `tty2printer` and `tty3printer` using the **`cupsdisable <printer_name>`** command. Test your results using the **`lpstat -p <printer_name>`** command.
8. Be sure to do this lab step as written. Print the files `/etc/hosts` and `/etc/shells` to both printers `tty2printer` and `tty3printer` by using the following commands:

```
lp -d tty2printer /etc/hosts ; lp -d tty2printer /etc/shells
lp -d tty3printer /etc/hosts/; lp -d tty3printer /etc/shells
```

9. Verify the jobs are in the queues using the **`lpstat -o`** command.
10. Print (**`lp`**) the file `/etc/passwd` to the (**`-d`**) `labclass` queue and verify the job has been printed (**`lpstat -o`**).

```
lp -d labclass /etc/passwd
lpstat -o
```

11. Prevent queues `tty2printer` and `tty3printer` from accepting print jobs by executing the **`cupsreject tty2printer`** and **`cupsreject tty3printer`** commands. Verify the results by executing the **`lpstat -p tty2printer`** and **`lpstat -p tty3printer`** commands.

12. Print the file /etc/group to printer tty2printer and class labclass. What happened? Why?

```
lp -d tty2printer /etc/group
Error: tty2printer not accepting jobs
```

13. Move all the print jobs in class labclass and tty3printer to tty2printer. Remember that tty2printer's queue is not accepting jobs, so you must fix that first. Once you are finished, check all the print queues:
    a. Execute **cupsaccept tty2printer** so the queue will start accepting jobs and verify the queue is accepting jobs.
    b. Execute **lpmove labclass tty2printer** and **lpmove tty3printer tty2printer**.
    c. Check the results with the **lpstat -o tty2printer** command.
14. Remove tty3printer from class labclass by executing the **lpadmin -p tty3printer -r labclass** command. Verify this by executing the **lpstat -c ttyprinter3** command.
15. Remove the printer tty3printer and class labclass:
    a. Execute the **lpstat -a -c** command.
    b. Execute the **lpadmin -x tty3printer; lpadmin -x labclass** command.
    c. Verify by executing the **lpstat -a -c** command.

Chapter Review

In this chapter, you discovered how to search for, add, modify, or remove hardware. You began by learning how the kernel discovers devices and writes configuration and statistical data to /sys/. You then learned how the /dev/ directory is built so users can access devices. During this process, you developed the skills to search for hardware information using the lsdev, lspci, lshw, systool, and udev commands.

You continued your discovery by learning about Bluetooth, Wi-Fi, and a variety of storage devices. You finished the chapter by learning how to add, modify, and delete printers and printer classes. Here are some key points from this chapter:

- A device is a system component capable of receiving or providing data.
- A bus is a system device used to transfer data between devices.
- A port is a physical connection to a bus.
- A driver is a file or group of files used to control a hardware device.
- Kernel space is memory accessible to the kernel.
- User space is memory accessible to users and user applications.

- Kernel information is made available to users via `/proc/` and `/sys/`.
- Major numbers designate a device class.
- `lsblk` prints a list of block devices.
- A device class contains devices that perform similar operations.
- The output of the `lspci -D` command is `Domain:Bus:Device:Function Class Vendor Name`.
- A host bus adapter is an expansion card used to connect multiple devices using a single controller to a computer system.
- Executing `lspci -nn | grep -i hba` or `systool -c <adapter_class>` displays host adapters.
- The `lsdev` command displays information about installed hardware
- Every device is assigned an interrupt (IRQ).
- `/proc/interrupts` displays active interrupts.
- Use the `lshw` (list hardware) command to display detailed hardware configuration information.
- To create a module alias, add `alias <alias_name> <module_name>` to a configuration file under `/etc/modprobe.d/`.
- `dmesg` is a command used to read and control the kernel ring buffer.
- To blacklist a module, add `blacklist <module_name>` to a configuration file under `/etc/modprobe.d/`.
- `lsusb` displays a list of USB devices.

Questions

1. Which directory contains device operational and statistical information discovered during the boot process?
   A. `/dev`
   B. `/proc/sys`
   C. `/sys`
   D. `/devices`
2. What of the following describe a bus? (Choose two.)
   A. A system device
   B. A system port
   C. A system driver
   D. Used to transfer data between devices

3. When are major and minor numbers discovered?
   A. During the device discovery process
   B. When creating an entry in `/dev`
   C. When a device is accessed
   D. When a device is created
4. Which of the following commands will display block devices? (Choose four.)
   A. `lsblk`
   B. `systool -c block`
   C. `lshw -short -class volume`
   D. `ls -l /sys/block`
   E. `lsblock`
5. Which of the following commands would display `uevents`? (Choose two.)
   A. `udevadm info`
   B. `udevadm monitor`
   C. `dmesg`
   D. `grep uevent /var/log/messages`
6. What will the command `dmesg -f kern -l notice | grep sdb` do?
   A. Display all `uevents` associated with `/dev/sdb`.
   B. Display kernel messages containing the string `sdb` generated by facility `kernel` and priority `notice`.
   C. Display all kernel events associated with `/dev/sdb`.
   D. Display all kernel messages.
7. Which of the following are the proper ways to blacklist the `joydev` module and assure it will not be installed as a dependency? (Choose two.)
   A. `echo "blacklist joydev" >> /etc/modprobe.d`
   B. `echo "blacklist joydev" >> /etc/modprobe.d/blacklist.conf`
   C. `echo "install joydev /bin/true" >> /etc/modprobe.d`
   D. `echo "install joydev /bin/true" >> /etc/modprobe.d /blacklist.conf`
8. Before writing a udev rule for a device, what command would you execute?
   A. `lsblk`
   B. `systools`
   C. `udevadm info`
   D. `udevadm reload`

9. Which file contains a list of active direct memory access channels?
   A. `/proc/interrupts`
   B. `/etc/dma`
   C. `/proc/dma`
   D. `/proc/memory`
10. To display a hierarchical view of USB devices, you would execute which command?
   A. `lsusb`
   B. `lsusb -t`
   C. `lsusb -D`
   D. `usbdev -t`
11. To manage CUPS using the browser interface, you would open your browser and enter which of the following?
   A. `:631`
   B. `631`
   C. `localhost:631`
   D. `localhost:cups`

Answers

1. **C.** During the boot process, kernel modules discover device information and populate `/sys`. Operational statistics are also stored in `/sys`.
2. **A, D.** A bus is a system device used to transfer data between devices.
3. **A.** The major and minor numbers are discovered during the kernel device discovery process. The major number is associated with the device class. The minor number is used by the device driver.
4. **A, B, C, D.** Each of these choices will display a listing of block devices.
5. **B, C.** The command `udevadmin monitor` can display both kernel and `udev` events associated with hardware discovery. The `dmesg` command may be used to display kernel events.
6. **B.** You can use the facility (`-f`) and priority (`-l`) filters found in syslog to filter the `dmesg` output. This question is asking to display the facility kernel and priority notice.
7. **B, D.** Modifying configuration files within `/etc/modprobe.d/*.conf` allows you to blacklist a module and keep it from being installed as a dependency, even when you set it as `/bin/true`.

8. **C.** `udevadm info` would provide you all the device attributes that can be used to write `udev` rules.
9. **C.** The file `/proc/dma` contains a list of active direct memory access (DMA) channels.
10. **B.** The command `lsusb -t` produces a hierarchical view of USB hubs and the devices attached to the hubs.
11. **C.** Port 631 is used to access the CUPS web tool. Entering `localhost:631` will start the CUPS web configuration tool.

CHAPTER 13

Writing Shell Scripts

In this chapter, you will learn about

- Advanced shell concepts
- Understanding shell script components
- Using control operators
- Processing text streams

Software is supposed to serve the human and not the other way around

—Gloria Washington, Howard University

This chapter covers how to create and control basic shell scripts on a Linux system. Shell scripts are text files that contain a variety of commands that can be used to automate tasks and process information. Scripts have features of many programming languages, including variables, operators, conditionals, looping, and more. Because these features are related to the Bash shell, details are found in the `bash` man page.

NOTE Most of the scripts found in this chapter can be found on the image provided with the book in the directory `/LABS/Chapter_13`.

Advanced Shell Concepts

A script is a series of commands that produces a specific result. When you run commands at the shell, you are intermittently acting like a script; the only difference is that the script groups the commands together within a file and executes the file.

To create your first script, run **`vi myscript.bash`** and type the following in the file:

```
#! /bin/bash                # define the interpreter
echo 'Hello World'          # Print to the screen "Hello World"
exit 0                      # Exit the program successfully (0=success)
~
~
~
```

Save the script by selecting **`Esc :wq <Enter>`**.

You can run your new script by executing one of the following commands: `source myscript.bash`, `. myscript.bash`, or `bash myscript.bash`. The script will execute if you have read permission on the file.

NOTE The `.bash` suffix is for your convenience so that you can recognize the file as a Bash script. GUIs use suffixes to determine the type of file, but Linux ignores them. To Linux, a suffix is simply part of the filename.

To make the script executable to everyone, run `chmod +x myscript.bash`. Once the script is made executable, supply the absolute path to the script. For example, enter `/home/student1/myscript.bash`.

To run a script using the relative path, tell Linux to look in the current directory by entering `./myscript.bash`.

Finally, you could set up the `PATH` variable to always look in your current directory "`.`" to run a command by entering `PATH=$PATH:.`, but this poses a security risk. If a hacker were to place a fake `passwd` program in your directory, then whenever you ran `passwd`, the hacker's program would run, steal your password, and compromise your system.

Knowledge of additional shell features will make you better at writing scripts. Here we will cover the advanced shell features of

- Globbing wildcard characters
- Sequencing commands
- Command substitution

Let's start by exploring wildcard characters called globs.

Globbing Wildcard Characters

Globbing wildcard characters allows users to list in their directory only the files that they want to see. For example, suppose the files in your directory appear like so:

```
purin $ ls
file     file14   file2    file7    note11   note17   note4
file1    file15   file20   file8    note12   note18   note5
file11   file17   file4    note     note14   note2    note7
file12   file18   file5    note1    note15   note20   note8
```

You can list only the files you want to see by using Bash shell pattern-matching characters listed and described in Table 13-1.

The following four entries display, respectively, how to list only files that start with `f` or `n` and end with `0`, only files that start with `f` and end in `1`, only files that have four characters, and only files `note12` through `note14`:

```
lafrance $ ls [nf]*0      # List files that start with f or n and end in 0 only
file20
note20
lafrance $ ls f*1         # List files that start with f and end in 1 only
file1
file11
```

Wildcard	Description	Example	Matches	Doesn't Match
*	Matches any number of characters, zero or more	And*	Andy, Andrew	WongAnd
?	Matches any single character	?art	cart, Cart	art
[ahp]	Matches single character within the set	Mar[kc]	Mark, Marc	mark, marc
[D-H]	Matches single character within the range	note[1-3]	note1, note2, note3	notes, note10
[!ahp]	Matches any single character not in the set	Ni[!c]k	Niak, Nijk	Nick
[!D-H]	Matches any single character not in the range	Evan[!4-6]	Evan1, Evan9	Evan4, Evan6

Table 13-1 Bash Shell Wildcard Characters

```
lafrance $ ls ????        # List files that are 4 characters only
file
note
lafrance $ ls note1[2-4]  # List note12, note13, and note14
note12
note14
```

NOTE To create a list of files similar to the preceding examples for practice, use the Bash shell feature called *brace expansion*. In a new, empty directory run:
`$ touch file note {file,note}{0..20}`

Sequencing Commands

You can sequence commands together with either the `&&`, `||`, or `;` metacharacters. The `&&` means run the next command only if the previous command was successful. The `||` means run the next command only if the previous command was unsuccessful. The `;` runs the next command whether the previous command was successful or not. Review the commands in the following demonstration; descriptions of each entry are stated in the comments:

```
nicholas $ ls -d . && ls -d ..    # Both results show since ls -d . succeeds
.
..
nicholas $ ls -d . || ls -d ..    # Only first result shows since ls -d . succeeds
.
nicholas $ ls -de . || ls -d ..   # Both results show since ls -de . fails
ls: invalid option - 'e'
..
nicholas $ ls -d . ; ls -d ..     # Both results show since ls -d . succeeds
.
..
nicholas $ ls -de . ; ls -d ..    # Both results show since ls -d . fails
ls: invalid option - 'e'
..
```

When a program exits successfully, it sends an exit code of 0; when unsuccessful it sends an exit code of 1. To see the exit code of the most recently run command, run echo $?.

Other examples of sequencing commands are discussed later in this chapter; for example, sequencing commands in a script can show whether a script exited successfully or not.

Command Substitution

Command substitution is a way of embedding the result of a command into an output. There are two methods of embedding a command: `<command>` or $(<command>). The backtick, `, is found on most keyboards in the top-left corner under the tilde, ~.

An example of command substitution may be found on line 7 of Figure 13-7. This command could have been written echo "Current time: `date +%m/%d/%y" "%R`" and the output results in Current time: 09/30/25 12:15, for example.

Understanding Shell Script Components

Scripts run a series of commands that are interpreted and executed by a shell. Scripts are composed of the following:

- Defining the interpreter with #!
- Commenting with #
- Defining variables
- Reading user input
- Using positional parameters
- Using functions

Defining the Interpreter with #!

The first line of a script, also called the *shebang* line, contains the absolute path to the command-line interpreter used when executing the script. For example, line 1 in Figure 13-1 indicates the script will use the Bash shell as the interpreter. When you define the interpreter, it must be the first line; otherwise, Linux uses a default interpreter defined by the login account.

The command chsh -l or cat /etc/shells displays a list of available command-line interpreters.

Figure 13-1 Shebang

```
1 #!/bin/bash
2
3 #This is a sample script
4 #which will display Hello World
5
6 echo "Hello World"      #The echo command will display Hello World
```

```
#!/bin/bash

# Declaring functions

timestamp()                                      #create function to display current date and time
{                                                #start function commands
echo "Current time $(date +%m/%d/%y" "%R)"       #display mm/dd/yyyy HH:MM
sleep 2                                          #idle for 2 seconds
clear                                            #clear scren
}

#Start of script

clear                                            #clear screen
timestamp                                        #call timestamp function

echo -n "Enter your first name: "; read          #input stored to read variable REPLY
echo -n "Enter your last  name: "; read lname    #input stored to variable lname


echo -e  " \v Full Name: $REPLY $lname \v\v"     #Vertical line feed and print value of variables REPLY and lname

timestamp                                        #call timestamp function
```

Figure 13-2 Comments

Commenting with

Comments are designed to explain purpose. Once you have specified the shell interpreter, you'll want to create a comment that details the purpose of the script.

Use comments liberally (see Figure 13-2). They are great reminders when you or another user must troubleshoot or add to a script several weeks after working with it. For example, when you edit a script, you should consider creating a comment that contains the date of and reason for the edit. All comments begin with the # symbol, which tells the interpreter to ignore all text to the right of the symbol to the end of the line.

Defining Variables

Variables store data. We will consider three variable types:

- `string` A string variable contains alphanumeric characters.
- `integer` An integer variable contains numbers that will be used in a mathematical expression.
- `constant` A constant variable may not be changed or removed (that is, unset).

A variable's type determines how the variable will be used. The variable type `string` contains alphanumeric characters and may not be used in mathematical expressions. The variable type `integer` contains only numbers. If a string is supplied as a value for an `integer` type variable, the value of the variable becomes 0. The last variable type is a `constant`. The variable type `constant` may be neither changed nor deleted.

The Bash interpreter does not assign a variable type when one is created. Bash considers a variable a `string` if its content contains an alphanumeric value. If the variable contains numbers, Bash will allow the variable to be used in arithmetic expressions.

Figure 13-3 Bash sum

```
1 # sum=100
2 # echo $sum
3 100
4 #
5 # sum=110
6 # echo $sum
7 110
8 #
9 # sum=Fred
10 # echo $sum
11 Fred
```

Figure 13-4 Assigning a variable type

```
1 # declare -i sum=100
2 # declare -p sum
3 declare -i sum="100"
4 # declare sum=110
5 # declare -p sum
6 declare -i sum="110"
7 # declare sum=Fred
8 # declare -p sum
9 declare -i sum="0"
```

The `declare` command enables you to assign a variable type to a variable. For example, the command `declare flower=rose` creates a local `string` variable named `flower` and assigns it a value of `rose`. To view the properties of a variable, execute the command `declare -p <variable_name>`.

You can use the command `echo $flower` to display the content of a variable. The `declare -p` command is more efficient because it will display any attributes assigned to the variable as well as the content. To create a variable of type `integer`, execute `declare -i <var_name>=<value>`.

Let's look at the difference between declaring a variable type and not declaring a variable type. In Figure 13-3 lines 1 and 5, we have assigned numerical values of `100` and `110`, respectively, to the variable `sum`. On line 9, we assign the variable `sum` a value of `Fred`.

In line 1 in Figure 13-4, we use the `declare` command to set the variable `sum` to type `integer`. On line 4 we change the value of the variable to `110`. On line 7 we change the value of the variable to `Fred`. Since the variable `sum` is assigned an `integer` type and we changed the value to a `string`, the value of the variable is changed to `0`.

Reading User Input

There are times when you need to prompt a user for a response and use the response in a script. The `read` command reads user input and assigns the value of the input to a variable specified by the argument in the `read` statement. If no variable name is supplied, the default variable `REPLY` is used.

In Figure 13-5, lines 1–7 contain the script `read_script.bash`, and lines 10–12 show the script executing.

Line 4 of the script requests user input but does not specify a variable; therefore, the user's first name will be stored to the variable `REPLY`. Line 5 assigns the user's input to the variable `lname`.

You can use the `-t` option to limit the time a user has to respond. The command `echo -n "Enter your name: " ; read -t 5` allows the user five seconds to reply or the script will terminate.

```
#!/bin/bash


echo -n "Enter your first name: "; read        #input stored to read variable REPLY
echo -n "Enter your last  name: "; read lname  #input stored to variable lname

echo "$REPLY $lname"

# bash read_statement
Enter your first name: George
Enter your last  name: Washington
George Washington
```

Figure 13-5 Using the `read` command

Using Positional Parameters

A command-line script can have up to nine arguments or positions, all of which can be identified numerically based on their position. For example, if you run

```
$ myscript.bash  fred  george  andrew
```

`fred` will save as argument `$1`, `george` as argument `$2`, and `andrew` as argument `$3`. Running the command `echo $2` displays `george`.

Let's modify the read script by using positional parameters. Notice in Figure 13-6 line 3 the script uses the `echo` command to display the first and second arguments of the command line.

Additional scripting information may be found by using parameter codes detailed in Table 13-2. Remember the `$` character is a metacharacter that may be interpreted as "the value of." Running `echo $*` displays all of the arguments, that is, `fred george andrew`. Running `$#` displays the number of arguments, or `3`.

```
1 #!/bin/bash
2
3 echo "$1 $2"   #Display the arguments entered in position 1 and position 2
4
5
6 # bash positional_parameters George Washington
7 George Washington
```

Figure 13-6 Positional parameters in a script

Table 13-2 Additional Parameter Shortcuts

Parameter	Description
`$0`	Name of command or script
`$#`	Number of command-line arguments
`$*`	List of command-line arguments
`$$`	Current process's PID
`$!`	PID of the last background job
`$?`	Command exit status code

```
1 #!/bin/bash
2
3 # Declaring functions
4
5 timestamp()                                      #create function to display current date and time
6 {                                                #start function commands
7 echo "Current time $(date +%m/%d/%y" "%R)"       #display mm/dd/yyyy HH:MM
8 sleep 2                                          #idle for 2 seconds
9 clear                                            #clear scren
10 }
11
12 #Start of script
13
14 clear                                            #clear screen
15 timestamp                                        #call timestamp function
16
17 echo -n "Enter your first name: "; read          #input stored to read variable REPLY
18 echo -n "Enter your last  name: "; read lname    #input stored to variable lname
19
20
21 echo -e  " \v Full Name: $REPLY $lname \v\v"     #Vertical line feed and print value of variables REPLY and lname
22
23 timestamp                                        #call timestamp function
```

Figure 13-7 Example of a function in a script

Using Functions

A function is a named section of a program that contains a series of commands designed to perform a specific task. Rather than writing the same code over and over, you can create a function and then have the script call (execute) the function.

A function is defined using `( )` and `{ }` as follows:

```
function_name()
     {
          <command>
          <command>
     }
```

Figure 13-7 displays the script `function_script.bash`. Lines 5–10 in Figure 13-7 define the function `timestamp`, which is called on lines 15 and 23.

Using Control Operators

Control operators change the flow of a script. In scripting, control operators are used to form test conditions and looping structures. In this section you will learn about

- Expression operators
- Testing with conditionals
- Using looping structures

Expression Operators

An expression uses operators to evaluate a condition and determine if the condition is true, which is exit status code `0`, or false, exit status code non-zero. Expression operators are available for text strings and integers.

String Operator	Description
=	Are both strings equal? `[ $a = $b ]`
>	Is the string on the left greater than the string on the right? `[ $a \> $b ]`
<	Is the string on the left less than the string on the right? `[ $a \< $b ]`

Table 13-3 String Operators

String Operators

String operators are used by expressions to test strings (see Table 13-3). The comparison is based on the ASCII character set.

NOTE The left and right brackets, `[ ]`, shown in the descriptions of Table 13-3, are the `test` command alternative, discussed later in this chapter.

Relationship Operators

Relationship operators are traditionally used for integers. Table 13-4 displays some relationship operators.

Table 13-4 Relationship Operators

Relationship Operator	Description
`-eq`	Equal to `[ $a -eq $b]`
`-ne`	Not equal to `[ $a -ne $b]`
`-ge`	Greater than or equal to `[ $a -ge $b]`
`-lt`	Less than `[ $a -lt $b]`
`-le`	Less than or equal to `[ $a -le $b]`
`<=`	Less than or equal to `(("$a" <= "$b"))`
`>`	Greater than `(("$a" > "$b"))`
`>=`	Greater than or equal to `(("$a" >= "$b"))`

NOTE The left and right double parentheses, `(( ))`, shown in the descriptions of Table 13-4, are the `test` command for integers, discussed later in the chapter.

Arithmetic Operators

With an arithmetic expression, you use one of the arithmetic operators shown in Table 13-5.

Boolean Operators

Boolean operators are used to join multiple expressions. In line 7 of Figure 13-8, we use the operator `-a`, the AND Boolean, to specify two conditions that must be true to make the expression true. Some of the Boolean operators are displayed in Table 13-6.

Table 13-5 Arithmetic Operators

Arithmetic Operator	Description
+	Add `a+b`
-	Subtract `a-b`
*	Multiply `a*b`
/	Divide `a/b`

```
1 #!/bin/bash
2
3 #Start of Script
4
5 if [ $EUID -ge 1000 ]; then                 #Test to see if the users effective user id is greater than or equal to 1000
6   echo "Regular User"                       #Display Regular Users
7    elif [ $EUID -gt 99 -a $EUID -lt 1000 ]  # If EUID was not 1000 but is greater than 99 and less than 1000
8     echo "System Account"                   #Display System Account
9    else                                     #If none of the conditions are true
10    echo "System Admin Account"             #Display System Admin Account
11 fi                                         # End of if statement
```

Figure 13-8 Using Boolean operators

Table 13-6 Boolean Operators

Boolean Operator	Description
`-a`	Boolean AND Both expressions must be true
`-o`	Boolean OR Either expression must be true
`!`	Boolean NOT Invert expression

File Test Operator	Description
-a or -e	Does the file exist? `[ -a /root/George ]`
-s	Is the file size greater than 0? `[ -s /etc/bashrc ]`
-f	Is the file a text file? `[ -f /etc/bashrc ]`
-d	Is the file a directory? `[ -d /etc ]`
-b	Is the file a block device? `[ -b /dev/sda ]`
-c	Is the file a character device? `[ -c /dev/tty1 ]`
-p	Is the file a named pipe? `[ -p /run/dmeventd-client ]`
-L or -h	Is the file a symbolic link?
-r	Does the file have read permissions for the user executing the test?
-w	Does the file have write permissions for the user executing the test?
-x	Does the file have execute permissions for the user executing the test?
-u	Does the file have SUID applied?
-g	Does the file have SGID applied?
-k	Does the file have sticky bit applied?
-O <username>	Is the file owned by the user specified by the argument <username>?
-G <group_name>	Is the file owned by the user specified by the argument <group_name>?

Table 13-7 File Test Operators

File Test Operators

File test operators (see Table 13-7) are used to test the properties of files. Permission and ownership tests are based on the user executing the script.

Figure 13-9 illustrates the script `file_test_operator_script.bash`, which contains an example of the file test expressions.

Testing with Conditionals

Conditionals are used to determine the flow of a script.

The `test` Command

The `test` command is a shell built in that allows you to evaluate conditions using the syntax `test <expression>`. Executing the command `test $EUID -eq 0;echo`

```
#!/bin/bash


#Script start

echo -e  "\v\vTesting -f /root/.bashrc \v"
if [ -f /root/.bashrc ]; then                    #Test to see if the file /root/.bashrc is a text file
 echo -e "true \v"
  else
   echo -e "not true \v"
fi

echo -e  "\v\vTesting -u /usr/bin/passwd \v"
if [ -u /usr/bin/passwd ]; then                  #Test to see if the file /usr/bin/passwd has suid applied
 echo -e "true \v"
  else
   echo -e "not true \v"
fi

echo -e  "\v\vTesting -d /etc \v"                #Test to see if /etc is a directory
if [ -d /etc ]; then
 echo -e "true \v"
  else
   echo -e "not true \v"
fi

echo -e  "\v\vTesting -b /dev/sda \v"
if [ -b /dev/sda ]; then                         #Test to see if /dev/sda is a block device.
 echo -e "true \v"
  else
   echo -e "not true \v"
fi
```

Figure 13-9 `file_test_operator_script.bash`

Figure 13-10 A `test` command script

```
#!/bin/bash

#start script

if test "$UID --eq 0"
  then
  echo "UID equals 0"
fi
```

`$?` on the command line would indicate if your effective user ID is `0`. This expression could also be written as `[ $EUID -eq 0 ];echo $?`.

NOTE When using the left and right brackets as the `test` command, remember to include a space after the left bracket and before the right bracket because a space is required after a command.

The `test` command may also be applied in scripts. The script `test_script.bash`, shown in Figure 13-10, displays an example of the `test` command.

`if then else` Statements

The `if` statement expands the use of the `test` command by allowing us to direct the flow of the script based on the exit status of the `test` statement. If the test condition evaluates to true, or exit status `0`, the command or commands directly under the `test` statement are executed.

```
#!/bin/bash


#Declare Variables

passwd_file=/etc/passwd                                 #set the value of the variable passwd_file

clear                                                   #clear the screen
read -p "Enter a username:" username                    #Ask the user to enter a username and place it in the variable username
grep ^$username $passwd_file > /dev/null                #Search /etc/passwd for the content of the variable username at the beginning of the line
status=$?                                               #Set the value of the variable status equal to the exit status of the previous command

if [ $status -eq 0 ]; then                              #Determine if the exit status of the previous command  is 0
  echo "User $username found in $passwd_file"           #Display user found
   else                                                 #Execute the command below if the exit status code was > 0
    echo "User $username is not found in $passwd_file"  #Display user not found
fi                                                      #End if statement
```

Figure 13-11 Sample `if_then_test_script_1.bash`

```
#!/bin/bash

#Start of Script

if [ $EUID -ge 1000 ]; then                      #Test to see if the users effective user id is greater than or equal to 1000
  echo "Regular User"                            #Display Regular Users
   elif [ $EUID -gt 99 -a $EUID -lt 1000 ]       # If EUID was not 1000 but is greater than 99 and less than 1000
    echo "System Account"                        #Display System Account
   else                                          #If none of the conditions are true
    echo "System Admin Account"                  #Display System Admin Account
fi                                               # End of if statement
```

Figure 13-12 `if then else` example

If the test condition evaluates to false, or exit status non-zero, one of two flow control elements may be used. The `else` statement indicates the commands to be executed if the original test condition is true. The `elif` statement opens another test condition. All `if` statements end in if spelled backwards, or `fi`, as shown here:

```
if [ $val -gt 100 ]
then
   echo $val is greater than 100
else
      echo $val is less than or equal to 100
fi
```

Figure 13-11, which shows `if_then_script_1.bash`, and Figure 13-12, which shows `multi-user_script.bash`, illustrate examples using `if`, `else`, and `elif`.

NOTE For a closer view of Figure 13-11 and other selected images from this chapter, download the full-resolution images from the online content for this book.

`case` Statements

Using `case` is a more efficient way of making choices as opposed to several nested `if` statements. It is similar to the JavaScript or C language `switch` statement, using the first argument or expression of the command line to determine what it will do.

```
1 #!/bin/bash
2
3 case $1 in                    #use the first argument of the command line as the string to match
4
5   start)                      #if the string is start execute this stanza
6    echo start
7   ;;                          #end of stanza
8
9   stop)                       #if the string is stop execute this stanza
10   echo stop
11  ;;                          #end of stanza
12
13  *)                          #if user has entered a string which does not match any of the strings in the case statement
14   echo "incorrect entry"
15  ;;
16
17 esac                         #end of case statement
```

Figure 13-13 Sample `case` statement

Figure 13-14 `case` script output

```
[root@localhost book]# bash case_script start
start

[root@localhost book]# bash case_script stop
stop

[root@localhost book]# bash case_script fred
incorrect entry
```

A `case` statement is broken into stanzas, where each selection ends in `;;`, and has the following structure ending in case spelled backwards, or `esac`:

```
case $variable in
green) echo you chose green ;;
*) echo you did not choose green;;
esac
```

The `case` statement examines the input argument against the string that begins a stanza. If the string matches, that stanza is executed. Notice that the very last stanza in Figure 13-13 (script `case_script.bash`, line 13) begins with `*)`. This entry is used to handle any user entry that does not match any of the strings in the `case` statement. Figure 13-14 shows the results of using a `case` statement.

Using Looping Structures

The `if/then/else` and `case` structures are called *branching structures.* Depending on how a condition evaluates, the script branches in one direction or another. You can also use *looping* control structures within a shell script. Looping structures come in three varieties: `while` loop, `until` loop, and `for` loop.

The `while` Loop

A `while` loop executes over and over until a specified condition is no longer true. The structure of a `while` loop is as follows:

```
while condition
do
     script commands
done
```

```
#!/bin/bash

#Declare variables

declare -i x=0

#Start Script

while [ $x -lt 10 ]                              #While the value of the variable x is less than 10
  do                                             #Execute the commands between do and done for each iteration
   x=$x+1                                        #Increment the value of x by 1
   echo "the variable x is less then 10"         #Display
  done                                           # End of commands for this iteration
```

Figure 13-15 The `while` loop

A `while` loop will keep processing over and over until the condition evaluates to false. Figure 13-15 shows `while_loop_script.bash` and illustrates the use of a `while` loop.

The `until` Loop

In addition to a `while` loop, you can also use an `until` loop in your script. It works in the opposite manner of the `while` loop. An `until` loop runs over and over as long as the condition is false. The structure for an `until` loop is as follows:

```
until condition
do
      script commands
done
```

NOTE The command bash -x <script_name> starts a script's debug mode.

The `for` Loop

You can also use a `for` loop, which operates in a different manner than `until` and `while` loops. The `until` and `while` loops keep looping indefinitely until the specified condition is met. A `for` loop, on the other hand, loops a specific number of times. The structure for the `for` loop is as follows:

```
for var in pattern1 pattern2 pattern3 … patternN
do
      script commands
done
```

It is very common to use the `seq` command within a `for` loop to create the sequence of numbers to determine how many times it will loop. There are three options for creating a number sequence with `seq`:

- If you specify a single value, the sequence starts at 1, increments by one, and ends at the specified value.

```
#!/bin/bash


#Start Script

for x in `seq 0 1 10`                          #Start sequence at 0 increment by 1 end at 10
 do
 echo "The current number is $x"
 done
```

Figure 13-16 `for_loop_seq.bash` script using `seq`

```
#!/bin/bash

#Start Script

for i in {0..10..1}                     #Replaces seq  start at 0 end at 10 increment by 1
  do
    echo "The current number is $i"
  done
```

Figure 13-17 `for` loop using { } for sequence

- If you specify two values, the sequence starts at the first value, increments by one, and ends at the second value.
- If you specify three values, the sequence starts at the first value, increments by the second value, and ends at the third value.

An example of a `for` loop script using `seq` is shown in Figure 13-16 (`for_loop_seq.bash` script).

You may also see scripts that use a different sequence notation. For example, `{0..10..1}` is the same as `seq 0 1 10`. Figure 13-17 (`for_loop_new_sequence.bash` script) illustrates the use of `{0..10..1}`.

EXAM TIP Make certain to have a good understanding of `while` loops, `if` statements, and `case` statements for CompTIA Linux+ exam scenario questions.

Exercise 13-1: Creating a Basic Shell Script

For Exercise 13-1, use the image provided with the book. Log on as user **root** using the password **password**. I have supplied the scripts used in this chapter in the directory `/LABS/Chapter_13/source` and duplicated the scripts in `/LABS/Chapter_13/work`.

VIDEO Please watch the Exercise 13-1 video for a demonstration on how to perform this task.

Follow these steps:

1. Log in as **student1** with password **student1**. Make sure you are in the home directory by typing the **cd** command.
2. Copy the `chooser.bash` script to your home directory, as follows:
   cp /LABS/Chapter_13/source/chooser.bash chooser.bash
3. Review the `chooser.bash` source code, and run the program as follows:
   more chooser.bash
   ./chooser.bash
   Enter **Ctrl-C** to exit the script.
4. Use `vi` or `gedit` to update the script with new features; for example:
   a. Execute the **vi chooser.bash** command.
   b. Add an option that shuts down the script using **q** or **Q**.
   c. Add a fourth option that will display the date and time.
   d. Change the `while` line from `[ ]` to the **test** command.
   e. Change option 2 to run the `top` command
5. View the solutions to Step 4 by running the following:
   less /LABS/Chapter_13/work/chooser.bash
6. Add any other features you desire. When you test the script, make certain to test based on the objectives you outlined before starting to write the script.

Enjoy!

Processing Text Streams

When processing text streams within a script or piping output at the shell prompt, you might need to filter the output of one command so that only certain portions of the text stream are actually passed along to the stdin of the next command. You can use a variety of tools to do this. In this part of the chapter, we'll look at using the following commands:

- `tr`
- `cut`
- `nl`
- `od`
- `sed`
- `awk`
- `sort`
- `split`
- `head`
- `tail`
- `uniq`
- `wc`

Let's begin by looking at the `tr` command.

The `tr` Command

The `tr` (translate) command is used to change or translate characters. The `tr` command accepts input from a command via an unnamed pipe, like so:

```
<command> | tr <option> <char_set_old> <char_set_new>
```

Figure 13-18 shows how you can translate lowercase letters to uppercase letters.

The `tr` command also assists with converting a Windows text file to a Linux text file. Lines in Windows text files end with a return and newline, like so: `\r\n`. Linux text files just end with a newline, `\n`. So that the Windows text file operates properly on a Linux system, the `\r` must be removed. This is done with `tr -d` option to *delete* a character as follows:

```
tr -d '\r' < winfile.txt > linuxfile.txt
```

The resulting `linuxfile.txt` file can be viewed properly on a Linux system with `cat`, `less`, `more`, or `vi`. There is also a command called `dos2unix` that performs the same function. The command `unix2dos` sets up a Linux text file to work on Windows.

Next, Figure 13-19 illustrates how to use the `tr` command to translate the letter `r` to `1`, `o` to `2`, and `t` to `3`.

The `tr` command can use the `-s` option to *squeeze* or replace multiple occurrences. In Figure 13-20, we use the squeeze option to remove multiple spaces between fields so there is only one space between fields. The command `who | tr -s "  " " "` replaces two contiguous spaces with one.

Figure 13-18 Using `tr` to translate lowercase to uppercase

```
[root@localhost ~]# grep root /etc/passwd | tr [a-z] [A-Z]
ROOT:X:0:0:ROOT:/ROOT:/BIN/BASH
OPERATOR:X:11:0:OPERATOR:/ROOT:/SBIN/NOLOGIN
```

Figure 13-19 Using `tr` to translate letters to numbers

```
# grep root /etc/passwd | tr rot 123
1223:x:0:0:1223:/1223:/bin/bash
2pe1a321:x:11:0:2pe1a321:/1223:/sbin/n2l2gin
```

Figure 13-20 `tr` squeeze option

```
[root@localhost ~]# who

root      :0          2019-05-16 13:48 (:0)
root      pts/0       2019-05-16 13:48 (:0)

[root@localhost ~]# who | tr -s "  " " "

root :0 2019-05-16 13:48 (:0)
root pts/0 2019-05-16 13:48 (:0)
```

Option	Description
-b	Extracts specific bytes from a file. By default, the character count starts at the beginning of a line. Here are some examples: `cut -b 1,3,5` will cut the first, third, and fifth bytes. `cut -b -3` will cut from the first to third byte. `cut -b 3-` will cut from the third byte to the end of the line. `cut -b 1-3` will cut the first three bytes.
-c	Extracts a character from a given position. Tabs are considered characters. Here are some examples: `cut -c 1,3,5` will cut the first, third, and fifth characters. `cut -c 1-3,7,8` will cut the first three characters and characters seven and eight.
-d	Specifies the delimiter used by `cut`. If a space is used as a delimiter, use " ".
-f	Extracts fields. Here's an example that extracts the first field of the file `/etc/passwd`: `cut -d : -f 1 /etc/passwd`

Table 13-8 `cut` Command Options

Figure 13-21 Using the `cut` command to extract fields

```
[root@localhost ~]# who

root     :0           2019-05-16 13:48 (:0)
root     pts/0        2019-05-16 13:48 (:0)

[root@localhost ~]# who | tr -s "  " " " |cut -d " " -f1,3
root 2019-05-16
root 2019-05-16
```

The `cut` Command

The `cut` command is used to print columns or fields that you specify from a file to the standard output. Table 13-8 shows options that can be used with `cut`.

In Figure 13-21, we execute the `who` command and then use the `tr -s` command to remove multiple contiguous spaces so there is only one space between the fields. The `cut` command, using a space as a delimiter, extracts the real username (field one) and time (field 3).

The `nl` Command

The common usage for `nl` is line numbering. This can be accomplished by executing the command `nl <filename>`.

When creating a text document, you can break the document up into three sections (header, body, and footer) and assign independent numbering schemes to each section. By default, `nl` only numbers the body section.

Table 13-9 shows the command-line option and the text file designator for a document marked up for `nl`. Figure 13-22 illustrates an example of dividing a document into sections with `nl` designators.

Table 13-9 nl Section Designators

Section	Option	Designator
Header	-h	\:\:\:
Body	-b	\:\:
Footer	-f	\:

Figure 13-22 Document formatted with nl designators

```
\:\:\:

This is the header section
To define line numbering for this section use the -h option

Line A

Line B
Line C


\:\:

This is the body  section
To define line numbering for this section use the -b option

Line A

Line B
Line C

\:

This is the footnote section
To define line numbering for this section use the -f option

Line A

Line B
Line C
```

The numbering schemes for each section are applied in the command line using the designator and one or more of the options shown in Table 13-10.

The syntax for a section would be `<-h|-b|-f> a`.

The command `nl -h a -b n -f t -v 20 nltest` will start the numbering of the file `nltest` at 20 (`-v 20`) and increment the numbers by two (`-i 2`). All lines in

Option	Description
a	Numbers all lines. By default, nl will not number empty lines. (Applied to section.)
-n	Formats line numbers using one of the following format codes: **ln** Left justified with no leading zeros (for example, `nl -nln <fname>`) **rn** Right justified with no leading zeros (for example, `nl -nrn <fname>`) **rz** Right justified with leading zeros (for example, `nl -nrz <fname>`) (Applied to document.)
-v #	Starting line number. Changes the starting line number of the document.

Table 13-10 nl Numbering Options

Figure 13-23 Numbering a document by section

```
[root@localhost book]# nl -h a  -b n -f t -v 20 -i 2 nltest

    20
    22  This is the header section
    24  To define line numbering for this section use the -h option
    26
    28  Line A
    30
    32  Line B
    34  Line C
    36
    38


       This is the body  section
       To define line numbering for this section use the -b option

       Line A

       Line B
       Line C



    40  This is the footnote section
    42  To define line numbering for this section use the -f option

    44  Line A

    46  Line B
    48  Line C
```

the header section will be numbered (`-h a`), none of the lines in the body section will be numbered (`-b n`), and the footer will not number empty lines (`-f t`). Figure 13-23 displays the output of the command.

The `od` Command

The `od` command converts the contents of a binary file into hex, octal, or decimal notation to the standard output device. The command is used to locate changes or unwanted characters in a file.

NOTE The file `helloworld.odt` can be found on your image in `/LABS/Chapter_13/source`.

The syntax for using `od` is `od <options> <filename>`. Here are some of the more commonly used options:

- **`-b`** Octal dump
- **`-d`** Decimal dump
- **`-x`** Hex dump
- **`-c`** Character dump

The od command is used by software developers to help reverse engineer compiled source code and by system administrators to find hidden characters like tabs or newlines. Next, we need to look at sed and awk.

The sed Command

sed is a data stream editor that reads one line of a file at a time into a buffer and makes a single change to a line at a time. sed does not change the content of the edited file. To save changes, you must redirect the output to a file.

The syntax of a sed command is sed <options> <address> <expression>. Some sed options are listed in Table 13-11.

The command sed '=' /etc/passwd will print the file /etc/passwd (see Figure 13-24). Each line will be preceded by a line number.

The command sed 1,3p /etc/passwd should print the range of lines from line 1 through line 3 of the file /etc/passwd. When viewing the output in Figure 13-25, it looks as if the whole file has been printed. However, what we are viewing is the pattern buffer.

Option	Description
-e	Expression. This option is used when placing more than one expression in a sed command.
-n	Does not print the pattern space.
-f <instruction_file>	Obtains sed filtering instructions from a file.
c	Appends text.
d	Deletes text.
i	Inserts a line.
a	Appends a line.
r <filename>	Reads in a file.
s	Substitutes one string pattern for another.

Table 13-11 sed Command Options

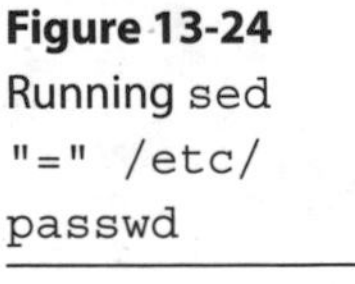

Figure 13-24 Running sed "=" /etc/passwd

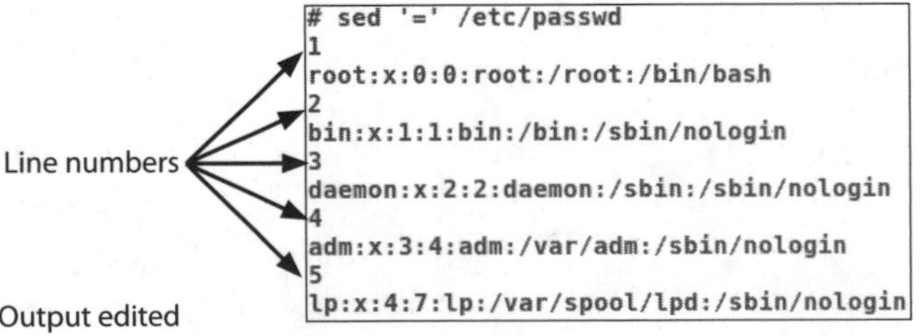
Line numbers
Output edited
sed '=' /etc/passwd
1
root:x:0:0:root:/root:/bin/bash
2
bin:x:1:1:bin:/bin:/sbin/nologin
3
daemon:x:2:2:daemon:/sbin:/sbin/nologin
4
adm:x:3:4:adm:/var/adm:/sbin/nologin
5
lp:x:4:7:lp:/var/spool/lpd:/sbin/nologin

Figure 13-25
The sed command printing without suppressing pattern space

```
[root@localhost proc]# sed 1,3p /etc/passwd
root:x:0:0:root:/root:/bin/bash
root:x:0:0:root:/root:/bin/bash
bin:x:1:1:bin:/bin:/sbin/nologin
bin:x:1:1:bin:/bin:/sbin/nologin
daemon:x:2:2:daemon:/sbin:/sbin/nologin
daemon:x:2:2:daemon:/sbin:/sbin/nologin
adm:x:3:4:adm:/var/adm:/sbin/nologin
lp:x:4:7:lp:/var/spool/lpd:/sbin/nologin
sync:x:5:0:sync:/sbin:/bin/sync
```

To prevent printing the pattern space, you must use the `-n` option, as shown in Figure 13-26.

You can print a number of lines from a starting address. The command `sed -n 3, +3p /etc/passwd` will begin printing from the third line of `/etc/passwd` and print the next three lines, as shown in Figure 13-27.

`sed` will only make one edit per line, as shown in Figure 13-28. The command `sed -n 's/root/fred/p' /etc/passwd` will search each line for the first instance of the string `root` and change the string to `fred`.

Figure 13-26
The sed command suppressing the pattern space

```
[root@localhost proc]# sed -n 1,3p /etc/passwd
root:x:0:0:root:/root:/bin/bash
bin:x:1:1:bin:/bin:/sbin/nologin
daemon:x:2:2:daemon:/sbin:/sbin/nologin

[root@localhost proc]#
```

Figure 13-27
The sed command printing three consecutive lines

```
# cat -n /etc/passwd | sed -n 3,+3p
     3  daemon:x:2:2:daemon:/sbin:/sbin/nologin
     4  adm:x:3:4:adm:/var/adm:/sbin/nologin
     5  lp:x:4:7:lp:/var/spool/lpd:/sbin/nologin
     6  sync:x:5:0:sync:/sbin:/bin/sync
```

Figure 13-28
Using sed to search and replace a single instance of a string per line

```
# sed -n 's/root/fred/p' /etc/passwd
fred:x:0:0:root:/root:/bin/bash
operator:x:11:0:operator:/fred:/sbin/nologin
```

Figure 13-29 Using sed to search and replace multiple instances of a string per line

```
# sed -n 's/root/fred/gp' /etc/passwd
fred:x:0:0:fred:/fred:/bin/bash
operator:x:11:0:operator:/fred:/sbin/nologin
```

Figure 13-30 Using sed with regular expressions

```
# sed -n 's/^root/fred/p' /etc/passwd
fred:x:0:0:root:/root:/bin/bash
```

In order to make multiple edits on a single line, add the g option to the end of the sed expression like so: sed -n 's/root/fred/gp' /etc/passwd. You can view the output in Figure 13-29.

You can use regular expressions as part of your search expression. The command sed -n 's/^root/fred/p' /etc/passwd will search for the string root at the beginning of the line in /etc/passwd and change it to fred, as shown in Figure 13-30.

We will use the file sedawk for the next few examples. Figure 13-31 displays the contents of sedawk.

The command cat sedawk | sed '/Jane/s/14/16' will search each line of the file sedawk for the string Jane. When it finds a line with the string Jane, it will search for the string 14 and replace it with the string 16 (see Figure 13-32).

Figure 13-31 The sedawk file

```
Jane     F        14       Algebra        90
George   M        13       French         88
Angela   F        14       Algebra        78
Jane     F        14       French         75
Bruce    M        15       Algebra        62
Bruce    M        15       French         89
George   M        13       Algebra        55
Angela   F        14       French         92
```

Figure 13-32 Using sed to search for a string in a line

```
# cat sedawk | sed /Jane/s/14/16/
Jane     F        16       Algebra 90
George   M        13       French  88
Angela   F        14       Algebra 78
Jane     F        16       French  75
Bruce    M        15       Algebra 62
Bruce    M        15       French  89
George   M        13       Algebra 55
Angela   F        14       French  92
```

Figure 13-33
Using sed to search a range of lines

```
# cat sedawk | sed 3,5s/Algebra/German/
Jane     F        14       Algebra 90
George   M        13       French  88
Angela   F        14       German  78
Jane     F        14       French  75
Bruce    M        15       German  62
Bruce    M        15       French  89
George   M        13       Algebra 55
Angela   F        14       French  92
```

The command `cat sedawk | sed 3,5s/Algebra/German` will search lines 3–5 for the string `Algebra` and replace it with the string `German`, as shown in Figure 13-33.

We can define multiple expressions. The command

```
sed -ne 's/Jane/Margaret/p' -e 's/Bruce/Bill/p' sedawk
```

will search the file `sedawk` and replace the name `Jane` with `Margaret` and the name `Bruce` with `Bill` (see Figure 13-34).

To insert a line, use the `i` option. The command `sed '3 i \This is an insert test'` as shown in Figure 13-35 will insert the text "`This is an insert test`" as the new line 3.

To append a line, use the `a` option. The command `sed '3 a \This is an append test'` (see Figure 13-36) will add the text "`This is an append test`" after line 3.

Figure 13-34
Using sed to make multiple edits

```
# sed -ne 's/Jane/Margaret/p' -e 's/Bruce/Bill/p' sedawk
Margaret       F       14      Algebra 90
Margaret       F       14      French  75
Bill     M      15      Algebra 62
Bill     M      15      French  89
```

Figure 13-35
Using sed to insert a line

```
# sed '3 i \This is an insert test' sedawk
Jane     F        14       Algebra 90
George   M        13       French  88
This is an insert test
Angela   F        14       Algebra 78
Jane     F        14       French  75
Bruce    M        15       Algebra 62
Bruce    M        15       French  89
George   M        13       Algebra 55
Angela   F        14       French  92
```

Figure 13-36
Using sed to append a line

```
# sed '3 a \This is an append test' sedawk
Jane     F        14       Algebra 90
George   M        13       French  88
Angela   F        14       Algebra 78
This is an append test
Jane     F        14       French  75
Bruce    M        15       Algebra 62
Bruce    M        15       French  89
George   M        13       Algebra 55
Angela   F        14       French  92
```

```
# cat sedawk | sed 3,5d
Jane    F       14      Algebra 90
George  M       13      French  88
Bruce   M       15      French  89
George  M       13      Algebra 55
Angela  F       14      French  92
```

Figure 13-37 Using sed to delete a range of lines

To delete a line, use the d option. The command cat sedawk | sed 3,5d (see Figure 13-37) will delete lines 3–5 of the file sedawk. Remember, sed will not change the file but instead displays the changes that would occur. To save the change, redirect the output to a file.

The awk Command

awk is an application used to process text files. The GNU implementation of awk is gawk. Either command, gawk or awk, may be executed. awk processes a single line at a time. It treats each line as a record that is divided into fields. Fields are separated by a delimiter. The default delimiter is a space or tab.

Table 13-12 lists some awk options.

awk also has a set of a built-in variables. A partial list of these variables is shown in Table 13-13.

awk uses the same escape sequences to do character insertions as the echo command. Some of these are listed in Table 13-14.

Option	Description
-f <instruction_file>	Obtains awk filtering instructions from the file specified by the argument <instruction_file>
-F <delimiter>	Uses the character(s) specified by the argument <delimiter> as the field delimiter

Table 13-12 awk Options

Table 13-13 awk Variables

Variable	Description
FILENAME	Filename of current input file
NF	Number of fields in a record
NR	Number of current record
FS	Current delimiter (input field separator)

Character	Description
\f	Inserts form feed (advance to next page)
\n	Inserts newline character (line feed and return cursor to the beginning of the line)
\r	Returns cursor to the beginning of the line
\t	Inserts tab

Table 13-14 Character Insertion Codes

Filtering Command Output

The next several commands use `awk` or `gawk` to filter the output of a command.

Most commands use a whitespace character to separate the columns of output. Each column, or field, is assigned a position number from `1` to `9`. We will use the position number to reference a specific output field.

In the following example, the output of the `ls -l` command is filtered by `awk` to display the first field of the output, or permissions, and the ninth field of the output, the filename.

```
# ls -l | gawk '{ print $1,$9 }'
total
-rw------- anaconda-ks.cfg
drwxr-xr-x Desktop
-rw-r--r-- install.log
-rw-r--r-- install.log.syslog
-rw-r--r-- sedawk
```

To make the output more readable, let's add spaces between the fields by adding several spaces surrounded by double quotes.

```
# ls -l | gawk '{ print $1 "        " $9 }'
total
-rw-------      anaconda-ks.cfg
drwxr-xr-x      Desktop
-rw-r--r--      install.log
-rw-r--r--      install.log.syslog
-rw-r--r--      sedawk
```

In the following illustration, we replace the spaces with a tab.

```
# ls -l | gawk '{ print "The file "$9" has the permissions " $1 }'
The file  has the permissions total
The file anaconda-ks.cfg has the permissions -rw-------
The file Desktop has the permissions drwxr-xr-x
The file install.log has the permissions -rw-r--r--
The file install.log.syslog has the permissions -rw-r--r--
The file sedawk has the permissions -rw-r--r--
```

Finally, we add descriptive text for clarity.

```
# ls -l | gawk '{ print $1,"\t" $9 }'
total
-rw-------        anaconda-ks.cfg
drwxr-xr-x        Desktop
-rw-r--r--        install.log
-rw-r--r--        install.log.syslog
-rw-r--r--        sedawk
```

Filtering the Content of a File

In the following example, we extract information from the file `/etc/passwd` and create formatted output. Notice the `-F` option is used to specify the colon (`:`) character as a delimiter.

```
#  gawk -F: '{ print "The user "$1 " has a userid of " $3"." }' /etc/passwd
The user root has a userid of 0.
The user bin has a userid of 1.
The user daemon has a userid of 2.
The user adm has a userid of 3.
The user lp has a userid of 4.
The user sync has a userid of 5.
The user shutdown has a userid of 6.
The user halt has a userid of 7.
```

The remainder of the examples use the file sedawk as a data source.

```
Jane    F    14    Algebra    90
George  M    13    French     88
Angela  F    14    Algebra    78
Jane    F    14    French     75
Bruce   M    15    Algebra    62
Bruce   M    15    French     89
George  M    13    Algebra    55
Angela  F    14    French     92
```

NOTE The sedawk file is available in the directory /LABS/Chapter_13/source.

In the following example, we are filtering for all female students ($2 =="F") who have grades greater than 80 ($5 > 80).

```
# cat sedawk | awk '$2 == "F" && $5 > 80 { print $1 " is passing." }'
Jane is passing.
Angela is passing.
```

In the next example, we are filtering for all students whose name begins with an A or B.

```
# cat sedawk | awk '/^[AB]/ { print $0 }'
Angela  F       14      Algebra 78
Bruce   M       15      Algebra 62
Bruce   M       15      French  89
Angela  F       14      French  92
```

Using a Script File

You can create awk script files and apply them to data. Figure 13-38 displays a script file called sedawkscript.

NOTE The file sedawkscript is available in the directory /LABS/Chapter_13/source.

Figure 13-38 The file sedawkscript

```
BEGIN{
        total_grade_n=0
        print " "
}
        {
        total_grade_n=total_grade_n + $5
        print "In " $4 " "$1 " received " $5
        }

END{
        print " "_
        print " "
        print NR " grades were reported."
        print "The average grade is " total_grade_n/NR "."
}
```

```
# cat sedawk | sort -k4,4 -k5,5nr | awk -f sedawkscript
Jane has achieved a grade of 90 in Algebra.
Angela has achieved a grade of 78 in Algebra.
Bruce has achieved a grade of 62 in Algebra.
George has achieved a grade of 55 in Algebra.
Angela has achieved a grade of 92 in French.
Bruce has achieved a grade of 89 in French.
George has achieved a grade of 88 in French.
Jane has achieved a grade of 75 in French.
The total number of grades reported equals 8
The average grade equals 78.625
```

Figure 13-39 Using `sedawkscript`

The script file is divided into three sections. Each section is enclosed within curly braces, { }. The `BEGIN` section is used to declare variables. The next section is a set of commands to process, and the `END` section is used to create a report.

The command

```
cat sedawk | sort -k4,4 -k5,5nr | awk -f sedawkscript
```

will sort the file `sedawk` by class and grade and then filter the result through the `awk` script, `sedawkscript` (see Figure 13-39). The report will produce the list of student grades, total number of grades reported, and the average grade.

EXAM TIP Make certain to have a good understanding of `tr`, `sed`, and `awk` for CompTIA Linux+ exam questions.

The `sort` Command

The `sort` command is used to sort a field or fields in output. Fields are sorted in the order they are presented on the command line. Table 13-15 describes some of the `sort` command's options.

The command `ls -l | sort -k 5,5n -k 9,9` (see Figure 13-40) will sort the output of the `ls -l` command on the file's size and then the file's name.

Option	Description
`-t <delimiter>`	Delimiter.
`-n`	Numeric sort.
`-r`	Reverse sort order.
`-k`	Specifies the field to sort on. Here are some examples: **`-k1`** or **`-k1,1`** Sorts on Field 1. **`-k 1.3,1.5`** Sorts on the third through fifth characters in Field 1.

Table 13-15 The `sort` Command Options

```
# ls -l | sort -k5,5n -k9,9
total 92
-rw-r--r-- 1 root root   176 Aug  5 16:31 sedawk
-rw-r--r-- 1 root root   236 Aug  5 16:31 sedawkscript
-rw------- 1 root root  1773 Jul 29 18:48 anaconda-ks.cfg
drwxr-xr-x 2 root root  4096 Jul 29 19:17 Desktop
drwxr-xr-x 4 root root  4096 Aug  6 02:08 labs
-rw-r--r-- 1 root root  5894 Jul 29 18:48 install.log.syslog
-rw-r--r-- 1 root root 33583 Jul 29 18:48 install.log
```

Figure 13-40 Using `ls` with `sort`

Option	Description
-l #	Defines the number of lines allowed per file. The default is 1,000 lines.
-b #	Defines the size of each file in bytes.

Table 13-16 The `split` Command Options

The `split` Command

The `split` command will split a large file into smaller pieces. Options used with the `split` command are explained in Table 13-16. The syntax for the `split` command is as follows:

```
split <-l | -b> <input_filename> <output_prefix>
```

The standard naming convention for the files created by `split` are `xaa`, `xab`, `xac`, and so on. The output prefix would replace the `x` with the argument specified in `<output_prefix>`. For example, if the `<output prefix>` argument is set to `sp`, the output files would be named `spaa`, `spab`, `spac`, and so on.

The `head` Command

The command `head <filename>` will print the first 10 lines of a file. The command `head -<n> <filename>` will display the first *n* lines of a file.

The `tail` Command

The command `tail<filename>` will print the last 10 lines of a file. The command `tail -<n> <filename>` will display the last *n* lines of a file.

The `uniq` Command

The `uniq` command reports or omits repeated lines that are right next to each other. The syntax is `uniq <options> <input> <output>`. You can use the following options with the `uniq` command:

- **-d** Prints only duplicate lines
- **-u** Prints only unique lines

For example, suppose our `lastnames` file contained duplicate entries:

```
1 Johnson
1 Johnson
2 Doe
3 Jones
```

You could use the uniq lastnames command to remove the duplicate lines. This is shown in the following example:

```
# uniq lastnames
1 Johnson
2 Doe
3 Jones
```

Again, the uniq command only works if the duplicate lines are adjacent to each other. If the text stream you need to work with contains duplicate lines that are not adjacent, use the sort command to first make them adjacent, and then pipe the output to the standard input of uniq.

Finally, let's look at the wc command.

The wc Command

The wc command prints the number of newlines, words, and bytes in a file. The syntax is wc <options> <filename>. You can use the following options with the wc command:

- **-c** Prints the byte counts
- **-m** Prints the character counts
- **-l** Prints the newline counts
- **-L** Prints the length of the longest line
- **-w** Prints the word counts

For example, to print all counts and totals for the firstnames file, you would use the wc firstnames command, as shown in this example:

```
# wc firstnames
 3 6 21 firstnames
```

The output means there were 3 lines, 6 words, and 21 characters.

Let's practice processing text streams in Exercise 13-2.

Exercise 13-2: Processing Text Streams

For this exercise, use the image supplied with the book. Log on as user **root** using the password **password**.

Here are the steps to follow:

VIDEO Please watch the Exercise 13-2 video for a demonstration on how to perform this task.

1. Use the command **cd /LABS/Chapter_13/work** to change to the directory that contains the scripts. Directory /LABS/Chapter_13 also contains a source directory. Those are originals you can copy to the work directory in case of an oops.

2. To display only the file owner, group owner, file size, and filename, use the following command:
   `ls -l | cut -d " " -f3,4,5,9`
3. Sort the output by file owner and file size:
   `ls -l | cut -d " " -f3,4,5,9 | sort -k3 -k9n`
4. Save the output of the command in Step 3 to `labfile` by executing this command:
   `ls -l | cut -d " " -f3,4,5,9 | sort -k3 -k9n >labfile`
5. To change the owner name of each file to `fred`, use the following command:
   `sed -n 's/root/fred/p' labfile`
6. Print the first line of the file `labfile` to determine its structure:
   `head -1 labfile`
7. Use `awk` to print "The file <filename> is owned by <owner>" using this command:
   `awk '{print "The file " $4 " is owned by " $1}' labfile`

Chapter Review

In this chapter, you learned how to create basic shell scripts on a Linux system. This chapter discussed how to set up control structures, such as `if` and `case` statements, to control the flow of a script, and how to use loops, such as `while`, `until`, and `for`, to repeat a series of commands for a specific period.

You also learned how to manipulate text using commands like `tr`, `cut`, `sed`, and `awk`. Shell scripts are text files that contain a variety of commands that can be used to automate tasks and process information.

Here are some key takeaways from this chapter:

- Bash shell scripts should begin with `#!/bin/bash` to specify that the Bash shell should be used to run the script.
- Include a comment, starting with #, at the beginning of each script that describes what it does.
- You can run shell scripts by using `/bin/bash <script_filename>` or by adding the execute permission to the script file.
- You can read user input in a script using `read <variable_name>`.
- To make a script that branches in two directions, you can use an `if/then /else` structure.
- You can use the `test` command in an `if/then/else` structure to test a condition.
- If you want more than two branches in your script, you can use the `case` structure.

- With a `case` structure, you can evaluate multiple conditions and execute a series of commands that are executed according to which condition is true.
- Looping structures come in three varieties: the `while` loop, the `until` loop, and the `for` loop.
- A `while` loop executes over and over until a specified condition is no longer true.
- An `until` loop runs over and over as long as the condition is false. As soon as the condition is true, it stops.
- To loop a specific number of times, you can use a `for` loop.
- You can process text streams to manipulate and modify text within a script or within a pipe.
- You can use the following utilities to process a text stream:
  - `cut`
  - `nl`
  - `od`
  - `sed`
  - `awk`
  - `head`
  - `tail`
  - `sort`
  - `split`
  - `tr`
  - `uniq`
  - `wc`
- Command substitution using `` ` ` `` or `$( )` allows you to run a command and have its output pasted back on the command line as an argument for another command.

Questions

1. Which of the following elements must be included at the beginning of every Bash shell script?

   A. `#Comment`

   B. `#!/bin/bash`

   C. `exit 0`

   D. `#begin script`

2. You've created a shell script named `myscript` in your home directory. How can you execute it? (Choose two.)
   A. Enter `/bin/bash ~/myscript` at the shell prompt.
   B. Enter `myscript` at the shell prompt.
   C. Select Computer | Run in the graphical desktop; then enter `~/myscript` and select `Run`.
   D. Enter `run ~/myscript` at the shell prompt.
   E. Enter `chmod u+x ~/myscript;` then enter `~/myscript` at the shell prompt.
3. Which command will create a new variable named `TOTAL` and set its type to be `integer`?
   A. `variable -i TOTAL`
   B. `declare -i TOTAL`
   C. `declare TOTAL -t integer`
   D. `TOTAL=integer`
4. You need to display the text "`Hello world`" on the screen from within a shell script. Which command will do this?
   A. `echo "Hello world"`
   B. `read Hello world`
   C. `writeln "Hello world"`
   D. `print "Hello world"`
5. From within a shell script, you need to prompt users to enter their phone number. You need to assign the value they enter into a variable named `PHONE`. Which command will do this?
   A. `read "What is your phone number?" $PHONE`
   B. `read $PHONE`
   C. `read PHONE`
   D. `? "What is your phone number?" PHONE`
6. Which command can be used from within an `if/then/else` structure to evaluate whether or not a specified condition is true?
   A. `eval`
   B. `==`
   C. `test`
   D. `<>`

7. Which command will evaluate to true within an `if/then/else` structure in a shell script if the variable `num1` is less than the variable `num2`?

   A. `eval num1 < num2`

   B. `test num1 < num2`

   C. `test num1 -lt num2`

   D. `test "num1" != "num2"`

8. In a shell script, you need to prompt the user to select from one of seven different options presented with the `echo` command. Which control structure would best evaluate the user's input and run the appropriate set of commands?

   A. A `while` loop

   B. A `for` loop

   C. An `until` loop

   D. `if/then/else`

   E. `case`

9. Which control structure will keep processing over and over until a specified condition evaluates to false?

   A. A `while` loop

   B. A `for` loop

   C. An `until` loop

   D. `if/then/else`

   E. `case`

10. Which control structures are considered to be branching structures? (Choose two.)

    A. A `while` loop

    B. A `for` loop

    C. An `until` loop

    D. `if/then/else`

    E. `case`

11. Which control structure will keep processing over and over as long as the specified condition evaluates to false?

    A. A `while` loop

    B. A `for` loop

    C. An `until` loop

    D. `if/then/else`

    E. case

12. Which control structure will process a specified number of times?
    - A. A `while` loop
    - B. A `for` loop
    - C. An `until` loop
    - D. `if/then/else`
    - E. case
13. Which command will delete the character `n` from the file called `file.txt`?
    - A. `tr -d n < file.txt`
    - B. `tr -d n file.txt`
    - C. `tr --delete n > file.txt`
    - D. `tr --delete n file.txt`
14. Which command can be used to print columns or fields that you specify from a file to the standard output using the tab character as a delimiter?
    - A. `cut`
    - B. `pr`
    - C. `fmt`
    - D. `sort`
15. The first column of the file `logfile.txt` contains last names. Which commands will sort the file by last names? (Choose two.)
    - A. `sort < logfile.txt`
    - B. `sort logfile.txt`
    - C. `sort < logfile.txt -o "screen"`
    - D. `sort < logfile.txt > screen`
    - E. `sort -n logfile.txt`
    - F. `cat /var/log/messages | awk 'syslog {print 6,7,8}'`
16. You need to search for and replace the word `June` with the word `July` in a file named `proj_sched.txt` in your home directory and send the output to a new file named `new_proj_sched.txt`. Which command will do this?
    - A. `cat ~/proj_sched.txt | sed s/June/July/`
    - B. `cat ~/proj_sched.txt | awk s/June/July/`
    - C. `cat ~/proj_sched.txt | awk s/June/July/ 1> new_proj_sched.txt`
    - D. `cat ~/proj_sched.txt | sed s/June/July/ 1> new_proj_sched.txt`

Answers

1. **B.** The `#!/bin/bash` element must be included at the beginning of every Bash shell script.
2. **A, E.** You can enter `/bin/bash ~/myscript` or `chmod u+x ~/myscript` to make the script execute.
3. **B.** The `declare -i TOTAL` command will create the `TOTAL` variable and type it as `integer`.
4. **A.** The `echo "Hello world"` command will display the text "`Hello world`" on the screen from within a shell script.
5. **C.** The `read PHONE` command in a shell script will assign the value entered by the user into a variable named `$PHONE`.
6. **C.** The `test` command can be used from within an `if/then/else` structure to evaluate whether or not a specified condition is true.
7. **C.** The `test num1 -lt num2` command will evaluate to true within an `if/then/else` structure if the variable `num1` is less than the variable `num2`.
8. **E.** The `case` structure is the best option presented to evaluate the user's choice of multiple selections and run the appropriate set of commands as a result.
9. **A.** A `while` loop will keep processing over and over until the specified condition evaluates to false.
10. **D, E.** The `if/then/else` and `case` structures are considered to be branching structures because they branch the script in one of several directions based on how a specified condition evaluates.
11. **C.** The `until` loop control structure will keep processing over and over as long as the specified condition evaluates to false.
12. **B.** The `for` loop control structure will process a specified number of times.
13. **A.** The `tr -d n < file.txt` command will remove all cases of the letter `n`. (The command `tr -delete n < file.txt` would also work.)
14. **A.** The `cut` command can be used to print columns or fields that you specify from a file to the standard output using the tab character as a delimiter.
15. **A, B.** The `sort < logfile.txt` command and the `sort logfile.txt` command will both send the contents of the `logfile.txt` file to the `sort` command to sort its lines alphabetically and display them on the screen.
16. **D.** The `cat ~/proj_sched.txt | sed s/June/July/ 1> new_proj_sched.txt` command will search the `proj_sched.txt` file for the word `June` and replace all instances with the word `July`. The output from `sed` will be written to a file named `new_proj_sched.txt`.

CHAPTER 14

Managing Linux Network Settings

In this chapter, you will learn about

- Understanding IP networks
- Configuring network addressing parameters
- Troubleshooting network problems
- Understanding network-based filesystems

I love robotics because of the connections I can make.

—Carlotta Berry, Rose-Hulman Institute of Technology

Up to this point in the book, we have focused on configuring and using Linux as a stand-alone computer system. However, Linux can also be configured to function in a networked environment. Unlike many operating systems, Linux was designed from the ground up with networking in mind.

One of Linux's greatest features is that most any distribution can be configured to fill a wide variety of roles on the network—all for little or no cost. For example, one can configure a Linux system as any of the following:

- A networked workstation
- A Secure Shell (SSH), file, and print server
- A database server
- A Dynamic Host Configuration Protocol (DHCP) server
- A Domain Name System (DNS) name server
- A web and Network Time Protocol (NTP) server
- An e-mail and virtual private networking (VPN) server
- A load balancing, clustering, or containers server
- A domain controller, logging, monitoring, and authentication server
- A Lightweight Directory Access Protocol (LDAP) directory server
- A gateway router and proxy server

- A packet-filtering, stateful, or application-level firewall
- A certificate authority (CA) server

With most other operating systems, you would have to pay lots of money to get these additional functionalities. In this chapter, we focus on enabling basic networking on your Linux system as well as how to set up a variety of Linux services.

EXAM TIP As a candidate, you should be very comfortable with Linux networking basics for the CompTIA Linux+ exam. Be sure to understand how Internet Protocol (IP) addressing works in IPv4 and IPv6.

Understanding IP Networks

For the CompTIA Linux+ exam, you need to be proficient with the IP protocol (both versions 4 and 6) and know how to configure the protocol such that a system can participate on the network. A brief review of IPv4 addressing and protocols follow:

- What is a protocol?
- How IPv4 addresses work
- How IPv4 subnet masks work

What Is a Protocol?

So, what exactly is a protocol? Strictly speaking, a *protocol* is a set of rules, and, in the context of networking, a protocol is the set of rules that governs communication between two systems. A good analogy for a protocol is a human language. Before two people can communicate, they must speak the same language; otherwise, no information can be transferred between them.

For the CompTIA Linux+ exam, you need to be familiar with the IP protocol, which is the networking protocol used on the Internet. IP works in conjunction with other protocols, such as the Transmission Control Protocol (TCP), the User Datagram Protocol (UDP), and the Internet Control Message Protocol (ICMP), to be discussed shortly.

NOTE The two versions of the IP protocol are called IPv4 and IPv6. We are going to discuss IPv4 first in this chapter and explore IPv6 later in the chapter.

To understand the TCP/IP protocol, you need to understand the Open Systems Interconnection (OSI) reference model. The OSI reference model was designed by delegates from major computer and telecom companies back in 1983. The goal was to design a network communications model that was modular so that products from different vendors could interoperate. Prior to this, networking solutions tended to be proprietary, forcing implementers to purchase all of their components from the same vendor. By defining the

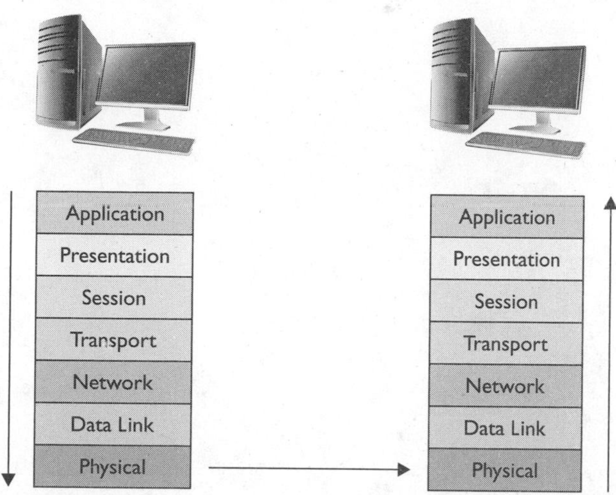

Figure 14-1 The OSI reference model

OSI reference model, the industry created a standard that allows administrators to pick and choose components from a variety of vendors.

The OSI reference model divides the communication process between two hosts into seven layers, as shown in Figure 14-1.

These layers break down the overall communication process into specific tasks. Information flows down through the layers on the sending system and then is transmitted on the network medium. The information then flows up the layers on the receiving side.

The OSI reference model layers are defined as follows:

- **Layer 1: Physical** Defines electrical formats between hosts. Devices include cables and hubs.
- **Layer 2: Data Link** Defines rules to access the Physical layer. Information received is organized into *datagrams*. Devices include switches and bridges.
- **Layer 3: Network** Enables the routing of the data to outside networks. Both IP and ICMP operate at this layer. Devices include routers and stateless firewalls.
- **Layer 4: Transport** Ensures *packet* integrity and reliability. TCP and UDP operate at this layer. Devices include packet-filtering firewalls.
- **Layer 5: Session** Responsible for maintaining connections between applications called *sessions*. This is how packets know their browser tab destination when five tabs are open.
- **Layer 6: Presentation** Responsible for ensuring that data is formatted and presented correctly. Most compression and encryption occur here.
- **Layer 7: Application** Where "apps" or applications such as FTP, SMTP, SSH, and Telnet operate. Devices include Application layer firewalls.

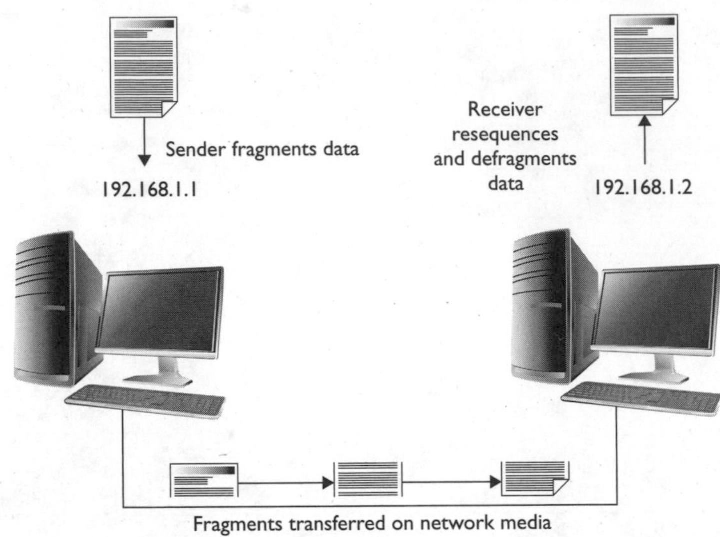

Figure 14-2 Transferring data with the IP protocol

The Internet Protocol itself is used only to make sure each packet arrives at the destination system and to reassemble and resequence it when it arrives at the destination system. This is shown in Figure 14-2.

TCP is one of the two original components of the IP protocol suite and provides a guaranteed connection, whereas UDP is considered *connectionless* because verification of packets reaching their final destination is not done.

Using TCP is like using signature confirmation with a shipping company. When one sends a package, the shipper requires the receiver to sign for the package, allowing the sender to verify that the package was received correctly.

TCP is used by applications that require a high degree of data integrity, including web servers, e-mail servers, FTP servers, and so on. With UDP, packets are sent unacknowledged. It assumes that error checking and correction are either not necessary or will be performed by the application, thus avoiding the processing overhead of TCP.

UDP is similar to sending a postcard through the mail. Essentially, the sender assumes that the mail carrier is reasonably reliable and that the data on the postcard is not important enough to require the receiver to sign for it. Some applications that make use of UDP include the following:

- Streaming audio and video
- Voice over IP (VoIP)

ICMP is another core protocol in the IP suite. It differs in purpose from TCP and UDP, which are transport protocols. The primary role of ICMP is to test and verify network communications between hosts. Commands that use the ICMP protocol are ping and traceroute.

For example, to test network connectivity, the `ping` utility will send ICMP echo request packets to a remote host. If the host receives them, it will respond to the sender, which verifies a successful connection. The `traceroute` utility is used to trace the router used by a packet from source to destination.

For the CompTIA Linux+ exam, you are required to understand the concept of IP ports, provided at the Transport layer. Ports allow a single host with a single IP address to provide multiple network services. Each service uses the same IP address but operates using a different port number.

For example, assume a network server with an IP address of 192.168.1.1. This system could be configured as both a web server and an FTP server, running at the same time. Each service will listen for requests. The web server listens on port 80, and the FTP server listens on ports 20 and 21. Therefore, requests sent to port 80 are handled by the web service, and data sent to ports 20 and 21 is handled by the FTP daemon.

NOTE The FTP service is somewhat unique in that it uses two ports. One is for the control connection (port 21) and the other (port 20) is for transferring data.

Port numbers can range from 0 to 65536. The way these ports are used is regulated by the Internet Corporation for Assigned Names and Numbers (ICANN). IP ports are lumped into three different categories:

- **Well-known ports** Reserved for specific services, well-known ports are those numbered from 0 to 1023. Here are some examples:
  - Ports 20 and 21: FTP
  - Port 22: Secure Shell (SSH, SCP, SFTP, STelnet)
  - Port 23: Telnet
  - Port 25: SMTP
  - Port 53: DNS
  - Port 80: HTTP
  - Port 110: POP3
  - Port 123: NTP (time synchronization)
  - Ports 137, 138, and 139: NetBIOS
  - Port 143: IMAP
  - Port 389: LDAP
  - Port 443: HTTPS
  - Port 514: Syslog remote logging
- **Registered ports** ICANN has reserved ports 1024 through 49151 for special implementations that organizations can apply for.

- **Dynamic ports** Dynamic ports are also called *private ports*. Ports 49152 through 65535 are designated as dynamic ports. They are available for use by any network service. They are frequently used by network services that need to establish a temporary connection.

How IPv4 Addresses Work

Every host on an IP-based network must have a unique IP address. An IP address is a Network layer (3) address that is logically assigned to a network host. Because the IP address is a logical address, it is not permanent.

The IP address is different from the MAC address. The MAC address is a Data Link layer (2) hardware address that is burned into a ROM chip on every network board sold in the world. The MAC address is hard-coded and cannot be changed; theoretically, every MAC address in the world is unique.

NOTE The Address Resolution Protocol (ARP) is used to map IP addresses to MAC addresses. ARP makes local area networks (LANs) faster. To view the current ARP table on your Linux system, simply run `arp -a`.

An IP address consists of four numbers, separated by periods. In decimal notation, each *octet* must be between 0 and 255. Here are some examples of valid IP addresses:

- 12.34.181.78
- 192.168.1.1
- 246.250.3.8

NOTE IPv4 addresses are sometimes called "dotted quad" addresses. Each number in the address is actually an 8-bit binary number called an *octet*. Because each octet is a binary number, it can be represented as 0's and 1's. For example, the address 192.168.1.1 can be represented in binary form as follows: 11000000.10101000.00000001.00000001

The fastest way to convert from decimal to binary, and vice versa, for the exam is to understand the decimal value of each binary field, as shown in Table 14-1. Note the only values that become part of the conversion to decimal are those with a 1. Once all the decimal values are determined, take the sum for the final conversion result. For example, use the table to determine the value of each bit in the binary number 10101011.

Field Value	*128*	*64*	*32*	*16*	*8*	*4*	*2*	*1*	**Total**
Binary	1	0	1	0	1	0	1	1	**10101011**
Decimal	128	0	32	0	8	0	2	1	**179**

Table 14-1 Binary-to-Decimal Conversion Calculator

Therefore, 10101011 = 128 + 0 + 32 + 0 + 8 + 0 + 2 + 1 = 179.

EXAM TIP In the real world, there are subnet calculators to perform these conversions, but you are not allowed to bring a calculator into the exam room.

Some IP addresses are reserved and cannot be assigned to a host. For example, the last octet in a host IP address cannot be the *lowest* subnet value, or 0. This is reserved for the address of the network segment itself that the host resides on. For example, the default network address for the host assigned an IP address of 192.168.1.1 is 192.168.1.0.

In addition, the last octet of an IP address assigned to a host cannot be the *highest* subnet value, or 255. This is reserved for sending a broadcast to all hosts on the segment. In the preceding example, the default broadcast address for a host with an IP address of 192.168.1.1 would be 192.168.1.255.

Every host on an IP-based network must have a *unique* IP address assigned to it. If the host resides on a public network, such as the Internet, it must use a *globally* unique IP address obtained from the IANA. Once an IP address is assigned, no one else in the world can use it on a public network.

This introduces an important problem with IP version 4. The 32-bit addressing standard allows for a maximum of 4,294,967,296 unique addresses. This seemed like a lot of addresses when IPv4 was originally defined. However, today the number of addresses is depleted.

One method to mitigate the shortage of IPv4 addresses is to utilize *network address translation (NAT)*. A NAT router can present a single registered IP address to a *public* network and hide thousands of *private* IP addresses on the network behind it. This is shown in Figure 14-3.

Within each class of IP address are blocks of addresses called *private* or *reserved* IP addresses. These addresses can be used by anyone who wants to use them. This allows administrators to use private addresses on their local network and still be able to connect to public networks, such as the Internet. All traffic from the private network appears to be originating from the registered IP address configured on the public side of the NAT router.

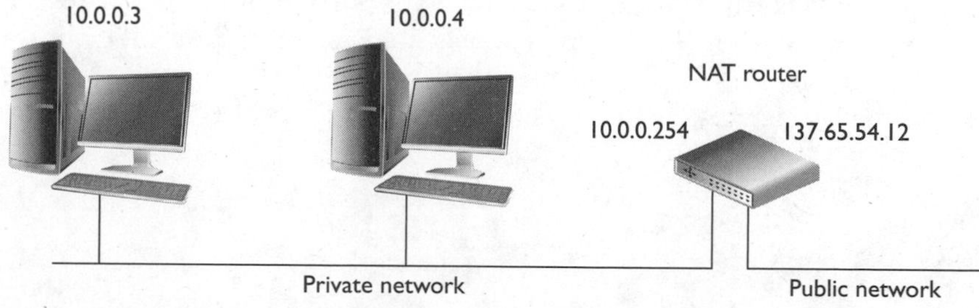

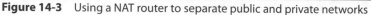

Figure 14-3 Using a NAT router to separate public and private networks

Here are the private IP address ranges:

- 10.0.0.0–10.255.255.255 (Class A)
- 172.16.0.0–172.31.255.255 (Class B)
- 192.168.0.0–192.168.255.255 (Class C)

These are nonroutable addresses, meaning that if you try to use them on a public network, such as the Internet, routers will not forward data to or from them. This allows anyone in the world to use these private IP address ranges without worrying about conflicts.

How IPv4 Subnet Masks Work

When configuring a system with an IP address, you must also assign a *subnet mask*. This parameter defines the network a system belongs to. The IP address is divided into two parts:

- Network address
- Node or host address

Part of an IPv4 address is used to identify the network the host resides on. The rest identifies a specific host (node) on the network. The key point to remember is that every system on the same network segment must have exactly the same numbers in the network portion of the address. However, they each must have a unique node portion. This is shown in Figure 14-4.

How much of the address is used for the network and how much is used for the node is defined by the *subnet mask*. Default subnet masks are divided into three classes, as defined next, in decimal and binary forms:

```
                 Decimal Notation  Binary Notation
Class A Mask:    255.0.0.0         11111111.00000000.00000000.00000000
Class B Mask:    255.255.0.0       11111111.11111111.00000000.00000000
Class C Mask:    255.255.255.0     11111111.11111111.11111111.00000000
```

Subnet mask octets with 1's identify the network portion of the IP address, and the 0's define the host portion. For example, an IP address of 192.168.1.1 with a mask of 255.255.255.0 specifies a subnet where the first three octets of the address are the network and the last octet is the node. This is shown in Figure 14-5.

192.168.1.1
Network | Node

Figure 14-4 Network vs. node in an IP address

```
11000000.10101000.00000001.00000001 (192.168.1.1)
11111111.11111111.11111111.00000000 (255.255.255.0)
          Network                  |  Node
```

Figure 14-5 Using the subnet mask to define the network and node portions of an IP address

IP addresses are divided into five different classes, with their own default subnet masks. You only need to be concerned with the first three address classes:

- **Class A** The decimal value of *the first octet must be between 1 and 126.* In a Class A address, the first octet is the network address and the last three octets are the node. Class A allows only 126 total possible networks, but offers 16.7 million possible node addresses.
- **Class B** The decimal value of the *first octet must be between 128 and 191.* In a Class B address, the first two octets are the network and the last two octets are the node address. Using Class B addressing allows 16,384 possible networks with 65,534 possible nodes each.
- **Class C** The decimal value of *the first octet must be between 192 and 223.* In a Class C address, the first three octets are the network address, while the last octet is the node address. A huge number of Class C networks are available at 2,097,152. However, only 254 hosts can exist on any given Class C network.

EXAM TIP To calculate the number of hosts per network, count the number of 0's, or *Z*, in the subnet. For example, there are eight 0's in a Class C network. The number of hosts per network, or *N*, is defined as follows:

$N = 2^Z - 2$

or

$254 = 2^8 - 2 = 256 - 1$ (the network address) $- 1$ (the broadcast address)

Subnet masks are often noted using a type of shorthand called *CIDR notation.* This is done by adding a slash (/) and the number of 1's used in the mask after the IP address (for example, 192.168.1.1/24). The /24 parameter indicates 24 bits are used for the subnet mask, which in longhand is 192.168.1.1/11111111.11111111.1111111.00000000, or in decimal is 192.168.1.1/255.255.255.0.

Default subnet masks are not required; for instance, you could define a mask of 255.255.255.0 for a Class A address or anything in between. For example, a subnet mask of 11111111.11111111.11111100.00000000, or a CIDR of 22, or 255.255.252.0 in decimal is allowed. This results in $N = 2^{10} - 2$, or 1,022 hosts per network. Network administrators perform this type of subnetting because debugging a 1,000-host network is much easier than troubleshooting a network of 16 million hosts.

Network ID	Available Addresses	Broadcast Address
10.0.0.0	10.0.0.1–10.0.3.254	10.0.3.255
10.0.4.0	10.0.4.1–10.0.7.254	10.0.7.255
10.0.8.0	10.0.8.1–10.0.11.254	10.0.11.255
10.0.12.0	10.0.12.1–10.0.15.254	10.0.15.255

Table 14-2 Creating Subnets with a 10-bit Subnet Mask

In this case, for a 10.0.0.0 network, the first subnet would range from

```
00001010.00000000.00000000.00000000 - 00001010.00000000.00000011.11111111
```

or in decimal from 10.0.0.0, the network ID, through 10.0.3.255, the broadcast address. Addresses from 10.0.0.1 through 10.0.3.254 are host addresses for the first subnet.

The next subnet would range from

```
00001010.00000000.00000100.00000000 - 00001010.00000000.00000111.11111111
```

or in decimal from 10.0.4.0 (the network ID) through 10.0.7.255 (the broadcast address). Addresses from 10.0.4.1 through 10.0.7.254 are host addresses for the second subnet.

The network administrator would continue assigning host addresses until they run out of systems or usable IP addresses. In the real world, subnetting calculators exist to complete this process. Two additional examples are shown in Table 14-2 for a subnet of 10.0.0.0/22.

Troubleshooting Subnet Network Configuration Issues

An important point to remember is that for two hosts on the same network segment to communicate, they need to have *exactly* the same network address, which means they must have *exactly* the same subnet mask. For example, suppose you have three systems, as shown in Figure 14-6.

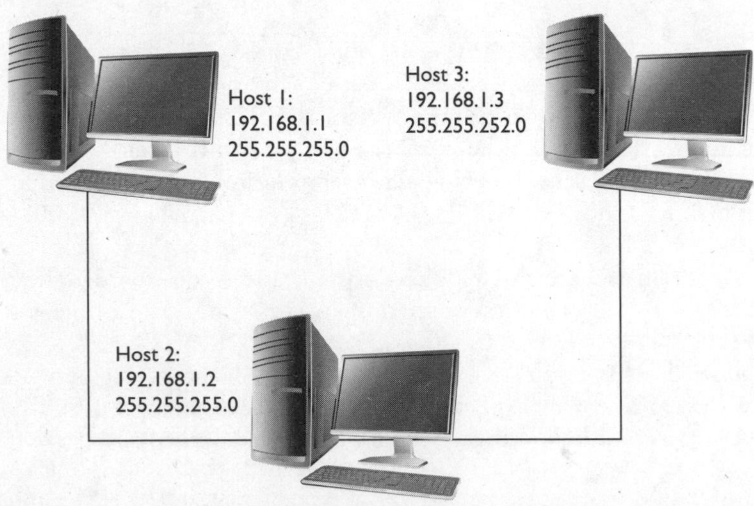

Figure 14-6 Hosts with wrong subnet masks

Host 1 and Host 2 both have the exact same network address and subnet mask, and therefore can communicate on the IP network segment. However, Host 3 uses a subnet mask of 255.255.252.0 instead of 255.255.255.0. Therefore, Host 3 has a different network address than Host 1 and Host 2 and will not be able to communicate with them without the use of a network router.

To fix this, change the netmask on Host 3 to match those of Host 1 and Host 2. In other words, modify the current subnet mask from 255.255.252.0 to 255.255.255.0, and then all three computers can communicate.

Configuring Network Addressing Parameters

Installing an Ethernet network interface in your system involves completing the following tasks:

- Assigning NIC nomenclature
- Configuring IPv4 parameters
- Configuring routing parameters
- Configuring name resolver settings
- Configuring IPv6

Assigning NIC Nomenclature

Linux's `systemd` uses *predictable network interface names.* One key benefit is that specific aliases can be permanently assigned to specific network interfaces. For example, an onboard network adapter is assigned the index number provided by the BIOS to construct the alias. A commonly assigned alias created using this parameter is `eno1`, where

- `en` is the Ethernet interface
- `o1` is the onboard device index number (in this case, device number 1)

At this point, the network interface is loaded and active.

Configuring IPv4 Parameters

Network interfaces can be configured using either a static IP address or a dynamic IP address. Table 14-3 highlights the advantages and disadvantages of each method.

To statically assign IP address parameters to a Linux system, use the `ifconfig` command or the newer `ip` command. Running `ifconfig` without any options displays the current status of all network interfaces in the system, as shown in Figure 14-7.

EXAM TIP `ifconfig` lists multiple interfaces, not just one. The extra interface labeled `lo` is the *loopback* interface and is usually assigned a special IP address of 127.0.0.1. This is a virtual interface, not an actual hardware interface. It is used for network testing, internal communications, diagnostics, and so on.

Option	Description	Advantages	Disadvantages
Static address assignment	Configure a network host with a nonchanging IP address.	Great for servers in the network.	The host consumes the address regardless of whether the system is on or off.
Dynamic address assignment	Linux contacts a DHCP server and assigns an available IP address for a specified *lease* time.	The system engages and gets an IP address. Once the system is powered off, the address can be reassigned to others.	You must have a DHCP server installed and configured before you can use this option.

Table 14-3 IP Address Assignment Options

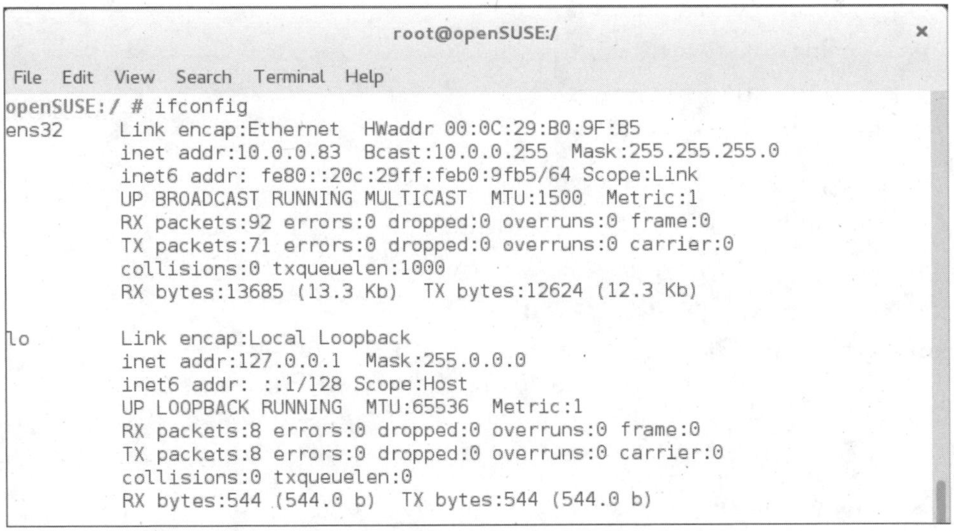

```
root@openSUSE:/
File  Edit  View  Search  Terminal  Help
openSUSE:/ # ifconfig
ens32     Link encap:Ethernet  HWaddr 00:0C:29:B0:9F:B5
          inet addr:10.0.0.83  Bcast:10.0.0.255  Mask:255.255.255.0
          inet6 addr: fe80::20c:29ff:feb0:9fb5/64 Scope:Link
          UP BROADCAST RUNNING MULTICAST  MTU:1500  Metric:1
          RX packets:92 errors:0 dropped:0 overruns:0 frame:0
          TX packets:71 errors:0 dropped:0 overruns:0 carrier:0
          collisions:0 txqueuelen:1000
          RX bytes:13685 (13.3 Kb)  TX bytes:12624 (12.3 Kb)

lo        Link encap:Local Loopback
          inet addr:127.0.0.1  Mask:255.0.0.0
          inet6 addr: ::1/128 Scope:Host
          UP LOOPBACK RUNNING  MTU:65536  Metric:1
          RX packets:8 errors:0 dropped:0 overruns:0 frame:0
          TX packets:8 errors:0 dropped:0 overruns:0 carrier:0
          collisions:0 txqueuelen:0
          RX bytes:544 (544.0 b)  TX bytes:544 (544.0 b)
```

Figure 14-7 Using `ifconfig` to view network interface information

Notice in Figure 14-7 that two network interfaces are displayed: `ens32` and `lo`. The `ens32` interface is the Ethernet network interface installed in the system. The `lo` interface is the local loopback virtual network interface. This interface is required for many Linux services to run properly.

Another utility you can use to manage IP addressing on a Linux system is the newer `ip` command. Practice using this command because it may supersede `ifconfig`, `route`, and others because it can also manage IPv6. This command is also available on Windows, Chrome, and macOS computers. To view the current configuration, enter `ip addr show` at the shell prompt, as shown here:

```
[root@localhost ~]# ip addr show
1: lo: <LOOPBACK,UP,LOWER_UP> mtu 65536 qdisc noqueue state UNKNOWN
   link/loopback 00:00:00:00:00:00 brd 00:00:00:00:00:00
```

```
    inet 127.0.0.1/8 brd 127.255.255.255 scope host lo
       valid_lft forever preferred_lft forever
    inet6 ::1/128 scope host
       valid_lft forever preferred_lft forever
2: ens32: <BROADCAST,MULTICAST,UP,LOWER_UP> mtu 1500 qdisc pfifo_fast
state UP qlen 1000
    link/ether 00:0c:29:b0:9f:b5 brd ff:ff:ff:ff:ff:ff
    inet 10.0.0.83/24 brd 10.0.0.255 scope global ens32
       valid_lft forever preferred_lft forever
    inet6 fe80::20c:29ff:feb0:9fb5/64 scope link
       valid_lft forever preferred_lft forever
```

EXAM TIP The `ethtool` command allows administrators to list and alter the hardware settings of the network card.

Some of the more important parameters include those shown in Table 14-4.

To use the `ip` command to configure IP addressing parameters, enter `ip addr add <ip_address> dev <interface>` at the shell prompt. For example, to set the IP address assigned to the `ens32` network interface to 10.0.0.84, enter the following:

```
[root@localhost ~]# ip addr add 10.0.0.84 dev ens32
```

NOTE The actual `ip` commands allow shortening the options, so
`# ip address add 10.0.0.84 dev ens32`
and even
`# ip a a 10.0.0.84 dev ens32`
are possible ways to run the command and get the same results.

To remove an IP address from an interface, just enter `ip addr del <ip_address> dev <interface>` at the shell prompt.

The `ip` command can also disable and enable a network interface. To disable an interface, enter `ip link set <interface> down` at the shell prompt. To bring a disabled interface back online, enter `ip link set <interface> up` at the shell prompt. Also, `systemctl` can restart the network interface. To do this, simply enter `systemctl restart network` on a Red Hat–class system or `systemctl restart networking` on a Debian-class system.

`ip addr` **Parameter**	**Description**
`link`	The MAC address of the network board
`inet`	The IPv4 address/mask assigned to the interface
`inet6`	The IPv6 address/mask assigned to the interface
`brd`	The broadcast address of the network segment

Table 14-4 `ip addr show` Output

Option	Description	Other Possible Values
`BOOTPROTO="static"`	Specifies that the interface use a static IP address assignment.	Set to `dhcp` to dynamically assign an address.
`IPADDR="192.168.1.81"`	Assigns an IP address of `192.168.1.10` to the interface with a subnet mask of `255.255.255.0`.	
`NETMASK="255.255.255.0"`	Assigns the `NETMASK` to CIDR /24.	`255.255.255.248` creates subnetworks of 6 systems.
`BROADCAST="192.168.1.255"`	Specifies the broadcast address.	`192.168.1.7` defines the broadcast address of the first subnet.

Table 14-5 Configuring Persistent Parameters for a Network Interface

This IP address assignment is not persistent. It will be lost on reboot. To make it persistent, configure the file `ifcfg-ens32` in the `/etc/sysconfig/network-scripts` directory. Sample parameters for the interface are shown here for this CentOS system:

```
[root@localhost ~]# cat /etc/sysconfig/network-scripts/ifcfg-ens32
BOOTPROTO='dhcp'
NAME='ens32'
NETMASK=''
NETWORK=''
```

Some other options available in this configuration file are listed in Table 14-5.

The lines for `IPADDR`, `NETMASK`, `NETWORK`, and `BROADCAST` are not required if `BOOTPROTO` is set to `dhcp`.

If the system DHCP leases are too short from the DHCP server, at the DHCP server, modify the `/etc/dhcpd.conf` file. Modify the `max-lease-time` variable to obtain longer lease times.

EXAM TIP The `/etc/hostname` file configures the Linux system's hostname and can be made persistent by using the `hostnamectl` command. Here's an example:

```
[root@localhost ~]#hostnamectl set-hostname server-one
```

The final network utility is the NetworkManager daemon, which has two interface utilities: `nmtui` and `nmcli`. The `nmtui` command provides a curses-based (that is, text user interface) with NetworkManager, as shown in Figure 14-8. The `nmcli` command is used to create, display, edit, delete, activate, and deactivate network connections with a command-line interface. What's great about both of these tools is that *they will*

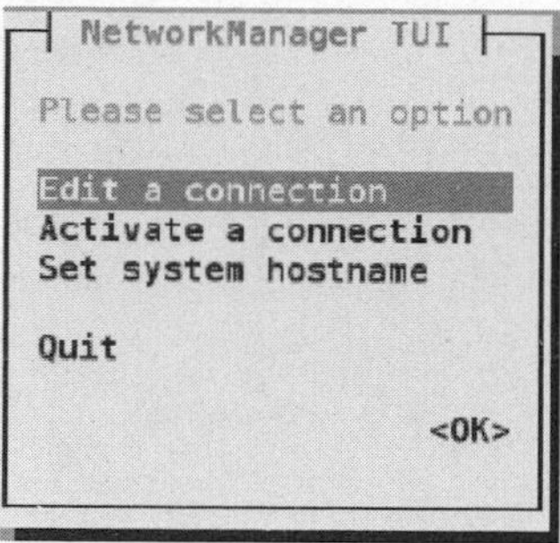

Figure 14-8 nmtui main screen

update the network-related configuration files automatically! To view the existing network connections, simply enter `nmcli con` or just `nmcli`, as shown here:

```
[root@localhost ~]# nmcli
ens32: connected to Wired connection 1
     "Intel 82540EM Gigabit Ethernet Controller (PRO/1000 MT Desktop Adapter)"
     ethernet (e1000), 08:00:27:6B:12:8C, hw, mtu 1500
     ip4 default
     inet4 10.0.2.15/24
     route4 169.254.0.0/16
     inet6 fe80::a00:27ff:fe6b:128c/64

lo: unmanaged
     loopback (unknown), 00:00:00:00:00:00, sw, mtu 65536

DNS configuration:
     servers: 10.153.10.100 10.153.10.103
     interface: ens32
```

To determine the IP address of the `ens32` connection, use the `show` option to `nmcli`:

```
[root@localhost ~]# nmcli con show ens32 | grep IP4.ADDRESS
IP4.ADDRESS[1]:                  10.0.2.15/24
```

To add an IP address alias on the `ens32` connection, use the `modify` option to `nmcli` and then activate the connection with the up option:

```
[root@localhost ~]# nmcli con modify ens32 +ipv4.addresses 10.0.2.14/24
[root@localhost ~]# nmcli con up ens32
Connection successfully activated
```

Again, use `modify` to remove the alias:

```
[root@localhost ~]# nmcli con modify ens32 -ipv4.addresses 10.0.2.14/24
[root@localhost ~]# nmcli con up ens32
Connection successfully activated
```

If the `BOOTPROTO` option is defined as DHCP and the DHCP server happens to be down when a request for an IP address is made, it is not necessary to reboot. Simply run `dhclient` at the shell prompt after the DHCP server is available. To acquire an address

```
root@openSUSE:/
File  Edit  View  Search  Terminal  Help
openSUSE:/ # dhclient ens32 -v
Internet Systems Consortium DHCP Client 4.2.5-P1
Copyright 2004-2013 Internet Systems Consortium.
All rights reserved.
For info, please visit https://www.isc.org/software/dhcp/

Listening on LPF/ens32/00:0c:29:b0:9f:b5
Sending on   LPF/ens32/00:0c:29:b0:9f:b5
Sending on   Socket/fallback
DHCPDISCOVER on ens32 to 255.255.255.255 port 67 interval 3
DHCPOFFER from 10.0.0.1
DHCPREQUEST on ens32 to 255.255.255.255 port 67
DHCPACK from 10.0.0.1
bound to 10.0.0.83 -- renewal in 41783 seconds.
```

Figure 14-9 Using `dhclient` to obtain an IP address lease

for a specific interface, enter `dhclient <interface>`. For example, `dhclient ens32` specifies that the interface get its IP address from the DHCP server. This is shown in Figure 14-9.

Exercise 14-1: Working with Network Interfaces

In this exercise, you practice using the `ifconfig` command to manage your network interface. You can perform this exercise using the CentOS virtual machine that comes with this book.

VIDEO Please watch the Exercise 14-1 video for a demonstration on how to perform this task.

Complete the following:

1. Boot your Linux system and log in as your **`student1`** user.
2. Open a terminal session.
3. Switch to your root user account by entering **`su -`** followed by the password.
4. At the shell prompt, enter **`ip addr show`**. Record the following information about your Ethernet interface:
    - MAC address
    - IP address
    - Broadcast address
    - Subnet mask

5. At the shell prompt, use the **cd** command to change to the /etc/sysconfig/network-scripts directory.
6. Use the **ls** command to identify the configuration file for your network board.
7. Use the **cat** command to view the contents of the configuration file for your Ethernet network interface board.
8. Bring your interface down by entering **ip link set enp0s17 down** at the shell prompt.
9. Bring your interface back up by entering **ip link set enp0s17 up** at the shell prompt.
10. Change the IP address assigned to your Ethernet network interface to 192.168.1.100 by entering **ip addr add 192.168.1.100 dev enp0s17** at the shell prompt.
11. Enter **ip addr show** again and verify that the change was applied.
12. Use the **ip addr show** command again to change your IP configuration parameters back to their original values.
13. If you have a DHCP server on your network segment, modify your network interface configuration to use DHCP and then dynamically assign an IP address to your Ethernet board by entering **dhclient enp0s17** at the shell prompt.

Configuring Routing Parameters

Within the IP protocol, routers do just what their name implies: they route data across multiple networks to deliver information to a destination. Routers operate at the Network layer and are used to connect various networks together.

Routers are usually implemented in conjunction with a gateway and need to be defined when setting a static network. The router hardware itself may be as simple as a computer system with two NICs installed, or it may be a specialized hardware appliance dedicated to routing.

Routers determine the best way to get data to the right destination by maintaining a routing table of available routes. Routers use an algorithm that evaluates distance, congestion, and network status to determine the best route to the destination. Even if not configured as a router, every Linux system maintains a routing table in RAM to determine where to send data on a network.

To configure the default router address on a Red Hat–class system, update the /etc/sysconfig/network-scripts/ifcfg-<interface> file with the GATEWAY parameter, as shown here:

```
[root@localhost ~]# tail -7 /etc/sysconfig/network-scripts/ifcfg-ens32
DEVICE=ens32
BOOTPROTO=static
ONBOOT=yes
IPADDR=192.168.1.81
NETMASK=255.255.255.0
BROADCAST=192.168.1.255
GATEWAY=192.168.1.1
```

To configure the default router address on a Debian-class system, update the `/etc/default/interfaces` file and add a line for the gateway, as shown here:

```
[root@localhost ~]# tail -7 /etc/network/interfaces
auto ens32
iface ens32 inet static
        address 192.168.1.81
        netmask 255.255.255.0
        broadcast 192.168.1.255
        ## default gateway for ens32
        gateway 192.168.1.1
```

NOTE Use IP addresses, not hostnames, in this file. If the DNS server were to go down or become unreachable, routing would be disabled.

After adding the gateway settings, simply restart the network, as shown here:

```
[root@localhost ~]# systemctl restart network
```

For the CompTIA Linux+ exam, you need be familiar with how to manage routes with the `route` command at the shell prompt. Use the `route` command to display or modify the routing table on the Linux host. If you enter `route` without options, it simply displays the current routing table, as shown in this example:

```
[root@localhost ~]# route
Kernel IP routing table
Destination     Gateway         Genmask         Flags Metric Ref    Use Iface
default         10.0.0.1        0.0.0.0         UG    0      0        0 ens32
10.0.0.0        *               255.255.255.0   U     0      0        0 ens32
loopback        *               255.0.0.0       U     0      0        0 lo
```

Note that the default gateway is 10.0.0.1 because it is listed under the Gateway setting, and the `G` is shown under Flags (the `U` means that the connection is up).

You can add routes to the host's routing table by entering

```
route add -net <network_address> netmask <netmask> gw <router_address>
```

For example, suppose you need to add a route to the 192.168.2.0/24 network through the router with an IP address of 10.0.0.254. In this case, you would enter the following:

```
[root@localhost ~]# route add -net 192.168.2.0/24 gw 10.0.0.254
```

To remove existing routes, use

```
route del -net <network_address> netmask <netmask> gw <router_address>
```

Here's an example:

```
[root@localhost ~]# route del -net 192.168.2.0/24 gw 10.0.0.254
```

Finally, to set the default route, enter `route add default gw <router_address>` at the shell prompt. For example, if you want to add 10.0.0.254 as your default gateway router, enter this:

```
[root@localhost ~]# route add default gw 10.0.0.254
```

NOTE Changes made with the `route` or `ip route` command are not persistent and are lost on reboot.

The `ip` command can also be used to manage routing. For example, to view the routing table, enter `ip route show` or simply `ip route` at the shell prompt, as shown here:

```
[root@localhost ~]# ip route
default via 10.0.0.1 dev ens32
10.0.0.0/24 dev ens32  proto kernel  scope link  src 10.0.0.83
127.0.0.0/8 dev lo  scope link
```

To add a static route to the routing table, enter the following at the shell prompt:

```
ip route add <network/prefix> via <router_ip_address> dev <interface>
```

The following example shows adding route 10.0.0.254 to the 192.168.5.0/24 network:

```
[root@localhost ~]# ip route add 192.168.5.0/24 via 10.0.0.254 dev ens32
[root@localhost ~]# ip route show
default via 10.0.0.1 dev ens32
10.0.0.0/24 dev ens32  proto kernel  scope link  src 10.0.0.83
127.0.0.0/8 dev lo  scope link
192.168.5.0/24 via 10.0.0.254 dev ens32
```

To remove a route from the routing table, enter `ip route del <network/prefix>` at the shell prompt. For example, to remove the 192.168.5.0/24 route, enter the following:

```
[root@localhost ~]# ip route del 192.168.5.0/24
```

Troubleshooting Routing Network Configuration Issues

After adding the default gateway, if you still cannot access the Internet, make certain the router is up by running the `route` command. If the default router does not appear and other computers cannot connect to the Internet, that means your router is down and needs to be either restarted or replaced.

Configuring Name Resolver Settings

When you open a browser window and enter http://www.google.com in the URL field, the browser, IP stack, and operating system have no clue where to go to get the requested information. To make this work, the local system needs to first resolve the domain name into an IP address.

In the old days, basic hostname-to-IP-address resolution was performed by the `/etc/hosts` file, which contains IP-address-to-hostname mappings.

NOTE The `/etc/hosts` file still exists on Linux systems. In fact, it is the first name resolver used by default. Only if a record for the requested domain name does not exist in the `hosts` file will the operating system then try to resolve the hostname using DNS. It is important to manage the `hosts` file very carefully because it can be exploited.

Malware attempts to rewrite the `/etc/hosts` file with name mappings that point to fake banking websites, but instead are elaborate pharming websites designed to steal the user's personal information.

The `hosts` file contains one line per host record. The syntax is

```
<IP_address>  <host_name>  <alias>
```

For example, consider the following `/etc/hosts` file entry:

```
192.168.1.1      mylinux.mydom.com      mylinux
```

This record resolves either the fully qualified DNS name of `mylinux.mydom.com` or the alias (CNAME) of `mylinux` to an IP address of 192.168.1.1. Usually this file contains only the IP address and hostname of the local system, but other entries may be added as well.

Using the `/etc/hosts` file to resolve hostnames works just fine; however, it really isn't feasible as the sole means of name resolution. The file would have to be huge in order to resolve all the domain names used by hosts on the Internet. In addition, an administrator would have to manually add, remove, and modify hostname mappings in the file whenever a domain name changed on the Internet. What a nightmare!

A better option is to submit the domain name to a DNS server. When a DNS server receives a name resolution request, it matches the domain name submitted with an IP address and returns it to the requesting system. The system can then contact the specified host using its IP address. Here's how it works:

1. The system needing to resolve a hostname sends a request to the DNS server it has been configured to use on IP port 53. If the DNS server is authoritative for the zone where the requested hostname resides, it responds with the appropriate IP address. If not, the process continues to step 2.

NOTE A DNS server is considered to be authoritative if it has a record for the domain name being requested in its database of name mappings.

2. The DNS server sends a request to a root-level DNS server. There are 13 root-level DNS servers on the Internet. Every DNS server is automatically configured with the IP addresses of these servers. These root-level DNS servers are configured with records that resolve to authoritative DNS servers for each top-level domain (`.com`, `.gov`, `.edu`, `.au`, `.de`, `.uk`, `.ca`, and so on).
3. The DNS server responds to the client system with the IP address mapped to the hostname, and the respective system is contacted using this IP address.

NOTE Once this process happens for a particular name mapping, most DNS servers will cache the mapping for a period of time. That way, if a resolution request for the same hostname is received again, the DNS server can respond directly to the client without going through this whole process again.

Therefore, to make this system work, the administrator must provide the system with the IP address of the DNS server to use. This is configured in the `/etc/resolv.conf` file. This file defines the search prefix and the name servers to use. Here is some sample content from a CentOS system's `/etc/resolv.conf` file:

```
search mydom.com
nameserver 8.8.8.8
nameserver 8.8.4.4
nameserver 192.168.2.1
```

As can be seen in this example, the file contains two types of entries:

- **`search`** Specifies the domain name that should be used to fill out incomplete hostnames. For example, if the system is trying to resolve a hostname of `WS1`, the name will be automatically converted to the fully qualified domain name of `WS1.mydom.com`. The syntax is `search <domain>`.
- **`nameserver`** Specifies the IP address of the DNS server to use for name resolution. You can configure up to three DNS servers. If the first server fails or is otherwise unreachable, the next DNS server is used. The syntax is `nameserver <DNS_server_IP_address>`.

Use the `/etc/nsswitch.conf` (name service switch) file to define the order in which services will be used for name resolution. Here are two lines of the file you need to be concerned with:

```
hosts:        files dns
networks:     files dns
```

These two entries specify that the `/etc/hosts` file (`files`) is consulted first for name resolution. If there is no applicable entry, the query is then sent to the DNS server (`dns`) specified in the `/etc/resolv.conf` file. To search `dns` first and then `files`, change the order within `/etc/nsswitch.conf` as shown here:

```
hosts:        dns files
networks:     dns files
```

Troubleshooting Name Resolution Failure

If you are having trouble accessing a website, first make sure your network connection is running correctly using `ping` and `traceroute`. Once the connection has been verified, double-check your entries within `/etc/resolv.conf` and `/etc/nsswitch.conf`.

If the `nameserver` field is undefined within `/etc/resolv.conf` or there is no `dns` entry within `/etc/nsswitch.conf`, that is likely the trouble. After making the corrections, you can validate success again using `ping` and `traceroute`.

Configuring IPv6

As mentioned earlier, the world's supply of registered IP addresses is exhausted. To address this issue, most organizations reduce the number of registered IP addresses that they need by implementing a NAT router. However, using a NAT router is a short-term solution. To fully address this issue, a new version of the IP protocol was released that handles the number of IP addresses the modern computing world needs.

To accomplish this, IP version 6 (IPv6) is rolling out around the world. IPv6 is expected to completely replace IPv4 over the next decade. Instead of 32 bits, IPv6 defines 128-bit IP addresses, which allows for 340,282,366,920,938,463,463,374,607,431,768,211,456 total unique IP addresses. (Hopefully, this will be enough!)

IPv6 addresses are composed of eight four-character hexadecimal numbers (called *hextets*), separated by colons instead of periods. Each hextet is represented as a hexadecimal number between 0 and FFFF. For example, a valid IPv6 address is 128 bits and appears like 35BC:FA77:4898:DAFC:200C:FBBC:A007:8973.

For an IPv6 address of 1:2:3:a:b:c:d:e, assume each hextet is led by zeros, so this address is the same as 0001:0002:0003:000a:000b:000c:000d:000e.

EXAM TIP Because IPv6 addresses are so long, they will frequently be abbreviated. If the address contains a long string of multiple zeros, omit them by specifying ::. If 0000 occurs more than once in an address, the abbreviation can only be used once. For example, the IPv6 address 2001:0000:3a4c:1115:0000:0000:1a2f:1a2b can be shown as either 2001::3a4c:1115:0000:0000:1a2f:1a2b or 2001:0000:3a4c:1115::1a2f:1a2b.

There are several configuration options when it comes to IPv6 addressing. The first is to use static assignment. As with IPv4, static IPv6 address assignments require you to manually assign the entire 128-bit IPv6 address and prefix to the host. This can be done from the shell prompt using a command-line utility such as `ifconfig` or `ip`. Alternatively, you can manually enter the address and prefix in the appropriate interface configuration file in `/etc/sysconfig/network` or use `nmcli`.

The final IPv6 address configuration option is to use DHCP. As with IPv4, IPv6 address assignments can be made automatically using an updated version of DHCP called DHCPv6.

Troubleshooting Network Problems

Getting the network interface installed is only half the battle. To enable communications, you need to use a variety of testing and monitoring tools to make sure the network itself is working properly. You need to understand the following topics to pass the CompTIA Linux+ exam:

- Using a standardized troubleshooting model
- Using `ping`
- Using `netstat`
- Using `traceroute`
- Using `nc`
- Using name resolution tools
- Synchronizing time on a network

NOTE If necessary, install these utilities by running the following on CentOS-class systems as `root`. This suite includes `net-tools` and `iproute2`:

```
# yum install nfs-utils nmap-ncat samba-client iproute
```

Using a Standardized Troubleshooting Model

Being a good troubleshooter is a key part of being an effective Linux system administrator. Some new administrators seem to have an intrinsic sense to troubleshoot problems; others turn five-minute solutions into five-hour puzzles. The reason for this is that troubleshooting is part art form, part science. Just as it is difficult for some to learn to draw, sculpt, or paint, it is also difficult for some to learn to troubleshoot.

There are three keys to troubleshooting effectively:

- Using a solid troubleshooting procedure
- Obtaining a working knowledge of troubleshooting tools
- Gaining a lot of experience troubleshooting problems

The last point is beyond the scope of this book. The only way to gain troubleshooting experience is to spend a couple years in the field. However, we can work with the first two points. In the last part of this chapter, we will focus specifically on troubleshooting network issues. However, the procedure we discuss here can be broadly applied to any system problem.

Many new system administrators make a key mistake when they troubleshoot system or network problems. Instead of using a methodical troubleshooting approach, they start trying to implement fixes before they really know what the problem is. The administrator tries one fix after another, hoping that one of them will repair the problem.

Even though troubleshooting models are not *covered on the CompTIA Linux+ exam,* here is a suggested troubleshooting model as a starting point for a new system administrator:

- **Step 1: Gather information.** This is a critical step. Determine exactly what has happened. What are the symptoms and error messages? How extensive is the problem?
- **Step 2: Identify what has changed.** In this step, identify what has changed in the system. Has new software or hardware been installed? Did a user change something?
- **Step 3: Create a hypothesis.** Develop several hypotheses that could explain the problem. Check FAQs and knowledgebases available on the Internet. Consult with peers to validate your hypotheses. Narrow the results down to one or two likely causes.
- **Step 4: Determine the appropriate fix.** Use peers, FAQs, and experience to identify the steps needed to fix the problem. Identify side effects of implementing the fix and account for them. Often, the fix may have side effects that are worse than the original problem.
- **Step 5: Implement the fix.** Note that in this troubleshooting model, much research is done before implementing a fix! This increases the likelihood of success. After implementing the fix, be sure to verify that the fix actually repaired the problem.
- **Step 6: Ensure user satisfaction.** Educate users as to how to keep the problem from recurring. Communicate with the users' supervisors and ensure they know that the problem has been fixed.
- **Step 7: Document the solution.** Finally, document the solution. If it occurs again a year later, the team can quickly identify the problem and know how to fix it.

Using this methodology, you can learn to be a very effective troubleshooter, gaining hands-on experience in the real world.

In addition to using a troubleshooting methodology, you also need to know how to use a variety of network troubleshooting tools for the CompTIA Linux+ exam.

Using `ping`

The `ping` utility is one of the handiest tools in the networking virtual toolbox. The `ping` command is used to test connectivity between hosts on the network. Ping works by sending an ICMP echo request packet from the source system to the destination. The destination system then responds with an ICMP echo response packet. This process is shown in Figure 14-10.

If the ICMP echo response packet is received by the sending system, you know three things:

- Your network interface is working correctly.
- The destination system is up and working correctly.
- The network hardware between your system and the destination system is working correctly.

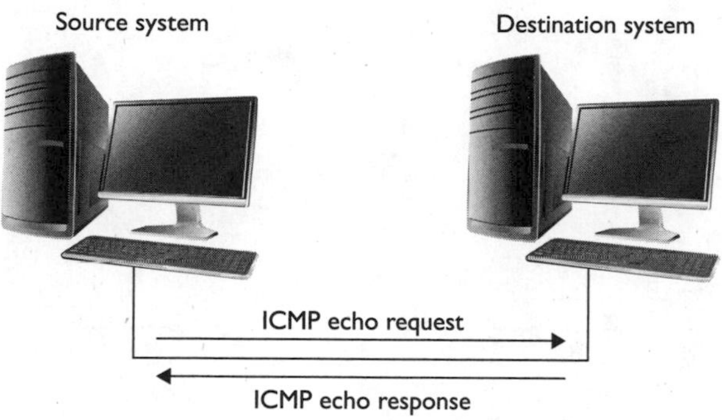

Figure 14-10 Using ping

CAUTION Be warned that many host-based firewalls used by many operating systems are configured by default to not respond to ICMP echo request packets. This is done to prevent a variety of denial of service (DoS) attacks that utilize a flood of ping requests. This configuration can give the false impression that the destination system is down.

The basic syntax for using ping is ping <destination_IP_address>. This causes ICMP echo request packets to be sent to the specified host. For example, enter ping 192.168.2.1 to test a host with this address. This is shown in Figure 14-11.

Notice in Figure 14-11 that the results of each ping sent are shown on a single line. Each line displays the size of the echo response packet (64 bytes), where it came from (192.168.2.1), its time-to-live value (63), and the round-trip time (4.25 ms to 1.01 ms).

NOTE The time-to-live (TTL) value specifies the number of routers the packet is allowed to cross before being thrown away.

By default, the ping utility will continue sending ping requests to the specified host until Ctrl-c is pressed to stop it. Use the -c option with the ping command to specify

```
root@openSUSE:/
File  Edit  View  Search  Terminal  Help
openSUSE:/ # ping 192.168.2.1
PING 192.168.2.1 (192.168.2.1) 56(84) bytes of data.
64 bytes from 192.168.2.1: icmp_seq=1 ttl=63 time=4.25 ms
64 bytes from 192.168.2.1: icmp_seq=2 ttl=63 time=2.52 ms
64 bytes from 192.168.2.1: icmp_seq=3 ttl=63 time=1.01 ms
64 bytes from 192.168.2.1: icmp_seq=4 ttl=63 time=1.07 ms
64 bytes from 192.168.2.1: icmp_seq=5 ttl=63 time=1.09 ms
```

Figure 14-11 Pinging a host by IP address

```
root@openSUSE:/
File Edit View Search Terminal Help
openSUSE:/ # ping www.google.com
PING www.google.com (74.125.239.144) 56(84) bytes of data.
64 bytes from nuq05s02-in-f16.1e100.net (74.125.239.144): icmp_seq=1 ttl=54 time=30.7 ms
64 bytes from nuq05s02-in-f16.1e100.net (74.125.239.144): icmp_seq=2 ttl=54 time=31.2 ms
64 bytes from nuq05s02-in-f16.1e100.net (74.125.239.144): icmp_seq=3 ttl=54 time=30.9 ms
64 bytes from nuq05s02-in-f16.1e100.net (74.125.239.144): icmp_seq=4 ttl=54 time=31.5 ms
64 bytes from nuq05s02-in-f16.1e100.net (74.125.239.144): icmp_seq=5 ttl=54 time=29.5 ms
```

Figure 14-12 Pinging by hostname

a number of times to ping. For example, enter `ping -c 10 192.168.2.1` to ping 10 times and then exit.

Pinging by hostname is shown in Figure 14-12.

Pinging with a hostname can be a valuable troubleshooting tool because it signals if there is a problem with the DNS server. For example, pinging by IP address works but pinging by hostname does not.

Using `netstat`

The `netstat` utility is another powerful tool in the virtual toolbox. This utility can do the following:

- List network connections
- Display the routing table
- Display information about the network interface

The syntax for using `netstat` is to enter `netstat <option>` at the shell prompt. Use the options listed in Table 14-6.

EXAM TIP The `ss` ("show sockets") command is the replacement command for `netstat` and has more functionality to better examine network status. Try running the command `ss -neopa` and observe the status from all sockets.

Table 14-6 `netstat` Options

`netstat` **Option**	**Description**
`-a`	Lists all listening and nonlistening sockets
`-i`	Displays statistics for your network interfaces
`-r`	Displays your routing table

Using `traceroute`

When information is sent to an IP host that does not reside on your local network segment, the packets will be sent to the default gateway router. This router will then use a variety of routing protocols to figure out how to get the packets to the destination. In the process, the packets are transferred from router to router to router to get them there, as shown in Figure 14-13.

This is the advantage of an IP-based network. A network administrator can connect multiple networks together using routers and transfer data between them. The routing protocols used by routers dynamically determine the best route for packets to take based on system load. The route taken can change as network conditions change.

The `traceroute` utility is used to trace the route a packet traverses through these routers to arrive at its destination. It does this using the same ICMP echo request and ICMP echo response packets used by the `ping` utility, but it manipulates the TTL parameter of those packets. As a result, an ICMP echo response packet is sent back to the source system from each router the packets cross as they work their way through the network to the destination host, providing a list that shows the route between the source and destination systems.

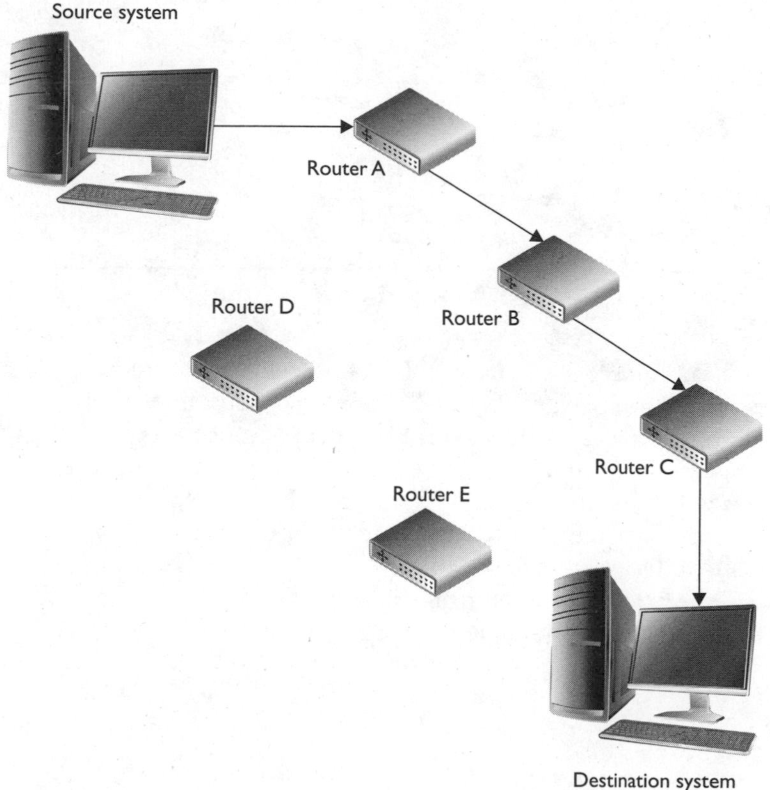

Figure 14-13 Routing in an IP network

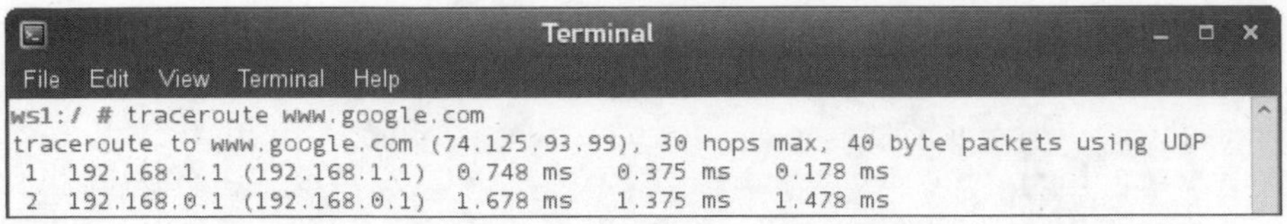

```
Terminal
File  Edit  View  Terminal  Help
ws1:/ # traceroute www.google.com
traceroute to www.google.com (74.125.93.99), 30 hops max, 40 byte packets using UDP
 1  192.168.1.1 (192.168.1.1)  0.748 ms   0.375 ms   0.178 ms
 2  192.168.0.1 (192.168.0.1)  1.678 ms   1.375 ms   1.478 ms
```

Figure 14-14 Using `traceroute`

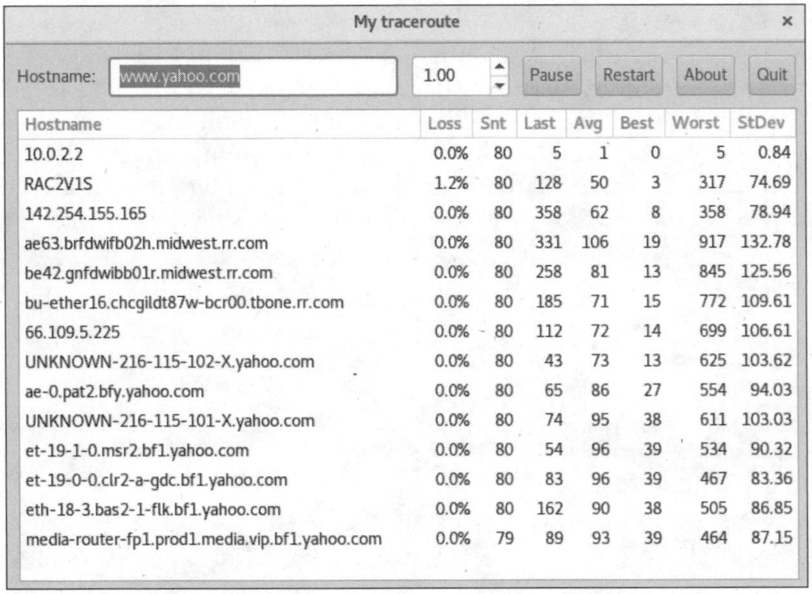

My traceroute

Hostname: www.yahoo.com 1.00 Pause Restart About Quit

Hostname	Loss	Snt	Last	Avg	Best	Worst	StDev
10.0.2.2	0.0%	80	5	1	0	5	0.84
RAC2V1S	1.2%	80	128	50	3	317	74.69
142.254.155.165	0.0%	80	358	62	8	358	78.94
ae63.brfdwifb02h.midwest.rr.com	0.0%	80	331	106	19	917	132.78
be42.gnfdwibb01r.midwest.rr.com	0.0%	80	258	81	13	845	125.56
bu-ether16.chcgildt87w-bcr00.tbone.rr.com	0.0%	80	185	71	15	772	109.61
66.109.5.225	0.0%	80	112	72	14	699	106.61
UNKNOWN-216-115-102-X.yahoo.com	0.0%	80	43	73	13	625	103.62
ae-0.pat2.bfy.yahoo.com	0.0%	80	65	86	27	554	94.03
UNKNOWN-216-115-101-X.yahoo.com	0.0%	80	74	95	38	611	103.03
et-19-1-0.msr2.bf1.yahoo.com	0.0%	80	54	96	39	534	90.32
et-19-0-0.clr2-a-gdc.bf1.yahoo.com	0.0%	80	83	96	39	467	83.36
eth-18-3.bas2-1-flk.bf1.yahoo.com	0.0%	80	162	90	38	505	86.85
media-router-fp1.prod1.media.vip.bf1.yahoo.com	0.0%	79	89	93	39	464	87.15

Figure 14-15 Output of the `mtr` command

This utility can be very useful in troubleshooting communication problems between networks, because it can track down which router is not working correctly. The syntax for using this utility is `traceroute <destination_hostname_or_IP_address>`. The `traceroute` command creates one line for each router the packets cross as they make their way to the destination. This is shown in Figure 14-14.

As you can see in Figure 14-14, the IP address of the router is displayed along with round-trip time statistics.

The `mtr` ("my traceroute") command is a network diagnostics tool that combines the functionality of `traceroute` and `ping`. To see `mtr www.yahoo.com` results, see Figure 14-15. The output displays the quality of the connections.

Using `nc`

The `nc` ("netcat") command is a very useful tool for testing network communications between hosts. It goes one step beyond the `ping` command and establishes a connection between two network hosts. One way to use this command is to open a listening socket on one host and then connect to that socket from another host. In the following example, the listening socket is enabled using the `-l` ("dash el") option using port 2388:

```
[root@10.0.0.83 ~]# nc -l 2388
```

With a listening socket established on the server, the client can connect to it using the `nc` command again, this time entering the IP address of the server and the listening port:

```
[root@fs5 ~]# nc 10.0.0.83 2388
```

Once the connection is established, any text typed at the prompt of the client system will appear on the netcat server, as shown here:

```
[root@fs5 ~]# nc 10.0.0.83 2388
This is a test.
[root@10.0.0.83 ~]# nc -l 2388
This is a test.
```

EXAM TIP Make sure the appropriate ports in the firewalls are open on both systems; otherwise, the test will fail!

Using Name Resolution Tools

Using DNS for name resolution works great—until it doesn't work! Fortunately, there are several tools available to troubleshoot name resolution on a network:

- `dig`
- `host`
- `nslookup`
- `resolvectl`

NOTE To install these utilities, run the following on CentOS-class systems as `root`:

```
# yum install bind-utils
```

`dig`

The Domain Information Groper, or `dig`, utility performs DNS lookups on the network and displays detailed information about the hostname being resolved from the DNS server, as configured in the `/etc/resolv.conf` file. The syntax is `dig <hostname>`, as shown in Figure 14-16.

The output from `dig` is considerably more extensive than that displayed by other DNS troubleshooting tools such as `nslookup` and `host` in that it displays more than just the IP address of the host. It also lists the authoritative name server for the host and zone.

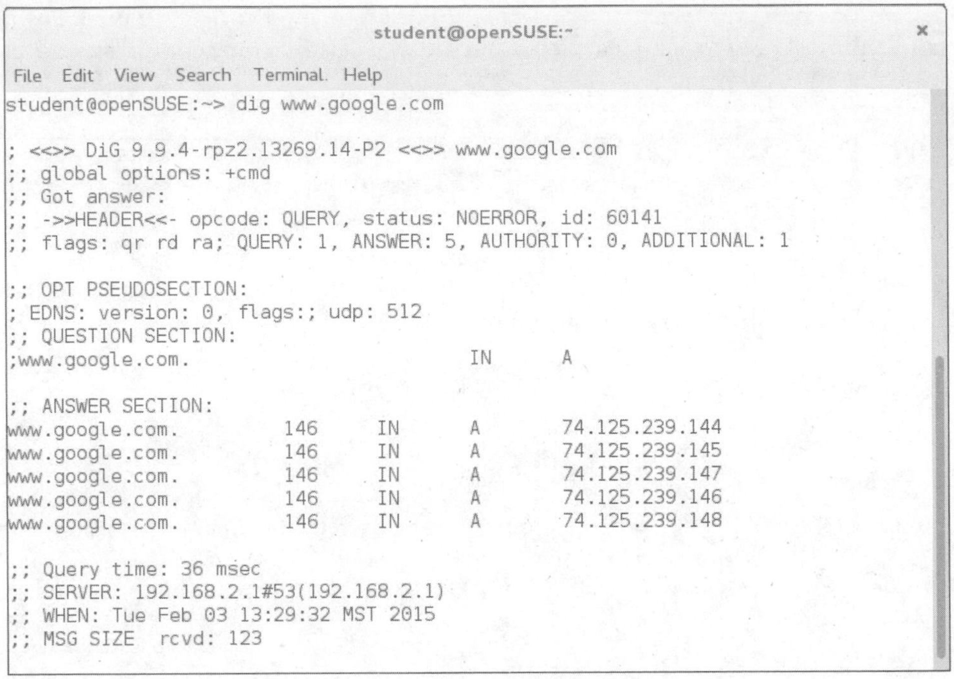

```
student@openSUSE:~
File  Edit  View  Search  Terminal  Help
student@openSUSE:~> dig www.google.com

; <<>> DiG 9.9.4-rpz2.13269.14-P2 <<>> www.google.com
;; global options: +cmd
;; Got answer:
;; ->>HEADER<<- opcode: QUERY, status: NOERROR, id: 60141
;; flags: qr rd ra; QUERY: 1, ANSWER: 5, AUTHORITY: 0, ADDITIONAL: 1

;; OPT PSEUDOSECTION:
; EDNS: version: 0, flags:; udp: 512
;; QUESTION SECTION:
;www.google.com.                   IN      A

;; ANSWER SECTION:
www.google.com.        146     IN      A       74.125.239.144
www.google.com.        146     IN      A       74.125.239.145
www.google.com.        146     IN      A       74.125.239.147
www.google.com.        146     IN      A       74.125.239.146
www.google.com.        146     IN      A       74.125.239.148

;; Query time: 36 msec
;; SERVER: 192.168.2.1#53(192.168.2.1)
;; WHEN: Tue Feb 03 13:29:32 MST 2015
;; MSG SIZE  rcvd: 123
```

Figure 14-16 Using `dig` to resolve a hostname

host

The `host` command resolves hostnames. Whereas the `dig` command provides extensive name resolution information, `host` provides simple, quick information. The syntax is similar to that of `dig`. Enter `host <hostname>` at the shell prompt. An example of using `host` is shown here:

```
[root@localhost ~]# host www.google.com
www.google.com has address 74.125.239.49
www.google.com has address 74.125.239.48
www.google.com has address 74.125.239.50
www.google.com has address 74.125.239.52
www.google.com has address 74.125.239.51
www.google.com has IPv6 address 2607:f8b0:4005:800::1011
```

nslookup

In addition to `host` and `dig`, `nslookup` can test name resolution, as shown here:

```
[root@localhost ~]# nslookup www.google.com
Server:          192.168.1.1
Address:         192.168.1.1#53

Non-authoritative answer:
Name:    www.google.com
Address:  172.217.8.196
```

`resolvectl`

The `resolvectl` command is a useful tool to display your DNS server. Here's partial output of the `resolvectl` (or optionally, `resolvectl status`) command:

```
openSUSE:~ # resolvectl
     <output omitted>
Current DNS Server: 192.168.1.1
       DNS Servers: 192.168.1.1
       <output omitted>
```

Use the `query` option to do a forward or reverse lookup of a domain, as shown here:

```
openSUSE:~ # resolvectl query www.jordanteam.com
www.jordanteam.com: 204.44.192.54
                    (jordanteam.com)
-- Information acquired via protocol DNS in 59.6ms
-- Data is authenticated: no
```

EXAM TIP Use the `whois` command to get ownership information of a website domain, if the owner has not blocked it. The command `whois <domain_name>` will list their name, phone number, and address.

Synchronizing Time on a Network

An option for network time synchronization is to use the Network Time Protocol (NTP) to sync time with a network time provider. If there is a time differential with the network time provider, NTP adjusts time gradually in small increments until time is eventually synchronized. The `ntpd` daemon on Linux synchronizes time with the NTP time provider and operates over IP port 123.

Here are several key NTP concepts that are *not* tested on the CompTIA Linux+ exam but are good to know as you set up your timeserver environment:

- **Stratum** NTP uses the concept of *stratum* to define a hierarchy of NTP servers:
  - **Stratum 1** Time servers that get their time from a reference time source, such as the Naval atomic clock; for example, `tick.usno.navy.mil` and `tock.usno.navy.mil`
  - **Stratum 2** Time servers that get their time from stratum 1 servers
  - **Stratum 3** Time servers that get their time from stratum 2 servers

To define your time server, modify `/etc/ntp.conf`. The first thing you need to do is ensure that the following entries exist for the local clock, which is used if the time server is not available:

```
OpenSUSE # cat /etc/ntp.conf
server 127.127.1.0 # local clock (LCL)
fudge 127.127.1.0 stratum 10 # LCL is unsynchronized
```

These directives tell the ntpd daemon to get time from the local clock in the event it can't reach any of the configured NTP time providers.

Next, add entries to the file for the network time providers to sync time with. Here is the syntax:

```
server <time_server_IP_address_or_DNS_name>
```

You can specify the IP address or DNS name of any NTP time provider you want to use. Visit https://support.ntp.org/Servers/WebHome to view a list of publicly available NTP time providers.

If you wish, use an *NTP pool time server* from the http://pool.ntp.org domain, which uses a DNS round robin to make a random selection from a pool of time providers who have volunteered to be in the pool. That way, no one public NTP server is overloaded with time synchronization requests. To use this, simply add the following server directive in /etc/ntp.conf:

```
server pool.ntp.org
```

To start ntpd, enter `systemctl start ntp` at the shell prompt. You can verify that it started correctly by entering `systemctl status ntp` at the shell prompt.

Once the ntpd daemon has started, you can use two commands to keep track of how the ntpd daemon is working:

- **`ntpq -p`** This command queries the status of the ntpd daemon. Here is an example:

```
openSUSE:~ # ntpq -p
     remote           refid      st t when poll reach   delay   offset  jitter
==============================================================================
*LOCAL(0)        .LOCL.          10 l   14   64    3    0.000    0.000   0.001
 helium.constant 18.26.4.105      2 u   12   64    1   96.614  -31.777   0.001
```

- **`ntptrace`** The ntptrace utility traces how the time consumer is receiving time from the provider. It lists the time provider's name, its stratum, and its time offset from the system clock on the local system.

Keeping Computer Clocks Accurate with chrony

The chrony utility uses two programs to keep clocks accurate, chronyd and chronyc. The chronyd utility is the background program for managing time, and chronyc is the user's command-line interface to track and verify time.

The chrony configuration file is /etc/chrony.conf, and an example is shown here:

```
openSUSE:~ # cat /etc/chrony.conf
server 0.pool.ntp.org
server 1.pool.ntp.org
server 2.pool.ntp.org
```

Start chrony by running systemctl start chronyd. To verify activity, run chronyc tracking. Partial output is shown here:

```
openSUSE:~ # chronyc tracking
Reference ID     : 481E2358 (t2.time.bf1.yahoo.com)
Stratum         : 3
Ref time (UTC)  : Sun Oct 16 02:48:24 2025
System time     : 1158969.000000000 seconds slow of NTP time
.
<output omitted>
.
```

The Reference ID represents the name and/or IP address of the time server. The Stratum is the number of hops away from a stratum 1 time server. Ref time is the UTC last measured from the time server.

One benefit of chrony over NTP is that it helps keep time for systems that normally are powered down or disconnected from the Internet.

Exercise 14-2: Working with Network Commands

In this exercise, you will practice using network commands to manage and troubleshoot your network interface. This exercise assumes that you have a connection to the Internet. You can perform this exercise using the CentOS virtual machine that comes with this book.

VIDEO Please watch the Exercise 14-2 video for a demonstration on how to perform this task.

Complete the following steps:

1. Boot your Linux system and log in as your **student1** user.
2. Open a terminal session.
3. Switch to your root user account by entering **su -** followed by the password.
4. Test connectivity by entering **ping www.google.com** at the shell prompt. Your system should resolve the hostname into an IP address and send ICMP echo request packets to it. (If your system isn't connected to the Internet, this step won't work.)

NOTE If you are unable to ping the remote website, verify that an IP address has been assigned using the ifconfig command. If an address has not been assigned, enter systemctl restart network to reload the network configuration.

5. Display summary information about your network interface by entering **netstat -s | more** at the shell prompt. Review the information displayed.

6. Trace the route to www.google.com by entering **`traceroute www.google.com`** at the shell prompt. Note the various routers crossed as your packets traverse the Internet to www.google.com.
7. Generate extended name resolution about www.google.com by entering **`dig www.google.com`** at the shell prompt.

Understanding Network-Based Filesystems

There are two network-based filesystems you need to be familiar with for the CompTIA Linux+ exam:

- Network File System (NFS)
- Samba

NFS allows users to mount network filesystems on vendor-neutral networks. Samba allows Linux systems to mount network filesystems on Windows-based networks. You should understand the basics of accessing these filesystems.

Network File System (NFS)

Most networks allow sharing of filesystems over NFS. In order for NFS to function properly, all systems need to run NFS. For Windows systems, this means installing PC-NFS. NFS Manager is built into macOS.

Once the NFS servers are properly set up, their "shares" are accessible to NFS clients. To view the possible shares, run the `showmount` command:

```
[root@localhost ~]# showmount -e system5
Export list for system5:
/music
/sales
/users
```

To access a shared NFS directory, use the `mount` command and the name of the NFS server (`system5`), as shown:

```
[root@localhost ~]# mkdir /mnt/sys5
[root@localhost ~]# mount -t nfs system5:/sales /mnt/sys5
```

There may be situations where an administrator attempts to mount a network filesystem but the remote system is down. NFS has a feature called *automounting* to alleviate this issue, which will automatically mount the remote filesystem once it becomes available.

Samba

For organizations that heavily rely on Windows systems, instead of installing PC-NFS on several Windows computers, they could take advantage of the SMB protocol available on

Windows networks. Once the Samba server is set up, the shared filesystems are viewable using the `smbclient` command:

```
[root@localhost ~]# smbclient -L win2 -U jim_angel

Server=[WIN2] User=[JIM_ANGEL] Workgroup=[WORKGROUP] Domain=[]

        Sharename       Type      Comment
        ---------       ----      -------
        ADMIN$          Disk      Remote Admin
        public          Disk      Public

        Music           Disk      Default share
        HPblack         Printer   HPblack
```

To access shared filesystems from Windows, use the `mount` command preceded by two forward slashes. This signifies that the mount is using SMB. An example follows from a system called `win2`:

```
[root@localhost ~]# mkdir /mnt/win2
[root@localhost ~]# mount //win2/Music /mnt/win2
```

NOTE Both NFS and Samba allow for shared directories to be available at boot time. Just add the shares to the `/etc/fstab` file.

Chapter Review

In this chapter, you learned how to set up networking on a Linux system. You will most likely work with Ethernet network boards and the IP protocol in most modern organizations.

The Internet Protocol (IP) works in conjunction with the Transmission Control Protocol (TCP) or the User Datagram Protocol (UDP) to fragment, transmit, defragment, and resequence network data to enable communications between hosts. We also looked at the Internet Control Message Protocol (ICMP), which is another core protocol in the IP protocol suite. The primary role of ICMP is to test and verify network communications between hosts.

Each host on the network must have a correctly configured, unique IP address assigned to it and the correct subnet mask assigned. The subnet mask defines how much of a given host's IP address is the network address. When viewed in binary form, any bit in the subnet mask that has a 1 in it represents a network address, and any bit with a 0 in it represents the host address. IP addresses are categorized into the following classes:

- **Class A** 255.0.0.0 = 11111111.00000000.00000000.00000000 binary
- **Class B** 255.255.0.0 = 11111111.11111111.00000000.00000000 binary
- **Class C** 255.255.255.0 = 11111111.11111111.11111111.00000000 binary

Hosts on the same network segment must have the same network address for them to communicate. Therefore, the same subnet mask must be assigned to each host.

To resolve domain names into IP addresses, the Linux system must also be configured with the IP address of the organization's DNS server. In addition, the system must be configured with the address of the default gateway to communicate with hosts on other network segments.

We also reviewed public and private IP addressing. Public networks are allowed on the Internet. Private networks are only allowed in local area networks (LANs). NAT routers hide a private network behind one or more public interfaces. IPv6 addresses are composed of eight four-character hexadecimal numbers, separated by colons instead of periods.

To assign the DNS server address or the default gateway address, edit the `/etc/resolv.conf` configuration file. To bring a network interface down, enter `ifdown` at the shell prompt. To bring it up, enter `ifup`. To use a DHCP server to dynamically assign IP address information to a Linux host, enter `dhclient <interface>` at the shell prompt.

This chapter discussed several command-line utilities you can use to test and monitor the network, such as `ping`, `traceroute`, and `mtr`.

The `nc` command establishes a connection between two hosts. First open a listening socket on one host and then connect to that socket from another host.

The tools to use to synchronize time via a network time server are NTP and `chrony`. Use `chrony` for systems that are often powered down.

Tools available for name resolution include `dig`, `host`, `resolvectl`, and `nslookup`. The `whois` command details the owner, phone number, and address of the domain owner.

Finally, the exam covers two utilities that allow remote mounts of filesystems. NFS is best for vendor-neutral environments, whereas Samba allows sharing from Windows systems.

Be sure you understand these key points about managing network settings:

- A protocol is a common networking language that must be configured for network hosts to communicate.
- The Internet Protocol (IP) works in conjunction with TCP or UDP to fragment, transmit, defragment, and resequence network data.
- The Internet Control Message Protocol (ICMP) is used to test and verify network communications between hosts with `traceroute` and `ping`.
- Ports allow a single host with a single IP address to provide multiple network services.
- Each host on an IPv4 network must have a unique IP address assigned as well as the correct subnet mask.
- The subnet mask defines how much of a given host's IP address is the network address and how much is the IP address.
- Hosts on the same network segment must have the same subnet mask and must be assigned to each host.
- A network host must be configured with the IP address of a DNS server to resolve domain names into IP addresses.

- A network host must be configured with the IP address of the segment's default gateway router for it to communicate with hosts on other network segments.
- IPv6 addresses are composed of eight four-character hexadecimal numbers, separated by colons instead of periods.
- Within each class of IP address are blocks of addresses called private or reserved IP addresses:
  - 10.0.0.0–10.255.255.255 (Class A)
  - 172.16.0.0–172.31.255.255 (Class B)
  - 192.168.0.0–192.168.255.255 (Class C)
- A NAT router hides a private network behind one or more public interfaces.
- You can enter `ifconfig` or `ip addr show` at the shell prompt to view the details of your installed network interfaces.
- To assign an IP address to a network interface, use `ifconfig` or `ip addr add` at the shell prompt.
- To make IP address assignments persistent, enter them in the appropriate file under the `/etc/` directory.
- Use the `ip` command to manage network interfaces.
- Enter the organization's DNS server address in the `/etc/resolv.conf` file.
- To dynamically assign an IP address to a Linux host, enter `dhclient <interface>` at the shell prompt.
- Use `ping` to test connectivity between systems. The syntax is `ping <destination_host>`.
- Use the `netstat` command to view a variety of network interface information using the `-a`, `-i`, and `-r` options.
- Use the `traceroute` utility to trace the route your packets follow to reach a remote system. The syntax is `traceroute <destination_host>`.
- The `mtr` command combines both `ping` and `traceroute` by displaying routes and how long it takes to reach them.
- Use the `route`, `ip route`, or `netstat -r` command to view your system's routing table.
- To test TCP or UDP communications, use the `nc` command.
- To synchronize time with a time server, use either NTP or `chrony`.
- Use the `route` or `ip route` command to add or remove routes from the route table.
- Use the `dig`, `host`, `resolvectl`, and `nslookup` commands to test DNS name resolution.
- The `whois` command provides domain ownership and IP address information.

Questions

1. Which of the following statements are true of the MAC address? (Choose two.)
   A. It is hard-coded in the network board.
   B. It is logically assigned by the operating system.
   C. It is globally unique.
   D. The network administrator can configure its value.
   E. It is used by the DNS server to resolve domain names.
2. Which transport protocol is used by network applications that need very low latency and can tolerate a certain degree of unreliability?
   A. User Datagram Protocol
   B. Transmission Control Protocol
   C. Internet Protocol
   D. Internet Control Message Protocol
3. Which layer of the OSI model enables the routing of data?
   A. Data Link
   B. Network
   C. Transport
   D. Session
   E. Application
4. You've just set up an e-mail server on your Linux system and enabled the SMTP and POP3 daemons to allow users to send and receive mail. Which ports must be opened in your system's host firewall to allow this? (Choose two.)
   A. 20
   B. 21
   C. 25
   D. 110
   E. 119
   F. 80
5. Which of the following are valid IP addresses that can be assigned to a network host? (Choose two.)
   A. 192.168.254.1
   B. 11.0.0.0
   C. 257.0.0.1
   D. 192.345.2.1
   E. 10.200.0.200

6. Your network interface has been assigned an IP address of 10.0.0.1. What is the binary equivalent of this decimal address?
   A. 10001010.00000000.00000000.00000001
   B. 00001010.00000001.00000001.00000001
   C. 10100000.00000000.00000000.00000001
   D. 00001010.00000000.00000000.00000001
7. You need to use `ifconfig` to assign an IP address of 176.23.0.12 and a subnet mask of 255.255.0.0 to your `eth0` interface. Which of the following commands will do this?
   A. `ifconfig eth0 176.23.0.12 netmask 255.255.0.0`
   B. `ifconfig 176.23.0.12 netmask 255.255.0.0`
   C. `ifconfig eth0 176.23.0.12 mask 255.255.0.0`
   D. `ifconfig dev=eth0 ipaddr=176.23.0.12 subnetmask=255.255.0.0`
8. You've opened your `/etc/resolv.conf` file in the `vi` editor. You want to specify a DNS server address of 10.200.200.1. Which of the following directives would you enter in this file to do this?
   A. `host 10.200.200.1`
   B. `resolver 10.200.200.1`
   C. `dnsserver 10.200.200.1`
   D. `nameserver 10.200.200.1`
9. You want to use your organization's DHCP server to dynamically assign an IP address to your `ens1` network interface. Which of the following commands would you enter at the shell prompt to do this?
   A. `dhcp ens1`
   B. `dhclient ens1`
   C. `get address dynamic ens1`
   D. `ip address=dhcp dev= ens1`
10. You need to verify that a remote host with a hostname of `fs1.mycorp.com` is up and running. Which of the following commands would you enter at the shell prompt to do this?
    A. `finger fs1.mycorp.com`
    B. `ping fs1.mycorp.com`
    C. `netstat -s fs1.mycorp.com`
    D. `verify fs1.mycorp.com`

11. Which commands can resolve domain names on a Linux system? (Choose four.)
    - **A.** `nslookup`
    - **B.** `dig`
    - **C.** `resolvectl`
    - **D.** `host`
    - **E.** `hosts`
12. Which `chronyc` option verifies time server activity?
    - **A.** `chronyc trackers`
    - **B.** `chronyc tracking`
    - **C.** `chronyc track`
    - **D.** `chronyc tracker`

Answers

1. **A, C.** MAC addresses are hard-coded into the firmware of every Ethernet network board. Theoretically, no two network boards in the world should have the same MAC address. However, a few types of network boards do allow you to manually configure the MAC address.
2. **A.** The User Datagram Protocol is an unacknowledged, connectionless protocol that sends packets without requesting a confirmation of receipt. This makes it ideal for network applications that need very low latency but can tolerate a certain degree of unreliability, such as streaming video.
3. **B.** The Network layer of the OSI model enables the routing of data between networks. In an IP network, this functionality is provided by the Internet Protocol (IP itself).
4. **C, D.** The SMTP daemon uses port 25 by default, whereas the POP3 daemon uses port 110 by default.
5. **A, E.** 192.168.254.1 and 10.200.0.200 are both valid IP addresses that can be assigned to network hosts.
6. **D.** The binary equivalent of the first octet (10) is 00001010. The binary equivalent of the second and third octets (0) is 00000000 each. The binary equivalent of the fourth octet (1) is 00000001.
7. **A.** The `ifconfig eth0 176.23.0.12 netmask 255.255.0.0` command will assign the IP address and subnet mask to the `eth0` interface.
8. **D.** The `nameserver 10.200.200.1` directive specifies a DNS server with an IP address of 10.200.200.1.

9. **B.** The `dhclient ens1` command will configure the `ens1` interface with IP address information from a DHCP server.
10. **B.** The `ping fs1.mycorp.com` command is the best to use to test the network.
11. **A, B, C, D.** There is no `hosts` command. `/etc/hosts` is a file for local domain name resolution.
12. **B.** The other options do not exist.

CHAPTER 15

Understanding Network Security

In this chapter, you will learn about

- Understanding how encryption works
- Implementing secured tunnel networks
- Configuring high-availability networking
- Understanding single sign-on
- Defending against network attacks
- Encrypting files with GPG

We came up with the standard to allow different CAD systems to communicate.

—Walt Braithwaite, Boeing

Unethical hackers have figured out that a minimal amount of information can yield huge profits, and they will stop at nothing to get it. As a result, ethical hackers must be obsessive about information security.

Network security is focused on protecting valuable electronic information of organizations and users. Therefore, the demand for IT professionals who know how to secure networks and computers is at an all-time high. Linux system administrators need to be very aware of the security issues affecting networks. In this chapter, we will cover how to use encryption to increase the security of Linux networks.

TIP Information security is a huge topic that cannot adequately be addressed in this book. I highly recommend that you enhance your career by getting the Security+ certification from CompTIA, or the CISSP certification from (ISC)². The IT world has become the modern equivalent of the Wild West from American history. CompTIA Linux+ certified engineers must know how to thoroughly protect data from malicious users!

Understanding How Encryption Works

Harken back to elementary school days when you may have passed notes to friends. To keep those notes secret, you may have used a code such as this:

```
Key:                ZABCDEFGHIJKLMNOPQRSTUVWXY
Plain Text:         ABCDEFGHIJKLMNOPQRSTUVWXYZ
```

NOTE This symmetric encryption technique is called a *letter shift*.

For example, the plain text "`JAKE LIKES DICEY`" would encrypt to the cipher "`IZJD KHJFR CHBDX`."

This basic concept of using keys to scramble and descramble messages can be used to encode network communications as well. In today's security-conscious world, the need to encrypt the contents of network communications is critical, as hackers listen to traffic for passwords, Social Security numbers, national insurance numbers, personal account numbers, and so on. Using network monitoring tools such as Wireshark, or the Linux command-line tools `tcpdump` and `tshark`, makes it relatively easy for hackers to sniff out network transmissions and read them.

To protect this information, network communications must be encrypted. Unlike simple codes used in the fourth grade, network cryptography today uses much more sophisticated encoding mechanisms. There are three general approaches:

- Symmetric encryption
- Asymmetric encryption
- Integrity checking via hashing

Symmetric Encryption

The fourth-grade encryption system just mentioned is an example of symmetric encryption, which uses a single private key. The key used to encrypt a message is the same key used to decrypt the message. This means the sender and the receiver must both have the exact same key, as shown in Figure 15-1. Symmetric algorithms include Blowfish, 3DES, and AES.

Figure 15-1 Symmetric encryption

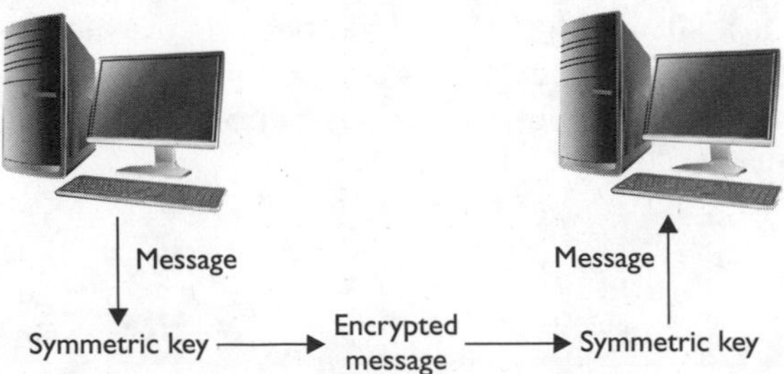

NOTE Symmetric encryption is sometimes called *secret key encryption*. Because of the high risk of the secret key being stolen, another encryption mechanism is commonly used today, called *asymmetric encryption*.

Asymmetric Encryption

Unlike symmetric encryption, asymmetric encryption uses two keys instead of one: a public key known by everyone, and a private key only known by the owner. Data encrypted with the public key is decrypted with the private key. Data signed with the private key is verified with the public key. Examples of asymmetric encryption include RSA, DSA, and Diffie-Hellman.

NOTE Digital signatures are not GIF or JPEG images of a written signature. They are codes that only each owner has. Because the data comes with the individual code (that is, the sender's private key), you can verify that the message came from that individual using the sender's public key.

Because of its high difficulty to break, public key cryptography is a widely used method for encrypting data. Online shopping only exists because of asymmetric encryption, keeping secret the customer's address, phone, and credit card number.

To verify that an online store is legitimate, such as `microbank.com`, a *certificate authority (CA)* is used, such as Verisign, Entrust, or DigiCert. The CA assures customers that they are banking at microbank.com, for example, and not a spoof site like fake-microbank.com, by providing the store with a signed certificate that only they own. The fake site appears to be microbank.com but is programmed to steal customers' private information. This asymmetric process is called *public key infrastructure (PKI)*.

To encrypt personally identifiable information (PII) such as account numbers, residential addresses, and tax identification numbers, website administrators deploy SSL/TLS. You'll know you're visiting a secure site because a small lock will display in the address bar of your browser. This is because you accessed the site using its https address, not the http setting.

To test your web server's SSL/TLS connection, use the `openssl` command. Running `openssl s_client -connect mywebsite.com:443` will help you ensure your connection has the correct encryption and hashing algorithms to satisfy your customers.

Administrators can mint their own certificates and use them to encrypt both network transmissions and files in the filesystem. These are called *self-signed* certificates.

NOTE Website administrators can acquire a *wildcard certificate* to save money. Instead of buying www.aaa.com and mail.aaa.com, they purchase only aaa.com, which can be used for www.aaa.com, mail.aaa.com, ssh.aaa .com, and so on.

Integrity Checking via Hashing

When downloading software, pictures, or music, how does the user know that the file has not been accidentally altered or intentionally modified? To validate that the file has not been altered, the user can use a technique called one-way encryption, or *hashing*. For example, when visiting OpenSUSE to download the operating system, you will also see a list of hash values, as shown here:

```
Filename: openSUSE-Leap-15.0-DVD-x86_64.iso
Path: /distribution/leap/15.0/iso/openSUSE-Leap-15.0-DVD-x86_64.iso
Size: 3.6G (3917479936 bytes)
Last modified: Wed, 16 May 2018 17:47:07 GMT (Unix time: 1526492827)
SHA-256 Hash: c477428c7830ca76762d2f78603e13067c33952b936ff100189523e1fabe5a77
SHA-1 Hash: 64b710bdb8e49d79146cd0d26bb8a7fc28568aa0
MD5 Hash: 5d4d4c83e678b6715652a9cf5ff3c8a3
BitTorrent Information Hash: 21b15d6ff16b245d2f48c5265a7a5463b2d9373b
```

NOTE You can reach OpenSUSE's link of mirror download sites by visiting https://opensuse.org. From there, click the link that states "Get the most complete Linux distribution" or "latest regular-release version" and then select "Pick Mirror."

In this case, three hash values are listed: SHA-256, SHA-1, and MD5.

File integrity checking is completed by ensuring the downloaded file hash matches the vendor's published hash value. There are several hashing tools, but the two most popular are MD5 and SHA. There are multiple versions of SHA, with SHA-256 being one of the best because it is less likely for two different files to calculate the same result, which is called a *collision*.

Hashes are like serial numbers for files. A specific file should only give one result. So, the MD5 hash for OpenSUSE v15.0 is `5d4d4c83e678b6715652a9cf5ff3c8a3`. If an administrator decides to download OpenSUSE v15.0 from a mirror, they have to ask themselves, is this a mirror we can trust? The administrator can verify the file by checking the hash with the `md5sum` command. This outputs a message digest, like so:

```
theogj@ws1:~> md5sum openSUSE-Leap-15.0-DVD-x86_64.iso
5d4d4c83e678b6715652a9cf5ff3c8a3
```

In this case, since the hash value matches the hash value on the OpenSUSE website, the administrator knows they have a clean download. If the value returned were any value other than `5d4d4c83e678b6715652a9cf5ff3c8a3`, then the administrator knows something is wrong with the downloaded file. In most cases, the user downloaded only a portion of the file and has to attempt the download again. In rare cases, a mismatch could signal the file has been altered with malware. A hash mismatch would look something like this:

```
ariaecj@ws1:~> md5sum openSUSE-Leap-15.0-DVD-x86_64.iso
7qwm66m390s9fkwilcm0909wwickj28d
```

The OpenSUSE website also lists SHA-1 and SHA-256 hash values. These can be verified using the `sha1sum` and `sha256sum` commands, respectively. Sometimes vendors will list the highest quality hashing value to date, SHA-512. In this case, use the `sha512sum` command to verify file integrity.

Implementing Secured Tunnel Networks

In the early days of UNIX/Linux, network connection tools between systems included `telnet`, `rlogin`, and `rsh`. Users would use `rcp` or FTP to copy files between systems. However, because of hackers, these utilities must never be used over public networks because they lack encryption.

These days, you can use the SSH package to accomplish these same tasks securely *with* encryption. In this section, the following topics are addressed:

- How SSH works
- Configuring SSH
- Logging in to SSH without a password
- Virtual private networks

How SSH Works

SSH provides the functionality of `telnet`, `rlogin`, `rsh`, `rcp`, and FTP, but with encryption. To do this, SSH provides the following encryption-enabled components:

- **`sshd`** This is the SSH daemon that runs on the server.
- **`ssh`** This is the SSH client used to connect to the SSH server from a remote system.
- **`scp`** This utility securely copies files between systems.
- **`sftp`** This utility securely copies files between systems, acting like FTP.
- **`slogin`** Like SSH, this utility is used to access the shell prompt remotely.
- **`ssh-keygen`** This utility is used to create users' public/private keys. It can also create self-signed certificates.

To establish a secure connection, SSH uses both asymmetric and symmetric encryption. First, the SSH client creates a connection with the system, where the SSH server is running on IP port 22. The SSH server then sends its public keys to the SSH client. The SSH server stores its keys in the following files:

- **Private key** `/etc/ssh/ssh_host_key`
- **Public key** `/etc/ssh/ssh_host_key.pub`

The client system receives the public key from the SSH server and checks to see if it already has a copy of that key. The SSH client stores keys from remote systems in the following files:

- `/etc/ssh/ssh_known_hosts`
- `~/.ssh/known_hosts`

By default, if the client does not have the server's public key in either of these files, it will ask the user to add it. Having done this, the client now trusts the server system and generates the symmetric key. It then uses the server's public key to encrypt the new secret key and sends it to the server. The server decrypts the symmetric key using its private key, and now both systems have the same secret key and can use faster symmetric encryption during the duration of the SSH session. The user is presented with a login prompt and can now authenticate securely because everything the user types is sent in encrypted format.

After this secure channel has been negotiated and the user has been authenticated through the SSH server, data can be securely transferred between both systems.

EXAM TIP By default, SSH is set up to use privileged port 22. This is defined in the `/etc/services` file. Hackers also know the default port is 22. Often, network administrators will use a port that is *not* 22 to make it harder for hackers to invade the network.

Configuring SSH

To use SSH, install the `openssh` package. This package includes both the `sshd` daemon and the `ssh` client. (SSH is usually installed by default on most Linux distributions.)

The process of configuring SSH involves configuring both the SSH server and the SSH client. Configure the `sshd` server using the `/etc/ssh/sshd_config` file. The `ssh` client, on the other hand, is configured using the `/etc/ssh/ssh_config` file or the `~/.ssh/config` file.

Let's look at configuring the SSH server first. There are many directives within the `/etc/ssh/sshd_config` file. The good news is that after you install the `openssh` package, the default parameters work very well in most circumstances. After making changes to this file, restart `sshd` as root by using `systemctl restart sshd`. Some of the more useful parameters in this file include those shown in Table 15-1.

Option	Description
`AllowUsers`	Restricts logins to the SSH server to only the users listed. Specify a list of users separated by spaces.
`DenyUsers`	Prevents users listed from logging in through the SSH server. Specify a list of users separated by spaces.
`PermitRootLogin`	Specifies whether `root` can authenticate through the SSH server. Set the value to `no` to disallow users from logging in as root.

Table 15-1 Options in the `/etc/ssh/sshd_config` File

Option	Description
`Port`	Specifies the port number to connect to on the SSH server system to initiate an SSH request
`User`	Specifies the user to log in to the SSH server as

Table 15-2 Options in the `/etc/ssh/ssh_config` File

EXAM TIP Set `PermitRootLogin` to `no` to disallow logging in as root.

The SSH client on a Linux system is configured using the `/etc/ssh/ssh_config` file. The `/etc/ssh/ssh_config` file is used to specify default parameters for all users running SSH on the system. A user can override these defaults using the `~/.ssh/config` file in their home directory. The precedence for configuring SSH client settings is as follows:

1. Any command-line options included with the `ssh` command at the shell prompt
2. Settings in the `~/.ssh/config` file
3. Settings in the `/etc/ssh/ssh_config` file

As with the `sshd` daemon, the default parameters used in the `/etc/ssh/ssh_config` file usually work without a lot of customization. Some of the more common parameters used to customize the SSH client are listed in Table 15-2.

EXAM TIP Before connecting to an SSH server, make sure port 22 is open on the host-based and network-based firewalls.

Figure 15-2 shows the YaST Firewall module on a SUSE Linux Enterprise Server, configured to allow SSH traffic.

After configuring the firewall, you can log in to the remote Linux system by entering

```
openSUSE:~ # ssh -l <user_name> <ip_address>
```

Figure 15-2 Configuring the firewall to allow SSH traffic

```
rtracy@openSUSE:~> ssh -l student fedora
The authenticity of host 'fedora (10.0.0.85)' can't be established.
RSA key fingerprint is 03:8f:61:c0:ba:3f:fc:00:3b:f1:03:1e:5f:f5:18:42.
Are you sure you want to continue connecting (yes/no)? yes
Warning: Permanently added 'fedora,10.0.0.85' (RSA) to the list of known hosts.
student@fedora's password:
Last login: Fri Jan 23 20:11:46 2015
[student@fedora ~]$ █
```

Figure 15-3 Connecting remotely via SSH

TIP Don't forget the `-l` parameter for logon name; otherwise, the SSH client will attempt to authenticate the user as `$USER` to the remote system. If the credentials are the same on both the client and server systems, authentication will be successful. But if they are not, authentication will be unsuccessful.

For example, to connect to a remote Linux system with a hostname of `fedora` (which has an IP address of 10.0.0.85) as the user `student` using the SSH client on a local computer system, enter `ssh -l student fedora` at the shell prompt, as shown in Figure 15-3.

Notice in Figure 15-3 that the user is prompted to accept the public key from the `fedora` host because this was the first connection to this SSH server. Once done, the user is authenticated to the remote system as the `student` user (notice the change in the shell prompt). Now the user has access to the `fedora` server and works as if they are sitting right at the console of `fedora`. To close the connection, just enter `exit` at the shell prompt.

TIP To enable *X11 forwarding* for your SSH session, connect to the SSH server using the `-X` option, like so: `ssh -X user@sshserver.example.com`

Exercise 15-1: Working with SSH

In this exercise, you set up an SSH server on a Linux system and then connect to it using an SSH client from another Linux system.

Set up at least two Linux systems for this and the remaining exercises in this chapter. Either use two live Linux systems, two Linux virtual machines, or a mixture of both.

VIDEO Watch the Exercise 15-1 video for a demonstration on how to perform this task.

Complete the following steps:

1. Configure the SSH server system by doing the following:
   a. Boot the Linux system that you want to function as an SSH server and log in as a standard user (for example, **student1**).
   b. Open a terminal session.
   c. Switch to your root user account by entering **su -** followed by your root user's password.
   d. At the shell prompt, use the package management utility of your choice to ensure the openssh package has been installed.
   e. At the shell prompt, enter **vi /etc/ssh/sshd_config**.
   f. Locate the PermitRootLogin setting. If it has been commented out, remove the # character from the beginning of the line.
   g. Press **Ins**; then set PermitRootLogin to a value of **no**.
   h. Press **Esc**; then enter **:x** to save your changes and exit the editor.
   i. At the shell prompt, enter **service sshd restart** to restart the SSH service and apply the change.
   j. If necessary, open port 22 in the host firewall of the system where the SSH server is running. The steps for doing this will depend on your particular distribution.
2. Create an SSH connection from a client system by doing the following:
   a. Start your second system, which will function as an SSH client, and log in as a standard user.
   b. Open a terminal session.
   c. Open an SSH session with the first Linux system by entering **ssh -l <user_name> <IP_address_of_SSH_server>** at the shell prompt. For example, to connect to a system with an IP address of 192.168.1.125 as the student1 user on that system, enter **ssh -l student1 192.168.1.125** at the shell prompt.
   d. If prompted, enter **yes** to accept the public key from the SSH server.
   e. Enter the password for the user you specified on the SSH server system.
   f. Enter **exit** at the shell prompt to log off from the remote system.
3. Practice working with SSH utilities from your client system by doing the following:
   a. Run the ifconfig command on the remote system using SSH by entering **ssh -l <user_name> <IP_address_of_SSH_server> /sbin/ifconfig** at the shell prompt.
   b. Enter the password of the remote user when prompted. You should see the networking configuration assigned to the various interfaces on the remote system. Notice that the connection automatically closed once the command finished running.

c. Copy a file using a secure SSH connection by doing the following:
   i. Create a new file in your user's home directory by entering **echo "This is my new file." > ~/mytestfile.txt** at the shell prompt.
   ii. Copy this new file to the home directory for your remote user account on your SSH server system by entering **scp ~/mytestfile.txt <user_name>@ <IP_address_of_SSH_server>:** at the shell prompt.
   iii. Enter the remote user's password when prompted. You should see that the file was copied.
   iv. Use the **ssh** command to establish an SSH connection again with your SSH server system using the same username you entered previously to copy the file.
   v. Verify that the file exists in the remote user's home directory.
   vi. Enter **exit** to close the connection.

d. Use the `sftp` command to copy the `mytestfile.txt` file down from the SSH server system to the local `/tmp` directory by doing the following:
   i. At the shell prompt of your workstation system, enter **sftp <user_name>@ <IP_address_of_SSH_server>**.
   ii. Enter the remote user's password when prompted.
   iii. At the `sftp>` prompt, enter **get mytestfile.txt /tmp/**.
   iv. At the `sftp>` prompt, enter **exit**.
   v. At the shell prompt, enter **ls /tmp**. You should see the `mytestfile.txt` file that was copied from the SSH server system.

Now that you know how to use the SSH server and SSH client, you're ready to advance your knowledge by learning how to tunnel unencrypted traffic through an SSH connection.

NOTE The `rsync` ("remote sync") utility is a great backup tool because it can upload file updates, not duplicates. Also, `ssh` is used to encrypt the transfers, like this: `# rsync -av /filesdir/* user@remote:/filesdir`

Logging In to SSH Without a Password

Administrators can also configure the SSH server to allow authentication without a password. For example, the system administrator Eric is setting up the system for encrypted remote backups using `scp` and wants to run these weekly. He decides running backups as a cron job is the best way to do this, but realizes that this will not work because `scp` always asks for a password. So, now he must inform the server that a *trusted* client needs access, so it should no longer ask for a password from this user at this client.

For this to work, the public key of the user on the client system must be stored at the server. The file on the server is called `~/.ssh/authorized_keys`. To do this, Eric needs to securely copy the public key from the client system to the server system and add it to `~/.ssh/authorized_keys`. (The private key, of course, remains on the client system.) Now Eric can use `scp` and SSH to log in to the server without a password; this is also known as *public key authentication.*

To configure public key authentication, first create the public/private key pair on the client system. This can be done using the `ssh-keygen` command by following these steps:

1. At the shell prompt of the client system, enter `ssh-keygen -t rsa` or `ssh-keygen -t dsa`, depending on which encryption method your SSH server supports. To be safe, simply use both commands to make two key pairs—one for RSA encryption and the other for DSA encryption.
2. When prompted for the file in which the *private* key will be saved, press `Enter` to use the default filename of `~/.ssh/id_rsa` or `~/.ssh/id_dsa`. The associated public key will be saved as `~/.ssh/id_rsa.pub` or `~/.ssh/id_dsa.pub`, respectively.
3. When prompted, enter a passphrase for the key. Assigning a passphrase to the key renders the key useless if someone does not know it.

At this point, the key pair is created. An example of creating an RSA key pair is shown here:

```
ejeff@ws1:~> ssh-keygen -t rsa
Generating public/private rsa key pair.
Enter file in which to save the key (/home/ejeff/.ssh/id_rsa):
Enter passphrase (empty for no passphrase):
Enter same passphrase again:
Your identification has been saved in /home/ejeff/.ssh/id_rsa.
Your public key has been saved in /home/ejeff/.ssh/id_rsa.pub.
The key fingerprint is:
ba:14:48:14:de:fd:42:40:f2:4b:c8:8b:03:a4:6d:fc ejeff@ws1
The key's randomart image is:
+--[ RSA 2048]----+
| .  +oo          |
|oo + = o         |
|o + = + o        |
| o + + o .       |
|  o E o S .      |
|   .   o .       |
|      o          |
|     . .         |
|      .          |
+-----------------+
ejeff@ws1:~>
```

Next, copy the public key just created to the SSH server. An easy (and secure) way to do this is to use the `scp` command. The syntax is

```
scp ~/.ssh/<key_name>.pub <user_name>@<address_of_SSH_server>:<filename>
```

In the example shown here, the RSA public key for the local ejeff user on WS1 is copied to the home directory of the ejeff user on WS3 and saved in a file named keyfile:

```
ejeff@ws1:~> scp ~/.ssh/id_rsa.pub ws3:keyfile
Password:
id_rsa.pub                                    100%  392     0.4KB/s   00:00
ejeff@ws1:~>
```

At this point, the contents of the key file just copied need to be appended to the end of the ~/.ssh/authorized_keys file in the home directory of the user connecting to the SSH server. An easy way to do this is to connect to the SSH server system using a standard SSH session and then use the cat command to append the contents of the key file to the end of the ~/.ssh/authorized_keys file. Here's an example:

```
ejeff@ws1:~> ssh -l ejeff ws3
Password:
Last login: Thu Jun  2 15:05:34 2022 from 192.168.1.84
ejeff@WS3:~> mkdir ~/.ssh
ejeff@WS3:~> cat keyfile » ~/.ssh/authorized_keys
ejeff@WS3:~>
```

Now test the configuration to see if public key authentication works by establishing a new SSH session with the server. In this case, Eric will be prompted for the key file's passphrase instead of a username and password. Once the passphrase is entered, Eric will be authenticated to the SSH server. Notice in the next example that no password was requested to establish the SSH session:

```
ejeff@ws1:~> ssh -l ejeff ws3
Last login: Thu Jun  2 16:13:39 2022 from 192.168.1.84
ejeff@WS3:~>
```

The final step is to use the ssh-agent command to eliminate the need to enter the passphrase every time an SSH connection is established, as detailed next. The ssh-agent command caches the keys once added to the agent with ssh-add.

1. At the shell prompt of the client system, enter ssh-agent bash.
2. At the shell prompt, enter ssh-add ~/.ssh/id_rsa or ssh-add ~/.ssh/id_dsa, depending on which key file was created.
3. When prompted, enter the key file's passphrase. You will be prompted that the identity has been added. An example follows:

```
ejeff@ws1:~> ssh-agent bash
ejeff@ws1:~> ssh-add ~/.ssh/id_rsa
Enter passphrase for /home/ejeff/.ssh/id_rsa:
Identity added: /home/ejeff/.ssh/id_rsa (/home/ejeff/.ssh/id_rsa)
ejeff@ws1:~>
```

Once this is done, the ssh-agent process stores the passphrase in memory and listens for SSH requests. It then automatically provides the key passphrase when requested.

Exercise 15-2: Configuring Public Key Authentication

In this exercise, you generate an RSA key pair on the client system and copy the public key to the SSH server to enable public key authentication.

You'll need at least two Linux systems for this exercise. Use either two live Linux systems, two Linux virtual machines, or a mixture of both.

VIDEO Watch the Exercise 15-2 video for a demonstration on how to perform this task.

Complete the following steps:

1. Generate an RSA key pair on your client system by doing the following:
    a. Log in to your client system as a standard user.
    b. Open a terminal session.
    c. Enter **ssh-keygen -t rsa** at the shell prompt.
    d. When prompted for the file in which the private key will be saved, press **Enter** to use the default filename of ~/.ssh/id_rsa.
    e. When prompted, enter a passphrase for the key.
2. Configure the server system to use public key authentication by doing the following:
    a. Copy the public key you just created to your SSH server system by entering the following:

```
scp ~/.ssh/id_rsa.pub <user_name>@<address_of_SSH_server>:mykeyfile
```

    b. Enter the remote user's password when prompted.
    c. Establish an SSH session with the remote system as the user you intend to authenticate as using public key authentication. Use the following command: **ssh -l <user_name> <address_of_SSH_server>**
    d. Enter the remote user's password when prompted.
    e. At the shell prompt of the remote system, check to see if the .ssh/ hidden directory already exists by entering **ls -la** at the shell prompt. If the .ssh/ directory doesn't exist, create it using the **mkdir ~/.ssh** command. Otherwise, go on to the next step.
    f. Enter **cat mykeyfile >> ~/.ssh/authorized_keys** at the shell prompt of the remote system.
    g. Enter **exit** at the shell prompt to close the SSH session.

3. Test the new configuration by doing the following:
   a. Enter **ssh -l <user_name> <address_of_SSH_server>** at the shell prompt of your client system.
   b. When prompted, enter the passphrase you assigned to your RSA private key. At this point, you should be automatically authenticated to the SSH server.
   c. Close the session by entering **exit** at the shell prompt.
4. Configure `ssh-agent` to remember your private key passphrase by doing the following:
   a. Enter **ssh-agent bash** at the shell prompt of your client system.
   b. At the shell prompt, enter **ssh-add ~/.ssh/id_rsa**.
   c. When prompted, enter the key file's passphrase. When you do, you should be prompted that the identity has been added.
   d. Enter **ssh -l <user_name> <address_of_SSH_server>** at the shell prompt of your client system. You should be automatically authenticated to the SSH server without being prompted for the private key passphrase.

Automatically Updating `authorized_keys`

The manual method to update `~/.ssh/authorized_keys` can be automated with `ssh-copy-id` if you already know the username and password of the remote system. Here's an example:

```
ejeff@ws1:~> ssh-copy-id ejeff@ws3
ejeff@ws3's password:
Number of key(s) added: 1
ejeff@ws1:~>
```

The `ssh-copy-id` command will automatically update the `authorized_keys` file on the SSH server.

Virtual Private Networks

A virtual private network (VPN) allows users to connect to remote servers over untrusted networks but make it appear that they are part of the internal network. To ensure the confidentiality of the network, encryption and tunneling protocols are used to create this private network. This security is provided through IP Security (IPSec). To reduce traffic congestion without sacrificing security, Datagram Transport Layer Security (DTLS) is implemented.

VPNs are used by employees to work from home and connect to the corporate office, for example. Figure 15-4 shows an example of a home office connecting to the corporate network via VPN.

VPN connections can be made either in transport mode or tunnel mode. Tunnel mode encrypts the headers and the message. Use tunnel mode when data is transported over public networks. Transport mode is used over trusted networks (for example, moving data from office to office). Transport mode only encrypts the message, not the headers.

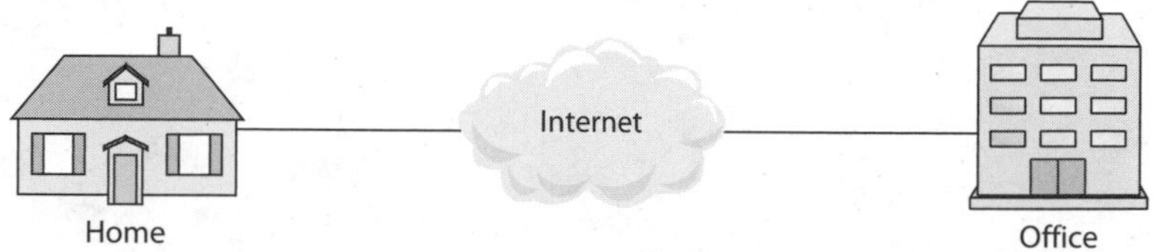

Figure 15-4 VPN connection from a home office to corporate headquarters

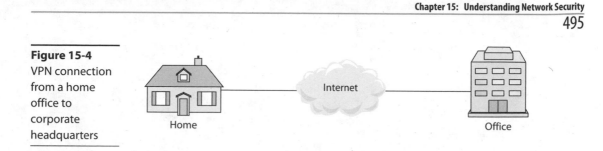

To set up the VPN client from Linux, click in the upper-right corner of the screen on the network icon, as shown in Figure 15-5.

Next, click Wired Settings (see Figure 15-6). Then click the + sign to the right of VPN to initiate the VPN connection, as shown in Figure 15-7.

After obtaining the credentials, save them to a file and import them into the VPN client for an easy connection to the VPN server.

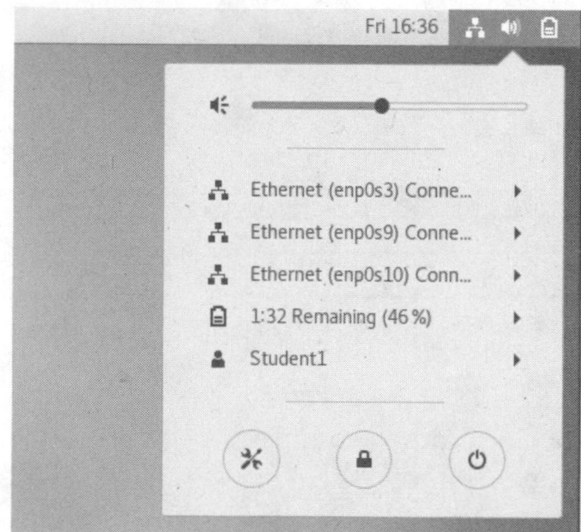

Figure 15-5 Step 1 of creating a VPN connection

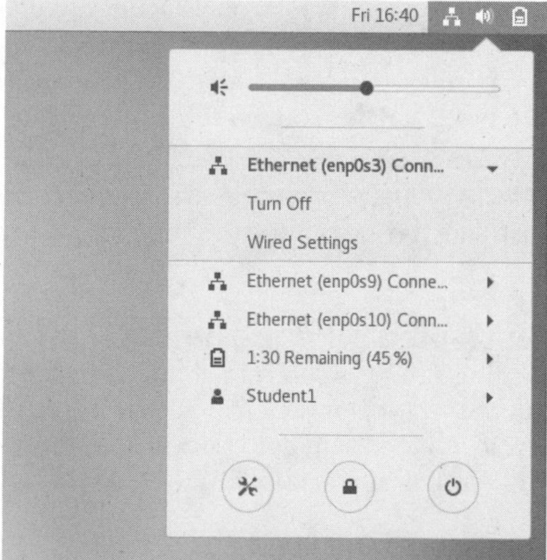

Figure 15-6 Step 2 of creating a VPN connection

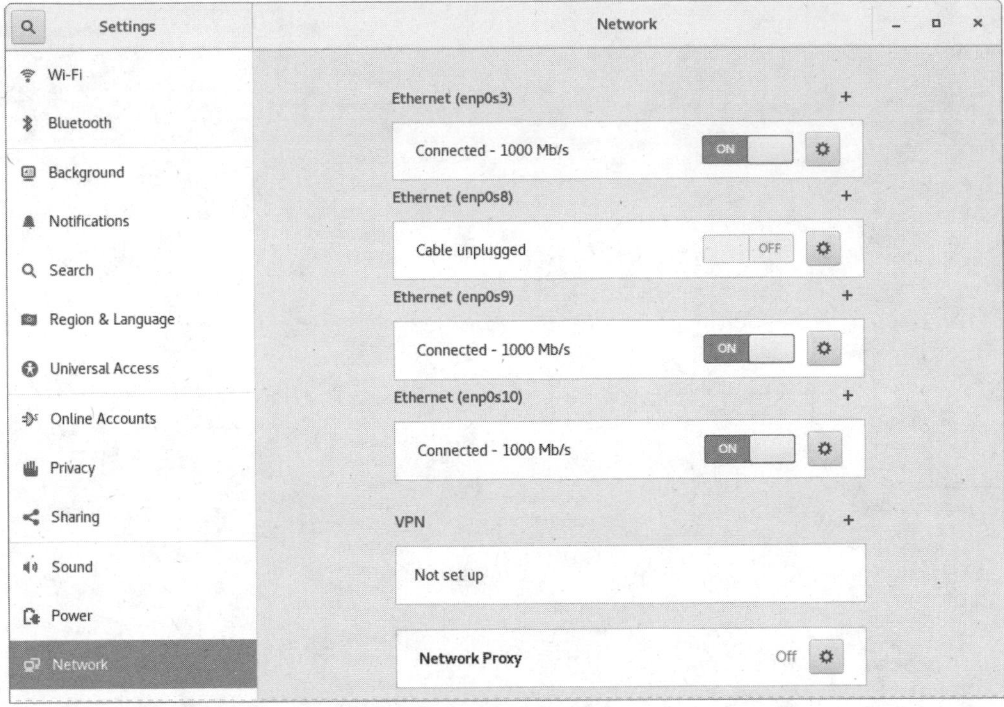

Figure 15-7 Step 3 of creating a VPN connection

NOTE A common command-line VPN client used on Linux systems is OpenVPN.

There are several implementations of VPNs. One type uses SSH, and another is the SSL VPN, which uses TLS as the encryption protocol (even though TLS replaced SSL, the name SSL VPN stuck so it hasn't changed). Some administrators find these easier to set up over IPSec-based VPNs because they can be deployed over a web browser.

EXAM TIP If the VPN settings are all correct and the system will not connect, make sure the proper ports are opened on the firewalls.

Securing Unencrypted Services with SSH Port Forwarding

SSH port forwarding allows you to tunnel unencrypted services over an encrypted SSH channel. For example, if you are servicing a web server in the DMZ via a jump server (a hardened server with intrusion detection that better services protocols running in the DMZ), access it by using the `-L` option of `ssh` to configure port forwarding as follows:

```
shakuntala@server$ ssh -L 80:website.server.com:80 jump.server.com
```

This allows you to securely connect to the jump server and forward connections to the web server securely.

Securing Unencrypted Services with SSH Dynamic Port Forwarding

SSH dynamic port forwarding allows you to open a proxy on your local machine by using the `-D` option. Run the following:

```
shakuntala@server$ ssh -D 55555 shah@ssh.server.com
```

Now you can configure a web browser to use port 55555, and all traffic originating from that location is directed via the SSH connections for port 55555.

Configuring High-Availability Networking

The consequence of not being able to access data is destruction. That is, if data is not available, it is as if it has been destroyed, so availability is an important component of security. Network availability can be enhanced by converting the local network adapter into a concept called *network bridging* or *bonding*. Bridging dual-homes two or more networks together for fault tolerance. Bonding dual-homes network segments to boost network throughput. Dual-homed networking is shown in Figure 15-8.

At this point, we will cover the two major types of redundant networks:

- Network bridge control
- Network bonding

For the CompTIA Linux+ exam, you need to understand the basics of bridging and bonding network interfaces.

NOTE Overlay networks allow administrators to give multiple IP addresses to a local network card. Fox example, running the following makes a single network card act like three network cards:

```
[root@cent71-5t dkosuth]# ifconfig eth0 inet
192.168.2.2
[root@cent71-5t dkosuth]# ifconfig eth0:0 inet
192.168.2.3
[root@cent71-5t dkosuth]# ifconfig eth0:1 inet
192.168.2.4
```

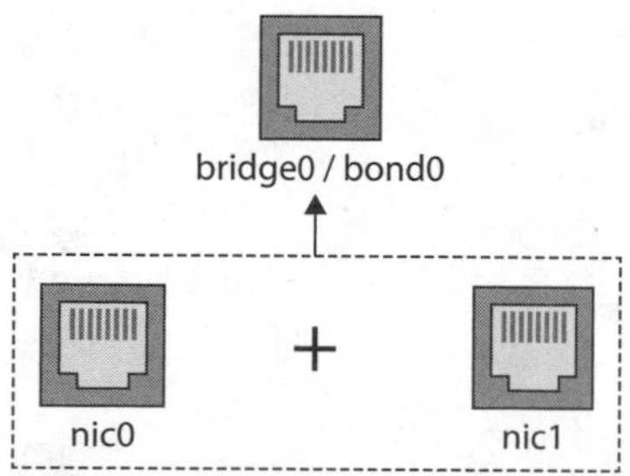

Figure 15-8 Setup for network bridging and bonding

Network Bridge Control

You set up bridging with the `brctl` command. Here is an example using the `addbr` function to create the bridge and `addif` to add interfaces to the bridge:

```
[root@cent71-5t dkosuth]# brctl addbr trilby
[root@cent71-5t dkosuth]# brctl addif trilby enp0s9 enp0s10
[root@cent71-5t dkosuth]# brctl show
bridge name bridge id         STP enabled interfaces
trilby      8000.0800271eb6e8 no          enp0s10
                                          enp0s9
```

Spanning Tree Protocol (STP) is not enabled by default, but when it is enabled, it provides methods to seek the shortest path between multiple network switches and prevents network loops when multiple bridges are on the network. To enable STP, run the following:

```
[root@cent71-5t dkosuth]# brctl stp trilby on
[root@cent71-5t dkosuth]# brctl show
bridge name bridge id         STP enabled interfaces
trilby      8000.0800271eb6e8 yes         enp0s10
                                          enp0s9
```

Network Bonding

Network bonding aggregates multiple network interface cards into a single bond interface that provides redundancy, increased throughput, and high availability. To construct the bond on CentOS, define the script file `/etc/sysconfig/network-scripts/ifcfg-bond0`:

```
[root@cent71-5t bertollini]# cat /etc/sysconfig/network-scripts/ifcfg-bond0
DEVICE=bond0
NAME=bond0
TYPE=Bond
BONDING_MASTER=yes
IPADDR=10.1.1.150
PREFIX=24
ONBOOT=yes
BOOTPROTO=none
BONDING_OPTS="mode=1 miimon=100"
```

The `BONDING_OPTS` setting describes the bonding mode, as listed in Table 15-3. The `miimon` parameter is the link check interval in milliseconds.

Policy	Mode	Description
Round-robin	0	Packets are sent in order across all NICs (the default policy).
Active-passive	1	One NIC sleeps and activates if another fails.
Aggregation	4	NICs act as one, which results in higher throughput.
Load balancing	5	Traffic is equally balanced over all NICs.

Table 15-3 Network Bonding Policies

Next, modify the network interface configuration files and add the bond definitions. Here is an example for interface `enp0s9`:

```
[root@cent71-5t bertollini]# cat /etc/sysconfig/network-scripts/ifcfg-enp0s9
TYPE=Ethernet
BOOTPROTO=none
DEVICE=enp0s9
ONBOOT=yes
HWADDR="08:a2:37:69:60:09"
MASTER=bond0
SLAVE=yes
```

The administrator would make similar settings for the other network interfaces that are part of the bond and then restart the network by running `systemctl restart network`.

NOTE The `ifcfg` command can be used to add, delete, or stop a network card instead of using `ifconfig`. For example, run `ifcfg enp0s3 stop` to disable the network card.

Understanding Single Sign-On

Single sign-on (SSO) is an identity management feature that allows a user to have one login and password to every system on the network. So, no matter if an engineer is working in the Austin, Texas, office or the Mumbai, Maharashtra, office, they can use the same login and password to access their data.

SSO systems have several features, including one-time passwords (OTPs). These systems provide the user a software token (e.g., FreeOTP) or a hardware token, as shown in Figure 15-9, that produces a random value every 30 seconds. When the user logs on to the system, to further authenticate themselves they must provide the updated random value. This provides an additional layer of security. If a hacker obtains the user's password but cannot guess the random value, they will still be locked out.

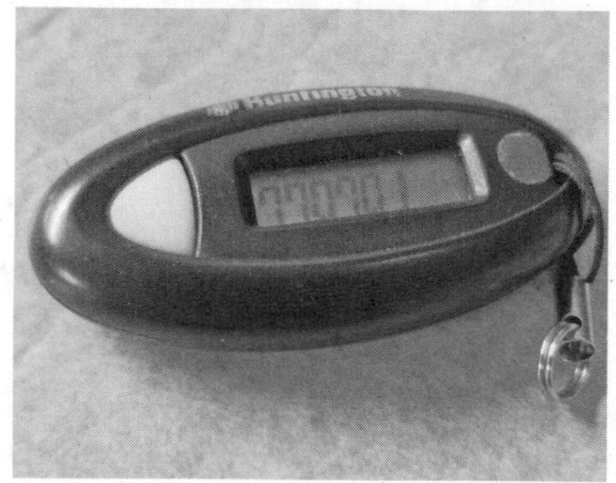

Figure 15-9 One-time password (OTP) hardware token

Several utilities provide SSO services, including the following:

- RADIUS
- LDAP
- Kerberos
- TACACS+

For the CompTIA Linux+ exam, you simply need to understand the basics of each single sign-on service.

EXAM TIP Every user must have a unique user ID that is not shared with anyone else. Shared accounts make it difficult to determine who caused a negative occurrence.

RADIUS

Remote Authentication Dial-In User Service (RADIUS) is an authentication protocol that allows local and remote users to connect via modems. Users log in and get authenticated by the RADIUS server. After the user is authenticated, they are granted an IP address and access to the network. Since RADIUS is an open standard, it is vendor neutral.

RADIUS uses ports 1812 and 1813. Figure 15-10 diagrams how users remotely access the RADIUS client to log on to the network.

LDAP

Lightweight Directory Access Protocol (LDAP) is an open source Active Directory service. LDAP is vendor neutral, so it can operate well in Linux, Windows, and macOS environments. The directory service follows the X.500 standard, which defines usernames, passwords, computers, networks, wireless devices, printers, and more.

LDAPv3 provides the most security, implementing TLS. LDAP uses ports 389, or port 636 if combined with SSL.

Kerberos

Kerberos is the name of the three-headed dog that guards Hades according to Greek mythology. The Kerberos utility for system administrators guards the network by providing strong authentication to protect the corporate network.

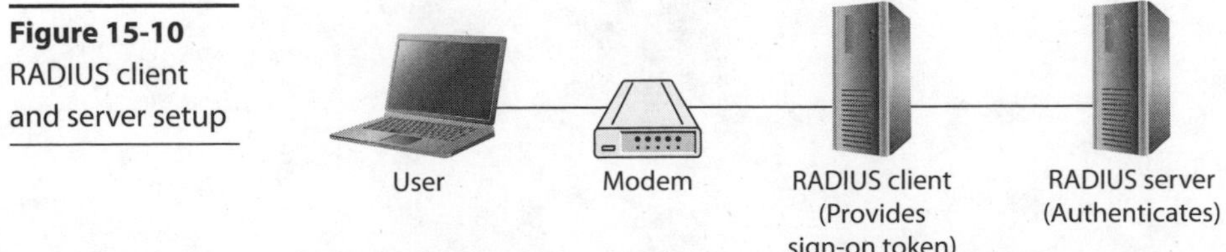

Figure 15-10 RADIUS client and server setup

Kerberos is the preferred system over public networks because users can access services such as e-mail and SSH *without* transmitting their password across the network. This way, hackers cannot even read the hashed version of the user's password. Kerberos uses a system called "tickets" to allow users access to services.

Kerberos tickets work similarly to tickets used to see a movie. For example, when you go to the movie complex, they may be showing 20 different titles. Let's say you want to see *Candace, Eric, Albert, and Edward: The Movie* at 2 P.M. You can only use the ticket for that movie at that time. When the movie ends, the ticket expires.

In a similar way, a user gets a ticket from Kerberos to access e-mail that starts now and expires in 60 minutes. Because encrypted tickets get passed instead of passwords, it makes it extremely difficult for a hacker to discover the credentials. Once the ticket expires, a new encrypted key with a new expiration can be requested.

Make sure the clocks match between the client and the server. If they are more than five minutes apart, Kerberos will fail. Kerberos will also fail if firewall port 88 is closed.

To initiate a Kerberos session, run `kinit <username>@<hostname>.com` and enter the user's password. To view the addresses associated with the current Kerberos tickets, run `klist -a`. To get details on current tickets, such as length, expiration times, renewal times, and so on, run `klist -v`.

TACACS+

Terminal Access Controller Access Control System Plus, or TACACS+ (pronounced "tack-us-plus" or "tack plus"), combines authentication, authorization, and accounting. TACACS+ is also more secure than other protocols, such as RADIUS, because not only is the password encrypted, but the entire transaction is encrypted. Also, TACACS+ can place authentication, authorization, and accounting on three different servers, unlike RADIUS, which combines authentication and authorization. TACACS+ is not compatible with its predecessor, TACACS.

TACACS+ uses TCP port 49 to operate. Because it uses TCP instead of UDP as RADIUS does, the connections are much more reliable. TACACS+ was originally designed for Cisco networks, but other vendors now support TACACS+.

NOTE Microsoft Windows systems use Active Directory for SSO. Linux provides the System Security Services Daemon (SSSD) to connect to Active Directory.

Defending Against Network Attacks

It would be nice if we lived in a world where we could connect networks together and be able to trust others to respect our systems. Unfortunately, such a world doesn't exist. If our Linux systems are connected to a network, we need to be concerned about network attacks. If our network is connected to a public network, such as the Internet, we need to be extremely concerned about network attacks.

As with most of the topics discussed in this book, network security is a huge topic that can fill many volumes. Therefore, we will discuss basic steps administrators can take to defend against network attacks. We will cover several important areas of the Linux+ exam, including the following:

- Mitigating network vulnerabilities
- Implementing a firewall with `firewalld`
- Implementing a firewall with `iptables`

Let's begin by discussing some steps to take to mitigate network vulnerabilities.

Mitigating Network Vulnerabilities

The good news is that there are some simple steps that system administrators can take to mitigate the threat to Linux systems from network attacks. These include the following:

- Disabling unused services
- Installing security updates

Let's first discuss staying abreast of current network threats.

Disabling Unused Services

One of the simplest steps administrators can take to mitigate threats from a network attack is to disable unused network services. Depending on the Linux distribution, there are probably a number of services running that do not need to operate. To view a list of installed services and whether or not they are running, enter `systemctl list-unit-files` at the shell prompt. This command will list each service and its status, as shown here:

```
[root@cent71-5t gwenj]# systemctl list-unit-files
UNIT FILE                                              STATE
exercises.mount                                        enabled
lcfileshare.mount                                      enabled
tmp.mount                                              disabled
brandbot.path                                          disabled
```

In addition to `systemctl`, you can also use the `nmap` command to view open IP ports on the Linux system. Again, each port that is open on the Linux system represents a potential vulnerability. Some open ports are necessary; others are not.

NOTE The `nmap` package is usually not installed by default.

The syntax for using `nmap` is `nmap -sT <host_IP_address>` for a TCP port scan and `nmap -sU <host_IP_address>` for a UDP port scan. In Figure 15-11, the `nmap` utility is used to scan for open TCP ports.

```
root@openSUSE:~
File  Edit  View  Search  Terminal  Help
openSUSE:~ # nmap -sT 10.0.0.3

Starting Nmap 6.40 ( http://nmap.org ) at 2015-01-20 19:33 MST
Nmap scan report for 10.0.0.3
Host is up (0.0011s latency).
Not shown: 982 filtered ports
PORT      STATE  SERVICE
22/tcp    open   ssh
80/tcp    open   http
113/tcp   closed ident
139/tcp   open   netbios-ssn
389/tcp   open   ldap
427/tcp   open   svrloc
443/tcp   open   https
445/tcp   closed microsoft-ds
524/tcp   open   ncp
631/tcp   open   ipp
636/tcp   open   ldapssl
5801/tcp  open   vnc-http-1
5901/tcp  open   vnc-1
5989/tcp  open   wbem-https
6901/tcp  open   jetstream
8008/tcp  open   http
8009/tcp  open   ajp13
```

Figure 15-11 Using nmap to scan for open ports

Figure 15-11 shows a number of services running on the host that was scanned. Use this output to determine what should be left running on the system. To disable a service, use systemctl disable <service_name> to ensure it will not start after reboot. Run systemctl stop <service_name> to disable the running service.

NOTE The legacy tool to manage services was called chkconfig. To check the status of all daemons, run chkconfig -l. To disable the service, run chkconfig <service_name> off.

The netstat utility also lists open ports. An example of using netstat with the -l option to view a list of listening sockets on a Linux host is shown in Figure 15-12.

Similar to netstat, using the -i option with lsof will also list network services and their ports, as shown here:

```
[root@cent71-5t gwenj]# lsof -i
COMMAND     PID   USER    FD    TYPE DEVICE SIZE/OFF NODE NAME
systemd       1   root    45u   IPv4  25466      0t0  TCP *:sunrpc (LISTEN)
systemd       1   root    46u   IPv4  25467      0t0  UDP *:sunrpc
systemd       1   root    47u   IPv6  25468      0t0  TCP *:sunrpc (LISTEN)
systemd       1   root    48u   IPv6  25469      0t0  UDP *:sunrpc
avahi-dae 3214  avahi    12u   IPv4  24455      0t0  UDP *:mdns
avahi-dae 3214  avahi    13u   IPv4  24456      0t0  UDP *:53940
rpcbind   3218    rpc     4u   IPv4  25466      0t0  TCP *:sunrpc (LISTEN)
rpcbind   3218    rpc     5u   IPv4  25467      0t0  UDP *:sunrpc
rpcbind   3218    rpc     6u   IPv6  25468      0t0  TCP *:sunrpc (LISTEN)
```

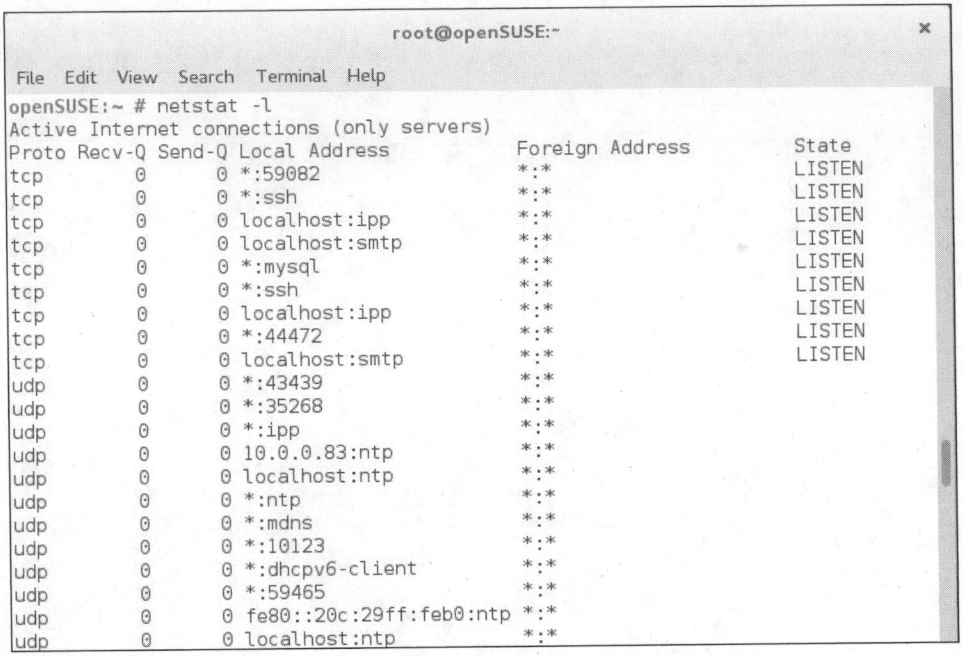

```
root@openSUSE:~
File  Edit  View  Search  Terminal  Help
openSUSE:~ # netstat -l
Active Internet connections (only servers)
Proto Recv-Q Send-Q Local Address           Foreign Address         State
tcp        0      0 *:59082                 *:*                     LISTEN
tcp        0      0 *:ssh                   *:*                     LISTEN
tcp        0      0 localhost:ipp           *:*                     LISTEN
tcp        0      0 localhost:smtp          *:*                     LISTEN
tcp        0      0 *:mysql                 *:*                     LISTEN
tcp        0      0 *:ssh                   *:*                     LISTEN
tcp        0      0 localhost:ipp           *:*                     LISTEN
tcp        0      0 *:44472                 *:*                     LISTEN
tcp        0      0 localhost:smtp          *:*                     LISTEN
udp        0      0 *:43439                 *:*
udp        0      0 *:35268                 *:*
udp        0      0 *:ipp                   *:*
udp        0      0 10.0.0.83:ntp           *:*
udp        0      0 localhost:ntp           *:*
udp        0      0 *:ntp                   *:*
udp        0      0 *:mdns                  *:*
udp        0      0 *:10123                 *:*
udp        0      0 *:dhcpv6-client         *:*
udp        0      0 *:59465                 *:*
udp        0      0 fe80::20c:29ff:feb0:ntp *:*
udp        0      0 localhost:ntp           *:*
```

Figure 15-12 Using `netstat` to view a list of listening sockets

```
rpcbind   3218     rpc    7u  IPv6  25469      0t0  UDP *:sunrpc
rpcbind   3218     rpc   10u  IPv4  24207      0t0  UDP *:844
rpcbind   3218     rpc   11u  IPv6  24210      0t0  UDP *:844
```

Installing Security Updates

One of the most important steps administrators can take to defend against network attacks is to regularly install operating system updates. A simple fact of life that we have to deal with in the IT world is that software isn't written perfectly. Most programs and services have some defects. Even the Linux kernel has defects that can represent serious security risks.

As software is released and used, these defects are discovered by system administrators, users, and hackers. As they are discovered, updates are written and released to fix the defects. Most distributions can be configured to automatically check and install updates. The tool used to update the system will vary depending on which Linux distribution you are using.

Implementing a Firewall with `firewalld`

Today, most organizations connect their corporate networks to the Internet. Doing so enhances communications and provides access to a wealth of information. Unfortunately, it also exposes their network to a serious security threat. If users can reach the Internet, an uninvited person from the Internet can also reach into their network. To keep this from happening, the organization needs to implement a firewall.

The two types are network-based firewalls and host-based firewalls. A *host-based firewall* controls traffic in and out of a single computer system, whereas a *network-based firewall* is used to control traffic in and out of an entire network.

In this part of the chapter, you spend some time learning how to use Linux in both capacities. We'll discuss the following topics:

- How firewalls work
- Implementing a packet-filtering firewall

How Firewalls Work

So what exactly is a firewall? A *firewall* acts like a gatekeeper between networks. Its job is to monitor the traffic that flows between the networks, both inbound and outbound. The firewall is configured with rules that define the type of traffic allowed. Any traffic that violates the rules is denied, as shown in Figure 15-13.

Firewalls can be implemented in a variety of ways. One of the most common types is a *packet-filtering firewall*, where all traffic moving between the private and public networks must go through the firewall. As it does, the firewall captures all incoming and outgoing packets and compares them against the access control list (ACL) configured by the network administrator.

The firewall ACL filters traffic based on the origin address, destination address, origin and destination ports, protocol used, or type of packet. If a packet abides by the rules, it is forwarded on to the next network. If it does not, it is logged and dropped, as shown in Figure 15-14.

Packet-filtering firewalls are considered *stateless* firewalls, which means they do not look at the state of the connection. *Stateful* firewalls maintain the state of the connection and are commonly used today. For example, if traffic is normally blocked from the Country of Belchre, traffic initiating from the Country of Belchre will be rejected.

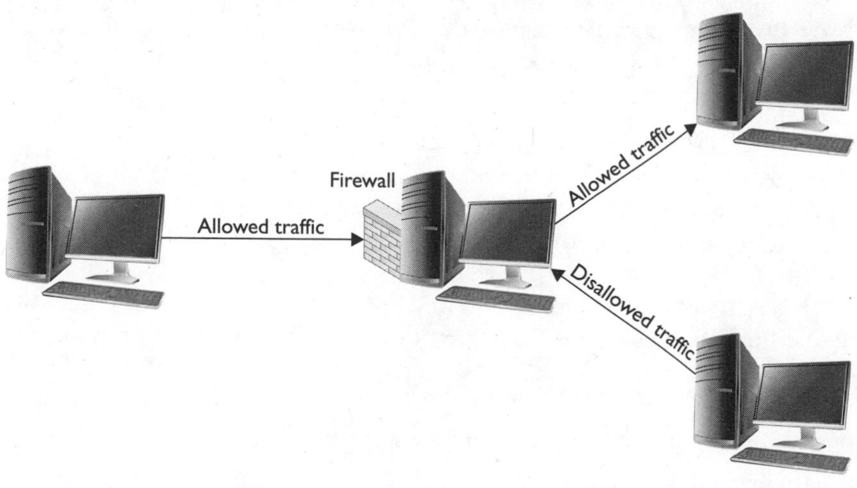

Figure 15-13 How a firewall works

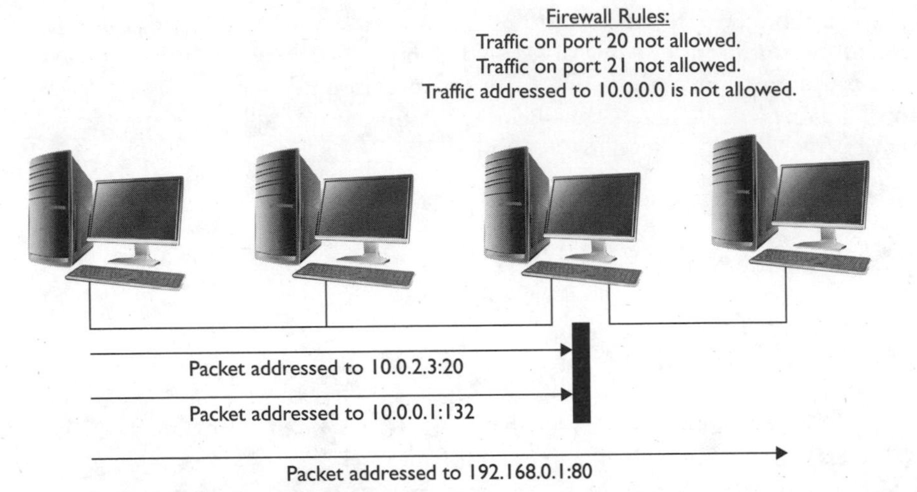
Firewall Rules:
Traffic on port 20 not allowed.
Traffic on port 21 not allowed.
Traffic addressed to 10.0.0.0 is not allowed.
Packet addressed to 10.0.2.3:20
Packet addressed to 10.0.0.1:132
Packet addressed to 192.168.0.1:80

Figure 15-14 Using a packet-filtering firewall

But if a trusted user within the LAN requests a connection with the Country of Belchre, they will be allowed, and traffic related to this connection will be allowed because it was initiated by an internal, trusted user. This takes a huge part of the workload off the network administrator. They no longer have to respond to hundreds of requests to adjust the ACL for users who justifiably need to reach normally banned websites.

But this also introduces *phishing* e-mails. If a hacker can trick a trusted user into clicking a link that forwards to a banned website in the Country of Belchre that the hacker controls, the hacker now has breached the firewall and now can attack the victims.

NOTE There are also kernel-proxy firewalls, web-application firewalls, application-level gateways, circuit-level next-generation firewalls, and so on. These operate higher up the OSI model and are beyond the scope of the CompTIA Linux+ exam.

Implementing a Packet-Filtering Firewall

A Linux system can be configured to function as many network devices, such as routers or firewalls. Currently, there are many firewall appliances on the market based on Linux. For our purposes, we will focus on creating a basic packet-filtering firewall using `firewalld` and the legacy tool `iptables`.

The first step in setting up a packet-filtering firewall on a Linux system is to design the implementation. Answer the following questions when designing the firewall:

- Will the firewall deny all incoming traffic except for specific allowed traffic?
- Will all outgoing traffic be blocked except for specific types or destinations?
- What ports must be opened on the firewall to allow traffic through from the outside? For example, is there a publicly accessible website behind the firewall? If so, then ports 80 and 443 must be opened.

Next, configure the firewall using the `firewalld` service. The `firewalld` service offers zone-based firewalling, making it easier to create common setups. The `firewalld` service supports IPv4 and IPv6 and is part of `systemd`. Also, permanent and temporary or runtime configurations are available.

To enable the `firewalld` service, use `systemctl`, as shown here:

```
[root@cent71-5t kimberli]# systemctl enable firewalld
[root@cent71-5t kimberli]# systemctl start firewalld
[root@cent71-5t kimberli]# systemctl status firewalld
firewalld.service - firewalld - dynamic firewall daemon
  Loaded: loaded (/usr/.../firewalld.service; enabled; vendor preset: en-
abled)
  Active: active (running) since Thu 2022-04-04 00:09:58 EDT; 1 day 22h ago
    Docs: man:firewalld(1)
Main PID: 3334 (firewalld)
   Tasks: 2
  CGroup: /system.slice/firewalld.service
          └─3334 /usr/bin/python -Es /usr/sbin/firewalld --nofork --nopid

Apr 04 00:09:56 cent71-5t systemd[1]: Starting firewalld - dynamic fire-
wall...
Apr 04 00:09:58 cent71-5t systemd[1]: Started firewalld - dynamic firewall
...
Hint: Some lines were ellipsized, use -l to show in full.
[root@cent71-5t kimberli]#
```

If there are multiple network interfaces, IP forwarding needs to be enabled, as shown next:

```
[root@cent71-5t kellij]# echo 1 > /proc/sys/net/ipv4/ip_forward
[root@cent71-5t kellij]# echo 1 > /proc/sys/net/ipv6/ip_forward
```

NOTE For IPv6 forwarding, set `/proc/sys/net/ipv6/conf/all/forwarding` to `1`. This will enable forwarding for all network interfaces enabled on the system.

The `firewalld` feature has several predefined zones of trust to manage IP packets. Table 15-4 lists some of the common zones available with `firewalld`.

Use the `firewall-cmd` tool to display available zones and to switch to a different default. For example, here's how to change from the home zone to `internal` zone:

```
[root@cent71-5t jake]# firewall-cmd --get-default-zone
home
[root@cent71-5t jake]# firewall-cmd --set-default-zone=internal
success
[root@cent71-5t jake]# firewall-cmd --get-default-zone
internal
[root@cent71-5t jake]#
```

To list all the configured services and interfaces allowed through the zone, run the `firewall-cmd --list-all` option, as shown here:

```
[root@cent71-5t edwina]# firewall-cmd --list-all
internal (active)
 target: default
```

Zone	Outgoing Connections	Incoming Connections
`work`	Allowed	SSH, IPP, and DHCPv6 client allowed
`home`	Allowed	SSH, IPP, multicast DNS, DHCPv6 client, and Samba client allowed
`internal`	Allowed	SSH, IPP, multicast DNS, DHCPv6 client, and Samba client allowed
`external`	Allowed and masqueraded to IP address of outgoing network interface	SSH allowed
`dmz`	Allowed	SSH allowed
`public`	Allowed	SSH and DHCPv6 client allowed
`trusted`	Allowed	Allowed
`drop`	Allowed	Dropped
`block`	Allowed	Rejected with `icmp-host-prohibited` message

Table 15-4 The `firewalld` Zones

```
icmp-block-inversion: no
interfaces: enp0s3
sources:
services: ssh mdns samba-client dhcpv6-client
ports:
protocols:
masquerade: no
forward-ports:
source-ports:
icmp-blocks:
rich rules:
```

After the system is rebooted, the firewall settings return to their default values. To add a service and make the runtime values permanent, use the `--permanent` flag:

```
[root@cent71-5t camilla]# firewall-cmd --permanent --add-service=telnet
success
[root@cent71-5t camilla]# firewall-cmd --reload
```

The `--reload` option makes it so that the change occurs immediately; otherwise, the change does not take effect until reboot.

NOTE Firewall issues can result from the `--reload` operation. It only loads the known existing service, so if you did *not* use `--permanent`, the `telnet` service would not be enabled. For example, `telnet` is not enabled after `--reload`:

```
[root@cent71-5t matia]# firewall-cmd --add-
service=http --zone=home
[root@cent71-5t matia]# firewall-cmd --reload
[root@cent71-5t matia]# firewall-cmd --list-services
--zone=home ssh \ mdns samba-client dhcpv6-client
```

Exercise 15-3: Implementing Network Security Measures with `firewalld`

In this exercise, you practice using `firewalld` settings by adding web services to the public zone. You can perform this exercise using the virtual machine that comes with this book. Complete the following steps:

VIDEO Please watch the Exercise 15-3 video for a demonstration on how to perform this task.

1. Boot your Linux system and log in as the `root` user. Install `firewalld` if necessary.
2. Set the firewall to use the `public` zone as follows:
```
firewall-cmd --set-default-zone=public
```
3. Add web services and secure web services to the `public` zone:
```
firewall-cmd --zone=public --add-service=http
firewall-cmd --zone=public --add-service=https
```
4. Confirm that you were successful in adding these services:
```
firewall-cmd --list-services --zone=home
```
5. Learn more about `firewalld` by running **`firewall-cmd --help`**.

Implementing a Firewall with `iptables`

The `firewalld` service is actually the front end to `iptables`, but `firewalld` can maintain existing connections even after a change in settings. Most Linux distributions include `iptables`, but if yours does not, you can download it from https://www.netfilter.org or from the vendor's repositories. The Linux kernel itself completes the packet-filtering tasks using `netfilter`.

The `netfilter` infrastructure uses the concept of "tables and chains" to create firewall rules. A *chain* is simply a rule that is implemented to determine what the firewall will do with an incoming packet. The `netfilter` infrastructure uses the *filter table* to create packet-filtering rules. Within the filter table are three default chains:

- **`FORWARD`** Contains rules for packets being transferred between networks through the Linux system
- **`INPUT`** Contains rules for packets that are being sent to the local Linux system
- **`OUTPUT`** Contains rules for packets that are being sent from the local Linux system

Each chain in the filter table has four policies:

- `ACCEPT`
- `DROP`
- `QUEUE`
- `REJECT`

To create a chain of multiple rules, each rule in a chain is assigned a number. The first rule you add is assigned the number 1. The `iptables` utility can add rules, delete rules, insert rules, and append rules. The syntax for using `iptables` is

```
iptables -t <table> <command> <chain> <options>
```

Use the following commands with `iptables`:

- **`-L`** Lists all rules in the chain
- **`-N`** Creates a new chain

You can work with either the default chains listed previously or create your own chain. You create your own chain by entering `iptables -N <chain_name>`. You can add rules to a chain by using the `-A` option. You can also use one of the other options listed here:

- **`-I`** Inserts a rule into the chain
- **`-R`** Replaces a rule in the chain
- **`-D`** Deletes a rule from the chain
- **`-F`** Deletes all the rules from the chain (called *flushing*)
- **`-P`** Sets the default policy for the chain

EXAM TIP You should be comfortable with the `iptables` options listed in Table 15-5.

You can also use the following options with `iptables`:

- **`-p`** Specifies the protocol to be checked by the rule. You can specify `all`, `tcp`, `udp`, or `icmp`.
- **`-s <ip_address/mask>`** Specifies the source address to be checked. If you want to check all IP addresses, use `0/0`.

- **-d <ip_address/mask>** Specifies the destination address to be checked. If you want to check all IP addresses, use 0/0.
- **-j <target>** Specifies what to do if the packet matches the rule. You can specify the ACCEPT, REJECT, DROP, or LOG action.
- **-i <interface>** Specifies the interface where a packet is received. This only applies to INPUT and FORWARD chains.
- **-o <interface>** Specifies the interface where a packet is to be sent. This applies only to OUTPUT and FORWARD chains.

NOTE The options presented here represent only a sampling of what can be done with iptables. To see all the options available, see the iptables man page.

The best way to learn how to use iptables is to look at some examples. Table 15-5 has some sample iptables commands to start with.

You can use iptables to create a sophisticated array of rules that control how data flows through the firewall. Most administrators use the -P option with iptables to set up the firewall's default filtering rules. Once the default is in place, use iptables to configure exceptions to the default behavior needed by the particular network.

Remember that any rules created with iptables are not persistent. If you reboot the system, they will be lost by default. To save the rules, use the iptables-save command to write firewall tables out to a file. Then use the iptables-restore command to restore the tables from the file created.

iptables Command	Function
iptables -L	Lists existing rules
iptables -D FORWARD 1	Deletes the first rule in the FORWARD chain
iptables -t filter -F	Deletes all rules from the filter table
iptables -P INPUT DROP	Sets a default policy for the INPUT chain that drops all incoming packets
iptables -P FORWARD DROP	Configures your FORWARD chain to drop all packets
iptables -A INPUT -s 0/0 -p icmp -j DROP	Configures the firewall to disregard all incoming ping packets addressed to the local Linux system
iptables -A INPUT -i eth0 -s 192.168.2.0/24 -j DROP	Configures the firewall to accept all incoming packets on eth0 coming from the 192.168.2.0 network

Table 15-5 Some iptables Commands

Exercise 15-4: Implementing Network Security Measures with `iptables`

In this exercise, you practice scanning for open IP ports and implementing a simple host-based firewall. Perform this exercise using the virtual machine that comes with this book.

VIDEO Please watch the Exercise 15-4 video for a demonstration on how to perform this task.

1. Boot your Linux system and log in as your **`student1`** user.
2. Open a terminal session and switch to your `root` user account by entering **`su -`** followed by the password **`student1`**.
3. Scan your system for open ports by completing the following steps:
   a. At the shell prompt, enter **`nmap -sT <your_IP_address>`**. What TCP/IP ports are in use on your system?
   b. At the shell prompt, enter **`nmap -sU <your_IP_address>`**. What UDP/IP ports are in use on your system?
4. Configure a simple firewall with `iptables` by doing the following:
   a. From a remote system, **`ping`** your Linux system and verify that it responds.
   b. Open a terminal session.
   c. At the shell prompt, **`su -`** to `root`.
5. Configure the kernel to use the `iptables` filter by entering **`modprobe iptable_filter`** at the shell prompt.
6. List the current rules for the filter table by entering **`iptables -t filter -L`** at the shell prompt.
7. At the shell prompt, enter **`iptables -t filter -A INPUT -s 0/0 -p icmp -j DROP`**. This command creates a rule that will drop all incoming packets using the ICMP protocol from any source destined for the local system.
8. View your new rule by entering **`iptables -t filter -L`** at the shell prompt. You should see the following rule added to your `INPUT` chain:

```
DROP       icmp --  anywhere             anywhere
```

9. Using your remote system, **`ping`** your Linux system's IP address. The packets should be dropped, as shown in this sample output:

```
Pinging 192.168.1.10 with 32 bytes of data:
Request timed out.
Request timed out.
```

Configuring a Firewall with UFW

The uncomplicated firewall (UFW) makes firewall configuration simple. After installing UFW, start with a simple set of rules:

```
[root@cent71-5t camilla]# ufw default allow outgoing
[root@cent71-5t camilla]# ufw default deny incoming
[root@cent71-5t camilla]# ufw allow ssh
[root@cent71-5t camilla]# ufw allow 80/tcp
```

This example blocks all incoming traffic except for SSH and HTTP. The `ufw status` command will show all the rules that are enabled as well as whether `ufw` is active or inactive. Default firewall policies can be defined within the file `/etc/default/ufw`, such as whether or not to enable IPv6 and whether to drop or reject packets.

To override the default `UFW` rules, create `before.rules` and `after.rules` files within the `/etc/ufw` directory. Before rules run before the user settings when `UFW` runs, such as adding ping or loopback features. After rules run after the administrator's command-line rules.

NOTE For IPv6 settings, there are also `before6.rules` and `after6.rules` files within `/etc/ufw`.

Firewall Configuration with `nftables`

The `nftables` firewall was developed by netfilter.org, the organization that maintains `iptables`, to fix performance and scalability issues that `iptables` firewalls run into. For example, `iptables` works great for IPv4, but a separate `ip6tables` was created for IPv6 firewall rules. `nftables` can handle both IPv4 and IPv6 networks.

If you used `iptables`, you can convert these rules to `nftables` by using the `iptables-translate` utility. Some example `nftables` rules follow.

To allow incoming SSH connections, run

```
nft add rule ip filter INPUT tcp dport 22 ct state new,established counter accept
```

To allow incoming HTTP and HTTPS traffic, run

```
nft add rule ip filter INPUT ip protocol tcp dport {80,443} ct state
new,established counter accept
```

Encrypting Files with GPG

Just as you can encrypt network transmissions between Linux systems using SSH, you can also use encryption to protect files in the Linux filesystem. There are a wide variety of tools to do this. Some are open source; others are proprietary. A great utility for encrypting files is the open source GNU Privacy Guard (GPG) utility. We'll discuss the following topics in this section:

- How GPG works
- Using GPG to encrypt files
- Using GPG to revoke keys

Let's begin by discussing how GPG works.

EXAM TIP Knowledge of GPG is *not* part of the requirements on the CompTIA Linux+ exam. This section was added for your information.

How GPG Works

GNU Privacy Guard (GPG) is an open source implementation of the OpenPGP standard (RFC 4880). It allows users to encrypt and digitally sign data and communications. For example, users can encrypt files and digitally sign e-mail messages.

GPG provides a cryptographic engine that can be used directly from the shell prompt using the `gpg` command-line utility. It can also be called from within shell scripts or other programs running on the system. For example, GPG is integrated into several Linux e-mail clients such as Evolution and KMail as well as instant messaging applications such as Psi.

GPG supports many encryption algorithms, including AES, 3DES, Blowfish, MD5, SHA, and RSA.

NOTE The `gpg.conf` file is also located in the `~/.gnupg` directory. You can use this file to customize the way GPG works on your system.

Using GPG to Encrypt Files

To encrypt a file using GPG, follow these steps:

1. Use GPG to generate your keys. To do this, enter `gpg --gen-key` at the shell prompt. An example is shown here:

```
cgreer@openSUSE:~> gpg --gen-key
gpg (GnuPG) 2.0.22; Copyright (C) 2013 Free Software Foundation, Inc.
This is free software: you are free to change and redistribute it.
There is NO WARRANTY, to the extent permitted by law.

Please select what kind of key you want:
   (1) RSA and RSA (default)
   (2) DSA and Elgamal
   (3) DSA (sign only)
   (4) RSA (sign only)
Your selection?
```

2. Select the type of key you want to create. Usually you will use the default option (`1`), which uses RSA and RSA. You are prompted to specify the size of the key, as shown here:

```
RSA keys may be between 1024 and 4096 bits long.
What keysize do you want? (2048)
```

3. Specify the size of key you want to create. Using the default size of `2048` bits is usually sufficient. You are prompted to configure the key lifetime, as shown here:

```
Please specify how long the key should be valid.
         0 = key does not expire
      <n>  = key expires in n days
      <n>w = key expires in n weeks
      <n>m = key expires in n months
      <n>y = key expires in n years
Key is valid for? (0)
```

4. Specify when the key will expire. As shown in step 3, you can specify that the key expire in a certain number of days, weeks, months, or years.
5. Construct your user ID for the key. The first parameter you need to specify is your real name. The name you specify is very important because it will be used later during the encryption process. In the next example, I entered `cgreer` for the real name:

```
GnuPG needs to construct a user ID to identify your key.
Real name: cgreer
```

6. When prompted, enter your e-mail address.
7. When prompted, enter a comment of your choosing. You are prompted to confirm the user ID you have created for the key. An example is shown here:

```
You selected this USER-ID:
    "cgreer <cgreer@openSUSE>"

Change (N)ame, (C)omment, (E)mail or (O)kay/(Q)uit?
```

8. If the information is correct, enter `O` to confirm the ID. You are prompted to enter a passphrase for the key.
9. Enter a unique passphrase for the key. After doing so, you are prompted to perform various actions on the system while the key is generated. An example is shown here:

```
We need to generate a lot of random bytes. It is a good idea to perform
some other action (type on the keyboard, move the mouse, utilize the
disks) during the prime generation; this gives the random number
generator a better chance to gain enough entropy.
+++.++++++++++.++++++++++.++++++++++.++++++++++..+++++.++++++++++>++++++++++
..................................>+++++...........................<+++++.
................................>+++++..........<+++++.......+++++
```

10. Move your mouse and type on the keyboard. GPG uses these actions to generate random numbers to make the key. If you are not doing enough, you'll be prompted to increase activity to generate enough entropy to create the key. An example is shown here:

```
Not enough random bytes available.  Please do some other work to give
the OS a chance to collect more entropy! (Need 137 more bytes)
```

At this point, the key pair has been generated! The key files are stored in the `~/.gnupg` directory in the user's home directory. The following files are created in this directory:

- **`secring.gpg`** The GPG secret keyring
- **`pubring.gpg`** The GPG public keyring
- **`trustdb.gpg`** The GPG trust database

To create a backup of your GPG key pair, enter the following at the shell prompt:

```
gpg --export-secret-keys -armor <key_owner_email_address>  >  <filename>.asc
```

This is shown in the following example:

```
gpg --export-secret-keys --armor cgreer@openSUSE > cgreer-privatekey.asc
cgreer@openSUSE:~> ls
addnum         firstnames       mytestfile.txt       cgreer-privatekey.asc
```

For security, do not leave this file on your hard disk. Instead, copy it to a USB flash drive and lock it away. This will allow you to restore the private key should the original get corrupted.

Now use the key pair to encrypt files and messages. For example, to encrypt a file in the Linux filesystem, do the following:

1. At the shell prompt, enter `gpg -e -r <key_user_name> <filename>`. As shown here, I encrypted `mytestfile.txt`. The `-e` option tells GPG to encrypt the file. Remember that I specified a key username of `cgreer` when I created the key user ID, so that's what I enter here.

   ```
   cgreer@openSUSE:~> gpg -e -r cgreer mytestfile.txt
   ```

2. Use the `ls` command to view the new encrypted file that GPG created. The original file is left intact. The new file will have the same filename as the original file with a `.gpg` extension added. In the example here, the name of the new file is `mytestfile.txt.gpg`.

Once the file has been encrypted, it can then be decrypted using the `gpg` command. The syntax is

```
gpg --output <output_filename> --decrypt <encrypted_filename>
```

For example, to decrypt the `mytestfile.txt.gpg` file created earlier, enter

```
gpg --output mytestfile.txt.decrypted --decrypt mytestfile.txt.gpg
```

This is shown in the following example:

```
cgreer@openSUSE:~> gpg --output mytestfile.txt.decrypted --decrypt   \
mytestfile.txt.gpg

You need a passphrase to unlock the secret key for
user: "cgreer (<cgreer@openSUSE>"
2048-bit RSA key, ID FB8BF16C, created 2023-01-24 (main key ID 9DF54AB2)
```

```
gpg: encrypted with 2048-bit RSA key, ID FB8BF16C, created 2023-01-24
     "cgreer (<cgreer@openSUSE>"
cgreer@openSUSE:~> cat mytestfile.txt.decrypted
This is a text file that I wrote.
cgreer@openSUSE:~>
```

At this point, you are able to encrypt and decrypt files on your local system. But what do you do if you need to exchange encrypted files with someone else and you want both of you to be able to decrypt them? To do this, you must exchange and install GPG public keys on your systems.

To do this, copy your public keys to a public key server on the Internet. This is done by entering `gpg --keyserver hkp://subkeys.pgp.net --send-key <key_ID>` at the shell prompt. Notice that this command requires you to know the ID number associated with your GPG public key. This number is displayed when you initially create the GPG key pair; you can generate it again from the command line by entering `gpg --fingerprint <key_owner_email>`, as shown here:

```
cgreer@openSUSE:~> gpg --fingerprint cgreer@openSUSE > key_ID.txt
cgreer@openSUSE:~> cat key_ID.txt
pub   2048R/9DF54AB2 2023-01-24
      Key fingerprint = AF46 4AB3 1397 B88E BC6A  FBDA 465F 82C4 9DF5 4AB2
uid                  cgreer        <cgreer@openSUSE>
sub   2048R/FB8BF16C 2023-01-24
```

In this example, the output was saved from the command to a file named `key_ID.txt` to keep it handy, but this is optional. The ID number of the key is contained in the first line of output from the command. The number needed appears in bold in this example.

Once you have the ID number, you can then copy your GPG public key to a public key server on the Internet. Using the preceding information for my system, enter the following at the command prompt:

```
gpg --keyserver hkp://subkeys.pgp.net --send-key 9DF54AB2
```

This option works great if you want to be able to exchange keys with a large number of other users. However, if you are only concerned about doing this with a limited number of people, just directly exchange keys between systems.

To do this, users can export public keys and send them to each other. To do this, enter the following at the shell prompt:

```
gpg --export --armor <key_owner_email>  >  <public_key_filename>
```

For example, to export the public key to the file named `gpg.pub` created earlier, enter the following:

```
cgreer@openSUSE:~> gpg --export cgreer@openSUSE > gpg.pub
```

Each user can then copy their key file to the other users. For example, to send a key to the `charly` user account on another Linux host named `fedora`, enter the following:

```
cgreer@openSUSE:~> scp gpg.pub charly@fedora:
```

Once this is done, each user can import the other users' public keys into their GPG keyring using the `gpg --import <public_key_filename>` command. For example, use `scp` to copy the public key file from the `openSUSE` system to the `fedora` system, and then use `gpg` to import the public key:

```
[charly@fedora ~]$ gpg --import gpg.pub
gpg: key 9DF54AB2: public key "cgreer <cgreer@openSUSE>" imported
gpg: Total number processed: 1
gpg:               imported: 1  (RSA: 1)
[charly@fedora ~]
```

Remember, each user needs to repeat this process. Then they can use each other's GPG keys to encrypt and decrypt files. You can view the keys in your GPG keyring by using the `gpg --list-keys` command, as shown in the following example:

```
[charly@fedora ~]$ gpg --list-keys
/home/charly/.gnupg/pubring.gpg
--------------------------------
pub   2048R/9DF54AB2 2023-01-24
uid                  cgreer <cgreer@openSUSE>
sub   2048R/FB8BF16C 2023-01-24
[charly@fedora ~]$
```

In this example, you can see that the public key created earlier on `openSUSE` is now imported into the `charly` user's GPG keyring on `fedora`. The keyring file itself is located in the `~/.gnupg/` directory within my home directory and is named `pubring.gpg`.

Using GPG to Revoke Keys

Before we end this chapter, we need to discuss the topic of *key revocation.* From time to time, you may need to revoke a key, which withdraws it from public use. This should be done if the key becomes compromised or gets lost, or if you forget the passphrase associated with the key.

To revoke a key, you create a *key revocation certificate.* As a best practice, you should create a key revocation certificate immediately after initially creating your key pair. This is done in case something gets corrupted and the revocation certificate can't be created should it be required for some reason later on. Creating the key revocation certificate doesn't actually revoke the key pair; only when you issue the key revocation certificate does the key get revoked. Therefore, the key revocation certificate is a placeholder just in case it's needed later.

To create (not issue) the key revocation certificate, enter the following at the shell prompt:

```
gpg --output revoke.asc --gen-revoke <key_ID>
```

Remember, use the `--fingerprint` option with the `gpg` command to view the key ID number. In the example that follows, a key revocation certificate is created for the GPG key pair generated for the `charly` user on the `fedora` system:

```
[charly@fedora ~]$ gpg --fingerprint charly@fedora
pub   2048R/899AB9E6 2023-01-24
      Key fingerprint = A469 942C F5C9 555A B4A4  F975 1B3A CB26 899A B9E6
uid                  charly <charly@fedora>
sub   2048R/A86F1A4B 2023-01-24
[charly@fedora ~]$ gpg --output revoke.asc --gen-revoke 899AB9E6
sec  2048R/899AB9E6 2023-01-24 charly <charly@fedora>
Create a revocation certificate for this key? (y/N) y
Please select the reason for the revocation:
  0 = No reason specified
  1 = Key has been compromised
  2 = Key is superseded
  3 = Key is no longer used
  Q = Cancel
(Probably you want to select 1 here)
Your decision? 1
Enter an optional description; end it with an empty line:
> This key has been compromised
>
Reason for revocation: Key has been compromised
This key has been compromised
Is this okay? (y/N) y
You need a passphrase to unlock the secret key for
user: "charly <charly@fedora>"
2048-bit RSA key, ID 899AB9E6, created 2023-01-24
ASCII armored output forced.
Revocation certificate created.
Please move it to a medium which you can hide away; if Mallory gets
access to this certificate he can use it to make your key unusable.
It is smart to print this certificate and store it away, just in case
your media become unreadable.  But have some caution:  The print system of
your machine might store the data and make it available to others!
```

Avoid keeping the key revocation certificate on your system's hard disk. Instead, copy it to the same flash drive as your key pair backup and lock it away! If someone were to get a hold of this file, they could revoke the certificate without the administrator's knowledge or consent.

NOTE Again, knowledge of GPG is *not* part of the requirements on the CompTIA Linux+ exam. This section was added for your edification.

So what should you do if the certificate actually does get compromised and you end up needing to revoke it? Import the revocation certificate in the same manner we discussed for standard certificates. Enter `gpg --import <revocation_certificate_filename>` at the shell prompt:

```
[charly@fedora ~]$ gpg --import revoke.asc
gpg: key 899AB9E6: "charly <charly@fedora>" revocation certificate imported
gpg: Total number processed: 1
gpg:    new key revocations: 1
gpg: 3 marginal(s) needed, 1 complete(s) needed, PGP trust model
gpg: depth: 0  valid:   1  signed:   0  trust: 0-, 0q, 0n, 0m, 0f, 1u
```

Once this is done, verify that the key was revoked by entering gpg --list-keys <key_ID> at the shell prompt. If you used the manual method discussed earlier in this chapter to distribute the public key, you must import the key revocation certificate on any other systems where your public key was imported.

If you are using a public key server on the Internet to distribute your keys to other users, you would need to issue the key revocation certificate there as well. Enter gpg --keyserver <public_key_server_URL> --send <key_ID> at the shell prompt. This lets everyone who is using your public key know that the key has been compromised and should no longer be used.

Exercise 15-5: Using GPG to Encrypt Files

In this exercise, you use GPG to encrypt a file and send it to a second Linux system. Then, you export the public key, copy it to the second Linux system, and decrypt the file that was sent. You'll need at least two Linux systems for this exercise. Use two live Linux systems, two Linux virtual machines, or a mixture of both.

VIDEO Please watch the Exercise 15-5 video for a demonstration on how to perform this task.

Complete the following steps:

1. Generate your GPG key pair by following these steps:
   a. Boot your first Linux system and log in as a standard user.
   b. Open a terminal session.
   c. Enter **gpg --gen-key** at the shell prompt.
   d. When prompted to select the type of key you want to create, press **Enter** to use the default option (1), which uses RSA and RSA.
   e. When prompted to specify the size of the key, press **Enter** to use the default size of 2048 bits.
   f. When prompted to specify when the key will expire, press **Enter** to select the default option (0), which specifies that the key never expires.
   g. Enter **y** when prompted to confirm this selection.

NOTE We're doing this for demonstration purposes. In the real world, you should configure your keys to expire after a certain length of time. That way, if your key ever gets compromised, it will become invalid after a period of time.

   h. Construct the user ID for the key by first specifying a username that is at least five characters long. Write down the username you entered because you will need it later.

i. When prompted, enter your e-mail address. Write down the e-mail address you entered because you will need it later.
j. When prompted, enter your full name as a comment.
k. When prompted to confirm the user ID you created for the key, enter **O** (the letter, not a zero) to confirm it.
l. When prompted to enter a passphrase for the key, enter a unique passphrase.
m. When prompted, move the mouse, type characters on your keyboard, or open and close your optical disc drive door. After you have done this, your key pair is generated!

2. Encrypt a file with GPG by doing the following:
   a. At the shell prompt, enter **gpg -e -r <key_user_name> mytestfile.txt**. Replace **<key_user_name>** with the real name you entered when creating your key. You created the `mytestfile.txt` file in Exercise 15-1. If you don't have this file, create a new one with this name.
   b. At the shell prompt, use the **ls** command to verify that the `mytestfile.txt.gpg` file was created.
3. Decrypt the file you just created by doing the following:
   a. Enter the following at the shell prompt to decrypt the file:
   ```
   gpg --output mytestfile.txt.decrypted --decrypt mytestfile.txt.gpg
   ```
   b. Use the **cat** command to display the contents of the **mytestfile.txt.decrypted** file and verify that it matches the content of the original file.
4. Send the encrypted file to a different system and decrypt it there by doing the following:
   a. Boot your second Linux system and log in as a standard user.
   b. Use the **ping** command to verify that the second Linux system can communicate over the network with the first Linux system, where you create the GPG key pair.
   c. Switch back to your first Linux system.
   d. From the shell prompt of your first Linux system, export your key by entering the following:
   ```
   gpg --export --armor <key_owner_email> > gpg.pub
   ```
   e. Use the **scp** command to copy the `gpg.pub` and `mytestfile.txt.gpg` files from your first Linux system to your second Linux system.
   f. Switch over to your second Linux system.
   g. Verify that the `gpg.pub` file was copied to your user's home directory.
   h. Import the public key from your first Linux system into the GPG keyring by entering **gpg --import ~/gpg.pub** at the shell prompt.

i. Verify that the public key was imported by entering **gpg --list-keys** at the shell prompt.

j. Decrypt the encrypted file you copied over from the first Linux system by entering the following at the shell prompt:

```
gpg --output mytestfile.txt.decrypted --symmetric mytestfile.txt.gpg
```

k. When prompted, enter the passphrase you assigned to the GPG key when you created it on the first system.

l. Use the **cat** command to display the contents of the **mytestfile.txt .decrypted** file and verify that it matches the content of the original file on the first Linux system.

5. Perform maintenance tasks on your GPG key pair by doing the following:

a. Create a backup of your GPG key pair by entering the following at the shell prompt:

```
gpg --export-secret-keys --armor <key_owner_email_address> > gpgkey.asc
```

b. Create a key revocation certificate by entering the following at the shell prompt:

```
gpg --output revoke.asc --gen-revoke <key_ID>
```

Remember, you can use the `--fingerprint` option with the `gpg` command to view the key ID number.

Chapter Review

This chapter covered how to use encryption to secure data on a Linux system and network security systems. We first looked at encrypting network communications with SSH, then explored high-available networks with bonding, and then reviewed defending networking attacks using `firewalld` and `iptables`.

Be familiar with the following key facts about network security:

- With symmetric encryption, the key used to encrypt a message is the same key used to decrypt the message. The sender and the receiver must both have the exact same key.
- Symmetric encryption processes much faster than asymmetric encryption.
- One of the difficulties associated with symmetric encryption is how to securely distribute the key to all the parties that need to communicate with each other.
- Asymmetric encryption uses two keys instead of one: the public key and the private key.
- Data that has been encoded with the public key can be decoded only with its private key. Data that has been signed with the private key can be verified only with its public key.
- A certificate authority (CA) is responsible for issuing and managing encryption keys.

- The private key is given only to the key owner.
- The public key can be made available to anyone who needs it.
- The primary role of the CA is to verify that parties involved in an encrypted exchange are who they say they are.
- Administrators can mint their own certificates, called self-assigned certificates.
- Hashing is used for file integrity checking. Hash values are unique to every file. When this fails, it is called a collision.
- Popular hash algorithms include MD5 and SHA.
- SSH uses private/public key encryption along with secret key encryption:
    - The SSH client first creates a connection with the system where the SSH server is running on IP port 22.
    - To use the SSH client on your local computer, connect to the `sshd` daemon on the remote Linux system by entering `ssh -l <user_name> <ip_address>` at the shell prompt.
- VPNs use IPSec in tunnel mode to provide encryption and authentication.
- Tunnel mode is best over untrusted networks, such as from home to the office.
- VPNs in transport mode use IPSec to encrypt packets and are a good solution over trusted networks.
- High-availability networks are implemented within Linux by way of bridging or bonding technologies.
- Network bridging provides fault tolerance.
- Network bonding boosts network throughput.
- Use the `brctl` command to set up a network bridge.
- Network bonding requires updating network scripts and enabling the bonding policy.
- Bonding options include active-passive, aggregation, and load balancing.
- Single sign-on (SSO) allows users the convenience of using one username and password to access their data within their entire organization.
- Popular SSO services include RADIUS with dial-up modem access, LDAP for vendor-neutral environments, Kerberos, which hides passwords by using tickets that expire, and TACACS+ for high availability and reliability.
- Linux systems can be configured as firewalls using `firewalld`, `iptables`, `netfilter`, `nftables`, or `ufw`.
- The `nmap`, `netstat`, and `lsof -i` utilities are used to examine vulnerable open IP ports.
- To enable IP forwarding, run `echo 1 > /proc/sys/net/ipv4/ip_forward`.

- The `firewalld` feature offers nine default zones, including `work`, `home`, `internal`, `external`, `dmz`, and `public`.
- Run `firewall-cmd --get-default-zone` to view the current zone setting.
- Run `firewall-cmd --permanent` to make runtime values permanent after reboot.

Questions

1. Which of the following statements are true of symmetric encryption? (Choose two.)
   - **A.** It uses a private/public key pair.
   - **B.** Both the sender and the recipient must have a copy of the same key.
   - **C.** RSA is a form of symmetric encryption.
   - **D.** Blowfish is a form of symmetric encryption.
2. Which tools can scan for open network ports? (Choose two.)
   - **A.** `tcpwatch`
   - **B.** `lsof`
   - **C.** `nmap`
   - **D.** `wireshark`
   - **E.** `webgoat`
3. Which host key files store the private keys used by the SSH version 2 server? (Choose two.)
   - **A.** `/etc/ssh/ssh_host_key`
   - **B.** `/etc/ssh/ssh_host_key.pub`
   - **C.** `/etc/ssh/ssh_known_hosts`
   - **D.** `/etc/ssh/ssh_host_rsa_key`
   - **E.** `/etc/ssh/ssh_host_dsa_key`
4. Which parameter in the `/etc/ssh/sshd_config` file specifies which version of SSH the `sshd` daemon should use?
   - **A.** `HostKey`
   - **B.** `Protocol`
   - **C.** `SSHVersion`
   - **D.** `ListenAddress`

5. Which parameter in the `/etc/ssh/sshd_config` file configures the SSH server to disable root logins?
   A. `RootAccess`
   B. `AllowRootLogin`
   C. `PermitRootLogin`
   D. `DenyRootLogin`
6. Which option to `iptables` will list the current firewall rules?
   A. `iptables -N`
   B. `iptables -L`
   C. `iptables -I`
   D. `iptables -R`
7. Which of the following shell commands will load the SSH client and connect as the `sseymour` user to an SSH server with an IP address of 10.0.0.254?
   A. `sshd -l sseymour 10.0.0.254`
   B. `ssh -u sseymour 10.0.0.254`
   C. `ssh -l sseymour 10.0.0.254`
   D. `sshd -u sseymour 10.0.0.254`
8. Which of the following are hashing algorithms? (Select two.)
   A. RSA
   B. DSA
   C. MD5
   D. SHA
9. You've just created a DSA private/public key pair for use with SSH public key authentication. What is the name of the public key file?
   A. `~/.ssh/id_rsa`
   B. `~/.ssh/id_dsa`
   C. `~/.ssh/id_rsa.pub`
   D. `~/.ssh/id_dsa.pub`
10. You've copied your RSA public key to the home directory of a user on an SSH server. Which file do you need to add the public key to in order to enable public key authentication?
    A. `~/.ssh/authorized_keys`
    B. `/etc/ssh/authorized_keys`
    C. `~/.ssh/id_rsa`
    D. `~/ssh_host_key.pub`

Answers

1. **B, D.** With symmetric encryption, both the sender and the recipient must have a copy of the same key. Blowfish is a form of symmetric encryption.
2. **B, C.** Use `nmap` and `lsof -i` to view open network ports on a system.
3. **D, E.** The private keys used by the SSH version 2 server are stored in `/etc/ssh/ssh_host_rsa_key` and `/etc/ssh/ssh_host_dsa_key`. The private keys for SSH version 1 are stored in `/etc/ssh/ssh_host_key`.
4. **B.** The `Protocol` parameter in the `/etc/ssh/sshd_config` file specifies which version of SSH the `sshd` daemon should use.
5. **C.** The `PermitRootLogin` parameter is set to `no` to disallow logging in as `root`.
6. **B.** Use `iptables -L` to list the current firewall ruleset with `iptables`.
7. **C.** The `ssh -l sseymour 10.0.0.254` command will load the SSH client and connect as the `sseymour` user to an SSH server with an IP address of 10.0.0.254.
8. **C, D.** The integrity checking algorithms include SHA and MD5. RSA and DSA are asymmetric encryption algorithms.
9. **D.** The `~/.ssh/id_dsa.pub` file is the DSA public key that can be used for SSH public key authentication.
10. **A.** You need to add the public key to the `~/.ssh/authorized_keys` file in the home directory of the user you want to authenticate as using public key authentication.

CHAPTER 16

Securing Linux

In this chapter, you will learn about

- Securing the system
- Controlling user access
- Managing system logs
- Enhancing group and file security

There were only about five of us, so we were not a threat. We were hardly noticed.

—Evelyn Boyd Granville, IBM

In today's world, security is a key issue in every organization. A Linux system administrator needs to be aware of the security threats affecting the architecture. This chapter covers how to increase the security of the Linux system.

EXAM TIP Computer system security is an ever-evolving topic. The security issues of recent years, such as ransomware and identity theft, teach us to prepare for the security incidents of tomorrow. This is reflected in your CompTIA Linux+ exam. Do not be overly concerned with specific security threats. Instead, focus on commands and key security principles.

Securing the System

One of the most important and most frequently overlooked aspects of Linux security is securing the system itself. Topics addressed here include

- Securing the physical environment
- Securing access to the operating system

Securing the Physical Environment

Convenience or security? That is the question. Many firms desire easy access to their computer systems. Organizations must balance security with convenience. If data on the system is mission critical or contains sensitive information, it should be less convenient to access, thus keeping it more secure.

Consider scenarios such as the following when determining physical access to Linux systems:

- A rogue supplier steals the hard drive from a server containing clients' tax identification numbers.
- A rogue employee steals week-old backup tapes from the shelf located outside the secure server room. The data contains customer logins and password hints.
- A passerby steals a pancake-style server from an unlocked closet, gleaning private health records of patients.

As a Linux administrator, one of the most important steps you can take is to limit who can access data-processing systems. Servers need the highest degree of physical security and should be locked in a server room. Access to the server room should be strictly controlled.

NOTE Passwords combined with biometric systems create multifactor authentication (MFA). Biometric systems scan retinas, match fingerprints, or observe voice patterns to control access to data.

In addition to controlling access to the office, you can further protect your organization's workstations and servers by securing access to the operating system.

Securing Access to the Operating System

After physically securing access to computer systems, the next line of defense is the access controls built into the Linux operating system itself. Of course, Linux provides user accounts and passwords to control who can do what with the system. This is an excellent feature, allowing users to protect their data no matter their level of responsibility or the criticality of the data. After the end users' work is complete, teach them to log out or lock their screen (a *session lock*, as shown in Figure 16-1) as a good security practice to protect their data.

CAUTION You should never leave a server logged in. If you do, at least use a screensaver that requires a password to resume operations. Otherwise, best security practice is that if the user is not using the server console, they should log out.

To allow users to log out and leave without killing an important process, use the `nohup` command to initially load the command. Any process loaded by `nohup` will ignore any hang-up signals it receives, such as those sent when logging out. The syntax for using `nohup` is `nohup <command> &`. For example, in Figure 16-2, the `find -name named &` command has been loaded using `nohup`, allowing the `find` command to continue to run even if the shell were logged out.

Finally, administrators need to also protect servers from data loss. Strategic plans could be leaked to competitors, harming the organization's image. One method to protect data

Figure 16-1 Locking the desktop

```
root@openSUSE:~
File Edit View Search Terminal Help
openSUSE:~ # nohup find / -name named &
[1] 2658
nohup: ignoring input and appending output to 'nohup.out'
```

Figure 16-2 Using `nohup`

leaks is to *disable USB ports.* In Linux you can do this by blocklisting or removing the USB module after Linux installation and every kernel update:

```
root# rm /lib/modules/$(uname -r)/kernel/drivers/usb/storage/usb-storage.ko.xz
```

Other Linux hardening security measures include

- Detecting threats through security scanning
- Avoiding threats by disabling or removing insecure services like Telnet and FTP
- Mitigating threats by removing unused packages and applications

- Blocking threats by configuring the host firewall, such as UFW
- Securing service accounts by enabling the `nologin` shell in `/etc/passwd`

Successful security practices boil down to end-user training. Social engineering attacks mitigate technical controls put in place by the system administrator to secure the network. If end users do not cooperate, corporate policies such as acceptable use policies and computer usage policies must be enforced.

Controlling User Access

A key aspect of both Linux workstation security and Linux server security is to implement and use user access controls to constrain what users can do with the system. Earlier in this book, we discussed how to create and manage users, groups, and permissions to do this. However, you can take additional measures to increase the security of your systems. In this section, we review the following:

- To root or not to root?
- Implementing a strong password policy
- Locking accounts after failed authentications
- Configuring user limits
- Disabling user login
- Security auditing using `find`

Let's begin by discussing the proper care and feeding of the *root* user account.

To Root or Not to Root?

As discussed earlier in this book, every Linux system, whether a workstation or a server, includes a default administrator account named `root`. This account has full access to every aspect of the system. As such, it should be used with great care. As a Linux+ candidate, you need understand the following:

- Proper use of the `root` user account
- Using `su`
- Using `sudo`
- Using `pkexec`

Proper Use of the `root` User Account

A key mistake made by new Linux users is excessive use of the `root` account. There's a time and a place when the `root` user account should be used; however, most of the work on a Linux system should be done as a non-root user. The rule of thumb is this: only use `root` when absolutely necessary. If a task can be completed as a non-root user, then use a non-root user account.

Why is the proper use of the root user account of concern? Imagine the havoc an intruder could wreak if they were to happen upon an unattended system logged in as root! All of the data on the system could be accessed and copied. Major configuration changes could be made to the daemons running on the system. Heaven only knows what kind of malware could be installed.

The point is that a system logged in as root represents a serious security risk. Everyone, including the system administrator, should have a standard user account that they always use to access the system. If the system administrator requires root privilege, they should temporarily use the privilege and then return back to normal privilege. Linux provides three ways to do this that are important for the CompTIA Linux+ exam: su, sudo, and pkexec.

Using su

The su command stands for "substitute user." This command allows you to change to a different user account at the shell prompt. The syntax is su <options> <user_account>. If no user account is specified in the command, su assumes switching to the root user account. Here are some of the more useful options you can use with su:

- **-** Loads the target user's profile. For example, when you use the su - command to switch to the root user account, this also loads root's environment variables.
- **-c <command>** Temporarily switches to the target user account, runs the specified command, and returns to the original account.
- **-m** Switches to the target user account but preserves the existing profile.

Everyone with the root password can use su to switch to the root user, but providing all users root privileges is a very poor security practice. Also, becoming root with su will not log the activities of the user. Sometimes users need root access temporarily to add a printer or a new network device. There must be a way to do this without having to locate the system administrator, and that method is with sudo.

Using sudo

Suppose there is a power user on a Linux system. This user might be a programmer, a project manager, or a database administrator. A user in this category may frequently need to run some root-level commands. To allow them to run a limited number of root-level commands, and to log their administrator activity, you can teach them to use sudo.

The sudo command allows a given user to run a command as a different user account. As with su, it could be any user account on the system; however, it is most frequently used to run commands as root. The sudo command reads the /etc/sudoers file to determine what user is authorized to run which commands. This file uses the following aliases to define who can do what:

- **User_Alias** Specifies the user accounts allowed to run commands
- **Cmnd_Alias** Specifies the commands that users can run
- **Host_Alias** Specifies the hosts that users can run commands on
- **Runas_Alias** Specifies the usernames that commands can be run as

```
root@openSUSE:~

File  Edit  View  Search  Terminal  Help
## sudoers file.
##
## This file MUST be edited with the 'visudo' command as root.
## Failure to use 'visudo' may result in syntax or file permission errors
## that prevent sudo from running.
##
## See the sudoers man page for the details on how to write a sudoers file.
##


##
## Host alias specification
##
## Groups of machines. These may include host names (optionally with wildcards),
## IP addresses, network numbers or netgroups.
# Host_Alias     WEBSERVERS = www1, www2, www3

##
## User alias specification
##
## Groups of users.  These may consist of user names, uids, Unix groups,
## or netgroups.
# User_Alias     ADMINS = millert, dowdy, mikef

"/etc/sudoers.tmp" 81L, 3009C                              1,1          Top
```

Figure 16-3 Editing /etc/sudoers with visudo

To edit the /etc/sudoers file, run either sudo -e /etc/sudoers, sudoedit /etc/sudoers or simply the visudo command as the root user. The /etc/sudoers file is loaded in using the default editor, which is usually vi but may be modified using the EDITOR, VISUAL, or SUDO_EDITOR environment variable. Your changes are written to /etc/sudoers.tmp until committed. This is shown in Figure 16-3.

NOTE To modify the default editor for programs like sudoedit, place the following line into the user's ~/.bashrc file:

```
EDITOR=/usr/bin/nano; export EDITOR
```

This example implements nano to be the default editor.

The /etc/sudoers file is configured by default such that users must supply their personal password when using sudo, instead of the root password like with su. This sudo feature makes the system more secure because the root password is shared with fewer users.

To configure the /etc/sudoers configuration file, modify User_Alias to define an alias containing the user accounts (separated by commas) allowed to run commands as root. The syntax is

```
User_Alias <alias> = <user1>, <user2>, <user3>, ...
```

For example, to create an alias named PWRUSRS that contains the cheryl, theo, and aria user accounts, you would enter the following in the /etc/sudoers file:

```
User_Alias PWRUSRS = cheryl, theo, aria
```

NOTE All alias names within /etc/sudoers must start with a capital letter!

Next use Cmnd_Alias to define the commands, using the full path, that you want the defined users to run. Separate multiple commands with commas; for example, if the users are programmers who need to be able to kill processes, define an alias named KILLPROCS that contains the kill command, as shown here:

```
Cmnd_Alias KILLPROCS = /bin/kill, /usr/bin/killall
```

Then use Host_Alias to specify which systems the users can run the commands on. For example, to allow them to run commands on a system named openSUSE, use the following:

```
Host_Alias MYHSTS = openSUSE
```

Finally, to glue the aliases together to define exactly what will happen, the syntax is this:

```
User_Alias Host_Alias = (user) Cmnd_Alias
```

For example, to allow the specified users to run the specified commands on the specified hosts as root, enter the following:

```
PWRUSRS      MYHSTS = (root) KILLPROCS
```

Now that the updates to /etc/sudoers are complete, exit visudo by pressing Esc and then enter :wq (this assumes that EDITOR is defined as /usr/bin/vi). The visudo utility will verify the syntax and, if everything is correct, will exit. At this point, the end users defined within /etc/sudoers can execute commands as the root user by entering sudo <command> at the shell prompt. For example, the cheryl user could kill a process named vmware-toolbox (owned by root) by entering sudo killall vmware-toolbox at the shell prompt. After the cheryl user supplies her password, *not* the root password, the process is killed.

You can also allow users to run sudo commands without a password. The following entry in /etc/sudoers allows the user amos to run the kill command without a password:

```
amos    ALL = NOPASSWD: /bin/kill, PASSWD: /usr/bin/lprm
```

User amos would still need a password to remove print jobs using the lprm command.

Using pkexec

Similar to the sudo command, the pkexec command, a PolicyKit feature, allows you to run a command as another user. PolicyKit is a toolkit used to define and handle authorizations. If the user liara wants to view the /etc/hosts file as user allen, she runs the following command:

```
[liara@localhost ~]$ pkexec -user allen cat /etc/hosts
127.0.0.1     localhost
::1           localhost
```

The /etc/hosts file is catenated after liara enters her password.

Implementing a Strong Password Policy

Another serious security weakness to organizations is the use of weak passwords. A weak password is one that can be easily guessed or cracked. Here are some examples:

- A last name
- A mother's maiden name
- A birthday
- Any word that can be found in the dictionary
- Using "password" as the password
- Blank passwords

These types of passwords are used because they are easy to remember. Unfortunately, they are also easy to crack. Administrators need to train their users to use strong passwords, such as passphrases. A strong password uses the following:

- Twelve or more characters (the longer the better!)
- A combination of numbers, special characters, and letters
- Upper- and lowercase letters
- Words not found in the dictionary

For example, a password such as M3n0v31273!! is a relatively strong password because it meets the criteria, but it is hard to remember. A passphrase such as To &3 or NOT to &3 is strong and easier to remember. The Linux password management utilities are configured by default to check user passwords to ensure they meet the criteria for strong passwords. For example, if you try to use a weak password with the passwd command, you are prompted to use a stronger one, as shown here:

```
[root@localhost ~]# passwd theo
New Password:BAD PASSWORD: it is WAY too short
BAD PASSWORD: is too simple
Retype new password:
```

In addition to requiring the use of strong passwords, administrators should also configure user accounts such that passwords expire after a certain period of time. This is called *password aging*. Why age passwords? The longer a user has the same password, the more likely it is to be compromised. Forcing users to periodically change passwords keeps intruders guessing. The length of time allowed for a given password varies from organization to organization. More security-minded organizations mandate password ages of 27–30 days. Less paranoid organizations use aging of 90 or more days.

NOTE NIST Special Publication 800-63B announced in March 2020 that if you are using two-factor authentication (2FA), annual password changes are sufficient in most circumstances.

Administrators can configure aging for passwords by using the `chage` command. The syntax for using `chage` is `chage <option> <user>`. The following options are available with `chage`:

- **`-m <days>`** Specifies the minimum number of days between password changes
- **`-M <days>`** Specifies the maximum number of days between password changes
- **`-W <days>`** Specifies the number of warning days before a password change is required

For example, in Figure 16-4, the `chage` command has been used to specify a minimum password age of 5 days, a maximum password age of 90 days, and 7 warning days for the `ksanders` user.

Social Engineering Threats

Administrators should also train users on how to deal with social engineering attempts. Social engineering is one of the most effective tools in the intruder's toolbox. Social engineering exploits human weaknesses instead of technical weaknesses in the system. Here's how a typical social engineering exploit works.

The intruder calls an employee of an organization, posing as another employee. The intruder tells the employee that he is "Fred" from Sales and is on the road at a client site. He needs to get a very important file from the server and cannot remember his password. He then asks the employee if he can use their password "just this once" to get the files he needs.

```
root@openSUSE:~
File  Edit  View  Search  Terminal  Help
openSUSE:~ # chage -m 5 -M 90 -W 7 ksanders
openSUSE:~ #
```

Figure 16-4 Using `chage` to set password aging

Most employees want to be team players and help out in an emergency. They are all too willing to hand out their password, granting the intruder easy access to the system.

Finally, administrators need to mitigate the flood of *phishing e-mails* plaguing organizations. Phishing e-mails appear to come from a legitimate organization, such as a bank, a friend, or an e-commerce website. They convince the user to click a link that takes them to a malicious website where they are tricked into revealing their password.

Train users to *hover* their mouse over a link (*without* clicking it) to see where the link actually leads. If the link is not pointing to a legitimate organization's URL, there's a pretty good chance the message is an exploit.

The best way to combat social engineering is end-user training. Enforce policies of not writing down passwords and not clicking e-mail links, as well as shredding sensitive data and forwarding any calls asking for passwords to the security office.

In addition to configuring password aging, you can also increase the security of your Linux systems by limiting logins and resources. Let's review how this is done next.

EXAM TIP Password security threat practices comprise a very important topic, but are not an area of focus for the CompTIA Linux+ exam. Be sure you know the columns and permissions of the `/etc/passwd` and `/etc/shadow` files.

Locking Accounts After Failed Authentications

Administrators can secure user account access using Pluggable Authentication Modules (PAM). PAM controls authentication of users for applications such as `login`, `ssh`, `su`, and others. For example, use PAM to enforce password strength by requiring specific password lengths and characters or to disallow users from logging in from specific terminals.

Linux locates the PAM configuration files in the `/etc/pam.d` directory. Configuration files for services such as `login`, `ssh`, and others are located here. Partial contents of `/etc/pam.d/sshd` appear as follows:

```
...
auth required pam_nologin.so
auth sufficient pam_ldap.so
account sufficient pam_ldap.so
password required pam_ldap.so
password required pam_limits.so
session required pam_selinux.so
session include password-auth
...
```

The first column represents authentication tasks, grouped by account, authentication, password, and session:

- **`account`** Provides account verification services (for example, whether the password has expired and whether the user is allowed access to a specific service)
- **`auth`** Used to authenticate the user, request a password, and set up credentials

- **`password`** Requests the user to enter a replacement password when updating the password
- **`session`** Manages what happens during setup or cleanup of a service (for example, mounting the home directory or setting resource limits)

The second column represents the control keyword to manage the success or failure processing:

- **`required`** If `required` fails, the entire operation fails after running through all the other modules.
- **`requisite`** The operation fails immediately if `requisite` fails.
- **`sufficient`** If successful, this is enough to satisfy the requirements of the service.
- **`optional`** Will cause an operation to fail if it is the only module in the stack for that facility.

The third column displays the module that gets invoked, which can take additional options and arguments. For example, `pam_ldap.so` provides authentication, authorization, and password changing to LDAP servers. The `pam_nologin.so` module prevents non-admin users from logging in to a system if the `/etc/nologin` file exists. The default security context permission is set with the `pam_selinux.so` module.

Using `pam_tally2` to Manage Failed Authentications

To deny access after three failed login attempts, add the following two lines to `/etc/pam.d/sshd`:

```
auth required pam_tally2.so deny=3 onerr=fail
account required pam_tally2.so
```

The `pam_tally2.so` module is the login counter. The argument `deny=3` sets the login counter for failed attempts, and `onerr=fail` will lock the account after three failures in this case.

To view the tally of failed logins, the `root` user can run the `/sbin/pam_tally2` command, as shown here:

```
[root@localhost ~]# pam_tally2
Login       Failures    Latest failure         From
malina      3           06/15/2024 12:12:13    localhost
```

After the security issue has been investigated, the `root` user can reset the account to allow logins, as follows:

```
[root@localhost ~]# pam_tally2 -u malina -r
Login       Failures    Latest failure         From
malina      3           06/15/2024 12:12:13    localhost
[root@localhost ~]# pam_tally2 -u malina -r
Login       Failures    Latest failure         From
malina      0
```

Using faillock to Manage Failed Authentications

The other utility used to view failed login attempts is faillock. The faillock command has the additional feature of tracking password attempts on screensavers. The following will display failed login attempts using faillock for user malina:

```
[root@localhost ~]# faillock --user malina
malina:
When                    Type        Source            Valid
2023-10-12 06:15:03     TTY         pts/0             V
```

To reset the failed-login counter for the user, run the following:

```
[root@localhost ~]# faillock --user malina --reset
```

Authentication utilities such as ssh and login need to use the pam_faillock.so module to implement the faillock capabilities.

Configuring User Limits

User limit settings allow for a better-tuned Linux system. For example, administrators can limit how many times users may log in, how much CPU time they can consume, how much memory they can use on a Linux system, and more. There are two ways administrators can restrict access to resources:

- Using ulimit to restrict access to resources
- Using pam_limits to restrict access to resources

Using ulimit to Restrict Access to Resources

Administrators use the ulimit command to configure limits on system resources. However, limits configured with ulimit are applied only to programs launched from the shell prompt. The syntax for using ulimit is ulimit <options> <limit>. You can use the following options with ulimit:

- **-c** Sets a limit on the maximum size of core files in blocks. If this option is set to a value of 0, core dumps for the user are disabled.
- **-f** Sets a limit on the maximum size (in blocks) of files created by the shell.
- **-n** Sets a limit on the maximum number of open file descriptors.
- **-t** Sets a limit on the maximum amount of CPU time (in seconds) a process may use.
- **-u** Sets a limit on the maximum number of processes available to a single user.

Use the -a option with ulimit to view the current value for all resource limits. This is shown in Figure 16-5.

```
root@openSUSE:~
File  Edit  View  Search  Terminal  Help
openSUSE:~ # ulimit -a
core file size          (blocks, -c) 0
data seg size           (kbytes, -d) unlimited
scheduling priority             (-e) 0
file size               (blocks, -f) unlimited
pending signals                 (-i) 11889
max locked memory       (kbytes, -l) 64
max memory size         (kbytes, -m) unlimited
open files                      (-n) 1024
pipe size            (512 bytes, -p) 8
POSIX message queues     (bytes, -q) 819200
real-time priority              (-r) 0
stack size              (kbytes, -s) 8192
cpu time               (seconds, -t) unlimited
max user processes              (-u) 11889
virtual memory          (kbytes, -v) unlimited
file locks                      (-x) unlimited
```

Figure 16-5 Viewing current resource limits with `ulimit`

Finally, use `ulimit` to set resource limits. For example, to set a limit of 250 processes per user, enter `ulimit -u 250` at the shell prompt. The user could then own no more than 250 concurrent shell processes.

Using `pam_limits` to Restrict Access to Resources

Administrators can also limit user access to Linux system resources using a PAM module called `pam_limits`, which is configured using the `/etc/security/limits.conf` file. This file contains resource limits defined using the following syntax:

```
<domain>    <type>    <item>    <value>
```

This syntax is described here:

- **`<domain>`** Describes the entity to which the limit applies. You can use one of the following values:
  - **`<user>`** Identifies a specific Linux user.
  - **`@<group_name>`** Identifies a specific Linux group.
  - **`*`** Specifies all users.
- **`<type>`** Defines a hard or soft limit. A hard limit cannot be exceeded, whereas a soft limit can be temporarily exceeded.
- **`<item>`** Specifies the resource being limited via values shown in Table 16-1.
- **`<value>`** Specifies a value for the limit.

Resource	Description
`core`	Restricts the size of core files (in KB)
`fsize`	Restricts the size of files created by the user (in KB)
`nofile`	Restricts the number of data files a user may have open concurrently
`cpu`	Restricts the CPU time of a single process (in minutes)
`nproc`	Restricts the number of concurrent processes a user may run
`maxlogins`	Sets the maximum number of simultaneous logins for a user
`priority`	Sets the priority to run user processes with
`nice`	Sets the maximum nice priority a user is allowed to raise a process to

Table 16-1 Configuring Resource Limits

For example, to configure the `aria` user with a soft CPU limit of 15 minutes, modify the `/etc/security/limits.conf` file in a text editor and enter the following:

```
aria      soft      cpu      15
```

This limit is useful for users running CPU-intensive programs that are hogging cycles away from other users.

Likewise, limit the `cheryl` user to a maximum of two concurrent logins by entering the following in the `/etc/security/limits.conf` file:

```
cheryl      hard      maxlogins      2
```

This would prevent any further logins to the system after two initial logins were successful for the `cheryl` user.

Disabling User Login

From time to time, it may be important to disable all logins to your Linux system (for example, if an administrator prefers a clean, total system data backup). To do this, all current users must log out. The `w` command lists all currently logged-in users and shows what they are doing. For example, in Figure 16-6, two users are currently logged in: `ksanders` and `rtracy`.

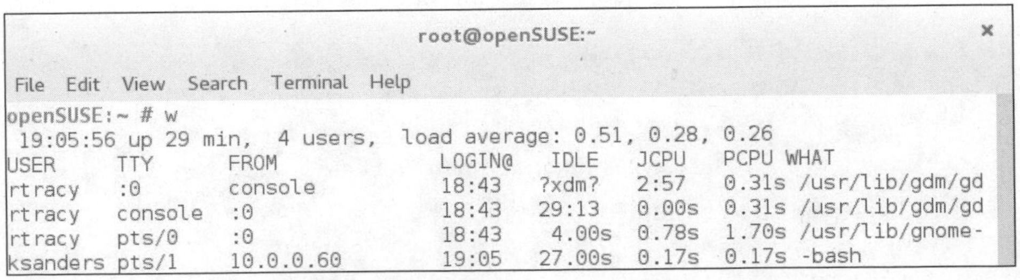

```
root@openSUSE:~
File  Edit  View  Search  Terminal  Help
openSUSE:~ # w
 19:05:56 up 29 min,  4 users,  load average: 0.51, 0.28, 0.26
USER     TTY      FROM             LOGIN@   IDLE   JCPU   PCPU WHAT
rtracy   :0       console          18:43   ?xdm?   2:57   0.31s /usr/lib/gdm/gd
rtracy   console  :0               18:43   29:13   0.00s  0.31s /usr/lib/gdm/gd
rtracy   pts/0    :0               18:43    4.00s  0.78s  1.70s /usr/lib/gnome-
ksanders pts/1    10.0.0.60        19:05   27.00s  0.17s  0.17s -bash
```

Figure 16-6 Generating a list of logged-in users

```
root@openSUSE:~
File  Edit  View  Search  Terminal  Help
openSUSE:~ # w
 19:05:56 up 29 min,  4 users,  load average: 0.51, 0.28, 0.26
USER     TTY      FROM              LOGIN@   IDLE   JCPU   PCPU WHAT
rtracy   :0       console           18:43   ?xdm?   2:57   0.31s /usr/lib/gdm/gd
rtracy   console  :0                18:43   29:13   0.00s  0.31s /usr/lib/gdm/gd
rtracy   pts/0    :0                18:43    4.00s  0.78s  1.70s /usr/lib/gnome-
ksanders pts/1    10.0.0.60         19:05   27.00s  0.17s  0.17s -bash
openSUSE:~ # pkill -KILL -u ksanders
openSUSE:~ # w
 19:10:10 up 33 min,  3 users,  load average: 0.13, 0.17, 0.21
USER     TTY      FROM              LOGIN@   IDLE   JCPU   PCPU WHAT
rtracy   :0       console           18:43   ?xdm?   3:21   0.31s /usr/lib/gdm/gd
rtracy   console  :0                18:43   33:27   0.00s  0.31s /usr/lib/gdm/gd
rtracy   pts/0    :0                18:43    2.00s  0.79s  2.16s /usr/lib/gnome-
```

Figure 16-7 Forcing a user to log off

Before you kick the users off the system, you may want to verify they are not doing anything important. To list which processes are running on a specific directory, use the `lsof` command, as shown here:

```
[root@localhost ~]# lsof +D /home
COMMAND    PID USER      FD   TYPE DEVICE  SIZE/OFF  NODE NAME
sleep    89881 ksanders  cwd   DIR  252,2     4096    131 /home/ksanders
sleep    89888 rtracy    cwd   DIR  252,2     4096    131 /home/rtracy
gedit    89913 ksanders  cwd   DIR  252,2     4096    131 /home/ksanders
gedit    89913 rtracy    mem   REG  252,2     6180   1982 /home/rtracy/.config/
```

After you politely ask the users to log off, you can brute-force log out users, and reasonably protect their jobs, using the `pkill -KILL -u <username>` command. For example, in Figure 16-7, the `pkill` command is used to log off the `ksanders` user.

Now, to disable all future logins, create a file in `/etc` named `nologin`. As long as this file exists, no one but `root` is allowed to log in. In addition, any text you enter in the `/etc/nologin` file will be displayed if a user attempts to log in. In the example shown in Figure 16-8, the text "The system is currently unavailable for login" is entered in the `/etc/nologin` file. Thus, when a user tries to log in, this is the error message displayed.

NOTE Administrators can enable a script to notify users of scheduled shutdowns. Within the script, they can use the `printf` command to send the message; for example:

```
printf  "System Going down for service at 5PM Today"
```

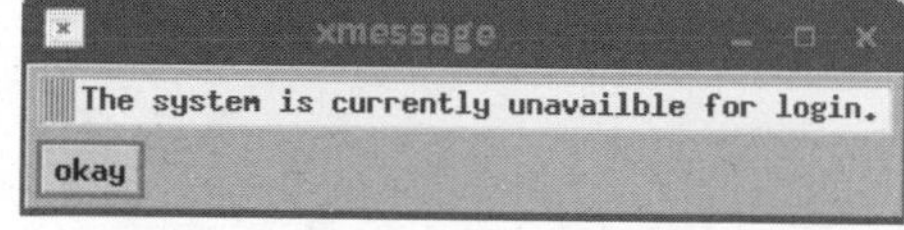
xmessage
The system is currently unavailble for login.
okay

Figure 16-8 "Login denied" message from `/etc/nologin`

This behavior is configured in the `/etc/pam.d/login` file, shown here:

```
[root@localhost ~]# cat /etc/pam.d/login
#%PAM-1.0
auth      requisite      pam_nologin.so
auth      [user_unknown=ignore success=ok ignore=ignore auth_err=die
default=bad]pam_securetty.so
auth      include        common-auth
account   include        common-account
password  include        common-password
session   required       pam_loginuid.so
session   include        common-session
session   required       pam_lastlog.so  nowtmp
session   optional       pam_mail.so standard
session   optional       pam_ck_connector.so
```

The line that reads `auth requisite pam_nologin.so` causes PAM to check whether a file named `nologin` exists in `/etc`. If it does, PAM does not allow regular users to log in.

After the full, clean backup is completed by the administrator, logins can be re-enabled by deleting or renaming the `nologin` file. For example, renaming it by entering the following at the shell prompt will still allow users to log in:

```
[root@localhost ~]# mv /etc/nologin /etc/nologin.bak
```

Let's next discuss how to audit files to locate files with the SUID or SGID permission set.

EXAM TIP Administrators can modify the "Message of the Day" file, or `/etc/motd`, so that maintenance messages appear on the end users' terminal at every login.

Security Auditing Using `find`

In addition to disabling user logins, another issue related to user security that you need to be familiar with is the need to audit files that have SUID `root` permissions set. As you learned in Chapter 6, SUID stands for "set user ID." When an executable file with the SUID permission set is run, the process is granted access to the system as the user who owns the executable file, not as the user who actually ran the command. *This is a serious issue if the file is owned by* `root`. When the `root` user owns a file with the SUID permission set, it allows the process created by the file to perform actions as `root`, which the user who started it is probably not allowed to do. The same issue applies to files owned by the `root` group that have "set group ID" (SGID) permission set.

Be aware that a small number of files owned by `root` on a Linux system do need to have these permissions set. However, other files owned by `root/root` that have the SUID/SGID permission set represent a security vulnerability on the system.

Many exploits are facilitated using files with this permission set. A file that has the SUID permission set appears as follows when listed with the `ls` command at the shell prompt:

```
-rwSr-xr-x
```

A file that has the SGID permission set appears as follows when listed with the `ls` command at the shell prompt:

```
-rw-r-Sr-x
```

Therefore, the administrator needs to consider running periodic audits to identify any files owned by `root` that have either of these permissions set. Any files beyond the minimal necessary files should be scrutinized carefully to make sure they are not part of some type of exploit. Administrators can search for files on Linux systems that have SUID permissions set using the following command at the shell prompt as the `root` user:

```
find / -type f -perm -u=s -ls
```

Here is an example:

```
[root@localhost ~]# find / -type f -perm -u=s -ls
36406    32 -rwsr-xr-x   1 root     root       31848 Sep  5  2024 /bin/su
30659    36 -rwsr-xr-x   1 root     root       35796 May  3  2022 /bin/ping
84596    20 -rwsr-xr-x   1 root     audio      20252 Jun 16  2021 /bin/eject
85643   324 -rwsr-xr-x   1 root     root      330420 Sep  5  2024 /bin/mount
30661    36 -rwsr-xr-x   1 root     root       35716 May  3  2022 /bin/ping6
85644   120 -rwsr-xr-x   1 root     root      121111 Sep  5  2024 /bin/umount
```

The `-perm` option tells `find` to match files that have the specified permission assigned to the mode; in this case, the `s` permission is assigned to the file's user (owner). You can also identify any files with the SGID permission set using the following command:

```
find / -type f -perm -g=s -ls
```

When you do, a list of all files with the SGID permission set is displayed. Here is an example:

```
[root@localhost ~]# find / -type f -perm -g=s -ls
94451    12 -rwxr-sr-x   1 root     tty        10588 May 18  2022 /opt/gnome/lib
85710    12 -rwxr-sr-x   1 root     tty        10404 Sep  5  2024 /usr/bin/wall
5867     12 -rwxr-sr-x   1 root     shadow      8800 Jun 16  2021 /usr/bin/vlock
85713    12 -rwxr-sr-x   1 root     tty         9024 Sep  5  2024 /usr/bin/write
93913    12 -rwxr-sr-x   1 root     maildrop   11300 Sep  5  2024 /usr/sbin/postdrop
93919    12 -rwxr-sr-x   1 root     maildrop   11668 Sep  5  2024 /usr/sbin/postqueue
26192     8 -rwxr-sr-x   1 root     tty         7288 Jun 16  2021 /usr/sbin/utempter
35720    24 -rwxr-sr-x   1 root     shadow     20672 Sep  5  2024 /sbin/unix_chkpwd
```

EXAM TIP Administrators can avoid disruptive server shutdowns by disabling Ctrl-Alt-Del as follows:

```
[root]#  systemctl mask ctrl-alt-del.target
[root]#  systemctl daemon-reload
```

Practice controlling user access to a Linux system in Exercise 16-1.

Exercise 16-1: Managing User Access

In this exercise, you practice setting age limits on user passwords. Also, you configure sudo to allow a standard user to kill processes on the system as the root user. Perform this exercise using the virtual machine that comes with this book.

VIDEO Watch the Exercise 16-1 video for a demonstration on how to perform this task.

Complete the following steps:

1. Boot your Linux system and log in as your **student1** user with a password of **student1**.
2. Open a terminal session.
3. Switch to your root user account by entering **su -** followed by a password of **password**.
4. Practice configuring age limits by completing the following steps:
   a. Use the **cat** or **less** utility to view the /etc/passwd file. Identify a user on the system who you want to configure password age limits for.
   b. Set the minimum password age to 3 days, the maximum password age to 60 days, and the number of warning days before expiration to 7 by entering **chage -m 3 -M 60 -W 7 <username>** at the shell prompt.
5. Configure sudo to allow a user on your system to kill processes as the root user by doing the following:
   a. Identify a user on your system to whom you want to grant the ability to kill processes as root.
   b. As your root user, enter **visudo** at the shell prompt. You should see the /etc/sudoers file loaded in the vi text editor.
   c. Scroll down to the lines shown in the example that follows and comment them out by inserting a **#** character at the beginning of each one.

```
Defaults targetpw   # ask for the password of target user i.e. root
ALL   ALL=(ALL) ALL   # WARNING! Only use with 'Defaults targetpw'!
```

   d. Add the following lines to the end of the sudoers file by pressing **G** and then **o**:

```
User_Alias PWRUSRS = your_user
Cmnd_Alias KILLPROCS = /bin/kill, /usr/bin/killall
Host_Alias MYHSTS = openSUSE
PWRUSRS MYHSTS = (root) KILLPROCS
```

e. Press **Esc** and then enter **:x** to save the changes to the sudoers file.

f. Run **top** at the shell prompt as your root user.

g. Open a new terminal session and (as your standard user) enter **ps -elf | grep top**. You should see a top process running that is owned by the root user.

h. Kill that process as your standard user by entering **sudo killall top** at the shell prompt.

i. When prompted, enter your user's password.

j. Enter **ps -elf | grep top** at the shell prompt again. You should see that the top process that was owned by the root user has been killed.

Managing System Logs

Log files are a gold mine of information for the system administrator. Log files are used to detect intruders into a system, troubleshoot problems, and determine performance issues within the system. Linux usually uses an audit trail system called auditd, but in this section, you will learn how to manage and use system log files with more advanced tools. We will discuss the following topics:

- Configuring log files
- Using log files to troubleshoot problems
- Using log files to detect intruders

Let's begin by discussing how to configure log files.

Configuring Log Files

System log files are stored in the /var/log/ directory, shown in Figure 16-9.

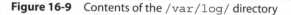

```
root@openSUSE:/var/log
File  Edit  View  Search  Terminal  Help
openSUSE:/var/log # ls
NetworkManager     btmp           mail.err                 pm-powersave.log
Xorg.0.log         cups           mail.info                samba
Xorg.0.log.old     faillog        mail.warn                speech-dispatcher
Xorg.1.log         firewall       messages                 warn
YaST2              gdm            messages-20141222.xz     wpa_supplicant.log
acpid              hp             mysql                    wtmp
alternatives.log   krb5           news                     zypp
apparmor           lastlog        ntp
audit              localmessages  pbl.log
boot.log           mail           pk_backend_zypp
```

Figure 16-9 Contents of the /var/log/ directory

Log File	Description
faillog	Contains failed authentication attempts.
firewalld	Contains firewall log entries.
kern.log	Contains detailed log messages from the Linux kernel.
lastlog	Contains the last login information for users.
maillog	Contains messages generated by the postfix and sendmail daemons.
messages	Contains messages from most running processes. This is probably one of the most useful of all the log files. Administrators can use it to troubleshoot services that won't start, services that don't appear to work properly, and so on.
secure	Contains messages related to authentication and authorization. The sshd process logs messages here, including unsuccessful login attempts.
wtmp	Contains a list of users who have authenticated to the system.

Table 16-2 Useful Log Files

Notice in this figure that there are a number of subdirectories in /var/log/ where system daemons, such as mysql, apparmor, audit, and cups, store their log files. Some of these log files are simple text files that can be read with text manipulation utilities. Others are binary files that require the use of a special utility, such as lastlog, which displays the most recent logins of users. As you can see in Figure 16-9, there are quite a number of files within /var/log/ and its subdirectories. As with most anything, some log files are much more useful than others. Table 16-2 contains a list of some of the more important log files.

NOTE The files shown in Table 16-2 are log files used on a SUSE Linux system. Other distributions may use different files by default. You can customize logging using the /etc/rsyslog.conf file.

How logging is implemented on Linux depends on the Linux distribution. For the CompTIA Linux+ exam, you need to be familiar with the following system logging configuration implementations:

- rsyslogd message logging
- Disk space management using log file rotation
- journald message logging

rsyslogd Message Logging

Logging on a Linux system that uses init is usually handled by the rsyslogd daemon. Instead of each daemon maintaining its own individual log file, most of your Linux services are configured to write log entries to /dev/log/ by default. This device file is maintained by the rsyslogd daemon. When a service writes to this

```
# Log all kernel messages to the console.
# Logging much else clutters up the screen.
#kern.*                                                 /dev/console

# Log anything (except mail) of level info or higher.
# Don't log private authentication messages!
*.info;mail.none;authpriv.none;cron.none                /var/log/messages

# The authpriv file has restricted access.
authpriv.*                                              /var/log/secure

# Log all the mail messages in one place.
mail.*                                                  -/var/log/maillog


# Log cron stuff
cron.*                                                  /var/log/cron

# Everybody gets emergency messages
*.emerg                                                 *

# Save news errors of level crit and higher in a special file.
uucp,news.crit                                          /var/log/spooler
./syslog.conf
```

Figure 16-10 The `/etc/rsyslog.conf` file

socket, the input is captured by `rsyslogd`. The `rsyslogd` daemon then uses the entries in the `/etc/rsyslog.conf` file, shown in Figure 16-10, to determine where the information should go.

NOTE Some Linux distributions use `syslog-ng` or `syslogd` instead of `rsyslogd` to manage logging.

The syntax for the `/etc/rsyslog.conf` file is

```
<facility>.<priority>        <file>
```

A `<facility>` refers to a subsystem that provides a message. Each process on your Linux system that uses `rsyslog` for logging is assigned to one of the following facilities:

- **`authpriv`** Facility used by services associated with system security and authorization
- **`cron`** Facility that accepts log messages from `cron` and `at`
- **`daemon`** Facility that can be used by daemons that do not have their own facility
- **`kern`** Facility used for all kernel log messages
- **`lpr`** Facility that handles messages from the printing system
- **`mail`** Facility for log messages from the mail MTA (for example, `postfix` or `sendmail`)

- **news** Facility for log messages from the news daemon
- **rsyslog** Facility for internal messages from the rsyslog daemon itself
- **user** Facility for user-related log messages (such as failed login attempts)
- **uucp** Facility for log messages from the uucp daemon
- **local0-7** Facilities used to capture log messages from user-created applications

In addition to facilities, the rsyslogd daemon also provides *priorities* to customize how logging occurs on the system. Prioritization is handled by the klogd daemon on most distributions, which runs as a client of rsyslogd. Use the following priorities with rsyslogd, listed from most to fewest messages:

- **debug** All information; normally used for debugging activities.
- **info** Informational and unremarkable messages.
- **notice** Issues of concern, but not yet a problem.
- **warn** Noncritical errors that can potentially cause harm.
- **err** Serious errors fatal to the daemon but not the system.
- **crit** Critical errors, but no need to take immediate action.
- **alert** Action must be taken immediately, but the system is still usable.
- **emerg** Fatal errors to the computer; system unusable.
- **none** Do not log any activity.

For example, review the /etc/rsyslog.conf file shown in Figure 16-10 and go down about 15 lines, where you will see the following:

```
# Log cron stuff
cron.*                          /var/log/cron
```

Here, the rsyslogd daemon directs messages of all priority levels (*) from the cron facility to the /var/log/cron file. If desired, an administrator could customize the /etc/rsyslog.conf file to split messages of different priority levels to different files, as shown here:

```
user.info                       /var/log/messages
user.alert                      /var/log/secure
```

The preceding definitions in /etc/rsyslog.conf will send all user-related info-level messages (and higher priorities) to the /var/log/messages file, and /var/log/secure will receive only user alert messages and higher.

Disk Space Management Using Log File Rotation

Linux distributions also include a utility named logrotate, which is run daily, by default, by the cron daemon. To customize how log files are rotated, modify the /etc/logrotate.conf file, as shown in Figure 16-11.

Figure 16-11 Configuring log file rotation in /etc/logrotate.conf

```
# see "man logrotate" for details
# rotate log files weekly
weekly

# keep 4 weeks worth of backlogs
rotate 4

# create new (empty) log files after rotating old ones
create

# use date as a suffix of the rotated file
dateext

# uncomment this if you want your log files compressed
#compress

# comment these to switch compression to use gzip or another
# compression scheme
compresscmd /usr/bin/bzip2
uncompresscmd /usr/bin/bunzip2

# former versions had to have the compressext set accordingly
#compressext .bz2

# RPM packages drop log rotation information into this directory
include /etc/logrotate.d

# no packages own wtmp and btmp -- we'll rotate them here
#/var/log/wtmp {
#    monthly
#    create 0664 root utmp
#       minsize 1M
#    rotate 1
#}
#
# /var/log/btmp {
#   missingok
#    monthly
#    create 0600 root utmp
#    rotate 1
#}
/etc/logrotate.conf lines 1-41/43 93%
```

The /etc/logrotate.conf file contains default global parameters used by logrotate to determine how and when log files are rotated. However, these defaults can be overridden for specific daemons using the configuration files located in the /etc/logrotate.d/ directory. For example, in Figure 16-12, the /etc/logrotate.d/apache2 file is used to customize logging for the apache2 daemon.

Also, the first line shown in Figure 16-12 means the /var/log/apache2/access_log file will be compressed. It can have a maximum age of 365 days, after which it will be removed (maxage 365). Old versions of the file will be archived using a date extension (dateext). The log file will go through 99 rotations before being removed (rotate 99). If the file grows larger than 4096 KB, it will be rotated (size=+4096k). The file will not be rotated if it is empty (notifempty). No error message will be generated if the file is missing (missingok). The file will be created with 644 permissions, will have the root user as the owner, and will be owned by the root group (create 644 root root). After a log file is rotated, the /etc/init.d/apache2 reload command will be run (postrotate /etc/init.d/apache2 reload).

Figure 16-12 Configuring Apache web server logging

```
/var/log/apache2/access_log {
    compress
    dateext
    maxage 365
    rotate 99
    size=+4096k
    notifempty
    missingok
    create 644 root root
    postrotate
     /etc/init.d/apache2 reload
    endscript
}

/var/log/apache2/error_log {
    compress
    dateext
    maxage 365
    rotate 99
    size=+1024k
    notifempty
    missingok
    create 644 root root
    postrotate
     /etc/init.d/apache2 reload
apache2 lines 1-25/69 38%
```

EXAM TIP You can test your logging configuration using the `logger` utility. This command-line tool allows you to manually make entries in your logging system. The syntax is as follows:

```
logger -p <facility>.<priority> "<log_message>"
```

`journald` Message Logging

Linux distributions that use the `systemd` daemon use the `journald` daemon for logging instead of `rsyslogd`. The `journald` daemon maintains a system log called the *journal*, located in `/run/log/journal/`. To view the journal, use the `journalctl` command. When you enter this command at the shell prompt with no parameters, the entire journal is displayed, as shown in Figure 16-13.

NOTE By default, journal log data is lost at reboot. To make it persistent, do the following:

```
# mkdir -p /var/log/journal
# systemd-tmpfiles --create --prefix /var/log/journal
```

One of the neat features of the `journald` daemon is the fact that you can use it to view system boot messages as well. To do this, enter `journalctl -b` at the shell prompt. The messages from the most recent system boot are displayed. In addition, you can use `journalctl` to view messages from previous system boots. This can be done in two different ways:

- Specifying the `-b` flag with the command followed by a positive number will look up messages from the specified system boot, starting from the beginning of the journal. For example, entering `journalctl -b 1` will display messages created during the first boot found at the beginning of the journal.

```
root@openSUSE:~
File Edit View Search Terminal Help
-- Logs begin at Thu 2015-01-22 16:56:49 MST, end at Thu 2015-01-22 17:08:25 MST
Jan 22 16:56:49 openSUSE systemd-journal[227]: Runtime journal is using 276.0K (
Jan 22 16:56:49 openSUSE systemd-journal[227]: Runtime journal is using 280.0K (
Jan 22 16:56:49 openSUSE kernel: Initializing cgroup subsys cpuset
Jan 22 16:56:49 openSUSE kernel: Initializing cgroup subsys cpu
Jan 22 16:56:49 openSUSE kernel: Initializing cgroup subsys cpuacct
Jan 22 16:56:49 openSUSE kernel: Linux version 3.11.10-21-desktop (geeko@buildho
Jan 22 16:56:49 openSUSE kernel: Disabled fast string operations
Jan 22 16:56:49 openSUSE kernel: e820: BIOS-provided physical RAM map:
Jan 22 16:56:49 openSUSE kernel: BIOS-e820: [mem 0x0000000000000000-0x0000000000
Jan 22 16:56:49 openSUSE kernel: BIOS-e820: [mem 0x000000000009f800-0x0000000000
Jan 22 16:56:49 openSUSE kernel: BIOS-e820: [mem 0x00000000000ca000-0x0000000000
Jan 22 16:56:49 openSUSE kernel: BIOS-e820: [mem 0x00000000000dc000-0x0000000000
Jan 22 16:56:49 openSUSE kernel: BIOS-e820: [mem 0x0000000000100000-0x000000005f
Jan 22 16:56:49 openSUSE kernel: BIOS-e820: [mem 0x000000005fef0000-0x000000005f
Jan 22 16:56:49 openSUSE kernel: BIOS-e820: [mem 0x000000005feff000-0x000000005f
Jan 22 16:56:49 openSUSE kernel: BIOS-e820: [mem 0x000000005ff00000-0x000000005f
Jan 22 16:56:49 openSUSE kernel: BIOS-e820: [mem 0x00000000e0000000-0x00000000ef
Jan 22 16:56:49 openSUSE kernel: BIOS-e820: [mem 0x00000000fec00000-0x00000000fe
Jan 22 16:56:49 openSUSE kernel: BIOS-e820: [mem 0x00000000fee00000-0x00000000fe
Jan 22 16:56:49 openSUSE kernel: BIOS-e820: [mem 0x00000000fffe0000-0x00000000ff
Jan 22 16:56:49 openSUSE kernel: NX (Execute Disable) protection: active
Jan 22 16:56:49 openSUSE kernel: SMBIOS 2.4 present.
lines 1-23
```

Figure 16-13 Viewing the journal with `journalctl`

- Specifying the `-b` flag with the command followed by a negative number will look up the messages from the specified system boot starting from the end of the journal. For example, entering `journalctl -b -2` will display system messages created two boots ago.

The `journalctl` command can also be used to display only log entries related to a specific service running on the system. The syntax is `journalctl -u <service_name>`. For example, to view all journal entries related to the SSH daemon running on the system, enter `journalctl -u sshd` at the shell prompt. An example is shown in Figure 16-14.

```
root@openSUSE:~
File Edit View Search Terminal Help
openSUSE:~ # journalctl -u sshd
-- Logs begin at Thu 2015-01-22 17:37:48 MST, end at Thu 2015-01-22 17:49:00 MST
Jan 22 17:38:53 openSUSE systemd[1]: Starting OpenSSH Daemon...
Jan 22 17:38:53 openSUSE systemd[1]: Started OpenSSH Daemon.
Jan 22 17:38:54 openSUSE sshd[2811]: Server listening on 0.0.0.0 port 22.
Jan 22 17:38:54 openSUSE sshd[2811]: Server listening on :: port 22.
lines 1-5/5 (END)
```

Figure 16-14 Viewing `sshd` journal events

The behavior of the `journald` daemon is configured using the `/etc/systemd/journald.conf` file. This file has many configurable parameters. Here are some of the more useful ones:

- **`ForwardToSyslog`** Configures `journald` to forward its log messages to the traditional `rsyslog` daemon.
- **`MaxLevelStore`** Controls the maximum log level of messages stored in the journal file. All messages equal to or less than the log level specified are stored, whereas any messages above the specified level are dropped. This parameter can be set to one of the following values:
  - `none`
  - `emerg (0)`
  - `alert (1)`
  - `crit (2)`
  - `err (3)`
  - `warning (4)`
  - `notice (5)`
  - `info (6)`
  - `debug (7)`

With this background in mind, let's next discuss how to view and use your log files.

Using Log Files to Troubleshoot Problems

As mentioned earlier in this chapter, log files can be an invaluable resource when troubleshooting Linux problems. If the kernel or a service encounters a problem, it will be logged in a log file. Reviewing these log files can provide a wealth of information that may not necessarily be displayed on the screen.

Some log files are binary files that must be read with a special utility; for example, the files in the `/run/log/journal/` directory are binary files read by `journalctl`. However, most log files are simple text files that are viewed with standard text manipulation utilities. Utilities like `cat`, `less`, `more`, and so on can be used to view text-based log files. However, there is a problem with these utilities: log files are huge!

For example, the `/var/log/messages` file, which logs generic system activity, may have 10,000 or more lines in it. That's a lot of text! The `less` utility displays only 24 lines at a time. You would have to press the spacebar a lot of times to get to the end of the file!

There are two strategies that can help. The first is to redirect the output of the `cat` command to the `grep` command to filter a specific term within a log file. For example, if you want to locate information within `/var/log/messages` related to logins, you would enter the following at the shell prompt:

```
[root@localhost ~]# cat /var/log/messages | grep login | more
```

Then, only entries containing the term "login" would be displayed from the /var/log/messages file. If the system uses systemd and a journal, the same could be done with the journalctl command:

```
[root@localhost ~]# journalctl | grep login | more
```

In addition to grep, you can also use the head and tail utilities to view log file entries. Understand that most log files record entries chronologically, usually oldest to newest. To view the beginning of a log file, enter head <filename> at the shell prompt to display the first lines of the file. For example, in Figure 16-15, the beginning of the /var/log/messages file has been displayed with head.

The tail utility works in a manner opposite of head. Instead of displaying the first 10 lines of a file, it displays the last 10 lines. This is very useful because, when troubleshooting, you only need to see only the last few lines of a log file. To do this, enter tail <filename> at the shell prompt. In Figure 16-16, the /var/log/messages file is being viewed using tail.

The tail utility provides the -f option, which is used often when troubleshooting. The -f option with tail will display the last lines of a log file as normal, but it monitors the file being displayed and displays new lines as they are added to the log file. For example, you could run the tail -f /var/log/messages command to monitor the system log file for error messages during the troubleshooting process. You can quit monitoring the file by pressing Ctrl-c.

```
root@openSUSE:~
File Edit View Search Terminal Help
openSUSE:~ # head /var/log/messages
2014-12-22T16:00:10.536035-07:00 openSUSE logrotate: ALERT exited abnormally wit
h [1]
2014-12-22T16:00:10.546737-07:00 openSUSE logrotate: error: skipping "/var/log/m
ysql/mysqld.log" because parent directory has insecure permissions (It's world w
ritable or writable by group which is not "root") Set "su" directive in config f
ile to tell logrotate which user/group should be used for rotation.
2014-12-22T16:00:10.549918-07:00 openSUSE logrotate: compress_ext is /usr/bin/xz
2014-12-22T16:00:10.551164-07:00 openSUSE logrotate: compress_ext was changed to
 .xz
2014-12-22T16:00:30.106794-07:00 openSUSE org.freedesktop.PackageKit[534]: Downl
oadProgressReportReceiver::start():http://download.opensuse.org/update/13.1/ --l
ibksba8;1.3.0-5.4.1;i586;repo-update
2014-12-22T16:00:33.767476-07:00 openSUSE org.freedesktop.PackageKit[534]: Downl
oadProgressReportReceiver::start():http://download.opensuse.org/update/13.1/ --n
tp;4.2.6p5-15.13.1;i586;repo-update
2014-12-22T16:00:58.500998-07:00 openSUSE /USR/SBIN/CRON[4257]: pam_unix(crond:s
ession): session closed for user root
2014-12-22T16:01:25.144933-07:00 openSUSE systemd[1]: Stopping Session 2 of user
 rtracy.
2014-12-22T16:01:25.157079-07:00 openSUSE systemd[1]: Stopped Session 2 of user
rtracy.
2014-12-22T16:01:25.213964-07:00 openSUSE systemd[1]: Stopping Stop Read-Ahead D
ata Collection 10s After Completed Startup.
```

Figure 16-15 Using head to view a log file

```
root@openSUSE:~
File Edit View Search Terminal Help
openSUSE:~ # tail /var/log/messages
2015-01-22T20:15:01.401866-07:00 openSUSE systemd[1]: Started Session 13 of user
 root.
2015-01-22T20:15:01.797227-07:00 openSUSE /USR/SBIN/CRON[4534]: pam_unix(crond:s
ession): session closed for user root
2015-01-22T20:22:38.598946-07:00 openSUSE gdm-password]: gkr-pam: unlocked login
 keyring
2015-01-22T20:23:54.017323-07:00 openSUSE systemd[1]: Mounting Arbitrary Executa
ble File Formats File System...
2015-01-22T20:23:54.089089-07:00 openSUSE systemd[1]: Mounted Arbitrary Executab
le File Formats File System.
2015-01-22T20:30:01.831200-07:00 openSUSE /usr/sbin/cron[4587]: pam_unix(crond:s
ession): session opened for user root by (uid=0)
2015-01-22T20:30:01.855247-07:00 openSUSE systemd[1]: Starting Session 14 of use
r root.
2015-01-22T20:30:01.858679-07:00 openSUSE systemd[1]: Started Session 14 of user
 root.
2015-01-22T20:30:02.096318-07:00 openSUSE /USR/SBIN/CRON[4587]: pam_unix(crond:s
ession): session closed for user root
2015-01-22T20:30:53.766809-07:00 openSUSE gdm-password]: gkr-pam: unlocked login
 keyring
```

Figure 16-16 Using `tail` to view a log file

The "follow" feature is also available with systems that use the `journald` daemon to manage logging. Run `journalctl -f` at the shell prompt, and the last few entries in the journal are displayed. The `journalctl` command then monitors the journal and prints new entries as they are added. Again, you can quit monitoring by pressing `Ctrl-c`.

You can check the system log files listed previously in Table 16-2 to troubleshoot problems, or other log files, including the following:

- **`cron`** Contains entries from the `cron` daemon
- **`dmesg`** Contains hardware detection information
- **`maillog`** Contains entries generated by the `sendmail` daemon
- **`secure`** Contains information about access to network daemons
- **`rpmpkgs`** Contains a list of installed `rpm` packages
- **`dpkg.log`** Contains a list of `deb` packages installed, upgraded, and removed

To troubleshoot problems associated with an application or service, check for a log file maintained specifically for that service. For example, check the `mail`, `mail.err`, `mail.info`, `mail.warn`, or `maillog` file to troubleshoot problems with the `postfix` or `sendmail` daemon. If there is trouble with the `mysqld` daemon, check the `mysqld.log` file within the `/var/log/mysql` directory. To troubleshoot problems with the Apache web server, investigate the various log files within the `/var/log/apache2` directory.

In addition to using log files to troubleshoot problems on the Linux system, use them to detect unauthorized intrusion attempts.

Using Log Files to Detect Intruders

Detecting intruders involves looking for clues they left behind in the system. One of the best resources in this regard is the log files in the Linux system. Much like a CSI detective, practice and experience are best to develop an intuitive sense that informs you when something looks suspicious. The best way to develop this intuition is to spend a lot of time reviewing log files, because then you'll have a baseline of "normal" for your system. Once you know what is normal, you can spot what is *not* normal.

An important log file to review to identify suspicious activities is the `/var/log/wtmp` file. This log file contains a list of all users who have authenticated to the system. The file is saved in binary format, so you cannot use `cat`, `less`, or a text editor such as `vi` to view it. Instead, you must use the `last` command at the shell prompt. Output from the `last` utility is shown in Figure 16-17.

The `last` utility displays the user account, login time, logout time, and where users authenticated from. When reviewing this file, look for activity that appears unusual—for example, logins that occurred in the middle of the night when no one is at work should be considered suspicious.

Also view the `/var/log/faillog` file, which contains a list of failed authentication attempts. This file is very effective at detecting dictionary attacks, which run through a list of dictionary terms, testing them as passwords for user accounts. Like `wtmp`, `faillog` is a binary file. To view it, use the `faillog` utility. This utility displays the user who tried to authenticate, how many times that user failed to log in, and when the last unsuccessful attempt occurred. Also, try the `-u` option to view login attempts for a specific user account—for example, `faillog -u malina`.

EXAM TIP The `lastb` command also lists bad login attempts by reading the log file `/var/log/btmp`, which contains all the bad login attempts.

```
root@openSUSE:~
File  Edit  View  Search  Terminal  Help
openSUSE:~ # last
rtracy   pts/0         :0                  Thu Jan 22 17:48   still logged in
rtracy   console       :0                  Thu Jan 22 17:42   still logged in
rtracy   :0            :0                  Thu Jan 22 17:42   still logged in
reboot   system boot   3.11.10-21-deskt    Thu Jan 22 17:37 - 20:48  (03:10)
(unknown :0            :0                  Thu Jan 22 17:39 - crash  (00:-1)
reboot   system boot   3.11.10-21-deskt    Thu Jan 22 17:37 - 20:48  (03:10)
rtracy   pts/0         :0                  Thu Jan 22 17:07 - 17:36  (00:28)
rtracy   console       :0                  Thu Jan 22 16:59 - 17:36  (00:36)
rtracy   :0            :0                  Thu Jan 22 16:59 - 17:36  (00:36)
reboot   system boot   3.11.10-21-deskt    Thu Jan 22 16:56 - 17:36  (00:40)
(unknown :0            :0                  Thu Jan 22 16:58 - crash  (00:-1)
reboot   system boot   3.11.10-21-deskt    Thu Jan 22 16:56 - 17:36  (00:40)
root     pts/2         :0.0                Tue Jan 20 19:39 - 19:58  (00:18)
root     pts/2         :0.0                Tue Jan 20 19:27 - 19:31  (00:03)
rtracy   pts/1         10.0.0.60           Tue Jan 20 19:13 - down   (01:17)
ksanders pts/1         10.0.0.60           Tue Jan 20 19:05 - 19:10  (00:04)
```

Figure 16-17 Using `last` to review login history

```
root            tty1                    Fri Jan  2 15:25:03 -0700 2015
rtkit                                   **Never logged in**
scard                                   **Never logged in**
srvGeoClue                              **Never logged in**
sshd                                    **Never logged in**
statd                                   **Never logged in**
svn                                     **Never logged in**
tftp                                    **Never logged in**
usbmux                                  **Never logged in**
uucp                                    **Never logged in**
wwwrun                                  **Never logged in**
dtracy                                  **Never logged in**
ksanders        pts/1    10.0.0.60      Tue Jan 20 19:05:29 -0700 2015
rtracy          :0       console        Thu Jan 22 17:42:15 -0700 2015
student         pts/1    10.0.0.60      Tue Nov 25 17:27:58 -0700 2014
mysql           _                       **Never logged in**
```

Figure 16-18 Using `lastlog` to view last login times

The next log file to analyze is `/var/log/lastlog`, which contains a list of all the users in the system and when they last logged in. As with the other log files we have reviewed, you cannot view `lastlog` with `less`, `cat`, or a text editor. To view `lastlog`, use the `lastlog` utility from the shell prompt, as shown in Figure 16-18.

The last type of log file can help you detect intrusion attempts. These are `/var/log/messages` and `/var/log/journal` (if your distribution uses them). As mentioned earlier, these log files contain messages from all services running on the system. As such, they contain plenty of data that may or may not be related to intrusion attempts. You can use `grep` to isolate relevant entries. For example, `grep login /var/log/messages | more` displays login-related entries in the files. The same can be done with the `journalctl` command.

In addition to viewing log files, you can use another command-line tool similar to w to see who is currently using the system, as discussed in Chapter 4. Use who to see who is currently logged into your system.

Enhancing Group and File Security

Security is considered a three-legged stool consisting of confidentiality, integrity, and availability. Linux systems are implemented with a priority of availability over confidentiality and integrity. This is called Discretionary Access Control (DAC). DAC systems allow users to set confidentiality rules at their own discretion. This is fine for most corporate environments where providing data as quickly as possible is important (for example, getting sales quotes out to prospects).

Military environments demand confidentiality be the priority. These environments utilize a system known as Mandatory Access Control (MAC). Figure 16-19 shows how MAC works. If a user has Confidential access, they are allowed to access documents in Unclassified, and Confidential; however, they are not allowed to access documents in Secret or Top Secret because their clearance is too low.

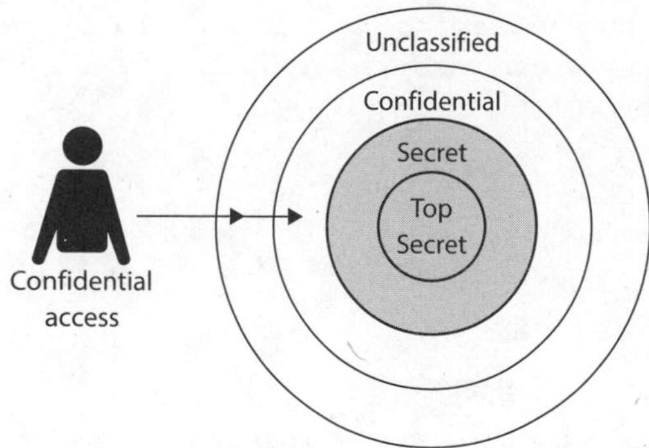

Figure 16-19 The Mandatory Access Control model

To enable MAC on Linux systems, install a Linux Security Module. There are several, but the Linux+ exam focuses on the following:

- Implementing SELinux
- Implementing AppArmor

Implementing SELinux

The U.S. National Security Agency (NSA) developed SELinux to provide security mechanisms above user/group/other and read/write/execute, which provide only DAC. The SELinux design restricts operations to the least privilege possible; actions not explicitly allowed are denied by default. Red Hat 7 and above, CentOS 7 and above, and derivatives come with SELinux incorporated into the kernel.

SELinux Contexts Permissions

SELinux is based on a *subject* (that is, a user or application) that needs to access an *object* (that is, a file, socket, or some other application). A *reference monitor,* also simply known as *monitor,* determines whether the subject has rights to the object depending on the context, or label defined onto the object, as shown in Figure 16-20. To view the context permissions of files, run the command `ls -Z`.

```
[root@localhost ~]# ls -Z
drwxr-xr-x. root root unconfined_u:object_r:admin_home_t:s0 adir
-rw-------. root root system_u:object_r:admin_home_t:s0 anaconda-ks.cfg
-rw-r--r--. root root system_u:object_r:admin_home_t:s0 initial-setup-ks.cfg
-rwxr-xr-x. root root unconfined_u:object_r:admin_home_t:s0 runme
[root@localhost ~]#
```

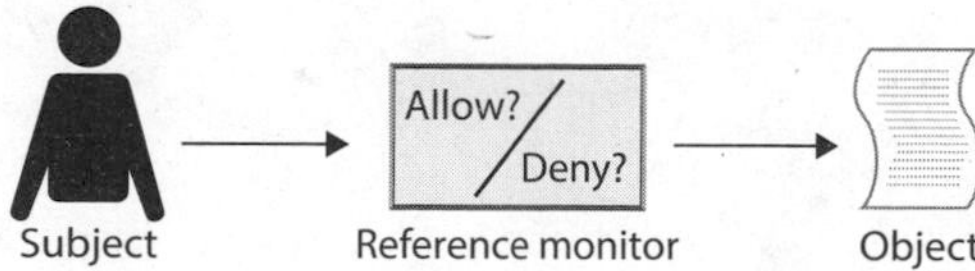

Figure 16-20 SELinux Reference Monitor System

The "dot" that appears at the end of the permissions (`-rw-r--r--.`) means that SELinux is enabled and the files have been defined a context. To view the context permissions of commands, run `ps -Z`:

```
[cheryl@localhost ~]$ ps -Z
LABEL                              PID TTY          TIME CMD
user_u:user_r:user_t:s0          22706 pts/0    00:00:00 bash
user_u:user_r:user_t:s0          22764 pts/0    00:00:00 sleep
user_u:user_r:user_t:s0          22773 pts/0    00:00:00 ps
[cheryl@localhost ~]$
```

The contexts are defined as `_u` for user, `_r` for role, and `_t` for type, and `s0` represents the sensitivity level. Rules of targeted policies are associated with `_t` contexts. Rules associated with multi-level security (MLS) levels are associated with the `s0` contexts. See Table 16-3 for a list of SELinux user context permission abilities.

NOTE SELinux also introduced `selinux-policy-minimum`, which allows users to interact with their Linux system in an unconfined state.

File contexts can be modified using the `chcon` command. To recursively change files in subdirectories, use the `-R` flag:

```
[root@localhost ~]# setenforce 0
[root@localhost ~]# ls -Zd adir
drwxr-xr-x. root root unconfined_u:object_r:admin_home_t:s0 adir
[root@localhost ~]# ls -Z adir
-rw-r--r--. root root unconfined_u:object_r:admin_home_t:s0 file1
-rw-r--r--. root root unconfined_u:object_r:admin_home_t:s0 file2
-rw-r--r--. root root unconfined_u:object_r:admin_home_t:s0 file3
[root@localhost ~]# chcon -R -r unconfined_r -t unconfined_t ./adir
[root@localhost ~]# ls -Z adir
-rw-r--r--. root root unconfined_u:unconfined_r:unconfined_t:s0 file1
-rw-r--r--. root root unconfined_u:unconfined_r:unconfined_t:s0 file2
-rw-r--r--. root root unconfined_u:unconfined_r:unconfined_t:s0 file3
[root@localhost ~]# ls -Zd adir
drwxr-xr-x. root root unconfined_u:unconfined_r:unconfined_t:s0 adir
```

User Context	Role Context	Type Context	GUI	sudo su	Execute in /home and /tmp	Network
unconfined_u	unconfined_r	unconfined_t	X	Both	X	X
sysadm_u	sysadm_r	sysadm_t	X	Both	X	X
staff_u	staff_r	staff_t	X	sudo	X	X
user_u	user_r	user_t	X		X	X
xguest_u	xguest_r	xguest_t	X			Firefox only
guest_u	guest_r	guest_t				

Table 16-3 SELinux User Context Permission Abilities

To return the filesystem to the default settings, either relabel the entire filesystem by running `touch /.autorelabel` and rebooting or use the `restorecon` command to change individual files and directories:

```
[root@localhost ~]# ls -Z adir
-rw-r--r--. root root unconfined_u:unconfined_r:unconfined_t:s0 file1
-rw-r--r--. root root unconfined_u:unconfined_r:unconfined_t:s0 file2
-rw-r--r--. root root unconfined_u:unconfined_r:unconfined_t:s0 file3
[root@localhost ~]# restorecon -R ./adir
[root@localhost ~]# ls -Z adir
-rw-r--r--. root root unconfined_u:unconfined_r:admin_home_t:s0 file1
-rw-r--r--. root root unconfined_u:unconfined_r:admin_home_t:s0 file2
-rw-r--r--. root root unconfined_u:unconfined_r:admin_home_t:s0 file3
```

Default contexts are defined in `/etc/selinux/targeted/contexts/files/file_contexts`. To modify the SELinux contexts, use the `semanage` command.

EXAM TIP It is good to know the following `semanage` options: `-s` specifies the user, and `-a` adds the constraining context permission to that user. These options provide more security because they force users to comply with SELinux policies:

```
[root@localhost ~]# semanage login -a -s user_u gosia
```

Enabling SELinux

SELinux can be implemented in three modes:

- Enforcing
- Permissive
- Disabled

Enforcing mode denies access to users based on the defined SELinux policies. Permissive access simply logs actions that would have been denied under enforcing mode; this is an excellent mode to use while tuning security policies. Disabled mode simply deactivates SELinux.

To see the current mode, use the `getenforce` command, and to set the SELinux mode, use `setenforce`:

```
[root@localhost ~]# getenforce
Enforcing
[root@localhost ~]# setenforce Permissive
[root@localhost ~]# getenforce
Permissive
[root@localhost ~]#
```

SELinux enforcement modes are defined in either `/etc/sysconfig/selinux` (on Red Hat, SUSE, and derivatives) or `/etc/selinux/config` (on Debian, Ubuntu, and derivatives).

SELinux's default policy is called "targeted," which allows administrators to define contexts in a fine-grained manner to targeted processes. This allows, for example, enforcing memory restrictions for all processes to minimize the vulnerability of buffer overflow attacks. For example, network services are targeted, but `systemd`, `init`, and user processes are not. The other policy mode is MLS, which uses the Bell-LaPadula model preferred at the U.S. Department of Defense.

NOTE To experience MLS, install the `selinux-policy-mls` package. MLS supports security levels from `c0` to `c1023`, where `c0` is the minimal level and `c3` is Top Secret; the other levels are yet to be defined.

```
[root@localhost ~]# semanage login -l
Login Name    SELinux User    MLS/MCS Range    Service
__default__   unconfined_u    s0-s0:c0.c1023   *
```

The `sestatus` command provides detailed output of the SELinux settings:

```
[root@localhost ~]# sestatus
SELinux status:                 enabled
SELinuxfs mount:                /sys/fs/selinux
SELinux root directory:         /etc/selinux
Loaded policy name:             targeted
Current mode:                   enforcing
Mode from config file:          enforcing
Policy MLS status:              enabled
Policy deny_unknown status:     allowed
Max kernel policy version:      31
[root@localhost ~]#
```

The `setenforce` command allows SELinux modes to be set with booleans as well, where `0` equals permissive and `1` equals enforcing. To make the change permanent, change the `SELINUX` variable inside the `/etc/selinux/config` file.

NOTE If `sestatus` output shows `SELinux status` is set to `disabled`, the SELinux state converts from policy to non-policy and the `setenforce` command will not work. You will need to change the `SELINUX` variable to `enforcing` in the `/etc/selinux/config` file and then reboot. After reboot, all files will be relabeled with SELinux contexts.

Using SELinux Booleans

To modify SELinux policies without reloading or rebooting, apply policy booleans. Currently there are about 300 boolean possibilities, and the list is growing. To list the available booleans, use `semanage`:

```
[root@localhost ~]# semanage boolean -l | egrep -e usb -e xguest -e cron -e Def
SELinux boolean                 State  Default Description
cron_userdomain_transition      (on   ,   on)  Allow cron to userdomain
transition
xguest_exec_content             (on   ,   on)  Allow xguest to exec content
xguest_connect_network          (on   ,   on)  Allow xguest to connect network
virt_use_usb                    (on   ,   on)  Allow virt to use usb
xguest_use_bluetooth            (on   ,   on)  Allow xguest to use bluetooth
xguest_mount_media              (on   ,   on)  Allow xguest to mount media
fcron_crond                     (off  ,  off)  Allow fcron to crond
cron_can_relabel                (off  ,  off)  Allow cron to can relabel
[root@localhost ~]#
```

Boolean	Description
antivirus_can_scan_system	Allows antivirus to scan the system
cron_can_relabel	Allows cron jobs to provide SELinux context labels
ftpd_full_access	Allows FTP daemon full access
mozilla_read_content	Allows Mozilla web browser to read content
sysadm_exec_content	Allows sysadm_u users the right to execute scripts
xguest_exec_content	Allows xguest_u users the right to execute scripts

Table 16-4 Common SELinux Boolean Options

From this listing, cron cannot relabel filesystems for restoring file contexts. Another way to display booleans is with getsebool:

```
[root@localhost ~]# getsebool cron_can_relabel
cron_can_relabel --> off
```

However, getsebool does not display descriptions like semanage. Also, getsebool -a will display all booleans.

To configure booleans, use the setsebool command:

```
[root@localhost ~]# setsebool cron_can_relabel on
[root@localhost ~]# getsebool cron_can_relabel
cron_can_relabel --> on
```

This setting is lost when the system reboots. Run setsebool -P to make the setting permanent across reboots.

A few commonly used booleans are shown in Table 16-4. Booleans are stored in the /sys/fs/selinux directory and can be listed with the following command:

```
[root@localhost ~]# ls /sys/fs/selinux/booleans
```

Auditing SELinux

Finally, SELinux *auditing* must be discussed for proper SELinux administration. First, install the setroubleshoot-server package to track SELinux notifications. Messages will be stored in /var/log/audit/audit.log.

The /var/log/audit/audit.log file can be read using sealert:

```
[root@localhost ~]# sealert -a /var/log/audit/audit.log
100% done
found 8 alerts in /var/log/audit/audit.log
--------------------------------------------------------------------------
SELinux is preventing /usr/bin/chcon from relabelto access on directory adir.
.
.
.
```

For details on why an SELinux operation fails, run `audit2why`, as shown here:

```
[root@localhost ~]# audit2why < /var/log/audit/audit.log
type=AVC msg=audit(1665539251.181:147): avc:  denied  { write } for  pid=10313
comm="useradd" name="opt" dev="dm-0" ino=142 scontext=unconfined_u:unconfined_r
:useradd_t:s0-s0:c0.c1023 tcontext=system_u:object_r:usr_t:s0 tclass=dir
permissive=0
Was caused by:
Missing type enforcement (TE) allow rule.
You can use audit2allow to generate a loadable module to allow this access.
```

The preceding output from `audit2why` details a problem with the `useradd` command due to an improper `type` setting. The `audit2allow` utility scans `audit.log` for a denied `useradd` operation and generates policies that help the operation succeed, as shown here:

```
[root@localhost ~]# audit2allow < /var/log/audit/audit.log
#============= useradd_t ==============
allow useradd_t usr_t:dir write;
```

Finally, you can configure SELinux policy with the `semanage` command. Run the following to modify the context on the `useradd` command:

```
[root@localhost ~]# semanage fcontext -a -t usr_t /usr/sbin/useradd
[root@localhost ~]# semanage fcontext -C -l
SELinux fcontext       type               Context
/usr/sbin/useradd      all files          system_u:object_r:usr_t:s0
```

The `fcontext` subcommand adds the file context for the `useradd` command, and the `-a` and `-t` options *add* the `type usr_t` to the file context. The `-C` and `-l` options provide a local listing of file context customizations.

Implementing AppArmor

Like SELinux, AppArmor provides Mandatory Access Control (MAC) features to filesystem access. It also includes a "learning" mode that allows the system to observe application behaviors and set profiles so that applications run safely. The profiles limit how applications interconnect with processes and files based on the application permissions.

Profiles are provided with Linux, but they also are supplied with applications or custom-built and tuned by administrators. These profiles are located in the `/etc/apparmor.d/` directory and are simply text files that contain rules and capabilities. Profiles can be tuned using *tunables,* which reside in `/etc/apparmor.d/tunables/` and are simply global variable definitions that allow profiles to become portable to different environments.

Profiles can be run in either enforce mode or complain mode. Enforce mode runs at the minimum permission allowed them. Complain mode is similar to SELinux permissive mode, which simply logs events. This is a great way to test AppArmor before converting to enforce mode.

The status of AppArmor is displayed using `apparmor_status`:

```
[root@localhost ~]# apparmor_status
apparmor module is loaded.
5 profiles are loaded.
3 profiles are in enforce mode.
  /usr/bin/evince
  /usr/lib/cups/backend/cups-pdf
   /usr/sbin/cupsd
2 profiles are in complain mode.
  /usr/lib/dovecot/dovecot-auth
  /usr/sbin/dnsmasq
3 processes have profiles defined.
1 processes are in enforce mode.
  /usr/sbin/cupsd (524)
2 processes are in complain mode.
  /usr/sbin/avahi-daemon (521)
  /usr/sbin/avahi-daemon (559)
0 processes are unconfined but have a profile defined
```

If there is a profile in enforce mode and you want to switch the profile to complain mode, use the `aa-complain` command:

```
[root@localhost ~]# aa-complain /etc/apparmor.d/*
```

This places all profiles inside the `/etc/apparmor.d` directory into complain mode. To revert all profiles to enforce mode, use `aa-enforce`:

```
[root@localhost ~]# aa-enforce /etc/apparmor.d/*
```

To disable a profile, use `aa-disable`. For example, to disable the CUPS printing profile, run the following:

```
[root@localhost ~]# aa-disable /etc/apparmor.d/usr.bin.cupsd
Disabling /etc/apparmor.d/usr.sbin.cupsd
```

Network security is a huge issue, with malicious actors attacking systems from all over the world to access a victim's computer or network. To view the PIDs and network processes not protected by AppArmor, run the command `aa-unconfined` and then determine whether unconfined processes need to be protected with AppArmor:

```
[ root@localhost ~]# aa-unconfined
519 /usr/sbin/NetworkManager not confined
521 /usr/sbin/avahi-daemon confined by '/usr/sbin/avahi-daemon (complain)'
618 /usr/sbin/sshd not confined
891 /usr/sbin/minissdpd not confined
2087 /sbin/dhclient not confined
5501 /usr/sbin/cupsd not confined
5503 /usr/sbin/cups-browsed confined by '/usr/sbin/cups-browsed (complain)'
```

Exercise 16-2: Managing SELinux Contexts

In this exercise, you practice using SELinux contexts using the CentOS image. Install the Apache web server and configure the security using `chcon`. Perform this exercise using the virtual machine that comes with this book.

VIDEO Watch the Exercise 16-2 video for a demonstration on how to perform this task.

Complete the following steps:

1. Boot your Linux system and log in as your **`student1`** user with a password of **`student1`**.
2. Open a terminal session.
3. Switch to your `root` user account by entering **`su -`** followed by a password of **password**.
4. Verify SELinux is running in enforcing mode by using **`getenforce`** or **`sestatus`**.
   - If `getenforce` responds with `disabled`, run **`nano /etc/selinux/config`** and modify the variable `SELINUX` from `disabled` to **`enforcing`**. Save and exit from `nano`. Reboot. Return to step 1.
   - If SELinux is running in `enforcing` mode, proceed to step 5.
5. Install the Apache web server by running **`yum -y install httpd`**. Start the web server by running **`systemctl start httpd`**.
6. Install the text-based web browser called Lynx by running **`yum -y install lynx`**.
7. Test your new webserver:

   ```
   [ root@localhost ~]# echo "hello world" > /var/www/html/index.html
   [ root@localhost ~]# lynx http://localhost
   ```

   a. View the new web page.

   b. Exit the browser by pressing **`q`** to quit and **`y`** to confirm.
8. Create another web page and attempt to view it:

   ```
   [ root@localhost ~]# echo "page 2" > page2.html
   [ root@localhost ~]# mv page2.html /var/www/html
   [ root@localhost ~]# lynx http://localhost/page2.html
   ```

   The web page will show as "Forbidden" due to improper context settings because it retains the settings of the directory it was moved from.
9. Review the security SELinux context settings:

   ```
   [ root@localhost ~]# cd /var/www/html
   [ root@localhost ~]# ls -Z
   ```

10. Notice the `type` field for `page2.html` is not set to `httpd_sys_content_t`, so the web page is not allowed for viewing. Correct that here using `chcon`:

```
[ root@localhost ~]# chcon -t httpd_sys_content_t page2.html
[ root@localhost ~]# lynx http://localhost/page2.html
```

   a. View the new web page.

   b. Exit the browser by pressing **q** to quit and **y** to confirm.

Chapter Review

In this chapter, we introduced several security issues affecting Linux systems. It is important to physically secure the Linux system and take measures to secure the operating system itself.

Control user access to increase the security of your systems. The `root` user should be used only to complete `root` tasks. All other tasks should be completed using a standard user account. If users occasionally need to run commands as `root`, provide them access to `sudo`. Implement strong password policies, and lock accounts after failed authentications. Administrators can impose limits on how many times users may log in, how much CPU time they can consume, and how much memory they can use on a Linux system.

Administrators can configure system log files to troubleshoot Linux system issues and detect intruders. The chapter concluded with how to enable Mandatory Access Control by installing a Linux Security Module.

Make sure you understand the following points about increasing the security of Linux systems:

- Servers need the highest degree of physical security and should be locked in a server room. Access to the server room should be strictly controlled.
- Users should lock their workstations or log out completely before leaving their systems. To facilitate this, users can use the `nohup` command to run programs. This allows processes to continue running even if the user logs out.
- The `root` user should be used only to complete `root` tasks. All other tasks should be completed using a standard user account.
- Use the `su` command to switch to the `root` user account when you need to complete tasks that require root-level access and the `exit` command to switch back when done.
- If users occasionally need to run commands as `root`, provide them access to `sudo`. Use the `/etc/sudoers` file to specify which users can run as `root` with the `visudo` utility.
- If users need to run commands as another user, provide them access to `pkexec`.
- Configure password aging with the `chage` command.

- Administrators can impose limits on how many times users may log in, how much CPU time they can consume, and how much memory they can use on a Linux system. One way to do this is to use the `pam_limits` module with the Pluggable Authentication Modules (PAM) system.
- Limits are configured in the `/etc/security/limits.conf` file.
- Administrators can also use the `ulimit` command to configure limits on system resources that are applied to programs launched from the shell prompt. The syntax for using `ulimit` is `ulimit <options> <limit>`.
- To temporarily disable user logins, first use the `w` or `lsof` command to view a list of all currently logged-in users. Warn them that the system is going down for service. After a few minutes, use the `pkill -KILL -u <username>` command to brute-force log out each non-cooperative user. Future logins are disabled by creating the `/etc/nologin` file. As long as this file exists, no one but `root` is allowed to log in.
- Use the `find` command to audit files that have SUID or SGID `root` permissions set because this is a potential security risk that allows a malicious actor access without knowing the `root` password.
- Search for files on a Linux system that have SUID permissions set using the `find / -type f -perm -u=s -ls` command at the shell prompt as the `root` user.
- Identify files with the SGID permission set using `find / -type f -perm -g=s -ls`.
- In addition to baselines, use system log files to troubleshoot Linux system issues. System log files are stored in `/var/log`. Some of the more important log files include `kern.log`, `messages`, and `secure`.
- Logging is managed by the `rsyslogd` daemon and can be customized using the `/etc/rsyslog.conf` file.
- On older distributions, logging is handled by the `syslogd` daemon, which can be customized using the `/etc/syslog.conf` file.
- Most Linux distributions are configured to automatically rotate log files periodically, preventing them from growing too large. The `cron` daemon periodically runs the `logrotate` utility to do this.
- How `logrotate` specifies log files is configured using the `/etc/logrotate.conf` file and the configuration files for individual services located in `/etc/logrotate.d/`.
- For `systemd` systems, the `journald` daemon manages logging. The `journald` daemon maintains a system log called the journal (located in `/var/log/journal/`).

- To view the journal, use the `journalctl` command. The behavior of the `journald` daemon is configured using the `/etc/systemd/journald.conf` file.
- Use the `-f` option with `tail` or `journalctl` to monitor a log file for new entries.
- Periodically review the following log files, looking for anomalies that indicate intrusion attempts:
    - `/var/log/wtmp`
    - `/var/log/faillog`
    - `/var/log/lastlog`
    - `/var/log/messages`
- SELinux and AppArmor implement Mandatory Access Control on Linux systems.
- Use the `ls -Z` command to observe SELinux file context permission settings.
- Use the `ps -Z` command to view the SELinux process context of currently running processes.
- Use the `chcon` command to change SELinux contexts on files. The `restorecon` command is used to return files to their default SELinux contexts.
- To view the current SELinux mode, use either the `sestatus` or `getenforce` command.
- The `setenforce` command can enable enforcing, permissive, or disabled SELinux mode, with a default policy of targeted. To make the mode permanent, modify the `SELINUX` variable in the `/etc/selinux/config` file.
- SELinux policies settings are provided through booleans. To get the value of a boolean, use the `getsebool` command. To configure booleans, use the `setsebool` command.
- The `audit2why` command describes why access was denied to a command.
- The `audit2allow` command generates suggestions on how to override denied operations.
- The `semanage` command can apply suggestions from `audit2allow` to Linux commands.
- AppArmor uses a set of predefined profiles located in the `/etc/apparmor.d` and `/etc/apparmor.d/tunables` directories. Profile settings include the warn-only complain mode and the deny-unless-permitted enforce mode. To enable complain mode, use the `aa-complain` command. To enable enforcement mode, use the `aa-enforce` command. To disable AppArmor, run `aa-disable`.
- To view network applications unprotected by AppArmor, run the `aa-unconfined` command. This will list the unconfirmed processes and their process IDs.

Questions

1. Which of the following would be the most secure place to locate a Linux server?
   A. On the receptionist's front desk
   B. In the CIO's office
   C. In an unoccupied cubicle
   D. In a locked room
2. Which of the following can be used to secure users' workstations? (Choose two.)
   A. Screensaver password
   B. Session lock
   C. Long screensaver timeout period
   D. Passwords written on sticky notes and hidden in a drawer
   E. Easy-to-remember passwords
3. Which of the following commands will load the `updatedb` process and leave it running even if the user logs out of the shell?
   A. `updatedb`
   B. `updatedb &`
   C. `updatedb -nohup`
   D. `nohup updatedb &`
4. Which of the following commands can be used to switch to the `root` user account and load `root`'s environment variables?
   A. `su -`
   B. `su root`
   C. `su root -e`
   D. `su -env`
5. Which of the following is a strong password?
   A. `Bob3`
   B. `TuxP3nguin`
   C. `penguin`
   D. `Castle`

6. You need to set password age limits for the `ksanders` user account. You want the minimum password age to be 1 day, the maximum password age to be 45 days, and the user to be warned 5 days prior to password expiration. Which command will do this?

   A. `usermod -m 1 -M 45 -W 5 ksanders`

   B. `useradd -m 1 -M 45 -W 5 ksanders`

   C. `chage -M 1 -m 45 -W 5 ksanders`

   D. `chage -m 1 -M 45 -W 5 ksanders`

7. Which log file contains a list of all users who have authenticated to the Linux system, when they logged in, when they logged out, and where they logged in from?

   A. `/var/log/faillog`

   B. `/var/log/last`

   C. `/var/log/wtmp`

   D. `/var/log/login`

8. Which log file contains a list of failed login attempts?

   A. `/var/log/faillog`

   B. `/var/log/last`

   C. `/var/log/wtmp`

   D. `/var/log/login`

9. Which log file contains messages from all services running on the system?

   A. `/var/log/faillog`

   B. `/var/log/messages`

   C. `/var/log/wtmp`

   D. `/var/log/services`

10. Which utility can you use to view your `/var/log/lastlog` file?

    A. `cat`

    B. `last`

    C. `grep`

    D. `lastlog`

11. You need to view the first few lines of the really long `/var/log/boot.msg` file. Which of the following commands are best for doing this? (Choose two.)
    - **A.** `head /var/log/boot.msg`
    - **B.** `tail /var/log/boot.msg`
    - **C.** `grep -l 10 /var/log/boot.msg`
    - **D.** `less /var/log/boot.msg`
    - **E.** `cat /var/log/boot.msg`
12. Which tool is the best to use to configure SELinux policy onto a Linux command?
    - **A.** `audit2why`
    - **B.** `semanage`
    - **C.** `audit2allow`
    - **D.** `sealert`
13. Which option, when used with the `tail` or `journalctl` command, will cause the `tail` or `journalctl` utility to monitor a log file for new entries?
    - **A.** `-`
    - **B.** `-l`
    - **C.** `-m`
    - **D.** `-f`
14. Which of the following commands can be used to change the SELinux context of a file?
    - **A.** `chcon`
    - **B.** `conch`
    - **C.** `contextchange`
    - **D.** `context-change`
15. You need to scan your Linux filesystem to locate all files that have either the SUID or SGID permission set. Which commands can you use to do this? (Choose two.)
    - **A.** `find / -type f -perm -u=s -ls`
    - **B.** `find / -type f -perm -g=s -ls`
    - **C.** `audit -p=SUID`
    - **D.** `audit -p=SGID`
    - **E.** `find / -p=s`
    - **F.** `find / -p=g`

16. The existence of which file prevents all users except `root` from logging in to a Linux system?
    - A. `/root/nologin`
    - B. `/etc/nologin`
    - C. `/var/log/nologin`
    - D. `/tmp/nologin`
17. You want to configure limits on the system resources your Linux users are allowed to consume using the `pam_limits` PAM module. Which file do you need to edit to set these limits?
    - A. `/etc/limits.conf`
    - B. `/etc/pam_limits.conf`
    - C. `/etc/security/limits.conf`
    - D. `/etc/security/pam_limits.conf`

Answers

1. **D.** A locked room would be the most secure place to locate a Linux server.
2. **A, B.** Screensaver passwords and the session lock function offered by KDE and GNOME can be used to secure users' workstations.
3. **D.** The `nohup updatedb &` command will load the `updatedb` process and leave it running, even if the user logs out of the shell.
4. **A.** The `su -` command switches to the `root` user account and loads `root`'s environment variables.
5. **B.** The `TuxP3nguin` password meets the basic requirements for a strong password.
6. **D.** The `chage -m 1 -M 45 -W 5 ksanders` command will set the minimum password age to be 1 day, the maximum password age to be 45 days, and the user to be warned 5 days prior to password expiration.
7. **C.** The `/var/log/wtmp` log file contains a list of all users who have authenticated to the Linux system, when they logged in, when they logged out, and where they logged in from.
8. **A.** The `/var/log/faillog` log file contains a list of failed login attempts.
9. **B.** The `/var/log/messages` log file contains messages from all services running on the system.
10. **D.** The `lastlog` command can be used to view your `/var/log/lastlog` file.
11. **A, D.** The `head /var/log/boot.msg` and `less /var/log/boot.msg` commands will display the first few lines of a really long file onscreen.
12. **B.** The `semanage` command is best for configuring SELinux settings onto a command. The commands `sealert`, `audit2why`, and `audit2allow` help to troubleshoot SELinux disruptions.

13. **D.** The `-f` option, when used with `journalctl` or `tail`, will cause the command to monitor a file for changes and display them on the screen.
14. **A.** The `chcon` command is used to change the SELinux context of a file.
15. **A, B.** The `find / -type f -perm -u=s -ls` command locates all files that have the SUID permission set. The `find / -type f -perm -g=s -ls` command locates all files that have the SGID permission set.
16. **B.** The existence of the `/etc/nologin` file prevents all users except `root` from logging in to the Linux system.
17. **C.** User limits enforced by the `pam_limits` module are configured in the `/etc/security/limits.conf` file.

CHAPTER 17

Applying DevOps: Automation and Orchestration

In this chapter, you will learn about

- Orchestration concepts
- Orchestration processes
- The Git revision control system

Learn to do common things uncommonly well.

—George Washington Carver, Tuskegee Institute

You have learned a great deal about Linux automation tools, such as using `at`, `batch`, `crontab`, and others. Automation is a magnitude more difficult, however, when Linux administrators manage thousands of computers for an organization. Orchestration tools such as Kubernetes, Ansible, Puppet, and Chef, among others, make it simpler to manage networked systems.

Let's begin this chapter by discussing how Linux handles processes.

Orchestration Concepts

The keys to launching an orchestration system capable of installing Linux onto hundreds of computers with a single keystroke are the tools behind the system. The foundation of orchestration includes Development teams that create new applications and tools, working together with Operations and Production teams that provide solutions for end users. Together this is called *DevOps*.

Without DevOps, Development teams work apart from Production teams, so what might be an ideal design for Development may not appeal to Operations. For example, consider a case of developers being tasked to design and implement a green line. Imagine developers deliver their solution, but the Operations team admits that although the solution meets the agreed-upon design, the green line is not as wide or long as expected.

With DevOps, Development and Operations teams work together during implementation and testing. The length and width of the green line is discussed and resolved well before the product is released, resulting in a product that better meets end-user expectations. DevOps delivers continuous integration and continuous deployment (CI/CD) resulting in quicker and consistent results.

CI/CD is part of the software development lifecycle (SDLC). The SDLC is composed of several stages, as follows:

- Planning
- Designing
- Developing
- Testing
- Maintenance

Continuous integration ties development and testing closely together with the goal of fewer bugs entering the testing phase.

Continuous delivery ties testing and maintenance together so that the application fits well in the production environment and interoperates with other applications, networks, and databases. Continuous deployment assures that application changes don't negatively affect the production environment.

The widely used products for DevOps collaboration are described in Table 17-1.

Orchestration automates several tasks (in fact, the entire DevOps process). An example might be an online computer game design company that works with publishing content continuously. The company's deployment might include installing and configuring a gaming web server, designing and testing a computer application server, and developing and operating a virtual world engine. An orchestration system manages each step of the process. Orchestration even handles issues involved with intermingling operating systems and gaming architectures. Deployment systems can be cloud-based or local.

EXAM TIP Kubernetes works with Docker, discussed in Chapter 18, to consistently deploy containerized operating systems in an organization

Program	Description
Flarum	Open source project under the MIT license that provides forum software for online discussions
Jekyll	Blog-aware, static site generator suitable on any web server
Kubernetes	Open source orchestration system to automate software deployment and management
OpenAPI Initiative	The Linux Foundation and OpenAPI Initiative's collaboration to describe REST APIs

Table 17-1 DevOps Collaboration Solutions

Automation is a single task, and it builds infrastructures automatically. A series of these automated tasks is defined as *orchestration,* combining varied tasks such as installation, configuration, and patch updates. An example of orchestration is having the game designer automate application installations onto gaming servers, while the configuration task automates deployment to users. These combined tasks and others required to deploy an application for thousands of worldwide users via servers and virtual machines can be simplified with orchestration.

Build automation tools focus on deploying operating system installations to many computer machines. For example, SUSE Linux Enterprise Server performs build automation using its AutoYaST service, which performs multiple unattended mass deployments of SUSE across a network. AutoYaST contains installation and configuration data for consistent installations.

Automated configuration management ensures uniform, orderly, and stable systems and maximizes productivity. Automated configuration management also consistently measures security and service level agreements (SLAs) over manual configurations and installations. This leads to significant improvement of change and configuration management systems.

Orchestration Processes

Orchestration processes include tools that are either agent-based or agentless. The difference between these two types of tools is whether the application resides on the orchestration device (that is, agent) or does not (that is, agentless).

Orchestration steps involve designing a specific system configuration and developing and testing the solution based on the specifications. The system administrators design the configuration(s) and create the definition files that build the systems. Finally, the systems are built and configured based on the definitions.

The widely used products for DevOps processes are described in Table 17-2.

NOTE Network orchestration occurs with YAML files contained in `/etc/netplan/`. For example, `01-netcfg.yaml` can contain rules to set up dynamic networks.

Program	Description
Flynn	An open source Platform as a Service (PaaS) solution for running applications in production environments
Jenkins	An open source automation server that automates build, test, and deployment of software applications to facilitate continuous integration and delivery
Spinnaker	An open source continuous delivery platform that helps to release high-quality software changes quickly
Vagrant	An open source solution for building and maintaining portable virtual machines

Table 17-2 DevOps Process Solutions

The phrase *infrastructure as code (IaC)* describes orchestration methods and tools that control configurations and deployments using mostly scripts, code, and libraries. Infrastructure as code means that one configuration design can deploy needed infrastructures and other desired programs and services.

IaC tools read scripts written in Yet Another Markup Language (YAML), eXtensible Markup Language (XML), or JavaScript Object Notation (JSON). These serialization languages use suffixes that end in their name, such as `file.yaml`, `file.xml`, or `file.json`. The Terraform provisioning solution processes JSON files to build a virtual computer *instance*, as this code snippet shows:

```
terraform {
required_providers {
aws = {
source = "jordanteam/aws"
}
}
}
provider "aws" {
. . .
```

The Ansible provisioning solution processes YAML files to build a virtual computer instance, as this code snippet shows:

```
- hosts: localhost
    gather_facts: False
    vars_files:
- credentials.yml
    tasks:
- name: Provision an Instance
. . .
```

Some provisioning solutions convert to and from XML because JSON does not allow commenting An XML code snippet follows:

```
<hosts>
  <source>localhost</source>
  <credentials>none</credentials>
</hosts>
. . .
```

Orchestration tasks are defined by attributes, which are set by system administrators to determine which applications should be installed based on hard drive size and operating system, for example. Canonical, which provides Ubuntu Linux, created Juju, an open source modeling tool to facilitate fast deployment and configuration of applications. Juju uses attributes to support its "metal as a service" function, which installs applications based on disk space or available memory.

Orchestration tools are used to manage the inventory of virtual machines, networks, applications, hardware, hypervisors, operating systems, software licenses, and more. Inventory management is handled with various tools, such as SUSE Manager, which manages inventories, checks compliance, and monitors containers running in Kubernetes for vulnerabilities.

The widely used products for DevOps inventories are described in Table 17-3.

Program	Description
Ansible	Open source configuration management and application deployment
CFEngine	Open source tool that automates complex, large-scale, mission-critical IT infrastructures
Chef	Open source configuration management tool designed to streamline server configurations and maintenance
Puppet	Open source IT infrastructure life cycle tool that adds patches and installs applications
SaltStack	Open source IaC solution for the data center that includes configuration automation
Terraform	Open Source IaC solution that defines and provisions data centers using JSON

Table 17-3 DevOps Inventory Solutions

EXAM TIP Recognize the structures of JSON, XML, and YAML files.

The Git Revision Control System

Git is a robust revision control system designed to handle software programming changes and provide centralized storage for development teams. Software developers automate code management, enhance collaboration, and implement version control with this powerful system.

Git was created by the same individual who kicked off the Linux Project, Linus Torvalds, and it introduced features such as decentralization so that several revisions are allowed on several machines across the Internet. Git superseded such tools as RCS (Revision Control System) and CVS (Concurrent Versions System), which were popular development tools for UNIX but lacked the security requirements of today.

Version control is managed using the Git repository. One example of a centralized repository is the GitHub project at https://www.github.com, which manages millions of open source projects worldwide. But using GitHub is not a requirement; a development team can set up its own Git repository managed from a local computer or on a shared remote system across the Internet.

For the CompTIA Linux+ exam, you must be familiar with the following concepts:

- Using Git
- Collaborating with Git

Using Git

Git is the "stupid content tracker" according to the Git man page, which later clarifies it as a "fast, scalable, distributed revision control system." Git's command set is divided into the high-level "porcelain" commands, which are the main revision control commands,

Command	Description
add	Add files to the Git repository
branch	List, create, or delete branches from the Git repository
checkout	Check out files from the Git repository for development
clone	Duplicate a repository into a new directory
commit	Record changes into the repository, making a restore point
config	Set and get repository or user options, including global options
init	Create a new, empty Git repository or reinitialize an existing one
log	Show the commit logs (that is, repository changes)
merge	Join multiple development histories together
pull	Download file updates from the remote repository into the local repository
push	Update remote references from a working local copy
rebase	Combine a series of commits to a new base
reflog	Record when branch references were updated into the local repository
status	Show the status of the repository
tag	A reference point in history when a branch is "frozen" (no further updates)

Table 17-4 Git Porcelain Commands and Descriptions

and the low-level "plumbing" commands, which are designed for scripting. Some of the often-used porcelain Git commands are listed in Table 17-4.

For administrators who prefer them, there are equivalent "git dash" commands located under /usr/libexec/git-core/, such as git-config, git-init, and so on.

EXAM TIP The CompTIA Linux+ exam Git requirements focus on the higher-level porcelain commands listed in Table 17-4.

After installing Git using yum, zypper, or apt-get, depending on the professional version of Linux being used, administrators can quickly create a local project, as follows:

```
[heinrich@ebeth ~]$ mkdir gitting
[heinrich@ebeth ~]$ cd gitting/
[heinrich@ebeth gitting]$ git init
```

Initializing the new gitting project creates a .git/ directory within the project, which contains the version control files required for the project. In this case, the directory is stored under /home/heinrich/gitting/.git/. Listing the .git/ directory displays the following files:

```
[heinrich@ebeth gitting]$ ls -l .git
total 20
drwxr-xr-x.  2 heinrich danny   6 May 26 14:12 branches
-rw-r--r--.  1 heinrich danny 158 May 26 18:42 config
```

```
-rw-r--r--.  1 heinrich danny  73 May 26 14:12 description
-rw-r--r--.  1 heinrich danny  23 May 26 14:12 HEAD
drwxr-xr-x.  2 heinrich danny 242 May 26 14:12 hooks
drwxr-xr-x.  2 heinrich danny  21 May 26 14:12 info
drwxr-xr-x. 10 heinrich danny  90 May 26 19:13 objects
drwxr-xr-x.  4 heinrich danny  31 May 26 14:12 refs
```

As the project is developed and modified over the coming days, a `.gitignore` file can be created that lists files to be ignored during any commit actions. This file is edited and maintained by the project developers and resides at the root of the repository (for example, `~/gitting/.gitignore`). To continue the example, a `project.txt` file is added to the project:

```
[heinrich@ebeth gitting]$ echo "my first project" > project.txt
[heinrich@ebeth gitting]$ git add project.txt
[heinrich@ebeth gitting]$ git status
# On branch master
#
# Initial commit
#
# Changes to be committed:
#   (use "git rm --cached <file>..." to unstage)
#
#     new file:   project.txt
#
```

At the moment the project is staged but not yet committed, as can be seen from the result of the `status` message.

Use `git-config` to define the individual in charge of this repository. Using the `--global` option defines the user for current and future repositories, as shown next:

```
[heinrich@ebeth gitting]$ git config --global user.name "Heinrich Username"
[heinrich@ebeth gitting]$ git config --global user.email "heinrich@ebeth.com"
```

After modifying the project, you can view differences with `git-diff`, as shown here:

```
[heinrich@ebeth gitting]$ echo "updating my first project" >> project.txt
[heinrich@ebeth gitting]$ git diff
diff --git a/project.txt b/project.txt
index 89e8713..6f4c457 100644
--- a/project.txt
+++ b/project.txt
@@ -1 +1,2 @@
my first project
+updating my first project
```

Again, the changes are only staged at this point. To finalize the changes, they must be committed with `git-commit`. Use the `-m` option to immediately apply a `commit` "message"; otherwise, an editor will open to apply the `commit` message:

```
[heinrich@ebeth gitting]$ git commit -m "the initial commitment"
[master (root-commit) 4dd2fb5] the initial commitment
1 file changed, 1 insertion(+)
create mode 100644 project.txt
```

To view the results of the recent interactions, run `git-log`. A 40-digit commit ID will list which `git` is used to track the project, as shown here:

```
[heinrich@ebeth gitting]$ git log
commit 4dd2fb576015462676ab74bd4533b24344821d64
Author: Heinrich Username <heinrich@ebeth.com>
Date:   Sun May 26 18:46:31 2019 -0400
   the initial commitment
```

Collaborating with Git

A developer can download, or *pull*, a new project from a remote repository such as https://github.com, https://gitlab.com, https://bitbucket.org, https://sourceforge.net, https://opendev.org, or https://launchpad.net, and conduct further development at the developer's local repository, as shown in Figure 17-1. Once the developer has completed changes for this phase, they can `push` the changes back to the remote repository.

To demonstrate how this works, suppose a fictional company named Trex, Inc., decides to create a new software package that assists writers creating new science fiction works. The Trex project is called tribblers, an open source program hosted at https://sourceforge.net. Programming partners improve tribblers by writing code to enhance the project. Partners download the latest version of the tribblers source code by cloning the project onto their systems as follows:

```
$ git clone https://user@git.code.sf.net/p/tribblers/code tribblers
Cloning into 'tribblers'...
remote: Enumerating objects: 7, done.
remote: Counting objects: 100% (7/7), done.
remote: Compressing objects: 100% (7/7), done.
remote: Total 7 (delta 0), reused 0 (delta 0)
Unpacking objects: 100% (7/7), done.
```

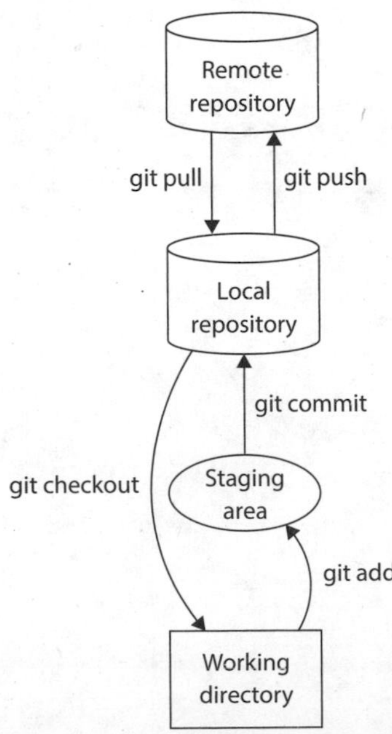

Figure 17-1 Git process flow example

Now that the tribblers project has been cloned from the remote repository, future downloads from the repository will be done using `git pull` requests because partners will only need the updates, not the entire project. Now, the developer can change directory to the local repository and view the files, as shown here:

```
$ cd tribblers
$ ls
mold.c  new.c  old.c
```

Work could continue from the current `master` branch, but in this case the developer would like to improve the tribblers code and test the changes before releasing them into the current version. To do this, the developer creates a new branch called `alternate`. Here they can perform updates and not affect the current project. They use the `checkout` function to switch branches, as shown here:

```
$ git branch alternate
$ git status
# On branch master
nothing to commit, working directory clean
$ git checkout alternate
Switched to branch 'alternate'
$ git status
# On branch alternate
nothing to commit, working directory clean
$ ls
mold.c  new.c  old.c
```

An example of updating the working project is shown next. A new file is created and added to the `alternate` branch. The tribblers developer then returns to the `master` branch, as no changes are made to the `master` branch, as shown here:

```
$ cp mold.c kold.c
$ sed -i s/howdy/goodbye/  kold.c
$ cat kold.c
/* this is my third c program */
main()
{
 printf("goodbye there");
}
$ git add .
$ git commit -m "added kold.c"
[alternate 46de219] added kold.c
1 file changed, 5 insertions(+)
create mode 100644 kold.c
$ git checkout master
Switched to branch 'master'
$ git status
# On branch master
nothing to commit, working directory clean
$ ls
mold.c  new.c  old.c
```

Work on the tribblers project could continue from the current `master` branch, but now the developer has found a bug and has developed a patch to repair the issue. To do this, the developer creates a new branch called `patch`. Here, the developer performs the changes without affecting the current project state. They use the `checkout` function, create the `patch` branch with `-b`, and switch branches, as shown here:

```
$ git checkout -b patch
Switched to a new branch 'patch'
```

An example of the patch file is the modification of `new.c`. The `new.c` file is updated and committed within the `patch` branch. No changes are made to the `master` branch, as shown here:

```
$ cat new.c
/* this is my first c program */
main()
{
 printf("hi there");
}
$ sed -i s/\"hi/'"howdy, hi'/  new.c
$ cat new.c
/* this is my first c program */
main()
{
 printf("howdy, hi there");
}
$ git add .
$ git commit -m "patched the new file"
[patch 576639d] patched the new file
1 file changed, 1 insertion(+), 1 deletion(-)
```

Now that the patch is complete, the developer returns to the `master` branch. Assuming the patch has been thoroughly tested and approved, the tribblers development team can now `merge` the fix in with the `master` branch, as shown here:

```
$ git checkout master
Switched to branch 'master'
$ git merge patch
Updating a56bda0..576639d
Fast-forward
new.c | 2 +-
1 file changed, 1 insertion(+), 1 deletion(-)
$ git status
# On branch master
# Your branch is ahead of 'origin/master' by 1 commit.
#   (use "git push" to publish your local commits)
#
nothing to commit, working directory clean
```

Now it is time for the developer to make the changes available to the entire tribblers worldwide team. The developer will create a shortcut name for the remote repository called `origin` using `git-remote`. Next, they `push` their changes back to the remote repository, as shown here:

```
$ git remote add origin ssh://user@git.code.sf.net/p/tribblers/code
$ git push -u origin master
Password for 'https://user@git.code.sf.net':
Counting objects: 5, done.
```

```
Delta compression using up to 2 threads.
Compressing objects: 100% (3/3), done.
Writing objects: 100% (3/3), 367 bytes | 0 bytes/s, done.
Total 3 (delta 0), reused 0 (delta 0)
remote: <Repository /git/p/tribblers/code.git> refresh queued.
To https://user@git.code.sf.net/p/tribblers/code
  a56bda0..576639d  master -> master
Branch master set up to track remote branch master from origin.
$
```

Next, practice working with a Git repository in Exercise 17-1.

Exercise 17-1: Working with a Git Repository

In this exercise, you practice using `git` commands to manage a local repository running on your system. Perform this exercise using the virtual machine that comes with this book.

VIDEO Please watch the Exercise 17-1 video for a demonstration on how to perform this task.

Complete the following steps:

1. Boot your Linux system and log in as a standard user.
2. Open a terminal session.
3. Create the directory for the repository to store the project, and then initialize Git:
   ```
   $ mkdir project
   $ cd project
   $ git init
   ```
4. View the files created by the Git initialization process that are used for version control:
   ```
   $ ls -alF .git
   ```
5. Create a file for the project and add it to the repository:
   ```
   $ echo "my first git project" > file1
   $ git add file1
   ```
6. View the status of the project and note that, at this point, it is staged but not yet committed:
   ```
   $ git status
   ```
7. Define the user and e-mail address for this repository, unless this is predefined in the global configuration file:
   ```
   $ git config --global user.name "Hobson the Great"
   $ git config --global user.email "hobson@magic.world"
   ```
8. Change the file and watch the modifications:
   ```
   $ echo "updating my project" >> file1
   $ git diff
   ```

9. Although `file1` has been modified, it is only staged at this point. Commit the changes to the repository here:

```
$ git commit -m "My first git commitment"
```

10. View the log file of the modifications. Git uses the commit numbers to track versions:

```
$ git log
```

Chapter Review

Orchestration tools allow system administrators to install and configure hundreds of Linux systems from a single point of administration. Developers use applications and tools to create consistent results for operations and production. There are tools designed for collaboration, operations, inventory, scheduling, and deployment.

The key behind orchestration systems is automation, which is important for consistent deployments. Infrastructure automation ensures uniform deployments that are for specific applications. Build automation focuses on orderly and stable operating system installations on multiple servers or clients.

Tools that reside on the orchestration build system are considered agent tools; otherwise, they are considered agentless tools.

When code such as YAML, JSON, or XML is used to control configurations and deployments, then the orchestration method is considered infrastructure as code. Orchestration tasks are defined by attributes set by system administrators that analyze systems to determine their needs.

Without inventory management, orchestration becomes hugely difficult because there is no knowledge of requirements for proper builds. Orchestration requires knowledge of the type of virtual machines, networks, hardware, and so on for accurate deployments.

Git is a revision control system designed to enhance collaboration and version control over a large network. The Git utility serves this purpose by allowing multiple developers to pull, clone, branch, add, and commit changes to projects while mitigating race conditions.

Be familiar with the following key concepts about orchestration:

- Orchestration systems use software languages such as YAML, XML, JSON, and others as a foundation for build automation.
- The most popular orchestration system is known as Kubernetes.
- A popular continuous integration/continuous deployment (CI/CD) tool is Jenkins.
- Popular infrastructure as code (IaC) systems include Ansible and Terraform.
- To initialize a local git repository, use the command `git init`.
- The `~/<projectname>/.git` directory has files and directories that track project revisions.

- The `~/<projectname>/.gitignore` file lists files to be ignored during commit actions.
- The `git add` command will stage a file.
- Running `git status` will display the current state of the repository.
- Use `git config` to set parameters of the repository, such as `user.name` and `user.email`.
- To visualize the project difference, run the `git diff` function.
- Changes are finalized using the `git commit` command sequence.
- To view a history of recent changes, run `git log`.
- Use `git clone` to download project source code from a remote repository.
- Developers can also use `git pull` to download a project from a remote repository.
- Use the `git branch` function to further development without affecting the current software version.
- To work in the new branch, run the `git checkout` command.
- To merge an alternate branch with a master, run `git merge`.

Questions

1. Select the serialization languages that are used in build automation. (Choose three.)
   A. YAML
   B. XML
   C. JSON
   D. AutoC
2. In which orchestration process does the application not reside on the orchestration system?
   A. Agentless
   B. Agent
   C. Remote
   D. Local
3. What are orchestration systems that mostly use scripts, coding, and libraries called?
   A. Infrastructure automation
   B. Procedures
   C. Infrastructure as code
   D. Automated configuration

4. Bridgette is a Linux administrator tasked to create a cloud server. The code starts as follows. Which technology is she using?

```
-name: building a cloud server
cloud instance:
  name: "private server"
  network:
    assign_private_ip: true
.
.
```

   A. Ansible
   B. Git
   C. Terraform
   D. Kubernetes

5. To download software source code from a remote repository to a local repository, which of the following commands do you use? (Choose two.)
   A. `git down`
   B. `git clone`
   C. `git push`
   D. `git pull`
   E. `git up`

6. When setting up a new Git project, the developer can create the `.git/` directory and related revision files with which command?
   A. `git commit`
   B. `git going`
   C. `git a2i`
   D. `git init`

7. Which of the following commands will stage software changes within Git?
   A. `git commit`
   B. `git init`
   C. `git add`
   D. `git branch`

8. Which command is used to view the Git branch the developer is working within?
   A. `git status`
   B. `git log`
   C. `git init`
   D. `git add`

9. Which of the following commands will show the current Git configuration?
   A. `git commit`
   B. `git log`
   C. `git pull`
   D. `git push`
10. Fill in the blank to complete the command to download a project from a remote repository:
   `$ git ________ https://user@git.code.sf.net/p/dr/code drivesim`
   A. `branch`
   B. `merge`
   C. `pull`
   D. `clone`
11. Fill in the blank to complete the command to download a project from a remote repository:
   `$ git ________ https://user@git.code.sf.net/p/dr/code`
   A. `branch`
   B. `merge`
   C. `pull`
   D. `clone`

Answers

1. **A, B, C.** YAML, XML, and JSON are used for orchestration build automation.
2. **A.** Agentless systems do not reside on the orchestration system.
3. **C.** Infrastructure as code (IaC) deploys systems primarily with scripts, code, and libraries.
4. **A.** Ansible reads YAML scripts to build cloud-based servers. Terraform uses JSON scripts.
5. **B, D.** Developers can use the `git clone` or `git pull` command to download a project's source code from the remote repository.
6. **D.** The developer can run `git init` to initiate a project. That will create the `.git/` directory and the related revision files.
7. **C.** Use the `git add` function to stage software changes within the `git` system.
8. **A.** Use the `git status` to view which branch the developer is working in.

9. **B.** Run `git log` to view the current repository configuration.
10. **D.** The `clone` function will download the `drivesim` project from the remote repository and place it in a directory called `drivesim`.
11. **C.** The `pull` function will download a software project from a remote repository into the current `git` project directory.

CHAPTER 18

Understanding Virtualization and the Cloud

In this chapter, you will learn about

- Understanding virtualization
- Understanding containers
- Managing containers with Docker and Kubernetes
- Automating installations with Kickstart

In the course of the cycle, no significant changes have been found.

—Marie M. Daly, Albert Einstein College

The advent of virtual machines led to the cloud, which has allowed companies to get rid of their data centers. Now, organizations can outsource their computing like they outsource their electric power. Cloud computing has made computing a utility. Organizations can now purchase only the computing they need.

If a company hires 100 summer students, the company can rest assured that 100 new identical systems can be built because of the cloud and virtual computing environments. Also, using features of orchestration, these systems can be built in minutes, instead of days, like in the 20th century.

This chapter dives into how virtualization led to the creation of containers and cloud computing. Then, you will learn how to control and secure these containers with Docker and Kubernetes. Let's first explore virtualization.

Understanding Virtualization

Virtualization creates a *virtual* computing environment that, to the operating system, appears to be a physical environment. Virtual environments sit on top of a physical environment, called the *host* computer. The virtual environments are considered *guest* computers. The guests are managed by a hypervisor.

In this section you will learn about the components related to virtual machines, including the following:

- Hypervisors
- Thin vs. thick provisioning
- Virtualization file formats
- Managing virtual machines with `virsh`
- Virtual networking
- BLOB storage
- Virtual machine shortcomings

Let's first learn about the role of the hypervisor.

Hypervisors

Hypervisors were initially created by IBM to provide programmers a method of debugging an application without risking the integrity of the operating system.

Hypervisors, also called virtual machine managers (VMMs), create a boundary between the computer operating system and a logically isolated instance of a guest operating system contained in a virtual machine (VM).

Hypervisors come in several types: embedded, Type 1, and Type 2. Since a VM only accesses the hypervisor, it is unaware of the hypervisor's type.

Type 1

A Type 1 hypervisor, also called a bare-metal hypervisor, is installed as part of an operating system and has direct access to system hardware. This is illustrated in Figure 18-1.

Each "guest" appears as a dedicated machine but in reality shares system resources with the "host" and other guest machines.

Examples of Type 1 hypervisors include the Linux Kernel-based Virtual Machine (KVM), Microsoft Hyper-V, and Linux Foundation Xen.

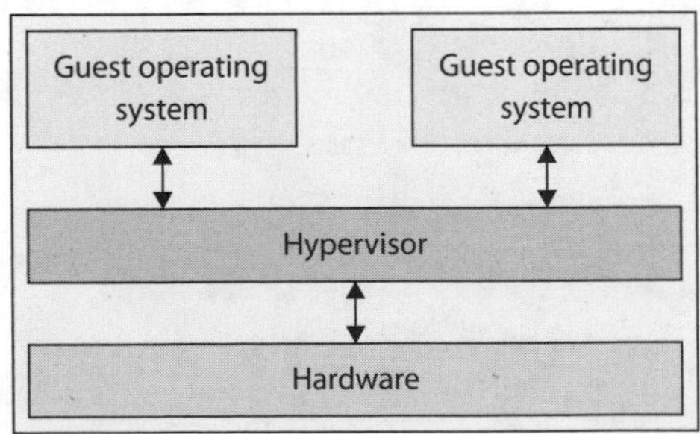

Figure 18-1 Type 1 (bare-metal) hypervisor configuration

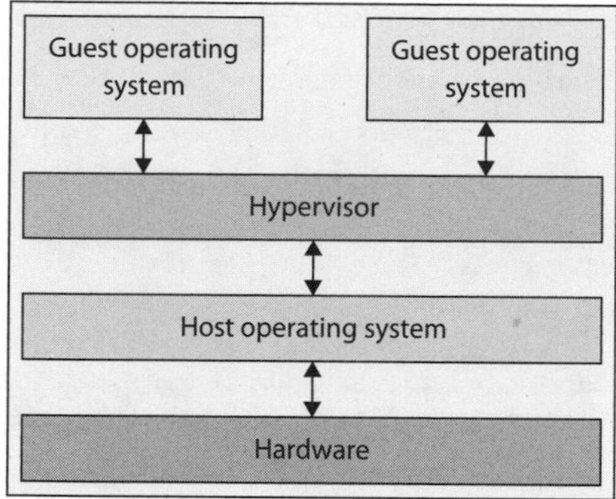

Figure 18-2 Type 2 (hosted) hypervisor configuration

Type 2

A Type 2 hypervisor, or hosted hypervisor, is an application installed on a host server, as illustrated in Figure 18-2. Guest machines use the installed hypervisor to access system resources via system calls.

Embedded Hypervisor

An embedded hypervisor is used in embedded systems. An embedded system is an independent or integrated device that contains a real-time operating system (RTOS), controller and application software designed to perform a task. (Some embedded systems will not have an RTOS.) An alarm or car automation system is an example of an embedded system.

An embedded hypervisor is programmed directly into a processor.

Thin vs. Thick Provisioning

Thick and thin provisioning define how storage space is allocated on a hard disk. When creating a virtual disk for a virtual machine, you have the choice of allocating the entire drive (thick provisioning) or dynamically allocating drive space as it is used (thin provisioning).

Thick provisioning is most efficient when the amount of storage allocated is close to the amount of space used.

Thin provisioning dynamically limits the size of a disk, but only allocates disk space as needed. Assume you have set a drive's size limit to 100MB and only used 20MB of storage. The drive size is only 20MB, but has the capability of growing to 100MB. Thin provisioning reduces the cost of storage space, but requires more monitoring.

Virtualization File Formats

Table 18-1 lists the formats to store virtual machine files.

Managing Virtual Machines with `virsh`

Red Hat designed `libvirt` as a management utility for multiple hypervisors (KVM, LXC, Microsoft Hyper-V, VirtualBox, VMware, and Xen). `libvirt` contains the command-line utility `virsh` and the `libvirtd` daemon, which are used to manage guest machines. Install the library and utilities by running `yum install libvirt`.

Format	Description
HDD	HDD is a virtual hard disk file used with the Parallels para-virtualization application.
OVA	Open Virtual Application (OVA) files are an archive (tar file) of an OVF file. VMware and Oracle Virtual Box support OVA files.
OVF	Open Virtualization Format (OVF) is a design standard created by the Distributed Management Task Force (DTMF) to provide a platform-independent method to archive and share VMs. An OVF file consists of a single directory that contains multiple configuration files. The directory includes a manifest file written in Extensible Markup Language (XML). The manifest file, or OVF descriptor file, contains network, storage, and other metadata used to configure a VM.
QCOW	QCOW, or QEMU copy-on-write, is a disk image file used by the QEMU open source hypervisor. QCOW has been succeeded by QCOW2.
VDI	VDI files are default Oracle VM VirtualBox storage files.
VMDK	VMDK was designed by VMware but is also used by VirtualBox and QEMU.
VHD	VHD is a virtual hard disk format designed and used by Microsoft. VHD was succeeded by VHDX.

Table 18-1 Virtual Machine File Formats

These management capabilities include the ability to stop, start, pause, save, and migrate virtual machines and manage system devices. `libvirt` also manages network interfaces, virtual networks, and storage devices.

Virtual Networking

When a virtual machine is initially created, it is usually operating in host-only mode, which means it is not connected to a network (but VMs can be created with networking as well). This section describes various configurations used with virtual machines to connect them to a network.

NAT

A typical network consists of multiple host machines with unique IP addresses. Rather than make these IP addresses public, you can create a private network with world access using network address translation (NAT) or IP masquerading. Both NAT and IP masquerading present one public address for a network. When a host on the private network wishes to communicate with the world, the source address in the packet is changed to the public IP address. The process is reversed when the packet returns.

NAT permits one connection to the public IP address at a time; IP masquerading permits multiple connections to the public IP address at a time.

Bridge

A bridge is used to connect multiple segments of a network. Network segments are used to split a network into subnetworks to improve security and performance.

A bridge differs from a router in that the bridge does not analyze, filter, or forward messages. Some routers also contain bridging functions.

Overlay Network

An overlay network is a computer network on top of another network using logical links.

Imagine a container pod in which the containers are hosts on the same virtual network, and a bridge attaches the virtual network to a physical network. The virtual network is an overlay network.

Dual-Homed Network

A dual-homed network contains multiple network interface cards (NICs) connected to the same network. Dual NICs are used to provide redundancy and therefore fault tolerance.

The simplest form of redundancy on a dual-homed network is two NICs (primary and secondary) configured as failover devices for each other. At any time, only one NIC is connected to the network. If one NIC fails, traffic is rerouted to the second NIC.

Bonding Interfaces

NIC redundancy is created by bonding two NICs. For example, assume two NICs, `enp0s1` and `enp0s2`, and the bonding module is available.

To set up the bonding interface, create a file in `/etc/sysconfig/network-scripts` named `ifcfg-<bond#>` where # is the number of the bond interface. For this example, we will use `bond0`:

```
DEVICE=bond0                   #Name of physical device
NAME=bond0                     #Interface Name
TYPE=Bond                      #Interface Type
BONDING_MASTER=yes             #Master Bond configuration file
IP_ADDRESS=                    #IP Address of interface
PREFIX=24                      #First 24 bits are network number
ONBOOT=yes                     #Activated on boot
BOOTPROTO=none                 #No boot protocol
BONDING_OPTIONS="mode 1"       #Space delimited list of bond options.
                              #Mode 1 is active e bonding
                                              #
NM_CONTROLLED=no               #Network Manager will not configure
```

Edit the configuration files `/etc/sysconfig/network-scripts/ifcfg-enp0s1` and `/etc/sysconfig/network-scripts/ifcfg-enp0s2` to attach them to `bond0` by adding or modifying the following entries:

```
BOOTPROTO=none
ONBOOT=yes
MASTER=bond0                   #Master
SLAVE=yes                      #Slave device to bond0
```

If you are using Network Manager, execute the command `nmcli con reload`. Restart the network by executing the command `systemctl restart network`. You can verify that the bond has been created by executing the command `cat /proc/net/bonding/bond#`.

Multi-homed networks have multiple NICs attached to different networks.

Virtual Switch

Network ports on virtual machines are associated with virtual network adapters, which are in turn associated with a virtual switch. The software-based virtual switch isolates and manages communications between VMs on the network.

BLOB Storage

A BLOB (binary large object) is a collection of binary data that is transmitted via HTTP. BLOBs are grouped into containers assigned to a user account.

There are several BLOB types: block, append, and page. Each BLOB type is used for a specific type of data storage, identified by a unique tag called an ETag.

Block BLOBs

Block BLOBs are designed for data streaming and storage. Each block has a unique ID and may store up to 100MB. A block BLOB can contain up to 50,000 blocks.

Block BLOBs may be updated by adding, replacing, or deleting data. In order for the changes to be made permanent, they must be committed. If the data has not been committed within a week, the data is removed.

Append BLOBs

Append BLOBs consist of a maximum of 50,000 4MB blocks and are used for logs. Existing blocks may not be deleted or modified. Data written to append BLOBs is always written to the end of the BLOB.

Page BLOBs

Page BLOBs consist of 512-byte pages and are used for random reads and writes. The maximum size of a page BLOB is 8TB.

Virtual Machine Shortcomings

Virtual machines can grow to become gigabytes and terabytes in size because each device provisioned is another computer image. Also, each VM can be slow to boot, and as more resources are used, each system can start performing poorly. To alleviate these and other issues, a new technology called *containers* was created, as discussed in the next section.

EXAM TIP A cloud VM instance is a single server located in the cloud. The `cloud-init` utility configures the cloud instance using the configuration file `/etc/cloud/cloud.cfg`.

Understanding Containers

Software developers create applications that support varied environments. A computer system or *node* could be a desktop, laptop, tablet, or smartwatch. Development is simplified when software developers do not need to consider the specific hardware or operating system on which the application will run. Containers make this possible by addressing the inconsistencies among various types of hardware and operating systems.

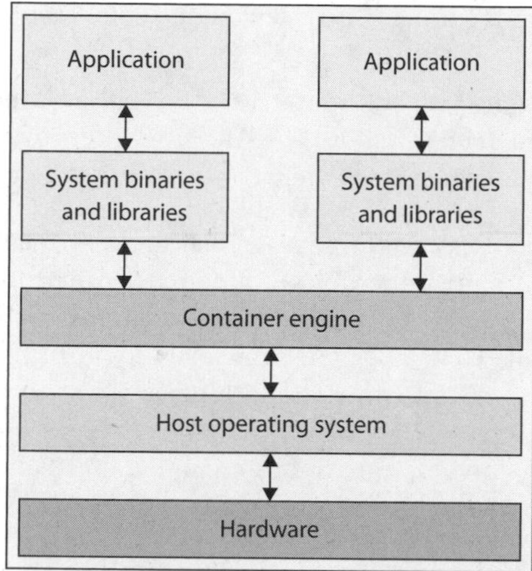

Figure 18-3 Container

A *container* is a runtime environment that consists of the files, libraries, dependencies, and configurations in a single instance (see Figure 18-3). Containers do not require a hypervisor; instead they share resources from the operating system and node. Examples of container platforms include LXC, LXD, LXCFS, LinuxKit, Docker, and Podman.

EXAM TIP The CompTIA Linux+ exam focuses on two container platforms, Docker and Podman.

Containers are isolated at the application level rather than at the operating system level. This means an error at the application level does not affect the host. Compared to VMs, containers are much smaller (only megabytes in size), much more efficient, much faster to start up and shut down, and can handle more applications.

At this point, you should understand the following overriding definitions for most container types before we proceed:

- Multiple processes, such as `sshd` or `httpd`, form a *container*; but ideally, they contain one process, for example, `sshd` only, for ease of updating and troubleshooting.
- Containers may need external helper services, which are called *ambassador containers.*
- Multiple containers form a *pod.* Containers within a pod share the network and other resources. Again, pods should ideally contain one container.

  For example, one container runs the `httpd` process, the other container the `sshd` process. Ideally, each container would launch from an independent pod, but they both could share a single pod.
- Pods may need helper containers, which are called *sidecars* because they ride alongside the pod's process.

- Multiple pods form a *deployment*. The deployment starts, monitors, and restarts pods that have died.
- Multiple nodes, for example, several servers and/or desktops networked together, form a *cluster*. The CPUs and RAM from the various nodes are pooled together, and deployments of pods are launched within the cluster.

A cluster controls multiple pods, which are managed by a container platform such as Docker or Podman; Kubernetes is a container platform that manages clusters utilizing Docker to duplicate clusters in multiple regions of the world and is covered later in this chapter. While CPU and RAM are shared within the cluster, file storage is cached, so when programs restart, the data no longer exists. To resolve this problem, persistent volumes must be created.

In this section you will learn about container components, including the following:

- Persistent volumes
- Container markup languages

Let's start with preserving data from the guest operating system into the host operating system with persistent volumes.

Persistent Volumes

In a container environment, a storage volume is a storage location (file) on the host system, which is removed when the container associated with the storage volume is removed. Persistent volume storage, which may be used by a container or pod, will remain after the container or pod is removed. This is like attaching an external hard drive to the cluster for the container to save data to.

Container Markup Languages

Configuration files for Docker and Kubernetes use either JSON (Docker) or YAML (Kubernetes) data files.

NOTE Kubernetes may use JSON, but best practices suggest the use of YAML.

JSON

JSON, or Java Script Object Notation, is a human-readable, text-based, data-serialization language designed to exchange data between a server and web applications. JSON files are stored as `<filename>.json`.

Data serialization converts data to a format that facilitates restoring data to its original structure. For example, JSON data may be converted into JavaScript objects.

An *object* is an independent structure that consists of a collection of related data. Although JSON is a subset of JavaScript, it may be used with other languages such as C, C++, Perl, Python, and Ruby. JSON does not support comments.

YAML

YAML, which stands for Yet Another Markup Language, is a human-readable data-serialization language that is a superset of JSON. An application that is a superset of another is an enhanced version of the "parent" application and contains all the features of the parent application.

YAML is found in programming languages such as Python and Ruby and is used to configure Docker and Kubernetes elements, which are stored as `<filename>.yaml` or `<filename>.yml`.

Managing Containers with Docker and Kubernetes

As previously mentioned, getting applications to run consistently over varied compute environments is resolved by using containers. Container images contain the libraries and dependencies an application needs to run in different environments.

To interact with containers, use the `podman` command or `docker` command. The subcommands and syntax are the same for both commands. Expect to see both commands on the CompTIA Linux+ exam. A few of their subcommands and descriptions are shown in Table 18-2.

Subcommand	Description
`attach`	Attach the pod to a running container
`build`	Build a container image from ContainerFile instructions
`commit`	Create new image based on a modified container
`images`	List container images that are loaded on the host computer
`inspect`	List object configuration details
`logs`	List container image logging details
`port`	Display port mappings
`pull`	Pull a container from an image registry
`push`	Push a container image to a specified location
`restart`	Restart one or more containers
`rm`	Remove one or more containers
`rmi`	Remove one or more container images from the host
`run`	Run a command in a new container
`save`	Save a container image to an archive
`start`	Start one or more containers
`stop`	Stop one or more containers
`top`	Display the running processes of a container image

Table 18-2 Subcommands for `podman` and `docker` Commands

The docker and podman command suite allows you to download images created by other users, simplifying your creation of containers.

In this section you will learn about container management, including the following:

- Getting started with Docker
- Deploying an existing container image
- Running a container image
- Configuring container persistent storage
- Removing containers
- Cluster management with Kubernetes

Let's start by pulling a custom container from a container repository.

Getting Started with Docker

Container image registries contain prebuilt containers for almost every purpose. These container registries are available at https://docs.docker.com/docker-hub, https://catalog.redhat.com/software/containers/explore, and many others.

To search the docker.io registry for available container images, use the search subcommand for podman or docker:

```
[root@localhost ~]# podman search docker.io
docker.io/library/debian
docker.io/library/mysql
docker.io/library/centos
docker.io/library/ubuntu
docker.io/library/alpine
. . .
```

To search for a specific container image, for example, mysql, run the following search with podman or docker:

```
[root@localhost ~]# docker search docker.io/mysql
NAME                                 DESCRIPTION
docker.io/library/mysql              MySQL is a widely used, open source...
docker.io/library/mariadb            MariaDB Server is a high performing...
docker.io/library/percona            Percona Server is a fork of the MyS...
docker.io/library/phpmyadmin         phpMyAdmin - A web interface for My...
. . .
```

Running podman search --no-trunc docker.io/mysql lists a more detailed description of the pod container image.

NOTE If you want to follow and continue along with this example, create an account at https://hub.docker.com.

Deploying an Existing Container Image

To pull an existing container image from one of the remote registries, authenticate and then pull the image as follows:

```
[root@localhost ~]# docker login docker.io
Username: bridgette
Password:
Login Succeeded!
[root@localhost ~]# podman pull docker.io/debian
Trying to pull docker.io/library/debian:latest...
Getting image source signatures
Copying blob 17c9e6141fdb done
Copying config d8cacd17cf done
Writing manifest to image destination
Storing signatures
d8cacd17cfdcf44e296b41c96f5dab7ae82024c28c4f45bd9181f3823bca639f
[root@localhost ~]#
```

To inspect the new image, run `podman inspect` or `docker inspect`. This lists metadata information about the container, including the architecture and operating system.

To view the newly installed container images, run the `podman images` or `docker images` command. Notice how operating systems such as Alpine, Debian, and Ubuntu are much smaller than a regular installation. That's the power of containers!

```
[root@localhost ~]# docker images
REPOSITORY                    TAG        IMAGE ID       CREATED        SIZE
docker.io/library/mysql       latest     2a04bf34fdf0   5 days ago     548 MB
docker.io/library/ubuntu      latest     a8780b506fa4   8 days ago     80.3 MB
docker.io/library/debian      latest     d8cacd17cfdc   2 weeks ago    129 MB
docker.io/library/alpine      latest     9c6f07244728   3 months ago   5.83 MB
[root@localhost ~]#
```

Finally, to create an alias for a new image, use the `tag` subcommand with `docker` or `podman` to help make tracking your images easier. To create the new alias, you match the alias name with the IMAGE ID of the container, as follows:

```
[root@localhost ~]# podman images debian
REPOSITORY                 TAG        IMAGE ID       CREATED       SIZE
docker.io/library/debian   latest     d8cacd17cfdc   2 weeks ago   129 MB
[root@localhost ~]# docker tag d8cacd17cfdc mydebian
[root@localhost ~]# podman images mydebian
REPOSITORY                 TAG        IMAGE ID       CREATED       SIZE
localhost/mydebian         latest     d8cacd17cfdc   2 weeks ago   129 MB
```

Running a Container Image

After you've found a container image that's going to allow you to administer Debian better or help you write that new application, it's time to connect to it using the `podman` or `docker run` subcommand, as shown here:

```
[root@localhost ~]# docker run -d d8cacd17cfdc
805a7c00e360369bdaeca6f1dedc7afe4a43ac21072753f896e39c641301c4e9
```

Using the `-d` option in this example runs the container in the background.

Running docker port or podman port exposes the ports used by the image. To access the *interactive terminal* of the container image, use the -i and -t options, as shown here:

```
[root@localhost ~]# podman run -it d8cacd17cfdc
root@bb0dabe4d118:/# cat /etc/os-release
PRETTY_NAME="Debian GNU/Linux 11 (bullseye)"
NAME="Debian GNU/Linux"
VERSION_ID="11"
VERSION="11 (bullseye)"
VERSION_CODENAME=bullseye
ID=Debian
HOME_URL="https://www.debian.org/"
SUPPORT_URL="https://www.debian.org/support"
BUG_REPORT_URL="https://bugs.debian.org/"
root@bb0dabe4d118:/# exit
[root@localhost ~]#
```

Once you run exit to exit from the container image, it stops. To start it again, use the docker start or podman start command with the -a and -i options to attach interactively, as shown here:

```
[root@localhost ~]# docker run -it --name=mydebimg d8cacd17cfdc
[root@localhost ~]# podman start -ai mydebimg
root@bb0dabe4d118:/#
```

In a separate terminal, you can view your running containers with the ps subcommand of docker and podman. The -a option lists all containers, including those that have exited, as shown here:

```
[root@localhost ~]# podman ps
CONTAINER ID  IMAGE           COMMAND   CREATED     STATUS          PORTS  NAMES
2110ddf094ad  library/debian  bash      1 day ago   Up 1 sec ago           jee
[root@localhost ~]# docker ps -a
CONTAINER ID  IMAGE           COMMAND   CREATED     STATUS          PORTS  NAMES
70dbf8914f5c  library/ubuntu  bash      2 days ago  Exited (0)             rev
639c92462e43  library/ubuntu  bash      2 days ago  Exited (0)             zen
b6ccf76f1cde  library/alpine  /bin/sh   2 days ago  Exited (0)             zen
. . .
```

Configuring Container Persistent Storage

To create persistent storage, you need to map a directory in the host to the container. To do this you use the --privileged option, as shown here:

```
[root@localhost ~]# podman run --privileged -it -v /media:/mnt \
docker.io/library/debian /bin/bash
root@b15c37b46588:/# cat > /mnt/persist.txt
okay, saving stuff
CTRL-D
root@b15c37b46588:/# exit
exit
[root@localhost ~]# cat /media/persist.txt
okay, saving stuff
[root@localhost ~]#
. . .
```

In the preceding example, /media is the host directory where the persistent storage will save to. The /mnt directory is the container's volume. Stepping through the example, you can see that data saved in the container file persist.txt using the cat command is preserved on the host.

Removing Containers

To remove a container, first stop it with the stop subcommand, and remove it with the rm subcommand. Finally, you need to remove the container image using the rmi subcommand, as follows:

```
[root@localhost ~]# docker stop d8cacd17cfdc
[root@localhost ~]# podman rm d8cacd17cfdc
d8cacd17cfdcf44e296b41c96f5dab7ae82024c28c4f45bd9181f3823bca639f
[root@localhost ~]# docker rm -a
81e494d06c2464743147e18329a757a18e91712e7f50e0abd26f3286161aa87c
b15c37b465888c8092c322e9e161ae3caa5bdd8951d457c3d7e9e8faed40d352
2110ddf094ad2d97aec0c03416a5b8bc963a183fd81df6a38a27d8984f98958d
bb0dabe4d11871f2c77f373b6518f4ee520035a045ec948073c8607c3f8e50fa
805a7c00e360369bdaeca6f1dedc7afe4a43ac21072753f896e39c641301c4e9
[root@localhost ~]# podman rmi d8cacd17cfdc
Untagged: docker.io/library/debian:latest
Deleted: d8cacd17cfdcf44e296b41c96f5dab7ae82024c28c4f45bd9181f3823bca639f
. . .
```

Cluster Management with Kubernetes

Kubernetes can manage a single node but works best with multi-container use cases, such as a shopping website offering thousands of various items. Also, Kubernetes can ease network communications of a cluster by enabling a *service mesh* that manages the traffic between services. The kubectl command allows you to run commands to manage the Kubernetes clusters.

Use kubectl to deploy applications, compose solutions to instances, and manage the cluster. Table 18-3 lists and describes some important kubectl subcommands for you to understand for day-to-day use—these are *not* part of the CompTIA Linux+ objectives.

To wrap up, let's take a look at automating the installation of a Red Hat node with Kickstart.

Table 18-3 Subcommands for the kubectl Command

Subcommand	Description
apply	Apply a configuration change to a resource
attach	Attach to a running container
convert	Convert configuration files to and from YAML and JSON
cp	Copy files to and from containers
create	Create a resource from a file
get	List cluster or container resources
logs	Display the logs for a container
run	Run an image within the cluster

Automating Installations with Kickstart

Automating your Red Hat installations is offered by a feature called Anaconda, which is a system installer for Red Hat class distributions. This section details one way you can implement automation in your environment. Anaconda and Kickstart are great knowledge to have as a Red Hat administrator, but these are *not* covered on the CompTIA Linux+ exam.

Anaconda is an installer written in Python for Red Hat and other Linux distributions. Anaconda identifies the architecture of a computer system and configures an operating system (devices, filesystems, software, etc.) based on the choices made on multiple install menus.

As part of the installation process, Anaconda stores configuration choices in the file `/root/anaconda-ks-cfg`. This file should be copied to the file `/root/ks.cfg`. The `ks.cfg` file may be used as-is to perform an automatic install, or it can be modified via text mode (`vi`) or the GUI Kickstart Configurator, `system-config-kickstart`.

NOTE Use the command `yum -y install system-config-kickstart` to install the Kickstart Configurator.

The Kickstart configuration file is made up of multiple sections that must be presented in a specific order. Most options within a section may be specified in any order.

The command `ksvalidator <config_file>` will validate the syntax of a Kickstart file, and the command `ksverdiff <config_file_1> <config_file_2>` will display the differences between two configuration files.

NOTE The command `yum -y install pykickstart` will install `ksvalidator` and `ksverdiff`.

Once the Kickstart file is created and validated, it may be made available via a drive connected to an install process, DVD, or network (including PXE). The instruction `inst.ks=<ks_file_location>` will specify the Kickstart location for the boot process. Network boots may require specifying the network address (`ip` option) or location of the repository (`inst.repo=`).

Chapter Review

This chapter described many of the configuration terms associated with virtual machines, hypervisors, storage, networks, containers, and clusters. Here are some key takeaways from this chapter that are important to the CompTIA Linux+ exam:

- Hypervisors were created by IBM as a debugging tool.
- Hypervisors are called virtual machine managers.
- Hypervisors isolate the host (resource provider) and guest machine.

- Type 1, or bare-metal, hypervisors have direct access to system hardware.
- Type 2 hypervisors are applications installed on the host.
- Thick provisioning allocates all the disk space when the disk is created.
- Thin provisioning dynamically allocates disk space.
- OVF is a file used to create virtual machines. It consists of a single directory that contains all the metadata needed to create a virtual machine.
- VDI is the default Oracle VirtualBox storage.
- VMDK was designed by VMware and is used by VirtualBox and QEMU.
- `virsh` uses `libvirtd`, the `libvirt` daemon, to access virtual machines from the command line.
- NAT, or network address translation, uses a single IP address to represent a private computer network.
- Bridging is a method of joining two networks as one to extend a network.
- Overlay is a method of having one network sit on top of another network.
- A dual-homed network uses multiple interfaces to attach to one network.
- Bonding is a method of creating a dual-homed network.
- `cloud-init` is a bootstrap utility for containers.
- Containers virtualize applications rather than machines.
- Persistent volumes are used for storing container data. Once the container is removed, data stored on persistent volumes will remain available.
- JSON and YAML are markup languages that may be used for data serialization.
- Use the `docker` or `podman` command to manage container images.
- Use the `kubectl` command to manage clusters.

Questions

1. Which command will list your container images?
   - **A.** `docker show`
   - **B.** `docker list`
   - **C.** `docker images`
   - **D.** `docker display`
2. Which method of storage provisioning allocates disk space dynamically?
   - **A.** Thin
   - **B.** Persistent
   - **C.** BLOB
   - **D.** Thick

3. Which virtualization file format is a single directory containing multiple configuration files?
   - **A.** HDD
   - **B.** OVA
   - **C.** OVF
   - **D.** VMDK
4. Which virtualization file format is a single directory containing an archive of an OVF file?
   - **A.** HDD
   - **B.** OVA
   - **C.** OVF
   - **D.** VMDK
5. Which command-line utility was developed by Red Hat as a management tool for the KVM hypervisor?
   - **A.** `libvirt`
   - **B.** `vboxmanage`
   - **C.** `virsh`
   - **D.** `vmware-cmd`
6. A container is an example of:
   - **A.** Type 1 virtualization
   - **B.** Type 2 virtualization
   - **C.** Embedded virtualization
   - **D.** None of the above
7. Persistent volumes are associated with which of the following?
   - **A.** Pods
   - **B.** Containers
   - **C.** Thick provisioning
   - **D.** Thin provisioning
8. Which of the following properties apply to an append BLOB? (Choose three.)
   - **A.** New data must be appended.
   - **B.** Existing data cannot be modified.
   - **C.** Existing data can be modified.
   - **D.** Existing data cannot be deleted.

9. Which BLOB type is used for random reads and writes?
   - **A.** Append
   - **B.** Page
   - **C.** Block
   - **D.** Bob Loblaw's Law Blog
10. Data serialization converts data to a format that facilitates restoring data to its original structure. Which tools provide data serialization? (Choose two.)
    - **A.** `vi`
    - **B.** YAML
    - **C.** JSON
    - **D.** `nano`
11. `cloud-init` is a bootstrap facility whose configuration file is:
    - **A.** `/etc/cloud.cfg`
    - **B.** `/etc/cloud/cloud.config`
    - **C.** `/etc/cloud.config`
    - **D.** `/etc/cloud/cloud.cfg`
12. Bonding is associated with which network type?
    - **A.** NAT
    - **B.** Bridge
    - **C.** Dual-homed
    - **D.** Overlay
13. An overlay network would be associated with:
    - **A.** Pods
    - **B.** Dual-homed network
    - **C.** NAT
    - **D.** Bridge

Answers

1. **C.** The `docker images` (or `podman images`) command will display the images that reside on the host computer.
2. **A.** Thin provisioning allocates disk space as necessary. Thick provisioning allocates all disk space. Persistent volumes are used with pods to ensure data remains once a pod closes. BLOB storage is block data storage accessed via HTTP or HTTPS.
3. **C.** OVF files contain a single directory that consists of configuration files used to configure a virtual machine.

4. **B.** The OVA file is an archive of the OVF file.
5. **C.** `virsh` is the command-line utility used to manage KVM. `virsh` is a part of `libvirt`. `libvert` is a set of tools used to manage virtual machines.
6. **A.** A container is an example of Type 1, or bare-metal, virtualization.
7. **A.** Persistent volumes are associated with pods. Pod is the name for a container or group of containers within Kubernetes.
8. **A, B, D.** An append BLOB is used for logging data. Existing data in append BLOBs may not be modified or deleted, and any new entries are appended to the end of the BLOB.
9. **B.** The page BLOB is used for random read and write operations.
10. **B, C.** YAML and JSON are markup languages that facilitate data serialization.
11. **D.** `/etc/cloud/cloud.cfg` is `cloud-init`'s configuration file.
12. **C.** A dual-homed network is used to provide network card redundancy on a single network. This is accomplished by bonding multiple NICs.
13. **A.** An overlay network is a network that sits on top of another network. In the Kubernetes environment, each container in a pod is assigned an IP address on a local network assigned to the pod. This network may sit on top of a physical network.

CHAPTER 19

Troubleshooting and Diagnostics

In this chapter, you will learn about

- A standardized troubleshooting model
- Troubleshooting computer problems
- Troubleshooting network problems

Humans must remain in the loop.

—Kerrie L. Holley, IBM

When it comes to system security, one of the biggest issues companies face is insider threats. In this chapter, we tell the story of FRMS Corp., a children's toy company. FRMS plans to merge with SGMF, Inc., which offers excellent packaging solutions for toys, and executives see the merger as a great fit.

As is often the case with such ventures, staff get nervous about what is going to happen to them, so they plan to protect their jobs at FRMS by any means necessary, thus making them *internal threats.*

A Standardized Troubleshooting Model

Mugabe has experience with mergers and acquisitions (M&A) and as a lead engineer for SGMF understands the issue of internal threats. His great patience, understanding of common vulnerabilities and exposures (CVEs), and real-world experience make him a great troubleshooter. Mugabe plans a seven-step approach to handling computer- and network-related issues similar to the approach mentioned in Chapter 14:

Step 1: Identify the problem. Mugabe determines what has happened by asking questions, detecting symptoms, and reviewing error messages.

Step 2: Determine recent change. Mugabe identifies the single change in the system, whether it's new software, new hardware, or a new configuration.

Step 3: Create a causal theory. Using information gathered from the previous steps, Mugabe develops a theory that could explain the problem.

Step 4: Select the fix. Mugabe usually works with a team of other SGMF engineers, including Jessica and Carlos, to arrive at a solution and discuss if the fix will cause other problems.

Step 5: Attempt and verify the fix. At this point, Jessica and Carlos work together to implement the fix, making sure the problem is solved and does not return. Before unveiling the fix to the customer, Mugabe verifies the repairs made by his team.

Step 6: Ensure customer satisfaction. Mugabe, Jessica, or Carlos verifies the client is happy. A final word is shared with their supervisor to let them know the problem is fixed.

Step 7: Complete the paperwork. Mugabe and his team document the solution within a ticketing database to quickly identify the issue if it occurs again.

EXAM TIP Knowledge of the seven-step troubleshooting steps is great for the CompTIA A+ exam but is not a requirement for the CompTIA Linux+ exam.

Troubleshooting Computer Problems

Mugabe starts by collecting an inventory of computer systems used by the FRMS staff. Fortunately, like SGMF, FRMS is a Linux-only environment, having learned years earlier that Linux is a high-quality, well-supported operating system with fewer vulnerabilities than closed-sourced operating systems.

Tomika, Davy, Gary, and other engineers at FRMS are working to disrupt the merger, providing Mugabe and his team with an inaccurate inventory. From past experience, Mugabe has learned to "trust, but verify." Therefore, Mugabe will verify and validate computer issues using the following approaches:

- Verify hardware configuration
- Verify CPU performance
- Verify memory performance
- Validate storage performance
- Validate other devices

NOTE The events, characters, and firms depicted in this scenario are fictitious. Any similarity to actual persons, living or dead, or to actual firms is purely coincidental.

Verify Hardware Configuration

Mugabe has a couple of tools in his toolbox to verify the configuration of a computer without opening the system. These tools are the `lshw` and `dmidecode` commands.

The `lshw` command will "list hardware" installed on a Linux system, reporting an exact memory configuration, firmware version, motherboard configuration, CPU details, CPU cache details, bus speeds, and more. The report provided by Gary, unhappy about the coming merger, shows that each computer is configured with 2GB of RAM and no CD-ROM drive.

Mugabe runs the `lshw` command using the `-short` option, as shown here:

```
[root@cent71-5t buddy]# lshw -short
H/W path            Device      Class        Description
=====================================================
                                system       VirtualBox
/0                              bus          VirtualBox
/0/0                            memory       128KiB BIOS
/0/1                            memory       1GiB System memory
/0/2                            processor    Intel(R) Core(TM) i7-6500U CPU @ 2G
/0/100                          bridge       440FX - 82441FX PMC [Natoma]
/0/100/1                        bridge       82371SB PIIX3 ISA [Natoma/Triton I]
/0/100/1.1           scsi1      storage      82371AB/EB/MB PIIX4 IDE
/0/100/1.1/0.0.0    /dev/cdrom  disk         CD-ROM
/0/100/2                        display      VirtualBox Graphics Adapter
/0/100/3            enp0s3      network      82540EM Gigabit Ethernet Controller
/0/100/4                        generic      VirtualBox Guest Service
/0/100/5                        multimedia   82801AA AC'97 Audio Controller
/0/100/6                        bus          KeyLargo/Intrepid USB
/0/100/6/1          usb2        bus          OHCI PCI host controller
<...etc... >
```

The report shows that each system actually has 1GB of RAM and a CD-ROM installed. Later, Mugabe will complete a physical inspection to validate his findings.

The other command at Mugabe's disposal is `dmidecode`, which lists the computer's BIOS while in multi-user mode. The output shown next uses the `--quiet` option and shows that the mainboard supports ISA, PCI, and CD-ROM booting:

```
[root@cent71-5t buddy]# dmidecode --quiet
BIOS Information
        Vendor: innotek GmbH
        Version: VirtualBox
        Release Date: 12/01/2006
        Address: 0xE0000
        Runtime Size: 128 kB
        ROM Size: 128 kB
        Characteristics:
                ISA is supported
                PCI is supported
                Boot from CD is supported
                Selectable boot is supported
                8042 keyboard services are supported (int 9h)
                CGA/mono video services are supported (int 10h)
                ACPI is supported

System Information
        Manufacturer: innotek GmbH
        Product Name: VirtualBox
<...etc...>
```

To support his case for the merger, Mugabe gathered information, identified changes, and finally documented his findings into the ticketing system.

Verify CPU Performance

Davy at FRMS is the kind of guy who never forgets anything, especially if it affects his job, so without any paperwork he assures Mugabe that the CPU load averages are greater than 50 percent! The load average defines how busy a CPU is; the more jobs that are ready to use the CPU (in other words, *runnable* jobs), the higher the load average.

To observe the CPU model, number of cores, and options, Mugabe can run `lscpu` or review the contents of the `/proc/cpuinfo` file to determine if it is underpowered, as follows:

```
[root@cent71-5t buddy]# more /proc/cpuinfo
processor    : 0
vendor_id    : GenuineIntel
cpu family   : 6
model        : 78
model name   : Intel(R) Core(TM) i7-6500U CPU @ 2.50GHz
stepping     : 3
cpu MHz      : 2592.002
cache size   : 4096 KB
physical id  : 0
siblings     : 2
core id      : 0
cpu cores    : 2
apicid       : 0
initial apicid    : 0
fpu.         : yes
fpu_exception     : yes
cpuid level  : 22
wp           : yes
flags        : fpu vme de pse tsc msr pae mce cx8 apic sep mtrr pge mca cmov
pat pse36 clflush mmx fxsr sse sse2 ht syscall nx rdtscp lm constant_tsc
rep_good nopl xtopology nonstop_tsc eagerfpu pni pclmulqdq ssse3 cx16 pcid
sse4_1 sse4_2 x2apic movbe popcnt aes xsave avx rdrand hypervisor lahf_lm
abm 3dnowprefetch fsgsbase avx2 invpcid rdseed clflush
opt flush_l1d
```

The CPU certainly looks capable enough for their applications, so to examine CPU load averages, Mugabe employs the `uptime`, `w`, and `sar` commands:

```
[root@cent71-5t buddy]# uptime
15:35:02 up  2:17,  2 users,  load average: 0.01, 0.04, 0.05
[root@cent71-5t buddy]# w
15:35:04 up  2:17,  2 users,  load average: 0.01, 0.04, 0.05
USER     TTY      FROM             LOGIN@   IDLE   JCPU   PCPU WHAT
buddy  :0        :0               13:21   ?xdm?   6:32   0.42s /usr/libexec/gn
buddy  pts/0     :0               13:21    0.00s 29.28s  9.29s /usr/libexec/gn
[root@cent71-5t buddy]# sar 2 5
Linux 3.10.0-957.10.1.el7.x86_64 (cent71-5t)      04/26/2019  _x86_64_   (2 CPU)
03:35:11 PM     CPU     %user     %nice   %system   %iowait    %steal     %idle
03:35:13 PM     all      3.79      0.00      0.25      0.00      0.00     95.96
03:35:15 PM     all      4.31      0.00      0.51      0.00      0.00     95.18
03:35:17 PM     all      3.03      0.00      0.25      0.00      0.00     96.72
03:35:19 PM     all      3.79      0.00      0.51      0.00      0.00     95.71
03:35:21 PM     all      4.30      0.00      0.51      0.00      0.00     95.19
Average:        all      3.84      0.00      0.40      0.00      0.00     95.75
```

The uptime command shows how long a system has been running, and it outputs system load averages. In this example, the load average displays 1 percent over the past minute, 4 percent over the past 5 minutes, and 5 percent over the past 15 minutes—nowhere near the 50 percent load averages stated by Davy.

The w command shows who is logged in and what commands they are running. Mugabe uses this output to determine which programs are loading the system and from which accounts.

Finally, sar is the "system activity reporter." This is an all-purpose tool that lists performance information for CPU, RAM, I/O, disk, communication ports, graphics, and so on. Running sar 2 5 will collect system activity data and display five lines of output, one for every two seconds. By default, the sar command lists CPU performance details, including user time, system time, iowait, steal, and idle states.

To support the case for the merger, Mugabe notes that system loads are less than 10 percent, nowhere near the 50 percent stated by the FRMS representatives.

NOTE The time command is a useful tool. Simply run time <program_name> to determine how much CPU time is used by an individual program.

Verify Memory Performance

Jessica indicates from FRMS reports that all their systems require memory upgrades. To review memory and swap performance, Jessica runs lsmem and examines the /proc/meminfo file to observe how much memory is being used and how much is available, and then she runs vmstat 2 5 to review memory performance, as shown here:

```
[root@cent71-5t buddy]#  more /proc/meminfo
MemTotal:          1014816 kB
MemFree:             98152 kB
MemAvailable:       154816 kB
Buffers:                52 kB
Cached:             207880 kB
SwapCached:          39000 kB
Active:             351388 kB
Inactive:           375428 kB
Active(anon):       269716 kB
Inactive(anon):     293084 kB
Active(file):        81672 kB
Inactive(file):      82344 kB
Unevictable:             0 kB
Mlocked:                 0 kB
SwapTotal:         1048572 kB
SwapFree:           740732 kB
Dirty:                  28 kB
Writeback:               0 kB
AnonPages:          499196 kB
Mapped:             113292 kB
Shmem:               43916 kB
Slab:                91300 kB
SReclaimable:        40868 kB
```

```
[root@cent71-5t buddy]# vmstat 2 5
procs ----------memory---------- --swap-- ----io---- -system-- ------cpu-----
r  b   swpd   free  buff  cache si   so   bi    bo   in   cs us sy id wa st
2  0 307840 100952    52 299136  6   14  329    58  123  140  2  1 97  0  0
0  0 307840 101112    52 299168  0    0    0     0  457  641  6  1 93  0  0
0  0 307840 101000    52 299168  0    0    0     0  263  316  4  0 95  0  0
0  0 307840 100988    52 299168  0    0    0     0  288  334  4  1 95  0  0
0  0 307840 101004    52 299168  0    0    0     0  195  275  3  0 96  0  0
```

The first record shows free memory and file cache averages since the system booted. Additional records list activity for the two-second sampling period Jessica defined. She notices from the output that there is no memory exhaustion for their applications.

As with the `sar` command, `vmstat 2 5` reports virtual memory statistics five times, every two seconds. The `vmstat` command displays the amount of memory utilized in swap space, how much is idle, the amount used as buffers, and the volume saved as cache. The command also shows how much data is swapped to and from disk.

Out of Memory Killer

The OOM Killer, or *Out Of Memory Killer,* is a process killer that engages from the Linux kernel when the system is critically low on memory due to too many applications running or memory leaks. If enough processes begin to use memory, there will not be enough to support them all. So, the kernel invokes the OOM Killer to review the processes and kills one or more of them to free up memory and keep the system running.

The OOM Killer reviews all processes and assigns a severity score based on memory utilization and the number of child processes. The process with the highest score is killed. For security, the root, kernel, and important system processes are given much lower scores. If killing a process does not free enough memory, the server will soon crash.

To find whether the OOM Killer was the reason why processes were killed, you would run the following command:

```
[root@cent71-5t buddy]# dmesg | grep -i "killed process"
host kernel: Out of Memory: Killed process 4121 (mysql).
```

In this case, `mysql` was killed, with a process identification number or PID of `4121`.

The OOM Killer only gets invoked when the system is critically low on memory. Consequently, to avoid it, you can either reduce memory requirements, increase the memory, or increase swap space.

Increasing Swap Space

Mugabe's years of experience in technology and management help him understand that there are quick ways to stop the OOM Killer, and he decides to mitigate the threat by increasing swap space. Swap space can be added by using an additional new swap hard drive, by using an additional swap partition, or by adding a swap file using the `swapon` command, as shown in Figure 19-1.

Figure 19-1 Additional swap space devices

/

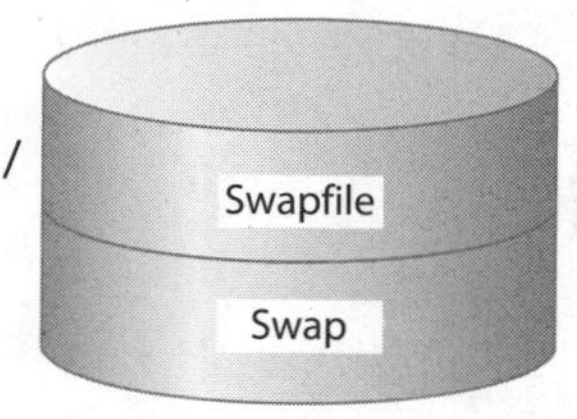

To view the current swap space status, look at the contents of the `/proc/swaps` file, run the `swapon` command with the `-s` option, or even try the `free` command to view memory and swap utilization, as shown here:

```
[root@cent71-5t buddy]#  more /proc/swaps
Filename                Type          Size          Used          Priority
dev/sda8                partition     1048572       298880        -2
[root@cent71-5t buddy]# swapon -s
Filename                Type          Size          Used          Priority
/dev/sda8               partition     1048572       298880        -2
[root@cent71-5t buddy]# free
           total       used        free      shared  buff/cache   available
Mem:     1014816     665656       73860       44400      275300      109660
Swap:    1048572     298880      749692
```

After the new swap device is created, it can be enabled using `swapon`. Tomika of FRMS intends to impede the merger by suggesting SGMF wait a month for new hard drives so they can be used as additional swap space. SGMF's Mugabe decides that the simplest way to proceed is to add a swap file.

Adding a new swap disk would require purchasing and installing a new hard drive. Addition of a swap partition is even tougher, as data must be backed up from an existing drive and repartitioned to increase the swap partition, and then the data must be restored. Adding a swap file simply requires creating an empty file using the `dd` command, assuming there is space available in the filesystem, as shown next:

```
[root@cent71-5t buddy]# dd if=/dev/zero of=~/swapfile bs=1M count=1024
1024+0 records in
1024+0 records out
1073741824 bytes (1.1 GB) copied, 1.52779 s, 703 MB/s
[root@cent71-5t buddy]#
```

After adding the swap file, you can enable it using the `swapon` command, as shown here:

```
[root@cent71-5t buddy]# swapon /home/buddy/swapfile
swapon: /home/buddy/swapfile: insecure permissions 0644, 0600 suggested.
```

Mugabe is warned that the permissions are insecure. This is fixed with `chmod` and `chown`, as shown here:

```
[root@cent71-5t buddy]# chown root:root /home/buddy/swapfile
[root@cent71-5t buddy]# chmod 600 /home/buddy/swapfile
```

Next, he ascertains that the swap file is added using the -s option to swapon. The Priority is set to -3, meaning it will be used after any Priority setting of -2 or -1 is filled. Once he has completed using the swap file, it can be disabled with swapoff and removed with rm, as shown here:

```
[root@cent71-5t buddy]# swapon -s
Filename                    Type          Size        Used        Priority
/dev/sda8                   partition     1048572     463708      -2
/home/buddy/swapfile        file          1048572     0           -3
[root@cent71-5t buddy]# swapoff /home/buddy/swapfile
[root@cent71-5t buddy]# rm /home/buddy/swapfile
```

Work with Mugabe to add a swap file in Exercise 19-1.

Exercise 19-1: Working with Swap Space

In this exercise, you practice using swap space commands to manage and troubleshoot memory utilization. Use the virtual machine that comes with the book.

VIDEO Please watch the Exercise 19-1 video for a demonstration on how to perform this task.

Complete the following steps:

1. Boot your Linux system and log in as the **student1** user.
2. Open a terminal session.
3. Switch to the root user account by entering **su -** followed by **student1** for the password.
4. Run **swapon -s** to review how much space there is currently.
5. Create a swap file using the dd command by running the following:
```
dd if=/dev/zero of=swapfile bs=1M count=250
mkswap swapfile
chown root:root swapfile
chmod 600 swapfile
```
6. Run **swapon swapfile** to enable your new swap space.
7. Run **swapon -s** to verify the space was added.
8. Run **swapoff swapfile** to disable the swap space.
9. Run **rm swapfile** to return the computer to its previous state.

Validate Storage Performance

Gary of FRMS informs Mugabe that disk drive performance is subpar and that they need to budget for better and faster hard drives. Mugabe puts on his thinking cap and realizes that tuning some simple kernel parameters can help improve performance *and* save time and money, expediting the merger.

Table 19-1 Disk Drive `scheduler` Settings

`scheduler` Setting	Description
none	Handles requests in order of submission.
mq-deadline	Each I/O request is on a timer and completes before it expires.
bfq	Higher-priority processes are served first.
kyber	A self-tuning scheduler designed to achieve low latency.

He looks at the result of the `scheduler` kernel variable found in the directory `/sys/block/<disk device>/queue/`, which can be set to `none`, `mq-deadline`, `kyber`, or `bfq`:

```
[root@cent71-5t buddy]# cat /sys/block/sda/queue/scheduler
[none] mq-deadline bfq kyber
```

Mugabe knows that hard drive I/O performance is application dependent and can improve depending on the setting, as shown in Table 19-1.

Bandwidth Fair Queuing, or `bfq`, is in general best for single-user systems such as desktops. The `none` `scheduler` is great for SAN or RAID systems because they provide their own scheduling. The `kyber` `scheduler` tunes itself to attain the lowest latencies. Finally, the `mq-deadline` `scheduler` is good for multi-user environments.

NOTE Knowledge of the `scheduler` features is *not* a CompTIA Linux+ exam requirement.

Mugabe analyzes I/O performance first using `iostat`, as shown next. For his analysis, he runs the corporate applications and uses the `-z` option to just observe drives that are in use. Also, measurements will take place over four seconds, and he only requires two outputs.

```
[root@cent71-5t buddy]# iostat -z 4 2 | tail -6
avg-cpu:  %user   %nice %system %iowait  %steal   %idle
          60.21    0.00   27.09    0.79    0.00   11.91

Device:            tps    kB_read/s    kB_wrtn/s    kB_read    kB_wrtn
sda             947.00     21978.00       776.50      87912       3106
```

The `iostat` output shows read and write activity per second and total I/O over the entire eight-second period on drive `/dev/sda`.

To test again and see performance results for `mq-deadline`, he changes the `scheduler` setting by updating the kernel value, as shown here:

```
[root@cent71-5t buddy]# echo mq-deadline > /sys/block/sda/queue/scheduler
[root@cent71-5t buddy]# cat /sys/block/sda/queue/scheduler
none [mq-deadline] bfq kyber
[root@cent71-5t buddy]# iostat -z 4 2 | tail -6
avg-cpu:  %user   %nice %system %iowait  %steal   %idle
          52.20    0.00   30.23    2.45    0.00   15.12
```

```
Device:            tps    kB_read/s    kB_wrtn/s    kB_read    kB_wrtn
sda             674.00      6889.00       281.12      27556       1124
```

Finally, he changes `scheduler` to `bfq` and then measures performance:

```
[root@cent71-5t buddy]# echo bfq > /sys/block/sda/queue/scheduler
[root@cent71-5t buddy]# cat /sys/block/sda/queue/scheduler
none mq-deadline [bfq] kyber
[root@cent71-5t buddy]# iostat -z 4 2 | tail -6
avg-cpu:  %user   %nice %system %iowait  %steal   %idle
          49.10    0.00   25.77    0.00    0.00   25.13

Device:            tps    kB_read/s    kB_wrtn/s    kB_read    kB_wrtn
sda               1.75         0.00        20.00          0         80
```

Another tool in Mugabe's tool case is the `ioping` command, which measures disk I/O latency in real time. Here are some examples. First he measures the disk I/O latency.

```
[root@cent71-5t buddy]# ioping /dev/sda
4 KiB <<< /dev/sda (block device 18 GiB): request=1 time=2.32 ms (warmup)
4 KiB <<< /dev/sda (block device 18 GiB): request=2 time=294.8 us
4 KiB <<< /dev/sda (block device 18 GiB): request=3 time=277.8 us
4 KiB <<< /dev/sda (block device 18 GiB): request=4 time=6.37 ms
4 KiB <<< /dev/sda (block device 18 GiB): request=5 time=280.8 us
^C
```

He uses the `-c` option to limit output so as not to use `^C` to complete the session:

```
[root@cent71-5t buddy]# ioping -c 5 /dev/sda
4 KiB <<< /dev/sda (block device 18 GiB): request=1 time=10.3 ms (warmup)
4 KiB <<< /dev/sda (block device 18 GiB): request=2 time=325.8 us
4 KiB <<< /dev/sda (block device 18 GiB): request=3 time=248.3 us
4 KiB <<< /dev/sda (block device 18 GiB): request=4 time=47.2 ms
4 KiB <<< /dev/sda (block device 18 GiB): request=5 time=288.3 us
```

Finally, he uses `ioping` to measure disk latency for the current (or other) directory, as shown here:

```
[root@cent71-5t buddy]# ioping -c 5 .
4 KiB <<< . (xfs /dev/sda5): request=1 time=2.08 ms (warmup)
4 KiB <<< . (xfs /dev/sda5): request=2 time=1.43 ms
4 KiB <<< . (xfs /dev/sda5): request=3 time=657.0 us
4 KiB <<< . (xfs /dev/sda5): request=4 time=216.3 us
4 KiB <<< . (xfs /dev/sda5): request=5 time=5.51 ms
```

In the end, Mugabe finds that simply tuning the disk drive's scheduling parameter saves the firm millions of dollars in hard drive upgrades and labor expenses, making the merger more amenable. To make the changes permanent, he uses features of `tuned` to enable the new scheduling value at boot time, as shown next.

NOTE Knowledge of the `tuned` features is *not* a CompTIA Linux+ exam requirement.

```
[root@cent71-5t buddy]# tuned-adm list
Available profiles:
- balanced                    - General non-specialized tuned profile
- desktop                     - Optimize for the desktop use-case
- latency-performance         - Optimize for performance but more power use
- network-latency             - Low latency network performance but power use
- network-throughput          - Optimize for streaming network throughput
- powersave                   - Optimize for low power consumption
- throughput-performance      - Broad tuning and performance over for workloads
- virtual-guest               - Optimize for running inside a virtual guest
- virtual-host                - Optimize for running KVM guests
Current active profile:
```

Since the "active profile" shows as `virtual-guest`, Mugabe modifies the `tuned.conf` file located in `/usr/lib/tuned/virtual-guest/`. (Other `tuned` profiles are defined in the `/usr/lib/tuned/` directory.) To make `bfq` the I/O scheduler at boot time, he uses

```
[root@cent71-5t buddy]# cat >> /usr/lib/tuned/virtual-guest/tuned.conf

[bootloader]
cmdline="elevator=bfq"

^D
```

where `elevator` is used to specify the desired I/O `scheduler`.

Validate Other Devices

Mugabe has several troubleshooting tools and tricks in his toolbox as well as several ways to run them. Most of the time he will run the commands within a pseudo-terminal, much like what is seen when logging in from a display manager (see Figure 19-2).

To see the pseudo-terminal value, he runs the `tty` command, as shown in Figure 19-2. In this case, Mugabe sends `HELLO THERE` from one pseudo-terminal to the other using the command `echo HELLO THERE > /dev/pts/0` from the `/dev/pts/1` pseudo-terminal. This allows him to send error messages to different locations during troubleshooting.

There are also six alternative virtual consoles. These can be accessed with the key triad of `Ctrl-Alt-F{2,3,4,5,6,7}`, where `Ctrl-Alt-F1` will return the user to the graphical desktop on Red Hat–class systems. On Debian-class systems, the key triad is `Ctrl-Alt-F{1,2,3,4,5,6}` and `Ctrl-Alt-F7` returns the user to a graphical desktop. Figure 19-3 shows the result of using `Ctrl-Alt-F6` and the result of the `tty` command, which shows Mugabe is using terminal `/dev/tty6`.

Virtual consoles are useful on systems when the display manager hangs due to a runaway process.

NOTE Many systems do not allow logging in as `root` by default. This setting is defined in `/etc/securetty`, which includes terminals where `root` is allowed to log in. Comment terminal lines using # to disallow logging in from that terminal.

Figure 19-2 Working with pseudo-terminals

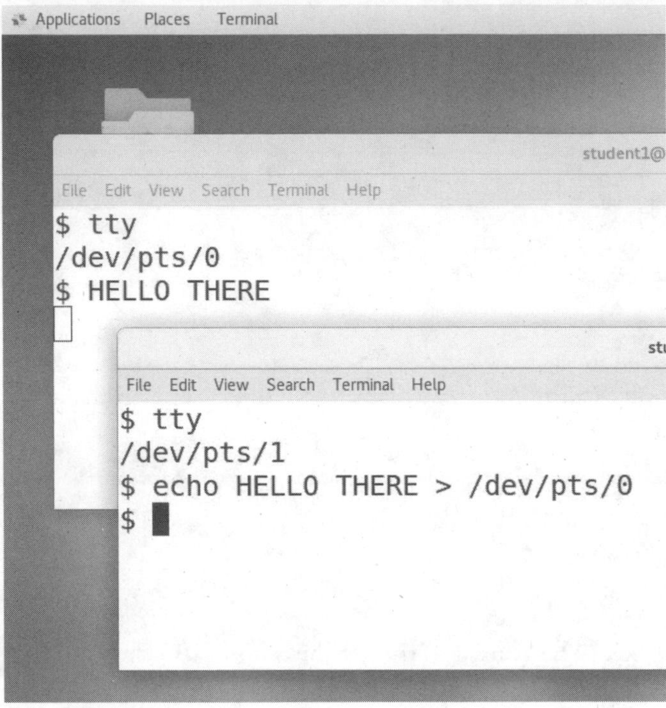

Figure 19-3 Using the virtual console

```
CentOS Linux 7 (Core)
Kernel 3.10.0-957.10.1.el7.x86_64 on an x86_64

cent71-5t login: student1
Password:
Last login: Mon May  6 13:44:53 on tty6
[student1@cent71-5t ~]$ tty
/dev/tty6
[student1@cent71-5t ~]$
```

Troubleshooting File-Related Issues

Robert, another FRMS internal threat, informs Mugabe that they are out of disk space because of an error message that says "cannot create new files" or something similar. When Mugabe runs `df`, he can clearly see that there is plenty of disk space left. Using `df -i` on an `ext4`-type filesystem shows him the real problem, which is the system is out of inodes:

```
[root@cent71-5t buddy]# df /boot
Filesystem      1K-blocks   Used         Available Use% Mounted on
/dev/sda1          487634        221068    236870        49%  /boot
[root@cent71-5t buddy]# df -i /boot
Filesystem      Inodes  IUsed  IFree IUse% Mounted on
/dev/sda1       524288  524288 0     100%  /
[root@cent71-5t buddy]# dumpe2fs /dev/sda1 | grep -i 'inode count'
dumpe2fs 1.42.9 (28-Dec-2013)
Inode count:                524288
```

To increase the inode count, the filesystem will need to be re-created by backing up all the data and then using `mkfs.ext4 -N 1000000 /dev/sda1` to double the inode count. Once the data is restored, users will be able to create new files. Meanwhile, Mugabe will work with management and determine if they can switch from an `ext4` to XFS filesystem, which automatically builds new inodes when required.

NOTE Administrators must externally label or banner backup tapes to know they are restoring the correct versions of files.

Troubleshooting Directory-Related Issues

An FRMS insider threat named Coughin made it so that anyone could remove anyone else's files from the shared `sales` directory folder. He was able to run `chmod -t sales`, which removes the sticky bit, and cause the trouble.

Mugabe must fix this and reenable the sticky bit. He simply uses the `chmod +t sales` command on this directory. Now, only file owners can remove their files; that is, if you don't own the file, you cannot remove the file.

Changing Keyboard Maps

A few frustrated staffers (also known as *internal threats*) concerned about the merger have decided to alter the keyboard maps to work well, but not great. Mugabe uses `localectl` to fix this issue. He notices the keymap is set to `us-mac` instead of `us`. He fixes this as follows:

```
[root@cent71-5t buddy]# localectl
  System Locale: LANG=en_US.UTF-8
      VC Keymap: us-mac
     X11 Layout: us-mac
[root@cent71-5t buddy]# localectl set-keymap us
[root@cent71-5t buddy]# localectl
  System Locale: LANG=en_US.UTF-8
      VC Keymap: us       X11 Layout: us
```

Troubleshooting Printers

Staff members at FRMS have never set up printers on Linux because they always failed to work. Mugabe does some research and finds that the printing service, CUPS, is not enabled. He fixes the issue and verifies that CUPS port 631 is listening by using `netstat` and `lsof`, as shown here:

```
[root@cent71-5t buddy]# systemctl status cups
• cups.service - CUPS Printing Service
  Loaded: loaded (/usr/lib/systemd/system/cups.service; disabled)
  Active: inactive (dead)
[root@cent71-5t buddy]# lsof -i tcp:631
[root@cent71-5t buddy]# netstat -a | grep ipp
[root@cent71-5t buddy]# systemctl start cups
[root@cent71-5t buddy]# lsof -i tcp:631
COMMAND  PID USER   FD   TYPE DEVICE SIZE/OFF NODE NAME
cupsd   8030 root   10u  IPv6  65928      0t0  TCP localhost:ipp (LISTEN)
```

```
cupsd    8030 root    11u  IPv4  65929      0t0  TCP localhost:ipp (LISTEN)
[root@cent71-5t buddy]# netstat -a | grep ipp
tcp        0      0 localhost:ipp           0.0.0.0:*               LISTEN
tcp6       0      0 localhost:ipp           [::]:*                  LISTEN
```

Finally, Mugabe ensures printing capability for future reboots by running `systemctl enable cups`, as shown next:

```
[root@cent71-5t buddy]# systemctl enable cups
Created symlink from /etc/systemd/system/multi-user.target.wants/cups.service to
/usr/lib/systemd/system/cups.service.
Created symlink from /etc/systemd/system/printer.target.wants/cups.service to
/usr/lib/systemd/system/cups.service.
Created symlink from /etc/systemd/system/sockets.target.wants/cups.socket to
/usr/lib/systemd/system/cups.socket.
Created symlink from /etc/systemd/system/multi-user.target.wants/cups.path to
/usr/lib/systemd/system/cups.path.
```

Verifying Graphics Cards

Several systems have NVIDIA graphics cards that are not functioning. Mugabe uses `lspci` and `lshw` to study the issue, as follows:

```
[root@cent71-5t buddy]# lspci -v | grep -i vga
00:02.0 VGA compatible controller: InnoTek Systemberatung GmbH VirtualBox
Graphics Adapter (prog-if 00 [VGA controller])
[root@cent71-5t buddy]# lshw -class display
 *-display
      description: VGA compatible controller
      product: VirtualBox Graphics Adapter
      vendor: InnoTek Systemberatung GmbH
      physical id: 2
      bus info: pci@0000:00:02.0
      version: 00
      width: 32 bits
      clock: 33MHz
      capabilities: vga_controller rom
      configuration: driver=vboxvideo latency=0
      resources: irq:18 memory:e0000000-e7ffffff
```

Since NVIDIA does not show in any of the output, it is clear to Mugabe what the issue is: the drivers have not been installed for the NVIDIA graphics cards. After he downloads the GPU drivers from NVIDIA and installs them, the cards function.

Troubleshooting Network Problems

Getting the network interface installed is only half the battle. To enable communications, network administrators use a variety of testing and monitoring tools to make sure the network is working properly.

As Mugabe continues with his system and network analysis, he will verify and validate network issues using the following approaches:

- Verify network performance
- Validate user connections
- Validate the firewall

Verify Network Performance

Again, Mugabe has several software tools in his tool case to configure, monitor, and troubleshoot networks. To view network status, he uses the ip command. For example, by running the command ip addr show, he can see the current network devices and their status, as shown here:

```
[root@cent71-5t buddy]# ip addr show
1: lo: <LOOPBACK,UP,LOWER_UP> mtu 65536 qdisc noqueue state UNKNOWN group default
qlen 1000
   link/loopback 00:00:00:00:00:00 brd 00:00:00:00:00:00
   inet 127.0.0.1/8 scope host lo
      valid_lft forever preferred_lft forever
   inet6 ::1/128 scope host
      valid_lft forever preferred_lft forever
2: enp0s3: <BROADCAST,MULTICAST,UP,LOWER_UP> mtu 1500 qdisc pfifo_fast state UP
group default qlen 1000
   link/ether 08:00:27:2a:00:2b brd ff:ff:ff:ff:ff:ff
   inet 10.0.2.15/24 brd 10.0.2.255 scope global noprefixroute dynamic enp0s3
      valid_lft 62516sec preferred_lft 62516sec
   inet6 fe80::ab6d:48ca:f676:aacf/64 scope link noprefixroute
      valid_lft forever preferred_lft forever
3: enp0s8: <NO-CARRIER,BROADCAST,MULTICAST,UP> mtu 1500 qdisc pfifo_fast state
DOWN group default qlen 1000
   link/ether 08:00:27:be:b6:ee brd ff:ff:ff:ff:ff:ff
4: enp0s9: <BROADCAST,MULTICAST,UP,LOWER_UP> mtu 1500 qdisc pfifo_fast state UP
group default qlen 1000
   link/ether 08:00:27:79:dc:91 brd ff:ff:ff:ff:ff:ff
   inet 192.168.1.82/24 brd 192.168.1.255 scope global noprefixroute dynamic
enp0s9
      valid_lft 585297sec preferred_lft 585297sec
   inet6 2605:a000:1401:21e::973/128 scope global noprefixroute dynamic
      valid_lft 585306sec preferred_lft 585306sec
   inet6 2605:a000:1401:21e:a95c:b673:538e:b1da/64 scope global noprefixroute
dynamic
      valid_lft 604778sec preferred_lft 604778sec
   inet6 fe80::712c:f509:edbe:18d1/64 scope link noprefixroute
      valid_lft forever preferred_lft forever
```

The ip command can also configure networking, routing, and tunnels, and has built-in features to configure IPv6 networks as well.

Mugabe can also use the ifconfig command to configure networks. Like the ip command, the ifconfig command can assign IP addresses, netmask addresses, broadcast addresses, and more. Plus, ifconfig provides interface error information, such as dropped packets, collisions, and link status, as shown here:

```
[root@cent71-5t buddy]# ifconfig enp0s3
enp0s3: flags=4163<UP,BROADCAST,RUNNING,MULTICAST>  mtu 1500
       inet 10.0.2.15  netmask 255.255.255.0  broadcast 10.0.2.255
       inet6 fe80::ab6d:48ca:f676:aacf  prefixlen 64  scopeid 0x20<link>
       ether 08:00:27:2a:00:2b  txqueuelen 1000  (Ethernet)
       RX packets 35  bytes 6843 (6.6 KiB)
       RX errors 0  dropped 0  overruns 0  frame 0
       TX packets 66  bytes 8459 (8.2 KiB)
       TX errors 0  dropped 0 overruns 0  carrier 0  collisions 0
```

Mugabe can run ip -s to get interface information.

To determine which driver to use with network cards, Mugabe uses the `lspci` command with the `-v` option. This provides more details about the network card, including model and IRQ setting, as shown here:

```
[root@cent71-5t buddy]# lspci -v | head -33 | tail -10
00:03.0 Ethernet controller: Intel Corporation 82540EM Gigabit Ethernet Cont
roller (rev 02)
     Subsystem: Intel Corporation PRO/1000 MT Desktop Adapter
     Flags: bus master, 66MHz, medium devsel, latency 64, IRQ 19
     Memory at f0000000 (32-bit, non-prefetchable) [size=128K]
     I/O ports at d010 [size=8]
     Capabilities: [dc] Power Management version 2
     Capabilities: [e4] PCI-X non-bridge device
     Kernel driver in use: e1000
     Kernel modules: e1000
```

The `lspci` command can also be used to discover high-performance networking cards (for example, those that are RDMA capable). RDMA (Remote Direct Memory Access) over Ethernet allows direct access to the memory of one computer from the memory of another without using the OS of either system, thus resulting in low latency and high throughput. If any of the network cards were RDMA capable, `lspci` would display the term `InfiniBand`. Since this does not appear in the preceding result, the FRMS computers do not support RDMA.

NOTE Performance can also be improved by using UNIX sockets. UNIX sockets are for interprocess communications to allow the exchange of processes on the same system, where IP sockets allow process communications over a network.

Troubleshooting Local Area Network Performance

Users complain to Carlos of long delays and high latency when accessing computers on the network. Their systems are named after vegetables to remind staff that personal health is of the utmost importance. When users `ssh` or `ping` systems named `tomato`, `cucumber`, `zucchini`, and so on, it takes at least five minutes to get a response.

Carlos first suspects the timeouts and high latency issues are due to network saturation. He runs `iftop` to monitor traffic bandwidth. The `iftop` command is similar to `top` in that it measures activity and automatically updates every two seconds. The results are shown in Figure 19-4 and indicate normal network activity.

EXAM TIP For command updates similar to `top` and `iftop`, try using the `watch` command. For example, try running `watch uptime` to visualize new uptime and load outputs every two seconds.

Another powerful network throughput measuring tool in Carlos' tool case is `iperf`. The `iperf` command evaluates bandwidth limitations over a specific path, so a server and client are required for the command to function successfully. In the following example,

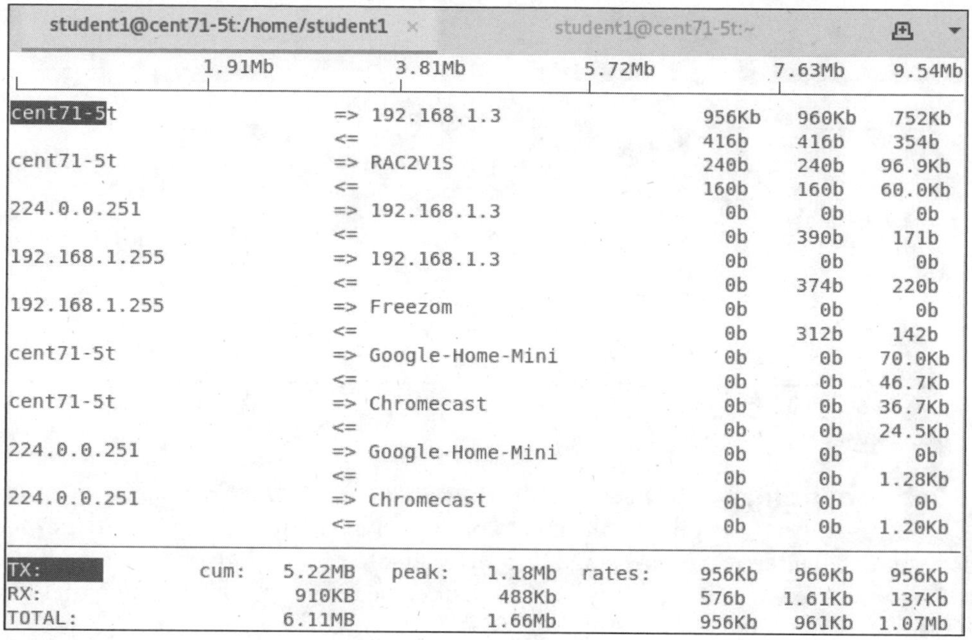

```
student1@cent71-5t:/home/student1    student1@cent71-5t:~
              1.91Mb          3.81Mb          5.72Mb          7.63Mb     9.54Mb
cent71-5t                 => 192.168.1.3                       956Kb   960Kb   752Kb
                          <=                                   416b    416b    354b
cent71-5t                 => RAC2V1S                           240b    240b    96.9Kb
                          <=                                   160b    160b    60.0Kb
224.0.0.251               => 192.168.1.3                       0b      0b      0b
                          <=                                   0b      390b    171b
192.168.1.255             => 192.168.1.3                       0b      0b      0b
                          <=                                   0b      374b    220b
192.168.1.255             => Freezom                           0b      0b      0b
                          <=                                   0b      312b    142b
cent71-5t                 => Google-Home-Mini                  0b      0b      70.0Kb
                          <=                                   0b      0b      46.7Kb
cent71-5t                 => Chromecast                        0b      0b      36.7Kb
                          <=                                   0b      0b      24.5Kb
224.0.0.251               => Google-Home-Mini                  0b      0b      0b
                          <=                                   0b      0b      1.28Kb
224.0.0.251               => Chromecast                        0b      0b      0b
                          <=                                   0b      0b      1.20Kb

TX:            cum:   5.22MB   peak:   1.18Mb  rates:   956Kb   960Kb   956Kb
RX:                   910KB            488Kb            576b    1.61Kb  137Kb
TOTAL:                6.11MB           1.66Mb           956Kb   961Kb   1.07Mb
```

Figure 19-4 Output of `iftop` command

Carlos evaluates the bandwidth, loss, saturation, and latency between the client and the DNS server. On the DNS server, he starts the `iperf` server program by running `iperf -s`, as shown in Figure 19-5.

On the client machine, he runs `iperf` in client mode and lets it run for a few seconds to measure network activity and latency, as shown in Figure 19-6. Again, Carlos sees that network performance is acceptable.

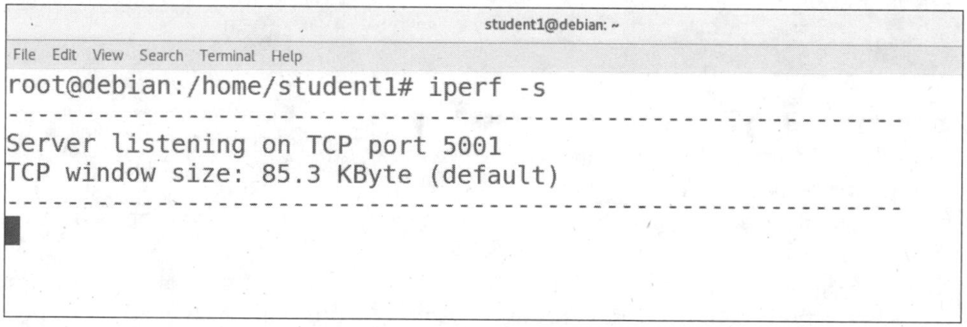

```
student1@debian: ~
File  Edit  View  Search  Terminal  Help
root@debian:/home/student1# iperf -s
------------------------------------------------------------
Server listening on TCP port 5001
TCP window size: 85.3 KByte (default)
------------------------------------------------------------
```

Figure 19-5 Starting the `iperf` server

```
root@cent71-5t:~
File  Edit  View  Search  Terminal  Help
[root@cent71-5t ~]# iperf -c 192.168.1.84
------------------------------------------------------------
Client connecting to 192.168.1.84, TCP port 5001
TCP window size:  434 KByte (default)
------------------------------------------------------------
[  3] local 192.168.1.82 port 59728 connected with 192.168.1.84 port 5001
[ ID] Interval       Transfer     Bandwidth
[  3]  0.0-10.0 sec  2.14 GBytes  1.84 Gbits/sec
[root@cent71-5t ~]# 
```

Figure 19-6 Running the `iperf` client

Troubleshooting Name Resolution Issues

Carlos remembers a similar case while working as a summer intern with the U.S. government. The system is checking DNS tables first to resolve domain names, and after a five-minute timeout, it performs local domain name resolution. He therefore modifies the `hosts` record in `/etc/nsswitch.conf`, changing it from

```
hosts:       dns   files
```

to

```
hosts:       files dns
```

so that the `/etc/hosts` file is checked before `/etc/resolv.conf` when resolving hostnames. Now users access their "salad ingredients" (that is, hosts named after vegetables) much faster. Carlos uses tools like `host`, `nslookup`, and `dig` to verify name server status.

EXAM TIP Knowledge of the `hosts:` record is the only entry of `/etc/nsswitch.conf` tested on the CompTIA Linux+ exam

Troubleshooting Dynamic IP Address Issues

Users complain to Jessica that they cannot get an IP address from the DHCP server. She asks the users to try releasing the address with the `dhclient -r` command and renewing the address by running `dhclient`. The users report back that they still cannot obtain an IP address.

She also dumps the `/var/lib/dhclient/dhclient.leases` file and sees there are no connections defined there. This explains part of the reason why users cannot get an IP address from the DHCP server.

Next Jessica modifies the `/etc/dhcp/dhclient.conf` file and alters how it communicates with the DHCP server to resolve the issue.

EXAM TIP Knowledge of the `/etc/dhcp/dhclient.conf` is good to know for the CompTIA Linux+ exam.

Troubleshooting Gateways with `sysctl`

As mentioned in Chapter 15, IP forwarding must be enabled for a Linux system to act as a network router or gateway. To verify whether IP forwarding has been enabled, run `cat /proc/sys/net/ipv{4,6}/ip_forward`, as shown here:

```
[root@cent71-5t buddy]# cat /proc/sys/net/ipv4/ip_forward
0
```

Alternatively, you can use the `sysctl` command (not to be confused with the `systemctl` command, which manages run levels), as follows:

```
[root@cent71-5t buddy]# sysctl -a | grep ipv4.ip_forward
net.ipv4.ip_forward = 0
```

The `sysctl` command is used to configure kernel parameters that tune the computer. Tuning can help improve computer performance by up to 50 percent, depending on the application. To view all the kernel tunables, use the `-a` option, as shown here:

```
[root@cent71-5t buddy]# sysctl -a
abi.vsyscall32 = 1
crypto.fips_enabled = 0
debug.exception-trace = 1
debug.kprobes-optimization = 1
debug.panic_on_rcu_stall = 0
dev.cdrom.autoclose = 1
dev.cdrom.autoeject = 0
dev.cdrom.check_media = 0
dev.cdrom.debug = 0
dev.cdrom.info = CD-ROM information, Id: cdrom.c 3.20 2003/12/17
dev.cdrom.info =
dev.cdrom.info = drive name:             sr0
dev.cdrom.info = drive speed:            32
dev.cdrom.info = drive # of slots:       1
dev.cdrom.info = Can close tray:         1
dev.cdrom.info = Can open tray:          1
dev.cdrom.info = Can lock tray:          1
dev.cdrom.info = Can change speed:       1
dev.cdrom.info = Can select disk:        0
<...etc...>
```

Once the system is satisfactorily tuned, make the new values permanent by modifying `/etc/sysctl.conf` or the `/etc/sysctl.d/` directory. Jessica wants to make the system a routable device as well as make it permanent at boot time. To accomplish this, she does the following:

```
[root@cent71-5t buddy]# cat >> /etc/sysctl.d/99-sysctl.conf
net.ipv4.ip_forward = 1
^D
[root@cent71-5t buddy]# reboot
```

Now the system can be used as a gateway device to other networks. (Updating `/etc/sysctl.conf` with the `cat` command, as previously mentioned, would have worked as well.)

After reboot, the system reports that IP forwarding is automatically enabled at boot time, as shown next:

```
[root@cent71-5t buddy]# sysctl -a | grep ipv4.ip_forward
net.ipv4.ip_forward = 1
[root@cent71-5t buddy]# cat /proc/sys/net/ipv4/ip_forward
1
```

Validate User Connections

Gary reports to Mugabe that several users are locked out of their login accounts. This just started happening when the FRMS systems merged with the SGMF network. Mugabe starts by testing whether users can log in locally without Kerberos or LDAP.

He scans the `/etc/passwd` file and finds the usernames are there, as they should be, and that there is an `x` in the second column so that the system knows to find passwords in `/etc/shadow`. He also verifies that users are listed in `/etc/shadow`. Next, he attempts logging in as various users using `su -` *<username>* and is successful. Since he is able to access user accounts locally, there must be an issue with remote or external directory services.

He glances at the `/etc/nsswitch.conf` file on the newer systems and notices that the passwd, shadow, and group fields only search `files` (`/etc/passwd`, `/etc/shadow`, and `/etc/group`), as shown here:

```
passwd:       files
shadow:       files
group:        files
```

Part of what will make the merger successful is that both companies, FRMS and SGMF, use LDAP directory services for remote authentication. They also have identical password policies in that passwords should be at least eight characters long, with two uppercase characters and one special character that is defined in PAM (introduced in Chapter 18). If this policy is violated, the account cannot be used.

NOTE The settings in `/etc/login.defs` only affect shadow utilities. The settings in `/etc/pam.d/passwd` affect a specific command. For example, the file `/etc/login.defs` specifies a minimum length for a user password. The PAM file `/etc/pam.d/passwd` overrides a password length defined in `/etc/login.defs`.

So that users can access the LDAP server to be authenticated, Mugabe updates `/etc/nsswitch.conf` as follows:

```
passwd:       files   ldap
shadow:       files   ldap
group:        files   ldap
```

Users who are following the policy are now able to log in successfully.

NOTE To join the Linux system to a Windows Active Directory domain, use the `winbind` directive within `/etc/nsswitch.conf`.

Validate the Firewall

Davy and Tomika of FRMS notify Carlos that he may have forgotten about the SSH issue users are having, but Davy has not forgotten about the issue and needs Carlos to give this some attention, as their policy requires response times within 24 hours.

Carlos' memory is not as good as Davy's, but he gets on the case because he wants a successful merger. He attempts using SSH as a FRMS user and reproduces the issue. He cannot log in via SSH.

EXAM TIP Poor firewall settings cause most network-related issues, especially if a service is not available.

He next moves to the SSH server and verifies SSH is running with `systemctl`, as shown here:

```
[root@cent71-5t ~]# systemctl status sshd
● sshd.service - OpenSSH server daemon
  Loaded: loaded (/usr/lib/systemd/system/sshd.service; enabled; vendor
preset: enabled)
  Active: active (running) since Tue 2023-05-07 23:06:25 EDT; 10 day 15h ago
    Docs: man:sshd(8)
          man:sshd_config(5)
Main PID: 4084 (sshd)
   Tasks: 1
  CGroup: /system.slice/sshd.service
          └─4084 /usr/sbin/sshd -D
May 07 23:06:25 cent71-5t systemd[1]: Starting OpenSSH server daemon...
May 07 23:06:25 cent71-5t sshd[4084]: Server listening on 0.0.0.0 port 22.
May 07 23:06:25 cent71-5t sshd[4084]: Server listening on :: port 22.
May 07 23:06:25 cent71-5t systemd[1]: Started OpenSSH server daemon.
```

The results show that the `sshd` service is enabled.

Next, he investigates the firewall. He runs `firewall-cmd` to investigate whether port 22 is open, as shown here:

```
[root@cent71-5t ~]# firewall-cmd --list-services
mdns samba-client dhcpv6-client
```

The results show that port 22 using the TCP protocol for the SSH service is blocked. Apparently, the ACL allows features like Samba and DHCP, but not SSH. The ACL is too restrictive. Carlos changes the rule using `firewall-cmd` to unblock port 22 and unblock the TCP protocol for this service, as follows:

```
[root@cent71-5t ~]# firewall-cmd --add-service ssh
success
[root@cent71-5t ~]# firewall-cmd --list-services
mdns samba-client dhcpv6-client ssh
[root@cent71-5t ~]# firewall-cmd --add-service ssh --permanent
success
[root@cent71-5t ~]# firewall-cmd --reload
success
[root@cent71-5t ~]# firewall-cmd --list-services
ssh mdns samba-client dhcpv6-client
```

Running `firewall-cmd --add-service ssh` opens port 22/TCP so that users can now access SSH. So that the port is open on following reboots, he runs the `firewall-cmd --add-service ssh --permanent` command string. SSH shows as one of the open ports when he runs the `firewall-cmd --list-services` command with options.

Finally, he tests whether users can log in to the system via SSH, and he finds that users from FRMS and SGMF can now access the SSH server. Case closed—and even Tomika is impressed.

Practice working with network troubleshooting and performance commands in Exercise 19-2.

Exercise 19-2: Troubleshooting Networking Issues

In this exercise, you practice using network and firewall commands to manage and troubleshoot a network connection. This exercise assumes two systems are connected, as follows:

- **`sysA`** IP address 10.1.1.2/24 (SSH server)
- **`sysB`** IP address 10.1.1.3/24

VIDEO Please watch the Exercise 19-2 video for a demonstration on how to perform this task.

Complete the following steps:

1. From `sysB`, test the network connection to `sysA` with the `ping` command:

   ```
   $ ping 10.1.1.3
   ```

2. From `sysA`, switch to the `root` user account by entering **`su -`** followed by **`password`** for the password.

3. Disable network activity at `sysA`:

```
sysA # systemctl stop network
```

4. From `sysB`, test the network connection to `sysA` with the `ping` command:

```
sysB $ ping 10.1.1.3
```

5. Re-enable network activity at `sysA`:

```
sysA # systemctl start network
```

6. Verify the SSH server is running on `sysA`:

```
sysA # systemctl status sshd
```

   If it is not running, start the SSH server with `systemctl`:

```
sysA # systemctl start sshd
```

7. Even though the SSH server is running, block access to the service by typing the following `firewall-cmd` at `sysA`:

```
sysA # firewall-cmd --remove-service ssh
```

8. From `sysB`, attempt to log in via SSH. This should fail because the SSH service is blocked by the firewall.

```
sysB $ ssh student1@10.1.1.2
```

9. Re-enable access to the service by typing another `firewall-cmd` at sysA:

```
sysA # firewall-cmd -reload
```

10. From `sysB`, attempt to log in via SSH. This should succeed because the firewall port is now opened.

```
sysB $ ssh student1@10.1.1.2
```

Chapter Review

This chapter focused on troubleshooting, diagnostics, and performance tuning of hardware and networks. There are several software tools available to test CPU performance, RAM usage, and disk drive efficiency. Many of the tools read hardware states from the `/proc` and `/sys` pseudo-directories. Administrators can learn details of CPU, RAM, IRQ settings, and more, by reviewing files in `/proc`.

With respect to RAM shortages, administrators can increase swap space to prevent the OOM Killer from killing programs. If a swap partition is not available, a swap file can quickly be created and added as swap space.

Hard drives are tunable through a setting called scheduler. The possible disk drive scheduler settings are `none`, `mq-deadline`, `kyber`, and `bfq`. Each organization needs to evaluate which setting is best for its environment. Once the organization determines which is best for its applications, it can make the setting permanent using the `tuned` utility.

Administrators use the `systemctl` command to enable and disable services on a Linux server, such as SSH, FTP, Telnet, and shared printers.

Several familiar tools are available for troubleshooting networks, but most of them are not IPv6 friendly. However, the relatively new `ip` command replaces many networking commands that are normally used, and it handles IPv6 setup and troubleshooting as well.

Unfortunately, too often a service is running and available but users are unable to access it. Most of the time this is due to the firewall blocking the service. The fix is straightforward, of course (open the port for the service), but troubleshooting these types of issues can take hours to diagnose.

Review the following key points for exam preparation:

- The `/proc/cpuinfo` file provides details of the CPU installed.
- The `uptime` command shows how long the system has been running and load averages.
- Run `watch uptime` to monitor uptime changes every two seconds.
- The `w` command shows who is logged in to the system and what they are doing.
- Running `sar` allows administrators to see performance info on CPU, disk, RAM, and so on. The `/proc/meminfo` file provides details of the RAM installed.
- Use the `dd` command to create a swap file.
- Run `mkswap` to configure the new file as swap space.
- Enable the new swap space with the `swapon` command.
- Swap space can be disabled using `swapoff`.
- To access the second virtual console, run `Ctrl-Alt-F2`.
- Where root users are allowed to log in is found in the `/etc/securetty` file.
- Running `df -i` will display the number of inodes available on a filesystem.
- Use the `lsof -i` command to list listening network ports.
- Use the `lspci -v` command to verify graphic card installs.
- Use `ip addr show` to display network card settings.
- Run the `dhclient -r` command to release an address from the DHCP server.
- If you have difficulty connecting to a DHCP server, validate settings within `/etc/dhcp/dhclient.conf`.
- The `iftop` command measures network activity, updated every two seconds.
- Use `sysctl` to change kernel settings, such as `/proc/sys/net/ipv4/ip_forward`.
- Modify `/etc/sysctl.conf` so that `ip_forward` is enabled at boot time.
- Name server settings can be added within `/etc/nsswitch.conf`, such as LDAP, Active Directory, and so on.

Questions

1. Which option to the `lshw` command will provide a hardware installation summary with device trees showing hardware paths?
   - **A.** `-X`
   - **B.** `-summary`
   - **C.** `-short`
   - **D.** `-s`
2. Which command lists the system's BIOS while in multi-user mode?
   - **A.** `dmidecode`
   - **B.** `biosview`
   - **C.** `bview`
   - **D.** `lsbios`
3. Commands like `w` and `uptime` only provide output once. Which command can be run with `uptime` or `w` to have the output automatically update every two seconds?
   - **A.** `look`
   - **B.** `watch`
   - **C.** `rerun`
   - **D.** `repeat`
4. Which system activity reporter function will list CPU, RAM, I/O, disk activity, and more, with five outputs displaying the result every two seconds?
   - **A.** `sar -A -s 2`
   - **B.** `sar -A -s 2 -i 5`
   - **C.** `sar -A 5 2`
   - **D.** `sar -A 2 5`
5. Which commands list memory performance information? (Choose two.)
   - **A.** `vmstat`
   - **B.** `memviewer`
   - **C.** `perfmonitor`
   - **D.** `lsram`
   - **E.** `sar`

6. Which command displays how much memory and swap are available on a Linux system?
   A. `free`
   B. `swapon -s`
   C. `dd`
   D. `lsram`
7. Which kernel variable can be changed to either `none`, `mq-deadline`, `kyber`, or `bfq` to change storage scheduling on drive `/dev/sda`?
   A. `/proc/block/sda/queue/scheduler`
   B. `/sysv/block/sda/queue/scheduler`
   C. `/sys/block/sda/queue/scheduler`
   D. `/sys/block/sda1/queue/scheduler`
8. Which command will display disk I/O latency?
   A. `pingio`
   B. `diskio`
   C. `lsdisk`
   D. `ioping`
9. Which commands display disk I/O rates? (Choose two.)
   A. `lssda`
   B. `sar`
   C. `iostat`
   D. `swapon`
10. Which command will block access to the SSH server?
    A. `firewall-cmd --del-service ssh`
    B. `firewall-cmd --remove-service ssh`
    C. `firewall-cmd --block-service ssh`
    D. `firewall-cmd --disable-service ssh`

Answers

1. **C.** The command `lshw -short` outputs hardware information showing hardware paths with a device tree.
2. **A.** The `dmidecode` command lists the system's BIOS while in multi-user mode.
3. **B.** The `watch` command will execute a program periodically, showing output in full screen.

4. **D.** The `sar` command collects, reports, and saves system activity information, and the syntax is `sar <interval count>`.
5. **A, E.** Both `sar` and `vmstat` monitor memory performance.
6. **A.** The `free` command displays how much memory and swap space are available on a computer.
7. **A.** Modify the `/proc/block/sda/queue/scheduler` kernel variable to either `none`, `mq-deadline`, `kyber`, or `bfq` to change storage scheduling on drive `/dev/sda`.
8. **D.** The `ioping` command will display disk drive latency performance output.
9. **B, C.** The `sar` and `iostat` commands are two commands that display disk I/O rates.
10. **B.** The command to close port 22 for SSH is `firewall-cmd --remove-service ssh` or `firewall-cmd --remove-service=ssh`.

CHAPTER 20

Installing and Configuring Linux

In this chapter, you will learn about

- Designing a Linux installation
- Installing Linux
- Configuring the X Window System
- Configuring locale settings
- Configuring time zone settings
- Configuring printing with CUPS
- Configuring e-mail
- Configuring SQL databases
- Configuring storage

The best way to make your dreams come true is to wake up.

—Mae Jemison, NASA

The CompTIA Linux+ certification exam objectives *do not require* candidates to know how to perform a clean installation of a Linux distribution or how to configure e-mail, printing, and databases. However, in order for you to practice the Linux features discussed in this chapter, I thought it important to explain how to set up and configure a Linux system. The CompTIA Linux+ exam covers the most common Linux distributions, but this chapter only instructs on how to install CentOS. I chose CentOS because it is similar to the version of Linux installed by most U.S. employers—Red Hat Enterprise Linux. The Debian and OpenSUSE installation process is similar to installing CentOS as well.

Linux has become dramatically easier to install in the last 20 years. The distributions available in the mid-1990s were challenging to install, and hardware support was limited. Fortunately, modern Linux distributions employ an easy-to-use graphical installation wizard to facilitate the installation process. To install Linux properly, spend some time planning the installation *before* starting the installation process.

NOTE Although there are hundreds of Linux distributions listed at https://distrowatch.com, this discussion focuses on Linux distributions tested on the CompTIA Linux+ exam.

Designing a Linux Installation

When organizations deploy systems for their production environments, proper planning is critical. Mistakes will lead to system outages, and outages cost organizations time and money.

For example, suppose a major networking software vendor wanted to implement a new application that would make its employees' jobs easier. When reviewing the system requirements, the design and installation team found that the application required a specific version of the Windows server software—one not currently owned. Implementing the application would first require a new server be installed. Rather than develop a plan for the new server deployment, the design and installation team moved forward without a plan. They ordered a new server and set up the software without communicating with the employees.

In the end, all the employees' critical data was saved on this server. Thousands of human hours representing millions of dollars were never backed up. Good communications and change management would ensure this does not happen.

In this part of the chapter, we discuss how to go about planning a Linux installation. The following topics are addressed:

- Conducting a needs assessment
- Selecting a distribution
- Checking hardware compatibility
- Verifying system requirements
- Planning the filesystem
- Selecting software packages
- Identifying user accounts
- Gathering network information
- Selecting an installation source

The first step in any deployment plan is to conduct a needs assessment. Let's discuss this topic next.

Conducting a Needs Assessment

Conducting a needs assessment is one of the most important aspects of creating a Linux deployment plan. This is the process of determining *why* the Linux deployment is being undertaken, *what* outcomes are expected, and *when* it is expected to be complete. Completing a needs assessment requires you to remove your technician hat and put on the project manager hat. In this role, you need to meet with different individuals and understand their needs. This needs assessment should contain the following information (at a minimum):

- **What are the goals of the project?** What problem will this installation fix? What will be the final result of the implementation?
- **Who are the stakeholders in this project?** As a part of your needs assessment, identify all individuals who will be impacted by the project.
- **When is the system needed?** A key question to ask is, when should the project be completed? Begin with the "end in mind."

Once you have answers to these questions, do a reality check against the schedule. Remember that what looks good on paper might not work in real life.

With your project scope defined, move on to the next component in the project plan—the Linux distribution.

Selecting a Distribution

As discussed, Linux is available in a wide variety of flavors called *distributions* or *distros.* One of the key parts of the deployment plan is specifying which distribution to use. Which distro is the best to use depends on your preferences. Most of the U.S. federal government prefers Red Hat Enterprise Linux (RHEL) or SUSE Linux Enterprise Server (SLES) because they offer corporate support plans, and both provide Mandatory Access Control (MAC). Ethical hackers prefer Kali with the Tor browser because they provide the best auditing tools. Here are some guidelines to use to select the right distribution.

Determine if the system will function as a workstation or server. Most operating systems are designed to function as one or the other, but Linux can function as either a workstation or a server. This is unique among operating systems. IBM's Red Hat provides Red Hat Enterprise Linux distribution, designed to provide network services for medium to very large organizations with heavy server utilization. Red Hat also provides distributions designed specifically for use as desktops.

Oracle Linux is an enterprise-class operating system and is easily converted to RHEL by purchasing Red Hat's support plan. Oracle Linux is open source and 100 percent binary compatible with RHEL for applications and patches.

CentOS and Fedora are both open source versions of RHEL designed for the casual user. It is not recommended to use Fedora or CentOS in an organization's production environment.

Likewise, EQT Partners sells multiple versions of SUSE Linux and provides OpenSUSE for the open source community. Its distributions span offerings for the cloud and even embedded systems.

There are also purpose-specific distributions to create Linux-based appliances using standard PC hardware. For example, you can create a powerful network firewall using distributions such as Untangle.

Before selecting a specific Linux distribution, evaluate whether the corporate applications will run and are supported by the operating system. Also, verify the distribution runs on the selected system hardware.

Checking Hardware Compatibility

Today, most vendors offer a Linux version of the drivers for their hardware. In addition, most of the drivers for common PC hardware are now included with the various Linux distributions, especially virtual machines. Linux installs on various types of hardware. To validate hardware compatibility, visit https://tldp.org/HOWTO/Hardware-HOWTO/ or consult the Linux vendor's system requirements for updated specifications.

Though rarely done, it is still a very good idea to check the distribution's website and verify that the system hardware is listed on the distribution's hardware compatibility list (HCL). Even though hardware support for Linux has become much better in the last decade, there are still some devices that are not supported. A good example is integrated wireless network interfaces used in many notebook systems. Check the distribution's HCL to verify that the system's devices are supported.

HCLs are usually available in two locations. First, Linux distributions include a list of supported hardware in a text file on the installation DVD. However, because it is a static document, it has not been updated since the disc image was created. If a device in the computer was released at some point after the disc image was created, the driver may be outdated.

Instead, use the HCL maintained on the distribution websites. This version of the HCL contains the most current data on supported hardware. For example, if you're installing the openSUSE distribution, access its HCL at https://en.opensuse.org/Portal:Hardware. Once there, search for the system hardware and see if it is supported. In Figure 20-1, the openSUSE HCL for wired network cards is displayed.

If you're choosing a Red Hat distribution, check the HCL on Red Hat's website (https://access.redhat.com/articles/rhel-limits) to verify the system hardware is supported.

NOTE Driver availability is one reason organizations prefer to use big-name, well-supported Linux distributions when deploying in a production environment. Linux system administrators must protect data and ensure systems run at maximum efficiency. In production environments, it is critical to use Linux-supported hardware.

In addition to checking the HCL, also check the distribution's system requirements.

Verifying System Requirements

When formulating the deployment plan, be sure to specify the hardware needed by the distribution selected. A key aspect of the system requirements is the computer's CPU architecture. When downloading the Linux distribution, be sure to select the architecture that matches the system's CPU.

Today, there are many hardware options available to system administrators. There are still x86 and Alpha architectures, and the newer 64-bit x86 architecture. In addition, Intel produces the IA-64 architecture used by its Core CPUs. Each of these architectures requires a different version of Linux. In fact, many Linux distributions have even been ported to run on the M2 chip architecture from Apple. Other distributions are

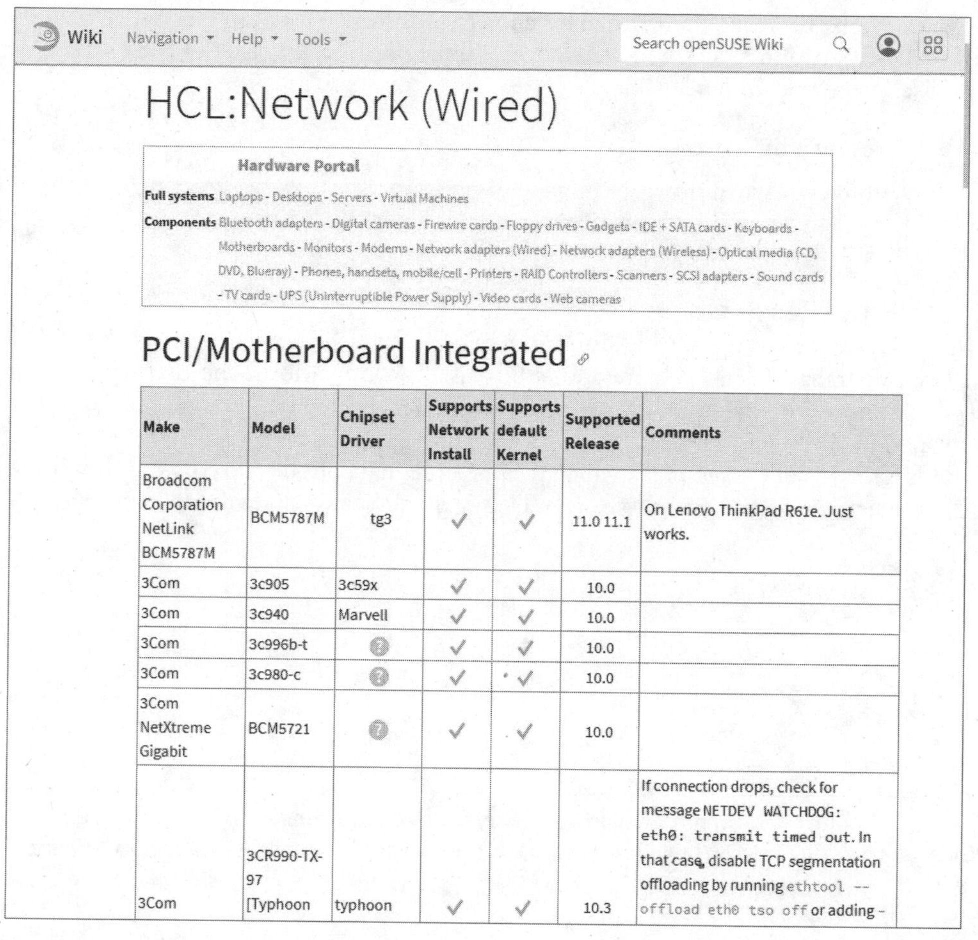

Wiki Navigation Help Tools Search openSUSE Wiki

HCL:Network (Wired)

Hardware Portal

Full systems Laptops - Desktops - Servers - Virtual Machines

Components Bluetooth adapters - Digital cameras - Firewire cards - Floppy drives - Gadgets - IDE + SATA cards - Keyboards - Motherboards - Monitors - Modems - Network adapters (Wired) - Network adapters (Wireless) - Optical media (CD, DVD, Blueray) - Phones, handsets, mobile/cell - Printers - RAID Controllers - Scanners - SCSI adapters - Sound cards - TV cards - UPS (Uninterruptible Power Supply) - Video cards - Web cameras

PCI/Motherboard Integrated

Make	Model	Chipset Driver	Supports Network Install	Supports default Kernel	Supported Release	Comments
Broadcom Corporation NetLink BCM5787M	BCM5787M	tg3	✓	✓	11.0 11.1	On Lenovo ThinkPad R61e. Just works.
3Com	3c905	3c59x	✓	✓	10.0	
3Com	3c940	Marvell	✓	✓	10.0	
3Com	3c996b-t	?	✓	✓	10.0	
3Com	3c980-c	?	✓	✓	10.0	
3Com NetXtreme Gigabit	BCM5721	?	✓	✓	10.0	
3Com	3CR990-TX-97 [Typhoon	typhoon	✓	✓	10.3	If connection drops, check for message `NETDEV WATCHDOG: eth0: transmit timed out`. In that case, disable TCP segmentation offloading by running `ethtool --offload eth0 tso off` or adding -

Figure 20-1 Using the openSUSE HCL

available for the Thinkpad T14s from IBM and Lenovo using Intel or AMD Ryzen CPUs. There are now even versions of Linux that have been ported to run on the Qualcomm Snapdragon architecture used by tablet devices and smartphones.

Regardless of which distribution is chosen, make sure to download the correct version for the system's architecture. If you choose the wrong version, the Linux installers will generate an error and cancel the installation.

Planning the Filesystem

When planning a Linux implementation, include specifications for how the filesystem will be created and maintained on the system's hard disk drive.

With Linux, however, there are more choices. Administrators can customize how the disk will be partitioned and what filesystem will be used. In this part of the chapter, we will discuss the following:

- Choosing a filesystem
- Planning the partitions

Let's begin by discussing filesystems.

Choosing a Filesystem

The drive is made up of multiple aluminum platters, each with two read-write heads that are used to transfer data. When conducting disk I/O operations, the operating system needs to know where data is stored, how to access it, and where it is safe to write new information.

This is the job of the *filesystem,* which reliably stores data on the hard drive and organizes it in such a way that it is easily accessible. Filesystem choices include the following:

- `ext3`
- `reiser`
- `ext4`
- `btrfs`
- `xfs`

NOTE Admins can also use many other filesystems with Linux, such as VFAT and NTFS filesystems. Don't use `ext2`, because it is a non-journaling filesystem.

The best supported filesystems are `reiser`, `ext4`, `btrfs`, and `xfs`. These filesystems can handle larger file sizes of much greater than 2TB, and filesystem partition sizes on the order of exabytes. Also, they manage system failures better because of journaling, being able to recover from system crashes in minutes instead of days with `ext2`.

Planning the Partitions

It is recommended to have at least two partitions (`/` and `swap`), and it's best to define these during the initial installation of the system. Changing disk partitions after system installation is possible, but it is somewhat challenging and time consuming. Therefore, best practice is to plan the partition layout before starting the installation process.

By default, Linux distributions propose multiple partitions during the installation process (see Figure 20-2):

- **`swap`** The appropriate size for the swap partition is larger than the amount of installed RAM, because in the event of a system crash, the entire RAM image will fit the swap partition. The kernel dump can later be analyzed to determine why the system faulted.

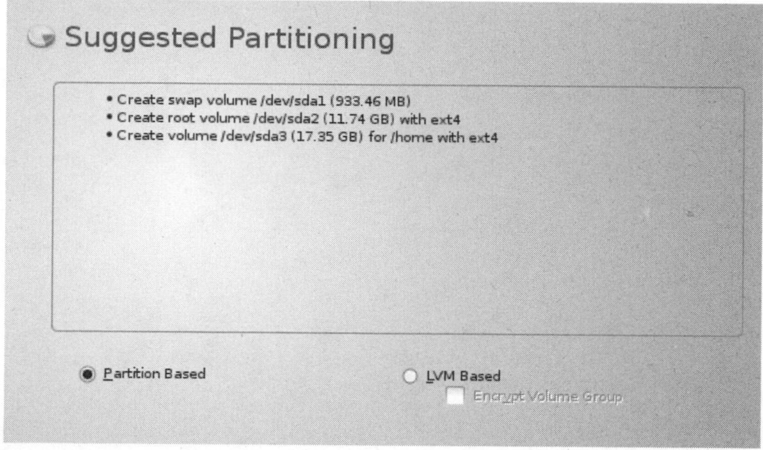

Figure 20-2 Default Linux partitioning

- `/` The slash partition is mounted at the root directory (/) of the Linux filesystem.
- `/boot` Files important to booting reside here, such as the kernel and the initial RAM disk. Filesystem corruptions recover faster when this partition resides on its own.

CAUTION The `/boot` partition must be created within the first 1,024 cylinders of the hard disk. A partition size of 250MB is plenty. To be safe, create this partition such that it begins with cylinder 0.

Using these recommended partitions will add stability to the system.

Selecting Software Packages

Linux includes a fairly extensive sampling of packages that administrators can choose to install with the operating system. Most distributions require multiple DVDs to store all the packages. OpenSUSE offers many different packages, as shown in Figure 20-3.

Another feature of graphical Linux installers is they automatically manage *dependencies,* which are specific software packages that other software packages need in order to run. Most Linux packages installed will have many dependencies associated with them.

In the early days of Linux, administrators had to manually manage dependencies and include them in the installation. This was a tough job because of the layers of dependencies, as shown in Figure 20-4. The job was even tougher when dealing with "circular" dependencies, where package A depends on package B, but package B also depends on package A!

Today, the installers covered on the CompTIA Linux+ exam automatically calculate package dependencies, include the necessary dependent packages in the installation, and manage circular dependencies.

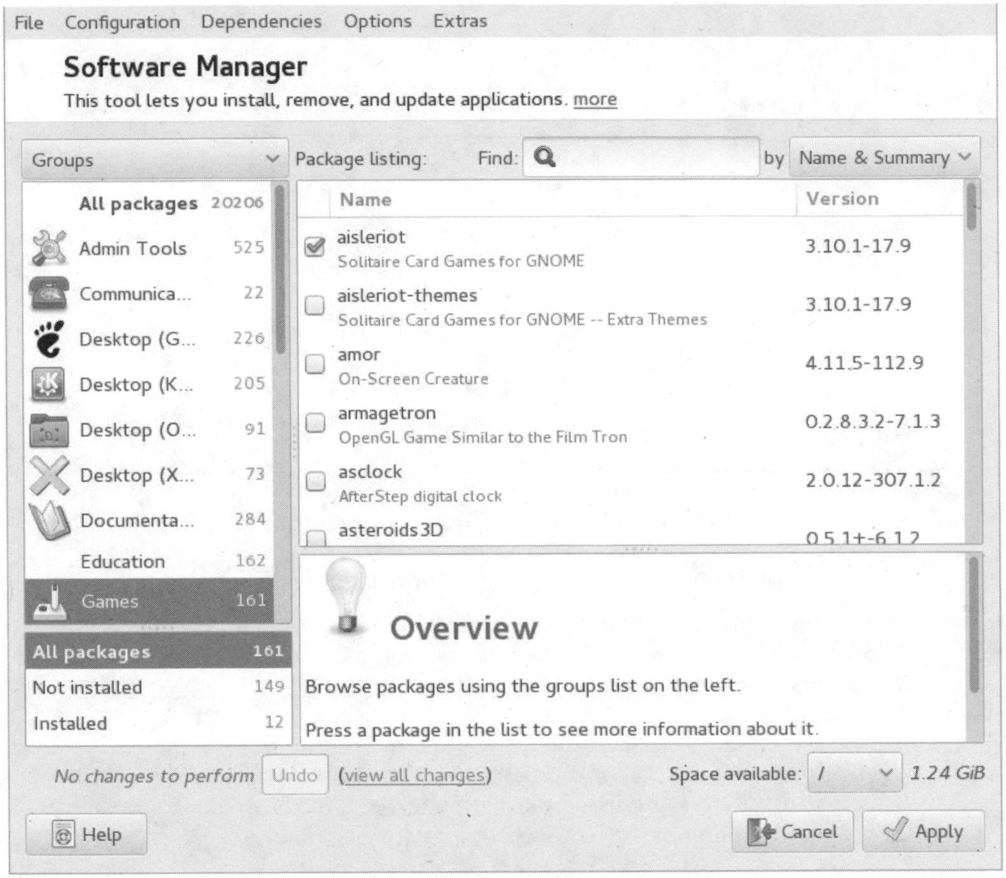

Figure 20-3 Installing software packages in openSUSE Linux

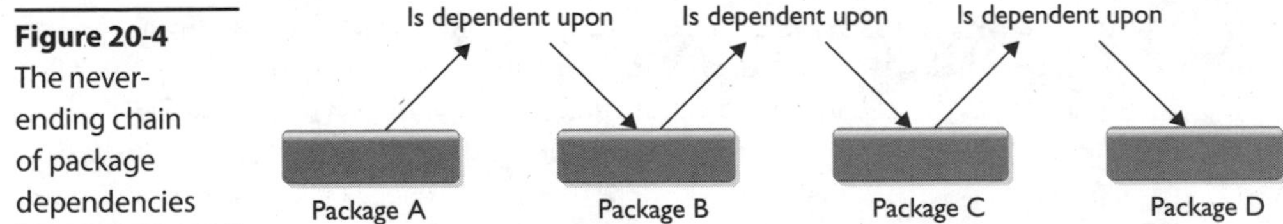

Figure 20-4 The never-ending chain of package dependencies

Identifying User Accounts

When you're planning the installation, determine the user accounts needed on the system. The installation utilities used by Linux distributions provide the ability to create these accounts during the installation process. No matter what distribution you use, you need to create the `root` user account during the installation, along with one standard user account.

Part of the installation process requires passwords be provided for each account. Make sure to use strong passphrases with at least 12 characters, upper- and lowercase letters, special characters, and numbers. Also at this stage of the installation, select which users have `sudo` rights.

Gathering Network Information

You need to gather the information necessary to connect to the network before starting the installation and include it in the deployment plan. Here are some key items to consider:

- Will the system have its networking configuration dynamically assigned or will it need to be manually configured?
- What hostname will be assigned to the system?
- What is the name of the DNS domain the system will reside in?
- Will the system need a host firewall configured?

Selecting an Installation Source

Linux provides multiple installation options, including the following:

- Installing locally from an optical disc or thumb drive
- Installing remotely from a network server
- Completing a remote installation using Virtual Network Computing (VNC)

Installing Locally from an Optical Disc or Thumb Drive

One of the more common methods for installing Linux is locally from a set of installation discs. Using this method, you simply insert the appropriate disc into the system's optical drive and boot the system from the disc. Alternatively, you can upload the image to a thumb drive and install from there.

Simply download the disc image(s) from the vendor's website. For example, to install Fedora, navigate to https://getfedora.org and select the "Download Now" button for Fedora Workstation or Fedora Server. After you choose server or workstation, select the Fedora Media Writer for your hardware, and the Fedora image downloads automatically. Plug in a 16+ GB thumb drive, and Fedora Media Writer will take you through the steps to create a bootable thumb drive.

To make a bootable optical disk, download the `.iso` file. These are known as *ISO images*. Once the ISO image is downloaded, burn it to a physical disc (or thumb drive) using Rufus, UNetbootin, or Universal USB Installer.

Installing Remotely from a Network Server

Another option for installing Linux is from a network server. This will work from installation sources using the SMB, NFS, HTTP, or FTP protocol. The key advantage of using a network is the capability to install a large number of systems at once.

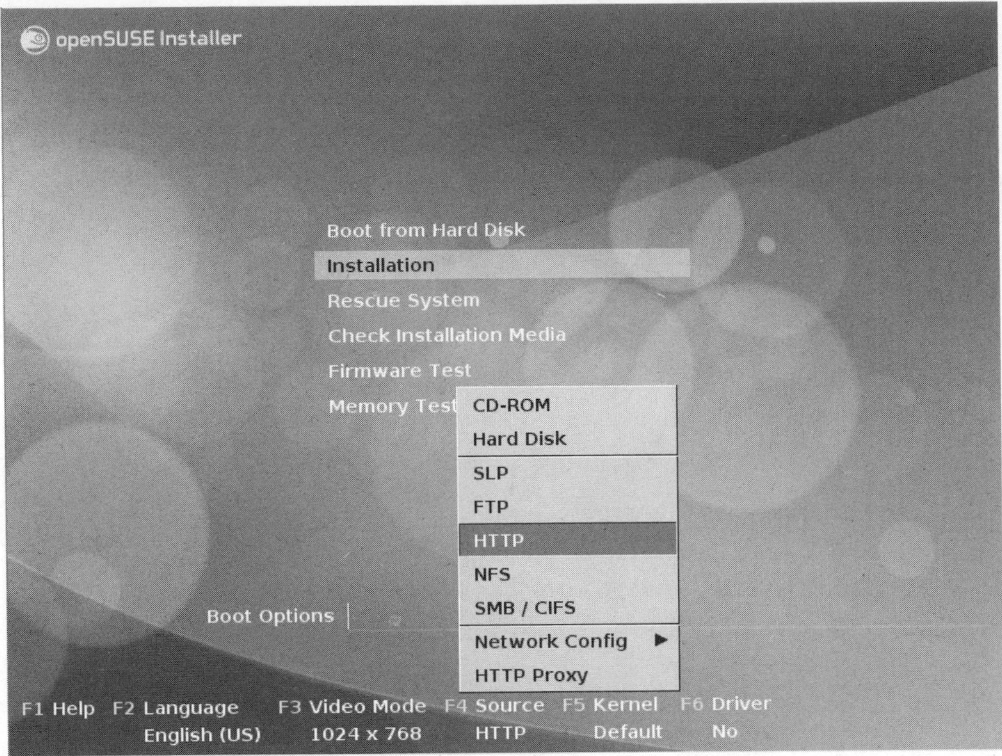

Figure 20-5 Selecting an installation source

NOTE Not all Linux distributions support a network-based installation. To complete a network installation, copy the Linux installation files to a directory on the server or mount a DVD for remote access. Then select the protocol for network access.

Once the installation source server is set up, download a network boot installation image. For example, to complete a network installation of SUSE Linux, navigate to http://opensuse.org, hover over Leap, and choose More Information > Install Leap > Download. In the page that is displayed, you can select a network boot image for download. Burn this image to disc and then boot the system from it. On the first installation screen, specify the installation source, as shown in Figure 20-5.

Completing a Remote Installation Using VNC

VNC allows video output to be redirected from one system to another system. Using the VNC protocol, you can start the installation on a target system but then use a web browser or VNC client software on another system to view the installation screens.

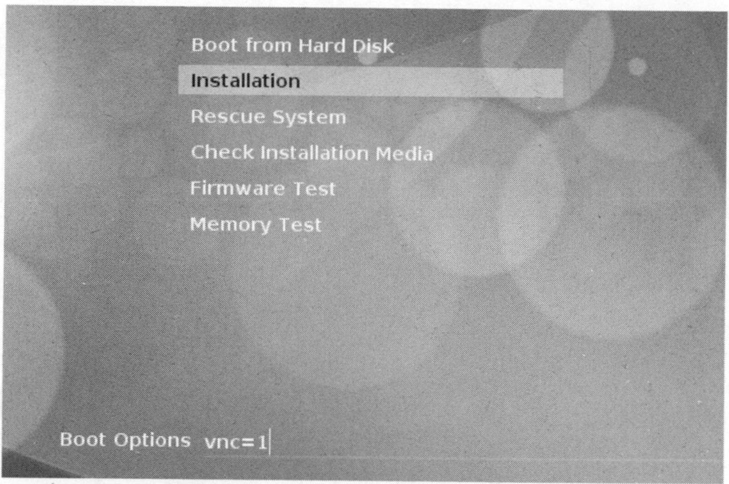

Figure 20-6 Configuring a VNC installation

On many distributions, such as openSUSE, you can enter `vnc=1` in the Boot Options field, as shown in Figure 20-6.

After you start the installation, prompts provide you with various network parameters needed to create a VNC connection. The installation system loads, and the IP address to access the system is displayed. The installation screens can be accessed remotely using either a web browser or VNC client software. For example, if the assigned IP address is 192.168.1.126 in the initial VNC configuration screen, a browser could access it by opening http://192.168.1.126:5801, as shown in Figure 20-7. Using this VNC connection, you can complete the installation process from the comfort of your home office.

NOTE The VNC server can also be accessed using the `vncviewer` utility. Alternatively, on Windows systems you can use VNC Viewer from RealVNC.

For the deployment plan, you need to determine the installation method and prepare the prerequisite systems if necessary. Once you have done so, the Linux deployment plan is complete. Now the data necessary to complete the installation is all gathered in an organized, efficient, and measurable manner. File the deployment plan in a safe place once installation is complete. This information can be an invaluable help for other system administrators who may need to work on the systems at some point.

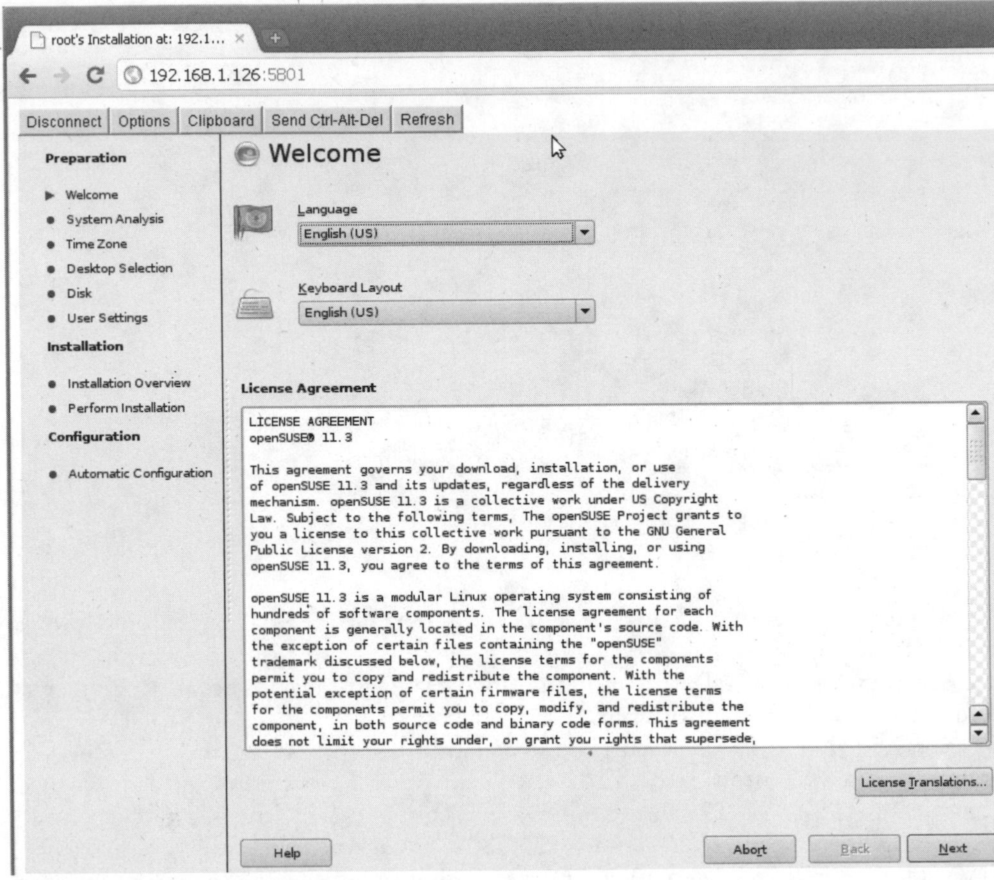

Figure 20-7 Completing the installation remotely in a browser

Installing Linux

When you're installing new systems, it is strongly recommended that you set up an isolated lab environment and install them there. This will allow you to collect a baseline and ensure that everything is working properly before releasing the systems into production.

As mentioned at the beginning of this chapter, there are simply too many different Linux distributions available to include them all on the CompTIA Linux+ exam or in this chapter. This chapter reviews how to install a CentOS workstation, and you practice installing a Linux system in Exercise 20-1.

Exercise 20-1: Installing a Linux System

In this exercise, we will first install the VirtualBox hypervisor and then CentOS Linux as a virtual machine. To follow along with the examples in the book, we will install CentOS 7 on top of VirtualBox 6.1.40.

VIDEO Please watch the Exercise 20-1 video for a demonstration on how to perform this task.

Complete the following steps:

1. On your computer, open a web browser and navigate to https://www.centos.org and select CentOS Linux > Download.
   a. Select x86_64 and choose a mirror that is near you for best download performance.
   b. Select CentOS-7-x86_64-Minimal-2009.iso.
   c. After the download completes, continue to step 2.
2. On your computer, open a web browser, navigate to https://www.virtualbox.org, and select Downloads on the left.
   a. Scroll down and select "VirtualBox older builds."
   b. Select VirtualBox 6.1 and then download VirtualBox 6.1.40 and initiate the installation.
   c. At the Welcome screen, click Next and then Next again at Custom Setup.
   d. Accept the defaults at the Options screen and click Yes for "Network Interfaces."
   e. Click Install at the "Ready to Install" screen, and then wait a few minutes for the software to install. If you're asked whether to install an Oracle device, choose Always Trust and then Install.
   f. Start VirtualBox by clicking Finish.
3. To install CentOS into the VirtualBox hypervisor, click New within VirtualBox.
   a. In the Name field, enter **CentOS-1**. The system should default to "Type: Linux" and "Version: Red Hat (64-bit)." If all checks out, click Next.

      If the version under "Type: Linux" shows as Red Hat (32-bit), you must select Cancel; then, shut down the host system, enter the *host* computer's BIOS, and enable virtualization.
   b. A memory size of 2048MB is fine. Click Next.
   c. Select "Create a virtual hard disk now" and click Create.
   d. VDI is fine for the "Hard disk file type" setting. Click Next.
   e. Choose "Dynamically allocated" and click Next.
   f. Set the hard drive size to 1.8TB and click Create.
   g. Click the down arrow next to Machine Tools and select Details. Then, click Display a few lines down and change Video Memory from 16MB to 128MB. Click OK.

4. Click the green Start button within VirtualBox.
    a. Under "Select start-up disk," click the yellow folder icon, and under Downloads, select CentOS-7-x86_64-Minimal-2009 (or similar), and click Open.
    b. Click Start.
    c. After the CentOS 7 window appears, click the up arrow to select Install CentOS 7 and press `Enter`; otherwise, the system will default to "Test this media."
    d. A couple of notification windows will appear at the top as the installation begins. Read the notices and then click the X to close them both.
    e. Press the right `Ctrl` key and `F` to enter full-screen mode. Read the notification box, choose not to show the message again, and click Switch.
5. The system is ready to install CentOS at this point. Click the blue Continue button in the lower-right area of the screen.
    a. Read the notification, select "Do not show this message again," and click Capture.
    b. Click the Continue button again.
    c. Click Date & Time if you need to change your time zone. Then click the blue Done button in the upper-left corner.
    d. Click Network & Host Name. Enable Ethernet by switching the OFF button to ON in the upper-right area of the screen. In the upper left, select the Done button.
    e. Click Installation Destination and then click Done.
    f. Click Begin Installation.
6. The installation will start. In the meantime, let's set up the users.
    a. Click Root Password and define a password for yourself. Click Done when this is complete. (You may have to click Done twice.)
    b. Click Create User and create **`student1`** with a password of **`student1`**.
    c. Click the option "Make this user administrator."
    d. Click Done twice.
7. Once the installation completes, click Reboot.
8. After the reboot process completes, log in as **`student1`**.
    a. Type the following command to install a graphical desktop:
    ```
    sudo yum groupinstall "GNOME Desktop" "Graphical Administration Tools"
    ```
    b. After you enter the password for student1, the installation will begin.
    c. After a moment, enter **y** to install the software. Return in about 10 minutes.
    d. Enter **y** to install the keys. Return in about five minutes.

e. Type the following command to convert the default runlevel to `graphics`:

```
sudo ln -sf /lib/systemd/system/runlevel5.target \
/etc/systemd/system/default.target
```

(A simpler method is to use `sudo systemctl set-default graphical.target`.)

f. Type **`sudo reboot`** to reboot.

9. Log in as **`student1`** to your new graphical desktop environment. Shortly, you will be asked to set up the language, keyboard, location, and so on. Select the appropriate options for you.

   Feel free to watch the "Getting Started" videos or close the window by clicking X in the upper-right corner.

10. Move the mouse to the upper right, hover over the speaker or battery icon, and click the "on/off" button in the applet. Select to install additional software updates and then select Power Off.

Congratulations! You now have a running CentOS Linux system. Installing other distributions, such as Debian, Ubuntu, Fedora, openSUSE, and others, follows a very similar process. Feel free to install these as additional virtual machines—as many as your hardware supports.

Regarding the VirtualBox hypervisor, practice with it a bit to maneuver to and from the guest and host computers. The main tip is that pressing the right `Ctrl` key will return you to the host machine. For the CentOS guest to take over, simply click into it with the mouse or enable "Mouse Pointer Integration" to switch systems by hovering the mouse pointer over them.

EXAM TIP Remote desktop tools available to Linux include VNC, XRDP, NX, and Spice.

Configuring the X Window System

Another great Linux topic to understand that is *not* part of the CompTIA Linux+ exam objectives is the X Window System, commonly called X11, or X for short. In practice, X configures itself pretty well as part of the installation process, so this section just explains how X works. In this part of the chapter, the following topics will be discussed:

- Configuring the X server
- Configuring the display manager
- Configuring accessibility

Configuring the X Server

Because the X server works directly with the video board and monitor, configuring it is critical. Use the correct settings; otherwise, the monitor could be damaged. Configuration can be done in two ways:

- By editing the X configuration file
- By using an X configuration utility

Let's look at the X configuration file first.

Editing the X Configuration File

Just like everything else in Linux, the X configuration is stored in a text file in the `/etc` directory.

NOTE A good friend of mine coined an appropriate axiom: "Everything in Linux is a file." All of your system and service configurations are stored in files. You even access hardware devices through a file.

Configuration settings are saved in `/etc/X11/xorg.conf`. Here is a portion of a sample `xorg.conf` file:

```
Section "InputDevice"
 Driver        "vmmouse"
 Identifier    "VMware Mouse"
 Option        "Buttons" "5"
 Option        "Device" "/dev/input/mice"
 Option        "Name" "ImPS/2 Generic Wheel Mouse"
 Option        "Protocol" "IMPS/2"
 Option        "Vendor" "Sysp"
 Option        "ZAxisMapping" "4 5"
 Option           "Emulate3Buttons"       "true"
EndSection

Section "Modes"
 Identifier    "Modes[0]"
 Modeline       "1024x768" 65.0 1024 1048 1184 1344 768 771 777 -hsync -vsync
 Modeline       "1024x768" 61.89 1024 1080 1184 1344 768 769 772
EndSection
```

NOTE Linux distributions that are based on `systemd` do not use the `xorg.conf` configuration file. Instead, the `X11` configuration is stored in a series of configuration files located in `/etc/X11/xorg.conf.d`.

Notice in this example that `xorg.conf` is broken into sections that begin with the `Section "<Name>"` directive and end with `EndSection`.

Let's look at commonly used sections in the `xorg.conf` file. First is the `"Files"` section. This section tells the X server where to find the files it needs to do its job, such as font files and input device files. Here is an abbreviated example of a `"Files"` section:

```
Section "Files"
 FontPath      "/usr/X11R6/lib/X11/fonts/misc:unscaled"
 FontPath      "/usr/X11R6/lib/X11/fonts/local"
 ...
 FontPath      "/usr/X11R6/lib/X11/fonts/xtest"
 InputDevices "/dev/input/mice"
EndSection
```

Next is the `"InputDevice"` section. This section configures the X server with the input devices it should use. You can use multiple `"InputDevice"` sections, such as one `"InputDevice"` section for the keyboard and another one for the mouse. Examples follow:

```
Section "InputDevice"
 Driver        "kbd"
 Identifier    "VMware Keyboard"
 Option        "Protocol" "Standard"
 Option        "XkbLayout" "us"
 Option        "XkbModel" "pc104"
 Option        "XkbRules" "xfree86"
EndSection

Section "InputDevice"
 Driver        "vmmouse"
 Identifier    "VMware Mouse"
 Option        "Buttons" "5"
 Option        "Device" "/dev/input/mice"
 Option        "Name" "ImPS/2 Generic Wheel Mouse"
 EndSection
```

The next section is the `"Modes"` section. The configuration file may have one or more of these sections. They define video modes the X server may use. Here is an example:

```
Section "Modes"
 Identifier    "Modes[0]"
 Modeline       "1024x768" 65.0 1024 1048 1184 1344 768 771 777 806 -hsync -vsync
 Modeline       "1024x768" 61.89 1024 1080 1184 1344 768 769 772 794
EndSection
```

The next section is the `"Screen"` section, which binds the video board to the monitor. Here is an example:

```
Section "Screen"
 Identifier    "Screen[0]"
   Device       "VMware SVGA"
   Monitor      "vmware"
   Subsection "Display"
       Depth        16
       Modes        "1024x768"
       ViewPort     0 0
   EndSubsection
```

```
    Subsection "Display"
        Depth       24
        Modes       "1024x768"
        ViewPort    0 0
    EndSubsection
EndSection
```

The last section we're going to look at is "ServerLayout". This section binds together one or more "Screen" sections and one or more "InputDevice" sections, as shown in the following example:

```
Section "ServerLayout"
 Identifier    "Layout[all]"
 Option        "Clone" "off"
 Option        "Xinerama" "off"
 Screen        "Screen[0]"
 InputDevice      "VMware Keyboard"        "CoreKeyboard"
 InputDevice "VMware Mouse"        "CorePointer"
EndSection
```

NOTE Wayland is the newer, improved version of X11, currently the default for Fedora Linux.

The DISPLAY variable

A keyboard, mouse, and monitor are defined as a DISPLAY. The first DISPLAY is defined as :0.0, in the form of *:display.screen*. For example, if you are running three screens from one computer, the left screen is defined as DISPLAY=:0.0, the middle screen as DISPLAY=:0.1, and the right screen as DISPLAY=:0.2.

If three separate systems are networked together, each with their own screen, keyboard, and mouse, the left screen is defined as DISPLAY=:0.0, the middle screen as DISPLAY=:1.0, and the right screen as DISPLAY=:2.0 because they are not sharing the keyboard and mouse as in the first example.

Using an X Configuration Utility

As with most Linux services, the X server configuration can be modified with a text editor such as vi. However, do not manually edit the file; instead, use the configuration utility under Settings | Displays, as shown in Figure 20-8. This applet allows you to configure screen resolution.

Enter Xorg -configure at the shell prompt to automatically detect all the hardware and create a configuration file named /root/xorg.conf.new. Then test the configuration before committing it by entering X -config /root/xorg.conf.new at the shell prompt. If everything looks correct, rename the file to /etc/X11/xorg.conf to start using the new configuration.

NOTE Use the xwininfo command to display information about open windows on your graphical desktop. The xdpyinfo command can be used to display the capabilities of an X server.

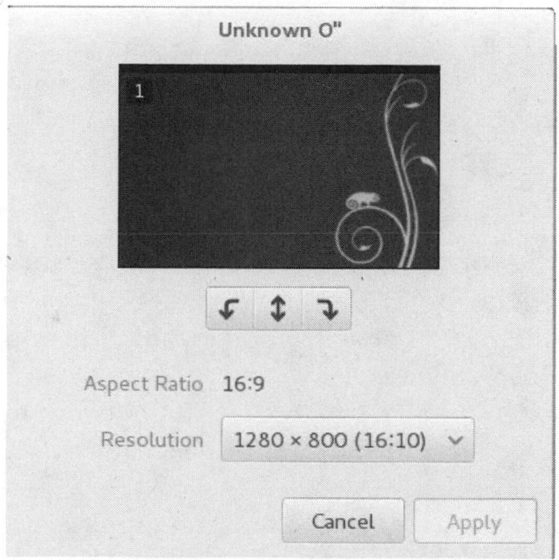

Figure 20-8 The Displays applet

Configuring the Display Manager

This section covers the following topics:

- Enabling and disabling the display manager
- Configuring the display manager
- Configuring remote access to the display manager

Enabling and Disabling the Display Manager

On many Linux distributions, the display manager is managed by the `xdm init` script located in the `/etc/init.d` directory. Other distributions may use the GNOME display manager (`gdm`) or the KDE display manager (`kdm`). To manually manage the display manager, enter `/etc/init.d/<init_script> stop` or `start` at the shell prompt.

EXAM TIP Graphical user interfaces (GUIs) available for Linux include Gnome, Unity, Cinnamon, MATE, and KDE.

Configuring the Display Manager

Configure the display manager by editing the appropriate configuration file:

- **xdm** `/etc/X11/xdm/xdm-config`
- **LightDM** The LightDM display manager is configured using several different files:
  - `/usr/share/lightdm/lightdm.conf.d`
  - `/etc/lightdm/lightdm.conf.d`
  - `/etc/lightdm/lightdm.conf`

- **kdm** The KDE display manager is actually based on `xdm` and usually uses the `xdm` configuration files. However, some distributions store your `kdm` settings in `/etc/kde/kdm` or `/etc/X11/kdm` instead. In this situation, you will use the `kdmrc` file in either of these directories to make most configuration changes.
- **gdm** `/etc/X11/gdm`

Configuring Remote Access to the Display Manager

Many organizations use thin-client systems for their end users. This implementation allows an organization to provide a full graphical desktop to all its users using a larger number of inexpensive thin clients.

To configure remote access to listen on the network for inbound connection requests from the X server software on the thin clients, run the `xhost +` command on the X server.

The thin clients simply need to `telnet` to the X server, enter their login and password, and run any X client. The X client will display to the thin clients.

NOTE Secure console redirection can be enabled via X11 with `ssh -X`, and running `ssh -L` can further enhance security with port forwarding.

Configuring Accessibility

To support a diverse workforce, administrators must learn to configure accessibility settings for physically, hearing, and visually impaired users. A few tools covered in this chapter include the following:

- Keyboard accessibility
- Mouse accessibility
- Screen readers

To access assistive technologies, search for and select Universal Access. The screen in Figure 20-9 is displayed.

Keyboard Accessibility

Universal Access allows you to configure the following:

- **StickyKeys** Allows users to lock keys such as `Ctrl` and `Shift` to complete keyboard tasks with just one finger that would normally require two or more fingers.
- **SlowKeys** This helps the user avoid sending accidental keystrokes.
- **BounceKeys and DelayKeys** Inserts a slight delay between keystrokes to prevent the keyboard from sending unintentional keystrokes.

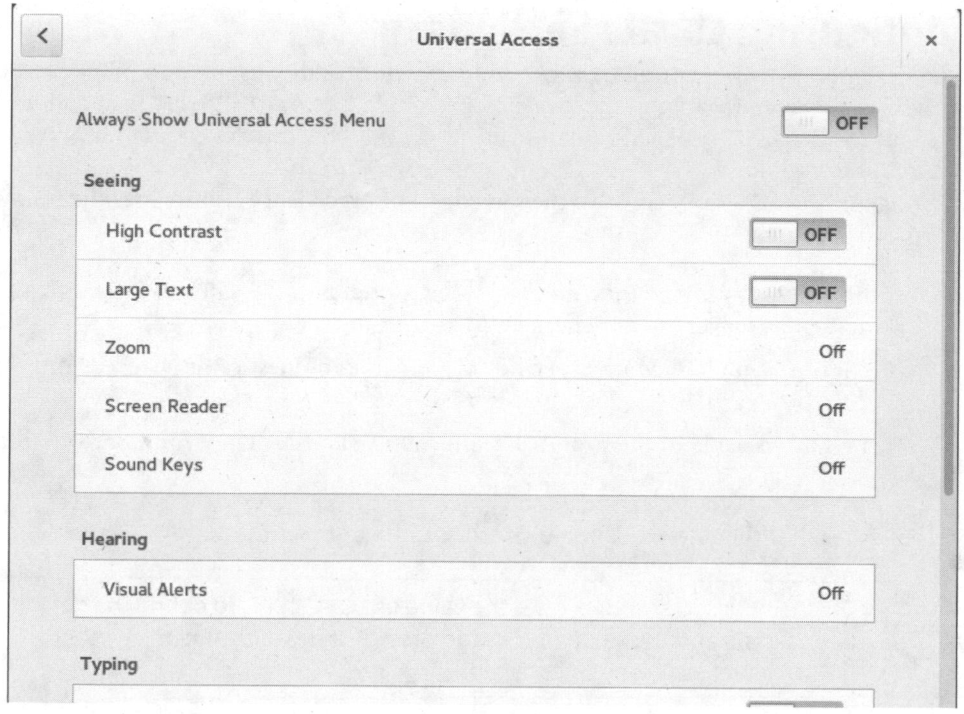

Figure 20-9 Enabling Assistive Technologies

For physically impaired users who are not able to use a traditional keyboard, Linux provides the option of using an onscreen keyboard, which allows users to use a mouse to select keys on a virtual keyboard. Commonly used onscreen keyboard applications include GOK (GNOME Onscreen Keyboard) and GTkeyboard.

Mouse Accessibility

In addition to keyboard accessibility, Assistive Technologies also provides mouse accessibility options for physically impaired users. For example, one can configure mouse options under Pointing and Clicking in the Universal Access panel. One such option is Simulated Secondary Click, which sends a double-click after holding the primary button down for a few seconds.

Screen Readers

One option available to visually impaired users is a screen reader, which "reads" the text displayed on the screen audibly for the user. The Orca application is probably the most commonly used screen reader. The other major screen reader is `emacspeak`.

Other accessibility utilities include screen magnifiers, braille devices, and high-contrast desktop themes.

Configuring Locale Settings

Administrators typically configure a system's *locale* during the installation process. They can also specify an encoding in the locale. For example, use en_US.UTF-8 to configure a default locale, or LC_, of U.S. English using UTF-8 character encoding (also known as *Unicode* encoding).

Not all of the LC_ variables have the same level of precedence. Linux uses the following rules:

- If the LC_ALL variable is defined, its value is used and the values assigned to all other LC_ variables are not checked.
- If LC_ALL is undefined, the specific LC_ variable in question is checked. If the specific LC_ variable has a value, it is used.
- If the LC_ variable in question has a null value, the LANG environment variable is used.

To define all of the LC_ variables to use the same value, set the LC_ALL variable.

NOTE Most distributions set the value of LC_CTYPE to define the default encoding and the value of LANG to provide a default value to all other LC_ variables.

To view the current locale settings, enter the /usr/bin/localectl or /usr/bin/locale command at the shell prompt. Here is an example:

```
openSUSE:~ # locale
LANG=POSIX
LC_CTYPE=en_US.UTF-8
LC_NUMERIC="POSIX"
LC_TELEPHONE="POSIX"
LC_MEASUREMENT="POSIX"
LC_IDENTIFICATION="POSIX"
LC_ALL=
```

In this example, only the LANG and LC_CTYPE variables are actually defined. The other LC_ variables are automatically populated with the value assigned to LANG.

Use the -a option with locale to generate a list of all available locales. Use the -m option with locale to view a list of available encodings. An example follows:

```
openSUSE:~ # locale -a
C
POSIX
aa_DJ
aa_DJ.utf8
aa_ER
aa_ER.utf8
....
ws1:~ # locale -m
ANSI_X3.110-1983
ANSI_X3.4-1968
ARMSCII-8
....
```

Be aware that changing encodings may result in issues viewing other files created using a different encoding. To convert from using one encoding to a new one, use the `iconv` command at the shell prompt. The syntax is as follows:

```
iconv -f <source_encoding> -t <destination_encoding> -o <output_filename> \
<input_filename>
```

NOTE Commonly used text encodings include iso8859 (also called Latin-9 encoding), which is designed for Western European languages; ASCII, which uses an English-based character-encoding scheme; and Unicode, which is designed to handle character sets from languages around the world.

Configuring Time Zone Settings

During the initial installation of your Linux system, you are prompted to specify the time zone the system is located in. To view the current time zone, enter `timedatectl` or `date` at the shell prompt, like so:

```
openSUSE:~ # date
Wed Feb  9 11:40:05 MST 2025
openSUSE:~ #
```

To change time zones on a Debian system, change the value of the `/etc/timezone` file. For other systems, modify the value of the `TZ` environment variable and then export it. This is useful in situations where you do not have the `root` password, or if you want to use a different time zone without changing the time zone used by other users. The syntax is `export TZ=<time_zone>`. A list of available time zones can be found in the `/usr/share/zoneinfo/` directory, as shown here:

```
openSUSE:~ # ls /usr/share/zoneinfo/
Africa       Canada   Factory   Iceland     MST7MDT   Portugal   Zulu
Antarctica   Cuba     GB-Eire   Iran        Mideast   Singapore  posix
Asia         EST      GMT+0     Jamaica     NZ-CHAT   UCT        right
Australia    Egypt    GMT0      Kwajalein   PRC       UTC
CET          Etc      HST       MET         Pacific   W-SU
ws1:~ #
```

This change is not persistent. Upon reboot, the system returns to the default time zone. To make the time zone persistent, add something similar to the following example to the `~<username>/.profile` file:

```
export TZ='America/Denver'
```

You can also change time zones by linking the `/etc/localtime` file with a zone file under `/usr/share/zoneinfo`. For example, to switch to the Mountain Standard Time zone, enter the following:

```
ws1:~ # ln -sf /usr/share/zoneinfo/MST /etc/localtime
```

Configuring Printing with CUPS

No matter what operating system you're using, one of the most important services it offers is the ability to send print jobs to a printer. Because of this, you need to be very familiar with Linux printing, even though it is *not* a requirement for the CompTIA Linux+ exam objectives. In this section, we cover the following topics related to printing in Linux:

- Configuring CUPS
- Using the Line Printer Daemon (`lpd`)

Let's begin by discussing how Linux printing works.

Configuring CUPS

All CUPS printers are defined in the `/etc/cups/printers.conf` file. Although you can manually edit this file, you really should use the CUPS web-based administration utility instead. You can either configure CUPS to service a locally attached printer (and optionally make it available to other network users) or connect to a CUPS printer over the network. For example, to configure CUPS to use a locally attached printer, do the following:

1. On your Linux system, start a web browser and navigate to http://localhost:631.
2. Select Administration.
3. Under Printers, select Add Printer.
4. When prompted, log in as the administrative user you created previously.
5. Select a locally attached printer type under Local Printers and then select Continue.

TIP You could also select a network printer on this screen. All broadcasting CUPS printers on other network hosts are listed under Discovered Network Printers. To send print jobs to one of these printers, just select it.

6. In the Name field, enter a name for the printer.
7. In the Description field, enter a description of the printer.
8. In the Location field, enter a location for the printer.
9. If you want to share the printer with other network users, mark Share This Printer.
10. Select Continue.
11. Select the printer manufacturer; then select Continue.
12. In the Model field, select your printer model; then select Add Printer.
13. Configure your default options for the printer, such as paper size, color model, media source, print quality, two-sided printing, and so on. When complete, select Set Default Options.

At this point, a page is displayed indicating your printer has been added. The current status of your printer is displayed.

From the Printer Status page, you can manage your CUPS printer. You can send a test page, stop the printer, kill a print job, modify the printer configuration, or delete the printer altogether.

At this point, you can send print jobs to the printer. If you're using a graphical X application, you can simply select File > Print, and then select the printer and click OK. You can also send print jobs from the command line to the printer. This is done using the `lp` command, which will send a specified file to the printer. The syntax is `lp -d <printer_name> <filename>`. For example, if I wanted to print the `myfiles` file in the current directory to the `HPLJ2` printer I just created, I would enter `lp -d HPLJ2 ./myfiles` at the shell prompt, as shown here:

```
openSUSE:~ # lp -d HPLJ2 ./myfiles
request id is HPLJ2-2 (1 file(s))
```

As you can see in this example, the job is created and assigned an ID (in this case, `HPLJ2-2`). The job is added to the print queue and sent to the printer. The `lp` utility includes a variety of options besides `-d` that you can use to create print jobs, including the following:

- **`-n x`** Prints *x* number of copies
- **`-m`** E-mails a confirmation message to the user's local user account when the job is finished printing
- **`-q x`** Sets the priority of the print job to *x*
- **`-o landscape`** Prints the file in landscape orientation instead of portrait
- **`-o sides=2`** Prints the file double-sided on a printer that supports duplexing

You can also configure other Linux systems to print to the CUPS printer. Simply configure a new printer, but specify that it listen for CUPS announcements. The CUPS printer you configured should be displayed within 30 seconds. After you select it, all print jobs sent to that printer will be redirected over the network connection to your CUPS printer.

In addition, if you've installed Samba on your system, your CUPS printers are automatically shared. You can connect to them from Windows workstations and submit print jobs. Now that's cool!

In addition to the CUPS web-based administration utility, you can also use a variety of command-line tools to configure CUPS. To view CUPS printer information, you can use the `lpstat` utility. One of the most useful options you can use with `lpstat` is `-t`. This will cause `lpstat` to display all information about all CUPS printers on the system, as this next example shows:

```
openSUSE:~ # lpstat -t
scheduler running
no system default destination
device for HPLJ2: parallel:/dev/lp0
HPLJ2 accepting requests since Fri 13 May 2025 10:57:13 AM MDT
printer HPLJ2 is idle.  enabled since Fri 13 May 2025 10:57:13 AM MDT
      Printer is now online.
```

This shows the default CUPS printer (`HPLJ2`), how it's connected (`/dev/lp0`), the print job currently being processed (if any), and a list of pending print jobs.

To cancel a pending print job, you can use the `cancel` command. The syntax is `cancel <job_ID>`. For example, suppose I sent a huge print job (a Linux user manual from `/usr/share/doc/manual/`) and it was assigned a print ID of `HPLJ2-4`. While printing, I decided that this was a real waste of paper. I could kill the job and remove it from the print queue by entering `cancel HPLJ2-4` at the shell prompt. This can also be done from within the CUPS web-based administration utility. Just go to the Jobs tab and select Show Active Jobs. Locate the job that needs to be canceled and select Cancel Job.

If you have more than one CUPS printer connected, you can use the `lpoptions -d <printer>` command to specify the default printer. For example, to set the `HPLJ5` printer as the default, I would enter `lpoptions -d HPLJ5`. This sets the default printer for all users on the system. Individual users can override this setting, however, by creating a file named `.lpoptions` in their home directory and adding the following directive:

```
default <printer_name>
```

If you want to view your printer's configuration settings, you can enter `lpoptions -l` at the shell prompt.

In addition to the `lpoptions` command, you can also use the `cupsaccept <printer_name>` or `cupsreject <printer_name>` command to enable or disable a printer's print queue. For example, I could enter `cupsreject HPLJ2` at the shell prompt to disable the printer's print queue, as shown in this example:

```
openSUSE:~ # cupsreject HPLJ2
openSUSE:~ # lpstat is -t
scheduler is running
system default destination: HPLJ2
device for HPLJ2: parallel:/dev/lp0
HPLJ2 not accepting requests since Fri 13 May 2025 11:03:07 AM MDT -
      Rejecting Jobs
printer HPLJ2 is idle.  Enabled since Fri 13 May 2025 11:03:07 AM MDT
      Rejecting Jobs
```

The printer itself will continue processing queued print jobs, but `cupsd` will not allow any new jobs to enter the queue. The `cupsdisable` command also includes the `-hold` option, which stops printing after the current job is complete. To enable the queue again, I would enter `cupsaccept HPLJ2` at the shell prompt.

To disable the printer itself, not the queue, I could enter `cupsdisable HPLJ2` at the shell prompt, as this example shows:

```
openSUSE:~ # cupsdisable HPLJ2
openSUSE:~ # lpstat is -t
scheduler is running
system default destination: HPLJ2
device for HPLJ2: parallel:/dev/lp0
HPLJ2 accepting requests since Fri 13 May 2025 11:15:28 AM MDT
printer HPLJ2 disabled since Fri 13 May 2025 11:15:28 AM MDT -
     Paused
```

Task	lpd Command-Line Utility
Print a document	lpr -P <printer_name> <filename>
View printer status	lpc status
View pending print jobs	lpq
Delete a pending print job from the queue	lprm <job_number>

Table 20-1 lpd Commands

The print queue will continue to accept jobs, but none of them will be printed until I enter `cupsenable HPLJ2` at the shell prompt. The `cupsenable` command also includes the `--release` option to release pending jobs for printing.

By far, CUPS is the preferred printing system for modern Linux distributions. Years ago, the preferred printing system was the Line Printer Daemon (`lpd`). Most of the `lpd` commands have functionality similar to that offered by CUPS, as shown in Table 20-1.

As an interesting side note, these commands will also work with `cupsd`. For example, enter `lpc status` at the shell prompt and it will return the status of the CUPS printers.

Configuring E-mail

Although configuring e-mail is an important task as a Linux administrator, it is *not* a requirement for the CompTIA Linux+ exam objectives. Let's first look at reading messages stored in your local mail transfer agent (MTA). When you log in to a shell session, you will receive a notification if there are mail messages waiting for you. You can read messages for local users from the local MTA directly from the command line using the `mail` command at the shell prompt. When you do, a list of messages is displayed.

NOTE Some services running on Linux are configured to send notification messages to the `root` user.

These messages are stored in the user's mail queue, which is located in `/var/spool/mail/`. The mail utility reads a user's messages from the user's queue file. Because the mail utility is on the same system where the queue resides, there is no need to configure POP3 or IMAP support. Enter the `mail` commands shown in Table 20-2 at the `?` prompt.

mail Command	Description
d	Delete a message by entering `d <message_number>` at the ? prompt.
n	Enter `n` to display the next message in the queue.
r	Reply to all recipients by entering `r <message_number>` at the ? prompt.
m	Send a new message by entering `m <recipient>` at the ? prompt.
q	Enter `q` to quit mail.

Table 20-2 Mail Commands

To send a message, enter mail <recipient_address> at the shell prompt. Then enter a subject line and the text of the message. Press Ctrl-D when done to actually send the message. Once done, the message is delivered to the other user's mail queue by the local MTA.

To view a list of unread messages in your mail queue, you can enter mailq at the shell prompt.

You can also configure aliases for the MTA running on a Linux system. Mail aliases redirect mail addressed to one user to another user's account. Use the /etc/aliases file to configure aliases. This file defines one alias per line. The alias you define must point to an existing e-mail address. The syntax for this file follows:

```
<alias>:  <list of real e-mail addresses, separated by commas>
```

For example, the following two aliases must be present in this file on most Linux distributions:

```
postmaster:  root
mailer-daemon:     postmaster
```

These aliases cause any e-mail messages sent to the postmaster to be automatically redirected to the root user. Likewise, any e-mail messages sent to mailer-daemon will be redirected to postmaster (which will then be redirected to root). Depending on your distribution, you will probably find that many aliases are defined for you by default. Here is an example:

```
# General redirections for pseudo accounts in /etc/passwd.
administrator:      root
daemon:             root
lp:           root
news:         root
gnats:        root
nobody:       root
# "bin" used to be in /etc/passwd
bin:          root
```

Of course, you can enter your own custom aliases if needed. Just open the /etc/aliases file in a text editor and add the appropriate aliases, one per line. When done configuring aliases, you must run the newaliases command at the shell prompt as root to enable them.

Also use the ~/.forward file to configure forwarding. Linux MTAs check for the existence of this file to configure forwarding of messages. Now e-mail will automatically be forwarded to the e-mail address in this file. To stop forwarding, delete this file.

NOTE The MTA will treat the addresses you enter in this file as an alias. This causes all e-mail to be forwarded to the forwarding e-mail address. Messages will *not* be delivered to the original user's mailbox.

Configuring SQL Databases

Another great Linux topic to understand that's *not* included in the CompTIA Linux+ exam objectives is how to configure SQL databases. A *database* is a collection of information organized so that data can be quickly selected and retrieved based on a search query created.

Database services run on a client/server model. Two database services are commonly implemented on Linux:

- MySQL
- PostgreSQL

By installing one of these database services, you install the software needed to run, operate, and manage the database using SQL (Structured Query Language), which is a standard language for accessing and manipulating databases.

Both of these database services are relational databases, which are hierarchical in nature. Relational databases are specialized to organize and store huge amounts of data. They are also designed to be highly scalable, allowing them to grow over time.

A relational database is organized using fields, records, and tables. A *field* is a single piece of information. A *record* is one complete set of fields, and a *table* is a collection of records. Each table is identified by a name, such as Customers. Each table contains records (each one a single row) that contain one or more fields, which in turn contain the actual database data. For example, suppose you defined a table called Customers and created the following three records:

```
Last      First     Address                City      State     Zip
Tracy     Leah      1234 W. Longfellow     Bone      Idaho     83401
Morgan    Ken       3456 W. 100 S.         Rigby     Idaho     83442
```

Using the SQL language, you could create queries that select and retrieve specific data from the database. For example, suppose you were to compose the following query:

```
SELECT Last FROM Customers
```

The database would return the following data:

```
Last
Tracy
Morgan
```

You can use the following commands to manage data in an SQL database:

- **`SELECT`** Retrieves information from a table
- **`UPDATE`** Modifies information in a table
- **`DELETE`** Removes information from a table
- **`INSERT INTO`** Adds new data to a table
- **`CREATE TABLE`** Creates a new table
- **`ALTER TABLE`** Modifies an existing table
- **`DROP TABLE`** Deletes an existing table

A key feature of relational databases is the fact that you can create *relationships* between tables, which allows you to create interrelated data sets.

In order to manage data on the MySQL server, you must connect to it using some type of SQL client. You can choose from a plethora of different clients. If you can manipulate SQL Server data with this utility, all the other clients will be a piece of cake for you to use.

The command-line MySQL client is run by entering `mysql` at the shell prompt. The syntax is `mysql -h <hostname> -u <username> -p`. For example, to connect to the MySQL service running on the local Linux system as `root`, you would enter the following command:

```
openSUSE:/usr/bin # mysql -h localhost -u root -p
Enter password:
Welcome to the MySQL monitor.  Commands end with ; or \g.
Your MySQL connection id is 7
Server version: 5.6.12 openSUSE package
Copyright (c) 2000, 2013, Oracle and/or its affiliates. All rights reserved.
Oracle is a registered trademark of Oracle Corporation and/or its
affiliates. Other names may be trademarks of their respective owners.
Type 'help;' or '\h' for help. Type '\c' to clear the current input statement.
mysql>
```

Configuring Storage

This section contains details on storage that are interesting to learn but are not requirements of the CompTIA Linux+ exam objectives. The following topics are discussed:

- GUID Partition Table (GPT) components
- Integrated Drive Electronics (IDE) drives
- Locating a device

GUID Partition Table Components

Let's look at the various sections of a disk device using GPT partitioning (see Figure 20-10).

Protective MBR (LBA 0)

The protective MBR is used to prevent MBR disk utilities from writing over the GPT partition. The MBR's bootloader is used so BIOS-based systems can benefit from GPT. GPT's MBR is modified to recognize GPT partitions.

GPT Header (LBA 1)

The GPT header contains information regarding the structure of the partition table.

Partition Table Entries (LBA 2 to 33)

This section contains partition table entries for up to 128 logical partitions. Table 20-3 illustrates the information stored for each partition.

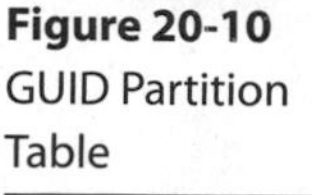

Figure 20-10 GUID Partition Table

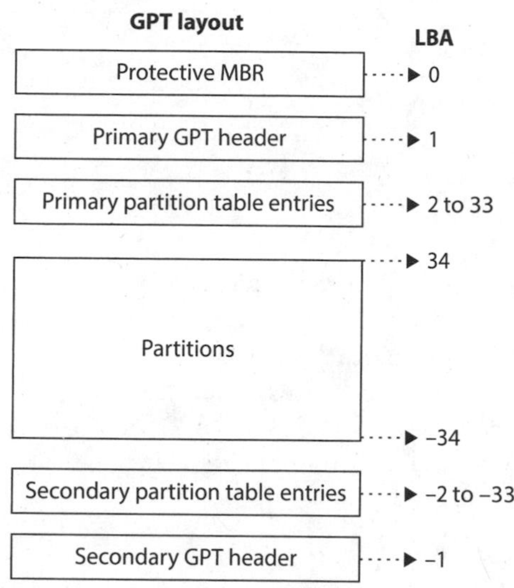

Table Entry	Definition
Partition type (GUID)	The entry indicates the type of partition. This replaces the partition code in MBR. Here are some examples: Boot: `83BD6B9D-7F41-11DC-BE0B-001560B84F0F` Home: `933AC7E1-2EB4-4F13-B844-0E14E2AEF915` Swap: `0657FD6D-A4AB-43C4-84E5-0933C84B4F4F` LVM: `E6D6D379-F507-44C2-A23C-238F2A3DF928` LUKS: `CA7D7CCB-63ED-4C53-861C-1742536059CC`
Unique GUID	Unique partition identifier (`ls -l /dev/disk/by-partuuid`).
Start LBA	Partition's starting block address.
End LBA	Partition's ending block address.
Attributes	A 64-bit number used to define partition attributes.
Partition name	Human-readable partition name (`ls -l /dev/disk/by-partlabel`).

Table 20-3 Partition Table Entries

Partitions (LBA 34 to –34) This section defines user-defined partitions.

Secondary (Backup) Partition Table Entries (LBA –33 to –2)

This is a backup to the partition table entries found in LBA 2 to 33.

Secondary (Backup) GPT Header (LBA 1)

This is a backup to the header entry found in LBA 1.

Table 20-4 IDE Drive Nomenclature

	Primary Disk	Secondary Disk
Primary channel	hda	hdb
Secondary channel	hdc	hdd

IDE Drives

An IDE interface does not contain device controllers. The controller for an IDE drive is built into the disk device. The interface consists of a primary and a secondary channel (see Table 20-4). Each channel supports two disk devices (primary and secondary). Within a specific channel, the primary device controls communications on the channel.

The `/dev/hda` is the name of the disk device attached to the IDE primary channel and is the primary disk device on the channel.

Locating a Device

When the system boots, it classifies a device, provides it a device name, and stores the device specifications. Next the operating system must provide a means of accessing a device. Let's take a brief look at that process.

Major and Minor Numbers

On boot, the Linux kernel detects and initializes devices by scanning each system bus. When the kernel discovers a device, it determines the device class and assigns the device a major and a minor number. The device class is used to look up the driver for the device. The Linux Assigned Name and Number Authority (LANANA) maintains a list of device classes.

Once the device class is determined, the kernel creates a device directory in `/sys` and stores the properties of the device in that directory. After boot, the kernel continuously scans system buses for device additions, changes, or removals.

NOTE `/sys` is the mount point for the `sysfs` pseudo-filesystem. `sysfs` provides device information to applications running in the system's user space.

Notice the output in Figure 20-11. Where the file size should be, you see two numbers (for example, `8, 0`). The first number is the major number, and the second number is the minor number. Using this information, you can see when you access device `sdb1` (Figure 20-11, line 6).The minor number of a disk device informs the device driver which logical device to communicate with.

The total number of partitions on a disk device is dependent on the drive type. IDE devices may have up to 63 partitions; SCSI devices may have up to 15 partitions.

Minor numbers for a device class are sequential. The first minor number of a SCSI disk device represents the entire drive. Minor numbers `0-15` are reserved for device `sda`, and the first minor number for device `sdb` is `16`.

Figure 20-11 Major and minor numbers

```
l# ls -l /dev/sd[ab]*

brw-rw----. 1 root disk 8,  0 Mar 31 09:19 /dev/sda

brw-rw----. 1 root disk 8, 16 Mar 31 09:19 /dev/sdb
brw-rw----. 1 root disk 8, 17 Mar 31 09:19 /dev/sdb1
brw-rw----. 1 root disk 8, 18 Mar 31 09:19 /dev/sdb2
brw-rw----. 1 root disk 8, 19 Mar 31 09:19 /dev/sdb3
brw-rw----. 1 root disk 8, 20 Mar 31 09:19 /dev/sdb4
brw-rw----. 1 root disk 8, 21 Mar 31 09:19 /dev/sdb5
brw-rw----. 1 root disk 8, 22 Mar 31 09:19 /dev/sdb6
brw-rw----. 1 root disk 8, 23 Mar 31 09:19 /dev/sdb7
brw-rw----. 1 root disk 8, 24 Mar 31 09:19 /dev/sdb8
```

`sdb`'s range of minor numbers is `16-31`. The first minor number of the sequence, `16`, is the logical unit number for the entire device (`sdb`). The second minor number (`17`) is the logical unit number for the first partition, or `sdb1`.

Device Tree Management with `udev`

It is possible that devices scanned during one boot process are not scanned in the same order in another boot process. Minor numbers influence the device name and are allocated sequentially, so this would cause a device's name to change. Although this does not affect the kernel's ability to access a device, an application trying to access a device by name would have a problem. This problem is solved by creating a path to a device in the systems device tree (`/dev`).

NOTE `/dev/disk/by-partlabel` and `/dev/disk/by-partuuid` are provided in addition to `/dev/disk/by-id`, `/dev/disk/by-uuid`, and `/dev/disk/by-path` as methods of accessing a disk device.

When the kernel discovers the addition, modification, or removal of a device on a system bus, it generates a `uevent`. The `uevent` informs `udev` of the addition, removal, or change. `udev` uses the class of the device, information stored in `/sys`, and `udev` rules to create, remove, or modify the system device tree, `/dev`.

`udev` rules define how a specific device may be added or deleted and any actions that should occur before or after the device is added, modified, or removed. This makes device configuration persistent.

`udev` rules are found in `/lib/udev/rules.d` or `/etc/udev/rules.d`. The rules found in `/lib/udev/rules.d` are system defaults, and those found in `/etc/udev/rules.d` are custom rules. Rules in `/etc/udev/rules.d` override the rules in `/lib/udev/rules.d`.

When enumerating a disk device, `udev` will create an entry in the following files:`/dev/disk/by-path, /dev/disk/by-id, /dev/disk/by-uuid, /dev/disk/by-partlabel (uefi)`, and`/dev/disk/by-partuuid (uefi)`.

`/dev/disk/by-path` The entries in `/dev/disk/by-path`, shown in Figure 20-12, provide a symbolic link between the physical path to the device and device name.

The path to a device is notated as `host:bus:target:lun` and detailed in Table 20-5.

```
# ls -l /dev/disk/by-path | sort -k9 | grep sdb
lrwxrwxrwx. 1 root root 10 Apr  4 16:09 pci-0000:00:0d.0-ata-1.0-part1 -> ../../sdb1
lrwxrwxrwx. 1 root root 10 Apr  4 16:09 pci-0000:00:0d.0-ata-1.0-part2 -> ../../sdb2
lrwxrwxrwx. 1 root root 10 Apr  4 16:09 pci-0000:00:0d.0-ata-1.0-part3 -> ../../sdb3
lrwxrwxrwx. 1 root root 10 Apr  4 16:09 pci-0000:00:0d.0-ata-1.0-part4 -> ../../sdb4
lrwxrwxrwx. 1 root root 10 Apr  4 16:09 pci-0000:00:0d.0-ata-1.0-part5 -> ../../sdb5
lrwxrwxrwx. 1 root root 10 Apr  4 16:09 pci-0000:00:0d.0-ata-1.0-part6 -> ../../sdb6
lrwxrwxrwx. 1 root root 10 Apr  4 16:09 pci-0000:00:0d.0-ata-1.0-part7 -> ../../sdb7
lrwxrwxrwx. 1 root root 10 Apr  4 16:09 pci-0000:00:0d.0-ata-1.0-part8 -> ../../sdb8
lrwxrwxrwx. 1 root root  9 Apr  4 16:09 pci-0000:00:0d.0-ata-1.0 -> ../../sdb
```

Figure 20-12 `/dev/disk/by-path`

Table 20-5 Device Path Notation

Element	Definition
`host`	Adapter (SCSI controller)
`bus`	SCSI bus address
`target`	Storage device
`lun`	Logical unit number (partition)

`/dev/disk/by-id` Each SCSI device is assigned a unique identifier called a World Wide Identifier (`WWID`) when the device is manufactured. The `/dev/disk/by-id` directory provides a symbolic link between the `WWID` of the device and the device name (see Figure 20-13). This allows applications to access a device even if the device path has changed.

The serial numbers in Figure 20-13 were created by VirtualBox.

`/dev/disk/by-uuid` A universally unique identifier (`UUID`) is a unique identification number applied to filesystem and system devices. A `UUID` number is assigned to each filesystem when it is created.

NOTE `UUID` numbers may also be applied to system devices such as network cards.

```
# ls -l /dev/disk/by-id | sort -k9 | grep sdb*
lrwxrwxrwx. 1 root root  9 Apr  4 16:09 ata-VBOX_HARDDISK_VB4c12c352-8137b90e -> ../../sdc
lrwxrwxrwx. 1 root root 10 Apr  4 16:09 ata-VBOX_HARDDISK_VBeb78d713-ad74ebc8-part1 -> ../../sdb1
lrwxrwxrwx. 1 root root 10 Apr  4 16:09 ata-VBOX_HARDDISK_VBeb78d713-ad74ebc8-part2 -> ../../sdb2
lrwxrwxrwx. 1 root root 10 Apr  4 16:09 ata-VBOX_HARDDISK_VBeb78d713-ad74ebc8-part3 -> ../../sdb3
lrwxrwxrwx. 1 root root 10 Apr  4 16:09 ata-VBOX_HARDDISK_VBeb78d713-ad74ebc8-part4 -> ../../sdb4
lrwxrwxrwx. 1 root root 10 Apr  4 16:09 ata-VBOX_HARDDISK_VBeb78d713-ad74ebc8-part5 -> ../../sdb5
lrwxrwxrwx. 1 root root 10 Apr  4 16:09 ata-VBOX_HARDDISK_VBeb78d713-ad74ebc8-part6 -> ../../sdb6
lrwxrwxrwx. 1 root root 10 Apr  4 16:09 ata-VBOX_HARDDISK_VBeb78d713-ad74ebc8-part7 -> ../../sdb7
lrwxrwxrwx. 1 root root 10 Apr  4 16:09 ata-VBOX_HARDDISK_VBeb78d713-ad74ebc8-part8 -> ../../sdb8
lrwxrwxrwx. 1 root root  9 Apr  4 16:09 ata-VBOX_HARDDISK_VBeb78d713-ad74ebc8 -> ../../sdb
lrwxrwxrwx. 1 root root 10 Apr  4 16:09 lvm-pv-uuid-qokTSF-xqlc-tWTd-8eXW-r9LG-M9ey-VUZ4DM -> ../../sdb3
lrwxrwxrwx. 1 root root 10 Apr  4 16:09 lvm-pv-uuid-X61Dh2-CukT-trKd-dfHM-Ow4a-9dE3-cC2ggV -> ../../sdb2
```

Figure 20-13 `/dev/disk/by-id` mappings to disk drives

```
#ls -l /dev/disk/by-uuid | sort -k9n | grep sdb

lrwxrwxrwx. 1 root root 10 Apr  9 06:40 a05ba7d2-1136-42e7-ad26-95daf6087a18 -> ../../sdb1
lrwxrwxrwx. 1 root root 10 Apr  9 06:40 ce81200d-04a3-4a45-b6f4-9eebc8ab97dd -> ../../sdb7
lrwxrwxrwx. 1 root root 10 Apr  9 06:40 e7d2409a-29c1-4673-a365-54ada40980ac -> ../../sdb5
lrwxrwxrwx. 1 root root 10 Apr  9 06:40 3bfcbdf2-2708-4009-8d87-fb2bb7fbd76c -> ../../sdb6
lrwxrwxrwx. 1 root root 10 Apr  9 06:40 88e1fb57-b587-4137-a5e8-3ff64d5c3592 -> ../../sdb8

# ls -l /dev/disk/by-uuid | sort -k9n | grep dm
ls: cannot access ls: No such file or directory
lrwxrwxrwx. 1 root root 10 Apr  9 06:40 b1645c67-b27a-43ef-bbf1-ec415d92d10c -> ../../dm-0
lrwxrwxrwx. 1 root root 10 Apr  9 06:40 e593e336-16cd-403c-bbe1-b0a2b0312546 -> ../../dm-1
```

Figure 20-14 `dev/disk/by/uuid` mappings to storage media

In Figure 20-14, you can see that `/dev/disk/by-uuid` contains symbolic links between a filesystem's `UUID` and the device name.

NOTE `dm-0` and `dm-1` in Figure 20-14 are LVM logical volumes. `dm` refers to device mapper.

`/dev/disk/by-partlabel` This file is only found using GPT partitioning. This directory contains files that are a symbolic link between the device partition label and the device.

`/dev/disk/by-partuuid` This file is only found using GPT partitioning. Each partition is assigned a `UUID`. This directory contains files that are a symbolic link between the partition's `UUID` and the device.

`/dev/mapper` `/dev/mapper` is a method of dividing a physical block device into virtual block devices. The commands `ls -lha /dev/mapper` and `dmsetup ls` will display a list of logical volume devices.

Recommended Swap Space Sizing

Each distribution may have its own swap space allocation suggestions. Table 20-6 is Red Hat's suggested swap space for systems that do not hibernate.

Based on the distribution's recommendations, it may be more efficient to divide swap space across multiple drives and set swap priorities so swap partitions act as a RAID stripe.

Table 20-6 Suggested Swap Space

RAM	Recommended Swap Size
< 2GB	Two times RAM
>2GB–8GB	Equal to RAM
>8GB–64GB	Minimum 4GB
>64B	Minimum 4GB

Restore a Damaged Superblock

One very useful feature of `e2fsck` is its ability to restore a damaged superblock on `ext2/3/4` filesystems. The superblock is the block at the beginning of the partition that contains information about the structure of the filesystem. Also, most Linux filesystems keep backup copies of the superblock at various locations in the partition.

If the superblock gets corrupted, you can restore it using one of these backup copies. The syntax is `e2fsck -f -b backup_superblock device`. The `-f` option tells `e2fsck` to force a check, even if the filesystem seems to be clean. The `-b` option tells `e2fsck` which copy of the superblock it should use.

If you cannot remember the location of the backup superblocks, execute the command `mkfs -n <device>`.

Kick Off Users from a Busy Filesystem

Sometimes users can get in the way of a proper shutdown. If users will not log out when the certified technician arrives to repair hardware, force them to log out using the `fuser` command.

Run either of the commands `fuser -k /<filesystem_name>` or `fuser -k -9 /<filesystem_name>`. For users that are in their home directory, run `fuser -k /home`. This will kill all of the user's jobs so that you can conduct a graceful shutdown. *Warning: this can harm user data.*

Chapter Review

This chapter covered Linux topics that are not part of the CompTIA Linux+ exam objectives but can be helpful to you as an administrator to set up servers and workstations. You learned how to perform a Linux installation and how to set up a graphical environment for users.

Next you learned how to configure a Linux system to connect and send print jobs to a printer, send and receive e-mails, and access storage devices like hard drives and thumb drives.

Some key points from this chapter include the following:

- If seeking employment in the United States, the most widely used enterprise-class version of Linux used is Red Hat Enterprise Linux, with SUSE Linux Enterprise Server being next.
- Linux installations support configurations for servers and workstations.
- The X Window and Wayland display variable is `DISPLAY`.
- Linux provides accessibility tools for users with physical impairments.
- To add a printer, use the Settings tool provided by the Linux vendor or visit the website http://localhost:631 to set up a CUPS printer.
- Linux can be set up as an e-mail server or e-mail client.
- Linux can be set up as an SQL server using `mysql`, `postgresql`, and others.
- Storage can be set up for hard drives, thumb drives, or SD cards.

Questions

1. When conducting a needs assessment prior to a Linux installation, what questions should you ask? (Choose two.)
   - **A.** What problem will this installation fix?
   - **B.** Which distribution should I use?
   - **C.** Where can I get the best price on a new server?
   - **D.** Who will be using the new system?
2. Which of the following is a properly stated goal in a needs assessment?
   - **A.** Mike's boss wants a new server, so we're going to install it.
   - **B.** We're going to install Linux on everyone's desktop.
   - **C.** We need a new Linux server.
   - **D.** The new Linux system will provide a network database to increase the documentation team's productivity by an anticipated 20 percent.
3. Suppose Karen from customer service approaches you and asks for a new Linux server for her team. Who else should you talk to as a part of your needs assessment? (Choose two.)
   - **A.** Karen's boss
   - **B.** Karen's coworkers
   - **C.** The technical support supervisor
   - **D.** Your hardware vendor
4. You're responsible for implementing five new Linux servers in your organization's technical support department. The technical support supervisor has asked that four additional servers be added to the project. Due to time constraints, the supervisor won't allow you to adjust the original schedule. Which of the following is the most appropriate response?
   - **A.** Ignore the request.
   - **B.** Inform the supervisor that additional resources will have to be added to the project.
   - **C.** Resign in protest.
   - **D.** Cheerfully agree to the request and then miss the deadline.
5. You're installing new Linux systems that will be used by software engineers to develop advanced computer-aided design applications. Which distributions would be the best choices for this deployment? (Choose two.)
   - **A.** Red Hat Enterprise Linux
   - **B.** Red Hat Enterprise Desktop
   - **C.** Red Hat Enterprise Linux Workstation
   - **D.** SUSE Linux Enterprise Server
   - **E.** SUSE Linux Enterprise Desktop

6. You're installing a new Linux system that will be used by an administrative assistant to type documents, create presentations, and manage e-mail. Which distributions would be the best choices for this deployment? (Choose two.)
   - **A.** Red Hat Enterprise Linux
   - **B.** Red Hat Enterprise Desktop
   - **C.** Red Hat Enterprise Linux Workstation
   - **D.** SUSE Linux Enterprise Server
   - **E.** SUSE Linux Enterprise Desktop
7. You're installing a new Linux server that will be used to host mission-critical database applications. This server will be heavily utilized by a large number of users every day. Which distributions would be the best choices for this deployment? (Choose two.)
   - **A.** Red Hat Enterprise Linux
   - **B.** Red Hat Client
   - **C.** Red Hat Enterprise Linux Workstation
   - **D.** SUSE Linux Enterprise Server
   - **E.** SUSE Linux Enterprise Desktop
8. You're planning to install Linux on a system that you've built out of spare parts. Several components in the system aren't listed on your distribution's HCL. This system will be used by your team's administrative assistant to manage employee schedules, send and receive e-mail, and track employee hours. What should you do?
   - **A.** Install the distribution anyway and hope for the best.
   - **B.** Install the distribution and then install the latest product updates.
   - **C.** Replace the incompatible parts with supported hardware.
   - **D.** Spend three days scouring the Internet looking for drivers.
9. You're planning to install Fedora on a system that uses a 32-bit CPU. Which distribution architecture should you download?
   - **A.** `IA-64`
   - **B.** `x86-Celeron`
   - **C.** `x86-64`
   - **D.** `x86`
10. You're planning to install Fedora on a system that uses a 64-bit AMD multicore CPU. Which distribution architecture should you download?
    - **A.** `IA-64`
    - **B.** `x86-AMD`
    - **C.** `x86-64`
    - **D.** `x86`

11. You're installing a new Linux system. This system will be used by a civil engineer to model the behavior of buildings and bridges during an earthquake. This system must run as fast as possible. It must protect the integrity of the data if the system goes down unexpectedly. If it does go down, the system needs to be backed up and running as quickly as possible. Which filesystem would be the best choice?

    A. `VFAT`

    B. `FAT32`

    C. `ext4`

    D. `ext3`

12. Which partition is used for virtual memory by a Linux system?

    A. `pagefile`

    B. `swap`

    C. `/swap`

    D. `/boot`

13. If your system has 1GB of RAM installed, how big should your swap partition be?

    A. 256MB

    B. 1GB

    C. 512GB

    D. Depends on what the system will be used for

14. Which of the following directories should have their own partition? (Choose three.)

    A. `/bin`

    B. `/boot`

    C. `/etc`

    D. `/usr`

    E. `/home`

    F. `/root`

    G. `/dev`

15. You're installing a new Linux server. This system will function as an e-mail server for your organization. What ports should you open on its host firewall? (Choose three.)

    A. 110

    B. 80

    C. 25

    D. 143

    E. 443

16. You need to install Linux on a workstation. The hard drive has been wiped and is ready for the new operating system. You insert your Linux installation DVD in the optical drive and boot the system. Instead of the installation routine starting, the screen displays an error message indicating that an operating system couldn't be found. What's the most likely cause of the problem?
    A. Your Linux DVD is damaged.
    B. The hard drive is failing and needs to be replaced.
    C. The DVD drive is malfunctioning.
    D. The boot device order is set incorrectly in the BIOS.
17. Your Linux system uses two SATA hard disk drives. Which of the following refers to the second SATA drive in the system?
    A. `/dev/sda`
    B. `/dev/sdc`
    C. `/dev/sdb`
    D. `/dev/sdd`
18. Your Linux system uses a single SATA hard disk drive. Which of the following refers to the first partition on the drive?
    A. `/dev/sda1`
    B. `/dev/sdb1`
    C. `/dev/sda2`
    D. `/dev/pdb2`
19. Your Linux system uses a single SATA hard disk drive. Which of the following refers to the second partition on the drive?
    A. `/dev/sda1`
    B. `/dev/hdb1`
    C. `/dev/sda2`
    D. `/dev/hdb2`
20. Your Linux system uses two SCSI hard disk drives. The first drive is assigned SCSI ID 0; the second drive is assigned SCSI ID 1. Which of the following refers to the first partition on the second SCSI drive in the system?
    A. `/dev/sda1`
    B. `/dev/sdc1`
    C. `/dev/sdb1`
    D. `/dev/sdd1`

21. Which locale environment variable configures your default character encoding?
    A. `LC_NUMERIC`
    B. `LC_CTYPE`
    C. `LC_MEASUREMENT`
    D. `LC_CHAR`
22. Which locale value specifies French Canadian using Unicode encoding?
    A. `en_US.UTF-8`
    B. `fr_CA.UTF-8`
    C. `fr_CA.ASCII`
    D. `en_CA.ASCII`
23. Which locale variable overrides all other locale variables?
    A. `LC_ALL`
    B. `LANG`
    C. `LANGUAGE`
    D. `LC_CTYPE--d MIN2300W --n 2 /home/tux/employees.txtlp --d MIN2300W /home/tux/employees.txt--d MIN2300Wlp default = MIN2300Wlpoptions`
24. Which CUPS component handles IPP printing requests from CUPS clients?
    A. CUPS Scheduler
    B. PDLs
    C. CUPS Backends
    D. PPDs
25. Your Linux system has an IP address of 192.168.1.20. What URL should you use in a browser to access the CUPS web-based administration utility?
    A. http://192.168.1.20
    B. https://192.168.1.20
    C. http://192.168.1.20:631
    D. http://192.168.1.20/cups
26. Which directive in the `/etc/cups/cupsd.conf` file specifies whether or not `cupsd` will announce its printers using broadcasts on the network?
    A. `BrowseAddress`
    B. `BrowseAllow`
    C. `Broadcast`
    D. `Browsing`

27. Which command can be used to set the hardware clock on a Linux system to the system time?
    A. `hwclock -w`
    B. `hwclock -s`
    C. `hwclock -set`
    D. `hwclock -r`
28. Which IP port does the NTP daemon use to synchronize time?
    A. 636
    B. 80
    C. 443
    D. 123

Answers

1. **A, D.** You should determine why the new Linux installation is needed and who will be using it.
2. **D.** This response clearly states the goal of the project and is measurable.
3. **A, B.** Karen's boss and her coworkers are key stakeholders in the project.
4. **B.** The best response to this situation is to have a frank discussion with the technical support supervisor and point out the consequences of the decision. Either the scale will have to be reduced or more resources must be added to the project to complete it in the same time frame.
5. **C, E.** Technically, any Linux distribution could be used in this role. However, RHEL Workstation and SUSE Linux Enterprise Desktop are specifically optimized for these kinds of tasks.
6. **B, E.** Red Hat Enterprise Desktop and SUSE Linux Enterprise Desktop are optimized for basic workstation tasks such as word processing.
7. **A, D.** Red Hat Enterprise Linux and SUSE Linux Enterprise Server are designed for high-demand network servers.
8. **C.** The best approach is to use supported hardware.
9. **D.** A 32-bit CPU uses the x86 architecture.
10. **C.** The 64-bit AMD CPU uses a 64-bit x86 architecture.
11. **C.** The `ext4` filesystem is the fastest, and it uses enhanced journaling to speed crash recovery while maintaining the overall integrity of the system.
12. **B.** Linux systems use a dedicated swap partition by default for virtual memory.
13. **D.** The optimal size of the swap partition depends on what the system will be used for. A workstation running lots of applications simultaneously will need a large swap partition. A server providing network services may not need one as large.

14. **B, D, E.** You should consider creating separate partitions for `/boot`, `/usr`, and `/home`.
15. **A, C, D.** Port 110 is used by the POP3 e-mail protocol. Port 25 is used by the SMTP e-mail protocol. Port 143 is used by the IMAP e-mail protocol.
16. **D.** The most likely cause of this problem is that the system is set to boot off the hard drive first. When it can't find the operating system on the hard drive, the error message is displayed.
17. **C.** `/dev/sdb` points to the second hard drive installed in a system.
18. **A.** `/dev/sda1` points to the first partition on the first hard drive in the system.
19. **C.** `/dev/sda2` points to the second partition on the first hard drive in the system.
20. **C.** `/dev/sdb1` points to the first partition on the second hard drive in the system.
21. **B.** The `LC_CTYPE` environment variable configures the default character encoding.
22. **B.** The `fr_CA.UTF-8` locale value specifies French Canadian using Unicode encoding.
23. **A.** The `LC_ALL` locale variable overrides all other locale variables.
24. **A.** The CUPS Scheduler handles IPP printing requests from CUPS clients.
25. **C.** The http://192.168.1.20:631 URL can be used to access the CUPS administration utility on a Linux system with an IP address of 192.168.1.20.
26. **D.** The Browsing directive in the `/etc/cups/cupsd.conf` file specifies whether `cupsd` will announce its printers using broadcasts on the network.
27. **A.** The `hwclock -w` command can be used to set the hardware clock on a Linux system to the system time.
28. **D.** Port 123 is used by the NTP daemon to synchronize time.

APPENDIX

Objective Map

Exam XK0-005

Official Exam Objective	Chapter No.
1.0 System Management	
1.1 Summarize Linux fundamentals.	
Filesystem Hierarchy Standard (FHS)	5
/boot	5
/proc	5
/sys	5
/var	5
/usr	5
/lib	5
/dev	5
/etc	5
/opt	5
/bin	5
/sbin	5
/home	5
/media	5
/mnt	5
/root	5
/tmp	5
Basic boot process	11
Basic input/output system (BIOS)	11
Unified Extensible Firmware Interface (UEFI)	11
Commands	11
mkinitrd	11
grub2-install	11

Official Exam Objective	Chapter No.
grub2-mkconfig	11
grub2-update	11
dracut	11
initrd.img	11
vmlinuz	11
Grand Unified Bootloader version 2 (GRUB2)	11
Boot sources	11
Preboot eXecution Environment (PXE)	11
Booting from Universal Serial Bus (USB)	11
Booting from ISO	11
Kernel panic	11
Device types in /dev	5
Block devices	5
Character devices	5
Special character devices	5
/dev/null	3
/dev/zero	7
/dev/urandom	7
Basic package compilation from source	10
./configure	10
make	10
make install	10
Storage concepts	7
File storage	7
Block storage	7
Object storage	18
Partition typo	7
Master boot record (MBR)	7
GUID [globally unique identifier] Partition Table (GPT)	7
Filesystem in Userspace (FUSE)	7
Redundant Array of Independent (or Inexpensive) Disks (RAID) levels	8
Striping	8
Mirroring	8
Parity	8

Official Exam Objective	Chapter No.
Listing hardware information	12
lspci	12
lsusb	12
dmidecode	12
1.2 Given a scenario, manage files and directories.	
File editing	13
sed	13
awk	13
printf	16
nano	2
vi(m)	2
File compression, archiving, and backup	8
gzip	8
bzip2	8
zip	8
tar	8
xz	8
cpio	8
dd	8
File metadata	5
stat	5
file	5
Soft and hard links	5
Copying files between systems	8
rsync	8
scp	15
nc	14
File and directory operations	5
mv	5
cp	5
mkdir	5
rmdir	5
ls	1
pwd	5
rm	5
cd	5

Official Exam Objective	Chapter No.
.	5
..	5
~	5
tree	5
cat	5
touch	5
1.3 Given a scenario, configure and manage storage using the appropriate tools.	
Disk partitioning	7
Commands	7
fdisk	7
parted	7
partprobe	7
Mounting local and remote devices	7
systemd.mount	7
/etc/fstab	7
mount	7
Linux Unified Key Setup (LUKS)	7
External devices	7
Filesystem management	7
XFS tools	7
Ext4 tools	7
Btrfs tools	7
Monitoring storage space and disk usage	7
df	7
du	7
Creating and modifying volumes using Logical Volume Manager (LVM)	8
Commands	8
pvs	8
vgs	8
lvs	8
lvchange	8
lvcreate	8
vgcreate	8
lvresize	8
pvcreate	8
vgextend	8

Official Exam Objective	Chapter No.
Inspecting RAID implementations	8
mdadm	8
/proc/mdstat	8
Storage area network (SAN)/ network-attached storage (NAS)	8
multipathd	8
Network filesystems	7
Network File System (NFS)	7
Server Message Block (SMB)/Common Internet File System (CIFS)	7
Storage hardware	8
lsscsi	8
lsblk	7
blkid	7
fcstat	8
1.4 Given a scenario, configure and use the appropriate processes and services.	
System services	9
systemctl	9
stop	9
start	9
restart	9
status	9
enable	9
disable	11
mask	11
Scheduling services	9
cron	9
crontab	9
at	9
Process management	9
Kill signals	9
SIGTERM	9
SIGKILL	9
SIGHUP	9
Listing processes and open files	9
top	9
ps	9

Official Exam Objective	Chapter No.
lsof	8
htop	9
Setting priorities	9
nice	9
renice	9
Process states	9
Zombie	9
Sleeping	9
Running	9
Stopped	9
Job control	9
bg	9
fg	9
jobs	9
Ctrl+Z	9
Ctrl+C	9
Ctrl+D	9
pgrep	9
pkill	9
pidof	9
1.5 Given a scenario, use the appropriate networking tools or configuration files.	
Interface management	14
iproute2 tools	14
ip	14
ss	14
NetworkManager	14
nmcli	14
net-tools	14
ifconfig	14
ifcfg	14
hostname	14
arp	14
route	14
/etc/sysconfig/network-scripts/	14

Official Exam Objective	Chapter No.
Name resolution	14
nsswitch	14
/etc/resolv.conf	14
systemd	14
hostnamectl	14
resolvectl	14
Bind-utils	14
dig	14
nslookup	14
host	14
WHOIS	14
Network monitoring	15
tcpdump	15
wireshark/tshark	15
netstat	14
traceroute	14
ping	14
mtr	14
Remote networking tools	14
Secure Shell (SSH)	15
cURL	15
wget	14
nc	14
rsync	8
Secure Copy Protocol (SCP)	15
SSH File Transfer Protocol (SFTP)	15
1.6 Given a scenario, build and install software.	
Package management	10
DNF	10
YUM	10
APT	10
RPM	10
dpkg	10
ZYpp	10

Official Exam Objective	Chapter No.
Sandboxed applications	10
snapd	10
Flatpak	10
AppImage	10
System updates	10
Kernel updates	10
Package updates	10
1.7 Given a scenario, manage software configurations.	
Updating configuration files	11
Procedures	11
Restart service	11
Reload service	11
.rpmnew	10
.rpmsave	10
Repository configuration files	10
/etc/apt.conf	10
/etc/yum.conf	10
/etc/dnf/dnf.conf	10
/etc/yum.repo.d	10
/etc/apt/sources.list.d	10
Configure kernel options	19
Parameters	19
sysctl	19
/etc/sysctl.conf	19
Modules	12
lsmod	12
imsmod	12
rmmod	12
insmod	12
modprobe	12
modinfo	12
Configure common system services	15
SSH	15
Network Time Protocol (NTP)	14
Syslog	12
chrony	14

Official Exam Objective	Chapter No.
Localization	3
timedatectl	3
localectl	3
2.0 Security	
2.1 Summarize the purpose and use of security best practices in a Linux environment.	
Managing public key infrastructure (PKI) certificates	15
Public key	15
Private key	15
Self-signed certificate	15
Digital signature	15
Wildcard certificate	15
Hashing	15
Certificate authorities	15
Certificate use cases	15
Secure Sockets Layer (SSL)/ Transport Layer Security (TLS)	15
Certificate authentication	15
Encryption	15
Authentication	16
Tokens	15
Multifactor authentication (MFA)	16
Pluggable authentication modules (PAM)	16
System Security Services Daemon (SSSD)	15
Lightweight Directory Access Protocol (LDAP)	15
Single sign-on (SSO)	15
Linux hardening	16
Security scanning	16
Secure boot	11
UEFI	11
System logging configurations	16
Setting default umask	6
Disabling/removing insecure services	16
Enforcing password strength	16
Removing unused packages	16
Tuning kernel parameters	19
Securing service accounts	16
Configuring the host firewall	16

Official Exam Objective	Chapter No.
2.2 Given a scenario, implement identity management.	
Account creation and deletion	4
Utilities	4
useradd	4
groupadd	4
userdel	4
groupdel	4
usermod	4
groupmod	4
id	4
who	4
w	4
Default shell	4
Configuration files	4
/etc/passwd	4
/etc/group	4
/etc/shadow	4
/etc/profile	3
/etc/skel	4
.bash_profile	3
.bashrc	3
Account management	4
passwd	4
chage	4
pam_tally2	16
faillock	16
/etc/login.defs	4
2.3 Given a scenario, implement and configure firewalls.	
Firewall use cases	15
Open and close ports	15
Check current configuration	15
Enable/disable Internet protocol (IP) forwarding	15
Common firewall technologies	15
firewalld	15
iptables	15
nftables	15
Uncomplicated firewall (UFW)	15

Official Exam Objective	Chapter No.
Key firewall features	15
Zones	15
Services	15
Stateful	15
Stateless	15
2.4 Given a scenario, configure and execute remote connectivity for system management.	
SSH	15
Configuration files	15
/etc/ssh/sshd_config	15
/etc/ssh/ssh_config	15
~/.ssh/known_hosts	15
~/.ssh/authorized_keys	15
/etc/ssh/sshd_config	15
/etc/ssh/ssh_config	15
~/.ssh/config	15
Commands	15
ssh-keygen	15
ssh-copy-id	15
ssh-add	15
Tunneling	15
X11 forwarding	15
Port forwarding	15
Dynamic forwarding	15
Executing commands as another user	16
/etc/sudoers	16
PolicyKit rules	16
Commands	16
sudo	16
visudo	16
su –	4
pkexec	16
2.5 Given a scenario, apply the appropriate access controls.	
File permissions	6
Access control list (ACL)	6
Set user ID (SUID)	6

Official Exam Objective	Chapter No.
Set group ID (SGID)	6
Sticky bit	6
Security-enhanced Linux (SELinux)	16
Context permissions	16
Labels	16
Autorelabel	16
System booleans	16
States	16
Enforcing	16
Permissive	16
Disabled	16
Policy types	16
Targeted	16
Minimum	16
AppArmor	16
Application permissions	16
Command-line utilities	6
chown	6
umask	6
chmod	6
getfacl	6
setfacl	6
ls	6
setenforce	16
getenforce	16
chattr	6
lsattr	6
chgrp	6
setsebool	16
getsebool	16
chcon	16
restorecon	16
semanage	16
audit2allow	16

Official Exam Objective	Chapter No.
3.0 Scripting, Containers, and Automation	
3.1 Given a scenario, create simple shell scripts to automate common tasks.	
Shell script elements	13
Loops	13
while	13
for	13
until	13
Conditionals	13
if	13
switch/case	13
Shell parameter expansion	13
Globbing	13
Brace expansions	13
Comparisons	13
Arithmetic	13
String	13
Boolean	13
Variables	13
Search and replace	5
Regular expressions	5
Standard stream redirection	3
|	3
||	13
>	3
>>	3
<	3
<<	3
&	9
&&	13
Redirecting	3
stderr	3
stdout	3
Here documents	3
Exit codes	13

Official Exam Objective	Chapter No.
Shell built-in commands	13
read	13
echo	13
source	13
Common script utilities	13
awk	13
sed	13
find	5
xargs	5
grep	5
egrep	5
tee	3
wc	13
cut	13
tr	13
head	5
tail	5
Environment variables	13
$PATH	13
$SHELL	3
$?	13
Relative and absolute paths	5
3.2 Given a scenario, perform basic container operations.	
Container management	18
Starting/stopping	18
Inspecting	18
Listing	18
Deploying existing images	18
Connecting to containers	18
Logging	18
Exposing ports	18
Container image operations	18
build	18
push	18
pull	18

Official Exam Objective	Chapter No.
list	18
rmi	18
3.3 Given a scenario, perform basic version control using Git.	
clone	17
push	17
pull	17
commit	17
add	17
checkout	17
branch	17
tag	17
•gitignore	17
3.4 Summarize common infrastructure as code technologies.	
File formats	17
YAML Ain't Markup Language (YAML)	17
JavaScript Object Notation (JSON)	17
Utilities	17
Ansible	17
Puppet	17
Chef	17
SaltStack	17
Terraform	17
Continuous integration/ continuous deployment (CI/CD)	17
Use cases	17
Advanced Git topics	17
merge	17
rebase	17
Pull requests	17
3.5 Summarize container, cloud, and orchestration concepts.	
Kubernetes benefits and application use cases	18
Pods	18
Sidecars	18
Ambassador containers	18
Single-node, multicontainer use cases	18
Compose	18

Official Exam Objective	**Chapter No.**
Container persistent storage	18
Container networks	18
Overlay networks	18
Bridging	18
Network address translation (NAT)	18
Host	18
Service mesh	18
Bootstrapping	18
Cloud-init	18
Container registries	18
4.0 Troubleshooting	
4.1 Given a scenario, analyze and troubleshoot storage issues.	7
High latency	7
Input/output (I/O) wait	7
Low throughput	7
Input/output operations per second (IOPS) scenarios	7
Low IOPS	7
Capacity issues	7
Low disk space	7
Inode exhaustion	5
Filesystem issues	7
Corruption	7
Mismatch	7
I/O scheduler	7
Device issues	7
Non-volatile memory express (NVMe)	7
Solid-state drive (SSD)	7
SSD trim	8
RAID	8
LVM	8
I/O errors	7
Mount option problems	7
4.2 Given a scenario, analyze and troubleshoot network resource issues.	
Network configuration issues	14
Subnet	14
Routing	14

Official Exam Objective	Chapter No.
Firewall issues	15
Interface errors	19
Dropped packets	19
Collisions	19
Link status	19
Bandwidth limitations	19
High latency	19
Name resolution issues	19
Domain Name System (DNS)	19
Testing remote systems	15
Nmap	15
openssl s_client	15
4.3 Given a scenario, analyze and troubleshoot central processing unit (CPU) and memory issues.	
Runaway processes	19
Zombie processes	9
High CPU utilization	19
High load average	19
High run queues	19
CPU times	19
steal	19
user	19
system	19
idle	19
iowait	19
CPU process priorities	9
nice	9
renice	9
Memory exhaustion	19
Free memory vs. file cache	19
Out of memory (OOM)	19
Memory leaks	19
Process killer	19
Swapping	19
Hardware	19
lscpu	19
lsmem	19

Official Exam Objective	Chapter No.
/proc/cpuinfo	19
/proc/meminfo	19
4.4 Given a scenario, analyze and troubleshoot user access and file permissions.	
User login issues	1
User file access issues	6
Group	6
Context	16
Permission	6
ACL	6
Attribute	6
Policy/non-policy	16
Password issues	1
Privilege elevation	4
Quota issues	7
4.5 Given a scenario, use systemd to diagnose and resolve common problems with a Linux system.	
Unit files	11
Service	11
Networking services	11
ExecStart/ExecStop	11
Before/after	11
Type	11
User	11
Requires/wants	11
Timer	9
OnCalendar	9
OnBootSec	9
Unit	9
Time expressions	9
Mount	11
Naming conventions	11
What	11
Where	11
Type	11
Options	11

Official Exam Objective	Chapter No.
Target	11
Default	11
Multiuser	11
Network-online	11
Graphical	11
Common problems	3
Name resolution failure	14
Application crash	10
Time-zone configuration	3
Boot issues	11
Journal issues	7
Services not starting on time	11

APPENDIX

About the Online Content

This book comes complete with TotalTester Online customizable practice exam software with 180 practice exam questions and other book resources including simulated performance-based questions, video demonstrations of select chapter exercises, and downloadable virtual machines.

System Requirements

The current and previous major versions of the following desktop browsers are recommended and supported: Chrome, Microsoft Edge, Firefox, and Safari. These browsers update frequently, and sometimes an update may cause compatibility issues with the TotalTester Online or other content hosted on the Training Hub. If you run into a problem using one of these browsers, please try using another until the problem is resolved.

Your Total Seminars Training Hub Account

To get access to the online content you will need to create an account on the Total Seminars Training Hub. Registration is free, and you will be able to track all your online content using your account. You may also opt in if you wish to receive marketing information from McGraw Hill or Total Seminars, but this is not required for you to gain access to the online content.

Privacy Notice

McGraw Hill values your privacy. Please be sure to read the Privacy Notice available during registration to see how the information you have provided will be used. You may view our Corporate Customer Privacy Policy by visiting the McGraw Hill Privacy Center. Visit the **mheducation.com** site and click **Privacy** at the bottom of the page.

Single User License Terms and Conditions

Online access to the digital content included with this book is governed by the McGraw Hill License Agreement outlined next. By using this digital content you agree to the terms of that license.

Access To register and activate your Total Seminars Training Hub account, simply follow these easy steps.

1. Go to this URL: **hub.totalsem.com/mheclaim**
2. To register and create a new Training Hub account, enter your e-mail address, name, and password on the **Register** tab. No further personal information (such as credit card number) is required to create an account.

   If you already have a Total Seminars Training Hub account, enter your e-mail address and password on the **Log in** tab.
3. Enter your Product Key: `0mxc-pknc-3v0q`
4. Click to accept the user license terms.
5. For new users, click the **Register and Claim** button to create your account. For existing users, click the **Log in and Claim** button.

   You will be taken to the Training Hub and have access to the content for this book.

Duration of License Access to your online content through the Total Seminars Training Hub will expire one year from the date the publisher declares the book out of print.

Your purchase of this McGraw Hill product, including its access code, through a retail store is subject to the refund policy of that store.

Restrictions on Transfer The user is receiving only a limited right to use the Content for the user's own internal and personal use, dependent on purchase and continued ownership of this book. The user may not reproduce, forward, modify, create derivative works based upon, transmit, distribute, disseminate, sell, publish, or sublicense the Content or in any way commingle the Content with other third-party content without McGraw Hill's consent.

Limited Warranty The McGraw Hill Content is provided on an "as is" basis. Neither McGraw Hill nor its licensors make any guarantees or warranties of any kind, either express or implied, including, but not limited to, implied warranties of merchantability or fitness for a particular purpose or use as to any McGraw Hill Content or the information therein or any warranties as to the accuracy, completeness, correctness, or results to be obtained from, accessing or using the McGraw Hill Content, or any material referenced in such Content or any information entered into licensee's product by users or other persons and/or any material available on or that can be accessed through the licensee's product (including via any hyperlink or otherwise) or as to non-infringement of third-party rights. Any warranties of any kind, whether express or implied, are disclaimed. Any material or data obtained through use of the McGraw Hill Content is at your own discretion and risk and user understands that it will be solely responsible for any resulting damage to its computer system or loss of data.

Neither McGraw Hill nor its licensors shall be liable to any subscriber or to any user or anyone else for any inaccuracy, delay, interruption in service, error or omission, regardless of cause, or for any damage resulting therefrom.

In no event will McGraw Hill or its licensors be liable for any indirect, special or consequential damages, including but not limited to, lost time, lost money, lost profits or good will, whether in contract, tort, strict liability or otherwise, and whether or not such damages are foreseen or unforeseen with respect to any use of the McGraw Hill Content.

TotalTester Online

TotalTester Online provides you with a simulation of the CompTIA Linux+ exam. Exams can be taken in Practice Mode or Exam Mode. Practice Mode provides an assistance window with hints, references to the book, explanations of the correct and incorrect answers, and the option to check your answer as you take the test. Exam Mode provides a simulation of the actual exam. The number of questions, the types of questions, and the time allowed are intended to be an accurate representation of the exam environment. The option to customize your quiz allows you to create custom exams from selected domains or chapters, and you can further customize the number of questions and time allowed.

To take a test, follow the instructions provided in the previous section to register and activate your Total Seminars Training Hub account. When you register, you will be taken to the Total Seminars Training Hub. From the Training Hub Home page, select your certification from the Study drop-down menu at the top of the page to drill down to the TotalTester for your book. You can also scroll to it from the list on the Your Topics tab of the Home page, and then click on the TotalTester link to launch the TotalTester. Once you've launched your TotalTester, you can select the option to customize your quiz and begin testing yourself in Practice Mode or Exam Mode. All exams provide an overall grade and a grade broken down by domain.

Other Book Resources

The following sections detail the other resources available with your book. You can access these items by selecting the Resources tab or by selecting **CompTIA Linux+ All-in-One Exam Guide, 2e (XK0-005)** from the Study drop-down menu at the top of the page or from the list on the Your Topics tab of the Home page. The menu on the right side of the screen outlines all of the available resources.

Performance-Based Questions

In addition to multiple-choice questions, the CompTIA Linux+ exam includes performance-based questions (PBQs), which, according to CompTIA, are designed to test your ability to solve problems in a simulated environment. More information about PBQs is provided on CompTIA's website. You can access the performance-based questions included with this book by navigating to the Resources tab and selecting Performance-Based Questions Quiz. After you have selected the PBQs, an interactive quiz will launch in your browser.

Virtual Machines

You can download the virtual machine files included with this book by navigating to the Resources tab and selecting Virtual Machines. Then select VM Setup Instructions to view detailed instructions on how to download and install the two virtual machine images provided.

Videos

Video MP4 clips from the authors of this book provide detailed demonstrations of select chapter exercises. You can access these videos by navigating to the Resources tab and selecting Videos.

Technical Support

For questions regarding the TotalTester or operation of the Training Hub, visit **www.totalsem.com** or e-mail **support@totalsem.com**.

For questions regarding book content, visit **www.mheducation.com/customerservice**.

INDEX

A

B

C

D

E

F

G

H

I

M

N

T

U

V